Reading C

READING CULTURE COMPANION WEB SITE

Reading Culture Online is a book-specific companion website designed to support *Reading Culture*, 4/E, by Diana George and John Trimbur. The companion website is an extension, and not a replication, of the book, and is designed to facilitate travel between the book and the world wide web. Material on the world wide web will be seen as culture in its own right, and careful consideration is given to different subjects such as evaluation of web design, chat room culture, newsgroups, and so on. The Student Resources section will contain chapter summaries, as well as features like those in the book: Checking out the Web, Visual Culture, and Mining the Archive. The Instructor Resources section of the website will contain cultural studies links, rhetoric and writing links, alternate syllabi, collaborative group projects, and additional fieldwork resources. You can visit the website at www.awl.com/george.

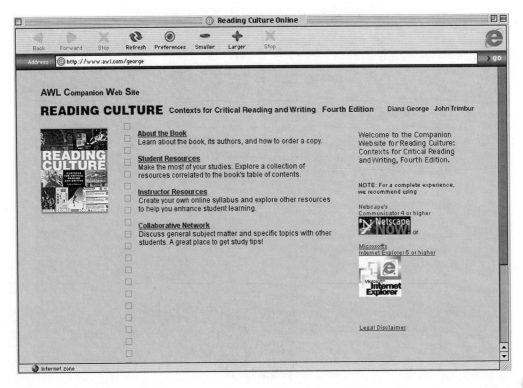

Reading Culture

CONTEXTS FOR CRITICAL READING AND WRITING

Fourth Edition

DIANA GEORGE
Michigan Technological University

JOHN TRIMBUR
Worcester Polytechnic Institute

Longman

New York San Francisco Boston
London Toronto Sydney Tokyo Singapore Madrid
Mexico City Munich Paris Cape Town Hong Kong Montreal

Editor-in-Chief: Joseph Terry
Acquisitions Editor: Lynn M. Huddon
Development Editor: Leslie Taggart
Marketing Manager: Carlise Paulson
Supplements Editor: Donna Campion
Production Manager: Ellen MacElree
Project Coordination, Text Design, and Electronic Page Makeup: Electronic Publishing Services Inc., N.Y.C.
Cover Designer/Manager: Wendy Ann Fredericks
Cover photos: Clockwise from top left: L.A. Mural, © Barbara Alper/Stock Boston; 50s family watching TV, © FPG; entrance sign at Mall of America, © Barbara Alper/Stock Boston; http://www.slashdot.org, © slashdot.com; professional rock climber, Utah, © Pete Saloutos/The Stock Market; paperback book cover *Beat, Beat, Beat* by William F. Brown, 1959, © John Hammer/Archive Photos; 10/16/68, extending gloved hands skyward in racial protest, U.S. athletes Tommie Smith (center) and John Carlos (right) stare downward during the playing of the Star Spangled Banner, © AP/Wide World Photos; and Women's Vietnam Memorial, © AP/World Wide Photos.
Photo Researcher: PhotoSearch, Inc.
Manufacturing Buyer: Roy Pickering
Printer and Binder: The Maple-Vail Book Manufacturing Group
Cover Printer: Phoenix Color Corps.

For permission to use copyrighted material, grateful acknowledgment is made to the copyright holders on pp. 554–559, which are hereby made part of this copyright page.

Library of Congress Cataloging-in-Publication Data
Reading culture : contexts for critical reading and writing / [edited by] Diana George, John Trimbur. —4th ed.
    p. cm.
    Includes bibliographical references and index.
    ISBN 0-321-08111-0 (pbk.)
    1. College readers. 2. English language—Rhetoric—Problems, exercises, etc. 3. Critical thinking—Problems, exercises, etc. 4. Academic writing—problems, exercises, etc. I. George, Diana, 1948– II. Trimbur, John.
PE1417 .R38 2001
808'.0427—dc21   00-042116

Please visit our website at http://www.awl.com

ISBN 0-321-08111-0

2 3 4 5 6 7 8 9 10—MA—03 02 01 00

Culture is ordinary;
that is where we must start.

Raymond Williams

Contents

CHAPTER 3   Schooling   108

CHAPTER 4 Images   173

CHAPTER 5 Style   230

CHAPTER 9 History   415

CHAPTER 10 Multicultural America   **488**

Visual Resources

Illustrations

Page Design

Murals, Graffiti, Signs

Paintings

Parodies/Rewrites

Alternate Contents

II. Academic and Critical Writing

Cross-Cultural Studies

Cultural and Social Criticism

Ethnography/Oral History

Rhetorical Contents

Comparison and Contrast

Illustration/Example

Definition

Problem Formulation/Solution

Evaluation

Argument

Deliberation/Reflection

Preface

Every edition of *Reading Culture* has opened with these words from Raymond Williams: "Culture is ordinary; that is where we must start." We start, then, with the world that surrounds us and the experience of everyday life. In *Reading Culture*, we ask students to look at culture as a way of life that organizes social experience and shapes the identities of individuals and groups. We will be using the term *culture* in this textbook to talk about how people make sense of their worlds and about the values, beliefs, and practices in which they invest their energies and allegiances. One of our central aims is to provide students with reading and writing assignments in their familiar ways of life, and to understand how these ways of life fit into the diverse, mass-mediated, multicultural realities of contemporary America.

Reading Culture assumes that students are already immersed in a wealth of cultural data and that their experiences of everyday life can usefully be brought to attention as material for reflection and deliberation. The reading and writing assignments in *Reading Culture* are designed to promote a critical distancing so that students can begin to observe and evaluate as well as participate in contemporary America. To this end, *Reading Culture* asks students to read in two ways. First we ask students to read carefully and critically the range of writing about culture we have assembled here. We ask student to identify the purposes and assumptions writers bring to the study of culture and the rhetorical patterns they use to enact their aims. Second, we ask students to read the social world around them, to identify the patterns of meaning in the commonplace, and to put into words their familiar experiences of everyday life that often go without saying.

Reading Culture is organized into ten chapters. The first chapter, "Reading and Writing About Culture: The Case of Daytime Talk TV," provides both a general introduction to the study of culture and a case study of daytime talk TV. The reading selections illustrate how writing about culture seeks to influence public opinion. The case study includes a step-by-step sequence of reading and writing activities that introduce students to a number of useful reading strategies—underlining, annotating, and summarizing—and writing strategies—exploratory writing, synthesis, and deliberative judgment. In addition, the case study includes critical strategies for watching daytime talk TV and guidelines for interviewing other viewers.

The chapters that form the main part of *Reading Culture*, as in past editions, are arranged under a number of broad topics. "Generations" and "Schooling" explore the personal experience of growing up and learning in contemporary America. "Images," "Style," and "Public Space" explore the ways values and ideals are conveyed in the popular media, as well as in clothing and hairstyles and in the way public space is organized. In the remaining chapters, "Storytelling," "Work," "History," and "Multicultural America," students can investigate how the narratives Americans tell themselves and those that are told about them come to be part of national mythmaking.

In the third edition of *Reading Culture*, we included two new features—*Visual Culture* and *Fieldwork*—that are now standard parts of the textbook. In each chapter, a *Visual Culture* section presents strategies for analyzing and interpreting films, photographs, television shows, ads, public health messages, page design, signs in public places, and other forms of visual communication. In addition, most chapters include a *Fieldwork* section that provides ways of studying culture through interviews, participant observation, questionnaires, audience studies, oral histories, and other forms of on-site research.

Reading Culture is designed to be used flexibly and creatively. Instructors may wish to ask students to work on the chapters in *Reading Culture* as they are arranged, but this is only one possible order. In the Alternate Contents, we have classified the reading selections in terms of genres and rhetorical modes, and the Instructor's Manual suggests ways to pair readings across chapters.

NEW TO THE FOURTH EDITION

This fourth edition includes new and expanded features to help students investigate contemporary and past cultures. These additions come in large part from discussions we've had with writing teachers who have used previous editions of *Reading Culture*.

- *Checking Out the Web* and the *Reading Culture Online* Website. With the expansion of the Internet and the dizzying proliferation of the Web, the way people communicate has changed dramatically in recent years. To take into account how the Web has become such a cultural force, we have expanded the feature *Checking Out the Web* to include a new section *Reading the Web*, with guidelines for analyzing websites and talk on the Web. In addition, *Reading Culture* now has its own website with links to the sites we discuss in the book and further activities and resources. See www.awl.com/george.

- *Mining the Archive*. To add historical depth to the topics presented in *Reading Culture* and to offer students further research opportunities, each chapter now includes the feature *Mining the Archive*. This feature sends students to various sources as repositories of historical materials, including old newspapers, textbooks, magazines, comic books and comic strips, court cases, and government reports—whether in libraries, special collections, or on websites. In addition, we ask students to see what they can find in local museums and historical societies, and to design a walking tour of a historical site.

- *Perspectives*. Many chapters now include paired readings so that students can see how writers go about developing different perspectives on a topic. In some cases the writers may outrightly disagree, but in others they may simply take up different points of views. These paired readings ask students to consider the various ways writers approach cultural analysis and the kinds of assumptions they bring to their interpretations.

The readings in *Reading Culture* draw on a variety of resources, including popular press features, academic scholarships, and news reports. Each reading selection is introduced by a headnote that provides a context for the reading and a Suggestion for Reading that directs students to notice particular themes or rhetorical features in the selection. The reading selections are followed by Suggestions for Discussion, which raise issues for students to talk about in class or in small collaborative groups. The Suggestions for Writing ask students to consider a range of angles on the issues presented in the reading selections. Typically these writing assignments ask students to interpret a key point or passage in the reading selection, to relate the reading selection to their own experience, and to connect the reading to other readings and to the cultural realities of contemporary America.

The fourth edition of *Reading Culture* offers opportunities extending across chapters to work with visual literacy, multiculturalism, and microethnography. The work you do with this text will, however, depend on your needs and your students' interests. We think that with this edition *Reading Culture* has become a more flexible resource for teaching writing and critical reading, and for asking students to write about, and in the culture of, contemporary America.

An Instructor's Manual is also available to adopters of this edition.

ACKNOWLEDGMENTS

There are a number of people we want to thank for their insight and advice. Robert Schwegler deserves credit for helping us conceptualize this project in its first edition. Joseph Trimmer explained how to make a textbook and offered useful suggestions as a reviewer and as a friend. Lynn Huddon and Leslie Taggart provided the editorial support for this edition. We appreciate as well the careful readings we received by reviewers of this book:

Akeel Al-Khakani; Purdue University
Jami Carlacio; University of Wisconsin, Milwaukee
Jane M. Creighton; University of Houston
Todd W. Deam; Southern Illinois University at Carbondale
Susan Dreghorn; College of DuPage
Sara Farris; University of Houston
Debra Fletcher; University of Michigan, Dearborn
Kevin Griffith; Capital University
Kathleen Kelly; Northeastern University
Lisa Langstraat; University of Southern Mississippi
Daniel Lowe; Community College of Allegheny County
Timothy Morales; University of Central Oklahoma
David D. Moser; Butler County Community College
Derrick G. Pitard; Slippery Rock University
Robert D. Sturr; Kent State University, Stark Campus
David Susman; Salt Lake Community College
Marianne Ware; Santa Rosa Junior College
Randy Woodland; University of Michigan, Darborn

We want to thank particularly the teachers who have used the first three editions of *Reading Culture*. The feedback, suggestions, and insights they have offered us over the years have enabled us to see the book in new ways and to plan the fourth edition with their ideas in mind. Thanks to Marguerite Helmers and the group of writing faculty from University of Wisconsin, Oshkosh, who shared their experience using the second edition. Stephen Ruffus and the writing faculty at Salt Lake Community College helped us see thematic strands in the book. We want to thank Bill Baller of Worcester Polytechnic Institute for help with readings on the Vietnam War and Clare Trimbur for showing us how to do close readings of English Only legislation. Diane Shoos, Stephen Jukuri, and Nancy Barron at Michigan Tech offered thoughtful advice as we wrote the third edition. Tim Fountain, now at St. Cloud State, taught an early draft of the daytime talk TV chapter, allowing us to learn from his students' experience. We want to give particular thanks to Libby Miles of the University of Rhode Island and to Lucia Trimbur of Yale University for their work on the *Reading Culture* website. We also thank our companions Chuck Harris (and Maggie) and Lundy Braun for their patience and faith that we could do this one more time. We thank our students at Michigan Tech and Worcester Polytechnic Institute, and Clare Trimbur, Lucia Trimbur, and Catherine Trimbur for the best confirmation of our intentions we could possibly receive: they recognized themselves and their peers in this project and let us know that the cultural resources we are seeking to tap are vitally important to students in contemporary America. Finally, with respect and sadness, we wish to thank Jim Berlin for convincing us this project was not only worthwhile but necessary. He taught the earliest versions of *Reading Culture* and helped us see what was useful and what was not. We miss him. We keep his voice of encouragement and healthy skepticism with us as we write and teach.

Diana George
John Trimbur

Introduction

READING CULTURE

culture: education, enrichment, erudition, learning, wisdom, breeding, gentility, civilization, colony, community, crowd, folks, group, settlement, society, staff, tribe, background, development, environment, experience, past, schooling, training, upbringing, customs, habits, mores, traditions

The British cultural historian Raymond Williams has written that culture "is one of the two or three most complicated words in the English language." This is so, Williams explains, because the term *culture* has acquired new meanings over time without losing the older meanings along the way. Therefore, writers sometimes use the term *culture* in quite different and incompatible ways. Even a simple list of synonyms, such as the one that opens this chapter, can illustrate the truth of Williams's observation.

For some, culture refers to great art in the European tradition—Beethoven's symphonies, Shakespeare's plays, Picasso's paintings, or Jane Austen's novels. In this manner, culture refers to something that you read; something that you see in a museum, an art gallery, or a theater; or something that you hear in a concert hall. This culture is often referred to as "high culture" and is closely linked to the idea of *becoming* cultured—of cultivating good taste and discriminating judgment. A cultured person, according to this sense of the term, is someone who has achieved a certain level of refinement and class.

We encounter this use of the term more frequently than some might imagine. For example, advertisers who want to invest their products with class will draw on this idea of culture, as in the Absolut Vodka campaign that pays homage to such artists as Vermeer, Rubens, and Modigliani.

Those who equate culture with high art would most likely think, for example, that pop stars like Britney Spears or rappers like Snoop Doggie Dogg do not belong in the domain of culture. They would not include popular entertainment like *NYPD Blue, All My Children, Monday Night Football,* the *National Enquirer,* the latest Harlequin romance, or music videos in that category either. In making a distinction between high and low art, this view of culture is largely interested in the classics and in keeping serious art separate from popular culture.

Others, however, take an alternative approach to the study of culture. Instead of separating high from low art, they think of culture in more inclusive terms. For them, culture refers not only to the literary and artistic works which critics have called masterpieces but also to the way of life that characterizes a particular group of

1

ABSOLUT HOFMEKLER.
HOMAGE TO JAN VERMEER

Ori Hofmeker is an artist on the staff of *Penthouse* magazine. For this ad campaign, he was asked to reproduce works of old masters, inserting an Absolut bottle in the ad as though it belonged in the original. Richard Lewis, *The Absolut Story.*

people at a particular time. Developed since the turn of the century by anthropologists, though it has now spread into common use, *culture* offers a way to think about how individuals and groups organize and make sense of their social experience—at home, in school, at work, and at play. Culture includes all the social institutions, patterns of behavior, systems of belief, and kinds of popular entertainment that create the social world in which people live. Taken this way, culture means not simply masterpieces of art, music, and literature, but a people's lived experience—what goes on in the everyday lives of individuals and groups.

Reading Culture explores the interpretation of contemporary American culture and how cultural ideas and ideals are communicated in the home, the workplace, the school, and through the media. When we use the term *culture,* we are using a definition that, as you might have guessed, is much closer to the second definition than to the first. We think that the distinction between high and low art is indeed an important one but not because high art is necessarily better or more "cultured" than popular entertainment. What interests us is how the two terms are used in an ongoing debate about the meaning of contemporary culture in the United States—about, say, what children should read in school, about the influences of popular media, or about the quality of Americans' popular tastes. We will ask you to explore these issues in the following chapters to see how arguments over media or schooling or our national identity tell stories of contemporary U.S. culture.

In short, the purpose of this book is not to bring you culture or to make you cultured but to invite you to become more aware of the culture in which you already live. According to the way we will be using the term, culture is not something you can go out and get. Rather, culture means all the familiar pursuits and pleasures that shape people's identities and that enable and constrain what they do and what they might become. Our idea is to treat contemporary American culture as a vast research project—to understand its ways of life from the inside as you live and observe them.

READING CULTURE

The following chapters offer opportunities to read, research, and write about contemporary culture. The reading selections group together writers who have explored central facets of American culture or who offer information and ideas for you to draw on as you do your own work of reading and writing about culture. Each chapter raises a series of questions about how American culture organizes social experience and how Americans understand the meaning and purpose of their daily lives.

In these chapters, we will be asking you to think about how the writers find patterns in U.S. culture and how they position themselves in relation to contemporary cultural realities. We will be asking you to read not only to understand what the writers are saying but also to identify what assumptions they are making about cultural issues such as schooling, the media, or national identity. We also will be asking you to do another kind of reading, where the text is not the printed word but the experience of everyday life in contemporary America. We will be asking you to read culture—to read the social world around you, at home and in classrooms, at work and at play, in visual images and public places.

Reading a culture means finding patterns in the familiar. In many respects, of course, you are already a skilled reader of culture. Think of all the reading that you do in the course of a day. You read not only the textbooks assigned in your courses or the books and magazines you turn to for pleasure. You probably read a variety of other "texts" without thinking about what you are actually reading. You read the clothes that people wear, the cars that they drive, and the houses that they live in to make guesses about their social status or about how you will relate to them. You read the way social experience is organized on your campus to determine who your friends will be, who the preppies are, the jocks, the hippies. You read all kinds of visual images in the media not only for the products advertised or the entertainment offered but for the lifestyles that are made attractive and desirable. Most of your reading takes place as you move through the daily reality of contemporary American life, and it often takes place below the threshold of consciousness. Often, people just take this kind of reading for granted.

To read culture means *not* taking for granted such readings of everyday life. Reading culture means bringing forward for analysis and reflection those commonplace aspects of everyday life that people normally think of as simply being there, a part of the natural order of things. Most likely you do some of that kind of reading occasionally when you stop to think through an ad or a history lesson or anything that makes you connect what you are seeing or reading with other ideas coming your way every day. Very likely, you do not accept without question all that you see and read. You probably turn a skeptical eye to much of it. Still, to read culture you will have to be more consistent as you learn to bring the familiar back into view so that you can begin to understand how people organize and make sense of their lives. To read culture in this way is to see that American culture is not simply passed down from generation to generation in a fixed form but rather is a way of life in which individuals and groups are constantly making their own meanings in the world of contemporary America.

We are all influenced by what cultural critics call mainstream culture, whether we feel part of it or not. Everyone to one extent or another (and whether they embrace or reject its tenets) is shaped by what is sometimes called the "American way of life" and the value that it claims to place on hard work, fair play, individual success, romantic love, family ties, and patriotism. After all, to grow up in the United States means, in part, learning what the mainstream values. This is, undoubtedly, the most mass-mediated culture in human history, and it is virtually impossible to evade the dominant images of America past and present—whether of the Pilgrims gathered at that mythic scene of the first Thanksgiving or of retired pro football players in a Miller Lite commercial.

Yet for all the power of the "American way of life" as it is presented by schools, the mass media, and the culture industry, U.S. culture is hardly monolithic or homogeneous. The culture in which Americans live is a diverse one, divided along the lines of race, class, gender, language, ethnicity, age, occupation, region, politics, and religion. America is a multicultural society, and, in part because of that diversity, the culture of contemporary America is constantly changing, constantly in flux. To read culture, therefore, is to see not only how its dominant cultural expressions shape people but also how individuals and groups shape culture—how their responses to and interpretations of contemporary America rewrite its meanings according to their own purposes, interests, and aspirations.

ASSIGNMENT

Work together with a group of classmates. Think of as many instances as you can where the term *culture* or *cultured* appears. For example, when do you hear other people that you know (family, friends, coworkers, neighbors, teachers, and so on) use the terms? When do you use them yourself? Where have you seen the terms in written texts or heard them used on radio and television or in the movies? Make a list of occasions when you have encountered or used the terms. Categorize the various uses of the terms. Are they used in the same way in each instance or do their meanings differ? Explain your answer. How do you account for the similarities and differences in the use of the terms? Compare the results of your group discussion to the results of other groups.

CHAPTER 1

Reading and Writing About Culture

THE CASE OF DAYTIME TALK TV

You're not anybody in America unless you're on TV. On TV is where we learn about who we really are, because what's the point of doing anything worthwhile if nobody's watching?
—*From the Gus Van Sant film* To Die For

As a fixture in most of our homes, television is one of the most pervasive communicators of U.S. culture today. Some estimates suggest Americans watch as many as eight hours of television programming daily. A commercial medium, television responds to current tastes or, at least, to what TV executives determine are current tastes. All of that makes television a very good place to begin thinking about what it means to read and write about culture.

Americans watch all kinds of television shows, from news to sports to sitcoms to cartoons. However, our discussion will focus on the world of daytime talk TV, which in recent years has been among the most popular and controversial programming on the air. In January 1996, *Time* magazine reported that approximately twenty-three hours in a week's worth of TV scheduling were devoted to daytime talk.

Daytime talk TV explores topics and issues that are common in the news media (teen pregnancy, drug abuse, AIDS, domestic violence, family values), but it does not pretend to be journalism as do TV news magazines like *60 Minutes, 20/20,* or *Dateline.* As viewers watch daytime talk, they might very well acquire information about, say, teenage sexuality, and yet the informants are not reporters or what we typically consider experts in the field. Instead, they are primarily teens and their parents—sometimes arguing, sometimes weeping, but always giving first-person testimony, a very different kind of expertise. An extremely popular type of programming, daytime talk TV comments on cultural events and issues addressing contemporary concerns about such topics as lifestyle choices, public and private morality, and the politics of personal appearance. That freedom to comment on so much that is important to the audience makes talk TV something worth paying close attention to.

This chapter is divided into four major sections: Visual Culture: Watching Daytime Talk TV; Fieldwork: Listening to Viewers; Reading About Daytime Talk TV; and Writing About Daytime Talk TV. The sections are sequenced to prepare you for writing about the culture of daytime talk television in particular, and more generally, for reading, researching, and writing about the other cultural issues and events throughout this text. First, we need to make it very clear what we mean by "daytime talk TV."

DAYTIME TALK SHOWS

Good Morning America
(7 a.m., Ch. 5, 6)
M: *Where the Jobs Are* series begins.
Tu: *Where the Jobs Are* series.
W: *Where the Jobs Are* series; entertainment report.
Th: Julia Child's 85th birthday; *Woman to Woman.*
F: A concert from Central Park.

Today
(7 a.m., Ch. 7, 10)
M: Gene Stallings and his new book on raising a son; Ryder Cup team announced; manicures and pedicures.
Tu: Interview with Sylvester Stallone; beauty aides; Dr. Joyce Brothers.
W: Interview with Ray Liotta.
Th: Gene Shalit; Dr. Bob Arnot on health; entertainment news with Jill Rappaport.
F: Interview with Alicia Silverstone; finances with Ray Martin; performance by Little Richard.

This Morning
(7 a.m., Ch. 12; 8 a.m., Ch. 4)
M: The investigation into the death of JonBenet Ramsey.
Tu: Mel Gibson and Julia Roberts (*Conspiracy Theory*).
W: Shaquille O'Neal; financial advice.
Th: Sylvester Stallone; the Jon-Benet Ramsey murder investigation; chef Henry Meer; a health report.
F: Gene Siskel reviews the movies of Elvis Presley.

Gordon Elliott
(9 a.m., Ch. 4, 12)
M: Teachers dealing with school violence. (R)
Tu: Parents dealing with a child's disappearance or unsolved murder. (R)
W: Mothers find dates for their sons. (R)
Th: People who have parlayed personal tragedy into a greater good. (R)
F: Sinbad joins a tribute to emergency medical technicians. (R)

Rolonda
(9 a.m., Ch. 5; 1 p.m., WPIX)
M: A panel discusses race relations. (R)
Tu: How *Playboy* magazine has changed the lives of celebrities including Pamela Lee; Jenny McCarthy and Marilyn Monroe. (R)
W: Advice for parents on how to talk to their teenagers about

JULIA ROBERTS and Mel Gibson visit *This Morning* on CBS Tuesday to promote *Conspiracy Theory.*

sex. (R) Pre-empted 1 p.m., WPIX.
Th: Victims of child abuse comment on the California chemical castration law for repeat offenders. (R)
F: Highlights from past shows that featured people whose experiences mirrored those of dramatic movies and television shows.

In Person With Maureen O'Boyle
(9 a.m., Ch. 6; 3 p.m., Ch. 4)
M: Troubled teens. (R)
Tu: Getting in shape for the summer; Joey Heatherton. (R)
W: A relationship counselor helps families in crisis. (R)
Th: Loved ones are asked to leave bad relationships. (R)
F: Memorable celebrity moments from the past season. (R)

Live — Regis & Kathie Lee
(9 a.m., Ch. 7, 10)
M: Matt Lauer, Billy Crystal, Tony Danza and Pierce Brosnan. (R)
Tu: Hanson and Spice Girls; Billy Corgan, Jewel and Erykah Badu.
W: Jerry Seinfeld, Jason Alexander and Michael Richards.
Th: Whoopi Goldberg, Mike Myers, Lisa Kudrow and Val Kilmer. (R)
F: Rosie O'Donnell and David Letterman, Alex Trebek. (R)

Rosie O'Donnell
(10 a.m., Ch. 5; 5 p.m., Ch. 25)
M: Mary Tyler Moore, Valerie Harper and Emily Mae Young. (R)
Tu: Ron Howard and Jennifer Connelly (*Inventing the Abbotts*),

Tanya Tucker, James McBride. (R)
W: Dennis Franz (*NYPD Blue*), Christopher Walken (*Excess Baggage*) and Lisa Vidal (*High Incident, Fall*), Joey Kola.
Th: Demi Moore (*G.I. Jane*), Robin Wright (*She's So Lovely*) and Patrick Swayze.
F: Chita Rivera, Alicia Silverstone (*Excess Baggage*), Rob Reiner (*I Am Your Child*), Chris Tucker (*Money Talks*).

Maury
(11 a.m., Ch. 10; 4 p.m., Ch. 4)
M: Incredible stories of twins, including interracial twins and twins born 95 days apart. (R)
Tu: Mothers who are distressed over their teenage daughters' clothes; make-overs for teased teenagers. (R)
W: Adults who appeared years ago as children on Art Linkletter's *Kids Say the Darndest Things* show segment. (R)
Th: To be announced.
F: To be announced.

Ricki Lake
(11 a.m., Ch. 64; 5 p.m., Ch. 25)
M: Ricki recalls unforgettable episodes of her show. (R)
Tu: To be announced.
W: To be announced.
Th: Women seeking to prove their children's paternity. (R)
F: To be announced.

Ricki Lake
(noon, Ch. 25)
M: Reuniting with former amazing lovers. (R)
Tu: People who have survived harrowing experiences have their dreams come true. (R)
W: Young men who want to marry older women. (R)
Th: Confessions of infidelity. (R)
F: Casey Kasem, Kim Coles and Erik Estrada. (R)

Geraldo Rivera
(1 p.m., Ch. 28; 3 p.m., Ch. 7)
M: The families of murdered children.
Tu: Parents spying on their teenage children. (R)
W: Children who overcame obstacles. (R)
Th: Children whose mothers use drugs. (R)
F: People who survived near-death experiences. (R)

Jenny Jones
(1 p.m., Ch. 56)
M: Sons following in their chauvinistic fathers' footsteps.

Tu: Teenage guests who live and act like vampires.
W: Viewers who want dates with former guests.
Th: Guests once teased because of their high-school demeanor show off their new look. (R)
F: Sitcom stars of the '70s.

Oprah Winfrey
(4 p.m., Ch. 5, 10)
M: One year after being exposed by the media, alcoholic parents describe their recovery. (R)
Tu: Minor acts of wrongdoing of which most people are guilty; humorist Dave Barry (*Dave Barry in Cyberspace*). (R)
W: Dick Clark; music trivia.
Th: The issue of whether or not inmates should be celibate; a professor and his students help free wrongly convicted men. (R) Pre-empted Ch. 5.
F: TV fans meet their favorite stars, including Rob Estes (*Melrose Place*), Brandy Norwood (*Moesha*) and *Ellen* co-stars Joely Fisher and David Anthony Higgins; Julio Iglesias visits. (R)

At press time, no information was available on the following programs:

Fox After Breakfast
(9 a.m., Ch. 25)

Leeza
(10 a.m., Ch. 7, 10)

Montel Williams
(10 a.m., Ch. 12, 25)

Fox After Breakfast
(10 a.m., Ch. 64)

Sally
(11 a.m., Ch. 5)

View
(11 a.m., Ch. 6)

Jerry Springer
(11 a.m., WPIX)

Charlie Rose
(noon, Ch. 44)

Jerry Springer
(noon, Ch. 56)

Sally
(4 p.m., Ch. 12)

AUGUST 10, 1997 | 21

DEFINING THE GENRE OF DAYTIME TALK TV

Talk television programming has been around for a long time and varies from late-night shows such as David Letterman's to star-centered chat shows such as Rosie O'Donnell's to shock-value shows such as Jerry Springer's to shows that take a more middle ground such as Oprah Winfrey's. Media analyst Bernard Timberg has noticed, however, that even though the shows might look somewhat different, they all share some "unspoken rules":

- *Talk television is host-centered.* The most important element of a talk show is the host, and many of the shows are named for that host: *Oprah, Maury Povich,* and *Jenny Jones,* to name a few.

- *Talk television is produced and experienced in the present tense.* Even though these shows are taped and played later, they must appear to be happening in the present so that, as

Timberg puts it, "host and guest and viewer *occupy the same moment*" in order for viewers to feel the intimacy the show is trying to achieve with its audience.

- *Talk show hosts speak intimately to millions.* The host may be speaking into a camera while the show is being taped but must appear to be speaking in a very personal way to viewers, in effect achieving a kind of false closeness with members of the viewing audience.

- *Talk shows are profitable.* Talk shows make money for the networks, and these shows primarily are supported by commercials. Any appeal to advertisers to pull their ads from talk shows can have a significant impact.

- *Talk television structures spontaneity.* Though they may appear to be occurring in the present and the host may appear to be talking to viewers as intimate friends, these shows try their best to control these "spontaneous" events. Guests are prepared to act surprised at whatever pops up, whether they expected it or not. (Even programs that do "ambush" episodes try their best to control whatever reaction might take place.)

Jane Shattuc, in *The Talking Cure: TV Talk Shows and Women,* her study of issue-oriented talk shows, discusses the talk show genre:

> The talk show is much more complex than its reputation as "simple" pop culture, and the daytime talk show is a subgenre of the form. The talk show is as old as American broadcasting and borrows its basic characteristics from those of nineteenth-century popular culture, such as tabloids, women's advice columns, and melodrama. Today the term *talk show* encompasses offerings as diverse as *Larry King Live,* the *Oprah Winfrey Show,* the *700 Club,* the *Tonight Show, Rush Limbaugh: The Television Show, Ricki Lake,* talk radio, *Good Morning America,* and a host of local shows that are united by their emphasis on informal or nonscripted conversation rather than the scripted delivery of the news.
>
> Nevertheless, the issue-oriented daytime talk show—the subject of this book—is what a majority of Americans mean when they speak of pre-1994 talk shows; that year the form started to change direction. It is distinguished from other types of talk shows by five characteristics. One, it is issue-oriented; content derives from social problems or personal matters that have a social currency such as rape, drug use, or sex change. Two, active audience participation is central. Three, it is structured around the moral authority and educated knowledge of a host and an expert, who mediate between guests and audience. Four, it is constructed for a female audience. Five, it is produced by non-network companies for broadcast on network-affiliated stations. The four shows top rated by A. C. Nielsen in the 1980s, the first generation of daytime talk shows, fit these generic traits: Geraldo, the Oprah Winfrey Show, the Phil Donahue Show, and Sally Jessy Raphael. Their similarity allows their treatment as a cultural group.

VISUAL CULTURE WATCHING DAYTIME TALK TV

Later in this chapter, you will be given strategies for gathering information, understanding what others write about issues, comparing how other writers position themselves and their readers in relation to issues, and considering how these writers help shape public opinion about an issue. This is the kind of reading you are probably most familiar with—reading and evaluating written texts—but messages are also conveyed through the images we see. Some are accompanied by written text; some are not. Television is primarily a visual medium, so in order to write about daytime talk TV you will first need to learn to pay attention to visual meaning. In the next few pages, we offer strategies for reading these image-based messages.

Visual images convey meaning in much the same way that language conveys meaning: through emphasis and arrangement and the careful selection of details. Of course, you already know quite a bit about reading images because those are the kinds of messages that surround all of us every day: billboards, advertisements, television, movies, photographs, and Web pages. Even if you do not watch much television or see many movies, you are surrounded by images every time you enter a large city or small town, every time you pick up a magazine or newspaper, every time you ride down the highway. These images ask us to buy products or give to charities or vote for candidates or make decisions on local and national issues. They might be as familiar and easily read as McDonald's golden arches on a highway sign or as enigmatic as a pair of hands reaching out from a billboard to empty space. No matter. Every image has the capacity to send a message.

Like words, nonverbal images are symbols or signs used to relay meanings that have come to be attached to them through historic use, through association with other things familiar, through cultural context, and through such media as books, magazines, billboards, film, and television. That is not to say that visual meaning is unchanging or that everyone who sees these signs reads precisely the same message. Visual language, like any language, continually shifts with time, circumstance, and use.

Still, the most quickly read messages are often those that carry with them expressions of typical cultural meanings or ideals, images that act as a kind of visual shorthand. It is fairly customary in the United States, for example, for television stations to sign off with the national anthem and a shot of the flag waving over a series of idealized images of American life. The station counts on viewers to recognize this as a patriotic message—one so common that even viewers from other cultures will understand it, as most countries have a flag ceremony and a national anthem. Of course, since this image is placed where it is—on late-night television as the station sign-off—it takes on a secondary meaning: If you fall asleep in front of your TV and wake up to that flag waving in the breeze, you are likely to know that you've slept through to the end of the broadcasting day. Through such use, that image has become a marker for the end of programming.

Viewing Strategies *Read by Monday*

Before you can begin your own writing on daytime talk TV, you will want to know how to read these shows. That means you will have to consider not only the structure and content of daytime TV but also how a show's appearance actually contributes to meaning, helps set daytime talk apart from other television programming, and lends those programs an authority to speak out on issues that may seem at once public and private. What's more, you'll want to consider how these shows convey cultural meaning or communicate certain cultural ideals.

We offer, then, a list of strategies for reading daytime talk TV. You should notice that the first strategies ask you to pay attention to content, guests, and audience (what the show is about, who the guests are, and who is in the audience while the show is being taped). The next focus is on what the show actually looks like (camera shots, visual space, and set design). The final suggestion asks you to note sponsors (one clue to the television viewing audience).

You can watch several different shows or focus on one particular show, though if you do watch only one show, you should either tape the program so that you can watch it more than once or make sure you watch more than one day's programming. As you view these programs, keep in mind the following suggestions and take notes on what you see. You won't be able to write everything down, but you will find that with practice you can note the general look of a show and even the important details to illustrate your discussion.

Content, Guests, and Audience

- *Write down the show's topic for the day.* As Shattuc explains, these are issue-oriented shows. The issues are often private ones, but they are also designed to shock or pull in audiences through such topics as "My Mother Is Sleeping with My Boyfriend."

- *Pay attention to who the guests are, how they are identified, and even how they are dressed.* When you watch daytime talk TV, spend some time taking note of who has been invited to speak. What is the age range, the racial mix, the gender balance? Can you identify their economic status (e.g., working class, or upper or lower middle class)? What characteristics identify these guests for you?

  In many daytime talk shows, the guests are frequently shown in close-up and identified with their names and a brief description of why they are on the show (e.g., "Bob Summers—Is dating his ex-girlfriend's mother"). What effect does such labeling have for the viewer?

- *Pay attention to the studio audience and how they react to what is said on stage.* As Shattuc explains, audience participation is crucial to daytime talk TV. Some audiences shout as guests are speaking. Some wait to be called on. Many take the opportunity to give advice or to pass judgment. Notice how the audience reaction to a guest affects your own response to that guest. Notice the composition of the audience. What is the general age, racial, and gender mix? Does the audience seem to dress or speak in a way that identifies them?

Set Design, Spatial Arrangement, and Camera Space

- *Pay attention to the appearance of the set.* Set design can give you some clues to the basic tenor of a show. In general, the more like a living room the set is portrayed, the more respect guests seem to get from a host. In a show where guest and host sit in overstuffed chairs or around a nice table arrangement, you'll notice that the guest is treated with a certain amount of credibility. In shows where guests are perched awkwardly on stools or lined up in functional chairs, the credibility drops. It is in these shows that guests may break out into shouting matches with each other, the host, and even the audience. (Would a host ever argue like this with a celebrity guest?) For example, you'll probably notice that *Oprah,* a show often described as taking "higher ground" in the daytime talk show line-up, looks very different from a show like *Sally Jessy Raphael.* Does the set on the show you are watching seem to make the guests comfortable or not? Does the set look like a living room or a bare stage with stools and not much more?

- *Pay attention to how subjects are arranged in the visual space.* Another way to determine what is important in a visual image is simply to pay attention to where things are placed within the visual space. For example, hosts Jay Leno and David Letterman sit behind a desk on the right side of the screen, where they take up most of the visual space and look somewhat higher than the guest sitting stage left. It is clear that the host occupies the most important position in the visual space. As well, that arrangement suggests a relationship between the host and the guest: This is an interview. The host sometimes leans toward the guest, which suggests closeness, or nods in agreement or makes friendly jokes, which suggests intimacy but not exactly equality. The host is still the important figure here. When a visual space has a left-to-right orientation (as when a host is interviewing a guest), it is common to see the newest or most important element placed on the right side of the space.

This type of visual arrangement is less common in daytime talk than it is in late-night shows. The *Rosie O'Donnell Show* uses the late-night arrangement, but in most of daytime talk, the host does not at all occupy the same visual space as the guest. As you consider such issues as why critics charge daytime talk with putting their guests on display, take note of where and how those guests are placed in the visual space and where and how the host is placed in relation to them.

- *Pay attention to camera space.* Camera space is composed of what you see and how close it appears to you. The director can ask for a close-up (head and shoulders), a medium close-up (chest, head, shoulders), a medium shot (waist on up), a full shot (head to toes), or a wide shot (the camera takes in the entire set or stage). Sometimes on daytime talk, you will also see an extreme close-up, a shot that takes in only the face or even just part of the face.

Generally, you might say that the closer the camera is to a subject, the more intimate the feeling, and of course the director is likely to put in close-up what is most important. Very often on daytime talk, the camera gets close enough to a guest telling a disturbing story for us to see tears or a trembling lip. If the camera gets too close, however, viewers are likely to feel uncomfortable, and the guest might look somewhat distorted. The opposite is true, as well. You might consider what it means if a guest breaks down in shoulder-shaking sobs, yet the camera remains at a distance. How might your reaction change when the camera refuses to move in?

The wide shot, the broadest view of the stage or set, is certainly the most impersonal of these shots. It provides a general overview of the stage or set, and it takes in as broad a view

A typical daytime talk TV host-guest arrangement.

as possible. When the camera shows a wide shot, take note of how guests are placed on the stage and the effect the wide shot has on the way you as a viewer relate to them.

Notice, as well, how the host normally is shot. Is there a difference when the host is talking intimately to the viewing audience, standing among the studio audience, or directing questions at guests?

On interview-based shows, either the host or the guest often takes up the entire camera space. This is especially true when guests are famous personalities. The director might use a technique like *shot/reverse shot,* in which the camera switches back and forth from one person speaking to the other. When this happens, each speaker is given the full attention of the camera. On the *Oprah* show, when Madonna appeared in her first interview after the birth of her child, the camera rarely took in both women at the same time. When Madonna told the story of losing her mother early in life, the camera slowly moved closer and closer to take in her face as the emotion of the story rose. As the story concluded, the camera slowly backed off to the more normal head and shoulders close-up. That kind of camera movement can indicate a certain empathy with the storyteller. It also allows the viewer to visually take the place of the interviewer (so it seems that Madonna is answering *our* questions, not Oprah's).

That sort of empathy is, however, much less common when the storyteller is not a celebrity, and it very rarely happens with a line-up of guests who are all telling their stories at the same time. Pay attention, then, to those times a guest you would identify as just an ordinary person is treated in the same way a celebrity is treated. How might that camera treatment affect the way you respond to the guest's story?

The Viewing Audience

- *Note the advertisers for these shows*. Different daytime talk shows carry different kinds of sponsors. The type of sponsor often indicates the general audience for the show. For example, if a show primarily is sponsored by baby products, this show's sponsors believe that the primary audience is made up of parents or caretakers (mostly mothers) who are home with young children. If the show has a series of psychic network ads, the show may be aiming at a different audience. That doesn't leave stay-at-home parents out. It just suggests there might be others, say young people watching between classes, or singles looking for something new or different in their lives.

- *Note the time of day the show airs*. Because daytime talk is often developed and marketed independently of networks, local stations make their own choices about when to air shows. The choices they make have much to do with the audience these stations think they will draw. A show that airs after school, for example, is going to have a better chance of having a teenaged audience than a show that airs at 9 A.M. A show that airs at or around noon can pick up students and office workers on break. Look for details such as these during your observation. You'll need to do further research in media publications like *Advertising Age* or in trade magazines like *Variety* if you really want to know who the industry has identified as the audience for a particular show.

SUGGESTIONS FOR VIEWING

1. Choose any daytime talk TV show that is issue-oriented. Watch the show and take notes using the suggestions above as a guide. You will find it useful if you break the show into timed segments and summarize what happens as you watch. Use the commercial breaks as the boundaries for

each segment, but be sure to note down how much time has elapsed during each segment. In the accompanying box, we have reproduced a sample program model from Jane Shattuc's *The Talking Cure*. Use it as a model for your own notes.

Program Model

Segment One, 13–17 min.	**Exposition:** Introduction of subject, the problem/conflict, the guests/characters (usually three parallel examples/narrative). Set up of archetypical structure. Host functions as perfect listener. The longest segment because of the amount of narrative detail.
Segment Two, 6–9 min.	**Establishment of Conflict:** The audience begins asking questions, fleshing out the conflict. They move from listeners to characters in the narrative by paralleling their experiences.
Segment Three, 4–6 min.	**Further Complication:** Divisions between guests and/or audience members grow. Expert is introduced. She/he complicates narrative by adding a new level of conflict/understanding.
Segment Four, 3–6 min.	**Questioning the Expert:** The audience begins to question the expert's interpretation. Often new guests are introduced on stage or in the audience, complicating the range of resolutions. The host may move from perfect listener to narrator/character by offering personal experiences.
Segment Five, 2–5 min.	**Beginning of Resolution:** The expert begins to offer a resolution. The guests/characters question and discuss the viability of expert's resolution. The host begins to support the expert's resolution. The audience begins to side or break with the expert's resolution.
Segment Six, 2–5 min.	**Resolution Development:** The resolution is discussed more and moves toward affirmation.
Segment Seven, ½–2 min.	**Coda:** Short speech by expert on answer to conflict or short statements by guests and/or audience members affirming their personal resolutions.

Source: Jane M. Shattuc, *The Talking Cure*, p. 77.

---

2. Write a brief description of how the show looks. (See the sample description.) Pay attention to what occupies the screen space. Where is the host in relation to the guests? How are guests shot? How are they arranged on the set? In this description, you won't be able to record everything you see, but try to describe what seems important to you about the way the show looks. It might help if you roughly sketch out relationships in visual diagrams.

Sample Description

I watched an episode of the show *In Person* with Maureen O'Boyle. It airs at 9 A.M. EST in my area. The show began with the host (O'Boyle) interviewing only one guest, a girl suffering from anorexia. They were seated in comfortable chairs angled toward one another (O'Boyle on the left side speaking to the guest on the right side of the screen). A small living room table was between them. Mostly, they were shot in close-up and medium close-up and only rarely did the camera show them both. It was usually a shot of the host and then a shot of the guest answering her questions (shot/reverse shot).

After the first break, O'Boyle moved from the stage into the audience, and the guest was seated in a much less comfortable-looking chair facing the host and audience. As the show progressed, more guests were brought on, each with a different eating disorder and accompanied by family and friends. They were all seated up on the stage lined up in the less comfortable chairs. The original chairs and table disappeared from the set entirely. O'Boyle never came back to the stage during the rest of the show. She stayed in the audience.

At one point late in the show, O'Boyle was shown standing in a spot somewhere above the audience and the stage. The camera was behind her shoulder so that viewers would see a wide shot of the stage with all of the guests lined up and part of the audience looking at them, giving the impression that home viewers were up above the audience standing next to the host who was looking down at the guests lined up below and in a distance.

3. Talk television does have its own predictable patterns, much in the same way that news programming, soap operas, sitcoms, public-television nature shows, or network television dramas have predictable patterns. You'll notice that in her program model, Jane Shattuc identifies a general pattern from the introduction of the problem or conflict through complications, the advice of experts, and the resolution. One of the tasks you might undertake, then, is to determine what the daytime talk TV pattern tends to be and what it tells viewers about what to expect from these shows. Is there a beginning, middle, and end to the show you watched? How is the problem or conflict resolved? If there is an expert (a child or family counselor, for example), what role does the expert play in drawing the program to a conclusion? For example, the pattern established by the O'Boyle show in our sample description introduced a problem (mothers and daughters with eating disorders), illustrated the problem with examples of women who were struggling with it, and concluded with the advice of experts telling the guests that there is a solution. (See the sample program summary.)

Sample Program Summary

The episode of *In Person* that I watched, "Mothers and Daughters with Eating Disorders," did conform closely to Shattuc's program model. It began with an exposition of the problem, set up conflicts with additional guests, complicated the conflict when the audience entered the discussion, called upon an expert to give advice, and moved toward resolution with the expert, audience, and host all giving the mothers and daughters advice.

Exposition: The program began with the host Maureen O'Boyle interviewing an anorexic teenage girl. This interview set the show and its topic up, and the girl was given a lot of time to talk about her problem, which she blamed on her parents and which she has now seemingly gotten some control of, though she is 5'3" and only weighs about 70 pounds. She talked about going into therapy and moving in with another family and about how serious this problem is for other girls. When the audience talked to her, they mostly congratulated her on her courage, said they would pray for her, or asked if she was continuing her psychotherapy. It was a friendly and supportive response that may have been encouraged by the host-guest set-up. Both were seated in comfortable chairs with the girl on the right side of the space, drawing attention to her as someone the audience should listen to.

Establishment of Conflict: After the first commercial break, O'Boyle had moved away from the girl to stand in the audience. The girl was alone on stage in a much less comfortable chair, looking very awkward. The host stood in the audience surrounded by people all looking at the girl and eager to ask questions or give advice if they were called on.

Further Complication: When the next series of guests came on, though, the atmosphere became very tense. These new guests were all lined up with their mothers, friends, and family members. The first was a 12-year-old girl who weighed 210 pounds and who couldn't stop eating. Her mother was accused by the audience and by other guests of not caring enough for the girl to help her. The next was a young mother of three who was bulimic, and she was given sympathy but warned that she had children to think of. Both the overeater and the bulimic acknowledged that they didn't know what to do about their problems. I did think the two women who were starving themselves were given more sympathy than the overeater. The comments people were making to the overeater and her mother (also an overeater) suggested that the audience thought they should just learn to control themselves.

Resolution: At the end of the show, the host called in a counselor to ask what these guests could do about their problems. The counselor only had about 5 minutes of the program time, but she gave each one a one- or two-line quick fix diagnosis that seemed to come down to the suggestion that they all needed to learn to like themselves better. The host ended the show by warning parents that they could be responsible for their children's problems.

Analyze your notes, and look for patterns. Write a summary of the show that indicates the pattern on which the show you watched relies.

4. Write your own response to the show or shows you have watched. Pay particular attention to what interests you about the show as well as what bothers you. Did you find yourself identifying with any of the guests or having trouble understanding their dilemmas? Did the show sometimes seem comic to you? Sometimes tragic? You don't need to answer these particular questions in your response, but you should do your best to explain how you have responded to the show you have been watching. (See the sample program response.)

Sample Program Response

When I watch a program like the *In Person* episode on eating disorders, I get sad and mad and uncomfortable and impatient all at once. I know that doesn't narrow my response very well, but it's accurate.

I do feel sad for the girl with the eating disorder. A 12-year-old who already weighs 210 pounds is going to have a rough time. Kids at school will be horrible to her. Clothes won't fit right. She'll just end up mad at everybody—herself probably most of all. But I'm also pretty mad at the moms, and I wonder how much the show set me up for that. If the only thing a mother can do is put a padlock on the refrigerator door but sneak in there herself to eat whatever she wants, that won't work. Besides, how can you control a kid when you can't control yourself? That's what the audience said, too, and that's what made me uncomfortable. The mothers were all targeted as the "cause" of their daughters' problems. They were being accused of being fat and letting their daughters get fat. There was no one (at least no one given the chance to speak up) who pointed out that, if the mothers had eating disorders, they also needed help. Accusing them of being bad mothers wasn't going to do much. And I was impatient with what I saw because you think you are going to hear some sympathy for the plight of women and girls with eating disorders. But the only sympathy on the show was for the girl who was anorectic. She got applause and congratulations for facing her problem. And her problem was treated as something very serious. The fat girls were just told to stop eating so much, as if that was such an easy thing to do. To me, it seemed the old stereotypes of thin women having control and heavy women being sloppy and out of control were just reinforced on a show that I thought was going to be about solutions.

This topic (mothers and daughters with eating disorders) made it easy for the host, the audience, and the guests to blame the mothers for their daughters' problems. There wasn't much of an attempt to deal with the mothers' problems. The mothers just came off as bad parents who set a bad example with their eating habits. The guest line-up also focused on this as a female problem and one related to self-esteem. It was interesting, though, that while the audience sympathized with the anorectic and the bulimic and told them they had to like themselves and not rely on others for approval, they suggested to the 12-year-old overeater that she would probably get a date if she would lose weight.

SUGGESTIONS FOR DISCUSSION

1. Share with several classmates the visual description and the pattern summary you wrote. Are shows significantly different in the way they look or in the patterns on which they rely? What are some of the similarities you and your classmates could note? What does the look of the show and the way it is structured indicate about who the viewers might be, how guests are treated, or how an audience might respond to the show's content?

2. How were the guests identified on the show you watched? Is the charge some critics make that these are freak shows that demean the guests and trivialize issues one that might be supported in the ways guests are visually arranged or described? Some television critics argue that daytime talk TV gives outcasts and working-class people a chance to talk. To what extent does the visual arrangement of guest/host/audience make that chance to speak possible?

3. Bring to class a list of the advertisers who sponsored the show you watched. With a group of classmates, discuss whom the sponsors seem to identify as a likely audience for each of the shows your group watched. In what way does the content or look of the show seem to be aimed at particular audiences?

4. Share the response you wrote with several of your classmates. How would you compare the way each of you sees daytime talk TV? How does your response, and the responses of classmates, help explain the popularity of these shows?

FIELD WORK — *LISTENING TO VIEWERS*

By using the strategies for reading daytime talk TV, you can come to your own conclusions about what you see and how you feel about that programming. That is a good start for writing about any topic, but if you really want to know what viewers think about daytime talk, you have to ask them by conducting interviews. Despite critics' charges of "trash TV," these shows must have a very large following or it simply would not profit networks to carry them. It can be very helpful then—especially if you are not a regular viewer yourself—to try to understand what people see in daytime talk and why they watch.

The kind of information you can get from interviews is different from the information you would get doing other kinds of research. What you are after in an interview is learning what appeals to individual viewers or draws even occasional viewers to this programming. While these viewers will not be able to speak for the entire viewing audience, they will give you insight into the variety of reasons people watch and the many ways they respond to these shows. What appeals to one will certainly not appeal to all. What seems funny to some will seem tragic to others. So, while you won't be able to take one person's view as representative of the entire audience, you will have a fuller understanding of the audience after you have interviewed a few people than you had when you were relying on your own observations and responses alone.

SUGGESTED ASSIGNMENT FOR LEARNING FROM VIEWERS

Locate three people who watch daytime talk shows. They don't have to be daily viewers, but they should be viewers who tune in somewhat regularly, catch the shows whenever they can, or have been viewers in the recent past. Following the suggestions outlined below, interview them and write a one-page summary for each interview.

Conducting Interviews

- *Choosing subjects to interview.* To get the best information from viewers of daytime talk, you need to choose people who actually watch or who have watched these shows. Don't bother interviewing people who just have an opinion about daytime talk TV. As you might have already discovered by talking with classmates, many people have opinions about this programming whether they watch it or not. Your aim in these interviews is to find out what viewers see in daytime talk. That doesn't mean the viewers you choose have to take daytime talk seriously. They might watch because they think it is high comedy. They might watch because they like certain hosts or programs that have famous guests. No matter. Just be sure, before you decide to interview them, that they are or have been daytime talk TV viewers.

- *Preparing your subject for the interview.* Make an appointment for the interview, and be on time. Choose a private place to conduct the interview so that you and your subject can concentrate and feel comfortable that others aren't listening in. Tell your subject how much time you will be spending on the interview. Give your subject a general idea of the kinds of questions you will be asking. Tell your subject why you want this information. If you plan to use the subject's name in class discussion or a paper, get permission and make arrangements to show your subject your summary from the interview or any other material that you will be using. That way, you can be sure that you are representing the interview as accurately as possible.

- *Preparing yourself for the interview.* Before you meet with the subject, make a list of questions you want to be sure to ask. Some will be obvious and require a very brief response. For example, you will want to know what show or shows the subject watches or has watched. You will also want to know how often the subject watches the programs. Most questions, however, should be open-ended—they should not lead to a yes or no response. You want to know why they watch, what they like, and how they respond to the situations or guests on the shows—information that is not necessarily easy even for a fan to explain. You might ask your subject to describe a show or scene from a show that they remember or respond to strongly. This type of interview prompt can jog the subject's memory and lead to useful discussion. To a large extent, then, whom you talk to and the show or shows you are discussing will determine what you ask.

- *Conducting the interview.* Ask open-ended questions. Listen. Don't interrupt. Ask follow-up questions. Take notes. Of course, that means you have to concentrate carefully on what your subject is saying and do your best to write down the substance of what you hear. You won't get as many direct quotes, but you may be able to focus much better on what is being said if you have to take notes. Be sure to occasionally restate what you hear just to check yourself. ("Are you saying that…?") Let the subject speak as much as possible. Wait and be willing to sit through silent moments while your subject thinks about how to answer your question. If the interview strays too far from your topic, be careful to bring the discussion back to the topic. You want useful information about what viewers see in and how they respond to this programming. Before you end your interview, take a few minutes to summarize the content of the interview. Recount important points in order to give the subject time to add or correct information. It will give you a chance to gather your thoughts on what you have learned.

   If you are worried that you aren't used to taking such careful notes, use a tape recorder as a back up. Remember that, while the recording will give you an accurate record of the interview, it may make your subject feel uncomfortable, and there is always a chance of mechanical failure. Don't count solely on the tape recording to capture the interview. Even if you tape, take notes and use the recording only to check your memory.

- *Writing up your notes.* Don't delay. Make sure that you make time right after the interview to go over your notes and write a summary of what you have heard. The longer you wait, the harder it will be to remember what you asked, why you asked it, and what some of the answers meant. This will be a good time to find places in your notes that need clarification. If you find such places, make sure you get back to the subject quickly to ask questions that will help you write the most accurate summary you can.

- *Conducting other interviews*. The first interview that you conduct will probably help you decide what you want to ask in future interviews. If you interview someone who watches and laughs at talk shows, for example, it will be useful to try to find someone who takes them more seriously or who watches for reasons that the first subject didn't mention. Remember that one important reason for interviewing more than one subject is to get as much information as possible. If you get conflicting stories about what appeals to viewers about daytime talk, the differences simply offer richer data.

Sample Interview Summary

Kelsey Young is a first-year student at Clemson University. She has watched most of the popular programs for several years but especially since she moved into the dorm with her friends. Her favorites are *Jerry Springer* and *Ricki Lake* because, as she says, "When you turn on these shows you can always count on a good laugh." That is her primary reason for watching daytime talk TV, and she says it is the reason her friends watch it too. When something especially outrageous is happening on one of these shows ("*Jerry Springer* always has at least one fist fight, one drag queen, and one prostitute on in a week," she says), she and her friends call each other. Even if it's early in the morning, they will wake each other up to see what is happening on the shows.

For Kelsey, "These shows are nothing but pure entertainment," especially for the college students she knows who watch them. She doesn't take the shows seriously, so she disagrees with anyone who wants to police the content of daytime talk TV. "People think that they are filthy trash that have no right to be on the air," she told me. "But as long as people continue to watch and the ratings continue to stay high, the TV talk show will live on." She doesn't reject the idea that the shows might be harmful for people who do take them seriously, especially younger children. Still, for Kelsey, the issue seems to be that different audiences see different things in these shows, and she and her friends see them as high comedy and as a part of their social world.

Presenting Your Findings

With a group of two or three of your classmates, share the interviews you have summarized. As a group, use these interviews for a report on the various purposes daytime talk TV serves for its audience. If anyone in your group draws information from the Internet, incorporate those findings into your report as well. You can write up the report as a group or present your findings to the class orally.

If you write the report, be sure to set aside enough time (at least one week) to collaborate with the members of your group. An oral report should take at least one class period to collaborate on the findings from individual interviews and approximately 10 to 15 minutes to present those findings to the class. In either written or oral reports, you will want to draw upon quotes or other specific references when they are especially useful for a point you want to make.

Suggestions for Group Presentations

When you are assigned a group report, it is tempting to ask each member of the group to report on their individual findings. That might seem to be the most efficient way to prepare your presentation, but it may not lead to the most effective way to present your material. As you probably discovered when you wrote your group paper, you will first have to identify what your separate findings have in common and what generalizations you can come to from all of the interview data. You won't be able to detail every interview individually, so you will want to draw on the most interesting, surprising, or provocative information resulting from the interviews. That means you will have to meet beforehand, agree on the central idea you want to convey, and choose details from your paper to demonstrate that idea. You might want to present an outline of your paper on an overhead projector or make use of interesting quotes so that your audience can follow exactly what you are reading. If you choose one person from the group to make the presentation, other group members should contribute fully in preparing the talk. More than one person can give a presentation like this, but it takes coordination. You should generally know what everyone is going to say and make sure you all agree about the point you want to get across in your presentation. Watch your time carefully, and don't overwhelm the class with handouts or compli- cated overheads.

READING ABOUT DAYTIME TALK TV

Now that you have watched daytime talk, interviewed others, and thought about how view- ers respond to this programming, you are ready to investigate public debates over the worth, appropriateness, and effects of daytime talk TV. In what follows, we have chosen a series of articles that present for you a short case study of the debate over tabloid TV as a conveyor of standards and tastes. They appeared in 1995–98 in magazines, newspapers, and book-length studies of television talk shows. If you were to do your own search of newspaper and maga- zine articles on daytime talk television, these are the kinds of articles you would easily dis- cover. Even a quick look through the *Reader's Guide to Periodic Literature* would take you to most of these sources and many others like them.

Much of what you would discover would be critical of talk TV, but not all. A good deal of what is written about talk TV is published in entertainment industry magazines like *TV Guide, People Weekly,* or *Variety,* where you can find information about shows' ratings, pro- files of the hosts, short favorable reviews, and previews of upcoming shows—information that can be very useful if you want to know more about how these shows are promoted by the industry and received by the viewing audience.

Reading Strategies

Before you begin reading, let's briefly summarize the reading strategies that we recommend you follow. You will be familiar with many of these strategies because you have used them throughout the course of your education, probably with varying degrees of success. Still, it can be useful to look at them again and very consciously work through these readings using strate- gies that help you get as much as possible from what you read. All of them involve writing,

If you have access to the Internet, you are very likely to find Web pages and chat lines dealing with many of the most popular daytime talk shows. For example, as of this writing, fans have put together a Richard Bey Unofficial Web page in which viewers claim they watch the show because it is the worst talk show on daytime TV. This page lists recent topics and the ten worst quotes from recent shows. The page even has images of guests or scenes from the show.

Many of the companies that distribute talk TV shows have Web pages, so you can also find official pages for such shows as *Ricki Lake, Jenny Jones,* or *Jerry Springer*. To locate pages on daytime talk TV, use a search engine like Yahoo and enter key words. By entering the words *talk+shows*, we found 234 sites for shows as varied as *Rosie O'Donnell* and *Talk Soup*. You can narrow your search by typing in a host's name; for example, *Jenny+Jones* will take you to the official *Jenny Jones* site. The words *Jerry+Springer* will take you to the official site and to several unofficial fan sites. By accessing these pages and locating chat lines discussing the shows, you can find even more information about what viewers are saying about daytime talk. Remember, though, that an "official" site is likely to be sponsored by the corporation sponsoring the show. Warner Brothers maintains the *Jenny Jones* site. Universal Studios maintains the *Jerry Springer* site. Such sites might offer chat lines or opportunities for fan feedback, but they are primarily there to promote the show and the personality. Fan sites might be more free wheeling, but those sites represent anything the fan wants to say and might include parodies or unsubstantiated rumors.

What you can get from all of these sites, however, is a good sense of what fascinates people about the shows and how the shows represent themselves. If you visit these sites, you can use the information you gather there to more fully explain fan response to and popularity of the shows. Use that information in your report on viewers.

and all of them can help you both to read more carefully and to write your way into the texts you're reading as you work to develop your own position or analysis.

1. *Underlining or highlighting:* Most students underline or highlight what they are assigned to read—whether it's a textbook, a journal article, or a novel. The purpose of this practice is to catch the key points or memorable passages so that you can return to them easily when you need to study for a test, write a paper, or simply review for yourself a writer's point. This strategy works best if you keep in mind that you are looking for key points or noteworthy moments in the writing. If you underline or highlight too much of a reading selection, the strategy isn't likely to work well at all.

2. *Annotating:* Sometimes as students underline, they also write comments in the margins of the book or article they are reading. This practice, annotation, is a more active kind of reading than underlining because it provides the reader with a written record of his or her experience of the text. It offers readers a technique to write their way into the text. Annotations might include one- or two-word paraphrases of the content, notes on how the writer has structured the piece of writing ("important transition" or "key supporting evidence" or "refutes opposing views"), reactions ("I don't think so"), or questions about difficult passages. Not everything you read, of course, is worth annotating. You can probably,

for example, read the press release below and simply use underlining. But for many kinds of writing, annotation can be a valuable way to read and keep track of what you are read-ing. You'll find that you are beginning to get a fuller understanding of what the writer is saying when you annotate as well as underline or highlight more difficult assignments.

3. *Summarizing:* Not many students who underline or annotate what they read take the next step to summarize. This is unfortunate because summarizing allows you to spend time thinking through what you have read. To do a good job, you will want to be faithful to what the writer has said as you briefly rewrite the assigned reading in your own words. In this way, writing summaries can take you a step beyond what you have gained by underlining and annotating. Summarizing builds on these activities by providing you with an accurate account of what you have been reading. This strategy can be enor-mously useful in order to understand the material that you are reading.

4. *Exploratory writing:* Many students use a reading notebook to gather their exploratory writ-ing, though it isn't necessary. Exploratory writing offers a way to think out loud—on paper—about what you have been reading. It allows you to go beyond summary and anno-tation and actually to begin to make decisions about what you have read, what else it con-nects to, how it helps you understand other issues, or how it seems to confuse an issue. One way to think about exploratory writing is that it offers a means to test your responses to the public issues about what you have been reading. With exploratory writing, you can experiment with ways of explaining and justifying your own reactions so that others will take them seriously, if not necessarily agree with them wholesale. If you have underlined, annotated, and summarized a reading selection, you might think of exploratory writing as a fuller expression of what you have already written. Through exploratory writing you will begin to bring that selection into focus, even to draw inferences from and stake out your own position in relation to it. Exploratory writing can sound quite personal in tone, but it isn't exactly private either. It is a kind of halfway house, in between the reactions you recorded in those annotations ("this is truly idiotic" or "I couldn't agree more") and the public voice you eventually will need to assume in a more formal, deliberative essay. We offer a sample of exploratory writing later in this chapter. As you will see, it is not the kind of writing you would give to a teacher for a grade, but it is a way of getting there.

5. *Synthesis:* When you do research, as in the case study we have set up for you on daytime talk TV, you not only need to explore your own responses to what individual writers have said and how they have said it. You also need to compare how these writers have written on the same topic, how they have positioned themselves in different ways in relation to what other writers have argued, or how they have identified a different set of issues to address within the topic at hand. Comparing writers' positions and per-spectives to see how they work in relation to one another is what we call *synthesis*. Syn-thesis literally means to combine several separate elements or substances in order to create something new. To synthesize the arguments from two or more writers, then, you are likely to look for places where the writers share common ground, where they depart from one another, and how one writer's position might help you understand the other writer's position. For example, when you read a number of articles on daytime talk TV, you will draw different ideas and positions from each individual article. To write about daytime talk TV in an informed and knowledgeable way means that you have the added task of comparing these separate ideas and positions in a piece of writing that actually charts the field of discussion so that you can figure out how you might enter into it— that is, how you can develop and convey your own position within the larger conver-sation that has already taken place.

Reading and Writing Exercises

We have developed the following reading and writing exercises as a sequence, but they don't necessarily have to be completed in the order we present here. Our intention is to introduce you to a number of strategies for reading and writing, but we certainly don't assume that all writers doing research will necessarily follow each of the steps in a predetermined order. These are flexible strategies that can be combined in a number of ways. We'll leave it up to you and your teacher to determine what you want to do with them.

Exercise One Read Bennett's "Announcing a Public Campaign Against Select Day-Time Television Talk Shows" and Abt and Mustazza's "Coming After Oprah: Cultural Fallout in the Age of the TV Talk Show." Note that we have underlined, annotated, and summarized the Bennett announcement. Underline, annotate, and summarize the excerpt from Abt and Mustazza.

Suggestions for Underlining

When the work you need to do is a matter of extracting information and getting the facts, details, and issues clear in your mind, it is of benefit to turn to underlining or highlighting what you are reading. It gives you a way to recall key points when you go back to a textbook to study for a test. As well, it's a good way to keep the details of the article straight as you read. Keep in mind, though, that you will defeat the purpose if you underline or highlight too much text. Underline key points, passages, or ideas that strike you as important, interesting, or just worth going back to for reference.

Suggestions for Annotating

You may have already experienced one problem when you have underlined text but not annotated. Very often the thoughts that made you want to underline or highlight a passage in the first place are very difficult to recall when you go back to the text later. Annotations help to anchor those underlinings to your ideas, your reactions, and your ways of understanding what is being said in a reading selection. As we mentioned earlier, the purpose of annotating is to give you a means of writing your way into a text. Annotations can be paraphrases (these are really brief one- or two-word summaries), reactions, questions, or observations on how the writer has structured the piece of writing and what assumptions are being made. There is no one right way to annotate readings, so with practice you will develop your own techniques—which makes annotating a useful and active way to write as you read.

Suggestions for Summarizing

Once you have underlined and annotated, you might feel you have done enough. After all, it's reasonable to assume that you can always go back to what you underlined if you want to remember what you have read. We recommend, however, that you take one further step and write a summary of what you have read. This, of course, will involve rereading and noticing what you underlined and perhaps what you may have missed during the first reading. You'll want the summary to be in your words, not the writer's, but you will also want your summary to be faithful to the article you have read. This isn't the place for you to record your reactions to the article. Reactions should come in an exploratory writing. This is the place for you to try your best to understand what the writer has said.

Announcing a Public Campaign
Against Select Day-Time Television Talk Shows

William Bennett

William Bennett has served as Secretary of Education and has been an outspoken proponent of such issues as promoting "family values" in the media. He helped lead the organization Empower America in its campaign to force Time Warner to divest of its interest in rap groups he and others in the organization considered pornographic or advocates of violence. On October 26, 1995, he joined Senator Joe Lieberman of Connecticut in a press conference to announce what Bennett called a "Resistance Operation" and Lieberman called "the revolt of the revolted," a move to ask advertisers and viewers to boycott those daytime talk TV programs Bennett and Lieberman labeled "giant cultural sleaze." We found his comments on the Internet through the site http://www.townhall.com, a conservative coalition website. Bennett's argument is clearly *adversarial* and confrontational. It announces a position and calls for action. Keep that in mind as you read.

Sample Summary

In his press conference announcement, William Bennett explains why he thinks daytime talk television shows are having a bad influence on the American public and why we should try to do something about that. Bennett begins by charging daytime television talk with being morally degrading, the worst that television has to offer. He calls them "the bottom of the television barrel" and lists Sally Jessy Raphael, Ricki Lake, and Jerry Springer as specific targets for his campaign.

Bennett then tells his audience that he and Senator Joe Lieberman will be issuing a call for sponsors, producers, advertisers, and viewers to pull their support from this programming that is, he writes, the "pollution of the human environment." Bennett concludes his announcement by linking his campaign both to religion and to patriotism and says that the campaign is about "the dignity of God's greatest creation."

[handwritten margin notes: "against the exploited daytime talk shows." / "Purpose? To stop watching these shows"]

[handwritten note below box: "calls 4 immediate attention"]

Notice in the sample that our underlinings and annotations helped us summarize Bennett's announcement. We did not include our reactions to the article because reactions are more appropriate for an exploratory writing where you will record your own response to what is written. We have also incorporated *brief quotes* into our summary. By quoting a few short passages, you are reminding yourself of those parts of a reading that you find the most important to recall and restate.

As you compose a comparable summary of the Abt and Mustazza article, make sure to incorporate brief quotes into your writing. Remember that Abt and Mustazza are writing a *critique* about the nature of much daytime talk TV. In your underlinings and annotations, pay attention to how Abt and Mustazza set up their argument and how the language they have chosen might shape public opinion.

First, I want to express my thanks to Senator Joe Lieberman. Senator Lieberman is the father of this idea. It was his suggestion that we continue to bring pressure -- public pressure -- on the perpetrators of cultural rot by calling attention to these shows.

Earlier this year, Senator Lieberman joined C. DeLores Tucker of the National Political Congress of Black Women and me in our campaign to urge Time Warner to sell their stake in Interscope Records, Inc. Today, we turn our attention to television. Now these days there is a lot of criticism directed at television the casual cruelty, the rampant promiscuity, the mindlessness of sit-coms and soap operas. Most of the criticisms are justified. But this is not the worst of it. The worst of television is the day-time television talk shows we have identified. In these shows, indecent exposure is celebrated as a virtue.

This is what I think. A lot of it is junk.

It is hard to remember now, but there was once a time when personal or marital failure, subliminal desires, and perverse taste were accompanied by guilt or embarrassment. But today, these conditions are a ticket to appear as a guest on the Sally Jessy Raphael show, the Ricki Lake show, the Jerry Springer show, or one of the dozen or so like them.

old enough to remember + wiser, + patriotic, + religious

I asked my staff to provide me with a list of some of the shows of some recent day-time talk-show topics. The list included "A Mother Who Ran Off with Her Daughter's Fianc ," "Women Who Marry Their Rapists," "I'm Marrying a 14-year old Boy," a woman who claims she got pregnant while making a pornographic movie; a 13-year-old guest who was urged to share her sexual experiences which began when she was 10; a woman eight months pregnant who boasted of having eight sexual partners during her first two trimesters; a 17-year-old girl who boasted of having slept with over a hundred men -- well, you get the idea. It is important here to point out who we are not talking about. We are not talking about shows like Oprah, or Regis and Kathie Lee. The shows which are the object of our criticisms are not close calls; they go way over the line of decency. They are at the bottom of the television barrel. Instead of simply lamenting the state of our popular culture, we think it's a good idea to try and do something about it. So here we are.

Does this mean he hasn't watched it himself? Then how would he know?

I wonder what else he'd put in that barrel.

Okay, like what!

[handwritten: very patriotic; Need to make our country more moral]

Our objectives are these: <u>to raise a hue and cry across the</u> *[handwritten: Sounds like the charge of the light brigade.]* <u>land</u>; to cast some light on what's being produced and distributed— "Sunlight is the best disinfectant," Justice Brandeis once wrote; and <u>to</u> <u>petition men and women of good will—producers, sponsors,</u> <u>advertisers, and viewers—to rethink their support and sponsorship,</u> <u>participation and promotion of these programs.</u>

[handwritten: good question—some of this seems liks an over reaction]

<u>What exactly is the harm being done by these programs?</u> In his "Letter from Birmingham City Jail," Martin Luther King, Jr. instructed us that that which "uplifts human personality" is just and that which "degrades human personality" is unjust. <u>Can anybody doubt that these</u> *[handwritten: degrade human personality?]* <u>shows degrade human personality?</u> Do the sponsors think not? If so, why not?

Let me try and put this campaign in a broader context of the state of our popular culture, our country, and our civilization. <u>What is</u> *[handwritten: What does this mean? I'd better look it up.]* <u>happening today is the pollution of the human environment</u>, a kind of <u>tropism</u> toward the sordid. This nation desperately needs more oppor- tunities for moral uplift. We believe that progress can be made through moral <u>suasion</u> and justifiable public discontent.

In a fundamental way, that is what this effort and efforts like it are all about. <u>So today we declare ourselves to be part of a Resistance,</u> *[handwritten: Again, talk of the revolution.]* <u>a Resistance Operation to the giant popular culture sleaze machine.</u> We welcome more volunteers to our ranks.

Let me conclude with a personal note. <u>Joe Lieberman is a Jew.</u> *[handwritten: God and patriotism evoked at the end.]* <u>I am a Catholic. Like most Americans, we believe in God</u>; we both believe men and women are His creation, made in His image. And so we believe that men and women should not be celebrated when they debase themselves. Finally, what we are talking about is human dignity, the dignity of God's greatest creation—and whether or not we still believe in it.

[handwritten: Writing to older people]

Coming After Oprah:
Cultural Fallout in the Age of the TV Talk Show

Vicki Abt and Leonard Mustazza

Vicki Abt is Professor of Sociology and American Studies at Pennsylvania State University at Abington. Her work on daytime talk TV first came to national atten- tion when she carried out a content analysis of several popular talk shows in

1991. As a result of her study, she was given a two-day appearance on *The Oprah Winfrey Show* at the opening of the 1994–95 television season to discuss her study published with Mel Seesholtz ("The Shameless World of Phil, Sally, and Oprah: Television Talk Shows and the Deconstruction of Society"). Leonard Mustazza, Distinguished Professor of English and American Studies at Penn State Abington, has published widely on popular culture and on English and American literature.

"Americans Despair of Popular Culture," reads the headline of an article by Elizabeth Kolbert in the Sunday, August 20, 1995, issue of the *New York Times*. The article notes that Americans worry about sex and violence on television and that "they believe there is a direct connection between the fictional world young people are exposed to and the way they behave in real life." "Fictions," or the stores we tell, certainly help create the social "blueprints" of our behavior in real life. What is interesting, however, is that while most Americans at least acknowledge the dangers of violent and sexual images on television and in the movies, they do not appear to be as concerned with the words and images that make up the deceptive world of "reality-based" talk television. The blurring of the worlds of fiction and reality is a recurring theme throughout this book. Surely long-term exposure to this genre has consequences for the way we judge ideas, behaviors, and "values" and the way we respond to "deviance" in terms of defining it, emulating it, or mitigating it. Toxic talk may not seem as obvious in its effects as brutal violence and impersonal sex on the screen, but we believe it is at least as devastating to society at large. Consider what we are watching when we tune in to talk TV:

- Lies, misinformation, and incomplete information about "guests" as instigated or "enabled" by the celebrity-host
- Extreme close-ups of highly personal moments, including family "reunions," surprise encounters, and "outings"
- Wild audience cheering and laughing at inane or "deviant" behavior and responses to questions
- Interruptions of emotionally devastating stories for commercial breaks
- Intimate tales of personal turmoil out of the context of the confessants' ordinary lives
- Audience and guest obsession with extreme, socially uncontrolled behavior
- Guests treated as categories or types in a gallery of social grotesques
- Obliviousness to major social and political issues in favor of "confession"
- Sound-bite pop psychology to address serious pathologies
- Contempt for intellectuals and intellectual debate
- Poor grammar, limited vocabulary, and cliché-ridden language
- Fact undifferentiated from unsupported opinion
- Ignorance of the relationships among manners, morals, and behavior
- The replacement of a sense of history with interest only in personal biography and/or autobiography
- "Victims" obsessed with themselves and seemingly unaware of norms of conduct or etiquette whose violations may contribute to their "victimization"
- Near-monopolistic empires built on our morbid fascination with the dysfunctional and defended on the grounds of "equality" and "free speech"

The deceptions and contradictions are perhaps best exemplified in a September 1995 promo for the 1995–96 season of *The Montel Williams Show*. With words and faces flashing on the screen, the announcer proclaims, "*racist, sexist, activist*...Montel brings us together. *Survivor, deceiver, believer*...It starts with talk; it ends with answers. Montel brings us together." One can only assume from this "message" that there are really no significant differences among us that can't be smoothed over by entertaining talk. (Montel must have been on to something as his show won the daytime Emmy for "best talk show of 1995.") In the 1995–96 season, Montel continued this "therapeutic vein" with a May 1996 program featuring men bragging about having had sex with underaged girls (the girls *and* their mothers were on stage). Messages were then broadcast during the commercial breaks asking, "Are you a teen girl whose parents have kicked you out of the house? If so, call Montel." We can only conclude from this solicitation that the viewing public can expect more shows about the entertaining topic of exploited underage girls.

Surely long-term exposure to these "entertainments" threatens to alter our experience of the reality of social life and ultimately to remake society in its own muddled image. Talk television represents one of the fastest-growing segments of the mass-entertainment market, reaching always lower for emotional jolts, blithely consumed daily by millions. Its subject matter is akin to what Hannah Arendt called "the banality of evil." What was originally shocking has become commonplace, and to achieve the same novel effect—the hook that gets people to watch what they were not intended to see or shouldn't see, at least publicly—legitimate producers have become, in effect, "the new pornographers." In this cultural context, "pornography" implies pandering and commercialism relating to the production and broadcast of material devoid of authentic emotional contexts and calculatedly designed to titillate. Sexual messages are not essential characteristics in this meaning, but rather the cynical distortion of culture for sale.

SUGGESTIONS FOR DISCUSSION

1. Compare with other members of your class the summary you have written of Abt and Mustazza's critique of daytime talk TV. To what extent are the summaries your classmates have written similar? To what extent do they differ? If they differ, how do you account for those differences? Don't assume that one summary is necessarily better or more accurate than another. Instead, try to identify the principles of selection each writer has used. In your discussion, take time to talk about how others' summaries change or add to your own understanding of what the authors are saying in their article.

2. With a group of your classmates, look back at the underlinings and annotations you made in this article. What details, language choices, or incidents seem to each of you particularly striking or crucial for following the argument?

3. Examine Abt and Mustazza's list of "what we are watching when we tune in to talk TV." What argument is that list making about daytime talk TV? What items from the list convince you that talk TV is problematic? What items would you consider not as convincing? With a group of your classmates, prepare your own list of "what we are watching when we tune in to talk TV." To what extent does your list correspond to Abt and Mustazza's? How would you differentiate your list (and the argument you are making with it) from Abt and Mustazza's?

Exercise Two   Read Donna Gaines's "How Jenny Jones Saved My Life: Why William Bennett Is Wrong About Trash TV," underlining and annotating as you read. Respond to the article in an exploratory writing.

Suggestions for Exploratory Writing

The reading strategies we have suggested so far—underlining, annotating, and summarizing—are techniques to gain some control over what a written text is saying and how it says it. These are ways to get to the heart of the matter, to see the writer's central idea, and to understand how writers position themselves in relation to their readers and material.

Exploratory writing, on the other hand, has a different set of purposes. It offers a way to position yourself and your own concerns in relation to what you've read. You might think of yourself as engaging in a kind of conversation with a reading selection—a conversation where you can ask questions, voice confusion, make connections, record ideas, even talk back to and contradict the text if you like.

When you do exploratory writing, you should feel free to take some of the ideas the writer has raised and run with them, even if it seems that this will take you far afield from the reading. You may choose to dwell at length on a particular detail or incident in the reading that strikes you for some reason or another, even if it isn't the main point you'd identify in a summary. You may find that a particular reading selection reminds you of something you know or something you've read in a different context. It can be valuable to record this kind of connection as you write in response to a reading selection. In any case, the point to keep in mind about exploratory writing is that it offers a way to locate your own ideas, attitudes, experiences, and knowledge in relation to what you have just read, to test out those responses and associations to see how they sound, and to decide which ones you might tap for a later, more public, writing.

Perhaps one of the best ways to explain the process is to give you a sample of exploratory writing, in this case written in response to William Bennett's announcement. You should notice how the exploratory writing, though it does pick up on ideas from the text, is much more engaged with the reader's more immediate and even personal response to the ideas represented in the article:

Sample Exploratory Writing

I would like to admit that when I read William Bennett's announcement, I went back and forth between agreeing with him about daytime talk television and wondering where he comes off telling everybody else what to think. I was especially put off by the fact that he asked his staff to make a list of some of the recent shows because that made me wonder if he had any firsthand experience watching them at all. Still, he is right when he suggests that these shows seem to be competing for the sleaziest programming they can possibly get away with.

The question I have, however, is whether or not bad taste is something that is worth spending so much time or thought regulating. And of course I would want to explore how close some of what Bennett says comes to outright censorship.

Finally, I thought it was odd that Bennett told his audience that he was Catholic and Senator Lieberman Jewish and that he linked his campaign to religion and patriotism in the way he did. What about all of those Americans who don't go to church at all? Is this a religious campaign, or is it a campaign that should involve the legislature—which is what I thought he was saying when he brought in Senator Lieberman and C. DeLores Tucker of the national Political Congress of Black Women? I am actually confused about which direction his campaign is taking us, and I would want to know more about what he is asking of the public and of legislators.

As you can see from our sample, exploratory writing does just that—it explores the reader's attitudes about a reading selection, it opens possible directions for further research and examination, and it allows the reader to begin moving toward a position on the subject at hand.

How Jenny Jones Saved My Life:
Why William Bennett Is Wrong About Trash TV

Donna Gaines

Donna Gaines writes for *The Village Voice,* where this article first appeared on November 21, 1995 (pp. 41–43). She holds a master's degree in social work and a PhD in sociology. A portion of her full-length study of teenage life, *Teenage Wasteland* (1990), appears later in this text (see *Generations*). Like Bennett's, Gaines's article takes an adversarial position that is identifiable immediately in her title. Gaines gets at her argument through personal testimony, very much like the testimony heard on much of daytime talk. As you read, pay attention to the way Gaines moves from personal story to her argument with Bennett.

He was the great love of my life, promised to me in the doowop songs of my childhood. He believed we were made of the same DNA, lovers from past lives, fated for all eternity. I was his the moment I saw him standing in the doorway like a young Marlon Brando in his black leathers, sucking a Marlboro. I adored him, wanted to marry him, cook his food, wash his clothes, have his babies. Roland, as I'll call him, is the only man I have ever loved like that.

But Roland also did every mean thing a man can do. He cheated, he lied, and he hurt me—emotionally and sometimes physically. If you ask him now, he'll say I drove him to it, that I did worse things to him, and his friends will back him up. He'll say I manipulated him, was arrogant, never satisfied, "a bitch." My friends thought he was dangerous, bad news. But I loved him. For over three years Roland was the center of my world.

Good chemistry, bad karma. At times I was so exhausted from our drama and fighting, I couldn't get out of bed. I stopped writing, hiking, cruising the Net, playing music, even oiling my guns. I grew out of touch with myself and my life. Eventually my friends and family got tired of hearing about it. They told me I needed help, that I was suffering from battered wife syndrome, and would end up like Nicole. But I knew he really loved me. We just needed time to build trust. My friends said I was in denial.

Dazed and depressed, isolated from the world, I started watching daytime TV talk shows, every day, all day long, back-to-back. *The Jenny Jones Show* was my favorite. I needed a strong woman I could bond with, one who would understand about Roland, be supportive but confrontational too. Ricki Lake had a snotty streak, Sally Jessy Raphael was too judgmental, and Oprah had gotten boring since she moved her show to "higher ground." I was too ashamed to tell my loved ones how bad things had gotten, and the idea of psychotherapy terrified me. But I could tell Jenny about it every day, even twice a day, for almost a year.

Sometimes I imagined myself on the show, sitting next to Roland, crying and holding hands. Jenny would stick up for me, she would ask how I let myself get this low. "You're an attractive, accomplished woman, why would you let someone pour beer over your head and throw you around like a rag doll?" She'd tell Roland, "It's wrong to hurt someone you love." Jenny would understand my pain, but she'd cut Roland some slack too.

After all, Roland and I were prime Jenny material for another reason. Roland was born one year after I graduated high school; he was eight years old when I got my master's degree. Though we both thought the age difference was meaningless, *Jenny Jones* woke me up; one day I tuned in and listened to the story of Jan and Tyler, a hot intergenerational couple who had recently ended their psychotic relationship. In Jan I saw my own capacity for sexual manipulation; in Tyler I saw Roland's vulnerability. Maybe the balance of power was skewed in my favor. Maybe that's what made Roland angry.

Like Jenny says, there's always another side to the story, and Roland and I had actually talked about going for couples counseling. But Jenny and her guests ultimately convinced me that once a guy hurts you, roughs you up, or cheats on you it's foolish to think it won't happen again. I'd watch her and her guests urging passive, defeated women who had been cheated on, beaten, or betrayed to think about their self-esteem. I'd hear the audience label the bad boyfriend a dog. "Kick him to the curb!" they'd yell. I'd hear the bullshit stories the nasty dog would weave, realizing, Hey, that's Roland's game.

Eventually, I saw enough bad relationships and poisoned hearts that I called a therapist (and a psychic). I'd rather not go into any more detail, but in the end Roland and I severed all ties. Without Jenny's support, and her audience invoking societal norms of decency, we might have ended up destroying each other.

Four months later conservative gadfly William Bennett is on TV denouncing my beloved Jenny. Bennett went full metal jacket against the shows, targeting her and Ricki as his least favorite. (Jenny has been an easy mark since last March, when John Schmitz, a male guest on her show, murdered Scott Amedure, who had gone on the air to proclaim his crush on Schmitz.) Pumped up after his assault on gangsta rap forced Time Warner to divest itself of its Interscope subsidiary, Bennett—along with senators Joseph Lieberman and Sam Nunn and C. DeLores Tucker, chair of the National Political Congress of Black Women—is hoping to purge the airwaves of these "culturally corrupt" television shows. He railed against "salacious and sensational accounts of sexual perversion, cruelty, violence, and promiscuity." Under attack were topics like "Women Who Marry Their Rapist" and "Housewives Versus Strippers." (Bennett even lit into one of my favorite *Jenny Jones* episodes, "I'm Marrying a 14-Year-Old Boy," a bittersweet case of an abused woman and a young boy who found True Love. The woman, attractive, in her mid thirties, had been a battered spouse, fearful of men, until her young lover showed her tenderness and respect. The kid was a streetwise throwaway teen, now back in school and off drugs—thanks to her, he says. But everyone came down on them anyway.)

Ground zero for the attack on daytime talk was the recent Talk Summit, a two-day conference in New York City sponsored by Population Communications International, a nonprofit family planning organization. Held at midtown's Millennium Broadway Hotel the summit was designed to bring together top daytime talk show hosts, producers, executives, and leading experts on social and health issues. The conference had been planned for quite a while but coincided with the Bennett blitz, taking place one day after his press conference.

I was supposed to hook up with Andy the *Voice* photographer, outside the hotel. Though camera crews and reporters were everywhere, and I had never met Andy, we located each other immediately in the crowd. I was the only person in leather and lace, and he was the only one with a good haircut, cool glasses, and black jeans. Everyone else was blandly professional-managerial class, ringers for the sartorial abominations I suffer at academic conferences. Andy said we were dressed like we had someplace better to go afterward, and we sure did. Slaves of *The Village Voice,* we were heading downtown later that night to cover a band.

Inside the hotel, the discourse was as creepy as the fashion statements on parade. Talk show host Jerry Springer fielded questions from broadcast TV reporters. How responsible are talk shows for catastrophes like the Amedure murder? How do they safeguard against severe human damage? How much money do the shows make anyway? And what about all the kids watching this sleaze? Springer said the kids always know what's right—whenever he does a show, the young people in his audience boo the cheater, the beater, the racist, and the sexually irresponsible. When they cheer the bad guys, that's when he'll worry. Besides, asked the former Cincinnati mayor, "Who is Washington, D.C., to preach to us about morality?" Springer believes the shows provide the average person with an arena for a celebrity-style tell-all. But that's a mixed blessing; being exposed on national television can leave someone feeling totally exploited. But satisfying the urge to purge has its merits. It's cathartic. Unlike me, not everyone is lucky enough to get paid for writing about their fucked-up situations.

Springer claimed media and government hostility to TV talk shows is elitist. "This is about taste, not morality," he said. And we all know that Bennett, the trench coat guys, the PCI membership don't hang out. They probably can't even dance. Besides, who cares what they think? By now, TV talk shows probably have greater cultural authority than government, schools, the media, the left, or the right. They operate at the level of everyday life where real people live and breathe. Interracial couples are presented as normative, without commentary—or defended when need be. On one *Jenny Jones* a pair of white parents threatened to place their daughter in foster care if she continued seeing her black boyfriend. Jenny confronted them: "Your hatred of blacks is stronger than your love for your daughter!" The audience supported the couple, pleading, "Love sees no color."

And when Bennett et al. blast the "sexual perversity" of daytime TV, it's tough not to wonder if they equate *perversity* and *homosexuality*—the afternoon airwaves are a virtual diorama of gay pride, which must make all the queer kids trapped in the gulag of heterosocialization feel a whole lot better. One of Jenny's festive makeover shows featured lesbians who thought their lovers were "too butch." While all this was in progress one guest stopped the show, got down on her knees, and turned to her mate. "I want to ask you something. I want to know if you will spend the rest of your life with me." I was in tears. Jenny was moved too; she ran the clip twice. Sometimes the audience snickers at moments like this. Maybe they see it as spectacle; maybe they're just nervous.

I had my own problems. After Roland, I met George, who was even younger. My psychic told me don't fight it, it's fated, they'll always be younger (Mars-Mercury conjunction). So I needed support against friends who tried to match me up with "appropriate men" from my generation. I watched Jenny's "Younger Men Who Date Older Women" for tips. Some of the guys were teenagers and that's too much, even for me; they gotta be old enough to drink in a bar legally. The audience judged the couples harshly, saying the women were sickos for being with "children." Younger women were hostile toward the younger men who simply prefer older women. Someone in the audience noted that if it were older men with younger women there would be no complaints. Then I saw some comforting statistics; one-third of the women in my age group, 35–44, are living with younger men. Forty-one percent of them will marry younger men; 23 percent of all American brides will, too. Thanks to Jenny now I know I'm just part of a growing trend.

Bennett's morality squad may see talk shows as carnival freak shows, but all that means is that the shows have the power to drag us statistical outcasts in from the margins. They also loosen things up for the majority of folks back in the dull normal range of the bell curve. But the shows do more than normalize deviance, particularly for young people. The same year Scott Amedure was killed, *Jenny Jones* won an award from the Advocates for Youth foundation for a special episode designed to educate teenagers about AIDS. Not one show goes by without an almost didactic plea to practice safe sex, to respect yourself and your body, to hold out on pregnancy and finish school, so you can see what else is out there in the world.

Back at the conference, I found myself pushed once again to the margins. Despite the publicist's earlier claims, access to the talk show producers was difficult. So I went scamming for free food, fine wine, and career opportunities. I gave out my business card to anyone I spoke to and plugged my book on teenage suicide. Eventually I recognized my true calling: I was Michael Musto's personal emissary to the conference. Everyone who saw my press affiliation asked me about the glamorous columnist and star of E! Network's *Gossip Show*. ("Oh, Musto isn't planning to attend? What's he up to?")

Aside from Musto's fans, I felt totally alienated; most of the reporters there believed, a priori, that talk shows are bad, and they went in with that agenda. One reporter was typical: he said he'd like to see the talk shows on after 10 p.m. He has a six-year-old kid and thinks the stuff is sleaze. Darlene Hayes, executive producer of the *Gabrielle* show, told me she thinks the news media is exploiting the situation to sell papers and boost ratings. They don't want to acknowledge that some Americans live differently. Another talk show representative, speaking off the record, says, "Broadcast news interests are envious of the popularity of talk shows cutting into their turf. They want in on the action."

Although the hot and heavy "expert panel" session was closed to the press "in the interest of uninhibited problem-solving," we had the opportunity to attend a dinner featuring keynote speaker Health and Human Services Secretary Donna Shalala, who recited a depressing list of teenage statistics (every day nearly 1400 teens drop out of school; more than 1000 give birth out of wedlock; approximately 25 are infected with HIV, etc.). She all but admitted that the adult authority structure has failed.

What Shalala couldn't bring herself to acknowledge is that TV talk shows are far more effective in dealing with these issues than anything else out there. Turn them into vehicles for William Bennett's political agenda and you'll alienate the very kids talk shows appeal to. Kids are blessed with bullshit detectors; they instinctively cringe at the formalized "help" adults peddle. Talk shows may be messy and sometimes appalling—*Gabrielle*'s Darlene Hayes, an industry long-timer who used to work for *Donahue,* thinks that the recent surge in talk competition has caused some of the younger producers to get reckless—but that's exactly why young people relate to them.

The day before the conference, talk show host Charles Perez told the *Daily News* that Bennett, a former Education Secretary, ought to "look in his own backyard," given the high number of young people in Perez's audience who can't string together grammatical sentences. It occurred to me then how much more these talk shows do for our nation's youth than any of these people with all their high-minded goals, programs, and good intentions. So I stalked the genuinely charming Perez to thank him for speaking out. He had had a rough time in his press conference and appreciated my support—it seems I was the only non-talk show person there who saw value in what he does.

As I was leaving, Andy introduced me to a talk show host contender, who gave me a demo copy of his *Billy Blank Show*. He had hoped to give his videotape to one of the producers but he was thrown out. Who but two kooks from *The Village Voice* would lend him a sympathetic ear? I promised to watch his video—a touching, sensitive if ditzy New Age talk show in which Billy asks people in the audience and the street if they are happy. What can we do to evolve as humans, to make the world a better place? he wonders. Billy Blank can be reached at 914-961-7302.

As the action died down, Jerry Springer was lurking nearby with Andy. I wanted to invite him and Charles Perez to join us at Squeezebox. We were checking out transexual punk rock legend Jayne County's show. I wondered, what would happen if all the bureaucratic functionaries of the State, the talk show hosts, their producers, the smug liberals, and the media running dogs went to see Jayne's magnificent performance? What if, for one night, they got to be the freaks in our TV show? Hours later as I stood at the foot of Jayne's thumping stage, drinking and dancing, exquisite drag queens, hot queer couples, and dirty girls like me were shaking it everywhere. I felt ecstatic, alive and kicking, and mighty real.

SUGGESTIONS FOR DISCUSSION

1. Gaines's article is easily identifiable as personal story or testimony. Bennett's statement is a much more direct call to action. At what points, and for what purposes does Bennett also draw on the personal?

2. With a group of your classmates, compare the exploratory piece you have each written in response to this selection. How do your responses differ? In what ways are they similar? What about Gaines's article might account for the ways you and members of your group have responded to her work?

3. Near the end of her article, Gaines writes that TV talk shows are more effective at dealing with the problems teens have today "than anything else out there. Turn [talk shows] into vehicles for William Bennett's political agenda and you'll alienate the very kids talk shows appeal to." With a group of your classmates, discuss what Gaines is saying about the worth of campaigns like Bennett's. To what extent do you accept her argument that "Kids are blessed with bullshit detectors"?

Exercise Three   Read Willis's commentary "Bring in the Noise." Summarize it, then write a synthesis of the articles by Bennett, Abt and Mustazza, Gaines, and Willis. In your synthesis, pay attention to the way each of these arguments touches on the discussions of the others. You will note, for example, that Willis mentions both Bennett and Gaines in her discussion. How would you say her argument places her, in some ways, in alliance with Bennett and Abt and Mustazza as well as with Gaines? Where does she depart from them? How would you position your own argument within the spectrum of discussion provided by these writers?

Suggestions for Writing a Synthesis

In preparation for this assignment, you will of course want to reread the articles, but you can also go back and look at those portions of the articles you have underlined as well as at the annotations you have written in margins. If you have summarized articles, those summaries will help you see what each of these writers is doing in their separate discussions. You might think of a synthesis as a place where you report on a conversation: Who said what? Where does each writer stand on the issues? What seems interesting or different? How do their arguments compare to and contrast with one another?

In a synthesis, you are trying to get a handle on how a topic or issue has been discussed by others. Don't offer your opinion on the issues or the way these writers have handled the issues. Later, you will have the opportunity to put forth your opinion. In a synthesis, you simply want to focus on analyzing how different writers have presented a position or an argument.

Bring in the Noise

Ellen Willis

> Ellen Willis writes commentary for *The Nation,* where this article first appeared on April 1, 1996 (pp. 19–23). Willis's commentary is a good example of *cultural analysis.* In writing analysis, Willis does not make a simple argument for or against an issue. Instead, she presents her position within the broader conversation that has already taken place about an issue, suggesting additional ways of talking about an issue or connecting the issue at hand with other related issues and events. As you examine Willis's article in relation to those of Bennett, Abt and Mustazza, and Gaines, you should begin to see how she has managed to demonstrate the complexity of an issue that seems for some writers to be very simple or straightforward.

Whenever the right and the left agree on some proposition about culture, I know it's time to grab my raincoat; and so it is with the incessant demonizing of popular culture and media. Everywhere they look—tabloid television, MTV, *Married...With Children, Pulp Fiction,* gangsta rap, saturation coverage of O. J. Simpson/the Bobbitts/Amy Fisher—politicians and high-minded journalists see nothing but sleaze and moral degradation.

The latest target is daytime TV talk shows. Rumblings began last year when Jonathan Schmitz murdered Scott Amedure, a gay man, after Amedure identified Schmitz as his "secret crush" on *Jenny Jones* [see Jonathan Taylor, "To Die For," *The Nation,* April 3, 1995]. Since then, William Bennett and Democratic Senator Joe Lieberman of Connecticut have called on talk-show advertisers to withdraw their support, N.E.A. nemesis Donald Wildmon's American Family Association has joined the cause with a full-page ad in *The New York Times* and Phil Donahue's retirement has touched off a round of head-shaking at the contrast between the now-respectable pioneer of the talk show and his degenerate successors. Commentators reveal the stop-the-presses news that the talk-show audience prefers sex and violence to analyses of health care and foreign policy. Beyond this indisputable fact the legions of outraged moralists have little enlightenment to offer, since they rarely bother to pay much attention to the reviled genre, let alone try to understand what's going on in the imagination of people who do.

The popularity of popular culture is a problem for its detractors: It would be a breach of American democratic etiquette, not to mention an implicit rebuke to free-market platitudes about supply and demand, for journalists or (especially) politicians simply to claim that their own cultural tastes are superior to those of the barbarian hordes (though they come close to doing this when the subject is black music). The solution is to rely heavily on the assumption that the media are a species of addictive drug, pushed on a vulnerable populace by corporations out to make a buck and/or infiltrated by a perverse New York and Hollywood cultural elite. The audience is often referred to as "our children," even when the medium in question is aimed at adults. Lieberman indignantly cites a report that claims "children aged 2 to 11 comprise six percent" of talk-show viewers nationally. The other 94 percent? Don't ask!

In the case of talk shows, the critic-audience gap is even wider than usual. I doubt that Lieberman and his fellow attack dogs got the idea for their crusade by actually watching Ricki Lake or Richard Bey or Sally Jessy Raphael. But what's more interesting is the paucity of sympathetic popcult critics who are talk-show fans: Donna Gaines, with her *Village Voice* testimonial that *Jenny Jones* saved her life, is the conspicuous exception. Like McDonald's, these shows are genuinely lowbrow; unlike Quentin Tarantino or Snoop Doggy Dogg, they can't be said to appeal to the so-called cultural elite. They resist hip readings—it's hard to watch a talk show ironically, even when you're sure it's as fake as a wrestling match. Anyway, the shows come on at the wrong time for the critical classes, right in the middle of the sacred working day.

I first saw the Ricki Lake show because my daughter had mentioned it, and I thought I should check it out. We watched a show together; the subject, as I recall, was women whose boyfriends had impregnated other women. There were moments that made me squirm, but not because I was worried that, as Lieberman would later put it, "the constant confrontations and emotional violence" would teach my 11-year-old "a perverse way to solve personal problems" or give her the impression "that is the way normal adults behave." Leaving aside the absurdity of the idea that "normal adults" don't have nasty fights, it took little in the way of probing discussion to confirm that my daughter could tell the difference between real life and stage-managed psychodrama. Anyway, from my own childhood encounters with horror comics, soap operas, graphic sex manuals and other crypto-pornography of the fifties, I know kids have more complicated filters than adults tend to give them credit for. The danger, it seemed to me, was exactly the opposite: that my child was seeing Ricki's guests, working-class people willing to spill the beans on TV, as alien and unreal. Or maybe I was afraid that's what I was doing.

Like other forms of popular culture, talk shows reflect the peculiar contradictions of today's social and political climate. While conservatives dominate the political system and control the terms of debate on economic issues, their drive to roll back the cultural changes of the sixties and seventies has had much more ambiguous results. The most telling success of the cultural right (and in that category I include social conservatives who are political liberals or leftists) has been the discrediting of the idea of a pro-freedom, pro-pleasure revolution in everyday life in favor of nostalgia for an idealized past: These days it's even harder to get a serious public hearing for a radical critique of the family than for a radical critique of capitalism. This repression of the utopian impulse has combined with economic insecurity to brew a protean anger that leaks out in various forms of sadism—physical, verbal, moral and vicarious. On the other hand, social conservatives have been notably unsuccessful at stemming the democratization of culture, the breakdown of those class, sex and race-bound conventions that once reliably separated high from low, "news" from "gossip," public from unspeakably private, respectable from deviant.

Talk shows are a product of this democratization; they let people who have been largely excluded from the public conversation appear on national TV and talk about their sex lives, their family fights, sometimes their literal dirty laundry. What's more taboo than the subject matter itself is the way it's presented—as personal revelation rather than social comment, and as spectacle mostly devoid of pretensions to redeeming social value: "In these shows," William Bennett complains, "indecent exposure is celebrated as a virtue....There was once a time when personal or marital failure...and perverse taste were accompanied by guilt or embarrassment." Talk shows are meant to entertain, to excite the nerve ends. This in itself is anathema to social conservatives, for whom the only legitimate function of popular culture is instructing the masses in the moral values of their betters.

It's not that morality is absent from talk shows. True, some guests flaunt "deviant" behavior without being condemned for it; but others indignantly defend conventional moral standards against wayward lovers or children. Talk-show hosts often lecture guests, especially teenagers—Sally Jessy has perfected a stern school-principal style, Ricki a more maternal-therapeutic approach—while members of the audience or other guests (the parents, wronged girlfriends and so on) may subject the (usually defiant) miscreant to verbal stoning. The catch is that their very complicity in a public free-for-all undermines their moral authority. And though therapists may be called on to give "expert" commentary or do a bit of ad hoc family counseling, they are about as relevant to the action as those trailers that used to introduce porn movies with homilies on the need for sex education. At the dramatic center of talk shows are mostly black, Latino and low-rent white guests who, by their very willingness to expose intimate, "shameful" matters and yell and scream at each other on the air, assert their lack of deference to middle-class norms.

I mean "dramatic" literally; talk shows are theater. Like most kinds of popular entertainment, especially on television, they rely on formula. There's the trial scenario—an accusation ("My ex-husband's wife abuses my kid"), a rebuttal ("I hit her because she's disrespectful, but I don't abuse her") and a parade of witnesses: the alleged victim ("I don't have to obey you, you're not my mother and you threw me downstairs!"), the nervous father who hasn't seen anything and is totally out of it, the "expert" who lectures that it's abusive to hit a kid, even your own. The judge/host presides, asking questions and being fair to all sides. The jury/audience gets into the act, berating the stepmother for overstepping her bounds, the kid for being disrespectful, the father for being out of it. What's missing is a unanimous verdict or any semblance of courtroom decorum.

Then there's the increasingly popular "surprise" show, where a guest is tricked into appearing. This ploy makes explicit the basic appeal of talk-show formulas: However often repeated, they're never totally predictable, but offer the exciting possibility that a situation will get out of control. An argument can lead to an outburst of violence; the woman who is proposed to can say no. The talk show is a dangerous ritual like boxing or bullfighting, an improvisatory performance that seems to blur the boundary between actors and audience, yet leaves the larger audience safe behind the barrier of the screen. And since talk shows traffic in subjects that have universal resonance—from infidelity, incest and juvenile rebellion to clothes ("My mom dresses like a tramp!")—I suspect that few people are entirely impervious to their crude power.

As a distant graduate of youth culture and mother of a soon-to-be-teenager, I'm riveted by shows that feature generational collisions. On a recent *Sally Jessy Raphael* episode, "I'm Ready to Divorce My Children," kids of 12 (has sex and steals) and 13 (throws ashtrays), hiding behind their bad-seed fright masks to ward off who knew what terrors, sullenly confronted their desperate, baffled mother. There was Dantesque torment in that encounter; it stayed with me for days. I'm sure a lot of guests invent or exaggerate their torments, with or without the connivance of producers. But in this case, I could swear the emotions were real. If not, the acting was surely marvelous.

I don't mean to romanticize talk shows. If they reflect a democratizing impulse, they're also a symptom of today's anti-utopian and anti-political mood. While great popular art tends to bring disparate groups together—the way the Beatles reached teeny-boppers and intellectuals, or Duke Ellington whites and blacks—talk shows are more likely to reinforce class and racial fragmentation [see Jill Nelson, "Talk Is Cheap," *The Nation*, June 5, 1995]: Though viewers from the same social milieus as the guests may identify with them and their problems, my hunch is that for many middle-class talk-show fans, the kick is feeling superior (or as my daughter put it when I posed the question, "lucky").

As for the guests themselves, in the absence of any other way to have an impact on history—which is to say, the absence of effective social movements—the opportunity to sound off on national television offers visibility, and therefore validation, to teenagers and people of color and working-class whites; in effect it's the culture's acknowledgment that they exist. But existence proved this way is existence on someone else's terms. Often guests are so vivid, or funny, or sure of their right to be who they are that they outflank the manipulative condescension of their producers and hosts. But often they don't, especially when the audience gangs up on them, or when they're set up to be surprised. The Schmitz murder is a disturbing commentary on talk-show tactics, not because "Jenny made him do it"—homophobia made him do it—but because the whole rationale of talk shows is bound up with risking such events. If a show becomes a flashpoint for the culture's free-floating sadism, or a conduit for politics by other means, is it truly an accident?

Finally, though, our problem is not the excesses of talk shows but the brutality and emptiness of our political culture. Popbashing is the humanism of fools: In the name of defending people's dignity it attacks their pleasures and their meager store of power. On talk shows, whatever their drawbacks, the proles get to talk. The rest of the time they're told in a thousand ways to shut up. By any honest reckoning, we need more noise, not less.

SUGGESTIONS FOR DISCUSSION

1. What would you say is Willis's central concern about daytime talk TV and the controversy surrounding those programs? How does it differ from the concerns of other writers that you have read throughout this chapter? In what ways is it similar?

2. Willis, like Gaines, writes that talk shows offer what she calls "visibility, and therefore validation, to teenagers and people of color and working-class whites." She adds, however, that although this is "the culture's acknowledgment that they exist," it is "existence on someone else's terms." In a discussion with a group of your classmates, explore what it might mean for a marginalized group to have existence on someone else's terms.

3. Willis writes, "In the case of talk shows, the critic-audience gap is even wider than usual. I doubt that Lieberman and his fellow attack dogs got the idea for their crusade by actually watching Ricki Lake or Richard Bey or Sally Jessy Raphael. But what's more interesting is the paucity of sympathetic popcult critics who are talk-show fans." In such passages, Willis is positioning herself as someone who has stepped outside the talk-show-bashing circle of critics and is willing at least to hear from those who consider themselves fans and especially those who actually watch talk TV. Point to places in the previous readings where the authors position themselves in relation to the topic of talk shows and public responsibility.

WRITING ABOUT THE CULTURE OF DAYTIME TALK TV

Many of the writers in this chapter would argue that daytime talk television seriously distorts, even demeans, the character of ordinary Americans. The overeater, as we have seen from an earlier example, is depicted as being out of control and unattractive. The twelve-year-old child who "can't stop sleeping around" is displayed as a fallen woman and reminded that she is risking not only her reputation but her life if she is having unprotected sex with a number of different partners. The "ordinary Americans" depicted on these shows, some critics would argue, are our stereotypes of lower-class Americans: out of work, out of luck, and unaware. By contrast, Donna Gaines tells us that daytime talk portrays a reality of American life that much of television never comes close to.

Your own position on the culture of daytime talk television has likely already begun to form as you watched, interviewed viewers, and read what the critics have said. Now it is time for you to formulate that position on your own. Your teacher might ask you to do further library research—research that would give you information about program topics, program ratings, continuing debates on daytime talk, and more. What you discover in your research will depend on how you decide to focus your deliberations. In what follows, we offer suggestions for exploration, but the paper you write will be determined primarily by your own interests and the turn your thinking has taken as you have done the work throughout this chapter.

SUGGESTIONS FOR WRITING

1. By all accounts, daytime talk TV has become a very popular kind of programming in the United States. Advertisers would most likely say that a program is popular because it appeals to current tastes and interests of the viewing public. In your own analysis, speculate on what it is in these shows that appeals to the viewing audience. What are the current tastes and interests the shows seem to be taking advantage of? You can draw upon any of the work you have done in this chapter as you write your essay. Don't forget the notes you took as you watched daytime programming or the interviews you and your classmates conducted to learn about viewers' responses to daytime talk TV.

2. Vicki Abt and Leonard Mustazza, Donna Gaines, William Bennett, and Ellen Willis all offer different positions on how tabloid television talk shows represent their guests. Abt and Mustazza, for example, charge this programming with encouraging "audience and guest obsession with extreme, socially uncontrolled behavior." Gaines, on the other hand, suggests television talk is the place for real people to speak out. After looking back over your own responses to the shows you watched and reviewing interview notes and the reading selections, write an essay in which you enter this discussion about talk show guests and how viewers see those guests. You do not have to argue with the writers above, although you might find yourself doing that. You can instead offer yet another way of thinking about how these guests are represented and what roles they play for viewers.

3. Much of the discussion about daytime talk TV is about the cultural and moral values that they seem to convey. Write an essay addressing this issue of values. You might consider, for example, what you believe are the values conveyed on talk shows. How are those values conveyed? Are they in line with values you recognize in your peers, or do they seem very different from your own world and your own experience? Or you might instead take issue with those who are concerned about the values presented on talk TV. Is talk TV supposed to convey values? What is its purpose?

EXTENDING YOUR INVESTIGATIONS:
TV TABLOID JOURNALISM

Daytime talk TV has frequently been called *tabloid* TV for its similarity to gossip magazines, grocery-store scandal sheets, and the distorted reporting of newspapers like the *National Enquirer* or *The Star*. More and more often, the term *tabloid* has begun to be applied to television news magazines like *20/20* or "reality" shows like *COPS*. What these shows have in common with their print counterparts seems to be a tendency to sensationalize the events of the day.

For many critics, the impact of what is sometimes called tabloid culture is less of a concern in such shows as *Jerry Springer* or *Ricki Lake* than it is in the kind of programming we consider more serious: TV news programming.

In his book-length study of television journalism *Breaking the News: How the Media Undermined American Democracy* (Pantheon 1996), James Fallows writes that the emergence and popularity of *60 Minutes* marked a change in television journalism that has increasingly influenced the way television reports the news. Fallows calls it "news as spectacle." By Fallows's account, "of the nearly 500 stories that *60 Minutes* aired between 1990 and 1994, more than one-third were celebrity profiles, entertainment-industry stories, or exposes of…'petty scandals'" (57).

View a selection of shows that might be considered TV tabloid journalism—*60 Minutes, Dateline, 20/20, COPS,* etc. Make a list of the stories these shows carry. What would you say marks them as tabloid journalism? To what extent do network news programs also carry tabloid stories? Use your investigations to write an essay on TV tabloid journalism in which you discuss what differentiates tabloid TV journalism from straight news reporting.

CONCLUSION

What you have been doing in the assignments throughout this chapter amounts to a kind of cultural analysis of daytime talk TV. The assignments have asked you to rely on your own observations, learn firsthand what others think, read what critics and analysts have written, and write your position on or analysis of those issues. As you have read, taken notes, summarized, and synthesized others' writing, you have been analyzing how writers seek to shape public opinion and how the media represent what is happening in American culture. This amounts to a *cultural analysis* of the role of the media and the press in at least one part of American life and thought. Through your reading, you have also encountered a series of related issues about popular entertainment, race, class, morality, and cultural values.

Throughout the chapters that follow, we will be presenting further opportunities to do this kind of cultural analysis—to read and write your way into some of the meanings of contemporary U.S. culture. Each chapter includes *reading selections, fieldwork assignments* like the interviews you conducted here, and potential *research questions* raised in sections called *Mining the Archives*. In addition, we have included special sections in each chapter on the *visual culture* of American life.

The work you do will be informed by what others have written, but it will also rely on your own knowledge of the culture you live in and on the observations you will be able to make from your own fieldwork. Often in this text, you will be asked to go beyond analysis to create your own rewritings of cultural texts. You are, after all, not only a reader of culture but a user and producer of that culture.

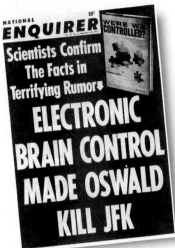

Tabloid front page.

Mining the Archive

PRINT TABLOIDS

Tabloid culture has been around for many generations. Elizabeth Bird in *Enquiring Minds: A Cultural Study of Supermarket Tabloids* (U of Tennessee Press, 1992) writes that the term *tabloid* is now "almost invariably used to refer to the 'sensational' tabloid—the paper whose stock in trade is in the human-interest, graphically told story, heavy on pictures and short, pithy, highly stereotyped prose" (8–9). We see these papers—featuring large, often distorted photos of celebrities or alien babies or suspected serial killers or 300 year-old men—as we check out at the grocery store. Despite the fact that they all seem the same, Bird's study indicated that tabloids have very different ways of handing those stories. She notes that the selection of stories displayed on the cover of each tabloid is the best indication of these differences.

Unfortunately, as Bird points out in the opening pages of her study, locating old tabloids is very difficult. This is an ephemeral genre—one that is more often tossed than archived. Because of the difficulty in locating old issues of tabloids, we have located and reprinted the front page of a past tabloid for you. Examine the front page reprinted here and compare it to the front pages of print tabloids available today in your local supermarkets. To what extent does your examination suggest that the older tabloid differs from those available on newsstands today?

CHAPTER 2

Generations

This is not your father's Oldsmobile. This is the new generation—of Olds.
—*1990 television commercial for Oldsmobile*

America is a nation of immigrants, and it is common to distinguish between first and second generations—between those who first traveled to and settled in the United States from Europe, Asia, Africa, or Latin America and their children who were born here. The two generations, of course, are biologically related to each other as well as to older generations of grandparents, great-grandparents, and great-great-grandparents, as far back as people can trace their ancestry. Yet first-generation and second-generation Americans often differ in the way they live their lives, in the hopes they have for themselves and their children, and in the ties they feel to the traditions and customs of their places of ancestry.

Individuals grow up as part of a biological generation that comes along every twenty years to continue their family's line. At the same time, however, individuals are also members of an historical generation. In cultural terms, generations are not only produced through biological descent. They are also formed out of a common history and the common experiences that people have growing up with others their age. To be a member of a generation, then, is to belong not only to a family. It also means belonging to a generation of people to whom you are related historically.

In this chapter, we will be asking you to read, think, and write about what it means to be a member of and a participant in your historical generation. Whether you are straight out of high school or returning to college, it can be valuable to consider how your

41

own personal experience has been shaped by growing up at a particular moment in a particular historical generation.

The term *generation* denotes change. It suggests new life and new growth—new styles, new values, and new ways of living. Americans hear generational voices all the time in everyday conversation, when young people tell their parents not to be "so old-fashioned" and their parents reply, "It wasn't like that when we were growing up." Advertising, too, as the Oldsmobile commercial at the beginning of this chapter indicates, likes to make us believe that the new generation of goods—not only cars but stereos, computers, household appliances—is smarter, better designed, and more high tech than its predecessors.

Each generation differs from those that came before. Cultural historian Raymond Williams says that "no generation speaks quite the same language as its predecessor. Each generation produces its own way of speaking and its own forms of cultural expression." Young people, for example, use slang to recognize friends, to distinguish between insiders and outsiders, to position themselves in relation to the older generation. Whether you say things are "phat" or "awesome" or "far out," the kind of music that you like to listen to, the way that you dance, your style of dress, where you go to hang out—all these things reveal something about you and your relation to the constantly changing styles of youth culture in contemporary America.

People's tastes in popular entertainment and their participation in fads, styles, and trends are not just personal matters, though they are often deeply felt by individuals. They also, quite literally, date individuals by tying people's personal experience to a particular time, when they first heard a song or saw a movie. How a generation looks at itself is inevitably entangled in the decisive historical events and the geopolitical changes of its day. The Depression, World War II, the Vietnam War, and the Reagan years have each influenced a generation profoundly. To understand what it means to belong to your generation, you will need to locate your experience growing up as a member of your generation in its historical times—to see how your generation has made sense of its place in American history and its relation to past generations.

From the invention of the American teenager and juvenile delinquency in movies like *Rebel Without a Cause* and *The Wild One* in the 1950s to grunge rock and MTV in the 1990s, American media have been fascinated by each new generation of young people. In America, a generation is always in part a media event, and to think about your generation, you will want to look at how the media have represented your generation and how these media representations have entered into your generation's conception of itself. Each generation seems to have its own characteristic mood or identity that the media try to capture in a label—whether the "lost" generation of the Jazz Age in the 1920s or the "silent" generation of the Eisenhower years in the 1950s. When people use these labels or refer to the "baby boomers" of the 1960s or the "yuppies" of the 1980s or the "slackers" of the 1990s, they not only are referring to particular groups of people. They are also calling up a set of values, styles, and images, a collective feeling in the air.

This is not to say that everyone in the same generation has the same experience and the same feelings. A generation is not, after all, a monolithic thing. In fact, every generation is divided along the same lines of race, class, gender, and ethnicity that divide the wider society. But a generation is not simply a composite of individuals either. To think about the mood of your generation—the sensibility that suffuses its lived experience—you will need to consider how the character of your generation distinguishes it from generations of the past, even if that character is contradictory or inconsistent.

READING THE CULTURE OF GENERATIONS

We begin this chapter with three reading selections that present various writing strategies to examine the relationship between generations. In the first, "Kiswana Browne," a chapter from the novel *The Women of Brewster Place*, Gloria Naylor uses fiction to explore the differences and continuities between an African American mother and her daughter. In the next selection, Dave Marsh writes a memoir recounting a moment of revelation while listening to Smoky Robinson sing "You Really Got a Hold on

Me." The third reading, "Youth and American Identity," an excerpt from Lawrence Grossberg's longer study *It's a Sin*, takes a broader, more analytical perspective on the way post–World War II America invested its hopes in the younger generation as the living symbol of national identity and the American Dream.

The next two selections look at conflicts and misunderstandings between generations. In "Teenage Wasteland," Donna Gaines writes as a sympathetic reporter who investigates a teenage suicide pact and the response of local officials in Bergenfield, New Jersey. Thomas Hine's "Goths in Tomorrowland" explores the fragmentation of teenage subcultures and the alienation of young people from adult society.

The final pair of readings, "Perspectives: Making Sense of the Littleton Shootings," offers perspective on the shootings at Columbine High School in Littleton, Colorado. In "The Gunfire Dialogues: Notes on the Reality of Virtuality," Thomas de Zengotita considers the relation between media and teenagers, while Jon Katz lets gamers, goths, geeks, and nerds talk for themselves in "More from the Hellmouth: Kids Tell About Rage."

As you read, think, talk, and write about the interpretations presented in this chapter, consider how you would characterize your own generation. What styles of cultural expression mark your generation from your predecessors? What is your generation's sense of itself? How is your generation portrayed in the media? These are some of the questions you will want to explore as you work your way through this chapter. Perhaps when you have completed your work, you will find a way to define the particular mood and character of your generation.

Kiswana Browne

Gloria Naylor

Gloria Naylor's highly acclaimed novel *The Women of Brewster Place* (1980) tells the stories of a number of African American women who live in a housing project in an unnamed city. We have selected the chapter "Kiswana Browne" because it presents a powerful account of the encounter between a mother and daughter that explores both their generational differences and the aspirations that they hold in common. Naylor's story reveals how the much-publicized generation gap of the 1960s is never simply a matter of differences in politics and lifestyle but rather is complicated by the intersecting forces of race, class, and gender. The cultural shift signified by Kiswana's change of name represents both a break with the past and, as Kiswana discovers, a continuation of her family's resistance to racial oppression.

SUGGESTION FOR READING

As you read, underline and annotate the passages where the story establishes conflict between the two characters and where (or whether) it resolves the conflict.

From the window of her sixth-floor studio apartment, Kiswana could see over the wall at the end of the street to the busy avenue that lay just north of Brewster Place. The late-afternoon shoppers looked like brightly clad marionettes as they moved between the congested traffic, clutching their packages against their bodies to guard them from sudden bursts of the cold autumn wind. A portly mailman had abandoned his cart and was bumping into indignant window-shoppers as he puffed behind the cap that the wind had snatched from his head. Kiswana leaned over to see if he was going to be successful, but the edge of the building cut him off from her view.

A pigeon swept across her window, and she marveled at its liquid movements in the air waves. She placed her dreams on the back of the bird and fantasized that it would glide forever in transparent silver circles until it ascended to the center of the universe and was swallowed up. But the wind died down, and she watched with a sigh as the bird beat its wings in awkward, frantic movements to land on the corroded top of a fire escape on the opposite building. This brought her back to earth.

Humph, it's probably sitting over there crapping on those folks' fire escape, she thought. Now, that's a safety hazard….And her mind was busy again, creating flames and smoke and frustrated tenants whose escape was being hindered because they were slipping and sliding in pigeon shit. She watched their cussing, haphazard descent on the fire escapes until they had all reached the bottom. They were milling around, oblivious to their burning apartments, angrily planning to march on the mayor's office about the pigeons. She materialized placards and banners for them, and they had just reached the corner, boldly sidestepping fire hoses and broken glass, when they all vanished.

A tall copper-skinned woman had met this phantom parade at the corner, and they had dissolved in front of her long, confident strides. She plowed through the remains of their faded mists, unconscious of the lingering wisps of their presence on her leather bag and black fur-trimmed coat. It took a few seconds for this transfer from one realm to another to reach Kiswana, but then suddenly she recognized the woman.

"Oh, God, it's Mama!" She looked down guiltily at the forgotten newspaper in her lap and hurriedly circled random job advertisements.

By this time Mrs. Browne had reached the front of Kiswana's building and was checking the house number against a piece of paper in her hand. Before she went into the building she stood at the bottom of the stoop and carefully inspected the condition of the street and the adjoining property. Kiswana watched this meticulous inventory with growing annoyance but she involuntarily followed her mother's slowly rotating head, forcing herself to see her new neighborhood through the older woman's eyes. The brightness of the unclouded sky seemed to join forces with her mother as it high-lighted every broken stoop railing and missing brick. The afternoon sun glittered and cascaded across even the tiniest fragments of broken bottle, and at that very moment the wind chose to rise up again, sending unswept grime flying into the air, as a stray tin can left by careless garbage collectors went rolling noisily down the center of the street.

Kiswana noticed with relief that at least Ben wasn't sitting in his usual place on the old garbage can pushed against the far wall. He was just a harmless old wino, but Kiswana knew her mother only needed one wino or one teenager with a reefer within a twenty-block radius to decide that her daughter was living in a building seething with dope factories and hangouts for derelicts. If she had seen Ben, nothing would have made her believe that practically every apartment contained a family, a Bible, and a dream that one day enough could be scraped from those meager Friday night paychecks to make Brewster Place a distant memory.

As she watched her mother's head disappear into the building, Kiswana gave silent thanks that the elevator was broken. That would give her at least five minutes' grace to straighten up the apartment. She rushed to the sofa bed and hastily closed it without smoothing the rumpled sheets and blanket or removing her nightgown. She felt that somehow the tangled bedcovers would give away the fact that she had not slept alone last night. She silently apologized to Abshu's memory as she heartlessly crushed his spirit between the steel springs of the couch. Lord, that man was sweet. Her toes curled involuntarily at the passing thought of his full lips moving slowly over her instep. Abshu was a foot man, and he always started his lovemaking from the bottom up. For that reason Kiswana changed the color of the polish on her toenails every week. During the course of their relationship she had gone from shades of red to brown and was now into the purples. I'm gonna have to start mixing them soon, she thought aloud as she turned from the couch and raced into the bathroom to remove any traces of Abshu from there. She took up his shaving cream and razor and threw them into the bottom drawer of her dresser beside her diaphragm. Mama wouldn't dare pry into my drawers right in front of me, she thought as she slammed the drawer shut. Well, at least not the bottom drawer. She may come up with some sham excuse for opening the top drawer, but never the bottom one.

When she heard the first two short raps on the door, her eyes took a final flight over the small apartment, desperately seeking out any slight misdemeanor that might have to be defended. Well, there was nothing she could do about the crack in the wall over that table. She had been after the landlord to fix it for two months now. And there had been no time to sweep the rug, and everyone knew that off-gray always looked dirtier than it really was. And it was just too damn bad about the kitchen. How was she expected to be out job-hunting every day and still have time to keep a kitchen that looked like her mother's, who didn't even work and still had someone come in twice a month for general cleaning. And besides...

Her imaginary argument was abruptly interrupted by a second series of knocks, accompanied by a penetrating, "Melanie, Melanie, are you there?"

Kiswana strode toward the door. She's starting before she even gets in here. She knows that's not my name anymore.

She swung the door open to face her slightly flushed mother. "Oh, hi, Mama. You know, I thought I heard a knock, but I figured it was for the people next door, since no one hardly ever calls me Melanie." Score one for me, she thought.

"Well, it's awfully strange you can forget a name you answered to for twenty-three years," Mrs. Browne said, as she moved past Kiswana into the apartment. "My, that was a long climb. How long has your elevator been out? Honey, how do you manage with your laundry and groceries up all those steps? But I guess you're young, and it wouldn't bother you as much as it does me." This long string of questions told Kiswana that her mother had no intentions of beginning her visit with another argument about her new African name.

"You know I would have called before I came, but you don't have a phone yet. I didn't want you to feel that I was snooping. As a matter of fact, I didn't expect to find you home at all. I thought you'd be out looking for a job." Mrs. Browne had mentally covered the entire apartment while she was talking and taking off her coat.

"Well, I got up late this morning. I thought I'd buy the afternoon paper and start early tomorrow."

"That sounds like a good idea." Her mother moved toward the window and picked up the discarded paper and glanced over the hurriedly circled ads. "Since when do you have experience as a fork-lift operator?"

Kiswana caught her breath and silently cursed herself for her stupidity. "Oh, my hand slipped—I meant to circle file clerk." She quickly took the paper before her mother could see that she had also marked cutlery salesman and chauffeur.

"You're sure you weren't sitting here moping and day-dreaming again?" Amber specks of laughter flashed in the corner of Mrs. Browne's eyes.

Kiswana threw her shoulders back and unsuccessfully tried to disguise her embarrassment with indignation.

"Oh, God, Mama! I haven't done that in years—it's for kids. When are you going to realize that I'm a woman now?" She sought desperately for some womanly thing to do and settled for throwing herself on the couch and crossing her legs in what she hoped looked like a nonchalant arc.

"Please, have a seat," she said, attempting the same tones and gestures she'd seen Bette Davis use on the late movies.

Mrs. Browne, lowering her eyes to hide her amusement, accepted the invitation and sat at the window, also crossing her legs. Kiswana saw immediately how it should have been done. Her celluloid poise clashed loudly against her mother's quiet dignity, and she quickly uncrossed her legs. Mrs. Browne turned her head toward the window and pretended not to notice.

"At least you have a halfway decent view from here. I was wondering what lay beyond that dreadful wall—it's the boulevard. Honey, did you know that you can see the trees in Linden Hills from here?"

Kiswana knew that very well, because there were many lonely days that she would sit in her gray apartment and stare at those trees and think of home, but she would rather have choked than admit that to her mother.

"Oh, really, I never noticed. So how is Daddy and things at home?"

"Just fine. We're thinking of redoing one of the extra bedrooms since you children have moved out, but Wilson insists that he can manage all that work alone. I told him that he doesn't really have the proper time or energy for all that. As it is, when he gets home from the office, he's so tired he can hardly move. But you know you can't tell your father anything. Whenever he starts complaining about how stubborn you are, I tell him the child came by it honestly. Oh, and your brother was by yesterday," she added, as if it had just occurred to her.

So that's it, thought Kiswana. That's why she's here.

Kiswana's brother, Wilson, had been to visit her two days ago, and she had borrowed twenty dollars from him to get her winter coat out of layaway. That son-of-a-bitch probably ran straight to Mama—and after he swore he wouldn't say anything. I should have known, he was always a snotty-nosed sneak, she thought.

"Was he?" she said aloud. "He came by to see me, too, earlier this week. And I borrowed some money from him because my unemployment checks hadn't cleared in the bank, but now they have and everything's just fine." There, I'll beat you to that one.

"Oh, I didn't know that," Mrs. Browne lied. "He never mentioned you. He had just heard that Beverly was expecting again, and he rushed over to tell us."

Damn. Kiswana could have strangled herself.

"So she's knocked up again, huh?" she said irritably.

Her mother started. "Why do you always have to be so crude?"

"Personally, I don't see how she can sleep with Willie. He's such a dishrag."

Kiswana still resented the stance her brother had taken in college. When everyone at school was discovering their blackness and protesting on campus, Wilson never took part; he had even refused to wear an Afro. This had outraged Kiswana because, unlike her, he was dark-skinned and had the type of hair that was thick and kinky enough for a good "Fro." Kiswana had still insisted on cutting her own hair, but it was so thin and fine-textured, it refused to thicken even after she washed it. So she had to brush it up and spray it with lacquer to keep it from lying flat. She never forgave Wilson for telling her that she didn't look African, she looked like an electrocuted chicken.

"Now that's some way to talk. I don't know why you have an attitude against your brother. He never gave me a restless night's sleep, and now he's settled with a family and a good job."

"He's an assistant to an assistant junior partner in a law firm. What's the big deal about that?"

"The job has a future, Melanie. And at least he finished school and went on for his law degree."

"In other words, not like me, huh?"

"Don't put words into my mouth, young lady. I'm perfectly capable of saying what I mean."

Amen, thought Kiswana.

"And I don't know why you've been trying to start up with me from the moment I walked in. I didn't come here to fight with you. This is your first place away from home, and

I just wanted to see how you were living and if you're doing all right. And I must say, you've fixed this apartment up very nicely."

"Really, Mama?" She found herself softening in the light of her mother's approval.

"Well, considering what you had to work with." This time she scanned the apartment openly.

"Look, I know it's not Linden Hills, but a lot can be done with it. As soon as they come and paint, I'm going to hang my Ashanti print over the couch. And I thought a big Boston Fern would go well in that corner, what do you think?"

"That would be fine, baby. You always had a good eye for balance."

Kiswana was beginning to relax. There was little she did that attracted her mother's approval. It was like a rare bird, and she had to tread carefully around it lest it fly away.

"Are you going to leave that statue out like that?"

"Why, what's wrong with it? Would it look better somewhere else?"

There was a small wooden reproduction of a Yoruba goddess with large protruding breasts on the coffee table.

"Well," Mrs. Browne was beginning to blush, "it's just that it's a bit suggestive, don't you think? Since you live alone now, and I know you'll be having male friends stop by, you wouldn't want to be giving them any ideas. I mean, uh, you know, there's no point in putting yourself in any unpleasant situations because they may get the wrong impressions and uh, you know, I mean, well…" Mrs. Browne stammered on miserably.

Kiswana loved it when her mother tried to talk about sex. It was the only time she was at a loss for words.

"Don't worry, Mama." Kiswana smiled. "That wouldn't bother the type of men I date. Now maybe if it had big feet…" And she got hysterical, thinking of Abshu.

Her mother looked at her sharply. "What sort of gibberish is that about feet? I'm being serious, Melanie."

"I'm sorry, Mama." She sobered up. "I'll put it away in the closet," she said, knowing that she wouldn't.

"Good," Mrs. Browne said, knowing that she wouldn't either. "I guess you think I'm too picky, but we worry about you over here. And you refuse to put in a phone so we can call and see about you."

"I haven't refused, Mama. They want seventy-five dollars for a deposit, and I can't swing that right now."

"Melanie, I can give you the money."

"I don't want you to be giving me money—I've told you that before. Please, let me make it by myself."

"Well, let me lend it to you, then."

"No!"

"Oh, so you can borrow money from your brother, but not from me."

Kiswana turned her head from the hurt in her mother's eyes. "Mama, when I borrow from Willie, he makes me pay him back. You never let me pay you back," she said into her hands.

"I don't care. I still think it's downright selfish of you to be sitting over here with no phone, and sometimes we don't hear from you in two weeks—anything could happen—especially living among these people."

Kiswana snapped her head up. "What do you mean, these people. They're my people and yours, too, Mama—we're all black. But maybe you've forgotten that over in Linden Hills."

"That's not what I'm talking about, and you know it. These streets—this building—it's so shabby and rundown. Honey, you don't have to live like this."

"Well, this is how poor people live."

"Melanie, you're not poor."

"No, Mama, *you're* not poor. And what you have and I have are two totally different things. I don't have a husband in real estate with a five-figure income and a home in Linden Hills—*you* do. What I have is a weekly unemployment check and an overdrawn checking account at United Federal. So this studio on Brewster is all I can afford."

"Well, you could afford a lot better," Mrs. Browne snapped, "if you hadn't dropped out of college and had to resort to these dead-end clerical jobs."

"Uh-huh, I knew you'd get around to that before long." Kiswana could feel the rings of anger begin to tighten around her lower backbone, and they sent her forward onto the couch. "You'll never understand, will you? Those bourgie schools were counterrevolutionary. My place was in the streets with my people, fighting for equality and a better community."

"Counterrevolutionary!" Mrs. Browne was raising her voice. "Where's your revolution now, Melanie? Where are all those black revolutionaries who were shouting and demonstrating and kicking up a lot of dust with you on that campus? Huh? They're sitting in wood-paneled offices with their degrees in mahogany frames, and they won't even drive their cars past this street because the city doesn't fix potholes in this part of town."

"Mama," she said, shaking her head slowly in disbelief, "how can you—a black woman—sit there and tell me that what we fought for during the Movement wasn't important just because some people sold out?"

"Melanie, I'm not saying it wasn't important. It was damned important to stand up and say that you were proud of what you were and to get the vote and other social opportunities for every person in this country who had it due. But you kids thought you were going to turn the world upside down, and it just wasn't so. When all the smoke had cleared, you found yourself with a fistful of new federal laws and a country still full of obstacles for black people to fight their way over—just because they're black. There was no revolution, Melanie, and there will be no revolution."

"So what am I supposed to do, huh? Just throw up my hands and not care about what happens to my people? I'm not supposed to keep fighting to make things better?"

"Of course, you can. But you're going to have to fight within the system, because it and these so-called 'bourgie' schools are going to be here for a long time. And that means that you get smart like a lot of your old friends and get an important job where you can have some influence. You don't have to sell out, as you say, and work for some corporation, but you could become an assemblywoman or a civil liberties lawyer or open a freedom school in this very neighborhood. That way you could really help the community. But what help are you going to be to these people on Brewster while you're living hand-to-mouth on file-clerk jobs waiting for a revolution? You're wasting your talents, child."

"Well, I don't think they're being wasted. At least I'm here in day-to-day contact with the problems of my people. What good would I be after four or five years of a lot of white brain-washing in some phony, prestige institution, huh? I'd be like you and Daddy and those other educated blacks sitting over there in Linden Hills with a terminal case of middle-class amnesia."

"You don't have to live in a slum to be concerned about social conditions, Melanie. Your father and I have been charter members of the NAACP for the last twenty-five years."

"Oh, God!" Kiswana threw her head back in exaggerated disgust. "That's being concerned? That middle-of-the-road, Uncle Tom dumping ground for black Republicans!"

"You can sneer all you want, young lady, but that organization has been working for black people since the turn of the century, and it's still working for them. Where are all those radical groups of yours that were going to put a Cadillac in every garage and Dick Gregory in the White House? I'll tell you where."

I knew you would, Kiswana thought angrily.

"They burned themselves out because they wanted too much too fast. Their goals weren't grounded in reality. And that's always been your problem."

"What do you mean, my problem? I know exactly what I'm about."

"No, you don't. You constantly live in a fantasy world—always going to extremes—turning butterflies into eagles, and life isn't about that. It's accepting what is and working from that. Lord, I remember how worried you had me, putting all that lacquered hair spray on your head. I thought you were going to get lung cancer—trying to be what you're not."

Kiswana jumped up from the couch. "Oh, God, I can't take this anymore. Trying to be something I'm not—trying to be something I'm not, Mama! Trying to be proud of my heritage and the fact that I was of African descent. If that's being what I'm not, then I say fine. But I'd rather be dead than be like you—a white man's nigger who's ashamed of being black!"

Kiswana saw streaks of gold and ebony light follow her mother's flying body out of the chair. She was swung around by the shoulders and made to face the deadly stillness in the angry woman's eyes. She was too stunned to cry out from the pain of the long fingernails that dug into her shoulders, and she was brought so close to her mother's face that she saw her reflection, distorted and wavering, in the tears that stood in the older woman's eyes. And she listened in that stillness to a story she had heard from a child.

"My grandmother," Mrs. Browne began slowly in a whisper, "was a full-blooded Iroquois, and my grandfather a free black from a long line of journeymen who had lived in Connecticut since the establishment of the colonies. And my father was a Bajan who came to this country as a cabin boy on a merchant mariner."

"I know all that," Kiswana said, trying to keep her lips from trembling.

"Then, know this." And the nails dug deeper into her flesh. "I am alive because of the blood of proud people who never scraped or begged or apologized for what they were. They lived asking only one thing of this world—to be allowed to be. And I learned through the blood of these people that black isn't beautiful and it isn't ugly—black is! It's not kinky hair and it's not straight hair—it just is.

"It broke my heart when you changed your name. I gave you my grandmother's name, a woman who bore nine children and educated them all, who held off six white men with a shotgun when they tried to drag one of her sons to jail for 'not knowing his place.' Yet you needed to reach into an African dictionary to find a name to make you proud.

"When I brought my babies home from the hospital, my ebony son and my golden daughter, I swore before whatever gods would listen—those of my mother's people or those of my father's people—that I would use everything I had and could ever get to see that my children were prepared to meet this world on its own terms, so that no one could sell them short and make them ashamed of what they were or how they looked—whatever they were or however they looked. And Melanie, that's not being white or red or black—that's being a mother."

Kiswana followed her reflection in the two single tears that moved down her mother's cheeks until it blended with them into the woman's copper skin. There was nothing and then so much that she wanted to say, but her throat kept closing up every time she tried to speak. She kept her head down and her eyes closed, and thought, Oh, God, just let me die. How can I face her now?

Mrs. Browne lifted Kiswana's chin gently. "And the one lesson I wanted you to learn is not to be afraid to face anyone, not even a crafty old lady like me who can outtalk you." And she smiled and winked.

"Oh, Mama, I..." and she hugged the woman tightly.

"Yeah, baby." Mrs. Browne patted her back. "I know."

She kissed Kiswana on the forehead and cleared her throat. "Well, now, I better be moving on. It's getting late, there's dinner to be made, and I have to get off my feet—these new shoes are killing me."

Kiswana looked down at the beige leather pumps. "Those are really classy. They're English, aren't they?"

"Yes, but, Lord, do they cut me right across the instep." She removed the shoe and sat on the couch to massage her foot.

Bright red nail polish glared at Kiswana through the stockings. "Since when do you polish your toenails?" she gasped. "You never did that before."

"Well…" Mrs. Browne shrugged her shoulders, "your father sort of talked me into it, and, uh, you know, he likes it and all, so I thought, uh, you know, why not so…" And she gave Kiswana an embarrassed smile.

I'll be damned, the young woman thought, feeling her whole face tingle. Daddy into feet! And she looked at the blushing woman on her couch and suddenly realized that her mother had trod through the same universe that she herself was now traveling. Kiswana was breaking no new trails and would eventually end up just two feet away on that couch. She stared at the woman she had been and was to become.

"But I'll never be a Republican," she caught herself saying aloud.

"What are you mumbling about, Melanie?" Mrs. Browne slipped on her shoe and got up from the couch.

She went to get her mother's coat. "Nothing, Mama. It's really nice of you to come by. You should do it more often."

"Well, since it's not Sunday, I guess you're allowed at least one lie."

They both laughed.

After Kiswana had closed the door and turned around, she spotted an envelop sticking between the cushions of her couch. She went over and opened it up; there was seventy-five dollars in it.

"Oh, Mama, darn it!" She rushed to the window and started to call to the woman, who had just emerged from the building, but she suddenly changed her mind and sat down in the chair with a long sigh that caught in the upward draft of the autumn wind and disappeared over the top of the building.

SUGGESTIONS FOR DISCUSSION

1. Gloria Naylor tells this story from Kiswana Browne's point of view. How would the story be different if Naylor had chosen to tell it from Kiswana's mother's point of view? What would be gained? What lost?

2. Consider how Naylor has organized this story—how she establishes a central conflict, leads up to the story's climax, and finally resolves the conflict. Does this kind of plot seem familiar? Does the story achieve a kind of closure or does it seem open ended? What kinds of satisfaction do readers derive from plots like this one? What, if anything, do such plots leave out or ignore?

3. Is Naylor making a judgment, whether implicit or explicit, of her characters? Explain your answer.

SUGGESTIONS FOR WRITING

1. Take the perspective of either Kiswana Browne or her mother and write an essay that explains how the character you have chosen sees the other. If you wish, write the essay in the voice of the character. Or you may choose to comment on the character's perceptions of the other and their generational differences in your own voice. In either case, be specific in your use of detail to define generational differences between the two women.

2. On one level, the chapter "Kiswana Browne" seems to be concerned with a "generation gap" between Kiswana and her mother. At the same time, other factors—race, class, and gender—affect the way generational differences are played out between the two characters. Write an essay that explains to what extent the chapter presents a version of the generation gap and to what extent other factors determine what happens between Kiswana and her mother. Do Kiswana and her mother have things in common, as well as generational differences? How do these factors influence the outcome of the story?

3. "Kiswana Browne" tells of the encounter between a young woman and her family and explores generational differences that have to do with issues such as lifestyle, names, and politics. Can you think of an encounter that you have had with your parents, or that someone you know has had with his or her parents, that involves such telling generational conflicts? (The conflict should be something that highlights differences in generational attitudes, values, or styles—not just "normal" disagreements about using the car or what time curfew should be.) Write an essay that explores such a conflict and explains what generational differences are at stake.

Fortunate Son

Dave Marsh

Dave Marsh is one of today's leading rock-and-roll critics. He is the author of books on Bruce Springsteen, Elvis Presley, and The Who. The following selection introduces *Fortunate Son,* a collection of Marsh's shorter critical essays and reviews. In his introduction, Marsh offers a memoir—a remembering—of his adolescence in Pontiac, Michigan, and how listening to rock and roll as a teenager in a working-class community led him to question "not just racism but all the other presumptions that ruled our lives."

SUGGESTION FOR READING

Notice that Marsh has divided his memoir into two parts. Part I tells the story of why Marsh's family moved from Pontiac to the suburbs, but Part II returns to Pontiac before the move. As you read, consider why Marsh has organized his memoir this way. How does Part II comment on what takes place in Part I? Where does Marsh explain the moment of revelation—or "epiphany"—that stands at the center of his memories?

INTRODUCTION I

This old town is where I learned about lovin'

This old town is where I learned to hate

This town, buddy, has done its share of shoveling

This town taught me that it's never too late

    Michael Stanley, "My Town"

When I was a boy, my family lived on East Beverly Street in Pontiac, Michigan, in a two-bedroom house with blue-white asphalt shingles that cracked at the edges when a ball was thrown against them and left a powder like talc on fingers rubbed across their shallow grooves. East Beverly ascended a slowly rising hill. At the very top, a block and a half from our place, Pontiac Motors Assembly Line 16 sprawled for a mile or so behind a fenced-in parking lot.

Rust-red dust collected on our windowsills. It piled up no matter how often the place was dusted or cleaned. Fifteen minutes after my mother was through with a room, that dust seemed thick enough for a finger to trace pointless, ashy patterns in it.

The dust came from the foundry on the other side of the assembly line, the foundry that spat angry cinders into the sky all night long. When people talked about hell, I imagined driving past the foundry at night. From the street below, you could see the fires, red-hot flames shaping glowing metal.

Pontiac was a company town, nothing less. General Motors owned most of the land, and in one way or another held mortgages on the rest. Its holdings included not only the assembly line and the foundry but also a Fisher Body plant and on the outskirts, General Motors Truck and Coach. For a while, some pieces of Frigidaires may even have been put together in our town, but that might just be a trick of my memory, which often confuses the tentacles of institutions that monstrous.

In any case, of the hundred thousand or so who lived in Pontiac, fully half must have been employed either by GM or one of the tool-and-die shops and steel warehouses and the like that supplied it. And anybody who earned his living locally in some less directly auto-related fashion was only fooling himself if he thought of independence.

My father worked without illusions, as a railroad brakeman on freight trains that shunted boxcars through the innards of the plants, hauled grain from up north, transported the finished Pontiacs on the first leg of the route to almost anywhere Bonnevilles, Catalinas, and GTOs were sold.

Our baseball and football ground lay in the shadow of another General Motors building. That building was of uncertain purpose, at least to me. What I can recall of it now is a seemingly reckless height—five or six stories is a lot in the flatlands around the Great Lakes—and endless walls of dark greenish glass that must have run from floor to ceiling in the rooms inside. Perhaps this building was an engineering facility. We didn't know anyone who worked there, at any rate.

Like most other GM facilities, the green glass building was surrounded by a chain link fence with barbed wire. If a ball happened to land on the other side of it, this fence was insurmountable. But only very strong boys could hit a ball that high, that far, anyhow.

Or maybe it just wasn't worth climbing that particular fence. Each August, a few weeks before the new models were officially presented in the press, the finished Pontiacs were set out in the assembly-line parking lot at the top of our street. They were covered by tarpaulins to keep their design changes secret—these were the years when the appearance of American cars changed radically each year. Climbing *that* fence was a neighborhood sport because that was how you discovered what the new cars looked like, whether fins were shrinking or growing, if the new hoods were pointed or flat, how much thinner the strips of whitewall on the tires had grown. A weird game, since everyone knew people who could have told us, given us exact descriptions, having built those cars with their own hands. But climbing that fence added a hint of danger, made us feel we shared a secret, turned gossip into information.

The main drag in our part of town was Joslyn Road. It was where the stoplight and crossing guard were stationed, where the gas station with the condom machine stood alongside a short-order restaurant, drugstore, dairy store, small groceries and a bakery. A few blocks down, past the green glass building, was a low brick building set back behind a wide, lush lawn. This building, identified by a discreet roadside sign, occupied a long block or two. It was the Administration Building for all of Pontiac Motors—a building for executives, clerks, white-collar types. This building couldn't have been more than three-quarters of a mile from my house, yet even though I lived on East Beverly Street from the time I was two until I was past fourteen, I knew only one person who worked there.

In the spring of 1964, when I was fourteen and finishing eighth grade, rumors started going around at Madison Junior High. All the buildings on our side of Joslyn Road (possibly east or west of Joslyn, but I didn't know directions then—there was only "our" side and every-where else) were about to be bought up and torn down by GM. This was worrisome, but it seemed to me that our parents would never allow that perfectly functioning neighborhood to be broken up for no good purpose.

One sunny weekday afternoon a man came to our door. He wore a coat and tie and a white shirt, which meant something serious in our part of town. My father greeted him at the door, but I don't know whether the businessman had an appointment. Dad was working the extra board in those years, which meant he was called to work erratically—four or five times a week, when business was good—each time his nameplate came to the top of the big duty-roster board down at the yard office. (My father didn't get a regular train of his own to work until 1966; he spent almost twenty years on that extra board, which meant guessing whether it was safe to answer the phone every time he actually wanted a day off—refuse a call and your name went back to the bottom of the list.)

At any rate, the stranger was shown to the couch in our front room. He perched on that old gray davenport with its wiry fabric that bristled and stung against my cheek, and spoke quite earnestly to my parents. I recall nothing of his features or of the precise words he used or even of the tone of his speech. But the dust motes that hung in the air that day are still in my memory, and I can remember his folded hands between his spread knees as he leaned forward in a gesture of complicity. He didn't seem to be selling anything; he was simply stating facts.

He told my father that Pontiac Motors was buying up all the houses in our community from Tennyson Street, across from the green glass building, to Baldwin Avenue—exactly the boundaries of what I'd have described as our neighborhood. GM's price was more than fair; it doubled what little money my father had paid in the early fifties. The number was a little over ten thousand dollars. All the other houses were going, too; some had already been sold. The entire process of tearing our neighborhood down would take about six months, once all the details were settled.

The stranger put down his coffee cup, shook hands with my parents and left. As far as I know, he never darkened our doorstep again. In the back of my mind, I can still see him through the front window cutting across the grass to go next door.

"Well, *we're* not gonna move, right, Dad?" I said. Cheeky as I was, it didn't occur to me this wasn't really a matter for adult decision-making—or rather, that the real adults, over at the Administration Building, had already made the only decision that counted. Nor did it occur to me that GM's offer might seem to my father an opportunity to sell at a nice profit, enabling us to move some place "better."

My father did not say much. No surprise. In a good mood, he was the least taciturn man alive, but on the farm where he was raised, not many words were needed to get a seri-ous job done. What he did say that evening indicated that we might stall awhile—perhaps there would be a slightly better offer if we did. But he exhibited no doubt that we would sell. And move.

I was shocked. There was no room in my plans for this...rupture. Was the demolition of our home and neighborhood—that is, my life—truly inevitable? Was there really no way we could avert it, cancel it, *delay* it? What if we just plain *refused to sell*?

Twenty years later, my mother told me that she could still remember my face on that day. It must have reflected extraordinary distress and confusion, for my folks were patient. If anyone refused to sell, they told me, GM would simply build its parking lot—for that was what would replace my world—around him. If we didn't sell, we'd have access privileges, enough space to get into our driveway and that was it. No room to play, and no one there to play with if there had been. And if you got caught in such a situation and didn't like it, then you'd really be in a fix, for the company wouldn't keep its double-your-money offer open forever. If we held out too long, who knew if the house would be worth anything at all. (I don't imagine that my parents attempted to explain to me the political process of condemnation, but if they had, I would have been outraged, for in a way, I still am.)

My dreams always pictured us as holdouts, living in a little house surrounded by asphalt and automobiles. I always imagined nighttime with the high, white-light towers that illuminated all the other GM parking lots shining down upon our house—and the little guardhouse that the company would have to build and man next door to prevent me from escaping our lot to run playfully among the parked cars of the multitudinous employees. Anyone reading this must find it absurd, or the details heavily derivative of bad concentration-camp literature or maybe too influenced by the Berlin Wall, which had been up only a short time. But it would be a mistake to dismiss its romanticism, which was for many months more real to me than the ridiculous reality—moving to accommodate a *PARKING LOT*—which confronted my family and all my friends' families.

If this story were set in the Bronx or in the late sixties, or if it were fiction, the next scenes would be of pickets and protests, meaningful victories and defeats. But this isn't fiction—everything set out here is as unexaggerated as I know how to make it—and the time and the place were wrong for any serious uproar. In this docile midwestern company town, where Walter Reuther's trip to Russia was as inexplicable as the parting of the Red Sea (or as forgotten as the Ark of the Covenant), the idea that a neighborhood might have rights that superseded those of General Motors' Pontiac division would have been regarded as extraordinary, bizarre and subversive. Presuming anyone had had such an idea, which they didn't—none of my friends seemed particularly disturbed about moving, it was just what they would *do*.

So we moved, and what was worse, to the suburbs. This was catastrophic to me. I loved the city, its pavement and the mobility it offered even to kids too young to drive. (Some attitude for a Motor City kid, I know.) In Pontiac, feet or a bicycle could get you anywhere. Everyone had cars, but you weren't immobilized without them, as everyone under sixteen was in the suburbs. In the suburb to which we adjourned, cars were *the* fundamental of life—many of the streets in our new subdivision (not really a neighborhood) didn't even have sidewalks.

Even though I'd never been certain of fitting in, in the city I'd felt close to figuring out how to. Not that I was that weird. But I was no jock and certainly neither suave nor graceful. Still, toward the end of eighth grade, I'd managed to talk to a few girls, no small feat. The last thing I needed was new goals to fathom, new rules to learn, new friends to make.

So that summer was spent in dread. When school opened in the autumn, I was already in a sort of cocoon, confused by the Beatles with their paltry imitations of soul music and the bizarre emotions they stirred in girls.

Meeting my classmates was easy enough, but then it always is. Making new friends was another matter. For one thing, the kids in my new locale weren't the same as the kids in my classes. I was an exceptionally good student (quite by accident—I just read a lot) and my neighbors were classic underachievers. The kids in my classes were hardly creeps, but they weren't as interesting or as accessible as the people I'd known in my old neighborhood or the ones I met at the school bus stop. So I kept to myself.

In our new house, I shared a room with my brother at first. We had bunk beds, and late that August I was lying sweatily in the upper one, listening to the radio (WPON-AM, 1460) while my mother and my aunt droned away in the kitchen.

Suddenly my attention was riveted by a record. I listened for two or three minutes more intently than I have ever listened and learned something that remains all but indescribable. It wasn't a new awareness of music. I liked rock and roll already, had since I first saw Elvis when I was six, and I'd been reasonably passionate about the Ronettes, Gary Bonds, Del Shannon, the Crystals, Jackie Wilson, Sam Cooke, the Beach Boys and those first rough but sweet notes from Motown: the Miracles, the Temptations, Eddie Holland's "Jamie." I can remember a rainy night when I tuned in a faraway station and first heard the end of the Philadelphia Warriors' game in which Wilt Chamberlain scored a hundred points and then found "Let's Twist Again" on another part of the dial. And I can remember not knowing which experience was more splendid.

But the song I heard that night wasn't a new one. "You Really Got a Hold on Me" had been a hit in 1963, and I already loved Smokey Robinson's voice, the way it twined around impossibly sugary lines and made rhymes within the rhythms of ordinary conversation, within the limits of everyday vocabulary.

But if I'd heard those tricks before, I'd never understood them. And if I'd enjoyed rock and roll music previously, certainly it had never grabbed me in quite this way: as a lifeline that suggested—no, insisted—that these singers spoke *for* me as well as to me, and that what they felt and were able to cope with, the deep sorrow, remorse, anger, lust and compassion that bubbled beneath the music, I would also be able to feel and contain. This intimate revelation was what I gleaned from those three minutes of music, and when they were finished and I climbed out of that bunk and walked out the door, the world looked different. No longer did I feel quite so powerless, and if I still felt cheated, I felt capable of getting my own back, some day, some way.

TRAPPED II

It seems I've been playing your game way too long

And it seems the game I've played has made you strong

Jimmy Cliff, "Trapped"

That last year in Pontiac, we listened to the radio a lot. My parents always had. One of my most shattering early memories is of the radio blasting when they got up—my mother around four-thirty, my father at five. All of my life I've hated early rising, and for years I couldn't listen to country music without being reminded almost painfully of those days.

But in 1963 and 1964, we also listened to WPON in the evening for its live coverage of city council meetings. Pontiac was beginning a decade of racial crisis, of integration pressure and white resistance, the typical scenario. From what was left of our old neighborhood came the outspokenly racist militant anti–school busing movement.

The town had a hard time keeping the shabby secret of its bigotry even in 1964. Pontiac had mushroomed as a result of massive migration during and after World War II. Some of the new residents, including my father, came from nearby rural areas where blacks were all but unknown and even the local Polish Catholics were looked upon as aliens potentially subversive to the community's Methodist piety.

Many more of the new residents of Pontiac came from the South, out of the dead ends of Appalachia and the border states. As many must have been black as white, though it was hard for me to tell that as a kid. There were lines one didn't cross in Michigan, and if I was shocked, when visiting Florida, to see separate facilities labeled "White" and "Colored," as children we never paid much mind to the segregated schools, the lily-white suburbs, the way that jobs in the plants were divided up along race lines. The ignorance and superstition about blacks in my neighborhood were as desperate and crazed in their own way as the feelings in any kudzu-covered parish of Louisiana.

As blacks began to assert their rights, the animosity was not less, either. The polarization was fueled and fanned by the fact that so many displaced Southerners, all with the poor white's investment in racism, were living in our community. But it would be foolish to pretend that the situation would have been any more civilized if only the natives had been around. In fact the Southerners were often regarded with nearly as much condescension and antipathy as blacks—race may have been one of the few areas in which my parents found themselves completely in sympathy with the "hillbillies."

Racism was the great trap of such men's lives, for almost everything could be explained by it, from unemployment to the deterioration of community itself. Casting racial blame did much more than poison these people's entire concept of humanity, which would have been plenty bad enough. It immobilized the racist, preventing folks like my father from ever realizing the real forces that kept their lives tawdry and painful and forced them to fight every day to find any meaning at all in their existence. It did this to Michigan factory workers as effectively as it ever did it to dirt farmers in Dixie.

The great psychological syndrome of American males is said to be passive aggression, and racism perfectly fit this mold. To the racist, hatred of blacks gave a great feeling of power and superiority. At the same time, it allowed him the luxury of wallowing in self-pity at the great conspiracy of rich bastards and vile niggers that enforced workaday misery and let the rest of the world go to hell. In short, racism explained everything. There was no need to look any further than the cant of redneck populism, exploited as effectively in the orange clay of the Great Lakes as in the red dirt of Georgia, to find an answer to why it was always the *next* generation that was going to get up and out.

Some time around 1963, a local attorney named Milton Henry, a black man, was elected to Pontiac's city council. Henry was smart and bold—he would later become an ally of Martin Luther King, Jr., of Malcolm X, a principal in the doomed Republic of New Africa. The goals for which Henry was campaigning seem extremely tame now, until you realize the extent to which they haven't been realized in twenty years: desegregated schools, integrated housing, a chance at decent jobs.

Remember that Martin Luther King would not take his movement for equality into the North for nearly five more years, and that when he did, Dr. King there faced the most strident and violent opposition he'd ever met, and you will understand how inflammatory the mere presence of Milton Henry on the city council was. Those council sessions, broadcast live on WPON, invested the radio with a vibrancy and vitality that television could never have had. Those hours of imprecations, shouts and clamor are unforgettable. I can't recall specific words or phrases, though, just Henry's eloquence and the pandemonium that greeted each of his speeches.

So our whole neighborhood gathered round its radios in the evenings, family by family, as if during wartime. Which in a way I guess it was—surely that's how the situation was presented to the children, and not only in the city. My Pontiac junior high school was lightly integrated, and the kids in my new suburban town had the same reaction as my Floridian cousins: shocked that I'd "gone to school with niggers," they vowed they would die—or kill—before letting the same thing happen to them.

This cycle of hatred didn't immediately elude me. Thirteen-year-olds are built to buck the system only up to a point. So even though I didn't dislike any of the blacks I met (it could hardly be said that I was given the opportunity to know any), it was taken for granted that the epithets were essentially correct. After all, anyone could see the grave poverty in which most blacks existed, and the only reason ever given for it was that they liked living that way.

But listening to the radio gave free play to one's imagination. Listening to music, that most abstract of human creations, unleashed it all the more. And not in a vacuum. Semiotics, the New Criticism, and other formalist approaches have never had much appeal to me, not because I don't recognize their validity in describing certain creative structures but because they emphasize those structural questions without much consideration of content: And that simply doesn't jibe with my experience of culture, especially popular culture.

The best example is the radio of the early 1960s. As I've noted, there was no absence of rock and roll in those years betwixt the outbreaks of Presley and Beatles. Rock and roll was a constant for me, the best music around, and I had loved it ever since I first heard it, which was about as soon as I could remember hearing anything.

In part, I just loved the sound—the great mystery one could hear welling up from "Duke of Earl," "Up on the Roof," "Party Lights"; that pit of loneliness and despair that lay barely concealed beneath the superficial bright spirits of a record like Bruce Channel's "Hey Baby"; the nonspecific terror hidden away in Del Shannon's "Runaway." But if that was all there was to it, then rock and roll records would have been as much an end in themselves—that is, as much a dead end—as TV shows like *Leave It to Beaver* (also mysterious, also—thanks to Eddie Haskell—a bit terrifying).

To me, however, TV was clearly an alien device, controlled by the men with shirts and ties. Nobody on television dressed or talked as the people in my neighborhood did. In rock and roll, however, the language spoken was recognizably my own. And since one of the givens of life in the outlands was that we were barbarians, who produced no culture and basically consumed only garbage and trash, the thrill of discovering depths within rock and roll, the very part that was most often and explicitly degraded by teachers and pundits, was not only marvelously refreshing and exhilarating but also in essence liberating—once you'd made the necessary connections.

It was just at this time that pop music was being revolutionized—not by the Beatles, arriving from England, a locale of certifiable cultural superiority, but by Motown, arriving from Detroit, a place without even a hint of cultural respectability. Produced by Berry Gordy, not only a young man but a *black* man. And in that spirit of solidarity with which hometown boys (however unalike) have always identified with one another, Motown was mine in a way that no other music up to that point had been. Surely no one spoke my language as effectively as Smokey Robinson, able to string together the most humdrum phrases and effortlessly make them sing.

That's the context in which "You Really Got a Hold on Me" created my epiphany. You can look at this coldly—structurally—and see nothing more than a naked marketing mechanism, a clear-cut case of a teenager swaddled in and swindled by pop culture. Smokey Robinson wrote and sang the song as much to make a buck as to express himself; there was nothing of the purity of the mythical artist about his endeavor. In any case, the emotion he expressed was unfashionably sentimental. In releasing the record, Berry Gordy was mercenary in both instinct and motivation. The radio station certainly hoped for nothing more from playing it than that its listeners would hang in through the succeeding block of commercials. None of these people and institutions had any intention of elevating their audience, in the way that Leonard Bernstein hoped to do in his *Young People's Concerts* on television. Cultural indoctrination was far from their minds. Indeed, it's unlikely that anyone involved in the process thought much about the kids on the other end of the line except as an amorphous mass of ears and wallets. The pride Gordy and Robinson had in the quality of their work was private pleasure, not public.

Smokey Robinson was not singing of the perils of being a black man in this world (though there were other rock and soul songs that spoke in guarded metaphors about such matters). Robinson was not expressing an experience as alien to my own as a country blues singer's would have been. Instead, he was putting his finger firmly upon a crucial feeling of vulnerability and longing. It's hard to think of two emotions that a fourteen-year-old might feel more deeply (well, there's lust ...), and yet in my hometown expressing them was all but absolutely forbidden to men. This doubled the shock of Smokey Robinson's voice, which for years I've thought of as falsetto, even though it really isn't exceptionally high-pitched compared to the spectacular male sopranos of rock and gospel lore.

"You Really Got a Hold on Me" is not by any means the greatest song Smokey Robinson ever wrote or sang, not even the best he had done up to that point. The singing on "Who's Loving You," the lyrics of "I'll Try Something New," the yearning of "What's So Good About Goodbye" are all at least as worthy. Nor is there anything especially newfangled about the song. Its trembling blues guitar, sturdy drum pattern, walking bass and call-and-response voice arrangement are not very different from many of the other Miracles records of that period. If there is a single instant in the record which is unforgettable by itself, it's probably the opening lines: "I don't like you/But I love you..."

The contingency and ambiguity expressed in those two lines and Robinson's singing of them was also forbidden in the neighborhood of my youth, and forbidden as part and parcel of the same philosophy that propounded racism. Merely calling the bigot's certainty into question was revolutionary—not merely rebellious. The depth of feeling in that Miracles record, which could have been purchased for 69¢ at any K-Mart, overthrew the premise of racism, which was that blacks were not as human as we, that they could not feel—much less express their feelings—as deeply as we did.

When the veil of racism was torn from my eyes, everything else that I knew or had been told was true for fourteen years was necessarily called into question. For if racism explained everything, then without racism, not a single commonplace explanation made any sense. *Nothing* else could be taken at face value. And that meant asking every question once again, including the banal and obvious ones.

For those who've never been raised under the weight of such addled philosophy, the power inherent in having the burden lifted is barely imaginable. Understanding that blacks weren't worthless meant that maybe the rest of the culture in which I was raised was also valuable. If you've never been told that you and your community are worthless—that a parking lot takes precedence over your needs—perhaps that moment of insight seems trivial or rather easily won. For anyone who was never led to expect a life any more difficult than one spent behind a typewriter, maybe the whole incident verges on being something too banal for repetition (though in that case, I'd like to know where the other expressions of this story can be read). But looking over my shoulder, seeing the consequences to my life had I not begun questioning not just racism but all of the other presumptions that ruled our lives, I know for certain how and how much I got over.

That doesn't make me better than those on the other side of the line. On the other hand, I won't trivialize the tale by insisting upon how fortunate I was. What was left for me was a raging passion to explain things in the hope that others would not be trapped and to keep the way clear so that others from the trashy outskirts of barbarous America still had a place to stand—if not in the culture at large, at least in rock and roll.

Of course it's not so difficult to dismiss this entire account. Great revelations and insights aren't supposed to emerge from listening to rock and roll records. They're meant to emerge only from encounters with art. (My encounters with Western art music were unavailing, of course, because every one of them was prefaced by a lecture on the insipid and worthless nature of the music that I preferred to hear.) Left with the fact that what happened to me did take place, and that it was something that was supposed to come only out of art, I reached the obvious conclusion. You are welcome to your own.

SUGGESTIONS FOR DISCUSSION

1. Marsh uses the Smokey Robinson and the Miracles' song "You Really Got a Hold on Me" to anchor his memoir. In fact, it is Marsh's recollection of listening to this song that provides the grounds for the "intimate revelation" or "epiphany" that Marsh sets up at the end of Part I and then explains more fully in Part II. What exactly is this revelation, and how does it emerge from Marsh's experience of listening to rock and roll?

2. In Marsh's view, racism is connected to the powerlessness of the white working-class community in Pontiac. Explain that connection. What does Marsh mean when he talks about racism as the "great trap"? How does Marsh's understanding of racism divide him from the older generation in Pontiac?

3. Marsh explains that rock-and-roll singers "spoke for as well as to me." Can you think of other examples of singers speaking for you or for some other individual or group? Explain what the singer gave voice to in your own or others' experience.

SUGGESTIONS FOR WRITING

1. Dave Marsh's memoir about growing up in Pontiac, Michigan, serves as the introduction to a collection of his essays and reviews of rock and roll. In this sense, the introduction is meant to present his reasons for writing about rock and roll. At the end of the memoir, Marsh says: "I reached the obvious conclusion. You are welcome to your own." Write an essay that explains what conclusions Marsh reaches and why. Do his conclusions seem persuasive to you? Assess how well Marsh enables you to understand his perspective on growing up in Pontiac. What conclusions do you draw?

2. One of the striking features of Dave Marsh's memoir about growing up in Pontiac is his attention to class. As Marsh shows, the sense of powerlessness rock and roll spoke to in his experience grows out of the relation between his working-class community in Pontiac and the dominant economic interests in society, represented by General Motors. Depending on class position, people's feelings can range from the sense of powerlessness which Marsh describes to the persistent anxieties of the middle classes about maintaining their socio-economic status to the

self-confidence of the economically secure and their sense of entitle-
ment to society's rewards. Write an essay that analyzes how the class
character of your family and the community in which you grew up has
shaped your own sense of power or powerlessness and your expectations about what you are entitled to in life. Note whether there are significant differences in expectations between generations. If there are,
how would you explain them? If not, how would you explain the continuity between generations?

3. As you have seen, Marsh uses the Smoky Robinson song "You Really Got
   a Hold on Me" to trigger the central revelation of the memoir, the
   moment when "the veil of racism was torn from my eyes" and everything
   "was necessarily called into question." Use an encounter that you have
   had with a song, an album, a live performance, a movie, or some other
   form of popular culture to write a memoir explaining such a moment of
   insight in your experience. The revelation doesn't have to change everything, as it does for Marsh, but it does need to indicate something
   notable—a new outlook, a shift in attitude, a discovery of one sort or
   another—that you can link to your encounter with music, the media, or
   popular culture. Following Marsh's example, your task is to tell a story in
   sufficient detail that explains how and why the encounter had such a
   powerful impact on you. What was it that gave the song, album, movie,
   etc., such force? What was it about the circumstances at the time that
   made you especially open to such influence?

Youth and American Identity

Lawrence Grossberg

Lawrence Grossberg is the Morris Davis professor of communication at the University of North Carolina–Chapel Hill. Grossberg is a cultural critic who writes
about popular culture and rock music. His essays have been collected in two volumes, *Bringing It All Back Home* and *Dancing in Spite of Myself* (1997). This selection appears in the latter volume. It is taken from "It's a Sin: Essays on
Postmodernism, Politics, and Culture," a study of the connections between politics and popular culture in the Reagan era. In the following excerpt, Grossberg
explains how young people came to be seen following World War II as a living
symbol of a unified national identity.

SUGGESTION FOR READING

As you read, notice that Lawrence Grossberg has organized this section from
his longer essay in a problem-and-solution format. To follow Grossberg's line
of thought, underline and annotate the passages where Grossberg defines
what he sees as the problem of American national identity and where he
explains how American young people were represented as the solution in the
post–World War II period.

The meaning of "America" has always been a problem. Except for rare moments, Americans have rarely had a shared sense of identity and unity. Rather, the United States has always been a country of differences without a center. The "foreign" has always been centrally implicated in our identity because we were and are a nation of immigrants. (Perhaps that partly explains why Americans took up anti-communism with such intensity—here at least was an "other," a definition of the foreign, which could be construed as non-American, as a threatening presence which defied integration.) It is a nation without a tradition, for its history depends upon a moment of founding violence which almost entirely eradicated the native population, thereby renouncing any claim to an identity invested in the land. And despite various efforts to define some "proper" ethnic and national origin, it is precisely the image of the melting pot, this perpetual sense of the continuing presence of the other within the national identity, that has defined the uniqueness of the nation. It is a nation predicated upon differences, but always desperately constructing an imaginary unity. The most common and dominant solution to this in its history involved constituting the identity of the United States in the future tense; it was the land of possibility, the "beacon on the hill," the new world, the young nation living out its "manifest destiny." Perhaps the only way in which the diversity of populations and regions could be held together was to imagine itself constantly facing frontiers. It is this perpetual ability to locate and conquer new frontiers, a sense embodied within "the American dream" as a recurrent theme, that has most powerfully defined a national sense of cultural uniqueness.

After what the nation took to be "its victory" in the second world war it anxiously faced a depressing contradiction. On the one hand, the young nation had grown up, taking its "rightful" place as the leader of the "free world." On the other hand, what had defined its victory—its very identity—depended upon its continued sense of difference from the "grown-up" (i.e., corrupt, inflexible, etc.) European nations. It was America's openness to possibility, its commitment to itself as the future, its ability to reforge its differences into a new and self-consciously temporary unity, that had conquered the fascist threat to freedom. The postwar period can be described by the embodiments of this contradiction: it was a time of enormous conservative pressure (we had won the war protecting the American way; it was time to enjoy it and not rock the boat) and a time of increasingly rapid change, not only in the structures of the social formation but across the entire surface of everyday life. It was a time as schizophrenic as the baby boom generation onto which it projected its contradictions. Resolving this lived dilemma demanded that America still be located in and defined by a future, by an American dream but that the dream be made visible and concrete. If the dream had not yet been realized, it would be shortly. Thus, if this dream were to effectively define the nation in its immediate future, if there was to be any reality to this vision, it would have to be invested, not just in some abstract future, but in a concrete embodiment of America's future, i.e., in a specific generation. Hence, the American identity was projected upon the children of those who had to confront the paradox of America in the postwar years. But if the dream was to be real for them, and if it were to be immediately realizable, people would have to have children and have children they did! And they would have to define those children as the center of their lives and of the nation; the children would become the justification for everything they had done, the source of the very meaning of their lives as individuals and as a nation.

The baby-boom created an enormous population of children by the mid-fifties, a population which became the concretely defined image of the nation's future, a future embodied in a specific generation of youth who would finally realize the American dream and hence become its living symbol. This was to be "the best fed, best dressed, best educated generation" in history, the living proof of the American dream, the realization of the future in the present. The American identity slid from a contentless image of the future to a powerful, emotionally invested image of a generation. America found itself by identifying its meaning with a generation whose identity was articulated by the meanings and promises of youth. Youth, as it came to define a generation, also came to define America itself. And this generation took up the identification as its own fantasy. Not only was its own youthfulness identified with the perpetual youthfulness of the nation, but its own generational identity was defined by its necessary and continued youthfulness. But youth in this equation was not measured simply in terms of age; it was an ideological and cultural signifier, connected to utopian images of the future and of this generation's ability to control the forces of change and to make the world over in its own images. But it was also articulated by economic images of the teenager as consumer, and by images of the specific sensibilities, styles and forms of popular culture which this generation took as its own (hence, the necessary myth that rock and roll was made by American youth). Thus, what was placed as the new defining center of the nation was a generation, an ideological commitment to youth, and a specific popular cultural formation. Obviously, this "consensus" constructed its own powerfully selective frontier: it largely excluded those fractions of the population (e.g., black) which were never significantly traversed by the largely white middle class youth culture. Nevertheless, for the moment, the United States had an identity, however problematic the very commitment to youth was and would become, and it had an apparently perpetually renewable national popular; it had a culture which it thought of as inherently American and which it identified with its own embodied image of itself and its future.

But this was, to say the least, a problematic solution to America's search for an identity, not merely because any generation of youth has to grow up and, one assumes, renounce their youthfulness, but also because "youth" was largely, even in the fifties, an empty signifier. As [Carolyn] Steedman says, "children are always episodes in someone else's narratives, not their own people, but rather brought into being for someone else's purpose." Youth has no meaning except perhaps its lack of meaning, its energy, its commitment to openness and change, its celebratory relation to the present, and its promise of the future. Youth offers no structure of its own with which it can organize and give permanence to a national identity. That is, youth itself, like America, can only be defined apparently in a forever receding future. How could this generation possibly fulfill its own identity and become the American dream— become a future which is always as yet unrealized and unrealizable? How could a generation hold on to its own self-identity as youthful, and at the same time, fulfill the responsibility of its identification with the nation? What does it mean to have constructed a concrete yet entirely mobile center for a centerless nation? Perhaps this rather paradoxical position explains the sense of failure that characterizes the postwar generations, despite the fact that they did succeed in reshaping the cultural and political terrain of the United States.

SUGGESTIONS FOR DISCUSSION

1. Define the problem of American national identity as Grossberg poses it early in this selection. How and in what sense did American young people become a "solution" to this "problem" in the post–World War II period?

2. Grossberg notes that the national commitment to youth set up its own "powerfully selective frontier," excluding, among others, young African Americans. Examine the claim that Grossberg makes here that the image of youth in the popular imagination after World War II was largely a white middle-class one—marked in the media as white "teenagers" but "black

youth." Explain why you do or do not find the claim persuasive. What further evidence could you offer, one way or the other? If you agree with the claim, does it still hold true?

3. At the end of this selection, Grossberg suggests that youth is a "problematic solution to America's search for identity." What makes the solution problematic? What is the "sense of failure that characterizes the postwar generations, despite the fact that they did succeed in reshaping the cultural and political terrain of the United States"?

SUGGESTIONS FOR WRITING

1. Lawrence Grossberg quotes Carolyn Steedman's remark that "children are always episodes in someone else's narratives, not their own people, but rather brought into being for someone else's purposes." Apply this quote to your own experience growing up. Write an essay that explains how your life might be seen as an "episode" in "someone else's narrative." You will need to take into account the hopes your parents and other significant adults invested in you and your future.

2. Grossberg opens this selection by saying that "the United States has always been a country of differences without a center." He describes American national identity as one "predicated upon differences, but always desperately constructing an imaginary unity." Write an essay that explains how you would describe America's national identity. To do this, you will need to consider whether you see a "shared sense of identity and unity" or whether, as Grossberg suggests, American identity should be characterized according to its diversity and the "continuing presence of the other within the national identity."

3. Gloria Naylor in "Kiswana Browne," Dave Marsh in "Fortunate Son," and Lawrence Grossberg in "Youth and American Identity" have written of the issue of generational identity, though in quite different ways. Naylor has written a fictional account, which is a chapter from her novel *The Women of Brewster Place,* while Marsh has written a memoir based on his own experience, and the selection from Grossberg's book *It's a Sin* takes an analytical perspective on the emotional and cultural investments made in American youth in the post–World War II period. Since each of these writers uses such a different writing strategy, they are likely to have somewhat different effects on their readers. Write an essay that compares the writing strategies. What do you see as the advantages and disadvantages of each writer's attempt to address the issue of generational identity? What effects are the writers' various strategies likely to have on readers?

Teenage Wasteland

Donna Gaines

Donna Gaines writes regularly for the *Village Voice.* She has worked as a social worker with teenagers and holds a PhD in sociology. She also writes for *Rolling Stone* and *SPIN* regularly, and teaches at Barnard College. The following selection is taken from Gaines's book *Teenage Wasteland,* an investigative report on the suicide pact carried out by four "heavy metal" kids in the working-class suburbs of northern New Jersey in 1987. As you will see, Gaines does not believe in the traditional neutrality of the reporter toward her subjects but instead aligns herself with the "burnouts" and takes on the task of telling their side of the story.

SUGGESTION FOR READING

This selection is set on the first anniversary of the suicide pact—a time of reckoning with the event and what it meant for the Bergenfield community. As you read, notice how Gaines treats the explanations of "why they did it" offered by various adults, journalists, and officials.

III

On the first anniversary of the suicide pact, a number of special follow-up news reports aired on local and national television. We saw many of the same faces—officials, loyal students of Bergenfield High School, mental health administrators. Over the year the town had gained a certain moral authority—it had survived the suicide pact as well as the media invasion. The community had learned something and had grown. By now, Bergenfield's representatives also knew how to work media.

On WABC's *Nightline,* we would learn of Bergenfield's "new awareness," its comprehensive battery of preventive services. We would see signs advertising "help" posted in store windows all over town, wherever kids might hang around. There was a hot line, and Bergenfield police were getting special training for suicide calls. Bergenfield High School would implement a "peer leadership" program. Parents would get involved at the school. There was an aggressive youth outreach program. The town would take pride in itself as a model for other towns to follow. Officials would seek out federal and state funding so that these programs could continue to help Bergenfield's youth. The town had been successful with its rational responses to a serious social problem. This is how Bergenfield would present itself to the television world.

On a local news program, there was a brief clip of a follow-up visit to Bergenfield High, on the anniversary of the suicide pact. Wholesome and alert students selected to represent the school sat around a table with their principal, Lance Rosza, and reiterated what had become *the* story about the Bergenfield suicide pact. The four kids "had nothing to do with the school." They had "chosen" to drop out. They committed suicide because they had "personal problems."

Police lieutenant Donald Stumpf, who had also served as school board president, admitted that Bergenfield was "weak on dropouts." A juvenile officer, Stumpf noted that once the kids drop out, "they go to never-neverland." Maybe that's where they came from, since the school took every opportunity to point out that it had nothing to do with its students' dropping out. Suddenly the "burnouts" appeared in this state of social dislocation, as if by magic. They had no involvement with the school or the town. By choice they turned their backs on all the available support, concern, and care. They were self-made outcasts, disengaged atoms floating in space somewhere over Bergenfield. There was no discussion of the process, only the product.

In the end, Bergenfield High School would be vindicated by its more devoted students, honored for its "involvement" with potential dropouts and their families. Supposedly, the town's "new awareness" and the preventive services had paid off: a few dropouts had been saved, or at least temporarily reprogrammed. In fact, Bergenfield officials had implemented programs so successfully they were now deemed worthy of replication in communities across America. And finally, everybody agreed Lisa, Cheryl, Tommy Rizzo, and Tommy Olton had committed suicide because they had *personal problems*.

Once the event was understood, explained under the banner of *personal problems,* entire sets of questions could be logically excluded. Yes, the four kids did have personal problems. But maybe there was more to it than that.

Some explanations for "why they did it" were formulated with compassion and sincerity, others were handed down contemptuously, callously. There was no organized conspiracy to keep "the burnouts'" own story silent. But it was kept silent—it was now outside the discourse which framed the event. In a sense, the burnouts' story, their view of things, was evacuated from the social text.

Once we all agreed that the four kids had banded together in a suicide pact because they had *personal problems,* we no longer needed to ask what "the burnouts" were alienating themselves from. Or what role their identification as "burnouts" played in the way they felt about themselves, their families, their school, or their town.

With the suicide pact explained away as the result of *personal problems,* it would be reasonable to believe that aided by Satan, drugs, and rock & roll, four "troubled losers" pulled each other down, deeper and deeper, into an abyss of misery until they finally idled themselves out of it.

If we understood the Bergenfield suicide pact as the result of *personal problems,* we would then have to remove the event from its social context. And once we did that, the story according to "the burnouts" would never be known; it would be buried with the four kids.

There were other reasons why "the burnouts" themselves weren't being heard. First, they had little access to the media. They weren't likely to be on hand when Bergenfield High School authorities needed bright, articulate youth to represent the school or the town to reporters. "Alienated youth" don't hang around teachers or shrinks any longer than they have to.

Second, to the chagrin of their caretakers, "burnouts" aren't particularly "verbal." The basic life-world shared by teenage suburban metalheads is action-oriented: best understood in context, through signs and symbols in motion. It would be hard to convey one's thoughts and feelings to reporters in the succinct lines that make up the news.

In the beginning "the burnouts" did talk to reporters, but things got twisted around— "the papers got the story all fucked up"—and besides, they really hated hearing their friends and their town maligned by strangers. So they clammed right up.

The kids everybody called burnouts understood this: Once you open the door, they've got you. You're playing their language game. Whatever you say can be held against you. At the very least, it changes meaning once it's out of the context created by you and your friends. Better to keep it to yourself. So programs existed in Bergenfield but "the burnouts" didn't dare use them. They may have been outcasts, but they weren't stupid. They knew to avoid trouble.

Kids who realize that they are marginal fear reprisals. Over and over again I was asked not to mention names. And no pictures. As a rule, teenagers love performing for the media. It's a game that lets adults think they understand "kids today," and it's fun. But "the burnouts" were now media wise. They knew better. They wanted complete control or they weren't saying shit.

So by design and by default, nobody really got to hear what "the burnouts" had to say. Like any other alienated youth since the conceptualization of "youth" as a social category, they don't like to talk to adults. About anything. After the suicide pact a few "burnouts" told reporters they were reluctant to confide in school guidance counselors because the counselors might tell their parents and "they'd be punished or even sent to a psychiatric hospital."

The idea of troubled youth doing themselves in was especially disturbing to a town that boasted over thirty active programs for its youth prior to the suicide pact of March 11. Yet Lieutenant Stumpf noted that the Bergenfield kids who most needed the services would not make use of them.

Authorities had acknowledged that the more "alienated" or "high-risk" youth of Bergenfield would not voluntarily involve themselves with the town's services. But the kids weren't talking about what it was that held them back, why they weren't looking to confide in the adults.

In the local papers, experts called in to comment on the tragedy referred to this as "the conspiracy of silence"—the bond of secrecy between teenage friends. While there was some acknowledgment that this reflected kids' terror of "getting in trouble," nobody questioned whether or not this fear might be rational.

Yet it was becoming clear that for Bergenfield's marginally involved youth, the idea of going to see a school guidance counselor or really "opening up" to parents, shrinks, and even clergy was inconceivable. It was apparent that even if they had done nothing wrong, they felt guilty.

On those rare occasions when "burnouts" spoke to reporters, it was obvious that any brush with authority carried the promise of trouble, fear of punishment, of getting snagged for *something*. Enemy lines were drawn. "Burnouts" articulated little confidence that they could be understood by their appointed caretakers, and they assumed that fair treatment was unlikely. Even being able to relate on any level of natural comfort was out of the question.

By now it was also apparent that the "burnouts," as a clique, as carriers of a highly visible "peer-regulated" subculture, posed a threat to the hegemony of parents, teachers, and other mandated "agents of socialization" in Bergenfield. The initial blaming of the suicide victims' friends for whatever had gone wrong did take some of the pressure off the parents and the school. This was predictable—after all, "Where'd you learn that from, your friends?" is a well-traveled technique adults use to challenge and suppress a kid's dissenting view.

While some "burnouts" did complain to reporters about feeling neglected by the town, the school, and their parents, some were just as happy to be left alone. This was a loosely connected network of friends and acquaintances who appeared to live in a world of their own, almost discontinuous from the rest of the town.

Readings of youth, from the *Rebel Without a Cause* 1950s to *The River's Edge* 1980s, have explored the young person's long-standing critique of the adult world: Nobody talks about what is really going on. Especially not parents, and never at school. The "burnouts" seemed to understand that very well. Yet the "insularity" of this group of outcasts frustrated adults everywhere. It annoyed them as much as "explosive inside views" might have titillated them.

These kids were actively guarding their psychic space because the adults controlled everything else. Yet the experts on the scene continued to urge the "burnouts" to purge. Forget about it. It's no secret, you give them an inch and they'll take a self. Bergenfield's alienated youth population already had a different way of seeing things. How *could* they reach out and speak up? When every day up until the suicide pact, and shortly thereafter, they were encouraged to suppress what *they* perceived to be reality? When living means having to deny what you feel, disassociating yourself to survive, you better stay close to your friends or you could start to believe the bullshit. Yes, the "burnouts" carried the news, they knew the truth. They all understood what that "something evil in the air" was. Alone, it made them crazy. Together, it made them *bad*.

SUGGESTIONS FOR DISCUSSION

1. Donna Gaines notes that school officials, mental health workers, and others from Bergenfield explained the suicide pact as the result of "personal problems." Why do you think this explanation became the dominant response to the suicides? Why would this explanation appeal to those in positions of authority? What, in Gaines's view, does this explanation of the suicides evade?

2. Gaines puts considerable emphasis on the suspicion of the "burnouts" toward the media, schools, and the world of adults in general. How does she explain this suspicion? To what extent does it seem reasonable or unreasonable?

3. The media have sensationalized teenage suicide by linking it to heavy-metal music and Satanism. Groups such as Black Sabbath, Ozzy Osborne, Iron Maiden, Judas Priest, and Metallica have been blamed for instigating suicides among heavy-metal fans. At the same time, teens such as the Bergenfield "burnouts" in part define their group identity as "metal-heads"—which sets up a classic case of young people versus adults. What do you know about heavy-metal music? Do you listen to it or know people who do? Why has heavy-metal music become so controversial? Work with two or three other students to answer these questions. Pool the information that you have about heavy-metal music. If you are not familiar with the music, you may want to interview a heavy-metal fan.

SUGGESTIONS FOR WRITING

1. One of Gaines's key points is that adults' tendency to explain the suicides as the result of "personal problems" evades some deeper questions about from what the "burnouts" are alienated and how their identities as "burnouts" shape their relations to each other, their families, their schools, and their communities. She wants us to think about them, in other words, not as isolated individuals but as a social phenomenon—a coherent subculture of "metalheads." Take Gaines's point seriously by using it to analyze a group or subculture of alienated teenagers whom you know something about. Follow Gaines's model for this assignment by writing an account that is sympathetic to troubled or marginalized young people. Imagine that your task is to explain to readers why the group of young people is alienated from the official system and what holds together their subculture.

2. The media have been fascinated by teenage suicide and its sensationalistic connection to heavy-metal music and Satanism. Do some research on how heavy-metal music is represented by adult culture. You might, for example, visit the website of the Parents Music Resource Group, which was established by Tipper Gore to monitor teenage listening preferences. Or you might investigate the 1990 trial in which a $6.2 million product liability suit charged Judas Priest with inspiring the suicides of two Nevada teenagers. (*Reader's Guide to Periodical Literature* should provide you with the sources that you need.) In any case, write a report that explains how

adult culture represents heavy-metal music and what, in your view, is at stake for the relationship between generations.

3. Gaines says that "burnouts" in Bergenfield systematically avoided social services and youth programs directed at "high-risk" young people. Their suspicion of adult culture was simply too high. Write an essay that explains what kinds of programs might succeed. How could they overcome young people's fears and suspicions? You don't have to limit yourself to the Bergenfield "burnouts" for this assignment. Draw on your knowledge, observations, and experience with troubled young people in other settings.

Goths in Tomorrowland

Thomas Hine

Thomas Hine is well known for his writing about architecture and design. He is the author of *Populuxe* (1987), a book on American design in the 1950s and 1960s, and *The Total Package* (1995), a study of brand names and packaging. The following selection comes from his most recent book, *The Rise and Fall of the American Teenager* (1999). As you will see, Hine explores the diversity of teen culture and its relation to adult society.

SUGGESTION FOR READING

Hine begins with an anecdote about the goth "invasion" of Disneyland in 1997 and the "zero tolerance" policy adopted by Disney's security forces. Notice that Hine wants to do more than just tell his story. He sees in it a larger issue about how the "mere presence of teenagers threatens us." As you read, keep in mind this general theme of the alienation of teenagers from adult society, how adults enforce it and how teenagers maintain it.

I feel stupid and contagious.

    Kurt Cobain, "Smells Like Teen Spirit" (1991)

In the summer of 1997, the security forces at Disneyland and the police in surrounding Anaheim, California, announced a "zero tolerance" policy to fend off a new threat.

Hordes of pale, mascaraed goths—one of the many tribes of teendom—were invading. It was an odd onslaught. Unlike their barbarian namesakes, they weren't storming the gates of the walled Magic Kingdom. They had yearly passes, purchased for $99 apiece. Many of them had not even been goths when their parents dropped them off at the edge of the parking lot. Rather, they changed into their black sometimes gender-bending garments, applied their white makeup accented with black eyeliner and gray blush-on. The punkier among them accessorized with safety pins and other aggressively ugly, uncomfortable-looking pierceables. And most important of all, they reminded themselves to look really glum. Once inside, they headed for Tomorrowland, Disneyland's most unsettled neighborhood, and hogged all the benches.

It was a sacrilege. Disneyland, said those who wrote letters to the editor, is supposed to be "the happiest place on earth," and these young people with their long faces clearly didn't belong. The presence of sullen clusters of costumed teens showed, some argued, that Disney had given up its commitment to family values. It was no longer possible to feel safe in Disneyland, came the complaints, and that was about the last safe place left.

Actually, the safety of Disneyland was part of the attraction for the goth teens. They told reporters that their parents bought them season passes because the theme park's tight security would assure nothing bad would happen to them. In the vast sprawl of Orange County, California, there are very few safe places where teens are welcome, and Disneyland has always been one of them.

Those who complained spoke of the goths as if they were some sort of an alien force, not just white suburban California teenagers. Only a few years earlier, they had been kids who were delighted to go with their parents to meet Mickey. And only a few years from now, they will be young adults—teaching our children, cleaning our teeth, installing our cable television. But now they insist on gloom. And the adult world could not find a place for them—even in Tomorrowland.

Unlike Minnesota's Mall of America—which became a battleground for gang warfare transplanted from Minneapolis and which eventually barred unescorted teenagers from visiting at night—the perceived threat to Disneyland was handled in a low-key way. Teenagers were arrested for even the tiniest infractions outside the park and forced by security guards to follow Disneyland's quite restrictive rules of decorum within the park. After all, the theme park's administrators had an option not available to government; they could revoke the yearly passes. While Disneyland doesn't enforce a dress code for its visitors, it can keep a tight rein on their behavior.

Yet, despite its lack of drama, I think the situation is significant because it vividly raises many of the issues that haunt teenagers' lives at the end of the twentieth century. It is about the alienation of teenagers from adult society, and equally about the alienation of that society from its teenagers. The mere presence of teenagers threatens us.

It is also a story about space. How, in an environment devoid of civic spaces, do we expect people to learn how to behave as members of a community? And it is about the future. Is a meaningful tomorrow so far away that young people can find nothing better to do than engage in faux-morbid posturing? (Even Disney's theme parks are losing track of the future; they are converting their Tomorrowlands into nostalgic explorations of how people used to think about the future a century and more ago.)

And even its resolution—a stance of uneasy tolerance backed by coercion and force—seems symptomatic of the way Americans deal with young people now.

Inevitably, a lack of perspective bedevils efforts to recount the recent past, but the problem is more than that. The last quarter of the twentieth century has, in a sense, been about fragmentation. Identity politics has led to a sharpening of distinctions among the groups in the society, and a suspicion of apparent majorities. Postmodern literary theory warns us to mistrust narratives. Even advertising and television, which once united the country in a common belief in consumption, now sell to a welter of micromarkets. Thus we are left without either a common myth, or even the virtual common ground of *The Ed Sullivan Show*.

It seems crude now to speak of teenagers and think of the white middle-class, heterosexual young people that the word "teenager" was originally coined to describe. The "echo" generation of teenagers, whose first members are now entering high school, is about 67 percent non-Hispanic white, 15 percent black, 14 percent Hispanic, and 5 percent Asian or American Indian. The proportion of Hispanic teens will grow each year, and the Census Bureau also reports significantly greater numbers of mixed-race teens and adoptees who are racially different from their parents.

Even the word "Hispanic" is a catch-all that conceals an enormous range of cultural difference between Mexicans, Cubans, Puerto Ricans, Dominicans, and other groups whose immigration to the United States has increased tremendously during the last quarter century. Urban school systems routinely enroll student populations that speak dozens of different languages at home.

Differences among youth do not simply involve differences of culture, race, income, and class—potent as these are. We now acknowledge differences in sexual orientation among young people. Today's students are also tagged with bureaucratic or medical assessments of their abilities and disabilities that also become part of their identities.

There are so many differences among the students at a high school in Brooklyn, Los Angeles, or suburban Montgomery County, Maryland, that one wonders whether the word "teenager" is sufficient to encompass them all. Indeed, the terms "adolescent" and "teenager" have always had a middle-class bias. In the past, though, working-class youths in their teens were already working and part of a separate culture. Now that the work of the working class has disappeared, their children have little choice but to be teenagers. But they are inevitably different from those of the postwar and baby boomer eras because they are growing up in a more heterogeneous and contentious society.

What follows, then, is not a single unified narrative but, rather, a sort of jigsaw puzzle. Many pieces fit together nicely. Others seem to be missing. It's easier to solve such a puzzle if you know what picture is going to emerge, but if I were confident of that, I wouldn't be putting you, or myself, to such trouble.

These discussions do have an underlying theme: the difficulty of forging the sort of meaningful identity that Erik Erikson described at midcentury. But if we look for a picture of the late-twentieth-century teenager in these fragments, we won't find it. That's because we're expecting to find something that isn't there.

The goths who invaded Tomorrowland are examples of another kind of diversity—or perhaps pseudo-diversity—that has emerged gaudily during the last two decades. These are the tribes of youth. The typical suburban high school is occupied by groups of teens who express themselves through music, dress, tattoos and piercing, obsessive hobbies, consumption patterns, extracurricular activities, drug habits, and sex practices. These tribes hang out in different parts of the school, go to different parts of town. Once it was possible to speak of a youth culture, but now there is a range of youth subcultures, and clans, coteries, and cliques within those.

In 1996 a high school student asked fellow readers of an Internet bulletin board what groups were found in their high schools. Nearly every school reported the presence of "skaters," "geeks," "jocks," "sluts," "freaks," "druggies," "nerds," and those with "other-colored hair," presumably third-generation punks. There were also, some students reported, "paper people," "snobs," "band geeks," "drama club types" (or "drama queens"), "soccer players" (who aren't counted as jocks, the informant noted), "Satanists," "Jesus freaks," "industrial preps," "techno-goths," and "computer dweebs." Several took note of racial and class segregation, listing "blacks," "Latinos," "white trash," and "wannabe blacks." There were "preppies," who, as one writer, possibly a preppie herself noted, "dress like the snobs but aren't as snobbish." "Don't forget about the druggie preps," another writer fired back.

This clearly wasn't an exhaustive list. Terms vary from school to school and fashions vary from moment to moment. New technologies emerge, in-line skates or electronic pagers for instance, and they immediately generate their own dress, style, language, and culture.

The connotations of the technologies can change very quickly. Only a few years ago, pagers were associated mostly with drug dealers, but now they've entered the mainstream. Pagers became respectable once busy mothers realized that they could use them to get messages to their peripatetic offspring. Young pager users have developed elaborate codes for flirtation, endearment, assignation, and insults. They know that if 90210 comes up on their pager, someone's calling them a snob, and if it's 1776, they're revolting, while if it's 07734, they should turn the pager upside down and read "hELLO."

Most of the youth tribes have roots that go back twenty years or more, though most are more visible and elaborate than they once were. Many of these tribes are defined by the music they like, and young people devote a lot of energy to distinguishing the true exemplars of heavy metal, techno, alternative, or hip-hop from the mere poseurs. Hybrid and evolutionary versions of these cultures, such as speed metal, thrash, or gangsta rap make things far more confusing.

One thing that many of these subcultures have in common is what has come to be known as modern primitivism. This includes tattooing, the piercing of body parts, and physically expressive and dangerous rituals, such as the mosh pits that are part of many rock concerts. Young people use piercing and tattoos to assert their maturity and sovereignty over their bodies.

"Can this be child abuse?" Sally Dietrich, a suburban Washington mother, asked the police when her thirteen-year-old son appeared with a bulldog tattooed on his chest. "I said, 'What about destruction of property?' He's my kid." Her son was, very likely, trying to signal otherwise. Nevertheless, Dietrich mounted a successful campaign to bar tattooing without permission in the state of Maryland, one of many such restrictions passed during the 1990s.

It may be a mistake to confuse visible assertions of sexual power with the fact of it. For example, heavy-metal concerts and mosh pits are notoriously male-dominated affairs. And the joke of MTV's "Beavis and Butt-head" is that these two purported metalheads don't have a clue about how to relate to the opposite sex. Those whose costumes indicate that they have less to prove are just as likely to be sexually active.

In fact, visitors to Disneyland probably don't need to be too worried about the goths, a tribe which, like many of the youth culture groups, has its roots in English aestheticism. As some goths freely admit, they're pretentious, and their morbid attitudes are as much a part of the dress-up games as the black clothes themselves.

The goth pose provides a convenient cover. For some males, it gives an opportunity to try out an androgynous look. The costumes, which emphasize the face and make the body disappear, may also provide an escape for young women and men who fear that they're overweight or not fit. Black clothes are slimming, and darkness even more so. "Until I got in with goths, I hadn't met other people who are depressed like I am and that I could really talk to," said one young woman on an Internet bulletin board. Another said being a goth allowed her relaxation from life as a straight-A student and a perfect daughter.

Although young people recognize an immense number of distinctions among the tribes and clans of youth culture and are contemptuous of those they regard as bogus, most adults cannot tell them apart. They confuse thrashers with metalheads and goths because they all wear black. Then they assume that they're all taking drugs and worshipping Satan.

The adult gaze is powerful. It classes them all as teenagers, whether they like it or not. The body alterations that young people use to assert that they are no longer children successfully frighten grown-ups, but they also convince them these weird creatures are well short of being adults. The ring through the lip or the nipple merely seems to demonstrate that they are not ready for adult responsibility. What they provoke is not respect but restrictions.

Tribes are about a yearning to belong to a group—or perhaps to escape into a disguise. They combine a certain gregariousness with what seems to be its opposite: a feeling of estrangement. The imagery of being alone in the world is not quite so gaudy as that of modern primitivism, yet it pervades contemporary youth culture.

While youthful exploration of the 1920s, 1940s, 1950s, or 1960s often took the form of wild dancing, more recently it has been about solitary posing. This phenomenon is reflected, and perhaps encouraged, by MTV, which went on the air in 1981. In contrast with the rudimentary format of *American Bandstand,* in which the viewer seemed simply to be looking in on young people having fun dancing with one another, MTV videos tend to be more about brooding than participation. They are highly subjective, like dreams or psychodramas. They connect the viewer with a feeling, rather than with other people.

And while the writhing, leaping, and ecstatic movement of the mosh pit seems to be an extreme form of *American Bandstand*-style participation, it embodies a rather scary kind of community. One's own motions have little relationship to those of others. And there's substantial risk of injury. The society implied by the dance is not harmonious and made up of couples. Rather, it is violent and composed of isolated individuals who are, nevertheless, both seeking and repulsing contact with others. If this sounds like a vision of American society as a whole, that's not surprising. Figuring out what things are really like is one of the tasks of youth. Then they frighten their elders by acting it out.

When a multinational company that sells to the young asked marketing psychologist Stan Gross to study teenagers around the country, he concluded after hundreds of interviews and exercises that the majority of young people embraced an extreme if inchoate individualism. Most believe that just about every institution they come in contact with is stupid. When asked to choose an ideal image for themselves, the majority selected a picture that depicted what might be described as confident alienation. The figure sits, comfortably apart from everything, his eyes gazing out of the image at something unknown and distant.

Such studies are done, of course, not to reform the young but to sell to them. And the collective impact of such knowledge of the young has been the proliferation of advertising that encourages young people not to believe anything—even advertising—and to express their superiority by purchasing the product that's willing to admit its own spuriousness.

The distance between spontaneous expression and large-scale commercial exploitation has never been shorter. Creators of youth fashion, such as Nike, go so far as to send scouts to the ghetto to take pictures of what young people are wearing on the streets and writing on the walls. Nike seeks to reflect the latest sensibilities, both in its products and its advertising. The company feeds the imagery right back to those who created it, offering them something they cannot afford as a way of affirming themselves.

One result of this quick feedback is that visual symbols become detached from their traditional associations and become attached to something else. Rappers, having made droopy pants stylish in the suburbs, began to wear preppie sportswear, and brand names like Tommy Hilfiger and Nautica became badges of both WASP and hip-hop sensibilities. Thus, even when the fashions don't change, their meaning does. Such unexpected shifts in the meaning of material goods cannot be entirely manipulated by adults. But marketers have learned that they must be vigilant in order to profit from the changes when they come.

More overtly than in the past, many of today's young are looking for extreme forms of expression. This quest is just as apparent in sports, for example, as in rock culture. The 1996 Atlanta Olympics began with an exhibition of extreme cycling and extreme skating. These and other extreme sports, categorized collectively as "X-Games," have become a cable television fixture because they draw teenage males, an otherwise elusive audience. "Extreme" was one of the catchwords of the 1990s, and it became, by 1996, the most common word in newly registered trade names, attached either to products aimed at youth or which sought to embody youthfulness.

Young people are caught in a paradox. They drive themselves to extremes to create space in which to be themselves. Yet the commercial machine they think they're escaping is always on their back, ready to sell them something new.

SUGGESTIONS FOR DISCUSSION

1. Thomas Hine uses the opening anecdote about goth teens and Disneyland to announce the theme of this passage. As Hine presents it, what is this story meant to represent about the relations between teenagers and adults? What further examples and evidence does Hine offer in the rest of the selection to reinforce his point?

2. Hine suggests that the terms "teenager" and "youth culture" no longer have one common meaning. If anything, he sees a diversity of teenagers and "tribes of youth" defined by different styles of dress, music, body ornamentation, extracurricular activity, drug use, and sexual practices, as well as racial and ethnic markers. Consider your high school and college. What "tribes" are represented? Develop a classification of the various groups. What do you see as the leading ways in which groups of young people define themselves? What are the meanings of the identities they take on? What are the relationships among the various groups?

3. Hine points to a social dynamic in which "extreme" forms of cultural expressions, such as tatooing, body piercing, music, and sports, are meant to affirm group identities but, from an adult perspective, only reinforce the view that young people "are not ready for adult responsibility." What is the lure, for young people, of such extreme expressions? How, from the perspective of adults, do the various forms of extreme style and behavior get lumped together?

SUGGESTIONS FOR WRITING

1. Write an essay that classifies the various groups (or "tribes") of youth culture at the high school you attended or your college. Describe the leading groups, their styles, behaviors, values, and attitudes. After you have offered readers an overview of the groups, explain their relationship to each other and to the adult society that surrounds them.

2. Hine suggests that some of the groupings of youth culture represent a threat to adult society. Consider what Hine thinks is the source of this fear. Why would adults be so worried about young people? What exactly is at stake in the fears and anxieties of the older generation?

3. At the end of this selection, Hine says that young people are "caught in a paradox": No matter how much they rebel against adult society in order to create a space for themselves, the "commercial machine" they're trying to escape from reincorporates their cultural styles in the form of new products and merchandise. Do you think this is a reasonable assessment? Why or why not? Write an essay that explains your answer—and whether you think young people can establish their own way of doing things, independent of the market and the workings of adult society.

The shootings at Columbine High School on April 20, 1999, left thirteen dead, twenty-three wounded, and the nation stunned. Once again, the unthinkable had happened, and Littleton, Colorado joined Pearl, Mississippi; West Paducah, Kentucky; Jonesboro, Arkansas; and Springfield, Oregon—the apparently peaceful small towns in the American heartland whose daily lives have been interrupted forever by the sound of gunfire.

Almost immediately, journalists, educators, psychologists, politicians, talk show hosts, religious leaders, and others started to search for explanations. What makes teenagers like Eric Harris and Dylan Klebold into killers? What is going wrong with the younger generation? Who is to blame? The reasons offered to explain the shootings ranged across the cultural landscape of contemporary America—hate websites, ultra-violent video games, black trenchcoats, goth culture, Marilyn Manson, the breakdown of family values, the lack of school discipline, the easy availability of guns, child abuse, high school cliques, and the social ostracism of geeks and nerds by the jocks and preps. At the same time, while adults were agonizing about the meaning of Littleton, many young people turned to the Internet and World Wide Web to make sense of the shootings from their own perspectives.

The following two reading selections not only offer different perspectives on the Littleton shootings, teenagers, and media violence. They also come from two different sources. Thomas de Zengotita's "Gunfire Dialogues: Notes on the Reality of Virtuality" appeared in the monthly magazine *Harper's*, while Jon Katz's "More from the Hellmouth: Kids Tell About Rage" appeared originally online at Slashdot.

The Gunfire Dialogues:
Notes on the Reality of Virtuality

Thomas de Zengotita

Thomas de Zengotita teaches at the Dalton School and New York University. "Gunfire Dialogues" was published in *Harper's* magazine in July 1999, a few months after the shootings a Columbine High School. As de Zengotita notes, media coverage of "senseless school shootings" has become an unsettlingly familiar event in which we all have a part to play. In "Gunfire Dialogues," de Zengotita is interested in how the "sheer amount of media" absorbed by teenagers influences not only those who commit violent acts but the vast majority who don't.

SUGGESTION FOR READING

At the beginning of the second section, Thomas de Zengotita asks whether "the influence of today's media [is] qualitatively different from yesterday's"— and then says the "answer is obviously yes." As you read, notice how de Zengotita explains what is new and different about the media and how they influence everyone—not just those who take part in violent acts.

The incident at Columbine High School on April 20 arrested our attention not only because fifteen people were killed but because it consolidated our sense that school shootings say Something Important About Society. As a media event, it is related somehow to O.J. and Di and Monica, but practical preoccupation with causal "factors" distracted us, and the possibility of general synthesis was sacrificed to the need to Do Something. The essentials emerged within days of the event but flattened into cliché as the buzz of commentary echoes across our virtual polis. Still, they can be recovered.

The boy appeared in a local-folks-react piece on one of the morning shows just days after the shootings. He was white-ethnicky, pudgy and pimply, with purple streaks in his dread-locked hair and a couple of studs in his face. He spoke with a defiant whine. He didn't con-done the shootings, and he wasn't into Hitler, but he had been harassed by jocks all his life, and those kids in Colorado "at least…took a stand." He thought a lot of other kids like him would kind of idolize the Trench-coat Mafia.

He was right. Saturday's *New York Times* covered online discussions of the Littleton mas-sacre. The tone was set by psychologists and website executives hyping virtual communi-ties, but quotes from the kids told the tale: "I would never personally do anything like that, but it did take guts" and "Even though I would never take someone else's life, maybe it will make people think before they open their mouths next time…." The cruelty of prep and jock "culture" toward those who didn't fit in was the underlying issue for these kids. Cookie Roberts made it official that Sunday morning, and *Rolling Stone* columnist Jon Katz's web-site became a polling resource for the mainstream. The floodgates opened and commenta-tors everywhere were publicly recalling their high school days. Cliques joined Kosovo on the national agenda.

Sally Satel, a Yale psychiatrist, had an op-ed piece about the busloads of "grief counselors" who are as much a feature of such scenes as are SWAT teams and flower shrines. She focused on the "commodification of grief," the "unholy therapeutic alliance" between the talk-through-your-feelings-and-get-to-closure counselor and the empathic servants of the twenty-four-hour news cycle. And can anyone doubt that stricken mourners, no matter how authentic their feelings, respond at some level to implicit expectations when the cameras roll! Especially since they have seen this show on TV before: now, suddenly, they are in it.

For it is very much a show, and not only in the trivial sense that anything covered by the media becomes a show. "Senseless school shooting" is now a genre with resonance across the country because it unites universality and specificity so compellingly. There is a set: the open space of parking lots and sports fields around the one- or two-level brick-and-concrete sprawl of buildings, the school name and colors and logo—all pretty much interchangeable across the exurban landscape. There is a cast: kids made for yearbook pictures, local law-enforcement and school officials rising, or not rising, to the occasion, local volunteers in emergency services likewise, and local religious and political leaders, too. An indefinable qual-ity of localness pervades the scene. It's the hair and mustaches, the jackets, hats and eyewear, the cars and trucks—you can feel the nearby malls and the traffic on the interstate at the edge of town. It isn't New York and it isn't L.A. It's the heartland, and everyone knows this plot: reconstructing the lives of the killers, tracking down accomplices, the community outpour-ing of support, the coming together, the healing process—and the rifts and recriminations as well. Likewise the spectators; we distinguish immediately between this genre and natural-dis-aster or horrors-of-war "shows." We know how to respond as an audience as surely as we would know how to play our roles if, God forbid, we suddenly landed a part.

"Shows" belongs in quotes because, like all things postmodern, this is a reflexive entity, and that reflexivity testifies, in its practical futility, to the power of the total phenomenon. No amount of media self-criticism makes a dent. For "*coverage* of senseless school shootings" is also a genre. The correspondents are in moved-to-the-breaking-point-but-professional mode. The expert guests and other commentators are also grave, but inexplicability is not their provenance, and I-told-you-so and now-maybe-you'll-listen drives their spin toward gun control or family values or psychological-intervention programs.

The point here is not exploitation of personal pain for commercial or political gain. We are not at that familiar level of criticism. Indeed, many in the media have been moved to even more reflexive contortions because of just such concerns: correspondents asking interviewees about their grief now also ask how they feel about being interviewed about their grief. No, the point is to call attention to an emergent level of culture that transcends issue-oriented efforts to solve a social problem.

The key to the success of the show is the way everyone can identify so specifically with the set, the characters, and the plot; that is why the outpouring spreads, and innumerable other local responses are organized, or erupt, under the sign of "could it happen here?" It is like a myth played out in "real time," embracing millions of people. That is how the personal becomes the political. That is why ideologies no longer cohere and issues fragment; they can't compete with such narratives.

We come closest to addressing the situation as a whole when asking how violence in the media influences behavior. Cultural conservatives focus on permissive standards related to content, and surely that content goes way beyond anything imaginable thirty years ago. People who commit these acts always show evidence of its influence. The Littleton shooters spent a lot of time with *Natural Born Killers* and goth CDs and hate websites, but libertarians point out that Charlie Starkweather was inspired by comics and rock and roll, and argue that agency must be attributed to the person, not the muse. So the debate resolves itself into this question: Is the influence of today's media qualitatively different from yesterday's?

The answer is obviously yes. What is shown makes a difference. Saturation and production values matter, too. Interactivity from the killer's point of view in a graphic video game goes right to the sensorimotor brain centers. High school cliques have always been with us and jocks have always bullied geeks; the geeks now have something besides the chess club to retreat to—they have games like Doom, entire environments of testosterone-stimulating violence in which they compensate virtually for physical inequities. And compulsions of mimesis among the psychotically inclined have thresholds. This can be denied only by pointing to the fact that overall violence among teenagers, in school or out, is dramatically lower than it used to be. But that just confirms that, in an age when the organized and ritualized Fifties fistfight seems quaint, conflict-resolution programs collaborate unwittingly with computer games to nudge violence into virtuality. It also tells us that healthier kids, who never act out, cope differently with the same stimulations. What it does not tell us is that those stimulations might have powerful effects on them, perhaps just as corrosive in subtler ways.

The sheer amount of media absorbed by kids who commit such acts, the variety and intensity of its modalities, and the recurrence of specific items on their personal-favorites list tell us that something comparable in force to the oral culture Plato attacked in *The Republic* has emerged among us. Comparable in force, but very different in context and functionality. The performative Homeric narrative of pre-literate Greece provided irresistible paradigms of behavior and evaluation in an essentially tribal society. To counter the momentum of so enveloping a tradition, Plato recommended the detachments of a rational philosophy. The post-literate fusion of act and fiction in multimedia narratives of our day are similarly enveloping, but we resist through detachments of knowingness and irony. Or most of us do. But, resistant or not, we all know what counts: being on the show.

The really decisive piece of media in the Columbine case was the tape the shooters and their friends made for a video-production course in their school. In the tape, the boys rehearsed the event they would one day—but what is the verb here? Enact? Perform? A word like that is needed. The model of plan followed by action will not apply. That model belongs to an age when events in the real world and accounts of those events in the media were essentially separate. That difference no longer exists. For the shooters knew what coverage they could expect in their second production of "school shootings." They were already and always "on"—just like the people in Hollywood and New York, pitching angles on this story to one another before the bodies were out of Columbine's library.

So we are faced with a new space for public culture somewhere between reality and simulation, between action and acting—and this holds not just for latent psychotics but for the rest of us as well. Saying, "Well, millions of kids listen to Marilyn Manson and never harm anyone" misses the point. *Those* kids are just as influenced in a *different* way by the totality that is this virtual space. They go ironic rather than psychotic. They are the "apathetic" ones, for whom politics is, at best, a field of self-expression in which certain people identify with certain issues and "promote awareness" of them—a politics in which issues have fans.

Think of it all as do followers of Nietzsche among French intellectuals. The brain and its structure, the body and its desires, meet culture directly. Inclinations and threshold are built into our neurochemistry, and stimulating content and forms of behavior are imposed by technologies of communication and the administration of daily life in routines of work and play. The more enveloping and penetrating the stimulations and routines, the more uniform and centerless the settings of our lives—and what else should we expect but occasional psychotic eruptions on a vast plain of disengagement sustained by an economy devoted to simulations?

Traditional opinion leaders don't want to see this phenomenon whole. Those in the mainstream have a piece of the action—their material interests are increasingly vested in the immaterial economy. They must see the new technologies as a force at least *potentially* for good. People on the left don't want to see it either, but, ironically, this is because the media seem to them not material enough! They cling to old bread-and-circuses, opiate-of-the-people critiques. They learned nothing from O.J. and Di and Monica. They can't believe that virtual reality is *real*. But the folks who are creating virtuality have a deeper understanding. From *The Truman Show* to *The Matrix*, a slew of recent movies is exposing the project built into these technologies. The wonder is that we don't let this surreptitious confession sink in. After all, don't these technologies have as their explicit purpose making representations more and more realistic (think computer graphics and animations) and making reality more and more representational (think Times Square and sanctioned graffiti)?

A few years ago, Benjamin Barber wrote a book that characterized posteverything culture as *Jihad v. McWorld*. He had principally in mind developments that preoccupy political thinkers—global corporate media vis-à-vis retribalization after the Cold War: Hutu killers in Nike paraphernalia and so on. Columbine showed that the phenomenon Barber described is not essentially residual, that a hybrid entity with a structuring life of its own has emerged on the planet, a life in which Serbian three-fingered salutes echo homey gangsta signs and Hitler's birthday and high school movies converge seamlessly with Trench-coat Mafia and twenty-four-hour coverage of "Terror in the Rockies." To Muslims and Christians add Hilfiger and piercing.

Half-convinced, perhaps, you ask, "What is to be done?" And the answer must be, "Don't ask *that* question so fast." For if, as a gigantic matter of historical fact, our world is becoming so intensely reflexive that distinctions between action and performance and reality and representation are eroding at every level of our lives, then that question, asked immediately, represses the realization that we are at an utter loss. And that realization might spur us to take up a challenge to our understanding, which we cannot afford to leave to prophetic digerati and deconstructing academics. Because this much can be said for certain: we are all in the show, and the show must go on.

More from the Hellmouth: Kids Tell About Rage

Jon Katz

Jon Katz is a visiting scholar at the First Amendment Center at Vanderbilt University and writes two weekly columns on digital technology, geek culture, and life on the Web for the Center's website: free! Freedom Forum Online. The following selection appeared originally at the online site Slashdot on April 28, 1999, just a week after the Littleton shootings. Katz has written extensively about the Littleton shooting and its aftermath.

SUGGESTION FOR READING

Notice how Jon Katz introduces his column and then turns it over to teenagers and others who wrote him e-mails about the Littleton shootings—and what they reveal about life at school for goths, gamers, geeks, and nerds. Consider in what sense these voices offer another perspective from what the mainstream media was saying at the time about the Littleton shootings.

The messages started coming in a trickle Friday afternoon, April 23, becoming a torrent by Monday. They were wrenching, sometimes astonishing, an electronic outpouring of anger and compassion. Some came via *free!*; most came from an open-source website I write for called Slashdot. They were all in response to the Littleton, Colo., tragedy, and many included pleas for the message to reach the mainstream media that life in America's schools can be a nightmare for the so-called geeks of the world, the alienated, individualistic, or different.

While some of the messages expressed sympathy for the killers in Littleton, hardly any advocated violence or excused it. Rather, they were an effort to describe how brutal and alienating life can be for kids who aren't "normal," who are subject to perpetual harassment, cruelty and exclusion. For these geeks—sometimes also labeled nerds, dorks, goth—life seems even bleaker after Littleton than it was before.

They perceive their tormentors—jocks, preps, popular kids—as the objects of great sympathy, while they are more resented than they already were. And journalism, as ever, responds to complex and difficult social issues in the most manipulative and simple-minded of ways: suggesting that video games turn kids into killers, or that violence among the young was born on the Internet. The kids know better, and the stories they read and see further disconnect them from what they sadly perceive as a clueless media culture.

These painful testimonials explained more, a lot more, about Littleton than all the vapid news stories about video violence, goths and game-crazed geeks. These kids well understand that video games don't turn kids into murderers. They see journalism as an alien culture that has no idea what their lives are like, and journalists as much too lazy to find out. I've gotten close to 3,000 of these messages in the last few days—2,000 by Monday night, six days after the tragedy, and more pouring in. One computer crashed just under the e-mail load.

For a writer, there's nothing more humbling than to be at a loss for words. I can't possibly do more justice to some of these posts than to let them speak for themselves.

Thousands of e-mails were about the Hellmouth—school. Nobody remembered it fondly. Some had unbearable memories. Some are still recovering. Many more are still there, suffering every day. Many people wrote me asking if they could help these kids. Others wondered if there was any way these stories might reach the mainstream media in some form.

I replied that they shouldn't worry about that. These columns and the responses to them are ricocheting all over the world, via e-mail, mailing lists, links, even faxes. There have been scores of requests to reprint them, especially by guidance counselors, high school newspaper editors and kids who have their own websites.

On the Net, ideas don't need to be pushed. They find their own audience and stand or fall of their own weight. Eventually, I will answer each e-mail, and am grateful for them.

Here are more of these voices from the Hellmouth, from some of its children:

From Eric near Littleton, Colo.:

"I live just a few miles north of the school between the same streets. I'm a geek under the skin. I was a state champ in the high jump, and the leading scorer on the track team, so I was not quite the outcast that some of the geeks are, but I understand what they are going through. I wasn't very popular despite being the big athlete on campus, but I at least had respect.

"I am very happy to see you carrying coverage of 'the other side' of the story; the side nobody else wants to look at. These outcast kids are now being swept under the rug at best, and prosecuted at worst."

From Josh, a Slashdot reader:

"I was much like those kids when I was in school—weird, cast out, not much liked, alienated, all that sort of thing....I used to imagine bringing weaponry to school and making the f—ers who made by life miserable beg for mercy. (I was never sure what to do then, though. Do I let them go? They won't have learned, and after that, I could never turn my back. Do I kill them? I really just wanted to be left alone....Remember the scene in "Ender's Game.") I think my parents and their support made a lot of difference to me."

From John in Austin:

"You can probably imagine the emotional scars that I still tote around with me at age twenty-six. I still have yet to go to college, I have shelves upon shelves of books that I have bought, read and committed to memory. From literature to computer programming, there is no one that I can't have a meaningful and informed conversation with.

"But to this day, the thought of entering another educational institution to prove that I have the facilities to be a 'meaningful' member of society makes the hair on the back of my neck stand on end and turns my stomach inside out.

"I am the father now, and as such I worry about the kind of life my son will lead, too much at times, I'm sure....A few weeks ago I was watching the TLC (The Learning Channel) or the Discovery channel, and there was a special on the social structure within the United State prison system. While I was watching it, I was thinking to myself just how similar it was to the social structure we find in schools."

From John, who's thirty-seven years old:

"What this really means to all my fellow young geeks out there? Endure. It may take a year, or two or five, but we will win....All those preps, jocks, etc., etc., will have their M.S. degrees, 2.5 kids, a job at Circuit City as an assistant manager, will be wondering where their life went, when we are coming into full bloom and taking over the world."

From Kevin, a parent:

"I am married, have two wonderful little kids, and am, by conventional measures, considered 'successful.' I'm also a computer geek, a nerd, and still have painful memories of the emotional and physical trauma I sustained in high school. I still attend counseling regularly. I still take antidepressants every day and will probably continue to do so for the rest of my life.

"Did I feel hate and rage for my attackers? Oh, yes. But I could never do anything about it and couldn't get anyone to help me. The only advice I got from my parents was to just ignore the bullies and eventually they'd leave me alone. Fortunately, I don't seem to be predisposed to violence or was too much of a coward to consider it. I can, however, see how the wrong kid in the wrong situation could go over the edge."

From Peter in Boston:

"I am a geek....I am beaten, spit on, pushed, jeered at. Food is thrown at me while teachers pretend not to see, people trip me. Jocks knock me down in the hallway. They steal my notes, call me a geek and a fag and a freak, tear up my books, have pissed in my locker twice. They cut my shirt and rip it. They wait for me in the boy's room and beat me up. I have to wait an hour to leave school to make sure they're gone.

"Mostly, I honestly think, this is because I'm smarter than they are, and they hate that.

"The really amazing thing is, they are the most popular people in the school, while everybody thinks I'm a freak for being online and playing computer games. The teachers just slobber all over them. Mostly, the other kids laugh, or walk away and pretend not to see it. The whole school cheers when they play sports. Sometimes, I picture how I'd do it. Wouldn't you? But unlike those guys in Littleton, I never will. I value my own life much more. When I read these messages, I would ask other geeks to try and remember that, no matter what. And get online and make contact."

From Rory in Chicago:

"Would you bring a kid abused by his family to counseling and call him the problem? If that kid expressed rage and anger toward the world, we would call it a product of his abuse, and try to help him with this rage, treating him as the victim. However when it is other kids abusing each other, we treat the abusees as the problem and ignore the abusers altogether. Hunting down and persecuting the abusees is only going to alienate them further—not only will their peers be persecuting them but so will their parents and teachers."

From Jason:

"Please take these e-mails...and take them to CNN, ABC, NBC, whoever, whatever. Make them heard, and stand up for all of us! Geeks=different, different=okay, if not better! Make my mother understand, sweeping problems under the rug, or simply not dealing with them, doesn't do jack s—! And there's a bigger problem, it's them!

"The people who think being different is bad, being geek is bad, TV, Games, the Internet, all bad! It will be hard, a minority against a majority! But please do it!"

From Evan:

"I'm twenty-four years old, and a successful professional now, but...fifteen years ago, I was in the Hellmouth. Just wanted to shout some small form of encouragement out to the kids fighting today. Take your fight for the right to be different to the people with power, and enlist your parents' help. Remember that if you can get your parents to understand your need to be creative, and nonconformist, because your brain is just plain bigger than the small world of middle and high school, your parents can make a fuss to school boards. But if they won't listen, go to the school boards yourself. Peacefully, but forcefully, assert your right to be different by speaking out against fear and oppression. Because that's what it is. It's all about the fear.

"People fear what they don't understand, and let's face it, the world of a geek isn't something most people can understand, if only because it's a complicated world filled with smart folks. And most people aren't complicated smart folks. You have GOT to break them of the fear. You gotta explain that it's an outlet, like racquetball or bridge. You have to explain it's not violent, it's colorful. You want violent? Look at football, look at sports. That's REAL ACTUAL violence, not the simulated, stylized, far from even looking-real violence of video games or D&D (Dungeons and Dragons). And for a real kicker, ask them how many geeks are arrested for violent crimes and misdemeanors when compared to popular athletes."

From Cory, a high school student:

"I go to a private high school and on Wednesday in religion class I told the class, because we were on the subject, that I could understand what would drive them (the killers in Littleton) to do it. They said that it couldn't happen at our school and I responded by saying that it could because back in my freshman year it was so bad (the jokes, abuse, etc.) that I wished I had had a gun at home. I am a Senior now and nine days from graduation. News got to the administration and I was suspended until I received an evaluation by a psychologist and was deemed safe to return to school. I have not been back to school since."

From MishtaE:

"I've been out of school for awhile (not very long) but I still physically shake, I feel adrenaline go through my system when I think about my own junior high experiences....The feeling of hopelessness, of knowing that you have no one to go to who can or will make it STOP is a very horrid feeling. It makes you consider irrational things, because the rational ones obviously don't apply.

"But make no mistake, the cruelty inflicted on kids doesn't magically go away when you graduate (or drop out and get your GED at sixteen as I did). You live with it, you learn to deal with it, but it is still there, and it does change you."

From LHRunkle, a self-described geek mother:

"My six-year-old wonders why he isn't popular on the block, but does not enjoy racing his bike, or playing soccer. (Soccer is becoming fun.) He also wonders why no one else is reading the books he is. The online community did not exist when I was in high school, but geek culture did. Dungeons & Dragons (the original three-booklet set) and science fiction saved me.

"How many scared parents have taken the time to introduce their child to the items that kept them sane in high school? How many high school libraries are even allowed to stock Theodore Sturgeon, or all of Robert Heinlein? Before we go to Net culture, we need to face local culture. How many schools enforce a respect-for-all policy, and enforce it fairly? I know that I have a budding geek, and if I can get him sane through the next thirteen years, there will be another decent adult on this planet."

From Simon:

"The mainstream is missing the point. All over the world, 'geeks' are standing up and saying 'This is horrible and I know what [causes] it' and all over the world people are saying 'Oh, my God! Another killer!' I'll spell it out: The killers are a symptom of the alienation of an unrecognized minority—the geeks. No, that doesn't make it right. No, that doesn't mean a thousand more killers are lurking in the computer rooms of your schools.

"Failure to understand this severely limits your ability to correct it. I read with dismay that geeks are being cut off from the Internet and violent online games so that they 'won't become killers.'

"Follow my logic here:

"Given: The killers were motivated in no small part by alienation. Reducing a person's contact with like-minded people increases their alienation. Reducing a person's sense of identity increases their sense of alienation. Geeks tend to communication with each other via the Internet and online games.

"Conclusion: Cutting geeks off from each other (Internet access) and their identity (choice of clothing) will increase rather than decrease the likelihood of violence.

"I've been wracking my brain to figure out what stopped me (from hurting someone). I've been asking myself 'What can I hand to people to fix this?' The answer is very simple. The faces are very clear in my memory of the few 'popular people' who took the time to talk to me and find out about me. There are maybe a half a dozen. They showed me that they were people too.

"I heard a report, it may not be true [It is.—Jon Katz] that one of the killers went and told one of his classmates before the killing, 'I like you. Go home.' If that happened, if you are that person, you know that your attitude saved your life. If there were a few more like you, maybe it would have saved everyone."

From Armadillo:

"I thought I had put this behind me but I obviously haven't. This whole past week has really torn me up inside because fifteen years ago, I was one of those kids. And you know what? I feel far more sympathy for the shooters than the victims. Because HS for me was sheer and utter Hell. I have no single memory that I can recall as being good.

"I have no single person who I can recall as a friend. Hell, even the OTHER rejects kicked me around. I feel like I'm seeing this all through the eyes of a refugee from a war, who by some circumstance is rescued, taken off to a land far from the conflict, far from the danger and death and constant fear and destruction.

"Years later, after having made some personal peace with the past, if not the people, they hear or see a report that their former home town or village has been bombed and the people they knew killed and it all comes flooding back.

"Why is it that we geeks, freaks, nerd, dorks, dweebs...have to suffer while the clueless, bow-headed, testosterone poisoned 'normal' people are allowed to get away with murder....I wonder just how many outcasts have been driven to suicide because of just one too many tauntings or practical jokes on a particular afternoon?

"Why do we murder the spirits of our most gifted and talented young people? THEY are the ones that are our future. THEY are the ones that are best equipped to build the world to their hopes and dreams. The prom queens and cheerleaders will have their fifteen minutes and then take their places among the teeming masses of consumers. They have already shown they want to be led around and are more than happy to let society tell them where to go and what do to."

From Nick:

"I'm a junior in high school in a suburb....I felt that in light of what happened last Tuesday and your recent article on Slashdot, I should respond. Recently, one of my friends, Chris, was suspended for three days. He's an athlete (football and shotput), but is no means considered a 'jock' as he plays computer games, reads fantasy novels, plays Warhammer 40K, etc. One person, Ryan, considered a 'nerd' by his peers, mislabeled him (Chris) as a jock and decided to taunt him verbally. Chris is normally a nice guy who's never been in a fight before, as he gets along with most students. This verbal abuse continued for almost the entire school year so far.

"Last Thursday, Chris slapped Ryan upside the head due to a particularly nasty thing that was said and Ryan picked up a chair, shouting death threats and swears. They were quickly broken up by the teacher and hall monitors, and were escorted to the dean's office.

"Normally, each would only get a one-day in-school suspension for what they did, but due to the incident in Colorado, each got three days and counseling by the school psychiatrist for the remainder of the year. The deans obviously overreacted, given the circumstances. What the main problem is here is that years of torment in people like Ryan's lives have led to such 'classes'—goths, nerds, freaks, preps, etc. People form together in cliques where people are distinctly filed into the social pecking order. The high school situation could lead to a French Revolution-esque 'class war' where social outcasts decide to say enough with the years of torment. Unfortunately, this is happening sooner than we think."

From Sally:

"The irony in the current coverage, at least to me, is that I remember my leather-jacketed, spiky-haired, combat-boot wearing friends as being for the most part peaceful, gentle, sensitive types—lots of vegetarians and anti-nuke people. Sure, there were a few who probably could have benefited from some therapy, but most of them were—and are—the nicest, kindest people I knew, despite their rather alarming appearance. After all, we had to be like that—we all knew what it felt like to be shoved in a locker, spit on, have stuff thrown at us, etc. I seem to remember the football players and other jocks as being a lot more violent and given to fits of rage and other displays of aggression.

"While I certainly agree that the two shooters in Littleton were deranged boys filled with hate, I also believe that there's not much chemical difference between a pair of angry nerds wanting to blow away jocks and a pair of arrogant jocks wanting to bash freaks and geeks. It's a fine line between a supposedly 'well-adjusted' teenager and a disturbed one."

From Matthew C. in Wisconsin:

"I, like many of the Slashdot audience, was one of those kids in high school, and junior high, and elementary school. I have suffered what those kids suffered, and continue to suffer. I made it through, but apparently not everyone does. The response to your article seems to suggest that there are many of us out there who want to help do something to curb the backlash to focus on the correct issue. I was wondering, in your surely large catalogue of responses to this column, have you found any hints of where we might send letters? Or who we might contact, to start telling people what the real problems are?

"I want to help. I want to write, to talk, to help ensure that geeks of today and tomorrow aren't further persecuted for pursuing differences from the norm. We have to spread the word far and wide, teachers, parents and people who should know better than to ban trench coats, take away computers, and further drive their kids into depression and isolation. How can we organize something meaningful?"

John Katz can be e-mailed at jonkatz@slashdot.org.

SUGGESTIONS FOR DISCUSSION

1. How does Thomas de Zengotita answer the question he raises about "how violence in the media influences behavior"? Take into account what de Zengotita calls the "healthier kids, who never act out," as well as those who commit violent acts. What evidence does he offer to explain his view? What assumptions does he seem to make in connecting the evidence to his claims about the influence of the media? How do you think the "voices from the Hellmouth" in Jon Katz's column would respond to de Zengotita? What do you see as the main points of difference between de Zengotita and Katz? Are there points on which they might agree?

2. Consider where each of these readings were originally published—the monthly magazine *Harper's* and Jon Katz's regular online column at www.slashdot.org. What do these places of publication tell you about the kinds of readers de Zengotita and Katz are writing to and the perspective each writer takes on the Littleton shootings? How, in turn, do these publications differ from newspapers or weekly news magazines like *Time* and *Newsweek*? To answer these questions, you'll need to do a bit of research. Go to your college library and look at the July 1999 issue of *Harper's* and the May 3, 1999, issue of *Newsweek*, with the cover story "Massacre at Littleton: Why?" Leaf through each magazine, noticing the kinds of articles and other features that appear along with coverage of Littleton. Make photocopies of the covers to bring to class discussion. Visit the website Jon Katz Columns at www.freedomforum.org/technology/katzcolumns.asp and the Freedom Forum's home page. Also visit www.slashdot.org, where "More from the Hellmouth" originally appeared. If you can, print hard copies of these websites and bring them to class. Use the material you've assembled to think about what the visual design of each publication tells you about it, what kind of people read it, and what you might expect from it. What do you see as the main differences among the publications? What do you see as the significance of these differences?

3. De Zengotita says that neither "people on the left" nor "traditional opinion leaders" believe that "virtual reality is *real*." What prevents them, in his view, from seeing the reality of virtuality? What divides his way of thinking from theirs? What do you see as the implications of these differences? What do you think Jon Katz and the "voices from the Hellmouth" would say to de Zengotita about his concern that the news media have blurred the boundaries between reality and representation?

SUGGESTIONS FOR WRITING

1. There's a joke going around that if you want to find someone to program your VCR or set up a new computer, look for an eleven-year-old. The comic recognition here is that there are profound generational differences in the way people understand and relate to the new communication technologies. Both de Zengotita and Katz seem to suggest as much in their response to the Littleton shootings. Write an essay that gives your view of these generational differences. Take into account the way "voices from the Hellmouth" explicitly identify themselves as "geeks" and "nerds." What is "geek" culture and what does it tell us about at least a subsection of young people today and their relationship to the new technologies?

2. At the very end of his essay, de Zengotita says that we should answer the question "What is to be done?" with the response "Don't ask *that* ques-

tion so fast." The issue, as he sees it, is first understanding the influence of the media and how it has dismantled the boundaries between "action and performance and reality and representation"—and not rushing to conclusions about what we should or should not do about it. Take his position seriously. Write an essay that first explains de Zengotita's point about the media collapsing these boundaries. Then offer further examples of the media and how they represent reality to develop your own perspective. Remember that de Zengotita is looking at the influence of the media not just on "latent psychotics" but on "the rest of us as well."

3. The May 3, 1999, issue of *Newsweek* published a special report on the "Massacre in Colorado." The question that jumps off the cover is "Why?" Read the *Newsweek* report "Why the Young Kill" by Sharon Begley. As you will see, Begley describes new theories that offer a biological basis for violent behavior. What might the appeal of such theories be? How do these theories compare to the perspectives in the two reading selections, as well as in other sources you know about? Write an essay that gives an overview of how the *Newsweek* article "Why the Young Kill" explains school shootings. Then consider how persuasive you find such biological theories. Do they provide adequate explanation? If you think so, explain why. If not, explain what you see as their limits. Use this discussion to set up your explanation of what happened at Columbine High.

CHECKING OUT THE WEB

Items about Littleton began to appear on the Web almost the moment the shootings took place. People followed the breaking news online, as well as on television and in the press. Before long, message boards and chat rooms were filled with talk about Littleton, why it happened, who is to blame, and what should be done. Parents and school officials searched online for advice from experts about how to talk to children about the shootings, how to recognize the warning signs of violent behavior, and how to keep schools safe. Individuals and groups put up websites as shrines to commemorate the Columbine High students who had been killed and wounded.

There are literally hundreds of websites devoted, in one way or another, to the Littleton shootings. The following three give some sense of the range of websites and the variety of purposes people have in putting them up. You can find links to these sites through the Reading Culture website URL. The box "Reading the Web" offers some suggestions about how to assess websites.

NATHANIEL CLARK'S HOME PAGE

Nathaniel Clark is a computer science major at Worcester Polytechnic Institute. As you can see, his home page is a typical collage of links, poems, and graphics that gives us a sense of who Nate is and how he has decided to represent himself on the Web. Nate's home page also tells us something interesting about how information circulates on the Internet. One of the links—"MIT professor defends reality"—came to him in an e-mail from a friend and then Nate turned it into a link.

CHECKING OUT THE WEB *continued*

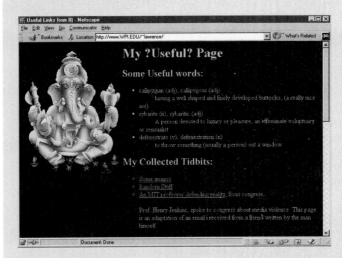

Check out Nate's home page, then click on the link. You'll find media studies professor Henry Jenkins's account of how, in the wake of the Littleton shootings, he testified before Congress about media violence and teenagers. Notice in the first part, where Jenkins describes what it was like testifying before Congress, his style and tone are informal and chatty. Notice, though, how the style and tone shift in the second part, where Jenkins reproduces the oral remarks he made. Consider what these differences in style and tone can tell us about Jenkins's relationship to these two audiences.

SCHOOL VIOLENCE AND THE LITTLETON TRAGEDY

"School Violence and the Littleton Tragedy" is a special Web page put up by the National Council of Teachers of English (NCTE), the leading professional association of language arts and English teachers in elementary and secondary schools. NCTE sponsors regional and national conferences, publishes books and journals, conducts research, issues reports and policy statements, and lobbies at the state and federal level. Like most other profes-

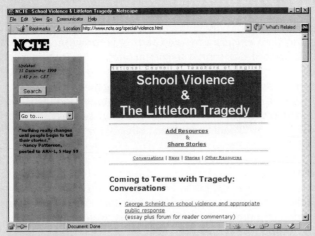

sional associations, businesses, government agencies, and colleges and universities, NCTE maintains its own website—and adds pages on special topics as needed.

Check out the NCTE page "School Violence and the Littleton Tragedy." As you will see, it consists of links to various resources, information, commentary, and news updates, as well as message boards, e-mail, stories, and readers' forums. Consider what NCTE's purpose seems to be in maintaining the page and how it selects links. You might compare the NCTE page to the Columbine Shrine (see below) in terms of the information each includes.

CHECKING OUT THE WEB *continued*

THE COLUMBINE SHRINE

The Columbine Shrine is self-described as a "sister site" of TSW: The Semicool World, a commercial entertainment website. The Columbine Shrine started as a one-page memorial with pictures of the victims of the Littleton shootings and a few items copied from other sites. Largely due to the interest of Webmaster Will, the site evolved into a multipurpose resource and memorial.

Visit the Columbine Shrine. Notice under the menu heading "Other Stuff," the option "Links." This will take you to a list of links to over thirty shrines and memorials. Take a look at a number of these commemorative websites. Consider their visual design and how they differ from other sites. What purposes do these sites seem to serve?

Guardian angels above, please keep watch over the survivors of this tragedy, and sit your 13 new doves by God's side in peace forever. Please leave me or the other passers-through a message and let me know what you think of this website. Residents of Littleton may see this, so please use descretion when writing.

READING WEBSITES

One of the attractions of the Web is that anyone with an Internet connection and a little technical knowledge can put up a site. There is little question that, despite the growing commercialization of the Web, it still provides broad access to the means of communication and a new forum for discussion and debate. At the same time, it is also important to understand that the information and perspectives that show up on the Web are largely unregulated—and can range from the thoroughly reliable to the utterly crackpot. That's part of the creative and chaotic anarchy of the Web and makes it so interesting and so much fun. But it also means that Web users need to learn to read in a somewhat new way, so that they can assess the various sites they visit—to identify who put them up, what their purposes are, and what you can expect from them in terms of the reliability of the information and ideas they contain.

What to Look For

Though there is great variation among website designs, a number of standard features have emerged that offer you a way to analyze websites. Here are things to look for in any website. You can use these features as clues to determine who put up the website, what its purposes are, how reliable and up-to-date its information is, and what its biases and attitudes are.

URL

The header at the top of your screen gives you the Web-page address or URL (Uniform Resource Locator). You can find out a good deal about a website from the URL alone. Take, for example, the URL of NCTE's page:

> www.ncte.gor/special/violence.html

There are two parts to the URL: the *host name* "www.ncte.org" and the *file path* "special/violence.html." The host name tells you the address of the server where the page is located (www), the organization that put up the Web page (ncte), and the domain (org). Domain names identify the kinds of organizations that sponsor websites: ".org" refers to nonprofit organizations, ".edu" to educational ones, ".gov" to government agencies, ".mil" to the military, and ".com" and ".net" to commercial enterprises. The file path enables a browser to find a particular page within a website.

Organizational Logo and Title

Web pages often feature an organization's logo or a common header at the top of each page. This feature helps to unify a website visually and to identify the sponsoring organization from page to page. The NCTE site, for example, makes the sponsor and theme easy to identify by featuring the organization's logo at top left and the title "School Violence The Littleton Tragedy" in large letters. In other cases, however, it is difficult or impossible to tell who is sponsoring the website.

Links

Links appear as text or graphics to help you navigate from place to place, both within a particular website and to Web pages at other sites. They may appear at the top or bottom of the page or both places. Many websites, such as the Columbine Shrine, include a menu of links in a column. But wherever they appear, links offer clues about the purpose of the site because they indicate the range and type of information and opinion the website considers relevant. Notice, for example, the inferences you can draw by looking at the links in Nate Clark's home page or the NCTE site on the Littleton shootings.

Signature and Credits

Signatures give the name and often the e-mail address of the person who maintains the Web page, information on when the Web page was established, when it was last updated, and those who have contributed to it. Sometimes individuals and organizations include further information such as their e-mail address, postal address, and phone number. Notice the NCTE page credits a number of people for contributing Other Sites/Resources.

Advertising

As the Web gets increasingly commercialized, more and more advertising appears. The type of products and services advertised can help give you a sense of the kind of website you're visiting, much as you can draw some inferences about how magazines see themselves and their readers from their ads. The absence of advertising, as in the case of websites like NCTE's, can also offer you information on how the organization wants to relate to its readers.

What Can You Do at the Site?

The possibilities that websites offer readers can give you further information to assess the site. Some, such as many of the Columbine memorials, want you simply to read the text and see the graphics that have been put up on the page as though you are visiting an actual shrine. Others give you more options—to navigate the site or follow links to other websites. Some invite you to sign a guest book, send e-mail, fill out surveys, enter contests, watch animation and videos, listen to music, or take part in message-board discussions. Commercial sites, of course, want you to buy something. Consider whether the website you're visiting provides you with choices about where you can go and whether it invites you to participate interactively. What purpose do these possibilities serve? What kind of relationship does the site seem to want to establish with people who visit it?

Analyzing Talk on the Web

As you can see from the reading selections "Gunfire Dialogues" and "More from the Hellmouth," the Littleton shootings prompted an outpouring of talk on the Internet as people tried to make sense of what happened. Analyzing the talk that appears on message boards, chat rooms, readers' forums, and e-mail links can give you further clues to the purposes of a website, the kind of visitors it wants to attract, and the type of online discussion it wants to foster.

Here are two threads of talk on the Web. The first example consists of two postings to the thread "Today in Colorado" on the listserv "NCTE-talk." This thread, which grew to over 200 messages, was put up as a link on NCTE's website on the Littleton shootings, along with a readers' forum. The second example comes from the message board linked to the Columbine Shrine website. It begins with the comment "I think it was an AWESOME PLAN" from ExuBiu and is followed by four responses, including one from Will the webmaster.

As you read, you will no doubt notice right away how different the two threads are. Consider what makes them so different. What seems to have prompted the various writers to talk on the Web? How does the anonymity of users such as ExuBiu or Angel influence the discussion? What role does the webmaster play in the second thread?

To: ncte-talk@serv1.ncte.org
Subject: Re: [ncte-talk] Today in Colorado
From: Pat King
Date: Tue, 20 Apr 1999 20:14:56 +0000

So sad. It makes me think of two things.

First. I have thought of what I would do if I were in that situation and remembered one day last week during a change in classes during the lunch mods when a kid put a firecracker in the trash can outside my room. When it exploded it did sound like a gun shot. I told the students to get to the back of the room and sit down. Could it have been a gun; I guess we were lucky. That school in Littleton wasn't.

Secondly several years ago, I had a student who sat in class and did nothing. His behavior was odd and he was into devil worship. He wore black and would write over his hands and arms. He and several of his friends murdered one of his friends for kicks. I watched that boy and knew he was a bomb waiting to explode. I talked to the guidance counselor, and it was thought he might be on drugs. His parents were a solid middle class who thought he was just going through a phase. He just seemed to hate the world. The boy he killed was a kind and generous kid who walked willingly into the trap thinking he was helping a "friend." I now see kids very differently than I did: and yes, I think this kind of violence can happen just about anywhere. Where is there a community that doesn't have guns in their homes and students who are misfits within the school population.

So sad!! What a horrible comment about our society.

To: ncte-talk@serv1.ncte.org
Subject: Re: [ncte-talk] Today in Colorado (4/27)
From: Vince
Date: Tue, 27 Apr 1999 13:47:44 +0600

This is getting more and more draining. Our school was basically "locked down" for the final period of the day. Nobody allowed in the halls. Undercover cops outside the building. Same plan is to be in effect for the next two weeks.

For the first time in several years, the thought came to me that I could change jobs.

TSW Message Boards
The Columbine Shrine
Comment
ExuBiu, Unregistered User (1/4/00 12:23:29 am)
I think it was an AWESOME PLAN!

I think what they did needed to be done. I think the way the media handled it was overrated. I think the way the media turns every negative things into something like a circus needs to stop. I think people need to stop feeling sorry for themselves and what happens. I think people need to @#%$ live their lives and forget about everyone else's business. I also think that, if the media didn't concentrate so heavily on the negative things, that there would be a lot more positive influence in the world, and then…no matter what music the kids listened to…or what games they played, they would have a positive outlook. It's the media's fault this @#%$ happens, and I think it's pathetic how weak we all are to feel sorry for the ones weak enough to break under the strain of @#%$ up societal views.

From: Will, webmaster
Re: I think it was an AWESOME PLAN!

Maybe the media over-did-it a little, but in no way are we to FORGET these people. We are remembering. And maybe you should learn to have a little sympathy and compassion. That's what this world needs…everyone talks of hate breeding hate…well that' s what you're doing now. Show some caring…I hope this doesn't have to happen again or at your school or to your best friend for you to realize just what you are saying is compassionless. I just pray to God that nothing like this EVER happens again. Step back and read what you wrote again from a 180 degree turn

bearden13, Unregistered User (1/5/00 10:10:58 am)
They were not right!!!

What these two boys did was not an awesome plan! No matter what is done to you, you don't have a right to kill innocent people. How could you even think that? Just because you're not part of the in-crowd doesn't mean you should go around killing people. Be yourself and don't worry about what people think about you. It's what you think that matters most.

From: angel, Unregistered User (1/6/00 10:29:51 pm)
Grow Up

I think what you are thinking is underrated, so many of you sickos just like eric and dylan are in this world and since you guys are getting so tough and taking a stand, I think WE should get tough and take a stand. No more just sitting on the couch thinking how sad. I can do something about this and I will. I don't know what your problem is but you think you can just go around shooting whoever you don't like because you're too immature to handle it. Grow up.

From: Mack1080, Unregistered User (1/13/00 4:25:59 pm)
They were merely pawns

Eric and Dylan were merely pawns in the sick lifestyle that the world calls high school. Can anyone remember what it felt like to be teased at school? Well try to live with that everyday before you condone what the boys did. They merely lashed out in the only way that they felt would be recognized. To me they were like modern day Robin Hoods who stole from the world future bigots and idiots and returned to us something to really consider. So before you judge and condone them, look at yourself and see if you know what they felt like. If you can honestly say that you can't then you would have been one of the tormentors. If you wish to give an intelligent reply to this then do so but I will not respond to the "holier-than-though" people who I know will write me.

VISUAL CULTURE
REPRESENTATIONS OF YOUTH CULTURE IN MOVIES

The identity of a generation takes shape in part through the movies. Since the 1950s, movies about teenagers and youth culture have explored generational identities and intergenerational conflicts. In *The Wild One, Blackboard Jungle,* and *Rebel Without a Cause* (1950s), *The Graduate* and *Easy Rider* (1960s), *Saturday Night Fever* and *American Graffiti*

Public Enemy. From left: Chuck D. Terminator X, and Flavor Flav. Sound track on Spike Lee's *Do the Right Thing.*

James Dean. *Rebel Without a Cause.*

(1970s), *River's Edge, The Breakfast Club,* and *Fast Times at Ridgemont High* (1980s), and *Do the Right Thing, Boyz'n the Hood, Slackers,* and *Clerks* (1990s), to name some of the best-known movies, Hollywood and independent filmmakers have fashioned influential representations of young people.

The purpose of this section is to consider how movies represent various youth cultures and their relations to adult culture.

John Travolta.
Saturday Night Fever.

A scene from Larry Clark's *KIDS.*

Juvenile Delinquency Films

James Gilbert

James Gilbert is an American historian at the University of Maryland. The following selection is taken from Gilbert's book *A Cycle of Outrage: America's Reaction to
Juvenile Delinquency in the 1950s.* Here, Gilbert traces the emergence in the 1950s
of juvenile delinquency films and popular responses to them. This selection consists of the opening paragraph of Gilbert's chapter "Juvenile Delinquency Movies"
and his analysis of *The Wild One, Blackboard Jungle,* and *Rebel Without a Cause.*

SUGGESTION FOR READING

Notice how Gilbert sets up his dominant theme in the opening paragraph,
when he explains that widespread public concern with juvenile delinquency
presents Hollywood with "dangerous but lucrative possibilities." Take note of
how Gilbert defines these "possibilities" in the opening paragraph and then
follow how he traces this theme through his discussion of the three films.

Whereas, shortly after the screening of this movie the local police had several cases in which
the use of knives by young people were involved and at our own Indiana Joint High School
two girls, while attending a high school dance, were cut by a knife wielded by a teen-age youth
who by his own admission got the idea from watching "Rebel Without a Cause."

Now Therefore Be It Resolved by the Board of Directors of Indiana Joint High School that said
Board condemns and deplores the exhibition of pictures such as "Rebel Without a Cause" and
any other pictures which depict abnormal or subnormal behavior by the youth of our country
and which tend to deprave the morals of young people.

Indiana, Pennsylvania, Board of Education to the MPAA, January 9, 1956

The enormous outpouring of concern over juvenile delinquency in the mid-1950s presented
the movie industry with dangerous but lucrative possibilities. An aroused public of parents,
service club members, youth-serving agencies, teachers, adolescents, and law enforcers constituted a huge potential audience for delinquency films at a time when general audiences for
all films had declined. Yet this was a perilous subject to exploit, for public pressure on the film
industry to set a wholesome example for youth remained unremitting. Moreover, the accusation that mass culture caused delinquency—especially the "new delinquency" of the postwar
period—was the focus of much contemporary attention. If the film industry approached the
issue of delinquency, it had to proceed cautiously. It could not present delinquency favorably;
hence all stories would have to be set in the moral firmament of the movie Code. Yet to be successful, films had to evoke sympathy from young people who were increasingly intrigued by
the growing youth culture of which delinquency seemed to be one variant.

Stanley Kramer's picture, *The Wild One,* released in 1953, stands in transition from the
somber realism of "film noir" pessimism and environmentalism to the newer stylized explorations of delinquent culture that characterized the mid-1950s. Shot in dark and realistic black
and white, the film stars Marlon Brando and Lee Marvin as rival motorcycle gang leaders who
invade a small California town. Brando's character is riven with ambiguity and potential violence—a prominent characteristic of later juvenile delinquency heroes. On the other hand,
he is clearly not an adolescent, but not yet an adult either, belonging to a suspended age that
seems alienated from any recognizable stage of development. He appears to be tough and

brutal, but he is not, nor, ultimately, is he as attractive as he might have been. His character flaws are appealing, but unnerving. This is obvious in the key symbol of the film, the motor-cycle trophy which he carries. He has not won it as the townspeople assume; he has stolen it from a motorcycle "scramble." Furthermore, he rejects anything more than a moment's tenderness with the girl he meets. In the end, he rides off alone, leaving her trapped in the small town that his presence has so disrupted and exposed. The empty road on which he trav-els leads to similar nameless towns; he cannot find whatever it is he is compelled to seek.

Brando's remarkable performance made this film a brilliant triumph. Its moral ambiguity, however, and the very attractiveness of the alienated hero, meant that the producers needed to invoke two film code strategies to protect themselves from controversy. The first of these was an initial disclaimer appearing after the titles: "This is a shocking story. It could never take place in most American towns—but it did in this one. It is a public challenge not to let it happen again." Framing the other end of the film was a speech by a strong moral voice of authority. A sheriff brought in to restore order to the town lectures Brando on the turmoil he has created and then, as a kind of punishment, casts him back onto the lonesome streets.

Aside from Brando's stunning portrayal of the misunderstood and inarticulate antihero, the film did not quite emerge from traditional modes of presenting crime and delinquency: the use of black and white; the musical score with its foreboding big-band sound; the rela-tively aged performers; and the vague suggestions that Brando and his gang were refugees from urban slums. Furthermore, the reception to the film was not, as some might have pre-dicted, as controversial as what was to come. Of course, there were objections—for example, New Zealand banned the film—but it did not provoke the outrage that the next group of juve-nile delinquency films inspired.

The film that fundamentally shifted Hollywood's treatment of delinquency was *The Blackboard Jungle,* produced in 1955, and in which traditional elements remained as a back-drop for contemporary action. The movie was shot in black and white and played in a slum high school. But it clearly presented what was to become the driving premise of subsequent delinquency films—the division of American society into conflicting cultures made up of ado-lescents on one side and adults on the other. In this film the delinquent characters are por-trayed as actual teenagers, as high school students. The crimes they commit are, with a few exceptions, crimes of behavior such as defying authority, status crimes, and so on. Of most symbolic importance is the transition in music that occurs in the film. Although it includes jazz numbers by Stan Kenton and Bix Beiderbecke, it is also the first film to feature rock and roll, specifically, "Rock Around the Clock" played by Bill Haley.

The story line follows an old formula of American novels and films. A teacher begins a job at a new school, where he encounters enormous hostility from the students. He stands up to the ringleader of the teenage rowdies, and finally wins over the majority of the students. In itself this is nothing controversial. But *Blackboard Jungle* also depicts the successful defiance of delin-quents, who reject authority and terrorize an American high school. Their success and their power, and the ambiguous but attractive picture of their culture, aimed at the heart of the film Code and its commitment to uphold the dignity of figures and institutions of authority.

Still cautious, the studio opened the film with a disclaimer. It also used a policeman as a voice of authority who explained postwar delinquency in this way: "They were six years old in the last war. Father in the army. Mother in a defense plant. No home life. No Church life. No place to go. They form street gangs....Gang leaders have taken the place of parents."

Despite this protective sermonizing, the film aroused substantial opposition. It did so for many reasons, but principally because it pictured a high school with unsympathetic administrators and teachers in the grip of teenage hoodlums. Given contemporary fears of just such a situation, and the belief that such was the case throughout the United States, the film's realistic texture was shocking. But other elements distressed some audiences. For example, the leading adolescent character is a black student, played with enormous sympathy and skill by Sidney Poitier. And the clash of cultures and generations, which later became standard in juvenile delinquency films, was in this, its first real expression, stated with stark and frightening clarity. For example, in one crucial scene, a teacher brings his precious collection of jazz records to school to play for the boys, hoping, of course, to win them over. His efforts to reach out to them fail completely. The students mock and despise his music and then destroy his collection. They have their own music, their own culture, and their own language.

Public response to *Blackboard Jungle* provided a glimpse of the audience division between generations and cultures. Attending a preview of the film, producer Brooks was surprised, and obviously delighted, when young members of the audience began dancing in the aisles to the rock and roll music. This occurred repeatedly in showings after the film opened. But other reactions were more threatening. For example in Rochester, New York, there were reports that "young hoodlums cheered the beatings and methods of terror inflicted upon a teacher by a gang of boys" pictured in the film. But box office receipts in the first few weeks indicated a smash hit, and in New York City the first ten days at Loew's State theater set a record for attendance.

Nevertheless, the film caused an angry backlash against the film industry. Censors in Memphis, Tennessee, banned it. It was denounced by legal organizations, teachers, reviewers like Bosley Crowther of the *New York Times,* and even by the Teenage Division of the Labor Youth League (a communist organization). The National Congress of Parents and Teachers, the Girl Scouts, the D.A.R., and the American Association of University Women disapproved it. The American Legion voted *Blackboard Jungle* the movie "that hurt America the most in foreign countries in 1955." And the Ambassador to Italy, Clare Booth Luce, with State Department approbation, forced the film's withdrawal from the Venice Film Festival.

Following swiftly on this commercial success was *Rebel Without a Cause*, a very different sort of film, and perhaps the most famous and influential of the 1950s juvenile delinquency endeavors. Departing from the somber working-class realism of *Blackboard Jungle, Rebel* splashed the problem of middle-class delinquency across America in full color. Moreover, its sympathy lay entirely with adolescents, played by actors James Dean, Natalie Wood, and Sal Mineo, who all live wholly inside the new youth culture. Indeed, this is the substantial message of the film: each parent and figure of authority is grievously at fault for ignoring or otherwise failing youth. The consequence is a rebellion with disastrous results.

Once the script had been developed, shooting began in the spring of 1955, during the height of the delinquency dispute and following fast on the heels of the box-office success of *Blackboard Jungle.* Warner Brothers approved a last minute budget hike to upgrade the film to color. In part this was a response to the box office appeal of the star, James Dean, whose *East of Eden* was released to acclaim in early April.

When it approved the film, the Code Authority issued two warnings. Geoffrey Shurlock wrote to Jack Warner in March 1955: "As you know, we have steadfastly maintained under the requirements of the Code that we should not approve stories of underage boys and girls indulging in either murder or illicit sex." He suggested that the violence in the picture be toned down. Furthermore, he noted: "It is of course vital that there be no inference of a questionable or homosexual relationship between Plato [Sal Mineo] and Jim [James Dean]." A follow-up commentary suggested the need for further changes in the area of violence. For example, Shurlock noted of the fight at the planetarium: "We suggest merely indicating that these high-school boys have tire chains, not showing them flaunting them."

Despite these cautions, the film, when it was released, contained substantial violence: the accidental death of one of the teenagers in a "chickie run"; the shooting of another teenager; and Plato's death at the hands of the police. Furthermore, there remained strong echoes of Plato's homosexual interest in Jim.

The film also took a curious, ambiguous position on juvenile delinquency. Overtly, it disapproved, demonstrating the terrible price paid for misbehavior. Yet the film, more than any other thus far, glorified the teenage life-styles it purported to reject. Adult culture is pictured as insecure, insensitive, and blind to the problems of youth. Teenagers, on the other hand, are portrayed as searching for genuine family life, warmth, and security. They choose delinquency in despair of rejection by their parents. Indeed, each of the three young heroes is condemned to search for the emotional fulfillment that adults deny: Dean for the courage his father lacks; Natalie Wood (as his girlfriend) for her father's love; and Plato for a family, which he finds momentarily in Dean and Wood. Instead of being securely set in adult society, each of these values must be constructed outside normal society and inside a new youth-created world. What in other films might have provided a reconciling finale—a voice of authority—becomes, itself, a symbol of alienation. A policeman who befriends Dean is absent at a decisive moment when he could have prevented the tragic ending. Thus no adults or institutions remain unscathed. The ending, in which adults recognize their own failings, is thus too sudden and contrived to be believable. It is as if the appearance of juvenile delinquency in such a middle-class setting is impossible to explain, too complex and too frightening to be understood in that context.

And also too attractive, for the film pictures delinquent culture as an intrusive, compelling, and dangerous force that invades middle-class homes and institutions. The producers carefully indicated that each family was middle class, although Plato's mother might well be considered wealthier than that. Teenage, delinquent culture, however, has obvious working-class origins, symbolized by souped-up jalopies, levis, and T-shirts that became the standard for youth culture. In fact, when Dean goes out for his fateful "chickie run," he changes into T-shirt and levis from his school clothes. Furthermore, the film presents this delinquent culture without judgment. There is no obvious line drawn between what is teenage culture and what is delinquency. Is delinquency really just misunderstood youth culture? The film never says, thus reflecting public confusion on the same issue.

A second tactic of the filmmakers posed a philosophic problem about youth culture and delinquency. This emerges around the symbol of the planetarium. In the first of two scenes there, Dean's new high school class visits for a lecture and a show. The lecturer ends his presentation abruptly with a frightening suggestion—the explosion of the world and the end of the universe. He concludes: "Man existing alone seems an episode of little consequence." This existential reference precedes the rumble in which Dean is forced to fight his new classmates after they puncture the tires of his car. The meaning is clear: Dean must act to establish an identity which his parents and society refuse to grant him. This is a remarkable translation of the basic premise of contemporary Beat poets, whose solitary search for meaning and self-expression tinged several of the other initial films in this genre also.

Another scene at the planetarium occurs at night, at the end of the film. The police have pursued Plato there after he shoots a member of the gang that has been harassing Dean. Dean follows him into the building, and, in a reprise of the earlier scene, turns on the machine that lights the stars and planets. The two boys discuss the end of the world. Dean empties Plato's gun, and the confused youth then walks out of the building. The police, mistaking his intent, gun him down. Once again tragedy follows a statement about the ultimate meaninglessness of life.

By using middle-class delinquency to explore questions of existence, this film undeniably contested the effectiveness of traditional family and community institutions. There is even the hint that Dean, Wood, and Mineo represent the possibility of a new sort of family; but this is only a fleeting suggestion. In the end it is family and community weakness that bring tragedy for which there can be no real solution. Without the strikingly sympathetic performances of Dean, Wood, and Mineo, this picture might have fallen under the weight of its bleak (and pretentious) message. As it was, however, *Rebel Without a Cause* was a box office smash, and Dean's short, but brilliant career was now assured.

As with *Blackboard Jungle,* the MPAA was the focus of furious reaction to the film. Accusations of copycat crimes, particularly for a stabbing in Indiana, Pennsylvania, brought condemnations and petitions against "pictures which depict abnormal or subnormal behavior by the youth of our country and which tend to deprave the morals of young people." The MPAA fought back against this accusation in early 1956 as Arthur DeBra urged an investigation to discover if the incident at the Indiana, Pennsylvania, high school had any relationship to the "juvenile delinquency situation in the school and community." As one writer for the *Christian Science Monitor* put it, "the new Warner Brothers picture will emerge into the growing nationwide concern about the effects on youth of comics, TV, and movies." This prediction was based upon actions already taken by local censors. The Chicago police had ordered cuts in the film, and the city of Milwaukee banned it outright.

On the other hand, much of the response was positive. As *Variety* noted in late 1955, fan letters had poured in to Hollywood "from teenagers who have identified themselves with the characters; from parents who have found the film conveyed a special meaning; and from sociologists and psychiatrists who have paid tribute to the manner in which child-parent misunderstanding is highlighted."

Quite clearly, the film became a milestone for the industry. It established youth culture as a fitting subject for films, and created some of the most pervasive stereotypes that were repeated in later films. These included the tortured, alienated, and misunderstood youth and intolerant parents and authority figures. It did not, however, lead to more subtle explorations of the connections between youth culture and delinquency. If anything, the opposite was true. For one thing, Dean was killed in an auto accident shortly after this enormous success. Furthermore, it was probably the seriousness of *Blackboard Jungle* and *Rebel* that provoked controversy, and the movie industry quickly learned that it could attract teenage audiences without risking the ire of adults if it reduced the dosage of realism. Thus the genre deteriorated into formula films about teenagers, made principally for drive-in audiences who were not particular about the features they saw.

SUGGESTIONS FOR DISCUSSION

1. Gilbert notes that *Rebel Without a Cause* became a "milestone" for the film industry, establishing youth culture as a fitting (and profitable) subject and creating stereotypes of alienated youth and intolerant adults that recurred in later movies. Consider to what extent these stereotypes continue to appear in movies. How would you update their appearance since the 1950s? List examples of movies that use the conventionalized figures of alienated youth and intolerant adults. What continuity do you see over time? In what ways have the portrayals changed?

2. Gilbert says that by "using middle-class delinquency to explore questions of existence," *Rebel Without a Cause* "contested the effectiveness of traditional family and community institutions." Explain what Gilbert means. Can you think of other films that "contest" family and community institutions?

3. Watch the three films Gilbert discusses—*The Wild One, Blackboard Jungle,* and *Rebel Without a Cause.* Work together with a group of classmates. First, summarize Gilbert's discussion of how each film handles the dilemma of evoking viewers' sympathy for young people while in no way presenting delinquency in a favorable light. Next, develop your own analysis of how (or whether) each film creates sympathy for young people in their confrontations with the adult world. To what extent do you agree with Gilbert's line of analysis? Where do you differ with or want to modify his analysis?

SUGGESTED ASSIGNMENT

Pick a film or group of films that in some way characterizes a generation of young people. For example, analyze how *The Graduate* captures something important about youth in the 1960s. Or look at how a cluster of three or four films portrays the "twentysomething" generation of the 1990s. (You can find youth-culture films from the 1950s to the present in many video stores.)

Write an analysis of how the film or films represent youth. Your task here is not to decide whether the portrayal is accurate but to analyze how it constructs a certain image of youth culture and what might be the significance of the representation.

Here are some suggestions to help you examine how a film represents youth culture:

- *How does the film portray young people?* What in particular marks them as "youth"? Pay particular attention to the characters' clothing, hairstyles, body posture, and ways of speaking.

- *How does the film mark young people generationally?* Are the characters part of a distinctive youth subculture? How would you characterize the group's collective identity? What is the relation of the group to the adult world and its institutions? What intergenerational conflicts figure in the film?

- *How does the film portray a particular historical moment or decade?* What visual clues enable viewers to locate the era of the film? What historical events, if any, enter into the film?

- *How does the sound track contribute to the representation of youth culture that is projected by the film?*

- *How do the "stars" of the film influence viewers' perceptions of youth culture?* Do they enhance viewers' sympathies? Are the main characters cultural icons like James Dean or Marlon Brando?

FIELD WORK   *ETHNOGRAPHIC INTERVIEWS*

Music is one of the keys to generational identities. Songs carry the emotional power to define for their listeners what it means to be alive at a particular moment. Singers and musicians evoke generations and decades—Frank Sinatra's emergence as a teen idol in the big band era of the 1940s; Elvis Presley, Little Richard, Buddy Holly, and early rock and roll in the 1950s; the Beatles, Rolling Stones, and Bob Dylan, Motown, and the Memphis sound of Aretha Franklin and Otis Redding in the 1960s; the funk of Parliament and War, disco, and punk bands like the Clash and Sex Pistols in the 1970s; the megastars Springsteen, Madonna, and Michael Jackson, the rap of Public Enemy and NWA, alternative, and the grunge groups of the 1980s and 1990s.

One way to figure out how individuals experience their lives as part of a generation is to investigate what music means to them. The fieldwork project in this chapter investigates how people across generations use music daily to create, maintain, or subvert individual and collective identities. The method is the ethnographic interview, a nondirective approach that asks people to explain how they make sense of music in their lives. "Ethnographic" means literally *graphing*—getting down in the record—the values and practices of the *ethnos,* the tribe or group.

My Music

Susan D. Craft, Daniel Cavicchi, and Charles Keil

The following three ethnographic interviews come from the Music in Daily Life Project in the American Studies program at the State University of New York at Buffalo. The project's goal was to use open-ended ethnographic interviews to find out what music means to individuals and how they integrate music into their lives and identities. Two undergraduate classes conducted the interviews and began with the question "What is music about for you?" (The classes settled on this question "so as not to prejudge the situation" and to give the respondents "room to define music of all kinds in their lives.") Then the interviews were edited, organized by age group, and published in the book *My Music.* The interviews that follow come from three generations—fifteen, thirty-three, and fifty-seven years old, respectively.

SUGGESTION FOR READING

Keep in mind that the interviews you are reading were not scripted but are the result of interviewers' on-the-spot decisions. As you read, notice how the interviewers ask questions and when they ask for more details or redirect the conversation.

EDWARDO

Edwardo is fifteen years old and is enrolled in an auto mechanics program at a vocational high school.

Q: What kind of music do you like to listen to?

A: Basically, I listen to anything. I prefer rap and regular...R and B and rock.

Q: What groups do you listen to when you get a choice?

A: When I'm by myself, I listen to rap like Eric B, MC Hammer, and KRS I. People like that. When I'm with my friends, I listen to Ozzie, and Pink Floyd, Iron Maiden, Metallica. You know, groups like that.

Q: Why do you listen to different stuff when you're by yourself? Different than when you're with your friends?

A: Usually when I'm over at their house they have control of the radio, and they don't like to listen to rap that much.

Q: What kind of things do you do when you are listening to music by yourself?

A: I lip-synch it in the mirror. I pretend I'm doing a movie. Kind of embarrassing, but I do that. And I listen to it while I'm in the shower. And…that's about all.

Q: Would you like to be a professional musician?

A: Kind of. Yeah.

Q: If you pictured yourself as a musician, how would you picture yourself? What kind of music would you play?

A: I'd probably rap. If I didn't, I'd like to play the saxophone.

Q: When you're walking along, do you ever have a song going through your head? Do you have specific songs that you listen to and, if not, do you ever make up songs?

A: Yes. I rap a lot to myself. I make up rhymes and have one of my friends give it a beat. Sometimes we put it on tape. Sometimes we don't.

Q: Could you give me an example of some of the stuff you have put together on your own?

A: I made up one that goes something like, "Now I have many mikes/stepped on many floors./Shattered all the windows/knocked down all the doors." That's just a little part of it. This is hard for me. I'm nervous.

Q: So what kind of things do you try to put together in your songs? What kinds of things do you try to talk about in your songs?

A: I make up different stories. Like people running around. Sometimes I talk about drugs and drinking. Most of the time I just brag about myself.

Q: Do you have any brothers and sisters who listen to the same sort of stuff?

A: Yes. My older brother…he's the one who got me into rap. We're originally from the Bronx, in New York, and he doesn't listen to anything else. My cousin, he listens to heavy metal but he's kind of switched to late-seventies, early-seventies rock. He listens to Pink Floyd and all them, so I listen with him sometimes. I listen with my friends. That's about all.

Q: How long have you been listening to rap?

A: For about seven or eight years.

Q: What kind of stuff were you listening to before that?

A: Actually, I don't remember. Oh yeah. We used to live in California and I was listening to oldies…like the Four Tops and all them. In California…the Mexicans down there, they only listen to the oldies and stuff like that.

Q: Why would you say you changed to rap?

A: When I came down here, everything changed. People were listening to different kinds of music and I was, you know, behind times. So I just had to switch to catch up.

Q: So you would say that your friends really influence you and the kind of music you listen to by yourself?

A: Yeah. I would say that.

Q: When you're listening to music by yourself, what kinds of things go through your mind? Are you concentrating on the words or what?

A: Sometimes I think about life, and all the problems I have. Sometimes I just dwell on the lyrics and just listen to the music.

Q: Do you ever use music as a way to change your mood? If you're really depressed, is there a record you put on?

A: No. Usually when I listen to music and it changes me is when I'm bored and I don't have anything to do or I just get that certain urge to listen to music.

RALPH

Ralph is thirty-three years old, an experienced truck driver who was working as a bus driver for a city transit authority when he was interviewed by a male friend.

I was weaned on the music of the fifties. My musical taste began to form in about...well, my first record album was Chubby Checker's *Let's Do the Twist*...that was 1961. I begged my mom for it. I saw it up at a grocery store here; I had to have it. So she bought it for me. I really dug that.

I still really dig those old rhythm and blues bands back then. I was mainly a product of the Beatles–Rolling Stones–Dave Clark Five era. You know, I never really cared for the Rolling Stones when they first came out. My big group was the Dave Clark Five. I thought they were it until I heard they died in a plane crash somewhere in France, which was a big rumor of the day; but two or three weeks later we found out they didn't die.

I was a Beatles generation kid. I can still remember most of the lyrics of most of the songs they put out. It's a result of constant repetition of it being drummed into my head constantly...just as I'm sure that like somebody who was born in the seventies...David Bowie...I'm sure that a teenager in the seventies would know the words to his songs—"Ziggy Stardust," the early Bowie stuff.

Did the Beatles direct me? Yes, they had some influence on my life. I hate to admit it, but they did. They always painted a rosy picture when I was growing up. It was all love and peace, the flower-child movement. But at that time someone who had a big influence on my musical life was my big brother. He was bringing home stuff like the Supremes at the A-Go-Go...blues...which I really think is the Lord's music. Today you can't find it anymore; there is very little of it coming out, if any.

Today's music just depresses me; it's like the doldrums between 1973 to about 1978...before the new pop or new wave scene arrived...the punkies, the pop stars. I can see things leading that way now too with all this techno-pop. Basically I was into jazz at the time; that's when I got my jazz influences with Monk, Bird, and Coltrane. I used to listen to those people heavily back in the early 1970s. I really loved groups like the Mahavishnu Orchestra. I love jazz fusion and Jeff Beck, but there's some people I really don't care for...Pat Metheny. I never cared for him; why, I don't know. Maybe he has no character in his guitar. It's like a bland speed shuffle. Whereas people like Larry Coryell and John McLaughlin and Jeff Beck, Jan Akkerman...it's just so distinct...their own personal signature. But guys like Pat Metheny and that guy who played with Chick Corea, Al Dimeola, they just don't sign their work; it's all just mumbo-jumbo to me. Other people like them; they sell, right? I don't know; that's my personal taste. I really appreciated any band with a truly outstanding guitarist, somebody you can say: Ah, now this is *him*... I really appreciate that, the signatures.

I like to hear music that I'm not going to hear anyplace else; judge it for myself. Another phase of my life I went through, I really appreciated the blues. From about '67 to '72 was really my blues era, when I was in college. Of course, a lot of people were blues addicts then. Everybody was getting drafted for Vietnam...the blues were very popular back then. You had a lot of English blues groups coming out, like the original Fleetwood Mac, Peter Green...who I thought was a phenomenal blues guitar player, phenomenal!...different groups like the Hedgehogs. A lot of groups shucked it off and went commercial; that really turned me off to them. I also happen to like Beach Boy music...all a rip-off of black history, all a rip-off of black music…but white fun…black fun translated into white fun. Surf music was big around '65 or '66. I'll admit it; we were punks.

Ah, let's see…punk. Where did punk start out? Malcolm McLaren? Malcolm McDowell in *Clockwork Orange*?…when he played the ultimate punk, Alex? Was it Richard Hell in 1974 in New York City with ripped T-shirts and safety pins? Punk is kind of a quaint way of expressing yourself. It hasn't come to murder yet; I wonder if it's gonna come down to murder-rock? You've got savage beating and stuff like that; I wonder if it's ever going to get there. It'll be interesting to see where it goes in the future…looking ahead.

These days I like to go into a bar with a quality jukebox…go in there, dump some quarters in the box, and listen to the old songs.

STEVE

Steve is fifty-seven years old and works as a salesman. He was interviewed by his daughter.

Q: Dad, what does music do for you?

A: What does music do for me? Well, music relaxes me. In order for me to explain, I have to go back and give you an idea exactly how my whole life was affected by music. For example, when I was five or six years old, my mother and father had come from Poland, so naturally all music played at home was ethnic music. This established my ethnic heritage. I had a love for Polish music. Later on in life, like at Polish weddings, they played mostly Polish music…since we lived in Cheektowaga and there is mostly Polish people and a Polish parish. My love for Polish music gave me enjoyment when I was growing up and it carried on all these years to the present time.

But naturally as I got educated in the English language I started going to the movies. I was raised during the Depression and, at that time, the biggest form of escape was musicals…people like Dick Powell, Ruby Keeler, Eddie Cantor, Al Jolson, and Shirley Temple. These were big stars of their day and in order to relax and forget your troubles…we all went through hard times…everybody enjoyed musicals, they were the biggest thing at that time. A lot of musicals were shows from Broadway so, as I was growing up in the Depression and watching movie musicals, I was also getting acquainted with hit tunes that came from Broadway. In that era, Tin Pan Alley was an expression for the place where all these song writers used to write and compose music, and these songs became the hits in the musicals.

Later on these writers went to the movies and it seemed as if every month there was a new hit song that everyone was singing. Some of the writers, like Irving Berlin, Gershwin, Jerome Kern, Harry Warren, and Sammy Kahn…some of these songs are the prettiest songs that were ever written. Even though I never played a musical instrument or was a singer, I was like hundreds of thousands of people in my era who loved music. In fact, radio was very popular at that time, so you heard music constantly on the radio, in the musicals, and all my life I could sing a song all the way through, knowing the tune *and knowing the words*.

Later on in life, when we get to W.W. II, music used to inspire patriotism, and also to bring you closer to home when overseas. For example, one place that just meant music was the Stage Door Canteen in Hollywood. All the stars of the movies and musicals used to volunteer their services and entertain everybody. Later on, as these stars went overseas and performed for the G.I.s, I had a chance to see a lot of these stars in person—stars that I really enjoyed, seeing their movies and listening to their music. So it was like bringing home to overseas. Of course, there was a lot of patriotic songs that stirred us…we were young…say, the Air Force song like "Praise the Lord and Pass the Ammunition."

There was sentimental songs like "There'll Be Blue Birds Over the White Cliffs of Dover," "I Heard a Nightingale Sing Over Berkeley Square." But it was actually music that helped you through tough times like W.W. II, the way music helped you feel better during the Depression…in days that I was younger.

When I came back from overseas…now I'm entering the romantic part of my life, in my early twenties…it was the era of the big bands. One of the greatest events in music history were bands like Glenn Miller and Benny Goodman, the Dorsey Brothers and Sammy Kaye…big bands were popular at the time you used to go to local Candy Kitchens and play the jukebox, and, just like some of the songs said, it was a wonderful time to be with your friends. Good clean entertainment; you listen to the jukebox, dance on the dance floor.

In the big band era, we get into the popular singers who used to sing with the big bands. They went on their own and the era of the ballads was born, and to me this was my favorite era of music in my life. I'll mention some of the big singers just to give you an idea of what I mean—singers like Bing Crosby, Frank Sinatra, Doris Day, Margaret Whiting, Jo Stafford, and Perry Como.

The time of your life when you meet the "girl of your dreams." I was fortunate that we had the Canadiana. It was just like the Love Boat of its time. They used to have a band, and you used to be able to dance on the dance floor. If they didn't have a dance band that night, they would play records, and you could listen to music riding on the lake at night under the stars and moon. It was unbelievable, that particular part of life. It's a shame the younger people of today couldn't experience, not only the boat, but a lot of the things we went through. We thought it was tough at that time, but it was the music that really made things a lot happier and the reason why it's so easy for someone like myself to hear a song and just place myself back in time, at exactly where I was. Was I in the Philippines, or Tokyo, or on the boat? What were the songs that were playing when I first met my wife, what were they playing when I was a young recruit in the Air Force? All I have to do is hear the songs and it'll just take me back in time and I will relive a lot of the parts of my life and, of course, you only remember the good parts! (laughing) You don't remember the bad.

Music to me is very important. One thought that I wanted to mention, about going back in time: when I was just five or six years old, my parents, because they were from the old country, played Polish music, so that when I did meet the girl I was going to marry…every couple has a favorite song and ours was one that was very popular at that time…it was a Polish song to which they put American lyrics. The song was "Tell Me Whose Girl You Are," and I think it was because my wife and I came from a Polish background that Polish music was still a very important part of our life.

Q: What music really did for you was to make you get through bad times and made you think of good things mostly, right?

A: Well, yes, and I would say that music became part of my personality. I use music to not only relax, I use it to relieve tension. About thirty percent of the time I am singing, and it has become part of my personality because it has given me a certain amount of assurance. Not only does it relax me but I think it also bolsters my confidence in being a salesman where you have to always be up. You can't be depressed. Otherwise, you're just going to waste a day. I think music to me is also something that bolsters my spirit.

Q: Does music amplify your mood or does it change your mood? For example, when you're in a depressed mood do you put on something slow or something happy to get you out of that mood?

A: Well, when I was single, if my love life wasn't going right, I used to play sad songs. Well, I guess like most young kids when their love life isn't going right they turn to sad music.

I know that after I'm married and have children and more experience, if I get in a depressed mood then I switch to happier music to change the mood.

Q: What do you think about today's music?

A: (laughing) I could give you enough swear words....No, seriously, I will answer you. I can do it right off the top of my head because I was in a restaurant this morning and I heard a song being played on the radio, which was supposedly a big hit by a new big star. Supposedly this fellow is just as big as Michael Jackson. I think his name is Prince, singing "All Night Long" [Lionel Richie], and, my God when I heard that record where they kept repeating the words over and over, I said to myself, "God, how terrible it is that these kids are not getting benefit of the music that we had when I was younger," because I can take one phrase and write a modern song. I could do the lyrics. And I'm not musical. Say, "Let's Go Mud Wrestling Tonight, Let's Go Mud Wrestling Tonight, You and I, Let's Go Mud Wrestling Tonight. We will be in the mud, we will be in the mud. After the day is over, it's night so Let's Go Mud Wrestling Tonight!"

I really felt very sorry because I realize that the music that I'm telling you about now...music of my era...not only gave me relaxation, not only gave me a certain amount of stimulation...the lyrics of the songs actually educated me. I would say thirty percent of what I know about life today was gleaned from songs. You remember what you learned from a song. Today I heard Paul Robeson singing "Ol' Man River," and I remember seeing the movie with Paul Robeson—the best singer of all time, and the story where it had a mixed marriage, things going on now...the problems of the black people. He sang, "take me away from the White Man Boss." That phrase stuck in my mind because as I heard the song today...and this song was sung thirty or forty years ago...I had also read in the editorial page why Reagan isn't the best candidate for the blacks because they are losing a lot of what they have gained, and I began to realize what a long struggle these people are having.

Q: So, in other words, some of the music you listen to taught you about the people singing it and gave you knowledge...?

A: Well, not only taught me about the people singing, but about life in general, conditions. For example, during the Depression there was a big hit, "Brother Can You Spare A Dime?" and the words went, "...once I built a railroad...now I'm asking for a hand-out."

It wasn't just the person singing the song but the times. For example, during the war era we sang songs that were not only patriotic, but they taught us a lot about what we were fighting for, what was so important about saving America. In a lot of cases, the songs weren't written by the religious but they had some religious overtones and brought in some sense of faith.

SUGGESTIONS FOR DISCUSSION

1. Edwardo's responses to the interviewer's questions are much shorter than Ralph's or Steve's. One senses the pressure that the interviewer must have felt to keep the conversation going. Ralph's interview, on the other hand, is one long response. Steve's contains an extended statement that is followed by question and answer. Take a second look at the questions that the interviewers ask of Edwardo and Steve. What do their purposes seem to be? Try to get a sense of how and why the interviewer decided to ask particular questions. What alternatives, if any, can you imagine?

2. Notice that the interviewees do not fall easily into one distinct musical subculture. Each talks about a range of music. How do Edwardo, Ralph, and Steve make sense of these various forms of musical expression?

3. Each of the interviewees relates his musical tastes to particular social groups or moments in time. How do they connect music to their relationship with others and/or their memories of the past?

FIELDWORK PROJECT

Work with two or three other students on this project. Each group member should interview three people of different ages to get a range of responses across generations. Use the opening question "What is music about for you?" from the Music in Daily Life project. Tape and transcribe the interview.

    As a group, assemble and edit a collection of the interviews and write an introduction that explains the purpose of the interviews and their significance.

A Note on Interviewing

Review the guidelines for interviews in Chapter 1. Remember that in many respects you control the agenda because you scheduled the interview and have determined the questions. The person you interview will be looking for guidance and direction. You are likely to have choices to make during the interview. The guidelines used by the Music in Daily Life Project note the following situation:

> Somebody says, "I really love Bruce Springsteen and his music, can't help it, I get weepy over 'Born in the USA,' you know? But sometimes I wonder if I haven't just swallowed the hype about his being a working-class hero from New Jersey with the symbolic black guy by his side, you know what I mean?" and then pauses, looking at you for some direction or an answer. A choice to make.

The choice concerns which thread in the conversation to follow—the person's love for Springsteen or his feeling of being hyped by the working-class hero image. You could do a number of things at this point in the interview. You could just wait for the person to explain, or you could say, "Tell me a little more about that," and hope the person that you are interviewing will decide on which thread to elaborate. Or you could ask a direct question—"Why do you love Springsteen's music so much?" "What makes you weepy about 'Born in the USA'?" "Why do you think you're being hyped?" (Notice that each of these questions involves a choice that may take the interview in a different direction.)

The point here is that a good interviewer must listen carefully during the interview. The goal is not to dominate but to give the other person some help in developing his or her ideas. Your task as an interviewer is to keep the conversation going.

Editing

An edited interview is not simply the transcribed tape recording. You want to capture the person's voice, but you also want the interview to be readable. Taped interviews can be filled with pauses, um's and ah's, incomplete or incoherent thoughts, and rambling associations. It is standard practice to "clean up" the interview, as long as doing so does not distort or change the person's meanings. Cleaning up a transcript may include editing at the sentence level, but you may also find that it can be helpful to leave out some of the taped material if it is irrelevant.

Writing an Introduction

In the introduction to the edited interviews, explain your purpose in asking people about the role that music plays in their lives. Follow this with some observations and interpretations of the results. Remember that the interviews you are presenting have a limited authority. They don't "prove" anything about the role of music in daily life and the formation of individual or group identity. But they can be suggestive—and you will want to point out how and why.

The Music in Daily Life Project emphasizes the verbs you can use to describe people's relationship to music:

> Is this person *finding* music to explore and express an identity or being *invaded* by music to the point of identity diffusion, *using* music to solve personal problems, *consuming* music to fill a void and relieve alienation and boredom, *participating* in musical mysteries to feel fully human, *addicted* to music and evading reality, *orienting* via music to reality?

As you can see, each verb carries a different interpretation.

Mining the Archive

LIFE MAGAZINE

During the 1940s and 1950s, *Life* was the most popular general magazine in the US, with an estimated readership of twenty million. Founded as a weekly in 1936, *Life* was the first American magazine to give a prominent place to the photo-essay--visual narratives of the week's news as well as special features about American life and culture. If anything, *Life* taught generations of Americans what events in the world looked like, bringing them the work of such noted photographers as Robert Capa, Margaret Bourke-White, and W. Eugene Smith in photojournalistic accounts of the farm crisis and labor conflicts in the Great Depression and of World War II.

In another sense, *Life* also taught Americans what the world should look like. After World War II, *Life* regularly featured families in postwar America, ordinary people in their new suburban homes, driving new cars on America's newly built freeway systems to work, school, and church. Perhaps no other source offers such a rich archive of what domestic life was supposed to be in the 1940s and 1950s, pictorial representations of white, middle-class nuclear families.

To get a sense of how *Life* pictured America in the early postwar period, check out the December 3, 1945 issue and the news story "U.S. Normalcy: Against the Backdrop of a Troubled World *Life* Inspects an American City at Peace." Published just four months after World War Two ended, *Life* juxtaposed images of international instability (the beginnings of the Cold War, the Nuremburg Trials, and child refugees in war-torn Europe and China) and of domestic turmoil (industrial strikes and unemployment) to the concerns of people in Indianapolis to return "their minds and energies to work, football games, automobile trips, family reunions and all the pleasant trivia of the American way of life."

Most college and public libraries will have *Life* in their collection. You will find many family portraits published in *Life* over the years. Take a look through a number of issues. There are various projects you could develop from this photojournalistic archive about "family values" in the postwar period, the role of women as homemakers, representations of teenagers, and the relation of domestic life to the Cold War. Keep in mind that the photo essays on the American family not only give us "slices of life" from the 1940s and 1950s. They also codify Americans' understanding of the ideal family and the American dream. Remember too that audiences did not read these photo-essays on the family in isolation from advertisements and other photo-essays. You might want to consider the overall "flow" of *Life* and how its messages about the family are connected to other messages.

Finally, you might think about why there is no longer a general magazine such as *Life* that claims to picture the "American way of life." The magazine industry today is thriving by attracting specialized readerships based on such interests as computers, skateboarding, mountain biking, and indie rock. The era of such general national magazines as *Life, Look, Colliers,* and the *Saturday Evening Post* has clearly been replaced by niche marketing and subcultural zines. What does this proliferation of specialized magazines suggest to you about the current state of American culture?

CHAPTER 3

Schooling

I wish first that we should recognize that education is ordinary; that is, before everything else, the process of giving to the ordinary members of society its full common meanings, and the skills that will enable them to amend these meanings, in the light of their personal and common experience.

    —*Raymond Williams*, Culture Is Ordinary

A Doll for Jane

"Hello, Father," said Dick.
"Jane will have a birthday soon.
Please get a new doll for Jane.
Get a baby doll that talks.
Please get a doll that talks."

By the time you read this chapter, it is quite likely that you will have already spent a considerable amount of time in school. Most Americans between the ages of five and seventeen or eighteen are full-time students whose daily lives revolve around their schooling. From the moment individuals enter school until they drop out, leave temporarily, graduate from high school, or go on to college, their intellectual and cultural growth is intimately connected to going to school and learning how to be students. Because so much of growing up takes place in them, schools are key agents of acculturation in America, the place where the younger generation not only learns how to read, write, and do mathematics but also gets its upbringing in literature, history, and civics. One of the purposes of all this schooling is to transmit bodies of knowledge from one generation to the next, and classrooms are the place where this intergenerational communication normally occurs, from teacher to student.

Americans have always put a lot of faith in educating the younger generation—to prepare them for the work of the future and to teach them what it means to be an American, a good citizen, and a productive member of society. But it is precisely because Americans put so much faith—and invest so many resources—in schooling that they worry and argue incessantly about what the schools are—or should be—accomplishing. Over the past decade, there has been mounting dissatisfaction with and criticism of the American education system

108

at the elementary, secondary, and college levels. Educational reformers have noted a variety of problems—ranging from declining standardized test scores and the "literacy crisis" to unimaginative teaching, passive learning, and outdated or irrelevant curriculum to skyrocketing college costs and the loss of careers in science, engineering, and mathematics. Critics have called attention to male biases in the curriculum and the neglect of race, ethnicity, and class in the study of history, culture, and literature. Others have argued that the way schools test and reward achievement favors middle-class students over working-class and poor students, whites over blacks, and males over females.

As a student, you are at the center of much of this controversy, and you are in a unique position to comment on schooling in your life and in the lives of others. The purpose of this chapter is to offer you opportunities to read, think, and write about the role of schooling in America today. You will be asked in the reading and writing assignments in this chapter to recall classroom episodes from your past and observe classroom life in the present. You will be asked to work your way from the everyday practices of schooling to the mission and function of education in contemporary America. We want to invite you to explore the world of schooling in order to identify how it has influenced you as a student, a learner, and a person. The writers we have gathered in this chapter will give you an idea of some of the questions educators are currently asking about schooling in America. By engaging the educational issues raised by the reading and writing assignments in this chapter, you can begin to develop your own analysis of the role of schooling in America.

One way to begin an investigation of the role of schooling is to ask what sounds like a very simple and innocent question: What have you learned in school? The answers you might get, however, may not be simple at all. You will need, for one thing, to consider the *formal curriculum* you have studied—the subjects you have taken, the teachers who have instructed you, and the knowledge you have acquired. You will want to think about why American schools teach what they do, why academic subjects are organized as they are, and what assumptions about the nature and function of education have shaped the formal curriculum.

The experience of going to school, of course, involves more than just learning the content of the courses. For students, schooling is not just a matter of the subjects they study. It is a way of life that shapes their sense of themselves and their life chances. Many people remember their first day in school because it marks, quite literally, the transition from home and play to classroom life and the world of schoolwork. The kind of knowledge students acquire when they learn how to be students and go to school forms what educators call the *hidden curriculum*. This part of the curriculum is just as structured as the lessons students study in the formal curriculum. The difference is that in the hidden curriculum the content remains unstated and gets acted out in practice. The hidden curriculum, therefore, refers to all the unspoken beliefs and procedures that regulate classroom life—the rules of the game no one writes down but that teachers and students have internalized in their expectations about each other.

Students learn the hidden curriculum from the early grades on, when they learn how to sit still, pay attention, raise their hands to be called on, follow directions, perform repetitive tasks, and complete work on time. Students learn what pleases teachers and what doesn't, what they can say to teachers and what they ought to keep to themselves. One of the functions of American schools has always been to instill the habits of discipline, punctuality, hard work, and the wise use of time in the younger generation—to teach them, as the old adage goes, that "there is a time for work and a time for play." We might describe the hidden curriculum as a training ground where students learn to work for grades and other symbolic rewards, to take tests and believe in their accuracy and fairness.

Examining the hidden curriculum offers a useful way to look at classroom life, in part because it demands that you research and bring into view the kinds of things that take place in school that teachers and students seem to take for granted. Bringing the familiar and the habitual into view can help generate questions about what you might otherwise accept without question. Why, for example, is the school day divided as it is, and what is the effect of moving from subject to subject in fifty-minute intervals? Why do students sit in rows? Who has the right to speak in class? Who gets called on by the teacher? Why do teachers ask questions when they already know the answer? You will be asked in the reading and writing assignments in this chapter to research questions such as these, to bring the hidden curriculum's unstated norms to light, and to assess their effects on students and on the role schooling plays in American culture.

READING THE CULTURE OF SCHOOLING

The reading and writing assignments in this chapter will ask you to draw on your memories of schooling and your current position as a student—to be a participant–observer of the education you are currently experiencing. The opening selection in the chapter—"What High School Is," Theodore R. Sizer's critical analysis of the typical high school day—offers some interesting leads to think about the goals of education at your high school or college. Sizer's portrait of a high school day comes from a longer study, *Horace's Compromise,* which offers a program to reform high school education. The next reading, however, Leon Botstein's "Let Teenagers Try Adulthood," suggests that high schools can't be reformed but should be abolished and replaced.

The selections from Mike Rose and Nicholas Lemann look at testing and how tests structure the success and failure of individual students. In "Crossing Boundaries," Mike Rose recounts the struggles and aspirations of returning adult learners and raises troubling questions about how schooling labels and stigmatizes individuals as being intellectually deficient—blaming the victim for school failure that has deeper social and political roots. Nicolas Lemann's "A Real Meritocracy" is the after-

word to *The Big Test*, his book-length study of the Educational Testing Service and the SATs. Lemann is interested in how testing fits into the larger educational system, how the system determines what counts as merit, and how it rewards merit.

The next selection is an excerpt from Margaret Finders's *Just Girls*, a study of how junior high school girls use reading and writing outside the official curriculum. "Note-Passing: Struggles for Status" traces one form of hidden literacy and how it (along with writing graffiti, yearbook signing, and reading teen 'zines) maintains social networks and hierarchies.

The last two reading selections—Min-zhan Lu's "From Silence to Words: Writing as Struggle" and June Jordan's "Nobody Mean More to Me Than You and the Future Life of Willie Jordan"—examine the relationship between the language of home and community and the language of the classroom.

What may emerge from the reading and writing assignments in this chapter is a picture of schooling as a way of life that sorts out students to prepare them for their future roles in society. How this sorting out takes place—how tracking assigns some students to college preparatory courses and others to vocational programs, how some students learn to be successful in school while others fail, how schooling confirms or undermines individual students' self-confidence—these are some of the questions you will be invited to explore. Your position as a participant–observer gives you a useful vantage point to raise such questions from the inside, to ask about the meaning of your own education and the role of schooling in American culture.

What High School Is

Theodore R. Sizer

> Theodore R. Sizer has been chairman of the Education Department at Brown University, headmaster of Phillips Academy, Andover, and Dean of the Graduate School of Education at Harvard. The following selection is a chapter from *Horace's Compromise,* Sizer's book-length study of American high schools. Sizer's book takes a critical look at high schools—at overworked teachers, undermotivated students, and the "assembly-line" educational practices that process people rather than educate them. Originally published in 1984, Sizer's study was one of a number of national reports that appeared in the 1980s and raised seri-

ous questions about the quality of American education. We have selected the opening chapter of *Horace's Compromise* because it looks at how the school day is organized and what it means to students to "take subjects."

SUGGESTION FOR READING

As you read, notice that Sizer gives a full account of Mark's day before he steps back to generalize about its significance. Underline and annotate this selection to indicate where Sizer begins to analyze the meaning of Mark's day and how Sizer goes on to develop a critical analysis of the typical high school day.

Mark, sixteen and a genial eleventh-grader, rides a bus to Franklin High School, arriving at 7:25. It is an Assembly Day, so the schedule is adapted to allow for a meeting of the entire school. He hangs out with his friends, first outside school and then inside, by his locker. He carries a pile of textbooks and notebooks; in all, it weighs eight and a half pounds.

From 7:30 to 8:19, with nineteen other students, he is in Room 304 for English class. The Shakespeare play being read this year by the eleventh grade is *Romeo and Juliet*. The teacher, Ms. Viola, has various students in turn take parts and read out loud. Periodically, she interrupts the (usually halting) recitations to ask whether the thread of the conversation in the play is clear. Mark is entertained by the stumbling readings of some of his classmates. He hopes he will not be asked to be Romeo, particularly if his current steady, Sally, is Juliet. There is a good deal of giggling in class, and much attention paid to who may be called on next. Ms. Viola reminds the class of a test on this part of the play to be given next week.

The bell rings at 8:19. Mark goes to the boys' room, where he sees a classmate who he thinks is a wimp but who constantly tries to be a buddy. Mark avoids the leech by rushing off. On the way, he notices two boys engaged in some sort of transaction, probably over marijuana. He pays them no attention. 8:24. Typing class. The rows of desks that embrace big office machines are almost filled before the bell. Mark is uncomfortable here: typing class is girl country. The teacher constantly threatens what to Mark is a humiliatingly girl future: "Your employer won't like these erasures." The minutes during the period are spent copying a letter from a handbook onto business stationery. Mark struggles to keep from looking at his work; the teacher wants him to watch only the material from which he is copying. Mark is frustrated, uncomfortable, and scared that he will not complete his letter by the class's end, which would be embarrassing.

Nine tenths of the students present at school that day are assembled in the auditorium by the 9:18 bell. The dilatory tenth still stumble in, running down aisles. Annoyed class deans try to get the mob settled. The curtains part; the program is a concert by a student rock group. Their electronic gear flashes under the lights, and the five boys and one girl in the group work hard at being casual. Their movements on stage are studiously at three-quarter time, and they chat with one another as though the tumultuous screaming of their schoolmates were totally inaudible. The girl balances on a stool; the boys crank up the music. It is very soft rock, the sanitized lyrics surely cleared with the assistant principal. The girl sings, holding the mike close to her mouth, but can scarcely be heard. Her light voice is tentative, and the lyrics indecipherable. The guitars, amplified, are tuneful, however, and the drums are played with energy.

The students around Mark—all juniors, since they are seated by class—alternately slouch in their upholstered, hinged seats, talking to one another, or sit forward, leaning on the chair backs in front of them, watching the band. A boy near Mark shouts noisily at the microphone-fondling singer, "Bite it...ohhh," and the area around Mark explodes in vulgar male laughter, but quickly subsides. A teacher walks down the aisle. Songs continue, to great applause. Assembly is over at 9:46, two minutes early.

9:53 and biology class. Mark was at a different high school last year and did not take this course there as a tenth-grader. He is in it now, and all but one of his classmates are a year younger than he. He sits on the side, not taking part in the chatter that goes on after the bell. At 9:57, the public address system goes on, with the announcements of the day. After a few words from the principal ("Here's today's cheers and jeers…" with a cheer for the winning basketball team and a jeer for the spectators who made a ruckus at the gymnasium), the task is taken over by officers of ASB (Associated Student Bodies). There is an appeal for "bat bunnies." Carnations are for sale by the Girls' League. Miss Indian American is coming. Students are auctioning off their services (background catcalls are heard) to earn money for the prom. Nominees are needed for the ballot for school bachelor and school bachelorette. The announcements end with a "thought for the day. When you throw a little mud, you lose a little ground."

At 10:04 the biology class finally turns to science. The teacher, Mr. Robbins, has placed one of several labeled laboratory specimens—some are pinned in frames, other swim in formaldehyde—on each of the classroom's eight laboratory tables. The three or so students whose chairs circle each of these benches are to study the specimen and make notes about it or drawings of it. After a few minutes each group of three will move to another table. The teacher points out that these specimens are of organisms already studied in previous classes. He says that the period-long test set for the following day will involve observing some of these specimens—then to be without labels—and writing an identifying paragraph on each. Mr. Robbins points out that some of the printed labels ascribe the specimens' names different from those given in the textbook. He explains that biologists often give several names to the same organism.

The class now falls to peering, writing, and quiet talking. Mr. Robbins comes over to Mark, and in whispered words asks him to carry a requisition form for science department materials to the business office. Mark, because of his "older" status, is usually chosen by Robbins for this kind of errand. Robbins gives Mark the form and a green hall pass to show to any teacher who might challenge him, on his way to the office, for being out of a classroom. The errand takes Mark four minutes. Meanwhile Mark's group is hard at work but gets to only three of the specimens before the bell rings at 10:42. As the students surge out, Robbins shouts a reminder about a "double" laboratory period on Thursday.

Between classes one of the seniors asks Mark whether he plans to be a candidate for schoolwide office next year. Mark says no. He starts to explain. The 10:47 bell rings, meaning that he is late for French class.

There are fifteen students in Monsieur Bates's language class. He hands out tests taken the day before: "*C'est bien fait, Etienne…c'est mieux, Marie…Tch, tch, Robert…*" Mark notes his C+ and peeks at the A− in front of Susanna, next to him. The class has been assigned seats by M. Bates; Mark resents sitting next to prissy, brainy Susanna. Bates starts by asking a student to read a question and give the correct answer. "*James, question un.*" James haltingly reads the question and gives an answer that Bates, now speaking English, says is incomplete. In due course: "*Mark, question cinq.*" Mark does his bit, and the sequence goes on, the eight quiz questions and answers filling about twenty minutes of time.

"Turn to page forty-nine. *Maintenant, lisez après moi…*" and Bates reads a sentence and has the class echo it. Mark is embarrassed by this and mumbles with a barely audible sound. Others, like Susanna, keep the decibel count up, so Mark can hide. This I-say-you-repeat drill is interrupted once by the public address system, with an announcement about a meeting for the cheerleaders. Bates finishes class, almost precisely at the bell, with a homework assignment. The students are to review these sentences for a brief quiz the following day. Mark takes notes of the assignment, because he knows that tomorrow will be a day of busywork in French class. Much though he dislikes oral drills, they are better than the workbook stuff that Bates hands out. Write, write, write, for Bates to throw away, Mark thinks.

11:36. Down to the cafeteria, talking noisily, hanging out, munching. Getting to Room 104 by 12:17: U.S. history. The teacher is sitting crosslegged on his desk when Mark comes in, heatedly arguing with three students over the fracas that had followed the previous night's basketball game. The teacher, Mr. Suslovic, while agreeing that the spectators from their school certainly were provoked, argues that they should neither have been so obviously obscene in yelling at the opposing cheerleaders nor have allowed Coke cans to be rolled out on the floor. The three students keep saying that "it isn't fair." Apparently they and some others had been assigned "Saturday mornings" (detentions) by the principal for the ruckus.

At 12:34, the argument appears to subside. The uninvolved students, including Mark, are in their seats, chatting amiably. Mr. Suslovic climbs off his desk and starts talking: "We've almost finished this unit, chapters nine and ten...." The students stop chattering among themselves and turn toward Suslovic. Several slouch down in their chairs. Some open notebooks. Most have the five-pound textbook on their desks.

Suslovic lectures on the cattle drives, from north Texas to railroads west of St. Louis. He breaks up this narrative with questions ("Why were the railroad lines laid largely east to west?"), directed at nobody in particular and eventually answered by Suslovic himself. Some students take notes. Mark doesn't. A student walks in the open door, hands Mr. Suslovic a list, and starts whispering with him. Suslovic turns from the class and hears out this messenger. He then asks, "Does anyone know where Maggie Sharp is?" Someone answers, "Sick at home"; someone else says, "I thought I saw her at lunch." Genial consternation. Finally Suslovic tells the messenger, "Sorry, we can't help you," and returns to the class: "Now, where were we?" He goes on for some minutes. The bell rings. Suslovic forgets to give the homework assignment.

1:11 and Algebra II. There is a commotion in the hallway: someone's locker is rumored to have been opened by the assistant principal and a narcotics agent. In the five-minute passing time, Mark hears the story three times and three ways. A locker had been broken into by another student. It was Mr. Gregory and a narc. It was the cops, and they did it without Gregory's knowing. Mrs. Ames, the mathematics teacher, has not heard anything about it. Several of the nineteen students try to tell her and start arguing among themselves. "O.K., that's enough." She hands out the day's problem, one sheet to each student. Mark sees with dismay that it is a single, complicated "word" problem about some train that, while traveling at 84 mph, due west, passes a car that was going due east at 55 mph. Mark struggles: Is it $d = rt$ or $t = rd$? The class becomes quiet, writing, while Mrs. Ames writes some additional, short problems on the blackboard. "Time's up." A sigh; most students still writing. A muffled "Shit." Mrs. Ames frowns. "Come on, now." She collects papers, but it takes four minutes for her to corral them all.

"Copy down the problems from the board." A minute passes. "William, try number one." William suggests an approach. Mrs. Ames corrects and cajoles, and William finally gets it right. Mark watches two kids to his right passing notes; he tries to read them but the handwriting is illegible from his distance. He hopes he is not called on, and he isn't. Only three students are asked to puzzle out an answer. The bell rings at 2:00. Mrs. Ames shouts a homework assignment over the resulting hubbub.

Mark leaves his books in his locker. He remembers that he has homework, but figures that he can do it during English class the next day. He knows that there will be an in-class presentation of one of the *Romeo and Juliet* scenes and that he will not be in it. The teacher will not notice his homework writing, or won't do anything about it if she does.

Mark passes various friends heading toward the gym, members of the basketball teams. Like most students, Mark isn't an active school athlete. However, he is associated with the yearbook staff. Although he is not taking "Yearbook" for credit as an English course, he is contributing photographs. Mark takes twenty minutes checking into the yearbook staff's headquarters (the classroom of its faculty adviser) and getting some assignments of pictures from his boss, the senior who is the photography editor. Mark knows that if he pleases his boss and the faculty adviser, he'll take that editor's post for the next year. He'll get English credit for his work then.

After gossiping a bit with the yearbook staff, Mark will leave school by 2:35 and go home. His grocery market bagger's job is from 4:45 to 8:00, the rush hour for the store. He'll have a snack at 4:30, and his mother will save him some supper to eat at 8:30. She will ask whether he has any homework, and he'll tell her no. Tomorrow, and virtually every other tomorrow, will be the same for Mark, save for the lack of the assembly; each period then will be five minutes longer.

Most Americans have an uncomplicated vision of what secondary education should be. Their conception of high school is remarkably uniform across the country, a striking fact, given the size and diversity of the United States and the politically decentralized character of the schools. This uniformity is of several generations' standing. It has, however, two appearances, each quite different from the other, one of words and the other of practice, a world of political rhetoric and Mark's world.

A California high school's general goals, set out in 1979, could serve equally well most of America's high schools, public and private. This school had as its ends:

- Fundamental scholastic achievement... to acquire knowledge and share in the traditionally accepted academic fundamentals...to develop the ability to make decisions, to solve problems, to reason independently, and to accept responsibility for self-evaluation and continuing self-improvement.
- Career and economic competence
- Citizenship and civil responsibility
- Competence in human and social relations
- Moral and ethical values
- Self-realization and mental and physical health
- Aesthetic awareness
- Cultural diversity

In addition to its optimistic rhetoric, what distinguished this list is its comprehensiveness. The high school is to touch most aspects of an adolescent's existence—mind, body, morals, values, career. No one of these areas is given especial prominence. School people arrogate to themselves an obligation to all.

An example of the wide acceptability of these goals is found in the courts. Forced to present a detailed definition of "thorough and efficient education," elementary as well as secondary, a West Virginia judge sampled the best of conventional wisdom and concluded that

> there are eight general elements of a thorough and efficient system of education: (a) Literacy, (b) The ability to add, subtract, multiply, and divide numbers, (c) Knowledge of government to the extent the child will be equipped as a citizen to make informed choices among persons and issues that affect his own governance, (d) Self-knowledge and knowledge of his or her total environment to allow the child to intelligently choose life work—to know his or her

options, (e) Work-training and advanced academic training as the child may intelligently choose, (f) Recreational pursuits, (g) Interests in all creative arts such as music, theater, literature, and the visual arts, and (h) Social ethics, both behavioral and abstract, to facilitate compatibility with others in this society.

That these eight—now powerfully part of the debate over the purpose and practice of education in West Virginia—are reminiscent of the influential list, "The Seven Cardinal Principles of Secondary Education," promulgated in 1918 by the National Education Association, is no surprise. The rhetoric of high school purpose has been uniform and consistent for decades. Americans agree on the goals for their high schools.

That agreement is convenient, but it masks the fact that virtually all the words in these goal statements beg definition. Some schools have labored long to identify specific criteria beyond them; the result has been lists of daunting pseudospecificity and numbing earnestness. However, most leave the words undefined and let the momentum of traditional practice speak for itself. That is why analyzing how Mark spends his time is important: from watching him one uncovers the important purposes of education, the ones that shape practice. Mark's day is similar to that of other high school students across the country, as similar as the rhetoric of one goal statement to others'. Of course, there are variations, but the extent of consistency in the shape of school routine for a large and diverse adolescent population is extraordinary, indicating more graphically than any rhetoric the measure of agreement in America about what one does in high school, and, by implication, what it is for.

The basic organizing structures in schools are familiar. Above all, students are grouped by age (that is, freshman, sophomore, junior, senior), and all are expected to take precisely the same time—around 720 school days over four years, to be precise—to meet the requirements for a diploma. When one is out of his grade level, he can feel odd, as Mark did in his biology class. The goals are the same for all, and the means to achieve them are also similar.

Young males and females are treated remarkably alike; the schools' goals are the same for each gender. In execution, there are differences, as those pressing sex discrimination suits have made educators intensely aware. The students in metalworking classes are mostly male; those in home economics, mostly female. But it is revealing how much less sex discrimination there is in high schools than in other American institutions. For many young women, the most liberated hours of their week are in school.

School is to be like a job: you start in the morning and end in the afternoon, five days a week. You don't get much of a lunch hour, so you go home early, unless you are an athlete or are involved in some special school or extracurricular activity. School is conceived of as the children's workplace, and it takes young people off parents' hands and out of the labor market during prime-time work hours. Not surprisingly, many students see going to school as little more than a dogged necessity. They perceive the day-to-day routine, a Minnesota study reports, as one of "boredom and lethargy." One of the students summarizes: School is "boring, restless, tiresome, puts ya to sleep, tedious monotonous, pain in the neck."

The school schedule is a series of units of time: the clock is king. The base time block is about fifty minutes in length. Some schools, on what they call modular scheduling, split that fifty-minute block into two or even three pieces. Most schools have double periods for laboratory work, especially in the sciences, or four-hour units for small numbers of students involved in intensive vocational or other work-study programs. The flow of all school activity arises from or is blocked by these time units. "How much time do I have with my kids" is the teacher's key question.

Because there are many claims for those fifty-minute blocks, there is little time set aside for rest between them, usually no more than three to ten minutes, depending on how big the school is and, consequently, how far students and teachers have to walk from class to class.

As a result, there is a frenetic quality to the school day, a sense of sustained restlessness. For the adolescents, there are frequent changes of room and fellow students, each change giving tempting opportunities for distraction, which are stoutly resisted by teachers. Some schools play soft music during these "passing times," to quiet the multitude, one principal told me.

Many teachers have a chance for a coffee break. Few students do. In some city schools where security is a problem, students must be in class for seven consecutive periods, interrupted by a heavily monitored twenty-minute lunch period for small groups, starting as early as 10:30 A.M. and running to after 1:00 P.M. A high premium is placed on punctuality and on "being where you're supposed to be." Obviously, a low premium is placed on reflection and repose. The student rushes from class to class to collect knowledge. Savoring it, it is implied, is not to be done much in school, nor is such meditation really much admired. The picture that these familial patterns yield is that of an academic supermarket. The purpose of going to school is to pick things up, in an organized and predictable way, the faster the better.

What is supposed to be picked up is remarkably consistent among all sorts of high schools. Most schools specifically mandate three out of every five courses a student selects. Nearly all of these mandates fall into five areas—English, social studies, mathematics, science, and physical education. On the average, English is required to be taken each year, social studies and physical education three out of the four high school years, and mathematics and science one or two years. Trends indicate that in the mid-eighties there is likely to be an increase in the time allocated to these last two subjects. Most students take classes in these four major academic areas beyond the minimum requirements, sometimes in such special areas as journalism and "yearbook," offshoots of English departments.

Press most adults about what high school is for, and you hear these subjects listed. *High school? That's where you learn English and math and that sort of thing.* Ask students, and you get the same answers. High school is to "teach" these "subjects."

What is often absent is any definition of these subjects or any rationale for them. They are just there, labels. Under those labels lie a multitude of things. A great deal of material is supposed to be "covered"; most of these courses are surveys, great sweeps of the stuff of their parent disciplines.

While there is often a sequence *within* subjects—algebra before trigonometry, "first-year" French before "second-year" French—there is rarely a coherent relationship or sequence *across* subjects. Even the most logically related matters—reading ability as a precondition for the reading of history books, and certain mathematical concepts or skills before the study of some physics—are only loosely coordinated, if at all. There is little demand for a synthesis of it all; English, mathematics, and the rest are discrete items, to be picked up individually. The incentive for picking them up is largely through tests and, with success at these, in credits earned.

Coverage within subjects is the key priority. If some imaginative teacher makes a proposal to force the marriage of, say, mathematics and physics or to require some culminating challenges to students to use several subjects in the solution of a complex problem, and if this proposal will take "time" away from other things, opposition is usually phrased in terms of what may be thus forgone. If we do that, we'll have to give up colonial history. We won't be able to get to programming. We'll not be able to read *Death of a Salesman*. There isn't time. The protesters usually win out.

The subjects come at a student like Mark in random order, a kaleidoscope of worlds: algebraic formulae to poetry to French verbs to Ping-Pong to the War of the Spanish Succession, all before lunch. Pupils are to pick up these things. Tests measure whether the picking up has been successful.

The lack of connection between stated goals, such as those of the California high school cited earlier, and the goals inherent in school practice is obvious and, curiously, tolerated.

Most striking is the gap between statements about "self-realization and mental and physical growth" or "moral and ethical values"—common rhetoric in school documents—and practice. Most physical education programs have neither the time nor the focus really to ensure fitness. Mental health is rarely defined. Neither are ethical values, save at the negative extremes, such as opposition to assault or dishonesty. Nothing in the regimen of a day like Mark's signals direct or implicit teaching in this area. The "schoolboy code" (not ratting on a fellow student) protects the marijuana pusher, and a leechlike associate is shrugged off without concern. The issue of the locker search was pushed aside, as not appropriate for class time.

Most students, like Mark, go to class in groups of twenty to twenty-seven students. The expected attendance in some schools, particularly those in low-income areas, is usually higher, often thirty-five students per class, but high absentee rates push the actual numbers down. About twenty-five per class is an average figure for expected attendance, and the actual numbers are somewhat lower. There are remarkably few students who go to class in groups much larger or smaller than twenty-five.

A student such as Mark sees five or six teachers per day; their differing styles and expectations are part of his kaleidoscope. High school staffs are highly specialized; guidance counselors rarely teach mathematics, mathematics teachers rarely teach English, principals rarely do any classroom instruction. Mark, then, is known a little bit by a number of people, each of whom sees him in one specialized situation. No one may know him as a "whole person"—unless he becomes a special problem or has special needs.

Save in extracurricular or coaching situations, such as in athletics, drama, or shop classes, there is little opportunity for sustained conversation between student and teacher. The mode is a one-sentence or two-sentence exchange: *Mark, when was Grover Cleveland president?* Let's see, was 1890...or something...wasn't he the one...he was elected twice, wasn't he? ...*Yes...Gloria, can you get the dates right?* Dialogue is strikingly absent, and as a result the opportunity of teachers to challenge students' ideas in a systematic and logical way is limited. Given the rushed, full quality of the school day, it can seldom happen. One must infer that careful probing of students' thinking is not a high priority. How one gains (to quote the California school's statement of goals again) "the ability to make decisions, to solve problems, to reason independently, and to accept responsibility for self-evaluation and continuing self-improvement" without being challenged is difficult to imagine. One certainly doesn't learn these things merely from lectures and textbooks.

Most schools are nice places. Mark and his friends enjoy being in theirs. The adults who work in schools generally like adolescents. The academic pressures are limited, and the accommodations to students are substantial. For example, if many members of an English class have jobs after school, the English teacher's expectations for them are adjusted, downward. In a word, school is sensitively accommodating, as long as students are punctual, where they are supposed to be, and minimally dutiful about picking things up from the clutch of courses in which they enroll.

This characterization is not pretty, but it is accurate, and it serves to describe the vast majority of American secondary schools. "Taking subjects" in a systematized, conveyer-belt way is what one does in high school. That this process is, in substantial respects, not related to the rhetorical purposes of education is tolerated by most people, perhaps because they do not really either believe in those ill-defined goals or, in their heart of hearts, believe that schools can or should even try to achieve them. The students are happy taking subjects. The parents are happy, because that's what they did in high school. The rituals, the most important of which is graduation, remain intact. The adolescents are supervised, safely and constructively most of the time, during the morning and afternoon hours, and they are off the labor market. That is what high school is all about.

SUGGESTIONS FOR DISCUSSION

1. The portrait of Mark that begins this selection, as Sizer notes, is "made up." It is a composite blending of a number of real students and real high schools—"somewhere," Sizer says, "between precise journalism and non-fiction fiction." As a composite of real students in real high schools, Sizer's portrait of Mark's school day must appear to be typical and recognizable for it to be persuasive and credible. Does Sizer's portrait achieve the kind of typicality he is trying for? Draw on your own experience and observations in high school to decide whether this is a fair portrait and what, if anything, it leaves out.

2. Sizer says, "Press most adults about what high school is for, and you hear these subjects listed. *High school? That's where you learn English and math and that sort of thing.*" How does Sizer answer his question, what is high school for? How would you answer it? Explain how you would account for differences and similarities between Sizer's answer and your own.

3. Do you agree with Sizer that there is a "lack of connection between stated goals" of high school education and "the goals inherent in school practice?" Sizer gives some examples of stated goals, such as the general goals for California high schools and the goals presented by a West Virginia judge, but he doesn't really say what the "goals inherent in school practice" might be. To answer this question you will need to decide what these unstated goals are and how they determine what actually takes place in the daily routines of American high schools.

SUGGESTIONS FOR WRITING

1. At the end of this selection, Sizer says "'Taking subjects' in a systematized, conveyer-belt way is what one does in high school." A few lines later he says, "students are happy taking subjects." Do you agree with Sizer? Are high school students, in your experience, happy "taking subjects," or do they feel something is missing? Write an essay that develops your own position. Begin by summarizing what Sizer views as "conveyer-belt" education. Then explain to what extent and why you agree or disagree with his sense that students are happy "taking subjects."

2. Sizer says, "Most schools are nice….The academic pressures are limited, and the accommodations to students are substantial. For example, if many members of an English class have jobs after school, the English teacher's expectations for them are adjusted, downward." Write an essay that describes the expectations of teachers in the high school you attended and explains what influence those expectations have had on you as a student, a learner, and a person. Take into account whether teachers' expectations varied and whether they held the same expectations for all students.

3. Use Sizer's composite portrait of Mark's school day as a model to write a portrait of a typical school day at the high school you attended or your college. You can draw on your own experience and memories, but keep in mind that in Sizer's portrait is a made-up character, not a real person. Similarly, in this writing task, you'll need to invent your own typical student and his or her experience of the school day.

In the late nineties, the website School Sucks appeared as a radical version of old "term paper mills," businesses that sell work to students for use in classes requiring research papers of any sort. In addition to inviting students to download papers free of charge, this page also asks students to submit their papers for others to download. School Sucks (http://www.schoolsucks.com) and other copycat pages like The Evil House of Cheat have become extremely popular, following outcries by college professors who charged the Web with encouraging students to cheat. In response, a site at http://www.plagiarism.org offers college professors the solution with TurnItIn.com, a site that "fingerprints" student papers. A teacher registers with the site. Students turn all of their papers in to the site. The site checks for "gross" plagiarism, and the site "guarantees" that a student's paper can never be used from the Web. One discussion of this phenomenon has been archived at http://www.dewey.lc.missouri.edu/~schoolsucks. Look for those pages and others that address this issue. Use your findings to discuss what it is that you know about schooling that has led to pages like School Sucks and other such means of challenging the culture of schooling.

Let Teenagers Try Adulthood

Leon Botstein

> Leon Botstein is the president of Bard College and author of *Jefferson's Children: Education and the Promise of American Culture*. The following selection appeared on the Op Ed page of the *New York Times* in May 1999, shortly after the school shootings in Littleton, Colorado. Botstein uses the shootings at Columbine High School to give a sense of urgency to his argument that "American high schools are obsolete and should be abolished." As you will see, however, the case he makes does not depend on the Littleton events alone. In Botstein's view, there are larger reasons for recognizing that high school is a failure not worth reforming.

SUGGESTION FOR READING

> Botstein makes his main point—namely that high schools are out of date and should be abolished—in the opening sentence. As you read, mark the reasons he offers to support this position.

The national outpouring after the Littleton shootings has forced us to confront something we have suspected for a long time: the American high school is obsolete and should be abolished. In the last month, high school students present and past have come forward with stories about cliques and the artificial intensity of a world defined by insiders and outsiders, in which the insiders hold sway because of superficial definitions of good looks and attractiveness, popularity, and sports prowess.

The team sports of high school dominate more than student culture. A community's loyalty to the high school system is often based on the extent to which varsity teams succeed. High school administrators and faculty members are often former coaches, and the coaches themselves are placed in a separate, untouchable category. The result is that the culture of the inside elite is not contested by the adults in the school. Individuality and dissent are discouraged.

But the rules of high school turn out not to be the rules of life. Often the high school outsider becomes the more successful and admired adult. The definitions of masculinity and femininity go through sufficient transformation to make the game of popularity in high school an embarrassment. No other group of adults young or old is confined to an age-segregated environment, much like a gang in which individuals of the same age group define each other's world. In no workplace, not even in colleges or universities, is there such a narrow segmentation by chronology.

Given the poor quality of recruitment and training for high school teachers, it is no wonder that the curriculum and the enterprise of learning hold so little sway over young people. When puberty meets education and learning in modern America, the victory of puberty masquerading as popular culture and the tyranny of peer groups based on ludicrous values meet little resistance.

By the time those who graduate from high school go on to college and realize what really is at stake in becoming an adult, too many opportunities have been lost and too much time has been wasted. Most thoughtful young people suffer the high school environment in silence and in their junior and senior years mark time waiting for college to begin. The Littleton killers, above and beyond the psychological demons that drove them to violence, felt trapped in the artificiality of the high school world and believed it to be real. They engineered their moment of undivided attention and importance in the absence of any confidence that life after high school could have a different meaning.

Adults should face the fact that they don't like adolescents and that they have used high school to isolate the pubescent and hormonally active adolescent away from both the picture-book idealized innocence of childhood and the more accountable world of adulthood. But the primary reason high school doesn't work anymore, if it ever did, is that young people mature substantially earlier in the late 20th century than they did when the high school was invented. For example, the age of first menstruation has dropped at least two years since the beginning of this century, and not surprisingly, the onset of sexual activity has dropped in proportion. An institution intended for children in transition now holds young adults back well beyond the developmental point for which high school was originally designed.

Furthermore, whatever constraints to the presumption of adulthood among young people may have existed decades ago have now fallen away. Information and images, as well as the real and virtual freedom of movement we associate with adulthood, are now accessible to every fifteen- and sixteen-year-old.

Secondary education must be rethought. Elementary school should begin at age four or five and end with the sixth grade. We should entirely abandon the concept of the middle school and junior high school. Beginning with the seventh grade, there should be four years of secondary education that we may call high school. Young people should graduate at sixteen rather than eighteen.

They could then enter the real world, the world of work or national service, in which they would take a place of responsibility alongside older adults in mixed company. They could stay at home and attend junior college, or they could go away to college. For all the faults of college, at least the adults who dominate the world of colleges, the faculty, were selected precisely because they were exceptional and different, not because they were popular. Despite the often cavalier attitude toward teaching in college, at least physicists know their physics, mathematicians know and love their mathematics, and music is taught by musicians, not by graduates of education schools, where the disciplines are subordinated to the study of classroom management.

For those sixteen-year-olds who do not want to do any of the above, we might construct new kinds of institutions, each dedicated to one activity, from science to dance, to which adolescents could devote their energies while working together with professionals in those fields.

At sixteen, young Americans are prepared to be taken seriously and to develop the motivations and interests that will serve them well in adult life. They need to enter a world where they are not in a lunchroom with only their peers, estranged from other age groups and cut off from the game of life as it is really played. There is nothing utopian about this idea; it is immensely practical and efficient, and its implementation is long overdue. We need to face biological and cultural facts and not prolong the life of a flawed institution that is out of date.

SUGGESTIONS FOR DISCUSSION

1. First, make a list of the reasons Botstein gives to support his view that "high school doesn't work anymore." Next, notice that what he calls "the primary reason" appears in paragraph six. Consider why he has organized his reasons in the order they appear. How does the order of reasons lead readers from one point to the next? What assumptions about schooling and American teenagers is Botstein asking readers to share?

2. Both Botstein and Theodore Sizer in the preceding selection, "What High School Is," are highly critical of American high schools. Their critiques, however, are quite different ones. Compare the analyses they offer of American high schools. What in particular do they focus on? Are they looking at the same things and drawing different conclusions, or do their differences begin with the things they are analyzing? How do these differences in perspective set up Botstein to argue for abolishing high school but Sizer to argue for reforming it?

3. Like Botstein, Thomas Hine in "Goths in Tomorrowland" (Chapter 2) is concerned about the alienation of American teenagers from adult society. Read (or reread) the selection from Hine. Compare the perspectives Hine and Botstein offer on the age segregation of American teenagers. What do they see as the larger implications of teenagers' alienation from adult society? Do you share their concern? Explain why or why not. Take into account what, if anything, you can say in favor of the kind of age segregation that takes place in high school.

SUGGESTIONS FOR WRITING

1. Write a letter to the editor of the *New York Times* that responds to Botstein's Op Ed piece. You can agree or disagree with his proposal to abolish American high schools or you can provide a different perspective on the issues of schooling he raises. In any case, you will need to explain your reasons for agreeing or the significance of the perspective you offer. To get a sense of the tone to use in such a letter and the approach to readers, take a look at some of the letters in a recent issue.

2. Assume that Botstein's plan to restructure American education actually takes place. In the new system, young people will leave secondary school at age sixteen. Some, as Botstein notes, will enter the world of work or national service, while others will go to college. For still others, however, we might devise what Botstein calls "new kinds of institutions, each dedicated to one

activity, from science to dance, to which adolescents could devote their energies while working together with professionals in those fields." Develop a proposal for one of these "new kinds of institutions." Include a rationale that explains why you think the particular activity the institution focuses on is worthwhile, what young people would do, and what the outcome might be.

3. Write an essay that develops your own position on what both Botstein and Thomas Hine talk about as the age segregation of young people in high school. First, explain the perspective each offers and the consequences they believe follow from age segregation. Then, explain your own point of view on the issue, indicating whether you think their concern about the alienation of teenagers from adult society is a justifiable one.

Crossing Boundaries

Mike Rose

Mike Rose is a professor of education at UCLA. He has worked for the past twenty years teaching and tutoring children and adults from what he calls America's "educational underclass"—working-class children, poorly educated Vietnam vets, underprepared college students, and adults in basic literacy programs. We have taken the following selection from the chapter "Crossing Boundaries" in Rose's award-winning book *Lives on the Boundary* (1989). This book is an intensely personal account of Rose's own life growing up in a Los Angeles ghetto and his struggles as an educator to make schooling more accessible to children and adults labeled "remedial," "illiterate," and "intellectually deficient." As the following selection indicates, throughout *Lives on the Boundary* Rose is especially interested in the "politics and sociology of school failure."

SUGGESTION FOR READING

You will notice that the following selection is separated into three parts. To help you think about how these parts combine to form a whole (or whether they do), underline and annotate as you read and note the focus of each section and how it provides a commentary on the other sections.

I myself I thank God for the dream to come back to school and to be able to seek the dream I want, because I know this time I will try and make my dream come true.

Each semester the staff of the Bay Area literacy program we're about to visit collects samples of their students' writing and makes books for them. You can find an assortment on an old bookshelf by the coordinator's desk. The booklets are simple: mimeographed, faint blue stencil, stapled, dog-eared. There are uneven drawings on the thin paper covers: a bicycle leaning against a tree, the Golden Gate Bridge, an Aubrey Beardsley sketch. The stories are about growing up, raising children, returning—sadly or with anticipation—to hometowns, to Chicago or St. Louis or to a sweep of rural communities in the South. Many of the stories are about work: looking for work, losing work, wanting better work. And many more are about coming back to school. Coming back to school. Some of these writers haven't been in a classroom in thirty years.

The stories reveal quite a range. Many are no longer than a paragraph, their sentences simple and repetitive, tenuously linked by *and* and *then* and *anyway*. There are lots of grammar and spelling errors and problems with sentence boundaries—in a few essays, periods come where commas should be or where no punctuation is needed at all: "It was hard for me to stay in school because I was allway sick. and that was verry hard for me." Or, "I sound better. now that my boys are grown." Papers of this quality are written, for the most part, by newcomers, people at the end of their first semester. But other papers—quite a few, actually—are competent. They tend to come from those who have received a year or more of instruction. There are still problems with grammar and sentence fragments and with spelling, since the writers are using a wider, more ambitious vocabulary. Problems like these take longer to clear up, but the writers are getting more adept at rendering their experience in print, at developing a narrative, at framing an illustration, at turning a phrase in written language:

> The kitchen floor was missing some of its tiles and had not been kissed with water and soap for a long time.

> The [teacher] looked for a moment, and then said, "All the students wishing to be accounted for, please be seated."

> A minute went by, then a tough looking Mexican boy got up, and walked to the teacher with a knife in his hand. When he got to the desk he said, "I'm here teacher! My name is Robert Gomez." With that he put the knife away, and walked over and found a seat.

> Back in the jaws of despair, pain, and the ugly scars of the defeated parents he loved. Those jaws he had struggled free of when he had moved out and away when he was eighteen years old.

> ...the wind was howling, angry, whirling.

A few new students also created such moments, indicators of what they'll be able to do as they become more fluent writers, as they develop some control over and confidence in establishing themselves on paper:

> [I used to have] light, really light Brown eyes, like Grasshopper eyes. which is what some peoples used to call me. Grasshopper, or Grasshopper eyes....I decided one Day to catch a Grasshopper. and look at its eye to be sure of the color.

> It was early in the morning just before dawn. Big Red, the sun hasn't showed its face in the heaven. The sky had that midnight blue look. The stars losing their shine.

There are about eight or ten of these stapled collections, a hundred and fifty or so essays. Five years' worth. An archive scattered across an old bookcase. There's a folding chair close by. I've been sitting in it for some time now, reading one book, then another, story after story. Losing track. Drifting in and out of lives. Wondering about grasshopper eyes, about segregated schools, wanting to know more about this journey to the West looking for work. Slowly something has been shifting in my perception: the errors—the weird commas and missing letters, the fragments and irregular punctuation—they are ceasing to be slips of the hand and brain. They are becoming part of the stories themselves. They are the only fitting way, it seems, to render dislocation—shacks and field labor and children lost to the inner city—to talk about parents you long for, jobs you can't pin down. Poverty has generated its own damaged script, scars manifest in the spelling of a word.

This is the prose of America's underclass. The writers are those who got lost in our schools, who could not escape neighborhoods that narrowed their possibilities, who could not enter the job market in any ascendent way. They are locked into unskilled and semiskilled jobs, live in places that threaten their children, suffer from disorders and handicaps they don't have the money to treat. Some have been unemployed for a long time. But for all that, they remain hopeful, have somehow held onto a deep faith in education. They have come back to school. Ruby, the woman who wrote the passage that opens this section, walks unsteadily to the teacher's desk—the arthritis in her hip goes unchecked—with a paper in her hand. She looks over her shoulder to her friend, Alice: "I ain't givin' up the ship this time," she says and winks, "though, Lord, I might drown with it." The class laughs. They understand.

It is a very iffy thing, this schooling. But the participants put a lot of stock in it. They believe school will help them, and they are very specific about what they want: a high school equivalency, or the ability to earn seven dollars an hour. One wants to move from being a nurse's aide to a licensed vocational nurse, another needs to read and write and compute adequately enough to be self-employed as a car painter and body man. They remind you of how fundamentally important it is—not just to your pocket but to your soul as well—to earn a decent wage, to have a steady job, to be just a little bit in control of your economic life. The goals are specific, modest, but they mean a tremendous amount for the assurance they give to these people that they are still somebody, that they can exercise control. Thus it is that talk of school and a new job brings forth such expansive language, as soaring as any humanist's testament to the glory of the word: "I thank God to be able to seek the dream I want...." For Ruby and her classmates the dream deferred neither dried up like a raisin in the sun, nor has it exploded. It has emerged again—for it is so basic—and it centers on schooling. "I admire and respect knowledge and those that have it are well blessed," writes another student. "My classmates are a swell group because they too have a dream and they too are seeking knowledge and I love them for that."

Sitting in the classroom with Ruby, Alice, and the rest, you think, at times, that you're at a revival meeting. There is so much testifying. Everybody talks and writes about dreams and goals and "doing better for myself." This is powerful, edifying—but something about it, its insistence perhaps, is a little bit discordant. The exuberance becomes jittery, an almost counterphobic boosting and supporting. It is no surprise, then, that it alternates with despair. In their hearts, Ruby and her classmates know how tenuous this is, how many times they've failed before. Somebody says something about falling down. Sally says, "I've felt that too. Not falling down on my legs or knees, but falling down within me." No wonder they sermonize and embrace. It's not just a few bucks more a week that's at stake; literacy, here, is intimately connected with respect, with a sense that they are not beaten, the mastery of print revealing the deepest impulse to survive.

When they entered the program, Ruby and Alice and Sally and all the rest were given several tests, one of which was a traditional reading inventory. The test had a section on comprehension—relatively brief passages followed by multiple-choice questions—and a series of sections that tested particular reading skills: vocabulary, syllabication, phonics, prefixes and roots. The level of the instrument was pretty sophisticated, and the skills it tested are the kind you develop in school: answering multiple-choice questions, working out syllable breaks, knowing Greek and Latin roots, all that. What was interesting about this group of test takers was that—though a few were barely literate—many could read and write well enough to get along, and, in some cases, to help those in their communities who were less skilled. They could read, with fair comprehension, simple news articles, could pay bills, follow up on sales and coupons, deal with school forms for their kids, and help illiterate neighbors in their interactions with the government. Their skills were pretty low-level and limited profoundly the kinds of things they could read or write, but they lived and functioned amid print. The sad thing is that we don't really have tests of such naturally occurring competence. The tests we do have, like the one Ruby and the others took, focus on components of reading ability tested in isolation (phonetic discrimination, for example) or on those skills that are school-oriented, like reading a passage on an unfamiliar topic unrelated to immediate needs: the mating habits of the dolphin, the Mayan pyramids. Students then answer questions on these sorts of passages by choosing one of four or five possible answers, some of which may be purposely misleading.

To nobody's surprise, Ruby and her classmates performed miserably. The tasks of the classroom were as unfamiliar as could be. There is a good deal of criticism of these sorts of reading tests, but one thing that is clear is that they reveal how well people can perform certain kinds of school activities. The activities themselves may be of questionable value, but they are interwoven with instruction and assessment, and entrance to many jobs is determined by them. Because of their centrality, then, I wanted to get some sense of how the students went about taking the tests. What happened as they tried to meet the test's demands? How was it that they failed?

My method was simple. I chose four students and had each of them take sections of the test again, asking them questions as they did so, encouraging them to talk as they tried to figure out an item.

The first thing that emerged was the complete foreignness of the task. A sample item in the prefixes and roots section (called Word Parts) presented the word "<u>un</u>happy," and asked the testtaker to select one of four other words "which gives the meaning of the underlined part of the first word." The choices were *very, glad, sad, not.* Though the person giving the test had read through the instructions with the class, many still could not understand, and if they chose an answer at all, most likely chose *sad,* a synonym for the whole word *unhappy.*

Nowhere in their daily reading are these students required to focus on parts of words in this way. The multiple-choice format is also unfamiliar—it is not part of day-to-day literacy—so the task as well as the format is new, odd. I explained the directions again—read them slowly, emphasized the sample item—but still, three of the four students continued to fall into the test maker's trap of choosing synonyms for the target word rather than zeroing in on the part of the word in question. Such behavior is common among those who fail in our schools, and it has led some commentators to posit that students like these are cognitively and linguistically deficient in some fundamental way: They process language differently, or reason differently from those who succeed in school, or the dialect they speak in some basic way interferes with their processing of Standard Written English.

Certainly in such a group—because of malnourishment, trauma, poor health care, environmental toxins—you'll find people with neurolinguistic problems or with medical difficulties that can affect perception and concentration. And this group—ranging in age from nineteen to the mid-fifties—has a wide array of medical complications: diabetes, head injury, hypertension, asthma, retinal deterioration, and the unusual sleep disorder called narcolepsy. It would be naive to deny the effect of all this on reading and writing. But as you sit alongside these students and listen to them work through a task, it is not damage that most strikes you. Even when they're misunderstanding the test and selecting wrong answers, their reasoning is not distorted and pathological. Here is Millie, whose test scores placed her close to the class average—and average here would be very low just about anywhere else.

Millie is given the word "<u>kilo</u>meter" and the following list of possible answers:

a. thousand

b. hundred

c. distance

d. speed

She responds to the whole word—*kilometer*—partially because she still does not understand how the test works, but also, I think, because the word is familiar to her. She offers *speed* as the correct answer because: "I see it on the signs when I be drivin'." She starts to say something else, but stops abruptly. "Whoa, it don't have to be 'speed'—it could be 'distance.'"

"It could be 'distance,' couldn't it?" I say.

"Yes, it could be one or the other."

"Okay."

"And then again," she says reflectively, "it could be a number."

Millie tapped her knowledge of the world—she had seen *kilometer* on road signs—to offer a quick response: *speed*. But she saw just as quickly that her knowledge could logically support another answer (*distance*), and, a few moments later, saw that what she knew could also support a third answer, one related to number. What she lacked was specific knowledge of the Greek prefix *kilo*, but she wasn't short on reasoning ability. In fact, reading tests like the one Millie took are constructed in such a way as to trick you into relying on common-sense reasoning and world knowledge—and thereby choosing a wrong answer. Take, for example, this item:

Cardio<u>gram</u>

  a. heart

  b. abnormal

  c. distance

  d. record

Millie, and many others in the class, chose *heart*. To sidestep that answer, you need to know something about the use of *gram* in other such words (versus its use as a metric weight), but you need to know, as well, how these tests work.

After Millie completed five or six items, I had her go back over them, talking through her answers with her. One item that had originally given her trouble was "<u>extra</u>ordinary": a) "beyond"; b) "acute"; c) "regular"; d) "imagined." She had been a little rattled when answering this one. While reading the four possible answers, she stumbled on "imagined": "I...im..."; then, tentatively, "imaged"; a pause again, then "imagine," and, quickly, "I don't know that word."

I pronounce it.

She looks up at me, a little disgusted: "I said it, didn't I?"

"You did say it."

"I was scared of it."

Her first time through, Millie had chosen *regular*, the wrong answer—apparently locking onto *ordinary* rather than the underlined prefix *extra*—doing just the opposite of what she was supposed to do. It was telling, I thought, that Millie and two or three others talked about words scaring them.

When we came back to "<u>extra</u>ordinary" during our review, I decided on strategy. "Let's try something," I said. "These tests are set up to trick you, so let's try a trick ourselves." I take a pencil and do something the publishers of the test tell you not to do: I mark up the test booklet. I slowly begin to circle the prefix *extra*, saying, "This is the part of the word we're concerned with, right?" As soon as I finish she smiles and says "beyond," the right answer.

"Did you see what happened there?" I said. "As soon as I circled the part of the word, you saw what it meant."

"I see it," she says. "I don't be thinking about what I'm doing."

I tell her to try what I did, to circle the part of the word in question, to remember that trick, for with tests like this, we need a set of tricks of our own.

"You saw it yourself," I said.

"Sure did. It was right there in front of me—cause the rest of them don't even go with 'extra.'"

I had been conducting this interview with Millie in between her classes, and our time was running out. I explained that we'd pick this up again, and I turned away, checking the wall clock, reaching to turn off the tape recorder. Millie was still looking at the test booklet.

"What is this word right here?" she asked. She had gone ahead to the other, more difficult, page of the booklet and was pointing to "<u>ego</u>centric."

I take my finger off the recorder's STOP button. "Let's circle it," I say. "What's that word? Say it."

"Ego."

"What's that mean?"

"Ego. Oh my." She scans the four options—*self, head, mind, kind*—and says "self."

"Excellent!"

"You know, when I said 'ego,' I tried to put it in a sentence: 'My ego,' I say. That's *me*."

I ask her if she wants to look at one more. She goes back to "<u>cardio</u>gram," which she gets right this time. Then to "<u>therm</u>ometer," which she also gets right. And "<u>bi</u>focal," which she gets right without using her pencil to mark the prefix. Once Millie saw and understood what the test required of her, she could rely on her world knowledge to help her reason out some answers. Cognitive psychologists talk about task representation, the way a particular problem is depicted or reproduced in the mind. Something shifted in Millie's conception of her task, and it had a powerful effect on her performance.

It was common for nineteenth-century American educators to see their mission with the immigrant and native-born urban poor as a fundamentally moral one. Historian Michael Katz quotes from the Boston school committee's description of social and spiritual acculturation:

> taking children at random from a great city, undisciplined, uninstructed, often with inveterate forwardness and obstinacy, and with the inherited stupidity of centuries of ignorant ancestors; forming them from animals into intellectual beings, and…from intellectual beings into spiritual beings; giving to many their first appreciation of what is wise, what is true, what is lovely and what is pure.

In our time, educators view the effects of poverty and cultural dislocation in more enlightened ways; though that moralistic strain still exists, the thrust of their concern has shifted from the spiritual to the more earthly realm of language and cognition. Yet what remains is the disturbing tendency to perceive the poor as *different* in some basic way from the middle and upper classes—the difference now being located in the nature of the way they think and use language. A number of studies and speculations over the past twenty-five years has suggested that the poor are intellectually or linguistically deficient or, at the least, different: They lack a logical language or reason in ways that limit intellectual achievement or, somehow, process information dysfunctionally. If we could somehow get down to the very basic loops and contours of their mental function, we would find that theirs are different from ours. There's a huge literature on all this and, originating with critics like linguist William Labov, a damning counterliterature. This is not the place to review that work, but it would be valuable to consider Millie against the general outlines of the issue.

Imagine her in a typical classroom testing situation. More dramatically, imagine her in some university laboratory being studied by one or two researchers—middle class and probably white. Millie is a strong woman with a tough front, but these would most likely be uncomfortable situations for her. And if she were anxious, her performance would be disrupted: as it was when she didn't identify *imagined*—a word she pronounced and knew—because she was "scared of it." Add to this the fact that she is very much adrift when it comes to school-based tests: She simply doesn't know how to do them. What would be particularly damning for her would be the fact that, even with repeated instruction and illustration, she failed to catch on to the way the test worked. You can see how an observer would think her unable to shift out of (inadequate) performance, unable to understand simple instructions and carry them out. Deficient or different in some basic way: nonlogical, nonrational, unable to think analytically. It would be from observations like this that a theory of fundamental cognitive deficiency or difference would emerge.

We seem to have a need as a society to explain poor performance by reaching deep into the basic stuff of those designated as other: into their souls, or into the deep recesses of their minds, or into the very ligature of their language. It seems harder for us to keep focus on the politics and sociology of intellectual failure, to keep before our eyes the negative power of the unfamiliar, the way information poverty constrains performance, the effect of despair on cognition.

"I was so busy looking for 'psychopathology,'..." says Robert Coles of his early investigations of childhood morality, "that I brushed aside the most startling incidents, the most instructive examples of ethical alertness in the young people I was getting to know." How much we don't see when we look only for deficiency, when we tally up all that people can't do. Many of the students in this book display the gradual or abrupt emergence of an intellectual acuity or literate capacity that just wasn't thought to be there. This is not to deny that awful limits still exist for those like Millie: so much knowledge and so many procedures never learned; such a long, cumbersome history of relative failure. But this must not obscure the equally important fact that if you set up the right conditions, try as best you can to cross class and cultural boundaries, figure out what's needed to encourage performance, that if you watch and listen, again and again there will emerge evidence of ability that escapes those who dwell on differences.

Ironically, it's often the reports themselves of our educational inadequacies—the position papers and media alarms on illiteracy in America—that help blind us to cognitive and linguistic possibility. Their rhetorical thrust and their metaphor conjure up disease or decay or economic and military defeat: A malignancy has run wild, an evil power is consuming us from within. (And here reemerges that nineteenth-century moral terror.) It takes such declamation to turn the moneyed wheels of government, to catch public attention and entice the givers of grants, but there's a dark side to this political reality. The character of the alarms and, too often, the character of the responses spark in us the urge to punish, to extirpate, to return to a precancerous golden age rather than build on the rich capacity that already exists. The reports urge responses that reduce literate possibility and constrain growth, that focus on pathology rather than on possibility. Philosophy, said Aristotle, begins in wonder. So does education.

SUGGESTIONS FOR DISCUSSION

1. What motivates students like Ruby, Alice, Sally, and Millie to return to school? What assumptions do they seem to make about the effects of education? Are these assumptions realistic? How do they compare to the assumptions you and your classmates make about the effects of education? Explain what you see as differences and similarities.

2. How does Rose explain poor performance and failure in school? Don't settle for generalizations such as "poverty and cultural dislocation." Look closely at how Rose analyzes Millie's experience with questions on a read-

ing comprehension test. Do you find Rose's explanations persuasive? What do these explanations imply about the nature and function of schooling in America?

3. Rose says that "nineteenth-century American educators" looked at their "mission" as a "fundamentally moral one." Later he suggests that such a "moralistic strain still exists" in the way Americans think about education and that it can "spark in us the urge to punish, to extirpate, to return to a precancerous golden age." What is the nature of the "moral terror" Rose talks about? Do you agree with him? Draw upon your experience in school to respond to this question.

SUGGESTIONS FOR WRITING

1. Write an essay that explains what Mike Rose sees as causes of failure in school. Compare his explanation to your own views on what causes students to fail. Draw on your own experience and what you have observed.

2. Most students have been "punished" at some point or another during their schooling. Write an essay that tells the story of a time when you were (or someone you know was) "punished" in school. What did you do? Did you break a rule? Was the rule fair? Was the "punishment" just or unjust? Your story should tell about what happened and how you felt about it. Then use the story to reflect on what the incident reveals about life in school and how students encounter and deal with the "rules" of schooling.

3. Rose says that "reports [of]...our educational inadequacies—the position papers and media alarms on illiteracy in America—" reduce "literate possibility and constrain growth." Write an essay that considers Rose's claim that such reports "focus on pathology rather than on possibility." You'll need to find a report or a media account of literacy and American education to use in this writing project. You can draw on reports from the past, such as *A Nation at Risk* (1993), which you will find in the library, or more recent ones online. Websites, such as Edweek (www.edweek.org/) and the American Federation of Teachers (www.AFT.org/edissues/standards99/index.htm), feature recent reports. Or you can use media accounts, such as *Newsweek*'s classic cover story "Why Johnny Can't Write" (December 1975) or more recent reporting on the "reading wars." (You can find overviews of the "reading wars" in "Reading: The First Skill" by Nick Anderson and Duke Helfand in the *Los Angeles Times*, September 13, 1998, and in "School from Start to Finish; Reading Wars, Take 2" by Karin Chenoweth in the *Washington Post*, May 16, 1999.) In any event, examine carefully the report or media coverage you've chosen to see how it describes an educational or literacy "crisis" and explains the causes and solutions. Use Rose's idea that reports too often rely on metaphors "of disease or decay or economic or military defeat" to analyze the report you've chosen. In the broadest sense, Rose is arguing that educational reports are alarmist and use fear to persuade readers. Is there a sense in which this is true of the report you're analyzing? If so, how? If not, what feeling does the report or media account try to tap in readers? How can you tell? Use examples from the report or media account to explain.

A Real Meritocracy

Nicholas Lemann

Nicholas Lemann is a staff writer at the *New Yorker* and the author a number of books, including the prizewinning *The Promised Land: The Great Black Migration and How It Changed America.* The following selection is taken from the afterword to his latest book, *The Big Test: The Secret History of the American Meritocracy*, a study of the rise of the Educational Testing Service (ETS) and the Scholastic Aptitude Test (SAT). Lemann shows that the original purpose of the SAT, in the view of its founding figures Harvard president James Bryant Conant and Henry Chauncey, was to use intelligence testing in order to create a democratic elite in postwar America based on merit—what Lemann calls "today's upper-middle-class American Mandarins"—to replace the older elite based on wealth and family background. As you will see, Lemann raises serious questions about whether the function of university education should be to confer such privileges and rewards on a small group of people.

SUGGESTIONS FOR READING

Lemann is offering both a critique of the current meritocracy—the selection of individuals for college and jobs based on talents and performance—and a proposal for a "real" meritocracy. As you read, notice the reasons he believes the current system is flawed and the changes in education he calls for.

"Meritocracy" is a curious word. Invented, by Michael Young, to denote a social order that he wanted to hold up as an object of horror, in the United States today it is received as the name of an inarguably sacred first principle: that our society rewards those who deserve and have earned advancement, rather than distributing reward by fiat in some way that involves the circumstances of birth. Moreover, people tend to assume casually that the system whose history I've given in these pages and in which we live our lives—a national regime of IQ-descended standardized tests that everyone takes and that lead the chosen few into the higher reaches of the university system—is the embodiment, and the only possible embodiment, of the principle of meritocracy.

Michael Young was dead set against the idea that giving rewards to the deserving could function as the premise of a good society. In the United States, equal opportunity for all seems far more worthy and workable as an ideal than it did to an English socialist in the 1950s. But from that it doesn't follow that the choice for Americans today is between a meritocracy organized around aptitude tests and "equality of result." There is much more space than we realize between the idea we've come to call meritocracy and the actual, specific American meritocracy we are living with.

The people at the top of a society almost always feel themselves to be genuinely superior to the rest, not just luckily born, and to have earned their place. Societies that we now think of as having been obviously more aristocratic than meritocratic—such as the United States between the world wars, or Victorian England—thought they were run by the people who deserved to be in charge. How could prosperous people in the past possibly have believed this about themselves? Usually they had participated in a limited-contest meritocracy, of the kind described, for example, in *Stover at Yale*: members of a small, highly restricted group compete all out for the best prizes, the winners feel justifiably entitled to them, and the great mass who could never enter the contest are off somewhere far away, invisible.

Today's upper-middle-class American Mandarins have taken on this set of attitudes. The notion that they are participating (and succeeding) in a great, broad, fair, open national competition is at the heart of their idea of themselves, and indeed you do have to be very intelligent and able to get the most prestigious of the billets distributed by the meritocratic machinery. Within every family, there is a variety of outcomes. But on the other hand the total range of possibilities for those born into the Mandarin class is pretty narrow, and so is the size of the opening to people who are not born in that class.

The advent of this particular system did not represent the country's embracing for the first time the idea of meritocracy—if meritocracy means equal opportunity, or rewards to the deserving, or careers open to talents. The idea of opportunity for everyone is woven deeply into the fabric of the United States, and it has been from the very beginning. Universal opportunity has been a theme in American writing and fable and rhetoric at every point in our history. The current system was a much more particular, even tendentious development, which in ensuing years we have wrongly conflated with the general principle.

The American meritocracy was founded on a linked chain of presumptions, which people aren't familiar with today because they weren't stated openly at the start. The first is that the system's main task should be to select a small number of people to form a new elite—the goal of giving opportunity to all Americans was added later, less as an essential element of the system's design than as a way of generating public support for it. The next presumption was that the means of selection should be intelligence tests, as a proxy for superior academic talent: the definition of "merit," in other words, is a purely intellectual, educational one. Finally, the purpose for which these students are being selected is to enter into the modern version of what Thomas Jefferson called "the offices of government"—that is, administrative and scholarly service to a modern bureaucratic state. What the founders of the system envisioned was closer to the elite civil-service system of a country like France or Japan than a meritocracy in the way the word is used today.

Over time the American meritocracy has evolved into a more general way of distributing opportunity to millions of people, fitting them into places in a highly tracked university system that leads to jobs and professions. And its assumed purpose has changed from being a way to obtain highly capable and well-trained public officials to a way of determining fairly who gets America's material rewards. These changes were, substantially, accidental, result of the expansionist impulses within both ETS and the universities and of the privatism of American culture, but they have altered the moral calculus.

Let us say you wanted to design, from scratch, a system to distribute opportunity in the fairest possible way. Would you design the American meritocracy as it now exists? You would only if you believed that IQ test scores and, more broadly, academic performance are the same thing as merit. That's a defensible position, but it ought at least to show itself openly to be debated, rather than being presumed. If it did, the arguments against it would quickly emerge. Merit is various, not unidimensional. Intelligence tests, and also education itself, can't be counted on to find every form of merit. They don't find wisdom, or originality, or humor, or toughness, or empathy, or common sense, or independence, or determination—let alone moral worth. Perforce they judge people on their potential, not on their actual performance over the long term at the work for which they're being selected.

Indeed, to take the exercise a step further, let us say you were given the task of designing a system that would distribute opportunity in the most unfair possible way. A first choice could be a system in which all roles were handed down explicitly by inheritance. That would be a pernicious system—one that, thankfully, has never existed in the United States. The second most unfair system, though, could well be one that allowed for competition but insisted that it take place as early in life as possible and with school as the arena. The influences of parentage, of background culture and class, are at their highest and most explicit during a person's student years; although at every school there is an academic competition whose net result is to give some people the chance to move dramatically beyond their original circumstances, schools can't possibly function generally, in the words of James Bryant Conant, "to reorder the 'haves and have-nots' every generation to give flux to our social order." Education offers the hope—a hope explicitly, energetically, taken up by parents—of transferring status between generations, not of altering or upending it.

That our universities have evolved into a national personnel department represents the striking of a complicated bargain. They have gotten out of it the chance to be big and important—to be treated by the public, and not wrongly, as an object of yearning, an all-powerful arbiter of fates. They have lost a certain apartness from the world, a commitment to pure learning and scholarship, a freedom from instrumentalism. Universities are now political and economic institutions. It isn't a happenstance that the question of who gets to attend them has become the subject of election campaigns and Supreme Court cases. Because of the peculiar circumstances of the founding of the American meritocracy—the lack of public debate or assent (therefore the lack of general understanding about its purpose), the heavy reliance on mental tests as a selection device, the steady imperceptible segue in orientation from leadership training to reward distribution—the system seems to be one whose judgments are mysterious, severe, and final. The natural impulse is not simply to accept these judgments as fair. That is why, instead, people worry and squabble over them almost obsessively.

Conant believed that the system he was helping to set up would have the effect of reviving "the American radical tradition in education"—an idea that today seems touchingly, or even laughably, naive. There is now a sturdy and well-established conservative defense of the system, which argues that, however odd its evolution, it now works just fine: we're right to assign economic destinies through education and test scores, because that's the fairest way and the one most likely to promote the quality of sheer brainpower that fuels the modern American economy.

Within the universities themselves, the main sentiment is probably a somewhat oxymoronic liberal elitism—a fierce, competitive protectiveness toward their privileged position combined with discomfort over their role as a generator of wondrous economic advancement for their graduates. The argument that would accompany this sentiment, if it were precisely expressed, would be that while the system doesn't work—because it uses too narrow a criterion, produces an elite too confined in race and class, and imposes too few public obligations on those it favors—it could be made to function well by being restored to its original purpose. Diversify the elite through affirmative action; de-emphasize test scores in choosing the members; make them serve their country (which, after all, substantially pays for the education that launches them, even when it's at private universities) for extended periods. The founders of the American meritocracy would surely not view any of this as a betrayal of their intentions.

The arguments of both sides have something important in common though, which is that they presume (as most discussions of meritocracy in America presume) that it's good for the country to have a designated, educationally derived elite. The question is whether to have one with a conservative or a liberal design. But there is another possibility, which would be for Americans to decline, to the greatest practicable extent, to use education to designate a national elite. Instead of our endeavoring to realize the dreams of Plato and Jefferson and Conant, we would reject those dreams as a workable basis of a good society, and side with John Adams: the ideal would be to have a society without a specially anointed group at the top of it. Adams was right to see immediately, when Jefferson suggested to him the idea of a natural aristocracy, that the project of picking just the right aristocrats for the United States is fundamentally quixotic, that it serves only to distract us from the obvious point: a democratic nation shouldn't have an aristocracy at all.

Every society of course has positions of authority and expertise that must be filled by people who can execute them well. But the central, original principle of the American meritocracy was different from this. It was that people should be chosen not for their suitability for specific roles but for their general worth, as if they were an updated Puritan elect. Hence it seemed right to select an American meritocracy by grades and test scores rather than by people's demonstrated abilities to do particular things, and to grant the high scorers a general, long-duration ticket to high status that can be cashed in anywhere. The reason for the crush at the gates of selective universities is that people believe admission can confer lifelong prestige, comfort, and safety, not just access to jobs with specific functions. To say that the project of picking the members of this elite properly, no matter how well it is done, cannot not confer an aura of justice on the whole society is not at all the same thing as to oppose selecting people for jobs on their merits. That is a good idea. So is the idea of a society that truly offers opportunity to all. But the idea of having a general-purpose meritocratic elite generated through university admissions is an idea we should abandon.

What would a United States that was a true meritocracy look like? It would be a society that gave everyone equal opportunity and gave jobs to those best able to perform them, but the restructuring that reaching these goals would entail would leave it looking quite different from the current American meritocracy. The essential functions and the richest rewards of money and status would devolve to people only temporarily, and strictly on the basis of their performances; there would be as little lifelong tenure on the basis of youthful promise as possible. The elite would be a group with a constantly shifting, rather than stable and permanent, membership. Successful people would have less serene careers, but this would give them more empathy for people whose lives don't go smoothly. Space in the Mandarin compound should be as small as possible and the space outside it as large as possible.

The institutions that would most dramatically change in this reimagining of what meritocracy means in America would be educational ones. John Gardner, in his little book entitled *Excellence*, published in 1961, a kind of manifesto for the current system, said in a tone of wondering disapproval: "There was a time—a fairly recent time—when education was not a rigorous sorting-out process." The present meritocracy was devised by educator-planners who couldn't imagine any disadvantage to setting up school as the arena for determining individual destinies: that looked to them far more practical, more just, more efficient, and more conducive to social harmony than it has turned out to be. Their goal was to construct a competitive race that would begin in elementary school and be substantially over by the time one graduated from college or professional school. This was supposed to be the embodiment of the principle of equal opportunity: better to have schools making decisions about people's lives than leaving it to the disorganized market. Here is John Gardner again:

> The sorting out of individuals according to ability is very nearly the most delicate and difficult process our society has to face. Those who receive the most education are going to move into virtually all the key jobs. Thus the question "Who should go to college?" translates itself into the more compelling question "Who is going to manage the society?" That is not the kind of question one can treat lightly or cavalierly. It is the kind of question wars have been fought over.

But surely our guiding principle regarding education and opportunity ought to be precisely the opposite of the one implied in that passage. The chief aim of school should be not to sort out but to teach as many people as possible as well as possible, equipping them for both work and citizenship. Those who like to think of American life as a great race should think of the race as beginning, not ending, when school has been completed. The purpose of schools should be to expand opportunity, not to determine results.

If we define the main objective in this way, then the main problem becomes obvious: in the bad bottom tier of public schools, the ones where students don't even learn to read, we don't come anywhere near to providing equal educational opportunity. Our meritocracy was devised so as to nationalize education for the few of great gifts, identifying the best test scorers and whisking them away to good colleges and universities all over the country, while leaving education local for everyone else. Localism works reasonably well for most people, but it works very badly for students in those worst schools, most of which are in poor, all-minority neighborhoods. Those schools should be (and in fact are being) taken over by mayors and governors who ensure that they confer literacy and numeracy on their students. Decent schooling, the absolute prerequisite to a decent life in America today, should be thought of as something that government guarantees to every citizen as a matter of right. It shouldn't be left to local authorities to screw up, any more than flight safety should.

College is not so absolutely essential as basic early education is, but it has become steadily more important; people who don't go to college are now losing access to a place in the middle class. We should adopt the goal of sending most people all the way through college, just as, a hundred years ago, we adopted the then much more distant goal of sending most people all the way through high school. But we must remember that our current meritocratic system was not set up to do this. Its founders believed that even the small college population of the 1930s needed to be reduced, and the meritocracy was designed to evade entirely the question of the quality and consistency of American high schools.

To get more people through college, we shall have to establish greater national authority over education. High schools should prepare their students for college by teaching them a nationally agreed-upon curriculum. Tests for admission to college should be on mastery of this curriculum—not the SAT or some dreamed-of better, fairer alternative test of innate abilities. Test-prep should consist of mastering the high-school curriculum, not learning tricks to outwit multiple-choice aptitude exams.

It occurred to Conant back in the 1940s that there was some danger that in setting up a mechanism for picking, educating, and giving power to a small group of highly intelligent people, we might engender in them some of the superiority and selfishness he so much hated in the elite of the 1930s. So he insisted:

> If we are to continue to have an essentially free and classless society in this country, we must proceed from the premise that there are no educational privileges, even at the most advanced levels of instruction….As far as possible there should be no hierarchy of educational discipline, no one channel should have a social standing above the other.

Of course, this is another dream that didn't come true. Admission to a selective college is treated by Americans largely as a matter of a competition for, precisely, "educational privileges" and "a social standing above the other," to an extent that would horrify Conant. The only way to undo the class-creating aspect of college admissions is to close the gap that Conant and his associates wanted to open, between the more and less selective colleges. The better and more equal the high schools are, the most universal college is, and the less territory in the posteducation world is reserved in advance for high-aptitude, high-grade Mandarins, the less important admission to a selective college will become.

It's a given by now that it matters a great deal *whether* you went to college; it doesn't, however, have to be supremely important *where* you went to college. Americans' preoccupation with admission to selective colleges has gone past the bounds of rationality. We don't have a radical undersupply of higher education, as in East Asia, and we don't have an informal tradition of the nation's best jobs being closed to people who didn't go to a certain handful of colleges, as in England. Nonetheless, the gap in graduates life-fates between all colleges and selective colleges is increasing. Closing it will make the United States a better country and one that more fully uses the talents of its people. The culture of frenzy surrounding admissions is destructive and anti-democratic; it warps the sensibilities and distorts the education of the millions of people whose lives it touches.

The idea of educating everyone at public expense ranks with political democracy as one of the United States' great original social contributions. Both ideas rest on a belief that ordinary people are capable of more than the leaders of previous societies would have thought possible. The best and most distinctive tradition in American education is the tradition of pushing to educate more people. That is what Thomas Jefferson was doing when he tried unsuccessfully to establish public elementary schools in Virginia; it is what Horace Mann did when he finally got taxpayers to support public schools in Massachusetts; it was the effect of the GI Bill.

Our apparatus of meritocracy is not part of this tradition. Rather, it belongs to an older, less distinctively American tradition of using tests and education to select a small governing elite. The founders of the American meritocracy were not supporters of an expanded, opportunity-oriented (rather than selection-oriented) educational system, and they were certainly not the originators of the idea of equal opportunity. They did, however, believe they were destroying a nascent class system and building a fluid, mobile society. In retrospect, this was vainglorious—you can't undermine social rank by setting up an elaborate process of ranking. Fifty years later, their creation looks more and more like what it was intended to replace.

SUGGESTIONS FOR READING

1. What problems does Lemann point to in the current meritocracy system of education? Notice that he is not opposed to meritocracy itself but to the way it distributes opportunities and rewards. List the shortcomings he sees. Do you agree with his assessment? Why or why not?

2. Lemann says that "the American meritocracy has evolved into a more general way of distributing opportunity to millions of people, fitting them into places in a highly tracked university system that leads to jobs and professions." What does he mean here by the term "highly tracked university system"? In what sense do colleges and universities represent different tracks in a larger system of higher education, ranging from more to less selective? In your experience, how does this system affect the way people perceive your college and others in your area? How does it affect the decisions high school seniors make about the colleges to which they apply?

3. Lemann argues that we "should adopt the goal of sending most people all the way through college." Currently about half of all high school graduates go on to college, and of this number (which does not include students who dropped out of high school) about half graduate from college. What changes in the educational system would be required to increase the number of college graduates? Do you think the goal of sending most people through college is a good one? Why or why not?

SUGGESTIONS FOR WRITING

1. Write an essay that explains your experience and that of other seniors at your high school applying to college. Use Lemann's notion of the American

meritocracy to analyze how you and other seniors approached the process of college application. What criteria did you and others use to decide which colleges to apply to? To what extent were these decisions influenced, as Lemann suggests, by the hope of long-term material rewards and social status in the American meritocracy? Consider the role, if any, that college admissions tests such as the SAT (not to mention preparation classes), letters of recommendation from teachers and others, and extracurricular activities such as athletics, school organizations, and community service played in the process.

2. Lemann asks us to reconsider the belief that test scores and academic performance are good measures of individual merit. Write a response to Lemann. Notice that he says equating academic performance with merit is "a defensible position" but one that is largely assumed rather than debated openly. If you believe academic performance is a good measure of merit, what reasons would you give to defend and explain your position? If you think the equation is a questionable one, explain why. What other measures do you think are better to determine merit?

3. Lemann mentions in passing the novel *Stover at Yale*, a 1911 classic of boy's fiction written by Owen Johnson. The novel, as Lemann remarks earlier in *The Big Test*, "follows the undergraduate career of Dink Stover, a clean-limbed boarding-school lad" and his crisis of conscience once he realizes how much family wealth and class background determine success at Yale. Read *Stover at Yale* (most college and larger public libraries will have a copy) and write an analysis of its vision of merit and success. Notice how it portrays college life, the role of academics, and the place of scholarship students. You may want to compare its representation of college life to the contemporary campus scene. What differences do you see and what significance do these differences hold?

Note-Passing: Struggles for Status

Margaret J. Finders

Margaret J. Finders is associate professor of English and education at Purdue University. The following selection is taken from her study *Just Girls: Hidden Literacies and Life in Junior High*. Finders focuses here on how a group of popular junior high girls (the "social queens") use reading and writing outside the official school curriculum—signing yearbooks, passing notes, writing bathroom graffiti, and reading teen 'zines. These "hidden literacies," Finders says, play key roles for these young women in defining their sense of self and maintaining group loyalties.

SUGGESTION FOR READING

Notice that Finders first describes the formal features of notes, then explains the social functions they perform, and finally generalizes three themes that emerge from "note-passing as a ritualized event." As you read, consider how her presentation of note-passing sets up the generalizations with which this passage ends.

Note-writing as a genre did not allow for much individual expression or originality. The girls all protested indignantly whenever I suggested such a notion: "You can write whatever you want." Yet the following notes illustrate the standards required for the genre of note-writing.

> Lauren,
>
> Yo! What's up? Not much here. I'm in math and it is BORING. Did you know that I like Nate a lot. But he'd probably never go out with me caz I'm too ugly. AND FAT. Oh, well though. I'm still going to try and get him to go with me caz I like him. I hope he goes with me before the football game Friday. I want to be going with him at the game. Are you and Ricky going to the game? I want to go somewhere after that. Maybe you could come over or I could come to your house. Don't show this to anyone. W-B [Write Back] Maggie

> Lauren,
>
> Hey. What's up? You don't need to ask Bill for me cause he won't go and he's just that way I guess. You can try but I know he's not going to go. Well I'm almost positive. I'm in social studies and I just got busted caz I had none of my homework done. Fun. My handwriting majorly Sucks. I hate it. Go to *Body Guard* at the mall and I'll say you need a ride home. Then you can spend the night at my house. Call me tonight. I will be at my mom's. S.S. [Stay Sweet or Stay Sexy] Carrie.

Notes regularly began with a common salutation, "Hey, what's up?" followed by a reference to where the note was written—"I'm in math." "I'm in social studies." Because notes were always written in school, this move positioned the queen in opposition to the institutional power by boldly announcing an act of defiance during one particular class and then adding a condemning judgment such as, "It's so boring." In this move, queens perceived themselves as powerful by defying authority. Yet that power was somewhat diffused as they often embedded in the body of the note a reference to themselves as inadequate: too fat, too ugly, my handwriting sucks. Often in notes, messages closed with "Sorry So Sloppy," which were sometimes shortened to S.S.S. For the most part, extreme care was taken to write neatly, at time dotting the i's with circles or hearts.

The content of notes was generally about making social arrangements for after-school activities and for requesting help in making romantic contacts. The notes carried highly coded messages such as N.M.H. (not much here) that limited the readership to those who were inside the circle of friends. The closing, as well, was most often highly coded—B.F.F. (best friends forever) W-B (write back)—to provide an insider quality to those who knew the codes. Britton (1970), noting the "with-it" language of adolescents, argues for the necessity of "drawing together members of a group or the set, and keeping outsiders out" (p. 235). The meaning behind S.S.S. evolved over time. At first it meant "Sorry So Sloppy," but over the course of the seventh-grade year, it came to carry a completely different meaning: "Stay Sweet and Sexy." The evolution of this one code illustrates the demands embedded within shifting social roles from girl to adolescent.

Although notes generally followed a standard format, a few did contain important unknown information such as the appropriate time to receive a call, an apology for flirting with a boyfriend, or guarded information about family problems. The queens attempted to control the circulation of their notes and regularly added to their messages, "Don't show this to anyone." For the most part, notes created boundaries around a group of friends. By creating a tangible document, girls created proof of their memberships.

As stated previously, girls all voiced the opinion that "you just write whatever you want," yet when someone outside the intimate circle of friends wrote a note to one of the most popular girls, she was criticized. As one girl described it, "Look at that. She doesn't even know how to write right." These teens were criticized for not recognizing or following the rules and rituals on note-writing, a primary rule being that notes could be passed only to friends of equal social status. The unstated rules of adhering to established social hierarchies were clearly enforced. If, for example, a girl did not know her place in the social hierarchy and wrote a note to a more popular girl, she became the object of ridicule and laughter within the higher circle.

This need for social sorting at the junior high was visible to teachers. Debra Zmoleck described the practice in this way:

> I think part of the way junior high kids feel good about themselves is they've got to have that ego, you know, it's a pecking order. They've got to have somebody that's down there that all the other chickens peck at, you know. And I don't know why, I guess it's just part of junior high.

The "pecking order" to which Debra referred was often documented in literate practices. Literacy was a tool used to document and maintain social position. In private interviews, Angie and Lauren both made statements in accord with Tiffany's own self-assessment.

> I don't write notes much so now I don't get 'em. Lauren gets the most because she writes the most. She's the most popular. Me, not so much.

Tiffany lost status because she didn't write as many notes as other girls and slowly over time received fewer and fewer, marking her as less popular. On the other hand, Lauren was perceived to be the most popular girl among her network of friends because "she has the most notes." She also received more notes from boys, which further served to document her high status among her friends.

In the fall of seventh grade, the number of notes passed increased until mid-November when a plateau was reached; January saw a sharp decline. When asked about this decline, the queens all relayed the fact that there just wasn't as much to write about; yet the events that they had written about all year—social arrangements, sports, and boys—had not decreased in their interest or in their activity. I contend that note-passing had served its purpose—to sort and select a hierarchy among the queens who had just entered a new arena in the fall. Arriving from different sixth-grade classrooms, the queens used literacies in the new school context to negotiate entry into new friendship networks. Through print sources, they maintained familiar ties in this strange new world, connecting at first with old sixth-grade friends and then negotiating their ways into other social groups. By January, new social positions were securely established, and note-passing decreased because jockeying for position was no longer an option for gaining status or entry into the social queens' network.

Note-passing was clearly a gendered activity. It functioned to control male voices and to try out women's voices. Circulation of notes was controlled exclusively by girls. Girls decided who was entitled to see, receive, or write a note. Boys did not write notes to boys, and they wrote to girls only when they were invited or instructed to do so by a girl directly or through a channeling system, where one girl wrote to another girl who would then write to a boy, thereby granting him permission to write to the first girl. This act of literacy bestowed power and control of romantic interactions exclusively to females. The hierarchical arrangement placed power firmly in the hands of the social queens, who controlled and regulated which boys wrote or received notes.

To guard the circulation of messages, the queens informed me that learning to fold a note properly was vital to ensure that it would not open if it were dropped. Notes were folded into small triangles or squares with edges tucked in, serving as a lock to protect messages from unauthorized eyes. Such skill in intricate folding was also used to gain status within the inner circle. One's knowledge of elaborate folds signaled one as a member in good standing. Again, literacy served to document status within the circle of friends. If one queen learned a new and extremely complex fold, she received high praise and then attained the honored position of teacher, instructing others in how to fold.

Note-folding was a crucial skill because passing the note was a fine game that required a small, streamlined object. A note could have no rough edges to catch in a pocket lining, and it must be easily manipulated in the palm of one hand in order to avoid detection as it slipped from hand to hand boldly under the nose of a teacher. Passing notes from one of the social queens to another under the sharp scrutiny of a teacher was seen by these girls as an act of defiance and a behavior to be admired. Girls wrote, circulated, and responded to notes while reading aloud, participating in classroom discussions, and completing written work. A girl, for instance, could participate in a large-group discussion while writing and then passing notes without skipping a beat as she actively engaged in the classroom discussion. Designed to fool the teacher into thinking one was paying attention, such a game documented allegiance to peers. Ironically, a queen had to pay extremely close attention to keep the game going in her favor, yet this game was played to make the teacher appear foolish and the teen powerful.

Whenever the risk became heightened by a teacher's reprimands or threats of posting notes on classroom walls, notes became a greater avenue of status-building. When the risks were greatest, girls began lacing their texts with obscene language to up the ante, for to have one such note confiscated would mean not only a disruption at school but disruption at home as well.

More often than not, the content of the note was inconsequential; meaning was conveyed in the passing of the note rather than within the text itself. The act of passing the note during class relayed the message, an act of defiance of adult authority. The message was modified not through words but through the creative manipulation of the passing. The closer one was to the teacher physically when the note was written or delivered, the more powerful the message. By mid-November, after the girls had grown to trust me, they would often dig into their pockets and notebooks and hand me unopened notes. They did not need to read the notes because the message was implicit in the process of passing: in clues such as who sent, who received, who was present during the passing, and how the note was transported.

After I examined note-passing as a ritualized event, several themes emerged: (1) Writing is a social event; (2) special status is ascribed to the girl who received the most notes, especially from boys; and (3) meaning often resides in the act of passing a note. Note-passing was a tool used to document and maintain social position. For the most part, notes were used to bestow power and patrol boundaries around a group of friends.

SUGGESTIONS FOR DISCUSSION

1. As Finders says in an earlier section, her study of junior high girls focuses on what Shirley Brice Heath calls "literacy events"—"any occasion in which a piece of writing is integral to the nature of participants' interactions and their interpretative processes." Finders is interested in how "literacy events" take place, the social functions they perform, and the meanings they have for participants. Consider the conclusions about the social role of reading and writing that Finders draws from this brief analysis of note-passing. How does her view of reading and writing differ from that of the official curriculum? What, if anything, does her perspective have to offer about reading and writing that you won't find in textbooks and classroom lessons?

2. Unlike the official curriculum, where students read and write on demand, note-passing is what you might call "self-sponsored" literacy, where the impetus comes from the student instead of the teacher. Make a list of the

many kinds of self-sponsored reading and writing that you do or have done in the past. As noted earlier, Finders pays particular attention to yearbook signing, note-passing, graffiti writing, and reading teen 'zines. These, of course, are not the only forms of reading and writing that fall outside the official curriculum. Others include writing journals, diaries, letters, e-mails, songs, poems, stories, raps, or petitions and reading sports, computer, car, music, or other nonfiction and popular novels (romance, science fiction, horror, mystery, and so on). Compare the list you compile with those of two or three other students. What do you see as the social functions of such self-sponsored literacy? In what sense do you and others use these forms of reading and writing to define a sense of self and maintain friendship or interest groups?

3. As Finders points out, note-passing involves certain risks. It takes place as an unsanctioned act of reading and writing outside the official curriculum. It is also done in opposition to the rules of schooling and, to be successful, must evade notice by the teacher. For Finders and other researchers who pay attention to what students actually do in school, note-passing is just one instance among many of how young people defy adult authority to carry on their own business. What other examples of such defiant behavior can you think of from your own experience or what you observed in junior high and high school? What risks were involved? What were the rewards from the student's point of view? What do you see as the implications?

SUGGESTIONS FOR WRITING

1. Write an essay on the functions of note-passing in school classrooms. Draw on you own experience and what you know and have observed about classroom life. You don't have to limit yourself to note-passing in junior high and high school. Note-passing takes place in college too, and it may be interesting to look at the role it plays there and whether it differs in function from note-passing in earlier education.

2. Consider the kinds of self-sponsored reading and writing you engage in. In what ways do they differ from what you are asked to do in school? Write an essay that focuses on one type of self-sponsored writing that is particularly important to you. Take into account the purposes this form of writing serves for you. To what extent are these purposes different from and similar to school-sanctioned purposes? Explain what you see as the significance of these differences and similarities.

3. It's a truism that students like to challenge the adult authority of schooling. Everyone can think of examples of how they or other students defied the powers that be in school, whether overtly or in more hidden ways. Choose a particularly revealing example of how you or another student or group of students sought to get away with something in school. First describe what happened and then analyze its meaning and significance. In your analysis, don't settle for easy generalizations such as the truism that young people will test limits and rebel against the older generation. Get inside the event from the student perspective. What exactly was at

stake for the student or group of students? How did the act of resisting or evading authority assert the identity and social allegiances of the student or students involved?

From Silence to Words: Writing as Struggle

Min-zhan Lu

Min-zhan Lu teaches English at Drake University. She has written many important articles about literacy and the teaching of writing. *Crossings*, a work of creative nonfiction, is about to be published as this edition of *Reading Culture* goes to press. The article included here, "From Silence to Words: Writing as Struggle," appeared in *College English* in 1987.

SUGGESTION FOR READING

Min-zhan Lu's literacy narrative uses autobiography to raise larger issues about the possible tensions between "home" and "school" languages. A good deal of the time, Lu seems simply to be telling the story of her experience growing up in China. Sometimes, though, she steps back to make sense of what happened. As you read, note those passages where Lu explains what she sees as the significance of her struggle with writing.

Imagine that you enter a parlor. You come late. When you arrive, others have long preceded you, and they are engaged in a heated discussion....You listen for a while, until you decide that you have caught the tenor of the argument; then you put in your oar. Someone answers; you answer him; another comes to your defense; another aligns himself against you, to either the embarrassment or gratification of your opponent, depending upon the quality of your ally's assistance. However, the discussion is interminable. The hour grows late, you must depart. And you do depart, with the discussion still vigorously in progress.
Kenneth Burke, The Philosophy of Literary Form

Men are not built in silence, but in word, in work, in action-reflection.
Paulo Freire, Pedagogy of the Oppressed

My mother withdrew into silence two months before she died. A few nights before she fell silent, she told me she regretted the way she had raised me and my sisters. I knew she was referring to the way we had been brought up in the midst of two conflicting worlds—the world of home, dominated by the ideology of the Western humanistic tradition, and the world of a society dominated by Mao Tse-tung's Marxism. My mother had devoted her life to our education, an education she knew had made us suffer political persecution during the Cultural Revolution. I wanted to find a way to convince her that, in spite of the persecution, I had benefited from the education she had worked so hard to give me. But I was silent. My understanding of my education was so dominated by memories of confusion and frustration that I was unable to reflect on what I could have gained from it.

This paper is my attempt to fill up that silence with words, words I didn't have then, words that I have since come to by reflecting on my earlier experience as a student in China and on my recent experience as a composition teacher in the United States. For in spite of the frustration and confusion I experienced growing up caught between two conflicting worlds, the conflict ultimately helped me to grow as a reader and writer. Constantly having to switch back and forth between the discourse of home and that of school made me sensitive and self-conscious about the struggle I experienced every time I tried to read, write, or think in either discourse. Eventually, it led me to search for constructive uses for such struggle.

From early childhood, I had identified the differences between home and the outside world by the different languages I used in each. My parents had wanted my sisters and me to get the best education they could conceive of—Cambridge. They had hired a live-in tutor, a Scot, to make us bilingual. I learned to speak English with my parents, my tutor, and my sisters. I was allowed to speak Shanghai dialect only with the servants. When I was four (the year after the Communist Revolution of 1949), my parents sent me to a local private school where I learned to speak, read, and write in a new language—Standard Chinese, the official written language of New China.

In those days I moved from home to school, from English to Standard Chinese to Shanghai dialect, with no apparent friction. I spoke each language with those who spoke the language. All seemed quite "natural"—servants spoke only Shanghai dialect because they were servants; teachers spoke Standard Chinese because they were teachers; languages had different words because they were different languages. I thought of English as my family language, comparable to the many strange dialects I didn't speak but had often heard some of my classmates speak with their families. While I was happy to have a special family language, until second grade I didn't feel that my family language was any different than some of my classmates' family dialects.

My second grade homeroom teacher was a young graduate from a missionary school. When she found out I spoke English, she began to practice her English on me. One day she used English when asking me to run an errand for her. As I turned to close the door behind me, I noticed the puzzled faces of my classmates. I had the same sensation I had often experienced when some stranger in a crowd would turn on hearing me speak English. I was more intensely pleased on this occasion, however, because suddenly I felt that my family language had been singled out from the family languages of my classmates. Since we were not allowed to speak any dialect other than Standard Chinese in the classroom, having my teacher speak English to me in class made English an official language of the classroom. I began to take pride in my ability to speak it.

This incident confirmed in my mind what my parents had always told me about the importance of English to one's life. Time and again they had told me of how my paternal grandfather, who was well versed in classic Chinese, kept losing good-paying jobs because he couldn't speak English. My grandmother reminisced constantly about how she had slaved and saved to send my father to a first-rate missionary school. And we were made to understand that it was my father's fluent English that had opened the door to his success. Even though my family had always stressed the importance of English for my future, I used to complain bitterly about the extra English lessons we had to take after school. It was only after my homeroom teacher had "sanctified" English that I began to connect English with my education. I became a much more eager student in my tutorials.

What I learned from my tutorials seemed to enhance and reinforce what I was learning in my classroom. In those days each word had one meaning. One day I would be making a sentence at school: "The national flag of China is red." The next day I would recite at home, "My love is like a red, red rose." There seemed to be an agreement between the Chinese "red" and the English "red," and both corresponded to the patch of color printed next to the word. "Love" was my love for my mother at home and my love for my "motherland" at school; both "loves" meant how I felt about my mother. Having two loads of homework forced me to develop a quick memory for words and a sensitivity to form and style. What I learned in one language carried over to the other. I made sentences such as, "I saw a red, red rose among the green leaves," with both the English lyric and the classic Chinese lyric—red flower among green leaves—running through my mind, and I was praised by both teacher and tutor for being a good student.

Although my elementary schooling took place during the fifties, I was almost oblivious to the great political and social changes happening around me. Years later, I read in my history and political philosophy textbooks that the fifties were a time when "China was making a transition from a semi-feudal, semi-capitalist, and semi-colonial country into a socialist country," a period in which "the Proletarians were breaking into the educational territory dominated by Bourgeois Intellectuals." While people all over the country were being officially classified into Proletarians, Petty-bourgeois, National-bourgeois, Poor-peasants, and Intellectuals, and were trying to adjust to their new social identities, my parents were allowed to continue the upper middle-class life they had established before the 1949 Revolution because of my father's affiliation with British firms. I had always felt that my family was different from the families of my classmates, but I didn't perceive society's view of my family until the summer vacation before I entered high school.

First, my aunt was caught by her colleagues talking to her husband over the phone in English. Because of it, she was criticized and almost labeled a Rightist. (This was the year of the Anti-Rightist movement, a movement in which the Intellectuals became the target of the "socialist class-struggle.") I had heard others telling my mother that she was foolish to teach us English when Russian had replaced English as the "official" foreign language. I had also learned at school that the American and British Imperialists were the arch-enemies of New China. Yet I had made no connection between the arch-enemies and the English our family spoke. What happened to my aunt forced the connection on me. I began to see my parents' choice of a family language as an anti-Revolutionary act and was alarmed that I had participated in such an act. From then on, I took care not to use English outside home and to conceal my knowledge of English from my new classmates.

Certain words began to play important roles in my new life at the junior high. On the first day of school, we were handed forms to fill out with our parents' class, job, and income. Being one of the few people not employed by the government, my father had never been officially classified. Since he was a medical doctor, he told me to put him down as an Intellectual. My homeroom teacher called me into the office a couple of days afterwards and told me that my father couldn't be an Intellectual if his income far exceeded that of a Capitalist. He also told me that since my father worked for Foreign Imperialists, my father should be classified as an Imperialist Lackey. The teacher looked nonplussed when I told him that my father couldn't be an Imperialist Lackey because he was a medical doctor. But I could tell from the way he took notes on my form that my father's job had put me in an unfavorable position in his eyes.

The Standard Chinese term "class" was not a new word for me. Since first grade, I had been taught sentences such as, "The Working class are the masters of New China." I had always known that it was good to be a worker, but until then, I had never felt threatened for not being one. That fall, "class" began to take on a new meaning for me. I noticed a group of Working-class students and teachers at school. I was made to understand that because of my class background, I was excluded from that group.

Another word that became important was "consciousness." One of the slogans posted in the school building read, "Turn our students into future Proletarians with socialist consciousness and education!" For several weeks we studied this slogan in our political philosophy course, a subject I had never had in elementary school. I still remember the definition of "socialist consciousness" that we were repeatedly tested on through the years: "Socialist consciousness is a person's political soul. It is the consciousness of the Proletarians represented by Marxist Mao Tse-tung's thought. It takes expression in one's action, language, and lifestyle. It is the task of every Chinese student to grow up into a Proletarian with a socialist consciousness so that he can serve the people and the motherland." To make the abstract concept accessible to us, our teacher pointed out that the immediate task for students from Working-class families was to strengthen their socialist consciousnesses. For those of us who were from other class backgrounds, the task was to turn ourselves into Workers with socialist consciousnesses. The teacher never explained exactly how we were supposed to "turn" into Workers. Instead, we were given samples of the ritualistic annual plans we had to write at the beginning of each term. In these plans, we performed "self-criticism" on our consciousnesses and made vows to turn ourselves into Workers with socialist consciousnesses. The teacher's division between those who did and those who didn't have a socialist consciousness led me to reify the notion of "consciousness" into a thing one possesses. I equated this intangible "thing" with a concrete way of dressing, speaking, and writing. For instance, I never doubted that my political philosophy teacher had a socialist consciousness because she was from a steelworker's family (she announced this the first day of class) and was a Party member who wore grey cadre suits and talked like a philosophy textbook. I noticed other things about her. She had beautiful eyes and spoke Standard Chinese with such a pure accent that I thought she should be a film star. But I was embarrassed that I had noticed things that ought not to have been associated with her. I blamed my observation on my Bourgeois consciousness.

At the same time, the way reading and writing were taught through memorization and imitation also encouraged me to reduce concepts and ideas to simple definitions. In literature and political philosophy classes, we were taught a large number of quotations from Marx, Lenin, and Mao Tse-tung. Each concept that appeared in these quotations came with a definition. We were required to memorize the definitions of the words along with the quotations. Every time I memorized a definition, I felt I had learned a word: "The national red flag symbolizes the blood shed by Revolutionary ancestors for our socialist cause"; "New China rises like a red sun over the eastern horizon." As I memorized these sentences, I reduced their metaphors to dictionary meanings: "red" meant "Revolution" and "red sun" meant "New China" in the "language" of the Working class. I learned mechanically but eagerly. I soon became quite fluent in this new language.

As school began to define me as a political subject, my parents tried to build up my resistance to the "communist poisoning" by exposing me to the "great books"—novels by Charles Dickens, Nathaniel Hawthorne, Emily Brontë, Jane Austen, and writers from around the turn of the century. My parents implied that these writers represented how I, their child, should read and write. My parents replaced the word "Bourgeois" with the word "cultured." They reminded me that I was in school only to learn math and science. I needed to pass the other courses to stay in school, but I was not to let the "Red doctrines" corrupt my mind. Gone were the days when I could innocently write, "I saw the red, red rose among the green leaves,". collapsing, as I did, English and Chinese cultural traditions. "Red" came to mean Revolution at school, "the Commies" at home, and adultery in *The Scarlet Letter*. Since I took these symbols and metaphors as meanings natural to people of the same class, I abandoned my earlier definitions of English and Standard Chinese as the language of home and the language of school. I now defined English as the language of the Bourgeois and Standard Chinese as the language of the Working class. I thought of the language of the Working class as someone else's language and the language of the Bourgeois as my language. But I also believed that, although the language of the Bourgeois was my real language, I could and would adopt the language of the Working class when I was at school. I began to put on and take off my Working class language in the same way I put on and took off my school clothes to avoid being criticized for wearing Bourgeois clothes.

In my literature classes, I learned the Working-class formula for reading. Each work in the textbook had a short "Author's Biography": "X X X, born in 19- in the province of X X, is from a Worker's family. He joined the Revolution in 19-. He is a Revolutionary realist with a passionate love for the Party and Chinese Revolution. His work expresses the thoughts and emotions of the masses and sings praise to the prosperous socialist construction on all fronts of China." The teacher used the "Author's Biography" as a yardstick to measure the texts. We were taught to locate details in the texts that illustrated these summaries, such as words that expressed Workers' thoughts and emotions or events that illustrated the Workers' lives.

I learned a formula for Working-class writing in the composition classes. We were given sample essays and told to imitate them. The theme was always about how the collective taught the individual a lesson. I would write papers about labor-learning experiences or school-cleaning days, depending on the occasion of the collective activity closest to the assignment. To make each paper look different, I dressed it up with details about the date, the weather, the environment, or the appearance of the Master-worker who had taught me "the lesson." But as I became more and more fluent in the generic voice of the Working-class Student, I also became more and more self-conscious about the language we used at home.

For instance, in senior high we began to have English classes ("to study English for the Revolution," as the slogan on the cover of the textbook said), and I was given my first Chinese-English dictionary. There I discovered the English version of the term "class-struggle." (The Chinese characters for a school "class" and for a social "class" are different.) I had often used the English word "class" at home in sentences such as, "So and so has class," but I had not connected this sense of "class" with "class-struggle." Once the connection was made, I heard a second layer of meaning every time someone at home said a person had "class." The expression began to mean the person had the style and sophistication characteristic of the Bourgeoisie. The word lost its innocence. I was uneasy about hearing that second layer of meaning because I was sure my parents did not hear the word that way. I felt that therefore I should not be hearing it that way either. Hearing the second layer of meaning made me wonder if I was losing my English.

My suspicion deepened when I noticed myself unconsciously merging and switching between the "reading" of home and the "reading" of school. Once I had to write a report on *The Revolutionary Family,* a book about an illiterate woman's awakening and growth as a Revolutionary through the deaths of her husband and all her children for the cause of the Revolution. In one scene the woman deliberated over whether or not she should encourage her youngest son to join the Revolution. Her memory of her husband's death made her afraid to encourage her son. Yet she also remembered her earlier married life and the first time her husband tried to explain the meaning of the Revolution to her. These memories made her feel she should encourage her son to continue the cause his father had begun.

I was moved by this scene. "Moved" was a word my mother and sisters used a lot when we discussed books. Our favorite moments in novels were moments of what I would now call internal conflict, moments which we said "moved" us. I remember that we were "moved" by Jane Eyre when she was torn between her sense of ethics, which compelled her to leave the man she loved, and her impulse to stay with the only man who had ever loved her. We were also moved by Agnes in *David Copperfield* because of the way she restrained her love for David so that he could live happily with the woman he loved. My standard method of doing a book report was to model it on the review by the Publishing Bureau and to dress it up with detailed quotations from the book. The review of *The Revolutionary Family* emphasized the woman's Revolutionary spirit. I decided to use the scene that had moved me to illustrate this point. I wrote the report the night before it was due. When I had finished, I realized I couldn't possibly hand it in. Instead of illustrating her Revolutionary spirit, I had dwelled on her internal conflict, which could be seen as a moment of weak sentimentality that I should never have emphasized in a Revolutionary heroine. I wrote another report, taking care to illustrate the grandeur of her Revolutionary spirit by expanding on a quotation in which she decided that if the life of her son could change the lives of millions of sons, she should not begrudge his life for the cause of Revolution. I handed in my second version but kept the first in my desk.

I never showed it to anyone. I could never show it to people outside my family, because it had deviated so much from the reading enacted by the jacket review. Neither could I show it to my mother or sisters, because I was ashamed to have been so moved by such a "Revolutionary" book. My parents would have been shocked to learn that I could like such a book in the same way they liked Dickens. Writing this book report increased my fear that I was losing the command over both the "language of home" and the "language of school" that I had worked so hard to gain. I tried to remind myself that, if I could still tell when my reading or writing sounded incorrect, then I had retained my command over both languages. Yet I could no longer be confident of my command over either language because I had discovered that when I was not careful—or even when I was—my reading and writing often surprised me with its impurity. To prevent such impurity, I became very suspicious of my thoughts when I read or wrote. I was always asking myself why I was using this word, how I was using it, always afraid that I wasn't reading or writing correctly. What confused and frustrated me most was that I could not figure out why I was no longer able to read or write correctly without such painful deliberation.

I continued to read only because reading allowed me to keep my thoughts and confusion private. I hoped that somehow, if I watched myself carefully, I would figure out from the way I read whether I had really mastered the "languages." But writing became a dreadful chore. When I tried to keep a diary, I was so afraid that the voice of school might slip in that I could only list my daily activities. When I wrote for school, I worried that my Bourgeois sensibilities would betray me.

The more suspicious I became about the way I read and wrote, the more guilty I felt for losing the spontaneity with which I had learned to "use" these "languages." Writing the book report made me feel that my reading and writing in the "language" of either home or school could not be free of the interference of the other. But I was unable to acknowledge, grasp, or grapple with what I was experiencing, for both my parents and my teachers had suggested that, if I were a good student, such interference would and should not take place. I assumed that once I had "acquired" a discourse, I could simply switch it on and off every time I read and wrote as I would some electronic tool. Furthermore, I expected my readings and writings to come out in their correct forms whenever I switched the proper discourse on. I still regarded the discourse of home as natural and the discourse of school alien, but I never had doubted before that I could acquire both and switch them on and off according to the occasion.

When my experience in writing conflicted with what I thought should happen when I used each discourse, I rejected my experience because it contradicted what my parents and teachers had taught me. I shied away from writing to avoid what I assumed I should not experience. But trying to avoid what should not happen did not keep it from recurring whenever I had to write. Eventually my confusion and frustration over these recurring experiences compelled me to search for an explanation: how and why had I failed to learn what my parents and teachers had worked so hard to teach me?

I now think of the internal scene for my reading and writing about *The Revolutionary Family* as a heated discussion between myself, the voices of home, and those of school. The review on the back of the book, the sample student papers I came across in my composition classes, my philosophy teacher—these I heard as voices of one group. My parents and my home readings were the voices of an opposing group. But the conversation between these opposing voices in the internal scene of my writing was not as polite and respectful as the parlor scene Kenneth Burke has portrayed (see epigraph). Rather, these voices struggled to dominate the discussion, constantly incorporating, dismissing, or suppressing the arguments of each other, like the battles between the hegemonic and counter-hegemonic forces described in Raymond Williams's *Marxism and Literature* (108–14).

When I read *The Revolutionary Family* and wrote the first version of my report, I began with a quotation from the review. The voices of both home and school answered, clamoring to be heard. I tried to listen to one group and turn a deaf ear to the other. Both persisted. I negotiated my way through these conflicting voices, now agreeing with one, now agreeing with the other. I formed a reading out of my interaction with both. Yet I was afraid to have done so because both home and school had implied that I should speak in unison with only one of these groups and stand away from the discussion rather than participate in it.

My teachers and parents had persistently called my attention to the intensity of the discussion taking place on the external social scene. The story of my grandfather's failure and my father's success had from my early childhood made me aware of the conflict between Western and traditional Chinese cultures. My political education at school added another dimension to the conflict: the war of Marxist-Maoism against them both. Yet when my parents and teachers called my attention to the conflict, they stressed the anxiety of having to live through China's transformation from a semi-feudal, semi-capitalist, and semi-colonial society to a socialist one. Acquiring the discourse of the dominant group was, to them, a means of seeking alliance with that group and thus of surviving the whirlpool of cultural currents around them. As a result, they modeled their pedagogical practices on this utilitarian view of language. Being the eager student, I adopted this view of language as a tool for survival. It came to dominate my understanding of the discussion on the social and historical scene and to restrict my ability to participate in that discussion.

To begin with, the metaphor of language as a tool for survival led me to be passive in my use of discourse, to be a bystander in the discussion. In Burke's "parlor," everyone is involved in the discussion. As it goes on through history, what we call "communal discourses"—arguments specific to particular political, social, economic, ethnic, sexual, and family groups—form, re-form and transform. To use a discourse in such a scene is to participate in the argument and to contribute to the formation of the discourse. But when I was growing up, I could not take on the burden of such an active role in the discussion. For both home and school presented the existent conventions of the discourse each taught me as absolute laws for my action. They turned verbal action into a tool, a set of conventions produced and shaped prior to and outside of my own verbal acts. Because I saw language as a tool, I separated the process of producing the tool from the process of using it. The tool was made by someone else and was then acquired and used by me. How the others made it before I acquired it determined and guaranteed what it produced when I used it. I imagined that the more experienced and powerful members of the community were the ones responsible for making the tool. They were the ones who participated in the discussion and fought with opponents. When I used what they made, their labor and accomplishments would ensure the quality of my reading and writing. By using it, I could survive the heated discussion. When my immediate experience in writing the book report suggested that knowing the conventions of school did not guarantee the form and content of my report, when it suggested that I had to write the report with the work and responsibility I had assigned to those who wrote book reviews in the Publishing Bureau, I thought I had lost the tool I had earlier acquired.

Another reason I could not take up an active role in the argument was that my parents and teachers contrived to provide a scene free of conflict for practicing my various languages. It was as if their experience had made them aware of the conflict between their discourse and other discourses and of the struggle involved in reproducing the conventions of any discourse on a scene where more than one discourse exists. They seemed convinced that such conflict and struggle would overwhelm someone still learning the discourse. Home and school each contrived a purified space where only one discourse was spoken and heard. In their choice of textbooks, in the way they spoke, and in the way they required me to speak, each jealously silenced any voice that threatened to break the unison of the scene. The homogeneity of home and of school implied that only one discourse could and should be relevant in each place. It led me to believe I should leave behind, turn a deaf ear to, or forget the discourse of the other when I crossed the boundary dividing them. I expected myself to set down one discourse whenever I took up another just as I would take off or put on a particular set of clothes for school or home.

Despite my parents' and teachers' attempts to keep home and school discrete, the internal conflict between the two discourses continued whenever I read or wrote. Although I tried to suppress the voice of one discourse in the name of the other, having to speak aloud in the voice I had just silenced each time I crossed the boundary kept both voices active in my mind. Every "I think..." from the voice of home or school brought forth a "However..." or a "But..." from the voice of the opponents. To identify with the voice of home or school, I had to negotiate through the conflicting voices of both by restating, taking back, qualifying my thoughts. I was unconsciously doing so when I did my book report. But I could not use the interaction comfortably and constructively. Both my parents and my teachers had implied that my job was to prevent that interaction from happening. My sense of having failed to accomplish what they had taught silenced me.

To use the interaction between the discourses of home and school constructively, I would have to have seen reading or writing as a process in which I worked my way towards a stance through a dialectical process of identification and division. To identify with an ally, I would have to have grasped the distance between where he or she stood and where I was positioning myself. In taking a stance against an opponent, I would have to have grasped where my stance identified with the stance of my allies. Teetering along the "wavering line of pressure and counter-pressure" from both allies and opponents, I might have worked my way towards a stance of my own (Burke, *A Rhetoric of Motives* 23). Moreover, I would have to have understood that the voices in my mind, like the participants in the parlor scene, were in constant flux. As I came into contact with new and different groups of people or read different books, voices entered and left. Each time I read or wrote, the stance I negotiated out of these voices would always be at some distance from the stances I worked out in my previous and my later readings or writings.

I could not conceive such a form of action for myself because I saw reading and writing as an expression of an established stance. In delineating the conventions of a discourse, my parents and teachers had synthesized the stance they saw as typical for a representative member of the community. Burke calls this the stance of a "god" or the "prototype"; Williams calls it the "official" or "possible" stance of the community. Through the metaphor of the survival tool, my parents and teachers had led me to assume I could automatically reproduce the official stance of the discourse I used. Therefore, when I did my book report on *The Revolutionary Family,* I expected my knowledge of the official stance set by the book review to ensure the actual stance of my report. As it happened, I began by trying to take the official stance of the review. Other voices interrupted. I answered back. In the process, I worked out a stance approximate but not identical to the official stance I began with. Yet the experience of having to labor to realize my knowledge of the official stance or to prevent myself from wandering away from it frustrated and confused me. For even though I had been actually reading and writing in a Burkean scene, I was afraid to participate actively in the discussion. I assumed it was my role to survive by staying out of it.

Not long ago, my daughter told me that it bothered her to hear her friend "talk wrong." Having come to the United States from China with little English, my daughter has become sensitive to the way English, as spoken by her teachers, operates. As a result, she has amazed her teachers with her success in picking up the language and in adapting to life at school. Her concern to speak the English taught in the classroom "correctly" makes her uncomfortable when she hears people using "ain't" or double negatives, which her teacher considers "improper." I see in her the me that had eagerly learned and used the discourse of the Working class at school. Yet while I was torn between the two conflicting worlds of school and home, she moves with seeming ease from the conversations she hears over the dinner table to her teacher's words in the classroom. My husband and I are proud of the good work she does at school. We are glad she is spared the kinds of conflict between home and school I experienced at her age. Yet as we watch her becoming more and more fluent in the language of the classroom, we wonder if, by enabling her to "survive" school, her very fluency will silence her when the scene of her reading and writing expands beyond that of the composition classroom.

For when I listen to my daughter, to students, and to some composition teachers talking about the teaching and learning of writing, I am often alarmed by the degree to which the metaphor of a survival tool dominates their understanding of language as it once dominated my own. I am especially concerned with the way some composition classes focus on turning the classroom into a monological scene for the students' reading and writing. Most of our students live in a world similar to my daughter's, somewhere between the purified world of the classroom and the complex world of my adolescence. When composition classes encourage these students to ignore those voices that seem irrelevant to the purified world of the classroom, most students are often able to do so without much struggle. Some of them are so adept at doing it that the whole process has for them become automatic.

However, beyond the classroom and beyond the limited range of these students' immediate lives lies a much more complex and dynamic social and historical scene. To help these students become actors in such a scene, perhaps we need to call their attention to voices that may seem irrelevant to the discourse we teach rather than encourage them to shut them out. For example, we might intentionally complicate the classroom scene by bringing into it discourses that stand at varying distances from the one we teach. We might encourage students to explore ways of practicing the conventions of the discourse they are learning by negotiating through these conflicting voices. We could also encourage them to see themselves as responsible for forming or transforming as well as preserving the discourse they are learning.

As I think about what we might do to complicate the external and internal scenes of our students' writing, I hear my parents and teachers saying: "Not now. Keep them from the wrangle of the marketplace until they have acquired the discourse and are skilled at using it." And I answer: "Don't teach them to 'survive' the whirlpool of crosscurrents by avoiding it. Use the classroom to moderate the currents. Moderate the currents, but teach them from the beginning to struggle." When I think of the ways in which the teaching of reading and writing as classroom activities can frustrate the development of students, I am almost grateful for the overwhelming complexity of the circumstances in which I grew up. For it was this complexity that kept me from losing sight of the effort and choice involved in reading or writing with and through a discourse.

Works Cited

Burke, Kenneth. *The Philosophy of Literary Form: Studies in Symbolic Action.* 2nd ed. Baton Rouge: Louisiana State UP, 1967.
———. *A Rhetoric of Motives.* Berkeley: U of California P, 1969.
Freire, Paulo. *Pedagogy of the Oppressed.* Trans. M. B. Ramos. New York: Continuum, 1970.
Williams, Raymond. *Marxism and Literature.* New York: Oxford UP, 1977.

SUGGESTIONS FOR DISCUSSION

1. In the opening paragraph, Lu notes that her understanding of her own education was "so dominated by memories of confusion and frustration" that she was unable to speak about them to her dying mother. How does Lu go on to explain what rendered her confused, frustrated, and silent? Does she want the reader to see her silence as peculiar to her own life or illustrative of something that affects many people?

2. Lu says that part of her problem was that she had adopted a view of language as a "tool for survival." Explain what she means by the term "tool for survival" and why she thinks it caused her to be passive and unable to participate in public discussions.

3. In place of the metaphor of language as a "tool for survival," Lu wants to substitute a metaphor of multiple "voices in my mind" contending for her allegiance and attention. Explain what Lu means by these contending voices. Then, test the metaphor of "voices in my mind" according to your own experience in and out of school. Can you think of instances in which you felt a struggle between the language of school and the language of home or some other group? How did you resolve or negotiate the struggle?

SUGGESTIONS FOR WRITING

1. Use Min-zhan Lu's essay as a model to think about how you became aware of the type of reading that is valued in English classes. Your experience, of course, will differ from Lu's, but all students in some fashion or another come to grips with teachers' expectations about what they should find in the reading assigned in English classes. Write an essay that explains your own understanding of what English teachers are looking for when students read literature, whether poems, plays, short stories, or novels. What are they supposed to notice and admire? What kinds of analyses are they supposed to perform when they read literary texts? Consider how this type of schooled reading fits with the way you read literature on your own. To what extent do you read for the same purposes that are called for when you are assigned literary works in school? How would you explain the differences and similarities?

2. Lu describes her experience learning to write in China, under an educational regime in which only certain forms of written expression were acceptable. The U.S. educational system is no doubt more open than the system in China when Lu was a schoolgirl. Nonetheless, there are certain conventions and formulas in place in American schools that students must observe when they write papers for their teachers. Write an essay that explains your own experience in high school English classrooms,

writing themes and papers for your teachers. Take into account how you were taught to write. Did your teachers introduce you to process writing or the five-paragraph theme? Did you exchange papers with other students to do peer response and review? What was the effect of these expectations and classroom practices on your development as a writer?

3. Lu's essay and the following selection by June Jordan, "Nobody Mean More to Me Than You and the Future Life of Willie Jordan," raise questions about the way people perceive spoken and written language, particularly in terms of how it conforms to standard usage and grammatical correctness. Notice in Lu's essay how, in the final section, her daughter is bothered by people who "talk wrong." Read (or reread) Jordan's essay with an eye to how people respond to nonstandard forms such as Black English. Can you think of an example from school or elsewhere when nonstandard, unofficial, or incorrect uses of language were judged unfavorably—as a sign of lack of intelligence or low social status? Write an essay that explains what was at stake in such an instance.

Nobody Mean More to Me Than You and the Future Life of Willie Jordan

June Jordan

June Jordan is a poet, playwright, essayist, and professor of English at the University of California, Berkley. The following selection, "Nobody Mean More to Me Than You and the Future Life of Willie Jordan," opens *On Call,* a collection of Jordan's political essays, published in 1985. In this essay, Jordan weaves two stories together, one concerning a class she taught on Black English and the other concerning Willie Jordan, a young black student in the class trying to come to terms with injustice in South Africa while facing the death of his brother through police brutality at home in Brooklyn. Jordan's story of how her students discovered the communicative power and clarity of Black English forms the backdrop for Willie Jordan's struggle to articulate his own understanding of oppressive power.

SUGGESTION FOR READING

Notice that there are many voices speaking in this essay—not just June Jordan the essayist and teacher, but also Alice Walker in *The Color Purple,* Jordan's students studying and translating Black English, and Willie Jordan in the essay that closes the selection. Underline and annotate passages in this essay to indicate who is speaking and where the voice shifts.

Black English is not exactly a linguistic buffalo; as children, most of the thirty-five million Afro-Americans living here depend on this language for our discovery of the world. But then we approach our maturity inside a larger social body that will not support our efforts to become anything other than the clones of those who are neither our mothers nor our fathers. We begin to grow up in a house where every true mirror shows us the face of somebody who does not belong there, whose walk and whose talk will never look or sound "right," because that house was meant to shelter a family that is alien and hostile to us. As we learn our way around this environment, either we hide our original word habits, or we completely surrender our own voice, hoping to please those who will never respect anyone different from themselves: Black English is not exactly a linguistic buffalo, but we should understand its status as an endangered species, as a perishing, irreplaceable system of community intelligence, or we should expect its extinction, and, along with that, the extinguishing of much that constitutes our own proud, and singular, identity.

What we casually call "English," less and less defers to England and its "gentlemen." "English" is no longer a specific matter of geography or an element of class privilege; more than thirty-three countries use this tool as a means of "intranational communication."[1] Countries as disparate as Zimbabwe and Malaysia, or Israel and Uganda, use it as their non-native currency of convenience. Obviously, this tool, this "English," cannot function inside thirty-three discrete societies on the basis of rules and values absolutely determined somewhere else, in a thirty-fourth other country, for example.

In addition to that staggering congeries of non-native users of English, there are five countries, or 333,746,000 people, for whom this thing called "English" serves as a native tongue.[2] Approximately 10 percent of these native speakers of "English" are Afro-American citizens of the U.S.A. I cite these numbers and varieties of human beings dependent on "English" in order, quickly, to suggest how strange and how tenuous is any concept of "Standard English." Obviously, numerous forms of English now operate inside a natural, an uncontrollable, continuum of development. I would suppose "the standard" for English in Malaysia is not the same as "the standard" in Zimbabwe. I know that standard forms of English for Black people in this country do not copy that of Whites. And, in fact, the structural differences between these two kinds of English have intensified, becoming more Black, or less White, despite the expected homogenizing effects of television[3] and other mass media.

Nonetheless, White standards of English persist, supreme and unquestioned, in these United States. Despite our multi-lingual population, and despite the deepening Black and White cleavage within that conglomerate, White standards control our official and popular judgments of verbal proficiency and correct, or incorrect, language skills, including speech. In contrast to India, where at least fourteen languages co-exist as legitimate Indian languages, in contrast to Nicaragua, where all citizens are legally entitled to formal school instruction in their regional or tribal languages, compulsory education in America compels accommodation to exclusively White forms of "English." White English, in America, is "Standard English."

This story begins two years ago. I was teaching a new course, "In Search of the Invisible Black Woman," and my rather large class seemed evenly divided among young Black women and men. Five or six White students also sat in attendance. With unexpected speed and enthusiasm we had moved through historical narration of the 19th century to literature by and about Black women, in the 20th. I then assigned the first forty pages of Alice Walker's *The Color Purple,* and I came, eagerly, to class that morning:

"So!" I exclaimed, aloud. "What did you think?" How did you like it?"

The students studied their hands, or the floor. There was no response. The tense, resistant feeling in the room fairly astounded me.

At last, one student, a young woman still not meeting my eyes, muttered something in my direction:

"What did you say?" I prompted her.

"Why she have them talk so funny. It don't sound right."

"You mean the language?"

Another student lifted his head: "It don't look right, neither. I couldn't hardly read it."

At this, several students dumped on the book. Just about unanimously, their criticisms targeted the language. I listened to what they wanted to say and silently marvelled at the similarities between their casual speech patterns and Alice Walker's written version of Black English.

But I decided against pointing to these identical traits of syntax, I wanted not to make them self-conscious about their own spoken language—not while they clearly felt it was "wrong." Instead I decided to swallow my astonishment. Here was a negative Black reaction to a prize-winning accomplishment of Black literature that White readers across the country had selected as a best seller. Black rejection was aimed at the one irreducibly Black element of Walker's work: the language—Celie's Black English. I wrote the opening lines of *The Color Purple* on the black-board and asked the students to help me translate these sentences into Standard English:

You better not never tell nobody but God. It'd kill your mommy.

Dear God,
     I am fourteen years old. I have always been a good girl. Maybe you can give me a sign letting me know what is happening to me.
     Last spring after Little Lucious come I heard them fussing. He was pulling on her arm. She say it too soon, Fonso. I aint well. Finally he leave her alone. A week go by, he pulling on her arm again. She say, Naw, I ain't gonna. Can't you see I'm already half dead, an all of the children.[4]

Our process of translation exploded with hilarity and even hysterical, shocked laughter: The Black writer, Alice Walker, knew what she was doing! If rudimentary criteria for good fiction include the manipulation of language so that the syntax and diction of sentences will tell you the identity of speakers, the probable age and sex and class of speakers, and even the locale—urban/rural/southern/western—then Walker had written, perfectly. This is the translation into Standard English that our class produced:

Absolutely, one should never confide in anybody besides God. Your secrets could prove devastating to your mother.

Dear God,
     I am fourteen years old. I have always been good. But now, could you help me to understand what is happening to me?
     Last spring, after my little brother, Lucious, was born, I heard my parents fighting. My father kept pulling at my mother's arm. But she told him, "It's too soon for sex, Alfonso. I am still not feeling well." Finally, my father left her alone. A week went by, and then he began bothering my mother, again: pulling her arm. She told him, "No, I won't! Can't you see I'm already exhausted from all of these children?"

(Our favorite line was "It's too soon for sex, Alfonso.")

Once we could stop laughing, once we could stop our exponentially wild improvisations on the theme of Translated Black English, the students pushed to explain their own negative first reactions to their spoken language on the printed page. I thought it was probably akin to the shock of seeing yourself in a photograph for the first time. Most of the students had never before seen a written facsimile of the way they talk. None of the students had ever learned how to read and write their own verbal system of communication: Black English. Alternatively, this fact began to baffle or else bemuse and then infuriate my students. Why not? Was it too late? Could they learn how to do it, now? And, ultimately, the final test question, the one testing my sincerity: Could I teach them? Because I had never taught anyone Black English and, as far as I knew, no one, anywhere in the United States, had ever offered such a course, the best I could say was "I'll try."

He looked like a wrestler.
     He sat dead center in the packed room and, every time our eyes met, he quickly nodded his head as though anxious to reassure, and encourage me.
     Short, with strikingly broad shoulders and long arms, he spoke with a surprisingly high, soft voice that matched the soft bright movement of his eyes. His name was Willie Jordan. He would

have seemed even more unlikely in the context of Contemporary Women's Poetry, except that ten or twelve other Black men were taking the course, as well. Still, Willie was conspicuous. His extreme fitness, the muscular density of his presence underscored the riveted, gentle attention that he gave to anything anyone said. Generally, he did not join the loud and rowdy dialogue flying back and forth, but there could be no doubt about his interest in our discussions. And, when he stood to present an argument he'd prepared, overnight, that nervous smile of his vanished and an irregular stammering replaced it, as he spoke with visceral sincerity, word by word.

That was how I met Willie Jordan. It was in between "In Search of the Invisible Black Women" and "The Art of Black English." I was waiting for departmental approval and I supposed that Willie might be, so to speak, killing time until he, too, could study Black English. But Willie really did want to explore contemporary women's poetry and, to that end, volunteered for extra research and never missed a class.

Towards the end of that semester, Willie approached me for an independent study project on South Africa. It would commence the next semester. I thought Willie's writing needed the kind of improvement only intense practice will yield. I knew his intelligence was outstanding. But he'd wholeheartedly opted for "Standard English" at a rather late age, and the results were stilted and frequently polysyllabic, simply for the sake of having more syllables. Willie's unnatural formality of language seemed to me consistent with the formality of his research into South African apartheid. As he projected his studies, he would have little time, indeed, for newspapers. Instead, more than 90 percent of his research would mean saturation in strictly historical, if not archival, material. I was certainly interested. It would be tricky to guide him into a more confident and spontaneous relationship both with language and apartheid. It was going to be wonderful to see what happened when he could catch up with himself, entirely, and talk back to the world.

September, 1984: Breezy fall weather and much excitement! My class, "The Art of Black English," was full to the limit of the fire laws. And in Independent Study, Willie Jordan showed up weekly, fifteen minutes early for each of our sessions. I was pretty happy to be teaching, altogether!

I remember an early class when a young brother, replete with his ever-present porkpie hat, raised his hand and then told us that most of what he'd heard was "all right" except it was "too clean." "The brothers on the street," he continued, "they mix it up more. Like 'fuck' and 'motherfuck.' Or like 'shit.'" He waited. I waited. Then all of us laughed a good while, and we got into a brawl about "correct" and "realistic" Black English that led to Rule 1.

Rule 1: *Black English is about a whole lot more than mothafuckin.*

As a criterion, we decided, "realistic" could take you anywhere you want to go. Artful places. Angry places. Eloquent and sweetalkin places. Polemical places. Church. And the local Bar & Grill. We were checking out a language, not a mood or a scene or one guy's forgettable mouthing off.

It was hard. For most of the students, learning Black English required a fallback to patterns and rhythms of speech that many of their parents had beaten out of them. I mean beaten. And, in a majority of cases, correct Black English could be achieved only by striving for incorrect Standard English, something they were still pushing at, quite uncertainly. This state of affairs led to Rule 2.

Rule 2: *If it's wrong in Standard English it's probably right in Black English, or, at least, you're hot.*

It was hard. Roommates and family members ridiculed their studies, or remained incredulous, "You studying that shit? At school?" But we were beginning to feel the companionship of pioneers. And we decided that we needed another rule that would establish each one of us as equally important to our success. This was Rule 3.

Rule 3: *If it don't sound like something that come out somebody mouth then it don't sound right. If it don't sound right then it ain't hardly right. Period.*

This rule produced two weeks of compositions in which the students agonizingly tried to spell the sound of the Black English sentence they wanted to convey. But Black English is, preeminently, an oral/spoken means of communication. And spelling don't talk. So we needed Rule 4.

Rule 4: *Forget about the spelling. Let the syntax carry you.*

Once we arrived at Rule 4 we started to fly, because syntax, the structure of an idea, leads you to the world view of the speaker and reveals her values. The syntax of a sentence equals the structure of your consciousness. If we insisted that the language of Black English adheres to a distinctive Black syntax, then we were postulating a profound difference between White and Black people, per se. Was it a difference to prize or to obliterate?

There are three qualities of Black English—the presence of life, voice, and clarity—that intensify to a distinctive Black value system that we became excited about and self-consciously tried to maintain.

1. *Black English has been produced by a pre-technocratic, if not anti-technological, culture:* More, our culture has been constantly threatened by annihilation or, at least, the swallowed blurring of assimilation. Therefore, our language is a system constructed by people constantly needing to insist that we exist, that we are present. Our language devolves from a culture that abhors all abstraction, or anything tending to obscure or delete the fact of the human being who is here and now/the truth of the person who is speaking or listening. Consequently, there is no passive voice construction possible in Black English. For example, you cannot say, "Black English is being eliminated." You must say, instead, "White people eliminating Black English." The assumption of the presence of life governs all of Black English. Therefore, overwhelmingly, all action takes place in the language of the present indicative. And every sentence assumes the living and active participation of at least two human beings, the speaker and the listener.

2. *A primary consequence of the person-centered values of Black English is the delivery of voice:* If you speak or write Black English, your ideas will necessarily possess that otherwise elusive attribute, voice.

3. *One main benefit following from the person-centered values of Black English is that of clarity:* If your idea, your sentence, assumes the presence of at least two living and active people, you will make it understandable, because the motivation behind every sentence is the wish to say something real to somebody real.

As the weeks piled up, translation from Standard English into Black English or vice versa occupied a hefty part of our course work.

Standard English (hereafter S.E.): "In considering the idea of studying Black English those questioned suggested—"

(What's the subject? Where's the person? Is anybody alive in here, in that idea?)

Black English (hereafter B.E.): "I been asking people what you think about somebody studying Black English and they answer me like this:"

But there were interesting limits. You cannot "translate" instances of Standard English preoccupied with abstraction or with nothing/nobody evidently alive, into Black English. That would warp the language into uses antithetical to the guiding perspective of its community of users. Rather you must first change those Standard English sentences, themselves, into ideas consistent with the person-centered assumptions of Black English.

Guidelines for Black English

1. *Minimal number of words for every idea:* This is the source for the aphoristic and/or poetic force of the language; eliminate every possible word.

2. *Clarity:* If the sentence is not clear it's not Black English.

3. *Eliminate use of the verb* to be *whenever possible:* This leads to the deployment of more descriptive and, therefore, more precise verbs.

4. *Use* be *or* been *only when you want to describe a chronic, ongoing state of things.*
   He *be* at the office, by 9: (He is always at the office by 9.)
   He *been* with her since forever.

5. *Zero copula:* Always eliminate the verb *to be* whenever it would combine with another verb, in Standard English.
   S.E.: She is going out with him.
   B.E.: She going out with him.

6. *Eliminate* do *as in:*
   S.E.: What do you think? What do you want?
   B.E.: What you think? What you want?

Rules number 3, 4, 5, and 6 provide for the use of the minimal number of verbs per idea and, therefore, greater accuracy in the choice of verb.

7. *In general, if you wish to say something really positive, try to formulate the idea using emphatic negative structure.*
   S.E.: He's fabulous.
   B.E.: He bad.

8. *Use double or triple negatives for dramatic emphasis.*
   S.E.: Tina Turner sings out of this world.
   B.E.: Ain nobody sing like Tina.

9. *Never use the* ed *suffix to indicate the past tense of a verb.*
   S.E.: She closed the door.
   B.E.: She close the door. Or, she have close the door.

10. *Regardless of intentional verb time, only use the third person singular, present indicative, for use of the verb* to have, *as an auxiliary.*
    S.E.: He had his wallet then he lost it.
    B.E.: He have him wallet then he lose it.
    S.E.: We had seen that movie.
    B.E.: We seen that movie. Or, we have see that movie.

11. *Observe a minimal inflection of verbs:* Particularly, never change from the first person singular forms to the third person singular.
    S.E.: Present Tense Forms: He goes to the store.
    B.E.: He go to the store.
    S.E.: Past Tense Forms: He went to the store.
    B.E.: He go to the store. Or, he gone to the store. Or, he been to the store.

12. *The possessive case scarcely ever appears in Black English:* Never use an apostrophe ('s) construction. If you wander into a possessive case component of an idea, then keep logically consistent: ours, his, theirs, mines. But, most likely, if you bump into such a component, you have wandered outside the underlying world view of Black English.
    S.E.: He will take their car tomorrow.
    B.E.: He taking they car tomorrow.

13. *Plurality:* Logical consistency, continued: If the modifier indicates plurality then the noun remains in the singular case.
   S.E.: He ate twelve doughnuts.
   B.E.: He eat twelve doughnut.
   S.E.: She has many books.
   B.E.: She have many book.

14. *Listen for, or invent, special Black English forms of the past tense, such as:* "He losted it. That what she felted." If they are clear and readily understood, then use them.

15. *Do not hesitate to play with words, sometimes inventing them:* e.g. "astropotomous" means huge like a hippo plus astronomical and, therefore, signifies real big.

16. *In Black English, unless you keenly want to underscore the past tense nature of an action, stay in the present tense and rely on the overall context of your ideas for the conveyance of time and sequence.*

17. *Never use the suffix* -ly *form of an adverb in Black English.*
   S.E.: The rain came down rather quickly.
   B.E.: The rain come down pretty quick.

18. *Never use the indefinite article* an *in Black English.*
   S.E.: He wanted to ride an elephant.
   B.E.: He wanted to ride him a elephant.

19. *Invariant syntax:* in correct Black English it is possible to formulate an imperative, an interrogative, and a simple declarative idea with the same syntax:
   B.E.: You going to the store?
   You going to the store.
   You going to the store!

Where was Willie Jordan? We'd reached the mid-term of the semester. Students had formulated Black English guidelines, by consensus, and they were now writing with remarkable beauty, purpose, and enjoyment:

> *I ain hardly speakin for everybody but myself so understan that.*
> *Kim Parks*

Samples from student writings:

> Janie have a great big ole hole inside her. Tea Cake the only thing that fit that hole....

> That pear tree beautiful to Janie, especial when bees fiddlin with the blossomin pear there growin large and lovely. But personal speakin, the love she get from starin at that tree ain the love what starin back at her in them relationship. (Monica Morris)

> Love a big theme in, *They Eye Was Watching God*. Love show people new corners inside theyself. It pull out good stuff and stuff back bad stuff....Joe worship the doing uh his own hand and need other people to worship him too. But he ain't think about Janie that she a person and ought to live like anybody common do. Queen life not for Janie. (Monica Morris)

> In both life and writin, Black womens have varietous experience of love that be cold like a iceberg or fiery like a inferno. Passion got for the other partner involve, man or women, seem as shallow, ankle-deep water or the most profoundest abyss. (Constance Evans)

> Family love another bond that ain't never break under no pressure. (Constance Evans)

> You know it really cold/When the friend you/Always get out the fire/Act like they don't know you/When you in the heat. (Constance Evans)

Big classroom discussion bout love at this time. I never take no class where us have any long arguin for and against for two or three day. New to me and great. I find the class time talkin a million time more interestin than detail bout the book. (Kathy Esseks)

As these examples suggest, Black English no longer limited the students, in any way. In fact, one of them, Philip Garfield, would shortly "translate" a pivotal scene from Ibsen's *A Doll's House,* as his final term paper.

> *Nora:* I didn't gived no shit. I thinked you a asshole back then, too, you make it so
>   hard for me save mines husband life.
> *Krogstad:* Girl, it clear you ain't any idea what you done. You done exact what I once
>   done, and I losed my reputation over it.
> *Nora:* You asks me believe you once act brave save you wife life?
> *Krogstad:* Law care less why you done it.
> *Nora:* Law must suck.
> *Krogstad:* Suck or no, if I wants, judge screw you wid dis paper.
> *Nora:* No way, man. (Philip Garfield)

But where was Willie? Compulsively punctual, and always thoroughly prepared with neat typed compositions, he had disappeared. He failed to show up for our regularly scheduled conference, and I received neither a note nor a phone call of explanation. A whole week went by. I wondered if Willie had finally been captured by the extremely current happenings in South Africa: passage of a new constitution that did not enfranchise the Black majority, and militant Black South African reaction to that affront. I wondered if he'd been hurt, somewhere. I wondered if the serious workload of weekly readings and writings had overwhelmed him and changed his mind about independent study. Where was Willie Jordan?

One week after the first conference that Willie missed, he called: "Hello, Professor Jordan? This is Willie. I'm sorry I wasn't there last week. But something has come up and I'm pretty upset. I'm sorry but I really can't deal right now."

I asked Willie to drop by my office and just let me see that he was okay. He agreed to do that. When I saw him I knew something hideous had happened. Something had hurt him and scared him to the marrow. He was all agitated and stammering and terse and incoherent. At last, his sadly jumbled account let me surmise, as follows: Brooklyn police had murdered his unarmed, twenty-five-year-old brother, Reggie Jordan. Neither Willie nor his elderly parents knew what to do about it. Nobody from the press was interested. His folks had no money. Police ran his family around and around, to no point. And Reggie was really dead. And Willie wanted to fight, but he felt helpless.

With Willie's permission I began to try to secure legal counsel for the Jordan family. Unfortunately, Black victims of police violence are truly numerous, while the resources available to prosecute their killers are truly scarce. A friend of mine at the Center for Constitutional Rights estimated that just the preparatory costs for bringing the cops into court normally approaches $180,000. Unless the execution of Reggie Jordan became a major community cause for organizing and protest, his murder would simply become a statistical item.

Again, with Willie's permission, I contacted every newspaper and media person I could think of. But the Bastone feature article in *The Village Voice* was the only result from that canvassing.

Again, with Willie's permission, I presented the case to my class in Black English. We had talked about the politics of language. We had talked about love and sex and child abuse and men and women. But the murder of Reggie Jordan broke like a hurricane across the room.

There are few "issues" as endemic to Black life as police violence. Most of the students knew and respected and liked Jordan. Many of them came from the very neighborhood where the murder had occurred. All of the students had known somebody close to them who had been killed by police, or had known frightening moments of gratuitous confrontation with the cops. They wanted to do everything at once to avenge death. Number One: They decided to compose a personal statement of condolence to Willie Jordan and his family, written in Black English. Number Two: They decided to compose individual messages to the police, in Black English. These should be prefaced by an explanatory paragraph composed by the entire group. Number Three: These individual messages, with their lead paragraph, should be sent to *Newsday.*

The morning after we agreed on these objectives, one of the young women students appeared with an unidentified visitor, who sat through the class, smiling in a peculiar, comfortable way.

Now we had to make more tactical decisions. Because we wanted the messages published, and because we thought it imperative that our outrage be known by the police, the tactical question was this: Should the opening, group paragraph be written in Black English or Standard English?

I have seldom been privy to a discussion with so much heart at the dead beat of it. I will never forget the eloquence, the sudden haltings of speech, the fierce struggle against tears, the furious throwaway, and useless explosions that this question elicited.

That one question contained several others, each of them extraordinarily painful to even contemplate. How best to serve the memory of Reggie Jordan? Should we use the language of the killer—Standard English—in order to make our ideas acceptable to those controlling the killers? But wouldn't what we had to say be rejected, summarily, if we said it in our own language, the language of the victim, Reggie Jordan? But if we sought to express ourselves by abandoning our language wouldn't that mean our suicide on top of Reggie's murder? But if we expressed ourselves in our own language wouldn't that be suicidal to the wish to communicate with those who, evidently, did not give a damn about us/Reggie/police violence in the Black community?

At the end of one of the longest, most difficult hours of my own life, the students voted, unanimously, to preface their individual messages with a paragraph composed in the language of Reggie Jordan. *"At least we don't give up nothing else. At least we stick to the truth: Be who we been. And stay all the way with Reggie."*

It was heartbreaking to proceed, from that point. Everyone in the room realized that our decision in favor of Black English had doomed our writings, even as the distinctive reality of our Black lives always has doomed our efforts to "be who we been" in this country.

I went to the blackboard and took down this paragraph dictated by the class:

YOU COPS!
WE THE BROTHER AND SISTER OF WILLIE JORDAN, A FELLOW STONY BROOK STUDENT WHO THE BROTHER OF THE DEAD REGGIE JORDAN. REGGIE, LIKE MANY BROTHER AND SISTER, HE A VICTIM OF BRUTAL RACIST POLICE, OCTOBER 25, 1984. US APPALL, FED UP, BECAUSE THAT ANOTHER SENSELESS DEATH WHAT OCCUR IN OUR COMMUNITY. THIS WHAT WE FEEL, THIS, FROM OUR HEART, FOR WE AIN'T STAYIN' SILENT NO MORE.

With the completion of this introduction, nobody said anything. I asked for comments. At this invitation, the unidentified visitor, a young Black man, ceaselessly smiling, raised his hand. He was, it so happens, a rookie cop. He had just joined the force in September and, he said, he thought he should clarify a few things. So he came forward and sprawled easily into a posture of barroom, or fire-side, nostalgia:

"See," Officer Charles enlightened us, "most times when you out on the street and something come down you do one of two things. Over-react or under-react. Now, if you under-react then you can get yourself kilt. And if you over-react then maybe you kill somebody.

Fortunately it's about nine times out of ten and you will over-react. So the brother got kilt. And I'm sorry about that, believe me. But what you have to understand is what kilt him: Over-reaction. That's all. Now you talk about Black people and White police but see, now, I'm a cop myself. And (big smile) I'm Black. And just a couple months ago I was on the other side. But it's the same for me. You a cop, you the ultimate authority: the Ultimate Authority. And you on the street, most of the time you can only do one of two things: over-react or under-react. That's all it is with the brother. Over-reaction. Didn't have nothing to do with race."

That morning Officer Charles had the good fortune to escape without being boiled alive. But barely. And I remember the pride of his smile when I read about the fate of Black policemen and other collaborators, in South Africa. I remember him, and I remember the shock and palpable feeling of shame that filled the room. It was as though that foolish, and deadly, young man had just relieved himself of his foolish, and deadly, explanation, face to face with the grief of Reggie Jordan's father and Reggie Jordan's mother. Class ended quietly. I copied the paragraph from the blackboard, collected the individual messages and left to type them up.

Newsday rejected the piece.

The Village Voice could not find room in their "Letters" section to print the individual messages from the students to the police.

None of the TV news reporters picked up the story.

Nobody raised $180,000 to prosecute the murder of Reggie Jordan.

Reggie Jordan is really dead.

I asked Willie Jordan to write an essay pulling together everything important to him from that semester. He was still deeply beside himself with frustration and amazement and loss. This is what he wrote, unedited, and in its entirety:

> Throughout the course of this semester I have been researching the effects of oppression and exploitation along racial lines in South Africa and its neighboring countries. I have become aware of South African police brutalization of native Africans beyond the extent of the law, even though the laws themselves are catalyst affliction upon Black men, women and children. Many Africans die each year as a result of the deliberate use of police force to protect the white power structure.
>
> Social control agents in South Africa, such as policemen, are also used to force compliance among citizens through both overt and covert tactics. It is not uncommon to find bold-faced coercion and cold-blooded killings of Blacks by South African police for undetermined and/or inadequate reasons. Perhaps the truth is that the only reasons for this heinous treatment of Blacks rests in racial differences. We should also understand that what is conveyed through the media is not always accurate and may sometimes be construed as the tip of the iceberg at best.
>
> I recently received a painful reminder that racism, poverty, and the abuse of power are global problems which are by no means unique to South Africa. On October 25, 1984 at approximately 3:00 p.m. my brother, Mr. Reginald Jordan, was shot and killed by two New York City policemen from the 75th precinct in the East New York section of Brooklyn. His life ended at the age of twenty-five. Even up to this current point in time the Police Department has failed to provide my family, which consists of five brothers, eight sisters, and two parents, with a plausible reason for Reggie's death. Out of the many stories that were given to my family by the Police Department, not one of them seems to hold water. In fact, I honestly believe that the Police Department's assessment of my brother's murder is nothing short of ABSOLUTE BULLSHIT, and thus far no evidence had been produced to alter perception of the situation.
>
> Furthermore, I believe that one of three cases may have occurred in this incident. First, Reggie's death may have been the desired outcome of the police officer's action, in which case the killing was premeditated. Or, it was a case of mistaken identity, which clarifies the fact that the two officers who killed my brother and their commanding parties are all grossly incompetent. Or, both of the above cases are correct, i.e., Reggie's murderers intended to kill him and the Police Department behaved insubordinately.

Part of the argument of the officers who shot Reggie was that he had attacked one of them and took his gun. This was their major claim. They also said that only one of them had actually shot Reggie. The facts, however, speak for themselves. According to the Death Certificate and autopsy report, Reggie was shot eight times from point-blank range. The Doctor who performed the autopsy told me himself that two bullets entered the side of my brother's head, four bullets were sprayed into his back, and two bullets struck him in the back of his legs. It is obvious that unnecessary force was used by the police and that it is extremely difficult to shoot someone in his back when he is attacking or approaching you.

After experiencing a situation like this and researching South Africa I believe that to a large degree, justice may only exist as rhetoric. I find it difficult to talk of true justice when the oppression of my people both at home and abroad attests to the fact that inequality and injustice are serious problems whereby Blacks and Third World people are perpetually short-changed by society. Something has to be done about the way in which this world is set up. Although it is a difficult task, we do have the power to make a change.

Willie J. Jordan Jr.
EGL 487, Section 58, November 14, 1984

It is my privilege to dedicate this book to the future life of Willie J. Jordan Jr., August 8, 1985.

Notes

1. *English Is Spreading, But What Is English?* A presentation by Prof. S. N. Sridhar, Department of Linguistics, SUNY, Stony Brook, April 9, 1985: Dean's Convocation Among the Disciplines.
2. Ibid.
3. *New York Times,* March 15, 1985, Section One, p. 14: Report on Study by Linguists at the University of Pennsylvania.
4. Alice Walker, *The Color Purple* (New York: Harcourt Brace Jovanovich, 1982), p. 11.

SUGGESTIONS FOR DISCUSSION

1. How does June Jordan intertwine the story of her class on Black English and the story of Willie Jordan? Would these stories have the same impact if they were presented separately? What, if anything, does Jordan accomplish by weaving them together?

2. Reread the passages where Jordan's students translate the opening of *The Color Purple* into Standard English and the scene from *A Doll's House* into Black English. Describe the qualities of Black expression that get lost in the first case and added in the second.

3. What are the advantages and disadvantages of Jordan's students' decision to write the preface to their individual messages to the police in Black English?

SUGGESTIONS FOR WRITING

1. Write an essay that explains the point June Jordan is making about the relationship between Black English and Standard English and what she thinks ought to be taught in school and why. Compare to your own views what Jordan says on how language should be taught in American schools.

2. Write an essay that explains what you see as the advantages and disadvantages of Jordan's students' decision to compose the introduction to their

letters to the police in Black English. You will want to arrive at your own evaluation of their decision, but before you do, it may help to explain how and in what sense the decision they had to make was a difficult one.

3. Choose a passage of dialogue in a novel or play you are familiar with, in which the speakers are speaking Standard English. Use Phil Garfield's translation of a scene from *A Doll's House* into Black English as a model. Translate the passage into some form of non-Standard English—whether the spoken language of your neighborhood, the vernacular of youth culture, or the dialect of a region.

VISUAL CULTURE

PICTURING SCHOOLDAYS

Visual images of teachers and children can be found in many places and put to use for many purposes. Photographs of one-room schoolhouses, for example, recapture the early days of American schooling and summon up nostalgia for tight-knit communities of the past. By the same token, Norman Rockwell's paintings of school scenes bring us pictures of lost innocence—a time when students were well-behaved and learned the three R's from strict but benevolent teachers. More recently, images of school have been used to illustrate the plight of American education, to argue for uniforms or dress codes, and to advertise new educational products.

Viewing images of schooling releases fond and not-so-fond emotional associations that schooling holds for people. Nearly everyone can remember what it was like to be in school and what their relationships were like with teachers and peers. The way we make sense of images of schooling, however, depends on more than just our personal experience. The composition of the images also gives us cues about how to respond to them.

The purpose of this section is to investigate the composition of photographs of school—to see how they represent teachers and students and to examine their relationship to each other and to the institution of schooling. We'll be looking in particular at how the composition of photographs uses vectors to establish relationships among the people in a photograph and perspective to establish the viewer's attitude toward what the photo represents.

VECTORS

When we look at visual images of schooling, such as the photographs assembled below, we turn these images into a story about what the people are doing and what their relationship to each other is. Because the photograph itself is a still shot, it can't record action that occurs over time. Viewers have to fill in the story based on their familiarity with the scene pictured and the cues they take from the photograph.

We can see how the composition of photographs enables us to fill in the story by looking at how the people and things in the photo are connected by *vectors,* or the diagonal lines viewers' eyes follow from one element of the photograph to another.

Take, for example, the first photograph—Francis Benjamin Johnston's picture of schoolchildren at the Hampton Institute saluting the American flag. It may seem, of course, that we recognize the flag salute right away because it is such a familiar part of schooling and civic life. (What may be puzzling is why the students' arms are outstretched in salute. The outstretched arm—or Roman salute—was the conventional way of saluting the flag until World War II, when it was

Francis Benjamin Johnston. "Pledging Allegiance." Library of Congress.

Vectors in "Pledging Allegiance."

changed because it reminded people of the Nazi salute to Hitler.) But the photograph also contains visual cues that enable us to recognize this familiar gesture. Notice in the schematic drawing how the outstretched arms and eyelines of the schoolchildren create a vector that connects them to the image of the flag and cues viewers to the interaction taking place.

PERSPECTIVE

Perspective is the angle of sight—or point of view—that a photograph offers a viewer. Viewers' attitudes toward what is represented in a photograph will vary depending on perspective. For example, a straight *frontal angle* promotes a high level of involvement and the sense that viewers are directly engaged with the image. A photograph shot from an *oblique angle* will give viewers a sense of detachment, as though they are simply looking on as a bystander. A *high angle,* in which the camera looks down on the people in the photo, gives the viewer a sense of power, while a *low angle,* in which the camera looks up, makes the people seem powerful.

Wallace Kirkland. "Jane Addams Reading at Hull House, Chicago, 1930's." Jane Addams
House Museum.

In the photograph of the New York Elementary School Classroom 1942, for example, notice
how the camera's perspective positions the viewer to look down on the classroom from a high
angle, as though it is our prerogative to observe what is going on.

SUGGESTIONS FOR DISCUSSION

1. Francis Benjamin Johnston's photograph of the schoolchildren saluting
   the flag at Hampton Institute can be an unsettling one that may provoke
   mixed feelings. How are we to respond to the photo? How do the outstretched arms, and their now unavoidable association with the Hitler
   salute, influence our attitude to the photograph? Are we being asked to
   admire the students' patriotism and the sense of order depicted, or does
   the image cast the students as victims of an authoritarian system? Could
   both, in some sense, be true? How does the fact that the students are
   African Americans at an all-black school in the time of segregated education enter into how you respond?

2. Notice how the children are grouped in the photos of Jane Addams and
   the New York classroom in relation to the adult or teacher. What do these
   groupings suggest about the children's relationship to each other and to
   the teacher? What vectors connect the participants, and what story do

"A New York Elementary School Classroom, 1942." All the Children: New York City School Report (1942–43).

Apple ad. © Apple Computer, Inc.

they tell? Follow the eyelines. What are the children observing? Do their eyelines point to an important focus of attention, or are they turned down to the children's work? Do the students look at each other? Is the teacher's gaze the dominant vector in the image?

3. In the Apple ad, we are looking directly at the teacher (or the model who plays the teacher) in the computer classroom instead of looking on from an oblique angle or from above or below. What effect does this frontal perspective have on the viewer? Compare the perspective in the Apple ad to the perspective in one or more of the other photographs. How do the different angles shape your attitude to the photo?

SUGGESTED ASSIGNMENT

What photographic image could tell the story of your classroom and the prevailing relationships among the students and between the teacher and the students? For this project, work in a group with two or three other students to take a photograph of your classroom.

When composing a photographic image, consider the following questions. How would students and the teacher be distributed and grouped in space? What vectors or eyelines would connect them? How would you want to position the viewer in relation to the classroom? How would you frame a shot that creates the point of view and angle of sight that you want for the viewer?

When you have decided on the shot you want, take the picture. This may involve posing students and the teacher in particular ways or asking them to do certain things that you want to capture on film. Everyone in class needs to cooperate on this project—whether you are taking the picture or being its subject.

When all the groups have developed the photos, bring them to class and discuss to what extent they portray different and similar stories. Identify the main vectors in each and how they establish the key relationships among the participants. Consider, too, how the photos create points of view and degrees of involvement on the viewer's part.

 CLASSROOM OBSERVATION

Most students know that being successful in school means understanding what teachers value and what they expect from students. This is sometimes called "psyching out" a teacher, and students learn to be good at it. They do this by evaluating the formal requirements of the course (e.g., reading assignments, labs, homework, tests, papers), by observing what takes place in the classroom (e.g., lectures, discussion, films, group work), and by learning the teacher's personality and eccentricities.

The purpose of this project is to investigate what it takes to be successful in a course in which you are enrolled and to draw some conclusions about the nature of teaching and learning. The method used is participant/observation. You are asked, in effect, to observe yourself, your teacher, and other students and to take detailed notes on what you do in and out of class.

A number of weeks will be needed for this project, so that you can accumulate a sufficient amount of entries in your field log to make your observations reliable and conclusions possible.

FIELD LOG

As a participant/observer, you need to keep a field log on the classes, reading assignments, papers, exams, sections or labs, if pertinent, study groups, and informal conversations outside of class.

Background

When you start this project, write a statement that summarizes what you know about the course at this time. Ask yourself the following questions:

1. *Why are you taking the class?* To fulfill a requirement, for personal interest, for some other motivation?

2. *Read the syllabus:* How does it describe the content of the course and what you will learn? What are the assignments? How will the course grade be determined?

3. *Describe the format of the class:* What size is the class? In what kind of room does it meet? Does it look like it will be mostly lecture, discussion, a combination of the two, something else? Keep track of attendance patterns. Note where students sit to see if patterns develop.

4. *From what you can tell so far, what will you need to do to get the grade you want?*

Field Notes

Field notes consist of the observations you record during and outside of class. Use these questions:

1. *Where do you sit in class?* Why?

2. *How do you actually spend your time in class*—taking notes, doodling, engaging in class discussion, looking around, writing notes to other students, daydreaming, talking to other students, working on something for another class, reading a newspaper or magazine?

3. *What does the teacher do in class?* Is it the same thing every day or does it change? How does the teacher run the class? Do individual class meetings have a routine format? Is there a set schedule (lecture Monday, discussion Wednesday, film Friday)? Who talks?

4. *What do other students do?*

5. *What do you do outside of class?* Keep track of the time devoted to various activities: reading assignments, reviewing or rewriting notes, studying for tests (alone or with others), attending lab sessions or section meetings, doing research, writing papers, meeting with the teacher or assistant, talking informally with other students about the class, etc.

ANALYSIS

Review your notes and look for patterns and key points. Here are some questions to consider:

1. *Compare what you know now about the course to what you wrote earlier on in your field log:* Have your responses changed? Does the course syllabus give an accurate forecast of what to expect or have you become aware in other ways of the "real" requirements of the class? Have you changed your mind about the grade you think you might get?

2. *What kinds of patterns emerge from notes on what you do in class?* Do you do the same thing in every class or does your activity vary? Have you changed what you do in class consciously? If so, why?

3. *Has the work returned to you so far (homework, tests, quizzes, papers, etc.) confirmed or revised what you thought it would take to do well in the course?* What have you learned about the teacher's expectations and preferences?

4. *How does the work you do outside of class figure in?* Could you skip class and still do well? Do you do all the work or only certain assignments? Do you have a system for deciding what to do and not do? If so, how did you develop it? Do you meet with or talk to the teacher, the teaching assistant, or other students about the class?

5. *What patterns emerge from your observations of other students?*

6. *What are the main differences and similarities in the courses you have observed?* What is their significance?

WRITING THE REPORT

For this project, use a version of the standard format for reports.

Introduction

Explain what you are investigating and the purpose of your research. Identify the class you observed, its enrollment, usual attendance, course requirements, and any other pertinent information. It can help readers to summarize this information in a diagram that accompanies your Introduction. (See Table 3.1.)

Method

Explain how you gathered data.

Observations

Summarize key points from your field log in order to establish patterns and to characterize your participation in the course. (See the sample Observations.)

Conclusions

Derive inferences and generalizations from your observations. (See sample Conclusions.)

Observations and Conclusions from "Cross-Curricular Underlife: A Collaborative Report on Ways with Academic Words"

Worth Anderson, Cynthia Best, Alycia Black,
John Hurst, Brandt Miller, and Susan Miller

> The following Observations and Conclusions come from a longer article written by a group of undergraduates at the University of Utah in an independent study course under the direction of Susan Miller, a faculty member in English and a prominent writing theorist. Following an introductory section, the article consists of observations and conclusions written by the various members of the research group.

SAMPLE OBSERVATIONS

Art History

On the first day of class, the professor urged us all to drop, said she was willing to dispense drop cards to everyone, launched into a lecture that filled the time, handed out a syllabus, and reminded us that it was not too late to drop. I promptly named her "Madame Battleaxe."

TABLE 3.1

Descriptions of Courses Observed

Student	Course Title	Enrollment and % Usual Attendance	Course Requirements and Student Interpretations of Them (MC = Multiple Choice)
Worth	Anthropology	90 (60%)	Pass 2 MC midterms = take notes, attend, study notes; 1-pg. extra credit paper.
	Common Medicines	150 (90%)	2 MC tests: drug names, uses = memorize, memorize; good notes are critical; final cramming will not do here.
	International Studies: Africa	55 (90%)	4 short ans. tests; 6-pg. paper. Study ugly stuff like population distribution.
	Art History	100 (95%)	Midterm and Final, both essay. Memorize names and dates; concepts not a problem.
Cynthia	Anthropology	76 (60%)	Read for weekly quizzes, watch films, pass MC midterm and final. 1-pg. book review for extra credit.
	Intellectual Trad. of the West (Medieval)	25 (90%)	Write 4 papers, essay midterm and final. Read, attend.
	Sociology	400 (50%)	3 MC tests. Read, take notes, watch films.
Alycia	Intellectual Trad. of the West (Medieval)	25 (80%)	1 paper; midterm, final with take-home essay. 150–200 pp./wk. reading.
	Critical Literature	22 (60–75%)	3 papers; response ¶s. 15–60 min. reading/night to practice analyzing.
	Law	20 (95%)	10 1-page papers; research on topic about church and state.
John	Astronomy	105 (60%)	MC tests. Attend, read text, extra credit for 1000-word report.
	Psychology	155 (70–75%)	MC tests. Attend, read text, extra credit for being a subject in dept. experiments.
	Basic Acting II	9 (100%)	Perform 2 scenes, one monologue; attend 3 plays, review 2 of them.
Brandt	Calculus	35 (80%)	Problem sets. Take notes; geometrically interpret concepts; review and keep up.
	Chemistry	450 (70%)	Problems sets and MC test; read to get high grades on tests.
	History of Science	20 (97%)	Essay midterm and final; paper. Take notes & refer to them when reading; research final paper (use Wr. 210 skills); do well on final by catching up.

It got worse. She was the embodiment of objectivist theories: "There are these facts. They constitute Truth. I will speak. You will listen. You will emerge with Truth." She spoke quickly, had some funky uses for the word "sensuous." I take notes very poorly, so I just sat and listened. A friend who sat beside me and played stenographer was frustrated by this, but for me I did better by just listening.

I realized that I was having trouble memorizing dates on pictures, so I went to see her. We got to talking about Charles V, and amazingly, I liked her. She reassured me about the test, and explained how highly she valued coherent writing, composed with an eye to history. I decided that she considered herself a historian, so her audience values would be in that community.

After our meeting, I was far more tolerant of her in class. On the midterm and final I wrote much more than anyone else, and emerged both times with the top grade. Serving up what she wanted worked.

Sociology

The teacher basically taught lecture one day—film one day—lecture one day....I believe that it's good to develop a routine, but not a rut! At first people groaned when they found out we were going to be watching another film. Once the students realized how the class would be taught, they began walking out during the films and lectures. One day I counted twenty-two people who walked out during a film. Later, the students developed a different routine. They would come to class and stay only if there was a film (so they could answer the test questions). But they would leave if the teacher was lecturing because they felt they could get more from reading the book.

The teacher lectured from an outline of key words on the overhead projector. Several people commented that his lectures were hard to follow, but I thought they weren't too difficult because he followed the book. In fact, at times he read straight from it! The professor had the habit of leaning on the lectern while he lectured and placing his hand on his chin. (It almost covered his mouth!) One day I observed, "Five people walked out of the lecture early. I assume from the time that had elapsed that it was after they'd copied the outline. I noticed people who simply copied the outline of key words and then just sat there in a kind of stupor."

In such a large class I noticed diverse student behaviors. One day during the film, as I counted the twelve people who left early, the girl to my left did homework for another class, the guy in front of me ate yogurt, and the guy to my right organized his Franklin Day Planner. I rarely took notes on the films because they were irrelevant, but some people took notes anyway. One girl's notes consisted of "Boring>>>>>>Big Time!"

Calculus

I would go early to hear students discuss assignments and compare solutions to take-home quizzes, but this seemed almost a formality rather than a concern over concepts. When the professor began to work rapidly on the board, the lead flew across my notebook. She may not be exceptionally exciting, but unless you pay attention, you get lost fast. There was only moderate interaction between students and instructor by way of questions. Amazingly few questions are raised about such complex material.

There were several overlapping communities of student interaction in this class. Although it was a small class, there were many students whose names I didn't know, and could barely recognize by sight. I think this was because math is an independent discipline. You only need to interact with a few students to find the right answer. I took notes the whole time. After class, I would talk to students who could explain concepts like double integration a little better than what I had understood.

Math is a very sequential subject. When I had had trouble understanding the last assignment, I knew it would only compound with a new one. Today's concepts would be based on what we learned yesterday, which was based on the day before. Students had a tough time when they hadn't been here. Dr. A. covers the new material by relating it to yesterday's material, which makes it easier. Dr. A. becomes a narrator for the strange mathematical figures that appear on the board.

When Dr. A. explained what kind of questions there would be on tests, she sometimes let us use a "cheat sheet," so we knew it would be hard. I would meet with other students to study.

SAMPLE CONCLUSIONS

A.

In ITW, I learned both on my own and in class. I learned as I read the assignments alone, and then my knowledge was expanded when the professor expounded on the material. Sections of this course are taught by teachers from different disciplines, so students who take more than one part of the sequence learn about ideas and about professors' specific fields. This section was actually "taught." The history professor who taught it connected ideas to historical background. But in Sociology, I learned the most from the text. The instructor's lectures were helpful, but I gained very little from the films. Ironically though, I preferred the films to the lectures. As I wrote one day, "I enjoyed the film simply because I didn't have to listen to another lecture." Anthropology was not "taught." The professor simply spouted facts each day. In considering where the learning occurred here, I've decided I learned most from the text. The films were informative and very helpful, but they were never shown at the right times. I really struggled with the professor's lectures, yet I learned from my notes because that's the only place that certain material was given.

School is a contract between a student and a teacher. Each must share a mutual respect for the other for learning to occur. In my liberal education courses, the teachers were not as concerned about the classes as they should have been. I got the impression that these teachers were being punished. They were bored because the material was so fundamental to their disciplines. But to the students, the material is new. If the professor shows excitement and projects a positive attitude, students will tend to be more interested in learning. Large classes require more effort from both students and teachers.

B.

Generally, the crucial part of learning in any classroom is digging up what the professor expects. I find that all classes require exceptional note-taking and analytical reading. Not all classes "require" attendance; in some I learn more from reading than from going to class. Poorly attended classes are those where the professor reads the text and gives no additional information. Well attended classes are taught by professors who enjoy the subject and make the students feel comfortable with it.

Although most of the students' learning must be done outside of class, an attitude toward learning is developed in the classroom. The professor's role is crucial because the students will be as active as the teacher is. Many of my peers say that the average student counts on having at least one "blow-off" class. If a teacher is strict, the students will make greater efforts and follow the teacher's guidelines. If a teacher is dull and doesn't include fun tidbits or allow us to express varying views, the students will find the material dull and difficult to study. But if the professor is excited, encourages us to voice different opinions, and interacts with us, the students will be excited about the subject and have an easier time.

A Doll for Jane

"Hello, Father," said Dick.

"Jane will have a birthday soon.

Please get a new doll for Jane.

Get a baby doll that talks.

Please get a doll that talks."

15

Mining the Archive

TEXTBOOKS FROM THE PAST

One way to get a sense of schooling in an earlier time is to take a look at the textbooks then in use. Two of the most famous and popular textbook series were designed to teach reading. *McGuffey's Eclectic Readers* taught millions of American children to read during the nineteenth century, just as the Dick and Jane primers did from the 1930s to the 1960s. Each series offers a fascinating view of how elementary school students learned to read and the kinds of social values their reading lessons transmitted. The McGuffey readers were anthologies of essays, poems, speeches, and stories filled with moral advice, patriotic ideas, and religious instruction. Heavily didactic in tone, the content of the readers was meant to be morally uplifting. The Dick and Jane readers, on the other hand, created a child's world of fun and surprise. Dick and Jane, along with their little sister Sally, dog Spot, and kitten Puff, lived in an American dream of white picket-fenced suburban homes, loving parents, laughter, and security. Most college and large public libraries will have copies of *McGuffey's Eclectic Reader* and some will have Dick and Jane readers as well. You can also find selections from the two textbook series in Elliot J. Gorn, ed., *The McGuffey Readers: Selections from the 1879 Edition* (Boston: Bedford, 1998) and Carol Kismaric and Marvin Heiferman, *Growing Up with Dick and Jane: Learning and Living the American Dream* (San Francisco: Collins Publishers, 1996). Researching these textbooks can lead to writing projects that focus on a range of topics. Here are a few examples. According to your interests, you can design your own.

- nineteenth-century reading instruction
- the Protestant middle-class values of the McGuffey readers
- gender stereotypes in Dick and Jane
- the postwar American dream in the Dick and Jane primers

CHAPTER 4

Images

Every day we move through a visual world of advertisements and newspapers, photographs and magazines, cinema and television: an optical empire that is regularly criticized for its power to shape our lives. This visual collage, accompanying us from morning to night, is a product of the three giant forces of the contemporary world: industrialization, capitalism, and urbanization. And the power of the images that these processes have produced…is inescapable. They are a part of daily vision, contributing to the way we look at and understand our world. We continually select images from the cinema, from fashion, from magazines, from adverts, from television. They stand in for 'reality,' become a reality; the signs of experience, of self.
— *Iain Chambers*, Popular Culture: The Metropolitan Experience

That an image can stand in for and even become reality, as Iain Chambers suggests, is something that advertisers count on as they produce the ads we see in print, on television, on billboards, on electronic signs, on buses, on rented movie videos, and most recently on the Web. In the United States, anyway, public images are inescapable. Because so much information competes for our attention wherever we turn, it is very often the image more than written text that must carry most of the message.

The image that conveys a message is hardly a new phenomenon. For centuries the images people created—paintings, drawings, designs, sketches, icons— did not simply decorate the insides of caves, temples, churches, palaces, and the like, but also recorded family and community history; taught lessons in religion, culture, and politics; and even gave directions to locations.

What is new in our experience of the image is not only the vast numbers and many kinds of images available or the ease with which they may be and are reproduced, copied, parodied, and reconstructed. What is new in our experience is something we might call the aggressive nature of the image. Unless we purposefully isolate ourselves from the industrial world, we have difficulty avoiding these images that daily insist on our attention. Thus most of us are so accustomed to this world of images that we read most of what we see without much thought.

Advertisers, of course, depend on the fact that we all already know a great deal about the messages that images convey. They are counting on the public being able to read very quickly a few generalized images as they speed down the highway, surf through TV channels, or flip through a magazine. We know some images simply because they have been around for so long. A full-color photo of a cowboy silhouetted on a horse at sunset is likely going to call to mind the Marlboro Man, whether or not it is in an ad for cigarettes. Because such scenes are so easily recognized, advertisers are sometimes able to use just a few words (Marlboro often uses the product's name and the obligatory FDA warning alone) to get the message across.

Then again the image can fool us, especially if the advertiser hasn't succeeded in linking the image directly to a product. Several years ago, the Whirlpool company ran a commercial that featured a bald eagle. The camera tracked the eagle in slow motion as it flew down toward impossibly still water, reached out, and snatched up a trout with a movement that was sure and elegant and surprising. The image was so appealing that even the advertisers couldn't resist showing it again. Viewers watched the eagle's catch once more—this time closer up and slightly slower. The image of the eagle is, in this country, one laden with the notions of patriotism, freedom, strength, and independence. The ad was beautiful to watch. The problem was that this image had so little obvious connection to the product (Whirlpool appliances) that viewers often could remember the ad but not the product. An effective ad image (like Maytag's lonely repairman) has a double burden: It must catch our attention, and it must link the image it uses to a particular product so that we think of the product the next time we are in a buying mood.

As you read this chapter, you will be asked to look at and read such messages—messages that rely on pictures or graphics more than on words to carry meaning. Many of the images we will discuss here are taken from print ads so that you will have easy access to images that you can study carefully for long periods of time. However, the power of the image to convey messages is, as Chambers points out, not at all limited to print advertising. Television, film, photographs, music videos, Web pages, even the very layout of the daily newspaper all signal an increased demand for us to become active readers and producers of visual text.

As we suggested in Chapter 1, the language of images is much like verbal language. In order to relay meaning, visual language depends on familiarity, patterns of use, composition, references to other images, and the context in which the image appears. Like verbal language, visual language does not convey simply one stable message to everyone who reads it. Meaning depends on the reader as well as the text. Still, the most quickly read messages are often those that carry with them expressions of common cultural ideas or ideals—images that act as a kind of visual shorthand.

We begin our discussion, then, with an illustration of that cultural shorthand. The poster below uses a simple design depicting a gagged George Washington above the words "Let Washington Speak. Congressional Voting Rights for D.C."

Even without the words beneath this picture, most individuals schooled in the United States are likely to read it as a message about the right to speak. This Gilbert Stuart portrait of Washington is the image most often copied when artists want to portray the first president of the United States. It appears on dollar bills, on postage stamps, and in elementary schoolrooms across the country. Moreover, Washington's image has come to be associated closely with issues of the American Revolution such as freedom of speech and the right of the people to determine their own form of government. The gagged mouth on Washington suggests forceful suppression of speech, perhaps by outlaws or thugs. Thus even without the text "Let Washington Speak. Congressional Voting Rights for D.C.," the image has within it the possibility of conveying a powerful message. The text, in this case, works to anchor a common reading of the image. It tells readers that this poster pertains to a particular issue in a particular political struggle. The text, then, helps limit the ways the image, on its own, might be read.

What the cultural shorthand cannot control is the additional meaning that readers are able to generate with an image such as this one. Though the artist who created the "Let Washington Speak" poster likely wanted to persuade voters that a vote against congressional voting rights for the District of Columbia was a vote against the principles upon which this nation was founded, a reader could conceivably look at the image and feel that it is about time the bigwigs of this country were finally gagged. That reader would be one who did not feel strongly persuaded by the image of Washington as a symbol of freedom but instead might see Washington as the first in a long line of patriarchal authority figures. Both readers are likely to understand the message about freedom of speech and constitutional rights, but their response to that message would differ depending on particular circumstances that may be determined by differences in gender, politics, social status, ethnicity, or economic background. Visual meaning, like all meaning, is dependent on both the message being sent and the receiver of that message.

To focus on the importance of the visual does not mean that we ignore the written text. Many images, like the "Let Washington Speak" poster,

Sitting Bull's great great great granddaughter, Jacqueline Brown-Smith, with her Coach Binocular Bag.

COACH
AN AMERICAN LEGACY

The Binocular Bag, No. 9853, $194. Enduring style, made of fine natural leather that becomes more beautiful with time. To order, or for a complimentary catalogue, call 800 262-2411. Also available at The Coach Stores, select department and specialty stores.

rely on pictures and words to carry meaning even when the words are few. In a text like the one we have been discussing or the following ad for Coach bags, words serve to anchor readers to a particular message. The first asks readers to vote yes for D.C. voting rights. The second, not as directly but just as assuredly, asks readers to buy Coach bags. And, yet, as we will see, words can also complicate readers' responses.

On its own, the visual image in the Coach ad is simple and commonplace: The attractive young woman posed in a rugged yet beautiful setting with her dog and her Coach bag is likely meant to associate the product with those things that appeal to us in the image. At the same time, the **ad copy** (what is written in the ad about the product) asks us to associate the product with more than natural beauty or rugged independence alone. The copy identifies the young woman as the great-great-great-granddaughter of Sitting Bull, the famous Hunkpapa

Sioux who resisted being placed on a reservation and whose name continues to call forth the image of Indian people as profoundly independent.

Such identification gives this image a cultural significance. That is, once the woman is identified as the direct descendant of Sitting Bull, we are no longer looking at her but through her, to her great-great-great-grandfather. Jacqueline Brown-Smith is thereby assigned special significance because of her relation to Sitting Bull. After discovering who she is, a reader is likely to look again at the image that has now taken on a different meaning. Naturally, the Coach bag is likely to pick up some of that meaning. In this ad, the bag is called "An American Legacy" like, we must assume, the legacy left by Sitting Bull and represented here in the image of his great-great-great-granddaughter, Jacqueline Brown-Smith.

Clearly, the ad puts Sitting Bull in a long line of famous and well-respected Americans. In fact, this particular campaign includes ads using the descendants of such luminaries as Albert Einstein, Jesse Owens, Gene Kelly, and George Washington, suggesting that Coach represents intelligence, endurance, priceless quality, good taste, and status. The bag Brown-Smith is carrying is a binocular case, which links her (and, by extension, her great-great-great-grandfather) to the natural world—to a rugged existence with an uptown taste.

Of course, readers might also find meanings in this ad, as in any ad, that the advertiser did not intend. They might question the reference to Sitting Bull—a man who clearly stood in opposition to U.S. government policies—to sell an expensive bag to what has become a consumer culture. Advertisers are aware of that possibility, which is why they must pitch ads differently to different groups of people.

Advertisers take advantage of cultural meanings every time they present an image as if it were representative of what everyone desires or understands. Take, for example, the Jeep ad reprinted below.

This ad uses a very simple design—the juxtapositioning of one image beside another—to convey a complex message. By placing the peace symbol ("International Symbol for Peace") beside the word Jeep ("International Symbol for Freedom"), the

INTERNATIONAL SYMBOL FOR PEACE.   INTERNATIONAL SYMBOL FOR FREEDOM.

Jeep

For more than half a century, Jeep 4x4s have led the way to freedom. Everything else just follows. For information,   contact us at 1-800-925-JEEP or www.jeep.com   THERE'S ONLY ONE

advertiser is asking us to connect one with the other. When we talk about the arrangement of images in relation to one another, we are describing the **visual syntax** of the ad. In other words, the images are arranged in such a way as to convey meaning. Cartoons, for example, use a sequencing of images to suggest an event unfolding over time. This ad simply juxtaposes one image with the other so that we might see a connection between the two images.

This particular ad has the potential to reach a number of different kinds of readers because of the cultural meanings the two images already carry. The peace symbol and the word Jeep are each depicted as if they could be worn on leather laces around the neck, so the retro look of the peace symbol might appeal to current fashion. The peace symbol continues to evoke a strong emotional response from those who were young during the Vietnam War, so the message is one that could elicit memories of youth and freedom from that generation. In addition, the Jeep is a vehicle that was made popular particularly during World War II, the war Studs Terkel and others have called the last "good war." As if to underscore this final connection, the ad copy at the bottom of the page reminds readers that, "For more than half a century, Jeep 4×4s have led the way to freedom. Everything else just follows." The Jeep name as an "international symbol for freedom" can, then, even appeal to a generation not entirely in sympathy with the peace movement of the sixties or the retro look of the nineties.

In fact, the fewer words an ad like this uses, the more likely it will draw a number of different readings—many of which will be positive and all of which will call up something of the reader's memories or desires or associations. Finally, with the statement "There's only one Jeep," the ad seems to acknowledge the possibility that there may be many responses to this juxtapositioning, but that there is only one product that can evoke all of those responses. Advertisers naturally hope that those associations eventually will lead readers to think of and then purchase the product after they have seen the ad.

On their own and depending on the individual, readers might still question the association of the peace symbol with the Jeep or wonder how the peace symbol could have changed from a political statement of the sixties to a fashion statement of the nineties. Such a reading, though, would threaten to interrupt the primary purpose of the ad, which is to sell Jeep cars and trucks. That kind of reading is certainly possible, but it must be done consciously, and most ads function at a more subconscious, even visceral level. They call on feelings and loyalties and fears and desires—responses most of us do not take much time to question.

Other kinds of visual images do the same: logos for sports teams, poster campaigns, graffiti, news photos, and family albums, for example. Some images are pure function: the icons that tell us to buckle our seat belts on planes, not to smoke in public places, which restroom door to walk through, and others of that sort. These are wholly visual, and many of them are multinational signs that tell a great deal in a simple design.

As you look at and consider the visual messages around you, remember that we don't have to be mindless consumers of visual culture. We are producers as well, and we can make our own visual messages. What bothers many people when they look at ads, for example, is the assuredness with which advertisers sell lifestyles and attempt to create new interests. Knowing that most people let ads go by without reading them closely, some activists will write over ads in public places so that the public at large might more easily see the alternative or oppositional readings possible in an ad campaign. The group of graffitists called the Billboard Using Graffitists Against Unhealthy Promotion (BUGAUP) are responsible for changing the text of the following Marlboro ad to accomplish that purpose.

The text of the original billboard read "New. Mild. And Marlboro." However, the BUGAUP group saw the original ad as one promoting an unhealthy product. They used the original text to rewrite the advertiser's message in order to send a message of their own.

The reading and rewriting by BUGAUP disrupted the ad's intended meaning by transforming "Mild" into "Vile" and "Marlboro" into "A Bore," thus challenging the Marlboro Man's image as well as the text that tried to reconcile cigarette smoking with health and independence. The tombstone drawn by BUGAUP in the background of the image used a traditional sign of the Western legend—Boot Hill—to subvert the code of the Western and to turn the text into a warning in the name of health.

Writing and rewriting in the hands of BUGAUP and similar groups like Canada's Adbusters or the many unnamed graffitists who carry on similar campaigns in small towns and major cities thus becomes a forceful tool of resistance to the messages that normally go unquestioned and often unnoticed in the public sector. Later in this chapter you will have the opportunity to rewrite and create images of your own, but before you do that you will want to understand how an image conveys meaning.

READING IMAGES

In this chapter, you will be reading articles by writers who have thought a great deal about the importance of the image, especially the advertising image. Stuart and Elizabeth Ewen dramatize just how much our lives are affected by a nearly unbroken stream of popular images. As you read the Ewens' article, begin to gather and think about images from your surroundings. A major part of reading images is the simple act of noticing what images are around us. The next selection, from Arthur Asa Berger's work on media literacy, should continue to provide you with skills to read visual messages. In particular, Berger's checklist of suggestions for reading visuals provides one set of guidelines for what to look for in almost any advertising image.

We follow Berger with a pair of essays. In the first, Jean Kilbourne argues the importance of understanding how advertising images convey cultural meaning and perpetuate cultural stereotypes. We have paired Kilbourne with the first in a series of visual essays designed to draw your attention to particular issues in reading images. Bearing in mind that Kilbourne's essay so strongly condemns advertisers' stereotypes of women, we use this first visual essay—"It's a Woman Thing"—to examine that stereotype and to raise questions about Kilbourne's discussion. The visual essay that follows—"Public Health Messages"—asks you to draw further on your experience with reading images to examine the multiple meanings embedded in such messages as public service announcements, posters, and health campaigns.

The next visual essay, on rewriting the image, encourages you to think about your own role as a producer of cultural meaning. At the beginning of this chapter, Iain Chambers tells us "the power of the images that these processes have produced…is inescapable. They are a part of daily vision, contributing to the way we look at and understand our world." We believe that the power of the image is something you can use to your advantage. The image doesn't have to be just another thing that works on you. You can use images to say what you want to say, to talk back to the images surrounding you.

Often when we talk about reading images, the images we think about are pictures: ads and television programs and films, for example. Our next visual essays are meant to extend your thinking about images to the very look of the text on a page—the layout, design, font, punctuation, and more. Ellen Lupton and J. Abbott Miller's visual essay "Period Styles" serves to open that discussion of how the look of the page is not a natural extension of writing or typing but, instead, results from new technologies as well as decisions made through time about such matters as how to mark natural pauses or breaks in a text, how to signal dialogue, and more.

Page layout and design are most obvious on the newsstands, so our visual essay on "The Look of the Page" offers an opportunity for you to look very carefully at popular print media. When the news daily *USA Today* began capturing a major market,

critics charged the paper with catering to a TV (or even an MTV) generation. We hear these charges quite often when the visual image competes successfully with the verbal text. We think these charges are interesting ones that can help us understand how a preference for or a reliance on the visual is often confused with immature thinking.

We conclude this chapter with a suggestion for archival research that allows you to trace for yourself the changing look of the page—the shifting balance of picture and text—that marks the history of design especially in magazine advertising. You can, of course, extend this research to other designs. Textbooks, newspapers, even tax forms have changed with our growing interest in the role visual design plays in the presentation of information. In this way, you can become knowledgeable consumers of images; more importantly, you become knowledgeable producers of images.

Some Suggestions for Collecting Images

As you work through this chapter, you will want to have a good selection of images of your own choosing to draw on for class discussions and for your own writing projects. That means you will have to start collecting those images right away. Don't limit yourself only to ad images. The more you pay attention, the more diverse images you are likely to find, so try to make your collection a rich one. Here are a few suggestions to start your collection:

- Clip ads from magazines.
- Videotape television programs and commercials.
- Photocopy pages and covers of textbooks and popular novels.
- Buy postcards of all sorts.
- Pay attention to the posters and other wall hangings you see at home, in dorm rooms, in apartments, and in offices.
- Notice what people put on their office doors.
- Photograph billboards, public murals, shop windows, road signs, shop and restaurant logos.
- Collect CD and audio tape covers.
- Notice T-shirts.
- Clip cartoons from newspapers and magazines.
- Rent films.
- Collect images from cereal boxes and other products with designs or pictures that interest you.
- Capture images from the Web.

- Collect news and entertainment magazine covers and the front pages of newspapers.
- Carry a small notebook with you so that you can describe the images you see but are unable to reproduce visually.

CHOOSING IMAGES

Your teacher might ask you to find specific types of images, like images that depict ethnicity or gender or status, but often when you begin a project like this you won't have that kind of direction. You can begin very simply by choosing images that strike you in some way, for whatever reason. You might like the colors or the design. You might feel you relate to the people in the image or that the image makes you angry or disgusted.

As you more clearly define your own projects for the chapter, your choices will become easier because they will be determined by those projects, but initially collect those images that catch your eye, that make you laugh or ask questions, and that seem typical of attitudes or fashions or values surrounding you. Don't worry if you cannot always explain why an image appeals to you. If it catches your eye for any reason, find a way to add it to your collection.

In the Shadow of the Image

Stuart and Elizabeth Ewen

Stuart and Elizabeth Ewen have written several books and articles on the history and meaning of popular culture. Cultural scholar Stuart Ewen's work includes *All Consuming Images: The Politics of Style in Contemporary Culture* and *Captains of Consciousness*. Historian Elizabeth Ewen's work includes *Immigrant Women in the Land of Dollars*. *Channels of Desire* (1982), from which the following selection is taken, is their first full-length collaboration. The Ewens argue that much of what Americans understand about self-image is actually a reflection of mass-media images. As this essay illustrates, ours is a culture living "in the shadow of the image," whether the image is present in advertising, news reporting, or popular television and film. Everywhere we go, we see images created for mass consumption but aimed at individuals. Sometimes consciously but mostly not, we measure our looks, our moods, our success or lack of it against the appearances that surround us daily.

SUGGESTION FOR READING

This series of vignettes describes the daily, often unconscious encounters Americans have with popular culture and especially with commercial images. As you read each vignette, take note of the effects these encounters seem to have on the characters the Ewens have created. If you begin to lose track of what is going on in this selection, skip to the final paragraphs where the point of the vignettes is explained, then go back and reread individual sections.

Maria Aguilar was born twenty-seven years ago near Mayagüez, on the island of Puerto Rico. Her family had lived off the land for generations. Today she sits in a rattling IRT subway car, speeding through the iron-and-rock guts of Manhattan. She sits on the train, her ears dazed by the loud outcry of wheels against tracks. Surrounded by a galaxy of unknown fellow strangers, she looks up at a long strip of colorful signboards placed high above the bobbing heads of the others. All the posters call for her attention.

Looking down at her, a blond-haired lady cabdriver leans out of her driver's side window. Here is the famed philosopher of this strange urban world, and a woman she can talk to. The tough-wise eyes of the cabby combine with a youthful beauty, speaking to Maria Aguilar directly:

Estoy sentada 12 horas al dia.

Lo último que necesito son hemorroides.

(I sit for twelve hours a day. The last thing I need are hemorrhoids.)

Under this candid testimonial lies a package of Preparation H ointment, and the promise *"Alivia dolores y picasonas. Y ayuda a reducir la hinchazón."* (Relieves pain and itching. And helps reduce swelling.) As her mind's eye takes it all in, the train sweeps into Maria's stop. She gets out; climbs the stairs to the street; walks to work where she will spend her day sitting on a stool in a small garment factory, sewing hems on pretty dresses.

Every day, while Benny Doyle drives his Mustang to work along State Road Number 20, he passes a giant billboard along the shoulder. The billboard is selling whisky and features a woman in a black velvet dress stretching across its brilliant canvas.

As Benny Doyle downshifts by, the lounging beauty looks out to him. Day after day he sees her here. The first time he wasn't sure, but now he's convinced that her eyes are following him.

The morning sun shines on the red-tan forehead of Bill O'Conner as he drinks espresso on his sun deck, alongside the ocean cliffs of La Jolla, California. Turning through the daily paper, he reads a story about Zimbabwe.

"Rhodesia," he thinks to himself.

The story argues that a large number of Africans in Zimbabwe are fearful about black majority rule, and are concerned over a white exodus. Two black hotel workers are quoted by the article. Bill puts this, as a fact, into his mind.

Later that day, over a business lunch, he repeats the story to five white business associates, sitting at the restaurant table. They share a superior laugh over the ineptitude of black African political rule. Three more tellings, children of the first, take place over the next four days. These are spoken by two of Bill O'Conner's luncheon companions; passed on to still others in the supposed voice of political wisdom.

Barbara and John Marsh get into their seven-year-old Dodge pickup and drive twenty-three miles to the nearest Sears in Cedar Rapids. After years of breakdowns and months of hesitation they've decided to buy a new washing machine. They come to Sears because it is there, and because they believe that their new Sears machine will be steady and reliable. The Marshes will pay for their purchase for the next year or so.

Barbara's great-grandfather, Elijah Simmons, had purchased a cream-separator from Sears, Roebuck in 1897 and he swore by it.

When the clock-radio sprang the morning affront upon him, Archie Bishop rolled resentfully out of his crumpled bed and trudged slowly to the john. A few moments later he was unconsciously squeezing toothpaste out of a mess of red and white Colgate packaging. A dozen scrubs of the mouth and he expectorated a white, minty glob into the basin.

Still groggy, he turned on the hot water, slapping occasional palmfuls onto his gray face.

A can of Noxzema shave cream sat on the edge of the sink, a film of crud and whiskers across its once neat label. Archie reached for the bomb and filled his left hand with a white creamy mound, then spread it over his beard. He shaved, then looked with resignation at the regular collection of cuts on his neck.

Stepping into a shower, he soaped up with a soap that promised to wake him up. Groggily, he then grabbed a bottle of Clairol Herbal Essence Shampoo. He turned the tablet-shaped bottle to its back label, carefully reading the "Directions."

"Wet hair."

He wet his hair.

"Lather."

He lathered.

"Rinse."

He rinsed.

"Repeat if necessary."

Not sure whether it was altogether necessary, he repeated the process according to directions.

Late in the evening, Maria Aguilar stepped back in the subway train, heading home to the Bronx after a long and tiring day. This time, a poster told her that "The Pain Stops Here!"

She barely noticed, but later she would swallow two New Extra Strength Bufferin tablets with a glass of water from a rusty tap.

Two cockroaches in cartoon form leer out onto the street from a wall advertisement. The man cockroach is drawn like a hipster, wearing shades and a cockroach zoot-suit. He strolls hand-in-hand with a lady cockroach, who is dressed like a floozy and blushing beet-red. Caught in the midst of their cockroach-rendezvous, they step sinfully into a Black Flag Roach Motel. Beneath them, in Spanish, the words:

Las Cucarachas entran…pero non pueden salir.

(In the English version: Cockroaches check in…but they don't check out.)

The roaches are trapped; sin is punished. Salvation is gauged by one's ability to live roach-free. The sinners of the earth shall be inundated by roaches. Moral tales and insects encourage passersby to rid their houses of sin. In their homes, sometimes, people wonder whether God has forsaken them.

Beverly Jackson sits at a metal and tan Formica table and looks through the *New York Post*. She is bombarded by a catalog of horror. Children are mutilated…subway riders attacked….Fanatics are marauding and noble despots lie in bloody heaps. Occasionally someone steps off the crime-infested streets to claim a million dollars in lottery winnings.

Beverly Jackson's skin crawls; she feels a knot encircling her lungs. She is beset by immobility, hopelessness, depression.

Slowly she walks over to her sixth-floor window, gazing out into the sooty afternoon. From the empty street below, Beverly Jackson imagines a crowd yelling "Jump!…Jump!"

Between 1957 and 1966 Frank Miller saw a dozen John Wayne movies, countless other westerns and war dramas. In 1969 he led a charge up a hill without a name in Southeast Asia. No one followed; he took a bullet in the chest.

Today he sits in a chair and doesn't get up. He feels that images betrayed him, and now he camps out across from the White House while another movie star cuts benefits for veterans. In the morning newspaper he reads of a massive weapons buildup taking place.

Gina Concepcion now comes to school wearing the Jordache look. All this has been made possible by weeks and weeks of afterschool employment at a supermarket checkout counter. Now, each morning, she tugs the decorative denim over her young legs, sucking in her lean belly to close the snaps.

These pants are expensive compared to the "no-name" brands, but they're worth it, she reasons. They fit better, and she fits better.

The theater marquee, stretching out over a crumbling, garbage-strewn sidewalk, announced "The Decline of Western Civilization." At the ticket window a smaller sign read "All seats $5.00."

It was ten in the morning and Joyce Hopkins stood before a mirror next to her bed. Her interview at General Public Utilities, Nuclear Division, was only four hours away and all she could think was "What to wear?"

A half hour later Joyce stood again before the mirror, wearing a slip and stockings. On the bed, next to her, lay a two-foot-high mountain of discarded options. Mocking the title of a recent bestseller, which she hadn't read, she said aloud to herself, "Dress for Success….What do they like?"

At one o'clock she walked out the door wearing a brownish tweed jacket; a cream-colored Qiana blouse, full-cut with a tied collar; a dark beige skirt, fairly straight and hemmed (by Maria Aguilar) two inches below the knee; shear fawn stockings, and simple but elegant reddish-brown pumps on her feet. Her hair was to the shoulder, her look tawny.

When she got the job she thanked her friend Millie, a middle manager, for the tip not to wear pants.

Joe Davis stood at the endless conveyor, placing caps on a round-the-clock parade of automobile radiators. His nose and eyes burned. His ears buzzed in the din. In a furtive moment he looked up and to the right. On the plant wall was a large yellow sign with THINK! printed on it in bold type. Joe turned back quickly to the radiator caps.

Fifty years earlier, in another factory, in another state, Joe's grandfather, Nat Davis, had looked up and seen another sign:

A Clean Machine Runs Better.

Your Body is a Machine.

KEEP IT CLEAN.

Though he tried and tried, Joe Davis' grandfather was never able to get the dirt out from under his nails. Neither could his great-grandfather, who couldn't read.

In 1952 Mary Bird left her family in Charleston to earn money as a maid in a Philadelphia suburb. She earned thirty-five dollars a week, plus room and board, in a dingy retreat of a ranch-style tract house.

Twenty-eight years later she sits on a bus, heading toward her small room in North Philly. Across from her, on an advertising poster, a sumptuous meal is displayed. Golden fried chicken, green beans glistening with butter and flecked by pimento, and a fluffy cloud of rice fill the greater part of a calico-patterned dinner plate. Next to the plate sit a steaming boat of gravy, and an icy drink in an amber tumbler. The plate is on a quilted blue placemat, flanked by a thick linen napkin and colonial silverware.

As Mary Bird's hungers are aroused, the wording on the placard instructs her: "Come Home to Carolina."

Shopping List

    paper towels

    milk

    eggs

    rice crispies

    chicken

    snacks for kids (twinkies, chips, etc.)

    potatoes

    coke, ginger ale, plain soda

    cheer

    brillo

    peanut butter

    bread

    ragu (2 jars)

    spaghetti

    saran wrap

    salad

    get cleaning, bank, must pay electric!!!

On his way to Nina's house, Sidney passed an ad for Smirnoff vodka. A sultry beauty with wet hair and beads of moisture on her smooth, tanned face looked out at him. "Try a Main Squeeze." For a teenage boy the invitation transcended the arena of drink; he felt a quick throb-pulse at the base of his belly and his step quickened.

In October of 1957, at the age of two and a half, Aaron Stone was watching television. Suddenly, from the black screen, there leaped a circus clown, selling children's vitamins, and yelling "Hi! boys and girls!" He ran, terrified, from the room, screaming.

    For years after, Aaron watched television in perpetual fear that the vitamin clown would reappear. Slowly his family assured him that the television was just a mechanical box and couldn't really hurt him, that the vitamin clown was harmless.

    Today, as an adult, Aaron Stone takes vitamins, is ambivalent about clowns, and watches television, although there are occasional moments of anxiety.

These are some of the facts of our lives; disparate moments, disconnected, dissociated. Meaningless moments. Random incidents. Memory traces. Each is an unplanned encounter, part of day-to-day existence. Viewed alone, each by itself, such spaces of our lives seem insignificant, trivial. They are the decisions and reveries of survival; the stuff of small talk; the chance preoccupations of our eyes and minds in a world of images—soon forgotten.

    Viewed together, however, as an ensemble, an integrated panorama of social life, human activity, hope and despair, images and information, another tale unfolds from these vignettes. They reveal a pattern of life, the structures of perception.

    As familiar moments in American life, all of these events bear the footprints of a history that weighs upon us, but is largely untold. We live and breathe an atmosphere where mass images are everywhere in evidence; mass produced, mass distributed. In the streets, in our homes, among a crowd, or alone, they speak to us, overwhelm our vision. Their presence, their messages are given; unavoidable. Though their history is still relatively short, their pre-history is, for the most part, forgotten, unimaginable.

The history that unites the seemingly random routines of daily life is one that embraces the rise of an industrial consumer society. It involves explosive interactions between modernity and old ways of life. It includes the proliferation, over days and decades, of a wide, repeatable vernacular of commercial images and ideas. This history spells new patterns of social, productive, and political life.

SUGGESTIONS FOR DISCUSSION

1. While many of the vignettes describe the effects of ad images on so many of us, others, like the story of Bill O'Conner, the story of the roach motel, and the story of Joe Davis, suggest something about the way information and even cultural attitudes are passed along or processed. Reread those sections and others like them and discuss what kind of information you unconsciously process in your daily life. In your discussion, take into account such things as the choices you make in what to wear, what to take when you have a cold, how to act around others, what to believe about political issues, and the like.

2. The grocery list intersperses generic items like paper towels with name brands that represent generics (like brillo for scouring pads). Consider the products you buy that are brand name. How would you say your own or your family's buying habits are influenced by what appears in newspapers, on television, on billboards, or on bus-stop ads? To what extent do you think those habits are influenced by loyalty or habit, like the Marshes' purchase of a new Sears washing machine?

3. Near the end of this selection the Ewens write, "As familiar moments in American life, all of these events bear the footprints of a history that weighs upon us, but is largely untold." After rereading this series of events, discuss what the authors mean by such a sweeping statement. How do you see that statement illustrated or not in the observations you have made about the way you and the people you know respond to living "in the shadow of the image"?

SUGGESTIONS FOR WRITING

1. Write a series of vignettes of your, your friends', and your family's daily encounters with ad images. Pay attention to how the Ewens' structure their piece. The vignettes lead to a kind of summary statement in which they tell their readers very quickly what the sequence of encounters might mean for them.

2. Make a list of images that you see on most days. The list might include posters, billboards, commercials, magazine and newspaper ads, cartoons, road signs, family and news photos, shop-window displays, for example. Write an essay in which you describe the kinds of images you encounter daily and what those images seem to be asking of you or telling you about the way people should look or act or feel.

3. Near the end of this selection the Ewens write, "The history that unites the seemingly random routines of daily life is one that embraces the rise of an industrial consumer society. It involves explosive interactions between modernity and old ways of life. It includes the proliferation, over days and decades, of a wide, repeatable vernacular of commercial images and ideas. This history spells new patterns of social, productive, and political life." Write an explanation of what you understand the authors to be saying in that statement. In your discussion, provide examples from your own experience or reading that help make the meaning clear for your readers.

Sex as Symbol in Fashion Advertising

Arthur Asa Berger

Arthur Asa Berger is a professor of Broadcast Communication Arts at San Francisco State University. His work on popular culture includes *The Comic Stripped American, The TV-Guided American,* and *Television as an Instrument of Terror.* Throughout his career, Berger has attempted to make accessible the language of media analysis and cultural critique. In this selection and the one that follows, which are taken from two book-length discussions of media analysis (published in 1982 and 1984), Berger provides an analysis of fashion and cosmetics advertisements and a checklist of what to look for when analyzing a visual image.

SUGGESTION FOR READING

Berger does not provide visuals with his analysis, which is based on a series of ads in a 1978 issue of *Vogue* magazine. Before you read this selection, it will be helpful to pick up a current issue of any wide-selling fashion magazine (*Vogue, Cosmopolitan, Elle, Vanity Fair*) and look at the advertisements for fashion and beauty items. You will notice that much of what Berger says about these 1978 ads for beauty items still holds true today.

While reading an issue of *Vogue* recently, I noticed that I was, somehow, taken by a number of the advertisements for fashions and cosmetics. Many of these advertisements contained striking photographs and suggestive (and in some cases rather overt) copy. I found myself absorbed by the advertisements. They had a remarkable power over me—to seize my attention and to stimulate, if only for a moment, fantasies of an erotic nature. It was not only the physical characteristics of the models that affected me; rather it was a kind of gestalt effect. There was the element of graphic design, of color, of light, and a host of other matters that "conspired" to excite me.

"What's going on?" I asked myself. That question led me to consider how magazine advertising works to stimulate desire and sell clothes, cosmetics, and everything else that is connected with beauty (in this case) or any product.

In analyzing an advertisement there are a number of factors that we must consider, such as the ambience, the design, the use of white space, the significant images and symbols, the use of language, the type faces used, and the item itself (and its role and function in society). We can also consider how the advertisement attempts to "sell" us and what roles it offers us to imitate, as well as examine how social phenomena might be reflected, indirectly. (Here I'm thinking about such things as alienation, boredom, conformism, generational conflict, and so on.) We can use whatever concepts we have at our command from history, psychology, sociology, anthropology, and any other disciplines to help us "dissect" the advertisement. In applying all of the above it is important to keep one cardinal principle in mind: The creators of any advertisement are trying to generate some kind of an effect or emotional response. So we must start with the effect and work backwards. What is the fantasy? And how is it induced?

SELLING MAGIC

I will answer these questions by examining some of the advertisements in the April 1978 issue of *Vogue* magazine. I've selected advertisements that, for some reason, caught my attention for a moment and that I think are interesting and worth examining closely.

Let me start with a double-page advertisement by Revlon for its Formula 2 cleanser and moisturizer. The left-hand page of the advertisement is devoted to an extreme close-up of a woman's face, but the face is rendered by using quarter-inch squares of various colors. We are, in fact, given an optical illusion. If we squint, or place the magazine fifteen feet away from us, the squares merge together and form a face. But at arm's length, the face is somewhat distorted and out of focus. It is also larger than life in size. From there we move over to the right-hand page, which has a great deal of white space and is formally designed, approximating axial balance. Generally speaking, large amounts of white space and axial balance (and formality) are associated with quality and "class" in most people's mind.

The copy of the ad stresses science and technology as opposed to nature. We find the following suggestive words and phrases in the advertisement:

Revlon Research Group

skincare system

natural electricity

formula

skincare that's simple, scientific

precision tip

beauty technology

hygiene

principle

All of these terms are signifiers for science and technology; we are led to think of scientists in laboratories discovering remarkable things that lead to "the New-Face Hygiene" and "beautiful life for your skin." A smaller photograph on this page shows two medicinal-looking bottles, in which the future-age Formula 2 cleanser and moisturizer are packaged.

Though this is something of a generalization, there seems to be a polar opposition in the public's mind that posits a world divided between culture (and with it science and technology) and nature. Thus the people who created the Revlon advertisement had two possibilities: to stress nature and all that's suggested by it, or to stress culture, in this case, science and technology. They chose the latter course and offered their readers a minicourse in science and technology: *This* principle leads to *those* results.

Ultimately what is being sold here—and what is being sold in most cosmetics ads—is magic, and that is where the large rendering of the woman's face comes in. It is an optical illusion that has two functions: First, it catches our attention because when we look at the face we see that it is really only a huge patchwork of squares. At first glance it seems out of focus and strange. But, if we squint or stare at it, magically it becomes a face, just the same way that Revlon Formula 2's "beauty technology of the future" gives you the gift of "life" (for your skin). Just as the law of closure forces us to complete that which is unfinished, we find ourselves obliged to make sense of the picture, and we visualize the woman's face even more completely than we find it. This act of visualization is what is asked of patrons or purchasers of the product. From the bits and pieces of their old faces they are asked (almost forced) to envision the new faces they will have with Formula 2.

Now that the face is taken care of, let us "finish off" the job (the law of closure once again) and take care of the entire body. For this we can use Benandré, which says it "will do for your body what a facial does for your face." This single-page advertisement has, like the Revlon advertisement, axial balance and a considerable amount of white space. It shows a woman in a glass bathtub bathing herself in "Mediterranean blue" water. A bit of greenery signifies the Mediterranean here. The woman's face is clearly shown, in profile, but her body is not. We see only a diffused figure in blue-green water. Benandré promises that its special form of collagen (a protein contained in the connective tissues and bones, which yields gelatin on boiling) helps the body retain moisture and helps it to restore moisture it loses during the day.

This matter of keeping the skin (and body) moist is interesting. A great deal of cosmetic advertising stresses wetness, moisture, and related concepts, as if the body were in danger of becoming an arid desert, devoid of life, dry, uninteresting, and infertile. These ads suggest that women fear, or should fear, losing their body fluids, which becomes the equivalent of losing their capacity to reproduce. This, in turn, is connected with sexuality and desirability. Anxiety over the body as a kind of wasteland is implicit in appeals in advertisements about retaining and restoring moisture. Dehydration is a metaphor for loss of sexual attractiveness and capacity, that is, desexualization.

Dry skin becomes, then, a sign of a woman who is all dried up and who is not sexually responsive—and who may also be sterile. This is because water is connected, in our psyches, with birth. It is also tied to purity, as in baptismal rites when sin is cleansed from a person. All of this suggests that words and images that picture a body of a woman as being dehydrated and losing water have great resonance.

In *Man and His Symbols,* Carl Jung (1968: 29) writes:

> Every concept in our conscious mind, in short, has its own psychic associations. While such associations may vary in intensity…they are capable of changing the "normal" character of that concept. It may even become something quite different as it drifts below the level of consciousness.
>
> These subliminal aspects of everything that happens to us may seem to play very little part in our daily lives. But in dream analysis, where the psychologist is dealing with expressions of the unconscious, they are very relevant, for they are the almost invisible roots of our conscious thoughts. That is why commonplace objects or ideas can assume such powerful psychic significance in a dream.

If we substitute "advertisements" for "dreams" in the above quotation, we can understand why and how we are affected so profoundly by images and words.

The copy in the Benandré ad is full of purple prose indicating power and luxury. Some of the more interesting words and phrases appear below:

lavished

unique

expensive

luxury

rare oils

prefer

enriching

treat yourself

beneficial

beauty treatment

This product is sold as a kind of indulgence for women. The copy hints at sex ("You'll make the skin of your body as nice to touch as the skin on your face. Just ask the one who touches you most."), which is always a strong selling point for beauty aids. But the pictorial element is connected with symbols of innocence—baptism, cleanliness, and so on. And the towel in the lower right-hand corner of the ad is a chaste white. From a psychoanalytic perspective, there is also something regressive about all this. It is almost as if the woman emerges with the skin of a baby. She also is quite undefined sexually; we are certain we are seeing a woman, but her sexuality has been subdued a great deal, which is in keeping with "class" as we have been taught to think of it.

Next let us move on to some clothes for our moist and soft-skinned beauty: Danskins. The advertisement for Danskins shows three female bodies lying down on a blue-green piece of fabric that may also be water—it is hard to say. What is interesting is the arrangement of the bodies, all horizontal and jammed together. Two of the models are lying with their heads on the left and the third is between them with her head to the right side of the picture. Although they touch one another, each seems unaware of any of the others—they all stare off into space in separate directions.

The Danskin ad is extremely simple and formal. It has three elements: a headline, the photograph of the three women, and an element containing six lines of copy, all in capitals. The product advertised is a "freestyle" leotard/swimsuit that comes in various "sensuous styles and colors." The large element of white space contrasts with the crowding in the photograph, a crowding that a Marxist would say reflects a diffuse alienation among the women, who are touching one another but do not seem to be aware of each other. They are all, we must assume, pursuing their private fantasies.

Finally, let us move on to an ad depicting a fully dressed woman in Calvin Klein separates. Here we find a model with her right hand on her hip, her left hand behind her head, and her left knee bent (in the "bashful knee pose") and prominently displayed. The background is gray and there is hardly any text. The shirt the model wears has a plunging neckline, but there is no cleavage showing, and there is a slit in the skirt, which enables her to display her knee.

We are given little textual information: the designer, Calvin Klein; the store where the outfit can be purchased, I. Magnin; and the fabric manufacturer, the Ideacomo group.

The model has long, curly hair. She has a rather cold look on her face, a look that is commonly seen in high-fashion advertising. And she is posed in a way that emphasizes her arms and legs rather than her breasts and hips. Thus attention is focused on her appendages, which are sexually undifferentiated. Yet there is something of a sexually alluring quality about this pose, which shows a lot of upper leg. It may have something to do with the tilt of the hips, the twist of the torso, and the neckline. Perhaps the unnaturalness of the pose is important, also.

BREAKING THE ADVERTISING CODE

The codes of simplicity, white space and formality, appear in the Calvin Klein advertisement just as they did in all the other advertisements discussed to this point. These "couture" codes are learned by people, who are taught, by advertisers, to associate simplicity, spaciousness, and formal structure with "class." In the same manner, we are taught the "meanings" of various typefaces and kinds of images. Soft focus signifies dream-like states, formal structure or design implies "classic" (whatever that means), and so on. All of these associations are carried around in our heads, so that all the advertiser has to do is "activate" us by striking the appropriate responsive chord. As Tony Schwartz (1974: 24–25) writes in *The Responsive Chord*:

> The critical task is to design our package of stimuli so that it resonates with information already stored with the individual and thereby induces the desired learning or behavioral effect. Resonance takes place when the stimuli put into our communication evoke *meaning* in a listener or viewer. That which we put into the communication has no meaning in itself. The meaning of our communication is what a listener or viewer *gets out* of his experience with the communicator's stimulus.

Culture, and "couture," which is part of culture, is a collection of codes we learn that provide us with meaning in the world. But how, specifically, do these codes work and how do we find meaning in advertisements (as well as other forms of communication)?

In a magazine (or other form of print) advertisement there are two ways that information is communicated—through the text and through pictorial and design elements. We can examine the text to determine what appeals are being pressed forward and what means are used to lead the reader/viewer to desire the product. Anxiety may be provoked. There may be inducements to self-gratifications of varying natures. Snobbery may be invoked. Any number of techniques of persuasion can be used here. And in the pictorial material there is also a "language" that may be employed to generate the desired feelings and fantasies. I have mentioned some of these techniques: design, size, color, grain, focus, and so on. And I have suggested that we learn to associate certain kinds of advertisements with certain kinds of fashions.

Can we take matters a step further? Can we explain how these associations are made and how the various signs and symbols generate the meanings they do? In some cases, yes. To do so we must expand our vocabulary of analysis. I would like to reintroduce some terms from semiology at this point:

metaphor: relationship by analogy (example: my love is a red rose)

metonymy: relationship by association (example: rich people and mansions)

icon: relationship by resemblance (example: photograph of an object)

index: relationship by implication (example: smoke implies fire)

symbol: relationship by convention (example: Star of David and Jews)

There is a problem in differentiating between metonymy and symbol that I find hard to solve. Neither are motivated or natural, but relationships by association seem to be stronger than relationships by convention. Anything can be a symbol once people learn to accept it as such. But the association between wealth and large mansions seems quite logical. Wealthy people, people with "class," tend to live in large houses, have a great deal of land and space for themselves, and are powerful. Thus spatiality becomes associated with wealth and class indirectly, through the matter of living space found in large homes.

In metonymy, then, the relationships are stronger than in symbols. One important form of metonymy is synecdoche, in which a part stands for a whole or vice versa. Monoca (1977: 135) in *How to Read a Film* suggests that in film "close shots of marching feet to represent an army" is synecdochic and "falling calendar pages" to indicate the passing of time are metonymic, and that it is through metonymy and synecdoche that Hollywood and films in general are able to communicate with people so quickly and powerfully. Thus, for example, sweat is an index of body heat (or nervous anxiety) that functions metonymically since "associated details invoke an abstract idea."

Magazine advertisements function in much the same way, using whatever devices they can to signify "abstract ideas"—what we call signifieds—such as passion, love, romance, and so on. Because these advertisements can use language, they can use metaphor, but more often they also wish to imply or suggest things (fantasies of exotic love, hopes for beauty) through pictorial elements that make use of the devices described above in various combinations.

With these terms we can do more than simply say that signs and symbols work on the basis of associations that people learn and that become codes by which they interpret the world and function in it. For example, let us consider our first advertisement, the one for Revlon's Formula 2 cleanser and moisturizer. Although there are many things going on in this advertisement it seems to me that the most important thing in the ad is the way it forces the reader to turn the optical illusion into a face, which suggests, perhaps subliminally, *magic*. Most cosmetic advertisements involve a belief in magic, but usually the appeals are verbal. In this advertisement, however, we are forced to do a great deal of work, work that "convinces" us that it is logical to believe in magic. Why not? We've just done something magical. We've seen that magic works, with our own eyes.

I see this process as indexical. The Revlon products promise beauty by magic just the way the square patches hold the promise of a face, once we learn how to see the patches correctly. The implication is that Revlon is magic and it will work for you the way your eyes work to figure out the optical illusion. There may also be an element of suggesting that beauty is an illusion and is attainable by all who can employ the correct magic. The picture of the woman in the ad is indexical, but the bottles are symbolic and rely upon the conventional look of medicinal products for their power. The stylishness of the advertisement, with its use of white space and simplicity, is also symbolic. There is nothing natural or logical about our associating white space and simplicity with "class." It is historical, part of our culture, and something that most of us learn.

In the Revlon advertisement and in all advertisements we find a kind of chain reaction taking place. The verbal and pictorial elements in the advertisement function as signifiers that generate feelings and beliefs or signifieds for those who look at and read the advertisement. These feelings and beliefs (and, we might add, hopes, fantasies, and the like) are based on codes (structured belief systems), which, in turn, operate via metaphor, metonymy, icon, index, and symbols in various combinations. Thus, in order to determine how advertisements and other forms of visual-verbal communication generate meaning, we can move beyond the notion of codes and see how the codes themselves function.

It is a fascinating business taking advertisements apart to see how they function and determining what they reflect about society. It is also a perilous business, for there is always the possibility that we are not examining society's fantasies, or those of the creators of the advertisements, but our own. In *The Strategy of Desire,* Ernest Dichter (1960: 11), one of the founding fathers of motivation research, writes:

> Human desire is the raw material we are working with. The strategy of desire is the tool of shaping the human factor, the most important aspect of our worldly arsenal. Human progress is a conquest of the animal within us. No conquest is possible without strategy.

Whether or not advertising and other tools of persuasion are leading us to higher levels of development is questionable. One thing seems quite evident—knowing the strategies used by the people who work at creating and shaping our desire is important, for then we can make more rational decisions and avoid manipulation. The person who is a slave to fashion is often also a slave to his or her own emotions—emotions that can be manipulated by the fashion advertising industry. But escape is possible.

Analyzing Signs and Sign Systems

Arthur Asa Berger

I would like to offer a checklist for analyzing photographs, advertisements, and frames from films in addition to less complicated signs. I am concerned with the various kinds of signs being used, how they generate meaning, how they relate to one another, what they reflect about our society and culture, and the problems they pose for the semiologist or other "interpreters" of signs.

Let us assume we are dealing with an advertisement in a magazine. We should be concerned with some or all of the following matters:

a. What is the general ambience of the advertisement? What mood does it create? How does it do this?

b. What is the design of the advertisement? Does it use axial balance or some other form? How are the basic components or elements of the advertisement arranged?

c. What is the relationship that exists between pictorial elements and written material and what does this tell us?

d. What is the spatiality in the advertisement? Is there a lot of "white space" or is the advertisement full of graphic and written elements (that is, "busy")?

e. What signs and symbols do we find? What role do the various signs and symbols play in the advertisement?

f. If there are figures (men, women, children, animals) in the advertisement, what are they like? What can be said about their facial expressions, poses, hairstyle, age, sex, hair color, ethnicity, education, occupation, relationships (of one to the other), and so on?

g. What does the background tell us? Where is the action in the advertisement taking place and what significance does this background have?

h. What action is taking place in the advertisement and what significance does this action have? (This might be described as the plot of the advertisement.)

i. What theme or themes do we find in the advertisement? What is the advertisement about? (The plot of an advertisement may involve a man and a woman drinking but the theme might be jealousy, faithlessness, ambition, passion, etc.)

j. What about the language used in the advertisement? Does it essentially provide information or generate some kind of an emotional response? Or both? What techniques are used by the copywriter: humor, alliteration, "definitions" of life, comparisons, sexual innuendo, and so on?

k. What typefaces are used and what impressions do these typefaces convey?

l. What is the item being advertised and what role does it play in American culture and society?

m. What about aesthetic decisions? If the advertisement is a photograph, what kind of a shot is it? What significance do long shots, medium shots, close-ups have? What about the lighting, use of color, angle of the shot?

n. What sociological, political, economic or cultural attitudes are indirectly reflected in the advertisement? An advertisement may be about a pair of blue jeans but it might, indirectly, reflect such matters as sexism, alienation, stereotyped thinking, conformism, generational conflict, loneliness, elitism, and so on.

SUGGESTIONS FOR DISCUSSION

1. Bring to class a recent issue of a fashion magazine. With a group of your classmates, look through the fashion and cosmetics ads and discuss which ads seem to be the most interesting or provocative and what makes them catch your eye. You won't all agree on the ads you find interesting, so make sure you take everyone's response into account in your discussion. How closely do the responses from your group correspond to the responses Berger describes?

2. At one point in his discussion Berger tells us, "there seems to be a polar opposition in the public's mind that posits a world divided between culture (and with it science and technology) and nature." How is that opposition reflected in the advertisements you have located, especially for cosmetic products?

3. Berger writes that in analyzing advertising "there is always the possibility that we are not examining society's fantasies, or those of the creators of the advertisements, but our own." How would you respond to that concern?

SUGGESTIONS FOR WRITING

1. With a group of three classmates, select one fashion or cosmetics ad from a current fashion magazine. Begin with the questions Berger poses early in this reading: "What is the fantasy? And how is it induced?" Using the checklist provided at the end of Berger's selection, write an analysis of the ad your group has chosen. Present your analysis to the rest of the class when it is completed. Make sure you have reproduced the ad so that the class can see what you are talking about during your presentation.

2. Berger writes that "In a magazine (or other form of print) advertisement there are two ways that information is communicated—through the text and through pictoral and design elements." Choose an advertisement from a current magazine and, using Berger's discussion of semiology, write an explanation of how the words and pictoral elements in the ad you have chosen work together to create a message. What is the message? How is it conveyed? What alternate meanings can you imagine readers might find in this ad, whether they are intended by the advertiser or not?

3. Art historian John Berger argues that advertising "proposes to each of us that we transform ourselves, or our lives, by buying something more." Choose any one of the ads presented in this chapter and write a brief essay in which you explain how the ad proposes to transform us with the purchase of the product being advertised. Be sure to pay attention to both the ad's image and the ad copy (the words in the ad) for your analysis.

Beauty...and the Beast of Advertising

Jean Kilbourne

Jean Kilbourne is a filmmaker and lecturer whose work primarily focuses on alcohol and cigarette advertising and gender stereotypes in the media. She is the creator of the award-winning *Still Killing Us Softly,* a film that examines images of women in advertising. In 1995, Kilbourne updated her discussion of gender in advertising with the film *Slim Hopes,* an examination of the connection between advertising images and eating disorders in young women. In the selection that follows, Kilbourne explains why it is important that we pay attention to the ways gender is portrayed in advertising today. This article originally appeared in 1989 in the media action magazine *Media & Values*. It was one of a two-part series of articles on images of women and men in the media.

SUGGESTION FOR READING

The essay by Kilbourne and the visual essay that follows have been paired so that you can test Kilbourne's argument against some current images of women in advertising. You can, of course, supplement the visual essay with images that you find in current magazines or images you see in television commercials, on billboards, on CD covers, or anywhere women are used in advertising today.

As you read the article, underline what you consider key points in Kilbourne's argument and note in the margins your own responses to what she is saying. Your response might, for example, include notes about ads that you think illustrate or contradict her position or questions and concerns her argument raises for you. Before you begin discussing this article with classmates, look back at your underlinings and notes, and write an exploratory response in which you record your own understanding of and reaction to what Kilbourne is saying.

To read any ad image, you will have to pay attention to the content of the ad and the actual "look" of the image. The ad images included in "It's a Woman Thing" are clearly not all alike in their representation of women. As you look at these ads, notice such detail as what is written in the ad copy, how the woman looks back at the viewer or not, how she is posed, what she seems to be doing, what effect is achieved with camera distance (close-ups, medium shots, etc.), and what product is being sold.

"You're a Halston woman from the very beginning," the advertisement proclaims. The model stares provocatively at the viewer, her long blonde hair waving around her face, her bare chest partially covered by two curved bottles that give the illusion of breasts and a cleavage.

The average American is accustomed to blue-eyed blondes seductively touting a variety of products. In this case, however, the blonde is about five years old.

Advertising is an over $100 billion a year industry and affects all of us throughout our lives. We are each exposed to over 2,000 ads a day, constituting perhaps the most powerful educational force in society. The average adult will spend one and one-half years of his/her life watching television commercials. But the ads sell a great deal more than products. They sell values, images and concepts of success and worth, love and sexuality, popularity and normalcy. They tell us who we are and who we should be. Sometimes they sell addictions.

Advertising's foundation and economic lifeblood is the mass media, and the primary purpose of the mass media is to deliver an audience to advertisers, just as the primary purpose of television programs is to deliver an audience for commercials.

Adolescents are particularly vulnerable, however, because they are new and inexperienced consumers and are the prime targets of many advertisements. They are in the process of learning their values and roles and developing their self-concepts. Most teenagers are sensitive to peer pressure and find it difficult to resist or even question the dominant cultural messages perpetuated and reinforced by the media. Mass communication has made possible a kind of nationally distributed peer pressure that erodes private and individual values and standards.

But what does society, and especially teenagers, learn from the advertising messages that proliferate in the mass media? On the most obvious level they learn the stereotypes. Advertising creates a mythical, WASP-oriented world in which no one is ever ugly, overweight, poor, struggling or disabled either physically or mentally (unless you count the housewives who talk to little men in toilet bowls, animated germs in drains or muscle-bound giants clad in white clothing). And it is a world in which people talk only about products.

HOUSEWIVES OR SEX OBJECTS

The aspect of advertising most in need of analysis and change is the portrayal of women. Scientific studies and the most casual viewing yield the same conclusion: Women are shown almost exclusively as housewives or sex objects.

The housewife, pathologically obsessed by cleanliness and lemonfresh scents, debates cleaning products with herself and worries about her husband's "ring around the collar."

The sex object is a mannequin, a shell. Conventional beauty is her only attribute. She has no lines or wrinkles (which would indicate she had the bad taste and poor judgment to grow older), no scars or blemishes—indeed, she has no pores. She is thin, generally tall and long-legged, and, above all, she is young. All "beautiful" women in advertisements (including minority women), regardless of product or audience, conform to this norm. Women are constantly exhorted to emulate this ideal, to feel ashamed and guilty if they fail, and to feel that their desirability and lovability are contingent upon physical perfection.

CREATING ARTIFICIALITY

The image is artificial and can only be achieved artificially (even the "natural look" requires much preparation and expense). Beauty is something that comes from without; more than one million dollars is spent every hour on cosmetics. Desperate to conform to an ideal and impossible standard, many women go to great lengths to manipulate and change their faces and bodies. A woman is conditioned to view her face as a mask and her body as an object, as things separate from and more important than her real self, constantly in need of alteration, improvement, and disguise. She is made to feel dissatisfied with and ashamed of herself, whether she tries to achieve "the look" or not. Objectified constantly by others, she learns to objectify herself. (It is interesting to note that one in five college-age women has an eating disorder.)

"When *Glamour* magazine surveyed its readers in 1984, 75 percent felt too heavy and only 15 percent felt just right. Nearly half of those who were actually underweight reported feeling too fat and wanting to diet. Among a sample of college women, 40 percent felt overweight when only 12 percent actually were too heavy," according to Rita Freedman in her book *Beauty Bound*.

There is evidence that this preoccupation with weight begins at ever-earlier ages for women. According to a recent article in *New Age Journal*, "even grade-school girls are succumbing to sticklike standards of beauty enforced by a relentless parade of waspwaisted fashion models, movie stars and pop idols." A study by a University of California professor showed that nearly 80 percent of fourth-grade girls in the Bay Area are watching their weight.

A recent *Wall Street Journal* survey of students in four Chicago-area schools found that more than half the fourth-grade girls were dieting and three-quarters felt they were overweight. One student said, "We don't expect boys to be that handsome. We take them as they are." Another added, "But boys expect girls to be perfect and beautiful. And skinny."

Dr. Steven Levenkron, author of *The Best Little Girl in the World,* the story of an anorexic, says his blood pressure soars every time he opens a magazine and finds an ad for women's fashions. "If I had my way," he said, "every one of them would have to carry a line saying, 'Caution: This model may be hazardous to your health.'"

Women are also dismembered in commercials, their bodies separated into parts in need of change or improvement. If a woman has "acceptable" breasts, then she must also be sure that her legs are worth watching, her hips slim, her feet sexy, and that her buttocks look nude under her clothes ("like I'm not wearin' nothin'"). This image is difficult and costly to achieve and impossible to maintain (unless you buy the product)—no one is flawless and everyone ages. Growing older is the great taboo. Women are encouraged to remain little girls ("because innocence is sexier than you think"), to be passive and dependent, never to mature. The contradictory message—"sensual, but not too far from innocence"—places women in a double bind; somehow we are supposed to be both sexy and virginal, experienced and naive, seductive and chaste. The disparagement of maturity is, of course, insulting and frustrating to adult women, and the implication that little girls are seductive is dangerous to real children.

INFLUENCING SEXUAL ATTITUDES

Young people also learn a great deal about sexual attitudes from the media and from advertising in particular. Advertising's approach to sex is pornographic; it reduces people to objects and de-emphasizes human contact and individuality. This reduction of sexuality to a dirty joke and of people to object is the real obscenity of the culture. Although the sexual sell, overt and subliminal, is at a fevered pitch in most commercials, there is at the same time a notable absence of sex as an important and profound human activity.

There have been some changes in the images of women. Indeed, a "new woman" has emerged in commercials in recent years. She is generally presented as superwoman, who manages to do all the work at home and on the job (with the help of a product, of course, not of her husband or children or friends), or as the liberated woman, who owes her independence and self-esteem to the products she uses. These new images do not represent any real progress but rather create a myth of progress, an illusion that reduces complex sociopolitical problems to mundane personal ones.

Advertising images do not cause these problems, but they contribute to them by creating a climate in which the marketing of women's bodies—the sexual sell and dismemberment, distorted body image ideal and children as sex objects—is seen as acceptable.

This is the real tragedy, that many women internalize these stereotypes and learn their "limitations," thus establishing a self-fulfilling prophecy. If one accepts these mythical and degrading images, to some extent one actualizes them. By remaining unaware of the profound seriousness of the ubiquitous influence, the redundant message and the subliminal impact of advertisements, we ignore one of the most powerful "educational" forces in the culture—one that greatly affects our self-images, our ability to relate to each other, and effectively destroys any awareness and action that might help to change that climate.

IT'S A WOMAN THING

Much discussion over the years has drawn the public's attention to the image of women in advertising. Our opening visual essay, "It's a Woman Thing," illustrates some of the ways women appear in ads today. The ads reprinted below offer a good illustration of how sophisticated advertisers can be as they draw on and challenge gender stereotypes. You will notice that, over a period of time, women have been portrayed in very different and yet somehow similar ways. If you look at the 1927 ad for Mum deodorant in "Mining the Archive" at the end of this chapter, you will see that the image of women has changed, but to what extent has the stereotype changed? Other ads reprinted here make a conscious attempt to overturn the meaning of femininity. The Don Diegos ad, for example, challenges the notion that cigars are for men alone. Of course, not all images of women are the same. You can quite easily extend and change this visual essay by collecting your own images from popular magazines.

As you look at images of people, you will notice that the way you as a viewer are being asked to relate to the person in the picture is often signaled by whether the person in the image is looking at or away from the camera (or you, as the imaginary viewer).

When the person in the image looks at you directly and at close range, a very different message is sent than when the person is depicted as looking down, away from, or beyond your gaze. Some images show the model only from behind, as if an imaginary viewer is looking at the model but the model is unaware of that intrusion (as in a lingerie ad). But if the person pictured from behind is clearly looking at and perhaps pointing to something else that we can see in the distance (like the Grand Canyon or a new car), the suggestion is that the viewer can also see that object and be delighted by it or desire it. In other words, you can put yourself in the place of the person in the ad.

In *Reading Images: The Grammar of Visual Design* (Routledge, 1996), their study of visual meaning, Gunther Kress and Theo van Leeuwen describe the position of the subject in an image as creating either an offer or a demand. They explain the difference between the two in this way (pp. 122–124):

> There is, then, a fundamental difference between pictures from which represented participants look directly at the viewer's eyes and pictures in which this is not the case. When represented participants look at the viewer, vectors, formed by participants' eyelines, connect the participants with the viewer. Contact is established, even if it is only on an imaginary level….[This representation] creates a visual form of direct address. It acknowledges the viewers explicitly, addressing them with a visual "you."…It is for this reason we have called this kind of image a "**demand**": the participant's gaze (and the gesture, if present) demands something from the viewer, demands that the viewer enter into some kind of imaginary relation with him or her. Exactly what kind of relation is then signified by other means, for instance by the facial expression of the represented participants. They may smile, in which case the viewer is asked to enter into a relation of social affinity with them; they may stare at the viewer with cold disdain, in which case the viewer is asked to relate to them, perhaps, as an inferior relates to a superior; they may seductively pout at the viewer, in which case the viewer is asked to desire them. The same applies to gestures. A hand can point at the viewer, in a visual "Hey, you there, I mean you", or invite the viewer to come closer, or hold the viewer at bay with a defensive gesture as if to say: stay away from me. In each case the image wants something from the viewers—wants them to do something (come closer, stay at a distance) or to form a pseudo-social bond of a particular kind with the represented participant….
>
> Other pictures address us indirectly. Here the viewer is not object but subject of the look, and the represented participant is the object of the viewer's dispassionate scrutiny. No contact is made. The viewer's role is that of the invisible

onlooker....we have called this kind of image an **"offer"**—it "offers" the represented participants to the viewer as items of information, objects of contemplation, impersonally, as though they were specimens in a display case.

As you examine the following collection of images, keep in mind how the woman in each image looks at or away from the viewer. This kind of close attention to detail can be useful when you read an image for how it is representing the people being depicted or how stereotypes are conveyed through images. It can also be useful when you make your own images.

Ripe Oregon strawberries are
especially selected as we

feel
it

best complements the rich cream
flavour of Häagen-Dazs.

Häagen-Dazs

FRESH CREAM ICE CREAM

Dedicated to Pleasure

Agnes, have you seen my
Don Diegos?

*A word of warning. Don't let your Don Diegos out of your sight. These hand-
crafted, rich-flavored, premium cigars have been known to disappear into thin air.*

She learned about life in a world of broken glass and blacktop. Where nothing is given. Especially to those trying to play a man's game. But she proved it was her game, too. And from grade school to high school to college, she's shown us that even on a court 100 feet long there's no limit to how far you can go. State Farm is a proud supporter of women's sports and women's dreams.

STATE FARM INSURANCE

Little girls have big dreams, too.

State Farm Insurance Companies ◆ Home Offices: Bloomington, Illinois ◆ www.statefarm.com

SUGGESTIONS FOR DISCUSSION

1. With a group of your classmates, look carefully at the ads reproduced here, paying particular attention to the manner in which each model is posed looking at or away from the viewer. What kind of relationship, as Kress and van Leeuwen describe it, is each image setting up with the viewer? How is that relationship likely to change if the viewer is a man or a woman? What else might determine the viewer's relationship to these images? Once you have examined the relationships established in each ad and how viewers are likely to respond to those relationships, write a group report on how these ads do or do not conform to the current stereotypes of women that you are familiar with.

2. In recent years, advertisers have begun selling what have traditionally been considered men's products to women. The Don Diego ad for cigars is an example. In such ads, men are obviously also a potential audience. In your group, discuss how the Don Diego ad addresses both men and women. How might the message change depending on who is reading it (men or women)?

3. How would you compare the women depicted in the ads reproduced here with Kilbourne's description of women in advertising? To what extent do these images conform to the stereotypes Kilbourne describes?

SUGGESTIONS FOR WRITING

1. Study the advertisements we have reprinted here, and collect additional advertising images that represent women. (You might need as many as ten to twenty collected images from which you can draw, but you won't need to write about all of them.) Now, write an essay that draws on Kilbourne's analysis but extends that analysis to further complicate her argument about gender roles in advertising. You don't have to disagree or agree with Kilbourne. Instead, you should be trying to find a wider range of representations than the one she discusses. In doing that, you will most likely propose a different argument entirely. Or your paper might not argue so much as it extends our thinking about these images beyond the "bad for us" or "good for us" formulation that Kilbourne seems to be working with. For example, you might want to consider how the message of these images changes depending on who is reading them. You will want to think about how the camera "treats" the woman being represented. (Is there a distancing between the viewer and the model? Does the model look at you straight on? What is the effect of that look? Does the model do anything in the ad, or is she just an object to be looked at?) You might also want to look for advertising that breaks from the stereotype Kilbourne describes. Don't dismiss Kilbourne's argument to create your own. As you form your own questions, you will probably want to return to the questions Kilbourne asks and the concerns she has about what these images say to women about themselves.

2. Kilbourne writes, "The aspect of advertising most in need of analysis and change is the portrayal of women." Some readers think that claim is much too narrow. Using Kilbourne's article as a starting place for your

 You have probably noticed that many advertisements today include website addresses. Check them out. Some sites simply tell you how to buy products, but others give you more information. Benetton's site, for example, reproduces all of the past Benetton ads and links you to information about the images, the photographers, and interviews with photographers. This site even summarizes much of the controversy about images that have appeared in Benetton ads. Also, if you want to explore a site that raises serious questions about advertising, try http://www.adbusters.org/adbusters/, where you will find the website for the magazine *Adbusters: Journal of the Mental Environment*.

thinking, begin collecting ads that focus on stereotypes other than images of women. (You might consider images of men, race, ethnicity, success, poverty, age, family, athletes, etc.) Once you have chosen a topic, make sure you collect as many as ten to twenty images. Collecting will be easier if, after you have scanned several magazines or watched commercials, you decide on a focus. For example, you might want to focus on the changing image of men in advertising. Or you might decide that, though there appears to be a change in the old image of men, that change is superficial and not much of a change at all. Sometimes it is easier to write about the stereotype when you find an image that breaks with that stereotype, so don't ignore images that at first do not seem to fit the argument you want to make.

3. In her article Kilbourne asks, "But what does society, and especially teenagers, learn from the advertising messages that proliferate in the mass media?" Write an essay in which you address that question. For this writing, you can draw on the work you have done collecting images, analyzing those images, and talking to your classmates about the images. You might also know particular friends, classmates, or brothers and sisters whom you could write about specifically in terms of Kilbourne's question. Of course, you won't be able to answer her question in a definitive way. Hers is a rhetorical question. She asks it in order to encourage her readers to think more about the problem of media influence. Your response to her question can only be made with reference to what you have experienced, what you have read, what you have noticed in the people around you, and your own analysis of media images and their potential influence on teens today.

Visual ESSAY — PUBLIC HEALTH MESSAGES

Public health campaigns take a number of forms, with messages that appear everywhere from billboards and subway posters to newspaper and magazine ads to public service announcements on radio and television. Like advertising, public health messages are intended to persuade readers, viewers, and listeners to do something. In the case of public health publicity, however, the pitch is not to buy a product but to live a healthy lifestyle—for instance, to eat a balanced diet, stop smoking, drink in moderation, avoid drugs, exercise regularly, use a condom, immunize your kids, have annual checkups.

Like advertising, public health publicity uses images that readers and viewers will recognize immediately to get its message across. As you can see, the Partnership for a Drug-Free America uses an image of happy, healthy children to play on parental fears that drug use could be lurking anywhere.

As is true in all advertising, agencies designing public health messages face decisions about how to sell the message: Should the publicity emphasize the negative consequences of unhealthy behavior or the positive benefits of a healthy lifestyle? The two anti-smoking ads on page 206 offer good examples of each approach.

Can You Find The Drug Dealer In This Picture?

You live in a nice middle-class neighborhood. You don't see drug dealers on the corner. Your kids are only in grade school. Why worry? Because drug dealers don't necessarily look like the ones on television. In fact, studies show that your kids are more likely to be pushed into using drugs by someone their own age – someone they think is their friend.

So tell your children that *anyone* who offers them drugs is not a friend. Next, be an informed parent. Call 1-800-624-0100 and ask for a free booklet called *Growing Up Drug-Free – A Parent's Guide To Prevention*. Then – and this is really important – get to know your kids' friends. And their parents. Because with you in the picture, chances are a drug dealer won't be.

Partnership for a Drug-Free America®

Some of the most interesting cases of how public health messages use images can be found in publicity concerning sexually transmitted diseases (STDs). In the following visual essay, we've assembled five examples:

- The first two posters were directed at men in the military during World War II.
- The third example is a poster from the 1930s, when many states began to require premarital blood tests.
- The fourth example is the cover of a recent pamphlet for teens on STDs.
- The final message is a bus-stop bench that was painted by the cartoonist Mike McNeilly in an "Art Attacks AIDS" program.

SUGGESTION FOR READING

As you look at these public health messages, consider how each uses a familiar image or images and whether it emphasizes negative consequences or positive benefits.

SUGGESTIONS FOR DISCUSSION

1. The first two posters were part of a World War II campaign to stem the spread of syphilis and gonorrhea—the most widespread STDs or "venereal diseases" (VD)—among allied forces. Notice how each poster portrays women. (In the first, a female death figure representing VD is accompanied by Hitler of Nazi Germany and Hirohito of Japan.) What assumptions do these posters seem to make about the role of women in spreading STDs? What assumptions do they seem to make about male sexual behavior?

2. Consider the third and fourth examples—the poster urging premarital testing and the cover of the pamphlet on STDs. Both use familiar images of romantic love, the wedding couple and the rose. How do the public health messages use these familiar images to get their point across? To what extent do the messages emphasize negative consequences or positive benefits?

3. The final example—the bus-stop bench by cartoonist Mike McNeilly—seems quite different from the other public health messages. How would you describe McNeilly's approach? How is it different from or similar to the other examples? Why do you think he has chosen this approach? Do you think it is effective? Why or why not?

SUGGESTIONS FOR WRITING

1. Work together in a group with two other classmates. Assemble a number of public health messages on STDs. (Your campus health center is a good resource, but also notice messages posted around campus or in other public places.) Analyze the kinds of images that appear in the public health publicity. Do your examples use familiar images? If so, are they used in expected or unexpected ways? Do the images seem to transmit messages about negative consequences or positive benefits (or some combination of the two)? How effective do you think the publicity is, given its intended audience? Prepare a report that explains your findings.

2. As you can see from the two "Attention Deficit" graphs reproduced here, anti-smoking media spending increased at the same time that the percentage of teenagers who smoke regularly increased. These figures raise some difficult questions about anti-smoking campaigns. Some critics have argued that the billboards and TV spots actually make smoking more attractive to teenagers, on the theory that anything adult culture tells teens not to do will appear to be cool and rebellious to at least some teens. The same has been said of "Just Say No" anti-drug campaigns. Write an essay that offers your own interpretation of why anti-smoking or anti-drug campaigns are persuasive to teenagers, or why they are not.

3. Design your own public health publicity. Choose any topic you find to be interesting and important (e.g., smoking, drugs, diet, exercise, STDs, alcohol). Decide on your intended audience—college students, teenagers, pregnant women, new mothers. Fashion your message so that it speaks to the particular audience you have in mind. Choose carefully the image or images that can best convey your message.

Attention Deficit

California has sharply increased its spending on anti-smoking campaigns. The stepped-up campaign, though, has failed to stem a rise in teen-age smoking in the state.

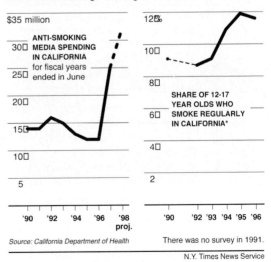

Source: California Department of Health

There was no survey in 1991.

N.Y. Times News Service

REWRITING THE IMAGE

Advertising doesn't just create "images," it constructs differences between men and women, which operate under the assumption that they reflect a universal timeless truth. And so it is never merely a case of a good image versus a bad image. Looking itself has to be rewritten....

It is time for some interventions in the belly of the beast.

There are many methods for upsetting the echelons of imagery. There is no one perfect way to intervene, not when the gospel of perfection is the very text being tampered with. From critiques to billboard activism, the creation of alternative imagery to boycotts and protests, strategic intervention is needed on all fronts. Humor and the unexpected are always good tools for deconstructing the codes the advertising world operates under.

Katherine Dodds, writing in Adbusters Magazine

In his book *Great Advertising Campaigns,* Nicholas Ind reports that in 1985 *Rolling Stone* magazine asked the Fallon McElligott ad agency to increase its total ad pages by 10 percent over 1984. At the same time, the Fallon group had just won the *Wall Street Journal* advertising account. According to Ind, many persons in the company felt that the accounts clashed so seriously (anti-establishment *Rolling Stone* vs. conservative, business-minded *Wall Street Journal*) that one of them would have to be dropped. The ad team had a different idea, however.

Perception.

Reality.

If your idea of a Rolling Stone reader looks like a holdout from the 60's, welcome to the 80's. Rolling Stone ranks number one in reaching concentrations of 18-34 readers with household incomes exceeding $25,000. When you buy Rolling Stone, you buy an audience that sets the trends and shapes the buying patterns for the most affluent consumers in America. That's the kind of reality you can take to the bank.

Instead of dropping either account, they came up with the "Perception and Reality" campaign. These were ads that had very little copy in comparison to the space taken up by visuals, and what copy there was spoke directly to potential advertisers. The ad reprinted here is typical of that campaign. It reads: "If your idea of a *Rolling Stone* reader looks like a holdout from the 60's, welcome to the 80's. *Rolling Stone* ranks number one in reaching concentrations of 18–34 readers with household incomes exceeding $25,000. When you buy *Rolling Stone*, you buy an audience that sets the trends and shapes the buying patterns for the most affluent consumers in America. That's the kind of reality you can take to the bank."

Clearly, these were ads meant to run in trade magazines like *Advertising Age.* By 1991, at the end of the campaign, advertising pages in *Rolling Stone* had increased 58 percent and ad revenues increased 224 percent. Ind writes that advertisers now identify *Rolling Stone* readers as young professionals rather than the counter-culture readers of an earlier generation. That was an important shift for ad revenues because the counter-culture set isn't the most profitable market for most advertisers.

The Perception/Reality campaign is a good one to keep in mind as you look at the images that follow. All of them, in one way or another, constitute a rewriting of the original. Corporations are very conscious of the power of the image, and they rewrite images whenever they think it is most useful for their purposes. The Perception and Reality campaign simply makes that corporate rewriting very easy to see.

Other advertisers habitually do the same. The Energizer Bunny ad campaign has made use of old films, other ad campaigns, and PBS-type nature story coverage to parody those other images and draw attention to its product image: the ever-so-reliable Energizer Bunny. The restaurant chain Boston Market used commercials that rewrote the black and white, somber, rail-thin model images in Calvin Klein ads. In one ad, a full-color promoter of Boston Market pokes his head up among all the black and white images and declares, "Here's a tip: Eat something! You know that burning sensation you sometimes feel inside? That's hunger." Although this ad parody critiques the body image that Kilbourne and Dodds find so damaging, it uses that critique not to warn against the influence of an image but to sell a product perhaps threatened by the too-thin ideal of the original ad.

Of course, learning to read the messages sent through such images and their rewrites is a useful task. No one wants to feel like a dupe of images—corporate or not. Even if you don't care about the messages corporate images send, just to learn how a message is visually conveyed can be an interesting lesson. Still, if you really want to have control of the visual message, then you'll have to do some of that writing and rewriting yourself.

Writing over or remaking an image is an idea that has been around for a long time, even beyond corporations and their advertising teams. Look, for example, at Marcel Duchamp's remake of Leonardo's *Mona Lisa.* The DaVinci portrait had been held up for so long as a masterpiece of Renaissance art that someone like Duchamp, trying to change the way we see the classics, did the unthinkable: He painted a mustache on the *Mona Lisa* (well, actually, on a reproduction of the *Mona Lisa*). It was, we might argue, one of the most effective acts of graffiti ever created, because at the same time that it shocked many in the art world and those who considered the masterpieces sacred, and while it made the public laugh, it also made a statement about how art had to change, how new voices had to be heard and new images had to be accepted.

In the same way, the Canadian-based organization Adbusters advocates rewriting ads that represent unhealthy products, products that promote stereotypes, and products that exploit workers. In the article from which Katherine Dodds's statement is taken, she writes of the importance of this act of taking control of advertising images, many of which you have read and written about in this chapter.

Sometimes, though, a rewrite isn't meant to change attitudes or attack stereotypes at all. Sometimes a rewrite is simply necessary, in a world so thick with images, if we are ever to say something new, or to revise the ways we see each other, or even to laugh at ourselves. Rewriting the image can be activism, as Dodds suggests, but it can also be a way of understanding how images function so that we aren't simply consumers but also producers of the image.

Of course, if we are going to complain about what's produced out there, then the best way to change it is to change it.

SUGGESTION FOR READING

Because parody depends on knowledge of the original to make its point, the message that results from the parody or rewriting threatens to change our response to the original. Duchamp, for example, certainly wanted to change the way viewers saw the *Mona Lisa*. As you look at the images below, make notes for yourself on how the rewrite makes you rethink the original image.

Marcel Duchamp, *L.H.O.O.Q.*

From *Adbusters Magazine*, a parody of KOOL cigarette advertising.

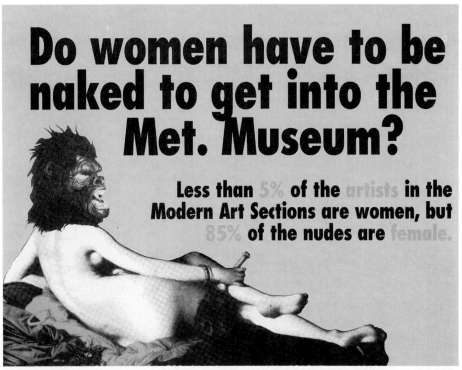

This poster designed by The Guerrilla Girls for the Public Art Fund in New York was rejected by PAF, so the activist group rented ad space on NYC buses to display their message.

Jean Auguste Dominique Ingres, *Odalisque.*

SUGGESTIONS FOR DISCUSSION

1. Some people are offended by the images that result in writing over classic paintings. Others find the rewrites to be funny or powerful statements about the originals. What is your response to the Guerrilla Girls' rewrite of Ingres's *Odalisque*? How would you account for your response?

2. As we mentioned in our introduction to these images, some ads parody other ads not in a direct attempt to comment on the ad but in an attempt to sell a different product (for example, the parody of Calvin Klein ads is used to sell Boston Market meals). What are some of the advantages and disadvantages of creating such a parody?

3. With a group of your classmates, choose a popular image to rewrite or parody. Present your rewrite to the class and explain what your group wanted to accomplish with the image that you created.

SUGGESTIONS FOR WRITING

1. Choose an advertisement or series of ads that illustrates Dodds's statement that advertising "constructs differences between men and women, which operate under the assumption that they reflect a universal timeless truth." Write a brief explanation of what Dodds means, then use your ad or ads to explain how, as Dodds suggests, "Looking itself has to be rewritten." To do that, you can write over the ads creating a parody or you can explain what a reader needs to understand in order to look at these images differently.

2. When you rewrite an advertisement as Adbusters suggests, your purpose usually is to bring to the surface what we have called the oppositional readings that are possible in any ad image. In the Adbuster ad, for example, the word *Kool* for Kool cigarettes is replaced by the word *Fool,* and the ad takes on a powerful new meaning. Find an ad image that you would like to rewrite for any reason, and redo the image in a way that clearly draws on the original yet brings to the surface a new and oppositional reading of the original.

3. Choose any kind of image that interests you: for example, T-shirts, posters, cereal boxes, magazine covers, commercials, famous paintings, covers from textbooks or novels. Rewrite the image so that you bring an alternate reading of that image to the surface meaning or that enables you to create an entirely new meaning (like Duchamp's rewrite of the *Mona Lisa*). To do that you will have to understand the original image, so pay attention to how the image conveys the meaning it carries at this time, and use the original to create your own image. The image you choose and the meaning you make with that image depends on your interests and on the interests of your intended audience. For whom are you making this image? Classmates? Parents? A "general audience" of readers in a particular age group?

Visual ESSAY

A GRAPHIC HISTORY OF PUNCTUATION

Graphic designers Ellen Lupton and J. Abbott Miller are the authors of *Design Writing Research,* from which the following selection has been reprinted. Lupton has served as curator of contemporary design at Cooper-Hewitt, National Design Museum. Together Lupton and Miller received the 1993 Chrysler Design Award for excellence in design. They are co-founders of Kiosk, an imprint of Princeton Architectural Press devoted to publishing works of history and criticism in the fields of graphic design, typography, fashion, and exhibitions. They have published widely on graphic design history, theory, and practice. The following essay, on the history of uses of punctuation, illustrates how choices in graphic design can be as important as words are to convey the meaning of a text.

SUGGESTION FOR READING

As you read, notice that Lupton and Miller use the design of the essay to illustrate the history of punctuation that they are outlining here. Make notes in the margins of the essay to designate for yourself the major changes Lupton and Miller trace in the way texts have been marked or punctuated throughout the history of text production.

Period Styles
A Punctuated History

Ellen Lupton and J. Abbott Miller

GREEKANDLATINMANUSCRIPTSWEREUSUALLYWRITTENWITHNOSPACE

BETWEENWORDS·UNTIL·AROUND·THE·NINTH·CENTURY·AD·ALTHOUGH·

ROMAN·INSCRIPTIONS·LIKE·THE·FAMOUS·TRAJAN·COLUMN·SOMETIMES·

SEPARATED·WORDS·WITH·A·CENTERED·DOT·   EVEN AFTER SPACING BECAME

COMMON IT REMAINED HAPHAZARD   FOREXAMPLE OFTEN A PREPOSITION

WAS LINKEDTO ANOTHER WORD EARLY GREEK WRITING RAN IN LINES

ALTERNATING FROM LEFT TO RIGHT AND RIGHT TO LEFT   THIS CONVENTION

WAS IT   SWOJP XO ƎHT SA ƏNINAƎM NO0ƎH4Ǝ4TSUO8 ꓒƎ⅃⅃AƆ SAW

CONVENIENT FOR LARGE CARVED MONUMENTS BUT BOUSTREPHEDON

HINDERED THE READING AND WRITING OF SMALLER TEXTS AND SO THE LEFT TO RIGHT DIRECTION BECAME DOMINANT A CENTERED DOT DIVID· ED WORDS WHICH SPLIT AT THE END OF A LINE IN EARLY GREEK AND LATIN MANUSCRIPTS IN THE ELEVENTH CENTURY A MARK SIMILAR TO THE MOD- ERN HYPHEN WAS INTRODUCED MEDIEVAL SCRIBES OFTEN FILLED ‡°/‡°(;](;] SHORT LINES WITH MARKS AND ORNAMENTS THE PERFECTLY JUSTIFIED LINE BECAME THE STANDARD AFTER THE INVENTION OF PRINTING THE EARLIEST GREEK LITERARY TEXTS WERE DIVIDED INTO UNITS WITH A HORIZONTAL LINE CALLED A PARAGRAPHOS PARAGRAPHING REMAINS OUR CENTRAL METHOD OF ORGANIZING PROSE AND YET ALTHOUGH PARAGRAPHS ARE ANCIENT THEY ARE NOT GRAMATICALLY ESSENTIAL THE CORRECTNESS OF A PARAGRAPH IS A MATTER OF STYLE HAVING NO STRICT RULES

LATER GREEK DOCUMENTS SOMETIMES MARKED PARAGRAPHS BY PLACING THE FIRST LETTER OF THE NEW LINE IN THE MARGIN THIS LETTER COULD BE ENLARGED COLORED OR ORNATE

TODAY THE OUTDENT IS OFTEN USED FOR LISTS WHOSE ITEMS ARE IDENTIFIED ALPHABETICALLY AS IN DICTIONARIES OR BIBLIOGRAPHIES ¶ A MARK CALLED CAPTULUM WAS INTRODUCED IN EARLY LATIN MANUSCRIPTS ¶ IT FUNCTIONED VARIOUSLY AS A POINTER OR SEPARATOR ¶ IT USUALLY OCCURRED INSIDE A RUNNING BLOCK OF TEXT WHICH DID NOT BREAK ONTO A NEW LINE ¶ IT ALSO PRESERVED THE VISUAL DENSITY OF THE PAGE WHICH EMULATED THE CONTINUOUS UNBROKEN FLOW OF SPEECH

BY THE SEVENTEENTH CENTURY THE INDENT WAS THE STANDARD PARAGRAPH BREAK IN WESTERN PROSE THE RISE OF PRINTING ENCOURAGED THE USE OF SPACE TO ORGANIZE TEXTS A GAP IN A PRINTED PAGE FEELS MORE DELIBERATE THAN A GAP IN A MANUSCRIPT BECAUSE IT IS MADE BY A SLUG OF LEAD RATHER THAN A FLUX IN HANDWRITING

EVEN AFTER THE ASCENDENCE OF THE INDENT THE CAPITULUM REMAINED IN USE FOR IDENTIFYING SECTIONS AND CHAPTERS ALONG WITH OTHER MARKS LIKE THE SECTION § THE DAGGER † THE DOUBLE DAGGER ‡ THE ASTERISK ＊ AND NUMEROUS LESS CONVENTIONAL ORNAMENTS § SUCH MARKS HAVE BEEN USED SINCE THE MIDDLE AGES FOR CITING PASSAGES AND KEYING MARGINAL REFERENCES † THE INVENTION OF PRINTING MADE MORE ELABORATE AND PRECISE REFERENCING POSSIBLE BECAUSE THE PAGES OF A TEXT WERE CONSISTENT FROM ONE COPY TO THE NEXT ‡

ALL PUNCTUATION WAS USED IDIOSYNCRATICALLY UNTIL AFTER THE INVENTION OF PRINTING WHICH REVOLUTIONIZED WRITING BY DISSEMINATING GRAMMATICAL AND TYPOGRAPHICAL STANDARDS BEFORE PRINTING PUNCTUATION VARIED WILDLY FROM REGION TO REGION AND SCRIBE TO SCRIBE THE LIBRARIAN AT ALEXANDRIA WHO WAS NAMED ARISTOPHANES DESIGNED A GREEK PUNCTUATION SYSTEM CIRCA 260 BC HIS SYSTEM MARKED THE SHORTEST SEGMENTS OF DISCOURSE WITH A CENTERED DOT · CALLED A COMMA · AND MARKED THE LONGER SECTIONS WITH A LOW DOT CALLED A COLON . A HIGH DOT SET OFF THE LONGEST UNIT ˙ HE CALLED IT

PERIODOS · THE THREE DOTS WERE EASILY DISTINGUISHED FROM ONE ANOTHER BECAUSE ALL THE LETTERS WERE THE SAME HEIGHT · PROVIDING A CONSISTENT FRAME OF REFERENCE · LIKE A MUSICAL STAFF ·

ALTHOUGH THE TERMS COMMA · COLON · AND PERIOD PERSIST · THE SHAPE OF THE MARKS AND THEIR FUNCTION TODAY ARE DIFFERENT · DURING THE SEVENTH AND EIGHTH CENTURIES NEW MARKS APPEARED IN SOME MANUSCRIPTS INCLUDING THE SEMICOLON ; THE INVERTED SEMI-COLON ; AND A QUESTION MARK THAT RAN HORIZONTALLY   A THIN DIAGONAL SLASH / CALLED A VIRGULE / WAS SOMETIMES USED LIKE A COMMA IN MEDIEVAL MANUSCRIPTS AND EARLY PRINTED BOOKS . SUCH MARKS ARE THOUGHT TO HAVE BEEN CUES FOR READING ALOUD ; THEY INDICATED A RISING , FALLING , OR LEVEL TONE OF VOICE . THE USE OF PUNCTUATION BY SCRIBES AND THEIR INTERPRETATION BY READERS WAS BY NO MEANS CONSISTENT , HOWEVER , AND MARKS MIGHT BE ADDED TO A MANUSCRIPT BY ANOTHER SCRIBE WELL AFTER IT WAS WRITTEN.

EARLY PUNCTUATION WAS LINKED TO ORAL DELIVERY, FOR EXAMPLE THE TERMS COMMA, COLON, AND PERIODOS, AS THEY WERE USED BY ARISTO-PHANES, COME FROM THE THEORY OF RHETORIC, WHERE THEY REFER TO RHYTHMICAL UNITS OF SPEECH, AS A SOURCE OF RHETORICAL RATHER THAN GRAMMATICAL CUES, PUNCTUATION SERVED TO REGULATE PACE AND GIVE EMPHASIS TO PARTICULAR PHRASES, RATHER THAN TO MARK THE LOGICAL STRUCTURE OF SENTENCES, MANY OF THE PAUSES IN RHETORICAL DELIVERY,

HOWEVER, NATURALLY CORRESPOND WITH GRAMMATICAL STRUCTURE: FOR EXAMPLE, WHEN A PAUSE FALLS BETWEEN TWO CLAUSES OR SENTENCES.

THE SYSTEM OF ARISTOPHANES WAS RARELY USED BY THE GREEKS, BUT IT WAS REVIVED BY THE LATIN GRAMMARIAN DONATUS IN THE FOURTH CENTURY A.D. ACCORDING TO DONATUS PUNCTUATION SHOULD FALL WHEREVER THE SPEAKER WOULD NEED A MOMENT'S REST; IT PROVIDED BREATHING CUES FOR READING ALOUD, SOME LATER WRITER MODIFIED THE THEORIES OF DONATURS, RETURNING TO A RHETORICAL APPROACH TO PUNCTUATION, IN WHICH THE MARKS SERVED TO CONTROL RHYTHM AND EMPHASIS. AFTER THE INVENTION OF PRINTING, GRAMMARIANS BEGAN TO BASE PUNCTUATION ON STRUCTURE RATHER THAN ON SPOKEN SOUND: MARKS SUCH AS THE COMMA, COLON, AND PERIOD SIGNALLED SOME OF THE GRAMMATICAL PARTS OF A SENTENCE. THUS PUNCTUATION CAME TO BE DEFINED ARCHITECTURALLY RATHER THAN ORALLY. THE COMMA BECAME A MARK OF SEPARATION, AND THE SEMICOLON WORKED AS A JOINT BETWEEN INDEPENDENT CLAUSES; THE COLON INDICATED GRAMMATICAL DISCONTINUITY: WRITING WAS SLOWLY DISTANCED FROM SPEECH.

RHETORIC, STRUCTURE, AND PACE ARE ALL AT WORK IN MODERN ENGLISH PUNCTUATION, WHOSE RULES WERE ESTABLISHED BY THE END OF THE EIGHTEENTH CENTURY. ALTHOUGH STRUCTURE IS THE STRONGEST RATIONALE TODAY, PUNCTUATION REMAINS A LARGELY INTUITIVE ART. A WRITER CAN OFTEN CHOOSE AMONG SEVERAL CORRECT WAYS TO PUNCTUATE A PASSAGE, EACH WITH A SLIGHTLY DIFFERENT RHYTHM AND MEANING.

THERE WAS NO CONSISTENT MARK FOR QUOTATIONS BEFORE THE SEV-
ENTEENTH CENTURY. DIRECT SPEECH WAS USUALLY ANNOUNCED ONLY BY
PHRASES LIKE HE SAID. „SOMETIMES A DOUBLE COMMA WAS USED IN MANU-
SCRIPTS TO POINT OUT IMPORTANT SENTENCES AND WAS LATER USED TO
ENCLOSED "QUOTATIONS." ENGLISH PRINTERS BEFORE THE NINETEENTH
" CENTURY OFTEN EDGED ONE MARGIN OF A QUOTE WITH DOUBLE COMMAS,
" THIS CONVENTION PRESENTED TEXT AS A SPATIAL PLANE RATHER THAN A
" TEMPORAL LINE, FRAMING THE QUOTED PASSAGE LIKE A PICTURE.
" PRINTING, BY PRODUCING IDENTICAL COPIES OF A TEXT, ENCOURAGED
" THE STANDARDIZATION OF QUOTATION MARKS. PRINTED BOOKS COM-
" MONLY INCORPORATED MATERIAL FROM OTHER SOURCES.

BOTH THE GREEK AND ROMAN ALPHABETS WERE ORIGINALLY MAJUS-
CULE: ALL LETTERS WERE THE SAME HEIGHT. greek and roman minuscule
letters developed out of rapidly written scripts called cursive, which were
used for business correspondence. minuscule characters have limbs
extending above and below a uniform body. Alcuin, advisor to Charle-
magne, introduced the "carolingian" minuscule, which spread rapidly
through europe between the eighth and twelfth centuries. during the dis-
semination of the carolingian script, condensed, black minuscule styles of
handwriting, now called "gothic," were also developing; they eventually
replaced the classical carolingian.

A carolingian manuscript sometimes marked the beginning of a
sentence with an enlarged letter. This character was often a majuscule,

presaging the modern use of minuscule and majuscule as double features of the same alphabet. Both scripts were still considered separate manners of writing, however.

"As he Sets on, he [the printer] considers
how to Point his Work,
viz. When to Set, where; where.· where to make ( ) where [ ]
and when to make a Break. . . .
When he meets with proper Names of Persons or Places
he Sets them Italick. . .
and Sets the first Letter with a Capital,
or as the Person or Place he finds
the purpose of the Author to dignifie, all Capitals;
but then, if he conveniently can,
he will Set a Space between every Letter. . .
to make it shew more Graceful and Stately."
Joseph Moxon 1683

In the fifteenth century, the Carolingian script was revived by the Italian humanists. The new script, called "lettera antica," was paired with classical roman capitals. It became the basis of the roman typefaces, which were established as a European norm by the mid-sixteenth century. The terms "uppercase" and "lowercase" refer to the drawers in a printing shop that hold the two fonts. Until recently, Punctuation was an Intuitive Art, ruled by convenience and Intuition. A Printer could Liberally Capitalize the Initial of Any word She deemed worthy of Distinction, as well as Proper Names. The printer was Free to set some Words entirely as C A P I T A L S and to add further emphasis with extra S P A C E S.

The roman typefaces were based on a formal script used for books. *The cursive, rapidly written version of the Carolingian minuscule was employed for business and also for books sold in the less expensive writing shops. Called "antica corsiva" or "cancelleresca," this style of handwriting was the model for the italic typefaces cut for Aldus Manutius in Venice in 1500. Aldus Manutius was a scholar, printer, and businessman. Italic script conserved space, and Aldus developed it for his internationally distributed series of small, inexpensive books. The Aldine italic was paired with Roman capitals. The Italian typographer Tagliente advocated Italic Capitals in the early sixteenth century. Aldus set entire books in italic; it was an autonomous type style, unrelated to roman.* In France, however, the roman style was becoming the neutral, generic norm, with *italic* played against it for *contrast*. The pairs UPPERCASE/lowercase and roman/*italic* each add an inaudible, non-phonetic dimension to the alphabet. Before *italic* became the official auxiliary of roman, scribes and printers had other techniques for marking emphasis, including enlarged, **heavy,** colored, or **gothic** letters. <u>Underlining</u> appeared in some medieval manuscripts, and today it is the conventional substitute for italics in handwritten and typewritten texts. S p a c e is sometimes inserted between letters to declare e m p h a s i s in Germany and Eastern European book t y p o g r a p h y. **Boldface** fonts were not common until the nineteenth century, when display advertising created a demand for **big, black** types. Most book faces designed since the early twentieth century belong to families of four: roman, *italic,* **bold roman**, and ***bold italic***. These are used for systematically marking different kinds of copy, such as headings, captions, body text, notes, and references.

Since the rise of digital production, printed texts have become more visually elaborate—typographic variations are now routinely available to writers and designers. Some recent fonts contain only ornaments and symbols; Carlos Segura's typeface Dingura (꙳ꙮ ꙮꙮꙮ ꙮꙮꙮ ꙮꙮꙮ) consists of mysterious runes that recall the era of manuscript production. During the e-mail incunabula, writers and designers have been using punctuation marks for expressive ends. Punctuated portraits found in electronic correspondence range from the simple "smiley" :) to such subtle constructions as $-) [yuppie] or :-I [indifferent].

SUGGESTIONS FOR DISCUSSION

1. Lupton and Miller write that "punctuation remains a largely intuitive art. A writer can often choose among several correct ways to punctuate a passage, each with a slightly different rhythm and meaning." To what extent do you believe that you have the freedom to choose the way you punctuate your writing? To what extent would you say you have no choice in the matter?

2. With a group of your classmates, discuss what Lupton and Miller mean when they say that gradually punctuation "came to be defined architecturally rather than orally" so that gradually writing became distanced from speech.

3. What effect do Lupton and Miller achieve with the design choices they have made for their essay?

SUGGESTIONS FOR WRITING

1. Write a brief autobiography of your own experience learning to use punctuation. To what extent have you ever considered punctuation a choice rather than a set of rules?

2. Find a book that you consider to be designed in a very traditional, academic, even dense manner—with rarely broken blocks of small print. Redesign a page of the book so that it is easier to read. In a brief discussion of your design, write an explanation of what you were aiming for and why you made the choices you made. You might want to include, for example, the audience you had in mind with your design.

3. Gather together four to seven books that represent for you a range of design types. This might include a school textbook, a children's book, a cookbook, a novel, a phone book, a "coffee table" book, and more. After looking at the design of the books, write an explanation of what design features identify each type of book. In your discussion, you may want to consider to what extent you recognize a type of book from its design alone.

Visual ESSAY

THE LOOK OF THE PAGE

Earlier in this chapter we suggested that reading the image entails looking at more than what might seem obvious: photos, ads, paintings, film, television, road signs, and the like. All of those kinds of images certainly warrant our attention. Also, it is worth thinking through the cultural messages (stereotypes, values, traditions, and more) that they send. However, pictures or icons are not the only visual texts that surround us.

Even the look of the printed page—the relationship set up between text and image in a book or magazine, the layout of newsprint, the font used, the white space or margins that separate and frame text—all of these constitute the elements of visual texts. The spatial organization of information in textbooks, in magazines, and on the front pages of newspapers already signals a visual knowledge that we draw on every time we choose which newspaper to read and for what purpose.

Moreover, in a highly industrialized, highly literate culture we are schooled to believe that verbal language is more important and more intellectual than visual language. Thus when *USA Today* became what has been called this country's first "national daily," critics charged the publication with "dumbing down" the news, catering to a TV generation, and not publishing serious journalism. By extension, those same critics were charging *USA Today* readers with anti-intellectualism.

The first image reprinted here is from an illuminated manuscript. If you look up the word *illuminate,* you'll see that it means to shed light on something, to make it clear, or to decorate. Although we often talk of words that explain or anchor what we see in a picture (as we did in our discussion at the beginning of this chapter of the Coach ad, for example), the picture in medieval manuscripts probably did just the opposite and more. Instead of the text explaining the image, the image (illumination) may have helped explain what was written. In the case of elaborate decoration, however, the illumination may not have illustrated what was in the text at all, but what it did was to make clear the importance of this text. In that way, the illumination became a part of the message being sent. The actual appearance of the page—how the page looked with image and text taken together—said something like this: What you are looking at is important; pay attention to it. It is something of high value. Treasure it.

Newspapers are not illuminated manuscripts, but they do convey visual meaning just the same. Of course, it is not the image alone that determines the sophistication of the text, but the image (in this case the visual layout of information) often signals intended audience. Nowhere is this more evident than on the front pages of newspapers.

SUGGESTIONS FOR READING

Below are a few general guidelines to help you read the image of the text.

- *Pay attention to the "gray space" of the page.* Although we often talk about "white space" (the amount of blank space surrounding a text or an image), newspaper readers often pay more attention to gray space, that is, the amount of unbroken or infrequently broken text that appears on the page. Gray space generally signals a serious paper, one not aimed primarily at casual readers looking for light entertainment.

- *Pay attention to the image-to-text ratio on the page.* By far, pages that are more image than text tend to be aimed at an audience interested in entertainment who would likely pick the paper up attracted by the photos.

- *Pay attention to the use of color vs. black and white images.* Black and white news photos surrounded by text tend to signal serious news or at least more traditional news formats.

- *Pay attention to the type and size of font used in headlines or with photos.* Big, bold headlines that extend across the front of any paper signal something important, catastrophic, or astounding. Words that are slanted or scattered across a page indicate a more informal, even intimate story being told. As you probably have discovered playing with the fonts on a word processor, the font often has an association all its own. That's why fonts have names like Vivaldi, New York, or Wide Latin.

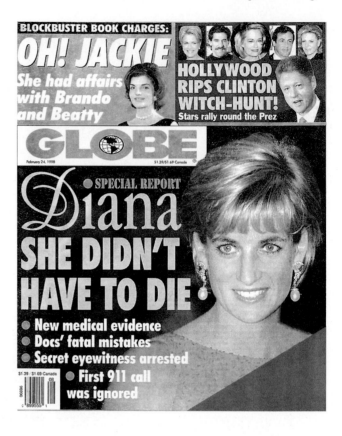

SUGGESTIONS FOR DISCUSSION

1. With a group of your classmates, spend some time examining the front pages of the newspapers that are reprinted here. What, in the visual presentation of the information, gives the impression that some display "serious news" and some do not?

2. What would happen to your impression of the *Wall Street Journal* if you were to take the very same stories, even the same headlines from this front page and give them the look of the *Globe*? (Could the tabloid front page be made to look like the *Journal*?) What particular visual details would you have to recreate to make the *Journal* take on the look of a tabloid?

3. If you were to encounter a text that looked like the illuminated manuscript page reprinted here, what would your impression be? With what do you associate such texts? How often do you encounter them? Where?

SUGGESTIONS FOR WRITING

1. Take a front page of the *New York Times* and create a different image for that paper. In a brief report, explain what type of audience you would like to attract, how the stories included on this page would have to be pre-

sented, and what selections you would have to make about font, image-to-text ratio, and story space to attract that audience.

2. *USA Today* has often been criticized for changing the look of major U.S. newspapers. The charge against this daily is that it is catering to visual tastes and that it is forcing other papers to do the same. What is the problem with appealing to visual tastes? Why do you think critics so harshly attack *USA Today's* appearance? In an exploratory writing, examine your own reasons for preferring one sort of look for newspapers over another. Do you judge people by what you see them reading in public? What purpose do you think a paper like *USA Today* serves to have made it such a popular newspaper in such a short time?

3. Find your own example of a front page from a newspaper other than the three that we have reprinted. Using the reading suggestions listed above, write an analysis of the paper in which you examine what the appearance of the text indicates about the paper. Who seems to be the audience? From its appearance, what kinds of stories do you expect this paper to cover? How much credibility does the paper convey with its appearance?

Mining the Archive

THE LOOK OF ADVERTISING THROUGH THE AGES

Locate old copies of any popular magazine. *Good Housekeeping*, for example, began publication in January 1900, so it represents a full century of magazine design. You'll see a dramatic change especially in advertising design over these years. Once you have found several ads ranging from the early to the mid to the late twentieth century, write a report on your findings, comparing the ad copy (written text) of older ads to current advertising. What role do pictoral elements play in those older ads? How would you describe the change in design over the years? This kind of report is easier to write if you choose one type of product for a focus—for example, cosmetics, bath soaps, laundry detergent, cigarettes.

CHAPTER 5

Style

I have been at odds with the hair on my head for most of my life.
—*Susan Brownmiller*, femininity

Americans live in a style-conscious culture in which even elementary school children know the difference between Airwalks and their generic imitations. That the label means so much even to children may seem surprising until you consider how often all of us characterize people in terms of their clothing, their hair, or their body type. Of course, just as we judge others, we are judged by others on what sociologist Erving Goffman has called our daily "performance." Like the actors in a stage play, we present ourselves to the public daily. Some, Goffman claims, are taken in by their own performance. They present themselves in the way that seems right for their group or social position, without being conscious of how their choices are influenced by the style and manner of those around them. Others are more cynical. They know they are dressing up or dressing down; their style is calculated for the effect it will have on the people they meet.

Although style refers to many things —the way you present yourself to others, your writing, your speech—we will limit our discussion of style to matters of personal appearance. The essays and images in this chapter focus on the hairstyles we select, the ways we choose to dress, and the body types many try to emulate, because those personal preferences in style are among the first choices individuals make as they decide who they are and how they want to appear to others. The hair on our heads, the length of our

"NICE ALTOIDS"
THE CURIOUSLY STRONG MINTS

skirts and shirts, the tight or loose fit of our jeans—all of these choices can absorb many of us, whether we will them to or not.

In many ways, it is certainly fair to say that such a concern for appearance or "stylishness" is trivial. After all, what does it really matter whether clothes or hair or cars or homes are up-to-date or old-fashioned? Why should anyone care? That is a difficult question to answer, and yet somehow many Americans do care. They care a great deal. The cosmetics and fashion industries thrive on such caring. Fashion designers, for example, depend on American consumers to care enough to change styles periodically. Sometimes it seems that manufacturers make those changes on their own and determine what the rest of us will buy, but style is not simply a product of manufacturers. Consumers make choices that have to do with everything from comfort and cost to status and tradition. In our own time, style has been at the center of animal rights controversies, a key to counterculture identities, the statement of teenagers wishing to declare themselves independent of their parents, and always, a guide to economic and social class. Style identifies.

Through close attention to style and the details of dress and look, men and women become visual objects. Furthermore, in our cultural consciousness we have a measure by which we might judge those details. Any one of us standing before the mirror can only evaluate the look reflected by measuring it against a more general look or style popular or unpopular in the culture at the time. Think of how often you judge others based on their clothing or hairstyle or makeup. Such judgment can be made only if you already have an idea of what the person ought to look like in a given situation. How ought a high school teacher or a business executive or a rock singer dress? Of course, not everyone will answer that question in the same way, but most of us share visual experiences that have shaped attitudes about personal as well as public styles. That doesn't mean we all accept the images we see. Style is just as often built on rebellion against the ordinary as acceptance of it.

For many, it is the label that signals class, so the most style-conscious among us shop not simply for look or quality but for designer names. The designer name labels the wearer as someone who can afford Calvin jeans or Tommy Hilfiger shirts. It is the label that promises acceptance. For the fashion industry, then, it is the label that determines cost, not the heft of the denim. Given recent revelations about sweatshop working conditions in overseas markets where much of this designer clothing is made, style can be a much more serious issue than it might initially seem.

Not everyone falls for the latest in high fashion. The look for some is to appear as uninterested in fashion as possible while still remaining hip or stylish. The *street look* does just that. Torn, worn jeans, jackets, and vests layered over rumpled secondhand shirts is one style that cuts across class lines and has many serious shoppers wandering through secondhand clothing stores and rummage sales.

You might feel that you do not want to be told how to dress or whom to impress. You might have already established a style that is yours, not your parents' style or even the style worn by the "fashionable" people you know. Even the most personal style, however, originates from the culture in which it is created. Even those styles that are outright rejections of that culture define themselves with reference to what seem to be mainstream styles. Some groups position themselves outside the values of the mainstream. These subcultures see themselves as offering alternatives to dominant ways of thinking and acting. In the 1980s, punks used dress, hair, makeup, language, music, and dance to declare a separateness. Still, much of what begins as a subculture's style—punked-out hair, rivet-laden jackets, makeup for men as well as women—often enters the fashion market later as popular, stylish dress. "Distressed" or torn jeans, for example, are no longer a symbol of poverty or defiance but a marker of wealth or hipness. Subculture styles that are incorporated into mainstream fashion are most often incorporated without the politics that motivated them. When that happens, the fashion generated by the subculture no longer carries with it the power of difference, so the subculture style will inevitably change.

READING STYLE

We open this chapter with the question of how style is linked to identity. Marjorie Garber's "The Clothes Make the Man" and Wendy Chapkis's interview with Joolz raise questions of what it means to break with convention when convention itself changes periodically. As Garber points out, before World War I, the color pink was coded as a "boy" color while blue was for girls. There is nothing natural about dressing baby girls in pink and baby boys in blue in hospital wards. It is just the current habit of mind. Joolz—a woman who made every effort to look different—tells us that she likes taking risks, looking strong. She doesn't want to look like all the secretaries in offices all over the city. Her story might serve to remind you of the decisions you have made or decisions you have seen others make in the way you and your friends look.

The next two selections, Henry Louis Gates's "In the Kitchen" and bell hooks's "Straightening Our Hair," make very clear how choices that we wish were private and personal can sometimes be political as well, especially for those whose looks do not conform to mainstream media images. In your writing assignments you will be asked to consider what it means in this or any culture to look different, not to conform to the standard model because of things you cannot control—ethnicity, race, body type, or simply the way you have been raised.

The selections that follow, John Molloy's "Dress for Success" and Dick Hebdige's "Style in Revolt: Revolting Style," explore the role fashion plays in determining how people are received by those in power or by what we think of as the mainstream. In his study of punk fashions, Hebdige examines the ways those who wish to defy the mainstream express their defiance through style. Molloy's text, on the contrary, assumes that we all want to look upper middle class and that to succeed, in the business world at least, we *must* look upper middle class.

In examining style as visual culture, we have included an excerpt on the male nude and body building ads, from a longer work by Richard Leppert. Although style is often represented as a female concern when it comes to discussions of body types, Leppert illustrates how that obsession with the impossibly perfect body is also a concern for men, especially when we think of the pumped-up look that is currently one very popular fashion.

As in the chapter on images, you will be asked to pay particular attention to visual detail and to choices that you make as you dress or buy a particular product or create a look for yourself or judge others based on the look they have chosen. You can begin by paying more careful attention than you normally do to such choices. Even if you have made a decision to ignore stylishness, you are making a decision about style and what it means in the larger culture. Why do you buy one pair of jeans and not another? Why do you wear your hair the way you do? Do you see models (the word means *example* or *prototype*) that you want to emulate? Do you want to be thinner, taller, fuller, darker—anything but what you are? Your answers to questions like these can help you sort out some of the notions you already hold about style and stylishness in this culture. You can very easily begin with yourself when you ask questions about style, but you need not remain focused on yourself for long. In fact, the questions become even more interesting when you ask them about entire groups or when you place them in more serious political contexts.

That style is a powerful motivator in this culture ought to be obvious from such recent phenomena as the boom in the designer clothing market or the push even in some public schools to adopt a school uniform, thus avoiding some of the schoolyard wars that have been waged over one kind of athletic shoe or another. But jeans, shoes, and uniforms are simply the most recent and most obvious manifestations of our obsession with style. The significance of this obsession must be understood in terms of its connection to an entire culture, not just one group of consumers.

Clothes Make the Man

Marjorie Garber

Marjorie Garber is the William R. Kenan Jr. Professor of English and director of the Center for Literacy and Cultural Studies at Harvard University. In her introduction to *Vested Interests: Cross-Dressing and Cultural Anxiety* (1992), from

which this selection is taken, Garber writes that an investigation of clothing—
especially the history of and our fascination with cross-dressing—can tell us
much about how "clothing constructs (and deconstructs) gender and gender
differences." Very generally, cross-dressing is the practice of men dressing like
women or women dressing like men. However, as Garber makes clear in her
study, what we identify as male or female has changed over the decades.

SUGGESTION FOR READING

After you have read this short selection, write a brief exploratory note in
which you discuss your own response to Garber's discussion of gender identity and clothing.

Although the logic of anatomy might suggest otherwise, skirts are the traditional garb of
women and pants the traditional garb of men—harem bloomers and kilts, the exceptions that
prove the rule.

    Boston Globe Magazine, *August 28, 1988*

When you meet a human being, the first distinction you make is "male or female?" and you
are accustomed to make the distinction with unhesitating certainty.

    Freud, "Femininity"[1]

Dressed as I am in jeans and a sweater, I have no idea to which sex the policemen will suppose
me to belong, and must prepare my responses for either decision. I feel their silent appraisal
down the corridor as I approach them, and as they search my sling bag I listen hard for a "Sir"
or a "Ma'am" to decide my course of conduct.

    Jan Morris, Conundrum: An Extraordinary Narrative of Transsexualism[2]

Many readers of the *New York Times* were startled recently to learn that one of their most
cherished assumptions about clothing and gender was, apparently, without ground.
Baby clothes, which since at least the 1940s have been routinely divided along gender
and color lines, pink for girls, blue for boys, were, said the *Times,* once just the other way
about. In the early years of the twentieth century, before World War I, boys wore pink ("a
stronger, more decided color," according to the promotional literature of the time) while
girls wore blue (understood to be "delicate" and "dainty"). Only after World War II, the *Times*
reported, did the present alignment of the two genders with pink and blue come into being.[3]

Few articles in the *Times* occasioned as much casual astonishment, at least among people of my acquaintance. It was generally known that infants and small children had for hundreds of years been dressed alike, in frocks, so that family portraits from previous centuries
made it difficult to tell the young boys from the girls. "Breeching," as a rite of passage, was a
sartorial definition of maleness and incipient adulthood, as, in later periods, was the all-
important move from short pants to long. Gender differentiation grew increasingly desirable
to parents as time went on.[4] By the closing years of the twentieth century the sight of little
boys in frilly dresses has become unusual and somewhat risible; a childhood photograph of
macho author Ernest Hemingway, aged almost two, in a white dress and large hat festooned
with flowers, was itself the focus of much amused critical commentary when reproduced in
a best-selling biography—especially when it was disclosed that Hemingway's mother had
labeled the photograph of her son "summer girl."[5]

Despite this general awareness of the mutability of infant style, the pink-blue reversal
came as something of a shock. In a society in which even disposable diapers had now been

gender-color-coded (pink for girls, blue for boys, with anatomically correct extra absorbency in the front or middle) the idea that pink was for boys was peculiarly destabilizing. Notice that it is the connotations of the colors, and not the perception of the genders, that has changed. But what was so particularly fascinating about this detail from the recent history of taste? I think, perhaps, the fact that it reversed a binarism—that it disconcerted not only feelings of tradition, continuity, and naturalness (rather than arbitrariness) of association, but also a way of reading.

The same kind of slightly comic consternation, still on the level of the gender-codes of the child, was produced by the recent discovery of a cross-dressed "Ken" doll ("Barbie's long-term boyfriend) in a sealed box sold by the Mattel corporation. Nattily attired in a pink tutu with lace flounces, a handbag slung over his shoulder, Ken stares cheerfully out from the plastic window of a box labeled "My first Ken—He's a handsome prince!" Above his head appears the legend, "So easy to dress!" Offered a regular Ken in exchange, the consumer, who collects Barbies and Kens, declined because she thought the cross-dressed version would be more valuable. Articles on what *Fortune* magazine called "the kinky Ken" made headlines in newspapers and magazines across the country.[6]

Nor, needless to say, are the gender ambiguities of color-coded dress limited to children. In the 1990s, now that television has made the red necktie *de rigueur* for male politicians and custom decrees it as a standard accessory for male professionals—lawyers, professors, and television anchormen—it is somewhat startling to learn that red ties not all that long ago declared their wearers to be homosexuals. The Chicago Vice Commission of 1909 reported that male homosexuals recognized each other by wearing red neckties, a fact that had already been noted in the streets of New York and Philadelphia by the sexologist Havelock Ellis.[7]

When I was in grade school in the 1950s it was *green*, not red, which was for some reason considered to be the "homosexual" color; to wear green inadvertently on a Thursday was to be the butt of jokes all the more tiresome for not being fully understood. These days it is lavender, or purple, that is the color that proclaims gay self-identification—lavender, and also pink, in the pink triangles used by the Nazis to label and stigmatize homosexual men, now defiantly "inverted" by gay activists on T-shirts and buttons as a sign of gay pride. In the period of less than a century the self-identification of gays and lesbians through what Ellis called "the badge of all their tribe"[8] has moved from a covert and localized practice aimed at mutual recognition to a global phenomenon with encompassing political implications. Pink, that "strong, decided" color for boys, now identifies—when they choose it to—gay men and lesbians. What goes around, comes around.

Notes

1. Sigmund Freud, "Femininity," in *New Introductory Lectures on Psycho-Analysis* (1933). *The Standard Edition of the Complete Psychological Works of Sigmund Freud,* general editor James Strachey (London: The Hogarth Press and The Institute for Psycho-Analysis, 1964), 22:113.

2. Jan Morris, *Conundrum: An Extraordinary Narrative of Transsexualism* (New York: Henry Holt and Co., 1974; 1986), 110.

3. Feminist Charlotte Perkins Gilman was one of the few to protest against "the premature and unnatural differentiation in sex in the dress of little children," arguing that "a little child should never be forced to think of this distinction." Charlotte Perkins Gilman, "Children's Clothing," *Harper's Bazaar,* January 1910, 24.

4. Kenneth S. Lynn, *Hemingway* (New York: Simon and Schuster, 1987), opposite 289. Lynn's captions for other childhood photographs of Hemingway point out that his mother raised him and his older

sister Marcelline as "twins," dressing them both in the clothing of the same gender, sometimes male, sometimes female. That Hemingway's youngest son Gregory should himself have become a cross-dresser (*Exposure* 3,2 [July 1990]: 109) is probably a coincidence—but nonetheless adds another twist to the fascinating and complex Hemingway story.

5. *Fortune*, August 27, 1990, 14.

6. Vern L. Bullough, *Sexual Variance in Society and History* (Chicago: University of Chicago Press, 1976), 610. Bullough speculates interestingly about "whether homosexuals had earlier adopted red as a color in Chicago or whether they wore red because Havelock Ellis told them it was the thing to do." Bullough, 611.

7. Havelock Ellis, *Studies in the Psychology of Sex* (New York: Random House, 1936), 1:299–300.

8. Sally Jacobs, "You Do What You Need to Do," *Boston Globe*, August 2, 1988, 2.

SUGGESTIONS FOR DISCUSSION

1. In your experience, how crucial is it that certain colors and certain clothing styles denote male or female?

2. One stock gag in popular film and television is the cross-dressed male forced for some reason beyond his control to dress like a woman—usually to infiltrate a place normally not accessible to men. With a group of your classmates, list a series of programs (for example, sitcoms like *The Drew Carey Show*) or films (like *Tootsie*) that you recall having used that gag. What makes it funny? Is it as funny when a woman dresses like a man? How do you account for the difference?

3. With a group of your classmates, make a list of celebrities (like Dennis Rodman, Madonna, Boy George, etc.) who have made it part of their media presence to defy gender-identifying styles—especially clothing, makeup, and hairstyles. How would you say the celebrities you have listed use their gender-bending styles to their advantage?

SUGGESTIONS FOR WRITING

1. Garber remembers schoolyard teasing when "green on Thursday" was the marker of difference. Write your own story of schoolyard teasing or of how you and your friends or others sorted people out or teased or identified with each other based on the styles popular when you were growing up.

2. A number of films (*Victor/Victoria, Tootsie, The Birdcage, La Cage aux Folles, Priscilla: Queen of the Desert, Mrs. Doubtfire, Some Like It Hot*, among others) use cross-dressing as the central plot line. Choose one of those films and write an analysis of how dressing and cross-dressing are used in the film to question or to reinforce gender identification.

3. Go back to the exploratory response you wrote after reading Garber. Use that response as a starting point for a paper in which you present your own position on how gender is or is not (or should or should not be) signaled by dress.

Dress as Success: Joolz

Wendy Chapkis

Wendy Chapkis began writing a journal to deal with the attacks she often experienced on the street. Men and children, in particular, felt comfortable laughing at or commenting on the fact that she has a "mustache." A woman, we all know, is not supposed to have a mustache. Through that experience, Chapkis began the book *Beauty Secrets: Women and the Politics of Appearance,* published in 1986, from which the following selection is taken. In *Beauty Secrets,* Chapkis writes of how cultural ideals of beauty are passed on to us through film, advertising, and even such self-help books as John Molloy's *Dress for Success,* from which a selection is reprinted later in this chapter. Chapkis's book also includes interviews with women who do not fit the customary idea of beauty. Joolz, the woman in the interview that follows, talks of what it meant to her to look different, to try to make a statement with her hair and clothes and tattoos. "My image," Joolz tells the interviewer, "may have more to do with fantasy than punk in the pure sense."

SUGGESTION FOR READING

As you read, keep in mind that this is an excerpt from an interview. The speaker is not analyzing punk fashion. Instead, she is telling her own story of wanting to look and to be different, wanting to show her "strength" through the way she looks.

Punks are rejecting their class position, but you have to be there before you can reject it.

Joolz

I was nineteen when I married a man who became a Satan's Slave. During the time I was with him, I looked pretty normal. Bikers don't like outrageous looking girls—at all. They do like "nice-looking" girls, though. And they prefer it if you have long hair. It fits with the heavy metal image.

You aren't to wear too much makeup or anything like that, and you wear jeans or trousers because you are on the bike so much. Though some of the girls did wear miniskirts which I always thought pretty stupid under the circumstances. The men clearly liked very girly girls. Oh, and they preferred blondes!

I never paid too terribly much attention to how I was supposed to look. I wore my hair short. It was more comfortable under the helmet. And I used to walk around in boy's clothes all the time. It was a bit of a problem for my husband in the club. But eventually they accepted me because they decided I was artistic and if I was an artist I was allowed to be eccentric. In general, the women were expected to be very domestic and they were.

The club is a close tribal community. Because my background had been so insecure, I found it very reassuring in the beginning. But after five years, I left. It had become too restrictive.

Even before I left my husband, I already had become interested in the punk image. I had already dyed my hair pink—something which didn't go down well in the club.

To dye your hair this color, you've got to first bleach it absolutely white, to strip it right down to the roots. I've had it this way for four years now. Pink was an easy first choice; it was a fashionable color, if you remember. Shocking pink and fluorescent green, those were the colors associated with punk. Nowadays, I have it colored a bright scarlet, Fire Red.

Even when I was a child I wanted colored hair. I remember wanting waist-length green hair because there was this puppet in a children's show on television, a mermaid who never spoke but was extremely beautiful and had long green hair.

I've always tended toward fantasy, the fantastic. In fact my image may have more to do with fantasy than punk in the pure sense. Punk started off anti-fashion. So you set out to make yourself look as anti-pretty as possible. But I've always been too insecure to do it properly. I worry too much about what I actually look like.

My mother is very beautiful—feminine, small and pretty in the magazine style. I take after my father who is big. When I was a child, my mother was very disappointed in me and was always trying to make me more presentable. Other people's mothers used to shout at them for wearing makeup; my mother used to shout at me for not wearing any.

When I was an adolescent, I suffered very badly from acne. I was also overweight. So I was sort of a tall, fat, spotty teenager. I had good teeth though. My mother used to tell me "you have good teeth; smile, it's your best feature."

Having been a hideous adolescent, I've always been too insecure to intentionally make myself more hideous. I tend to sort of go to the "glam" side of punk rather than the anarchy end. I always wanted a Mohican, but I never quite had the nerve to shave my head. I did have very, very short hair at one point, and I looked like a dog. And being big as well I was mistaken for a boy all the time. There are lots of things I wish I had the nerve to do with myself, but I just can't.

It's relative, of course. I suppose the way I look appears pretty outrageous to other people. Something like having a pierced nose I don't even think about anymore. But a lot of people seem to find it shocking.

My tattoos draw a lot of attention too. I got tattooed for the first time when I was about nineteen. I had one on my wrist and another around my ankles. I thought they were alright at the time—a sort of bracelet of flowers. But I only recently met a really good tattooist and have had new tattoos done over the old ones. These are in the Celtic style and are much better and much more extensive. Tattoos and tattooing fascinate me.

There are moments, though, when you get tired of it all. Everybody who looks this different feels that way sometimes, even if they don't admit it. There are mornings when I wake up and know I have to go down to the shops and wish that I looked like a perfectly ordinary person. But they are not often enough for me to want to change anything.

Not too long ago, for a giggle, I borrowed a plain brown wig off a friend and put it on. It looked pretty convincing. I didn't put on much makeup and went to a gig that way. People who have known me for months and months didn't recognize me.

It was tremendous. But after a while, I didn't find it tremendous at all. I found it extremely unpleasant. I actually entered a state of panic. I was so relieved to take the wig off and be myself again. I felt I had lost my whole personality. My whole statement was gone and I really hated it.

The tattoos are the big thing actually. The scarlet hair you can just cut off if you get tired of it. But when you take the step of having big tattoos so close to the hands, you really make a permanent statement, especially as a woman.

I always wear long skirts and I always wear black. I don't wear jeans anymore because I wore them for so long when I was biking that I just got sick of them. They feel constricting to me. Same with underwear.

Despite all the black and the tattoos and the skull rings, some of my stage costumes, made of lycra and sequins, are extremely glam. I love feather boas and fans. But always with studs;

say a studded belt at the waist. It is the combination that appeals to me. To be too completely glam would be tiresome. I like to confuse the eye.

The most important statement I am making through what I look like is one of strength. I have a strong personality and want to indicate that straight away. Especially in the business I am in, it is important to have a strong image. Not just from the point of selling your records, but more importantly so that from the moment you walk into a venue you are noticed by the sound crew, the security men, everyone. They've got to know right away you are not someone to be messed with. This is particularly true for a woman. The rock business is totally sexist. If you are not a strong person, they will walk all over you.

Of course sometimes the way I look frightens people I have no reason to want to impress with my strength. I was taking a train recently that was absolutely full—people were standing in the corridors—and there was an empty seat next to me but nobody would sit in it. People will often stare, but they don't want to get too close and only rarely will they try to make contact.

Sometimes it seems that people feel that if you look "odd" it is a license for them to abuse you or threaten you; it's as if the normal rules of politeness in society don't apply anymore. You've given up straight looks, therefore you've given up any right to be treated with respect.

A lot of people, particularly middle class people, look at punk and think it is a working class thing. But actually there are few working class punk rockers. Only children of the middle class can afford to look ragged. It is a class statement, but not in the way people tend to assume. Punks are rejecting their class position, but you have to be there before you can reject it. And I am not saying that rejecting everything that's expected of you is easy.

It is, in fact, very difficult to actually put yourself outside of society; to appear so different that you are beyond the normal relationships most women have. I don't blame girls who are secretaries during the day and backcomb their hair a bit at night to come to the clubs. For those girls, punk is just fashion.

In a way, I am jealous of them because, in the end, they can become normal. They can submerge themselves in the great stream of weddings and tumble dryers. But I also think that, somewhere inside them, they're disappointed. They know they have experienced a failure of nerve.

I have my hair done by a woman named Lorraine. She works in a very small salon in the suburbs. Every time I go in there, I see this row of ladies with The Perm under the dryers just having had The Cut—whichever one it is at the time. I once asked Lorraine "don't you ever get tremendously sick of doing this?" And she said "If another woman comes in who wants that Perm I'll scream and go mad!" But of course she'd then go and start rolling up the next woman's hair....

The clients watch her working on me and they are fascinated. They'll come over and feel my hair and ask questions. It must be tremendously tempting for them to say "the hell with it; make mine scarlet too!"

SUGGESTIONS FOR DISCUSSION

1. What Joolz accomplishes in this interview is something that isn't easy. She tells the story of her own decisions to look the way that she does. Most of us are probably not as aware as Joolz seems to be about why we have made personal decisions about our "style." With a group of your classmates, recap Joolz's story. About how many of your own style decisions could you talk this openly? Why is it difficult for many people to talk openly about such decisions?

2. Joolz talks about wanting to show strength in her looks and about wanting to be different, but there are also people in her life who seem to have influenced the way she looks. In what ways did her husband, her parents, and the people she sees in the beauty shop have something to do with the decisions she has made?

3. Joolz tells us, "Sometimes it seems that people feel that if you look 'odd' it is a license for them to abuse you or threaten you; it's as if the normal rules of politeness in society don't apply anymore. You've given up straight looks, therefore you've given up any right to be treated with respect." With a group of your classmates, discuss the kind of situation Joolz is talking about. When, if ever, have you witnessed the kind of attitude she identifies? To what extent do you think public approval accounts for the ways many people dress or wear their hair or makeup?

SUGGESTIONS FOR WRITING

1. Write your own autobiography of why you dress or look the way that you do. As you write, you'll want to think through how you make choices about your own appearance (including what chances you will and won't take with your appearance). Are there people or events that you can identify as having had an influence on how you look? Are there changes you'd like to make? Your autobiography can be fairly brief—three to four pages—but it should be thoughtful in the same way that Joolz is thoughtful about the choices she has made and the consequences of some of those choices.

2. Interview someone you see as breaking with convention in the way that person chooses to look. (See Chapter 1 for more information on interviewing.) In preparation for your interview, team up with a group of four to five classmates to make a list of questions you might ask to determine how the person you interviewed made choices pertaining to his or her appearance. Make sure you also cover some of the issues Joolz brings up—issues such as how others react to this person's appearance and how that makes the person feel about fitting in or not. Using Joolz as a model, write up your interview as a biography of personal style.

3. Interview someone you suspect would not approve of the way Joolz or others like her break with social conventions in the way they choose to look. (See Chapter 1 for more information on interviewing.) In this interview, make sure that you try to understand why the person you have chosen to interview holds these opinions. What style choices does this person make that he or she can easily talk about? What does this person consider to be out of bounds and why? Write a summary of this interview; then bring it to class to share with a group of your classmates. In your groups, prepare a report on your findings to present to the class. In your presentation, include the opinions held by the people your group has interviewed as well as the group's conclusions about how style has the potential to identify us.

 For a glimpse of some of the wildest current styles and trends, try checking out the Web. You can find Web pages on tattooing, body piercing, body building, high-fashion models, and more. These pages can become a useful resource for you, so take note of Web addresses to share with other classmates or for your own work as you continue to think and write about the culture of style. You can find many such sites simply by using a search engine like Lycos, Yahoo!, or AltaVista and entering the words body + art or body + building or simply tattoos. To take a closer look at some of this "Body Art," use the search tool Image Surfer, which will lead you to collections of images that you can use to supplement your writing about current styles.

PERSPECTIVES: THE POLITICS OF STYLE

Style is, as we all know, a personal choice, and most of the time we not only don't want to think very much about that choice but we probably don't want others challenging us on our choices, as Joolz makes clear in her interview. Yet even the choices we make about appearance can sometimes be unexpectedly political, and they are certainly personal. They are about how we grew up, who we wanted to be, who we admired, and what we notice going on around us.

In the sixties, African American men and women were confronted with one of those unexpected political challenges about private choices: As a statement about African American heritage and beauty, they were being challenged to stop straightening their hair. Yet as both of the writers below make clear, the very ritual of hair straightening has remained with them as a powerful and pleasant memory.

We have paired the following essays because they complement each other so well in the way each author deals with the same topic. However, the essays are not the same, and the two writers—though they may hold many opinions in common—do not come to the same conclusions about this topic. Both are, however, writing of a situation that is at once a very private and public one.

In the Kitchen

Henry Louis Gates, Jr.

Henry Louis Gates Jr. is the W. E. B. DuBois Professor of Humanities at Harvard University. He writes extensively on issues of race and culture for such publications as the *New York Times, Harper's Magazine,* and the *Village Voice.* His essay "In the Kitchen" is excerpted from Gates's memoir *Colored People* (1994), a book that begins with a letter to his children. In it he writes, "I have written to you because of the day when we were driving home and you asked your mother and me just exactly what the civil rights movement had been all about and I pointed to a motel on Route 2 and said that at one time I could not have stayed there. Your mother could have stayed there, but your mother couldn't have stayed there with me. And you kids looked at us like we were telling you the biggest lie you had ever heard."

SUGGESTION FOR READING

As you read, underline and annotate the many different meanings Gates gives the word *kitchen*. After your reading, write a short explanation of the title of this essay, taking into account the annotations you made throughout.

We always had a gas stove in the kitchen, though electric cooking became fashionable in Piedmont, like using Crest toothpaste rather than Colgate, or watching Huntley and Brinkley rather than Walter Cronkite. But for us it was gas, Colgate, and good ole Walter Cronkite, come what may. We used gas partly out of loyalty to Big Mom, Mama's mama, because she was mostly blind and still loved to cook, and she could feel her way better with gas than with electric.

But the most important thing about our gas-equipped kitchen was that Mama used to do hair there. She had a "hot comb"—a fine-toothed iron instrument with a long wooden handle—and a pair of iron curlers that opened and closed like scissors: Mama would put them into the gas fire until they glowed. You could smell those prongs heating up.

I liked what that smell meant for the shape of my day. There was an intimate warmth in the women's tones as they talked with my mama while she did their hair. I knew what the women had been through to get their hair ready to be "done," because I would watch Mama do it to herself. How that scorched kink could be transformed through grease and fire into a magnificent head of wavy hair was a miracle to me. Still is.

Mama would wash her hair over the sink, a towel wrapped round her shoulders, wearing just her half-slip and her white bra. (We had no shower until we moved down Rat Tail Road into Doc Wolverton's house, in 1954.) After she had dried it, she would grease her scalp thoroughly with blue Bergamot hair grease, which came in a short, fat jar with a picture of a beautiful colored lady on it. It's important to grease your scalp real good, my mama would explain, to keep from burning yourself.

Of course, her hair would return to its natural kink almost as soon as the hot water and shampoo hit it. To me, it was another miracle how hair so "straight" would so quickly become kinky again once it even approached some water.

My mama had only a few "clients" whose heads she "did"—and did, I think, because she enjoyed it, rather than for the few dollars it brought in. They would sit on one of our red plastic kitchen chairs, the kind with the shiny metal legs, and brace themselves for the process. Mama would stroke that red-hot iron, which by this time had been in the gas fire for half an hour or more, slowly but firmly through their hair, from scalp to strand's end. It made a scorching, crinkly sound, the hot iron did, as it burned its way through damp kink, leaving in its wake the straightest of hair strands, each of them standing up long and tall but drooping at the end, like the top of a heavy willow tree. Slowly, steadily, with deftness and grace, Mama's hands would transform a round mound of Odetta kink into a darkened swamp of everglades. The Bergamot made the hair shiny; the heat of the hot iron gave it a brownish-red cast. Once all the hair was as straight as God allows kink to get, Mama would take the well-heated curling iron and twirl the straightened strands into more or less loosely wrapped curls. She claimed that she owed her strength and skill as a hairdresser to her wrists, and her little finger would poke out the way it did when she sipped tea. Mama was a southpaw, who wrote upside down and backwards to produce the cleanest, roundest letters you've ever seen.

The "kitchen" she would all but remove from sight with a pair of shears bought for this purpose. Now, the kitchen was the room in which we were sitting, the room where Mama did hair and washed clothes, and where each of us bathed in a galvanized tub. But the word has another meaning, and the "kitchen" I'm speaking of now is the very kinky bit of hair at the back of the head, where the neck meets the shirt collar. If there ever was one part of our

African past that resisted assimilation, it was the kitchen. No matter how hot the iron, no matter how powerful the chemical, no matter how stringent the mashed-potatoes-and-lye formula of a man's "process," neither God nor woman nor Sammy Davis Jr. could straighten the kitchen. The kitchen was permanent, irredeemable, invincible kink. Unassimilably African. No matter what you did, no matter how hard you tried, nothing could dekink a person's kitchen. So you trimmed it off as best you could.

When hair had begun to "turn," as they'd say, or return to its natural kinky glory, it was the kitchen that turned first. When the kitchen started creeping up the back of the neck, it was time to get your hair done again. The kitchen around the back, and nappy edges at the temples.

Sometimes, after dark, Mr. Charlie Carroll would come to have his hair done. Mr. Charlie Carroll was very light-complected and had a ruddy nose, the kind of nose that made me think of Edmund Gwenn playing Kris Kringle in *Miracle on 34th Street*. At the beginning, they did it after Rocky and I had gone to sleep. It was only later that we found out he had come to our house so Mama could iron his hair—not with a hot comb and curling iron but with our very own Proctor-Silex steam iron. For some reason, Mr. Charlie would conceal his Frederick Douglass mane under a big white Stetson hat, which I never saw him take off. Except when he came to our house, late at night, to have his hair pressed.

(Later, Daddy would tell us about Mr. Charlie's most prized piece of knowledge, which the man would confide only after his hair had been pressed, as a token of intimacy. "Not many people know this," he'd say in a tone of circumspection, "but George Washington was Abraham Lincoln's daddy." Nodding solemnly, he'd add the clincher: "A white man told me." Though he was in dead earnest, this became a humorous refrain around the house—"a white man told me"—used to punctuate especially preposterous assertions.)

My mother furtively examined my daughters' kitchens whenever we went home for a visit in the early eighties. It became a game between us. I had told her not to do it, because I didn't like the politics it suggested of "good" and "bad" hair. "Good" hair was straight. "Bad" hair was kinky. Even in the late sixties, at the height of Black Power, most people could not bring themselves to say "bad" for "good" and "good" for "bad." They still said that hair like white hair was "good," even if they encapsulated it in a disclaimer like "what we used to call 'good.'"

Maggie would be seated in her high chair, throwing food this way and that, and Mama would be cooing about how cute it all was, remembering how I used to do the same thing, and wondering whether Maggie's flinging her food with her left hand meant that she was going to be a southpaw too. When my daughter was just about covered with Franco-American SpaghettiOs, Mama would seize the opportunity and wipe her clean, dipping her head, tilted to one side, down under the back of Maggie's neck. Sometimes, if she could get away with it, she'd even rub a curl between her fingers, just to make sure that her bifocals had not deceived her. Then she'd sigh with satisfaction and relief, thankful that her prayers had been answered. No kink...yet. "Mama!" I'd shout, pretending to be angry. (Every once in a while, if no one was looking, I'd peek too.)

I say "yet" because most black babies are born with soft, silken hair. Then, sooner or later, it begins to "turn," as inevitably as do the seasons or the leaves on a tree. And if it's meant to turn, it *turns,* no matter how hard you try to stop it. People once thought baby oil would stop it. They were wrong.

Everybody I knew as a child wanted to have good hair. You could be as ugly as homemade sin dipped in misery and still be thought attractive if you had good hair. Jesus Moss was what the girls at Camp Lee, Virginia, had called Daddy's hair during World War II. I know he played that thick head of hair for all it was worth, too. Still would, if he could.

My own hair was "not a bad grade," as barbers would tell me when they cut my head for the first time. It's like a doctor reporting the overall results of the first full physical that he has given you. "You're in good shape" or "Blood pressure's kind of high; better cut down on salt."

I spent much of my childhood and adolescence messing with my hair. I definitely wanted straight hair. Like Pop's.

When I was about three, I tried to stick a wad of Bazooka bubble gum to that straight hair of his. I suppose what fixed that memory for me is the spanking I got for doing so: he turned me upside down, holding me by my feet, the better to paddle my behind. Little *nig-ger,* he shouted, walloping away. I started to laugh about it two days later, when my behind stopped hurting.

When black people say "straight," of course, they don't usually mean "straight" literally, like, say, the hair of Peggy Lipton (the white girl on *The Mod Squad*) or Mary of Peter, Paul and Mary fame; black people call that "stringy" hair. No, "straight" just means not kinky, no matter what contours the curl might take. Because Daddy had straight hair, I would have done *anything* to have straight hair—and I used to try everything to make it straight, short of getting a process, which only riffraff were dumb enough to do.

Of the wide variety of techniques and methods I came to master in the great and chal-lenging follicle prestidigitation, almost all had two things in common: a heavy, oil-based grease and evenly applied pressure. It's no accident that many of the biggest black compa-nies in the fifties and sixties made hair products. Indeed, we do have a vast array of hair grease. And I have tried it all, in search of that certain silky touch, one that leaves neither the hand nor the pillow sullied by grease.

I always wondered what Frederick Douglass put on *his* hair, or Phillis Wheatley. Or why Wheatley has that rag on her head in the little engraving in the frontispiece of her book. One thing is for sure: you can bet that when Wheatley went to England to see the Countess of Huntington, she did not stop by the Queen's Coiffeur on the way. So many black people still get their hair straightened that it's a wonder we don't have a national holiday for Madame C. J. Walker, who invented the process for straightening kinky hair, rather than for Dr. King. Jheri-curled or "relaxed"—it's still fried hair.

I used all the greases, from sea-blue Bergamot, to creamy vanilla Duke (in its orange-and-white jar), to the godfather of grease, the formidable Murray's. Now, Murray's was some *seri-ous* grease. Whereas Bergamot was like oily Jell-O and Duke was viscous and sickly sweet, Murray's was light brown and *hard*. Hard as lard and twice as greasy, Daddy used to say when-ever the subject of Murray's came up. Murray's came in an orange can with a screw-on top. It was so hard that some people would put a match to the can, just to soften it and make it more manageable. In the late sixties, when Afros came into style, I'd use Afro-Sheen. From Murray's to Duke to Afro-Sheen: that was my progression in black consciousness.

We started putting hot towels or washrags over our greased-down Murray's-coated heads, in order to melt the wax into the scalp and follicles. Unfortunately, the wax had a curious habit of running down your neck, ears, and forehead. Not to mention your pillowcase.

Another problem was that if you put two palmfuls of Murray's on your head, your hair turned white. Duke did the same thing. It was a challenge: if you got rid of the white stuff, you had a magnificent head of wavy hair. Murray's turned kink into waves. Lots of waves. Frozen waves. A hurricane couldn't have blown those waves around.

That was the beauty of it. Murray's was so hard that it froze your hair into the wavy style you brushed it into. It looked really good if you wore a part. A lot of guys had parts cut into their hair by a barber, with clippers or a straight-edge razor. Especially if you had kinky hair—in which case you'd generally wear a short razor cut, or what we called a Quo Vadis.

Being obsessed with our hair, we tried to be as innovative as possible. Everyone knew about using a stocking cap, because your father or your uncle or the older guys wore them whenever something really big was about to happen, secular or sacred, a funeral or a dance, a wedding or a trip in which you confronted official white people, or when you were trying to look really sharp. When it was time to be clean, you wore a stocking cap. If the event was really a big one, you made a new cap for the occasion.

A stocking cap was made by asking your mother for one of her hose, and cutting it with a pair of scissors about six inches or so from the open end, where the elastic goes up to the top of the thigh. Then you'd knot the cut end, and behold—a conical-shaped hat or cap, with an elastic band that you pulled down low on your forehead and down around your neck in the back. A good stocking cap, to work well, had to fit tight and snug, like a press. And it had to fit that tightly because it was a press: it pressed your hair with the force of the hose's elastic. If you greased your hair down real good and left the stocking cap on long enough—*voilà:* you got a head of pressed-against-the-scalp waves. If you used Murray's, and if you wore a stocking cap to sleep, you got a *whole lot* of waves. (You also got a ring around your forehead when you woke up, but eventually that disappeared.)

And then you could enjoy your concrete 'do. Swore we were bad, too, with all that grease and those flat heads. My brother and I would brush it out a bit in the morning, so it would look—ahem—"natural."

Grown men still wear stocking caps, especially older men, who generally keep their caps in their top drawer, along with their cuff links and their see-through silk socks, their Maverick tie, their silk handkerchief, and whatever else they prize most.

A Murrayed-down stocking cap was the respectable version of the process, which, by contrast, was most definitely not a cool thing to have, at least if you weren't an entertainer by trade.

Zeke and Keith and Poochie and a few other stars of the basketball team all used to get a process once or twice a year. It was expensive, and to get one you had to go to Pittsburgh or D.C. or Uniontown, someplace where there were enough colored people to support a business. They'd disappear, then reappear a day or two later, strutting like peacocks, their hair burned slightly red from the chemical lye base. They'd also wear "rags" or cloths or handkerchiefs around it when they slept or played basketball. Do-rags, they were called. But the result was *straight* hair, with a hint of wave. No curl. Do-it-yourselfers took their chances at home with a concoction of mashed potatoes and lye.

The most famous process, outside of what Malcolm X describes in his *Autobiography* and maybe that of Sammy Davis Jr., was Nat King Cole's. Nat King Cole had patent-leather hair.

"That man's got the finest process money can buy." That's what Daddy said the night Cole's TV show aired on NBC, November 5, 1956. I remember the date because everyone came to our house to watch it and to celebrate one of Daddy's buddies' birthdays. Yeah, Uncle Joe chimed in, they can do shit to his hair that the average Negro can't even *think* about—secret shit.

Nat King Cole was *clean.* I've had an ongoing argument with a Nigerian friend about Nat King Cole for twenty years now. Not whether or not he could sing; any fool knows that he could sing. But whether or not he was a handkerchief-head for wearing that patent-leather process.

Sammy Davis's process I detested. It didn't look good on him. Worse still, he liked to have a fried strand dangling down the middle of his forehead, shaking it out from the crown when he sang. But Nat King Cole's hair was a thing unto itself, a beautifully sculpted work of art that he and he alone should have had the right to wear.

The only difference between a process and a stocking cap, really, was taste; yet Nat King Cole—unlike, say, Michael Jackson—looked good in his process. His head looked like Rudolph Valentino's in the twenties, and some say it was Valentino that the process imitated. But Nat King Cole wore a process because it suited his face, his demeanor, his name, his style. He was as clean as he wanted to be.

I had forgotten all about Nat King Cole and that patent-leather look until the day in 1971 when I was sitting in an Arab restaurant on the island of Zanzibar, surrounded by men in fezzes and white caftans, trying to learn how to eat curried goat and rice with the fingers of my right hand, feeling two million miles from home, when all of a sudden the old transistor radio sitting on top of a china cupboard stopped blaring out its Swahili music to play "Fly Me to the Moon" by Nat King Cole. The restaurant's din was not affected at all, not even by half a decibel. But in my mind's eye, I saw it: the King's sleek black magnificent tiara. I managed, barely, to blink back the tears.

Straightening Our Hair

bell hooks

"Straightening Our Hair" originally appeared in 1988 in *Z Magazine*. A Distinguished Professor of English at the City University of New York, bell hooks is the author of more than a dozen books on the politics of race, class, and gender. Her more recent work includes the books *Killing Rage, Teaching to Transgress,* and *Outlaw Culture.* In the essay reprinted below, hooks writes of her decision, during the Black Power Movement of the sixties, to stop straightening her hair, even though it took her a long time to feel comfortable with nonprocessed hair. Like Gates's memory piece, hooks's discussion of the politics of African American women straightening their hair is one that must be read with that historical and political context in mind. She made her decision when it was the decision that seemed most honest for her to make.

SUGGESTION FOR READING

As you read, you will notice that hooks writes of a dilemma that is at once a very private and public one. Underline and annotate those passages in her essay where hooks touches on this issue of the political nature of private choices.

On Saturday mornings we would gather in the kitchen to get our hair fixed, that is straightened. Smells of burning grease and hair, mingled with the scent of our freshly washed bodies, with collard greens cooking on the stove, with fried fish. We did not go to the hairdresser. Mama fixed our hair. Six daughters—there was no way we could have afforded hairdressers. In those days, this process of straightening black women's hair with a hot comb (invented by Madame C. J. Walker) was not connected in my mind with the effort to look white, to live out standards of beauty set by white supremacy. It was connected solely with rites of initiation into womanhood. To arrive at that point where one's hair could be straightened was to move from being perceived as child (whose hair could be neatly combed and braided) to being almost a woman. It was this moment of transition my sisters and I longed for.

Hair pressing was a ritual of black women's culture—of intimacy. It was an exclusive moment when black women (even those who did not know one another well) might meet at home or in the beauty parlor to talk with one another, to listen to the talk. It was as important a world as that of the male barber shop—mysterious, secret. It was a world where the images constructed as barriers between one's self and the world were briefly let go, before they were made again. It was a moment of creativity, a moment of change.

I wanted this change even though I had been told all my life that I was one of the "lucky" ones because I had been born with "good hair"—hair that was fine, almost straight—not good enough but still good. Hair that had no nappy edges, no "kitchen," that area close to the neck that the hot comb could not reach. This "good hair" meant nothing to me when it stood as a barrier to my entering this secret black woman world. I was overjoyed when mama finally agreed that I could join the Saturday ritual, no longer looking on but patiently waiting my turn. I have written of this ritual: "For each of us getting our hair pressed is an important ritual. It is not a sign of our longing to be white. There are no white people in our intimate world. It is a sign of our desire to be women. It is a gesture that says we are approaching womanhood....Before we reach the appropriate age we wear braids, plaits that are symbols of our innocence, our youth, our childhood. Then, we are comforted by the parting hands that comb and braid, comforted by the intimacy and bliss. There is a deeper intimacy in the kitchen on Saturdays when hair is pressed, when fish is fried, when sodas are passed around, when soul music drifts over the talk. It is a time without men. It is a time when we work as women to meet each other's needs, to make each other feel good inside, a time of laughter and outrageous talk."

Since the world we lived in was racially segregated, it was easy to overlook the relationship between white supremacy and our obsession with hair. Even though black women with straight hair were perceived to be more beautiful than those with thick, frizzy hair, it was not overtly related to a notion that white women were a more appealing female group or that their straight hair set a beauty standard black women were struggling to live out. While this was probably the ideological framework from which the process of straightening black women's hair emerged, it was expanded so that it became a real space of black woman bonding through ritualized, shared experience. The beauty parlor was a space of consciousness raising, a space where black women shared life stories—hardship, trials, gossip; a place where one could be comforted and one's spirit renewed. It was for some women a place of rest where one did not need to meet the demands of children or men. It was the one hour some folk would spend "off their feet," a soothing, restful time of meditation and silence. These positive empowering implications of the ritual of hair pressing mediate but do not change negative implications. They exist alongside all that is negative.

Within white supremacist capitalist patriarchy, the social and political context in which the custom of black folks straightening our hair emerges, it represents an imitation of the dominant white group's appearance and often indicates internalized racism, self-hatred, and/or low self-esteem. During the 1960s black people who actively worked to critique, challenge, and change white racism pointed to the way in which black people's obsession with straight hair reflected a colonized mentality. It was at this time that the natural hairdo, the "afro," became fashionable as a sign of cultural resistance to racist oppression and as a celebration of blackness. Naturals were equated with political militancy. Many young black folks found just how much political value was placed on straightened hair as a sign of respectability and conformity to societal expectations when they ceased to straighten their hair. When black liberation struggles did not lead to revolutionary change in society the focus on the political relationship between appearance and complicity with white racism ceased and folks who had once sported afros began to straighten their hair.

In keeping with the move to suppress black consciousness and efforts to be self-defining, white corporations began to acknowledge black people and most especially black women as potential consumers of products they could provide, including hair-care products. Permanents specially designed for black women eliminated the need for hair pressing and the hot comb. They not only cost more but they also took much of the economy and profit out of black communities, out of the pockets of black women who had previously reaped the material benefits (see Manning Marable's *How Capitalism Underdeveloped Black America,* South End Press). Gone was the context of ritual, of black woman bonding. Seated under noisy hair dryers black women lost a space for dialogue, for creative talk.

Stripped of the positive binding rituals that traditionally surrounded the experience, black women straightening our hair seemed more and more to be exclusively a signifier of white supremacist oppression and exploitation. It was clearly a process that was about black women changing their appearance to imitate white people's looks. This need to look as much like white people as possible, to look safe, is related to a desire to succeed in the white world. Before desegregation black people could worry less about what white folks thought about their hair. In a discussion with black women about beauty at Spelman College, students talked about the importance of wearing straight hair when seeking jobs. They were convinced and probably rightly so that their chances of finding good jobs would be enhanced if they had straight hair. When asked to elaborate they focused on the connection between radical politics and natural hairdos, whether natural or braided. One woman wearing a short natural told of purchasing a straight wig for her job search. No one in the discussion felt black women were free to wear our hair in natural styles without reflecting on the possible negative consequences. Often older black adults, especially parents, respond quite negatively to natural hairdos. I shared with the group that when I arrived home with my hair in braids shortly after accepting my job at Yale my parents told me I looked disgusting.

Despite many changes in racial politics, black women continue to obsess about their hair, and straightening hair continues to be serious business. It continues to tap into the insecurity black women feel about our value in this white supremacist society. Talking with groups of women at various college campuses and with black women in our communities there seems to be general consensus that our obsession with hair in general reflects continued struggles with self-esteem and self-actualization. We talk about the extent to which black women perceive our hair as the enemy, as a problem we must solve, a territory we must conquer. Above all it is a part of our black female body that must be controlled. Most of us were not raised in environments where we learned to regard our hair as sensual or beautiful in an unprocessed state. Many of us talk about situations where white people ask to touch our hair when it is unprocessed then show surprise that the texture is soft or feels good. In the eyes of many white folks and other non-black folks, the natural afro looks like steel wool or a helmet. Responses to natural hairstyles worn by black women usually reveal the extent to which our natural hair is perceived in white supremacist culture as not only ugly but frightening. We also internalize that fear. The extent to which we are comfortable with our hair usually reflects on our overall feelings about our bodies. In our black women's support group, Sisters of the Yam, we talk about the ways we don't like our bodies, especially our hair. I suggested to the group that we regard our hair as though it is not part of our body but something quite separate—again a territory to be controlled. To me it was important for us to link this need to control with sexuality, with sexual repression. Curious about what black women who had hot-combed or had permanents felt about the relationship between straightened hair and sexual practice I asked whether people worried about their hairdo, whether they feared partners touching their hair. Straightened hair has always seemed to me to call attention to the desire for hair to stay in place. Not surprisingly many black women responded that they felt uncomfortable if too much attention was focused on their hair, if it seemed to be too messy. Those of us who have liberated our hair and let it go in whatever direction it seems fit often receive negative comments.

Looking at photographs of myself and my sisters when we had straightened hair in high school I noticed how much older we looked than when our hair was not processed. It is ironic that we live in a culture that places so much emphasis on women looking young, yet black women are encouraged to change our hair in ways that make us appear older. This past semester we read Toni Morrison's *The Bluest Eye* in a black women's fiction class. I ask students to write autobiographical statements which reflect their thoughts about the connection between race and physical beauty. A vast majority of black women wrote about their hair. When I asked individual women outside class why they continued to straighten their hair, many asserted that naturals don't look good on them, or that they required too much work. Emily, a favorite student with very short hair, always straightened it and I would tease and challenge her. She explained to me convincingly that a natural hairdo would look horrible with her face, that she did not have the appropriate forehead or bone structure. Later she shared that during spring break she had gone to the beauty parlor to have her perm and as she sat there waiting, thinking about class reading and discussion, it came to her that she was really frightened that no one else would think she was attractive if she did not straighten her hair. She acknowledged that this fear was rooted in feelings of low self-esteem. She decided to make a change. Her new look surprised her because it was so appealing. We talked afterwards about her earlier denial and justification for wearing straightened hair. We talked about the way it hurts to realize connection between racist oppression and the arguments we use to convince ourselves and others that we are not beautiful or acceptable as we are.

In numerous discussions with black women about hair one of the strongest factors that prevent black women from wearing unprocessed hairstyles is the fear of losing other people's approval and regard. Heterosexual black women talked about the extent to which black men respond more favorably to women with straight or straightened hair. Lesbian women point to the fact that many of them do not straighten their hair, raising the question of whether or not this gesture is fundamentally linked to heterosexism and a longing for male approval. I recall visiting a woman friend and her black male companion in New York years ago and having an intense discussion about hair. He took it upon himself to share with me that I could be a fine sister if I would do something about my hair (secretly I thought mama must have hired him). What I remember is his shock when I calmly and happily asserted that I like the touch and feel of unprocessed hair.

When students read about race and physical beauty, several black women describe periods of childhood when they were overcome with longing for straight hair as it was so associated with desirability, with being loved. Few women had received affirmation from family, friends, or lovers when choosing not to straighten their hair and we have many stories to tell about advice we receive from everyone, including total strangers, urging us to understand how much more attractive we would be if we would fix (straighten) our hair. When I interviewed for my job at Yale, white female advisers who had never before commented on my hair encouraged me not to wear braids or a large natural to the interview. Although they did not say straighten your hair, they were suggesting that I change my hairstyle so that it would most resemble theirs, so that it would indicate a certain conformity. I wore braids and no one seemed to notice. When I was offered the job I did not ask if it mattered whether or not I wore braids. I tell this story to my students so that they will know by this one experience that we do not always need to surrender our power to be self defining to succeed in an endeavor. Yet I have found the issue of hairstyle comes up again and again with students when I give lectures. At one conference on black women and leadership I walked into a packed auditorium, my hair unprocessed wild and all over the place. The vast majority of black women seated there had straightened hair. Many of them looked at me with hostile contemptuous stares. I felt as though I was being judged on the spot as someone out on the fringe, an undesirable. Such judgments are made particularly about black women in the United States who choose to wear dreadlocks. They are seen and rightly so as the total antithesis of straightening one's hair, as a political statement. Often black women express contempt for those of us who choose this look.

Ironically, just as the natural unprocessed hair of black women is the subject of disregard and disdain we are witnessing return of the long dyed, blonde look. In their writing my black women students described wearing yellow mops on their heads as children to pretend they had long blonde hair. Recently black women singers who are working to appeal to white audiences, to be seen as crossovers, use hair implanting and hair weaving to have long straight hair. There seems to be a definite connection between a black female entertainer's popularity with white audiences and the degree to which she works to appear white, or to embody aspects of white style. Tina Turner and Aretha Franklin were trend setters; both dyed their hair blonde. In everyday life we see more and more black women using chemicals to be blonde. At one of my talks focusing on the social construction of black female identity within a sexist and racist society, a black woman came to me at the end of the discussion and shared that her seven-year-old daughter was obsessed with blonde hair, so much so that she had made a wig to imitate long blonde curls. This mother wanted to know what she was doing wrong in her parenting. She asserted that their home was a place where blackness was affirmed and celebrated. Yet she had not considered that her processed straightened hair was a message to her daughter that black women are not acceptable unless we alter our appearance or hair texture. Recently I talked with one of my younger sisters about her hair. She uses bright colored dyes, various shades of red. Her skin is very dark. She has a broad nose and short hair. For her these choices of straightened dyed hair were directly related to feelings of low self-esteem. She does not like her features and feels that the hairstyle transforms her. My perception was that her choice of red straightened hair actually called attention to the features she was trying to mask. When she commented that this look receives more attention and compliments, I suggested that the positive feedback might be a direct response to her own projection of a higher level of self-satisfaction. Folk may be responding to that and not her altered looks. We talked about the messages she is sending her dark-skinned daughters—that they will be most attractive if they straighten their hair.

A number of black women have argued that straightened hair is not necessarily a signifier of low self-esteem. They argue that it is a survival strategy; it is easier to function in this society with straightened hair. There are fewer hassles. Or as some folk stated, straightened hair is easier to manage, takes less time. When I responded to this argument in our discussion at Spelman by suggesting that perhaps the unwillingness to spend time on ourselves, caring for our bodies, is also a reflection of a sense that this is not important or that we do not deserve such care. In this group and others, black women talked about being raised in households where spending too much time on appearance was ridiculed or considered vanity. Irrespective of the way individual black women choose to do their hair, it is evident that the extent to which we suffer from racist and sexist oppression and exploitation affects the degree to which we feel capable of both self-love and asserting an autonomous presence that is acceptable and pleasing to ourselves. Individual preferences (whether rooted in self-hate or not) cannot negate the reality that our collective obsession with straightening black hair reflects the psychology of oppression and the impact of racist colonization. Together racism and sexism daily reinforce to all black females via the media, advertising, etc. that we will not be considered beautiful or desirable if we do not change ourselves, especially our hair. We cannot resist this socialization if we deny that white supremacy informs our efforts to construct self and identity.

Without organized struggles like the ones that happened in the 1960s and early 1970s, individual black women must struggle alone to acquire the critical consciousness that would enable us to examine issues of race and beauty, our personal choices, from a political stand-point. There are times when I think of straightening my hair just to change my style, just for fun. Then I remind myself that even though such a gesture could be simply playful on my part, an individual expression of desire, I know that such a gesture would carry other impli-cations beyond my control. The reality is: straightened hair is linked historically and cur-rently to a system of racial domination that impresses upon black people, and especially black women, that we are not acceptable as we are, that we are not beautiful. To make such a ges-ture as an expression of individual freedom and choice would make me complicit with a politic of domination that hurts us. It is easy to surrender this freedom. It is more important that black women resist racism and sexism in every way; that every aspect of our self-repre-sentation be a fierce resistance, a radical celebration of our care and respect for ourselves.

Even though I have not had straightened hair for a long time, this did not mean that I am able to really enjoy or appreciate my hair in its natural state. For years I still considered it a prob-lem. (It wasn't naturally nappy enough to make a decent interesting afro. It was too thin.) These complaints expressed my continued dissatisfaction. True liberation of my hair came when I stopped trying to control it in any state and just accepted it as it is. It has been only in recent years that I have ceased to worry about what other people would say about my hair. It has been only in recent years that I could feel consistent pleasure washing, combing, and caring for my hair. These feelings remind me of the pleasure and comfort I felt as a child sitting between my mother's legs feeling the warmth of her body and being as she combed and braided my hair. In a culture of domination, one that is essentially anti-intimacy, we must struggle daily to remain in touch with ourselves and our bodies, with one another. Especially black women and men, as it is our bodies that have been so often devalued, burdened, wounded in alienated labor. Celebrating our bodies, we participate in a liberatory struggle that frees mind and heart.

SUGGESTIONS FOR DISCUSSION

1. With a group of your classmates, look back at these two essays. Make notes comparing each writer's position and noting the stories they tell. Where do you think Gates and hooks are saying much the same thing? In what ways do their discussions differ?

2. At the end of his essay, when he tells of his reaction to hearing Nat King Cole in a Zanzibar restaurant, Gates reveals how powerful our memories can be. His memories of Cole and his straightened hair are obviously good ones, without any negative associations. hooks, as well, begins and ends her essay with powerful personal memories that are not negative, despite her position on straightening African American hair. What would you say the effect of such stories is for a reader? How did you respond to them as you read?

3. Most people probably think of hairstyle as a trivial concern, yet hooks and Gates both connect hairstyle with serious political choices. hooks tells us that, though she has not straightened her hair for many years, it took her a very long time to actually take pleasure from leaving her hair in its nat-ural state. Gates, as well, connects style to politics. He writes, "Murray's to Duke to Afro-Sheen: that was my progression in black consciousness." What do you think both writers have lost and gained from the choices they have made?

4. Both essays seem to suggest that hairstyle, especially for African Ameri-cans, plays a substantial role in presenting a public image. In a discussion of what importance this culture, in general, places on an individual's hair-

style, consider how that general bias toward hair affects either your own choices or the way that you see others.

5. How might the stories told by hooks and Gates be meaningful for readers who aren't convinced that straightening African American hair is such a negative choice or by readers who don't at all deal with that issue in their lives?

SUGGESTIONS FOR WRITING

1. In Gates's memoir, he writes of his mother checking his first child's hair to see if it was "good": "Sometimes, if she could get away with it, she'd even rub a curl between her fingers, just to make sure that her bifocals had not deceived her. Then she'd sigh with satisfaction and relief, thankful that her prayers had been answered. No kink…yet. 'Mama!' I'd shout, pretending to be angry. (Every once in a while, if no one was looking, I'd peek, too.)" Near the end of her essay, hooks addresses the ambivalence that Gates describes when she writes: "Individual preferences (whether rooted in self-hate or not) cannot negate the reality that our collective obsession with straightening black hair reflects the psychology of oppression and the impact of racist colonization. Together racism and sexism daily reinforce to all black females via the media, advertising, etc. that we will not be considered beautiful or desirable if we do not change ourselves, especially our hair." Review hooks's essay, especially with that passage in mind, and then write a one- to two-page explanation of what hooks is getting at in this passage. Consider supporting your discussion with examples from your own experience with or observations of mainstream attitudes toward beauty and race.

2. bell hooks asks her classes to write "autobiographical statements which reflect their thoughts about the connection between race and physical beauty." Write your own autobiographical position statement. Begin with a memory or a personal observation. Use that memory or observation to develop your own position on the connection between beauty and race in the U.S. media. Remember that your experience with style, beauty, and race may be very different from hooks's experience, just as your attitude toward processed hair may be very different from hers because of your age or experience or politics or personal preference.

3. Both hooks and Gates remind us that, even though we do develop our own personal preferences in the way we choose to look, the media and media personalities offer attractive or powerful models that help shape those preferences. Those preferences often fall into line with mainstream ideals. Spend some time looking through magazines, and think about your favorite musicians or actors or anyone in the media with whom you identify as having an influence on the way people choose to look today. In what ways do the looks these stars strive for reflect racial or ethnic backgrounds, class affiliations, social status, sexuality, generational ties, and/or a desire to break with or accept conventions? In your writing, focus on one style that might prompt you to address these questions. Be sure to include visuals with your paper so that you can point to very specific style markers. When it seems useful, refer back to Garber, Chapkis, Gates, and hooks to help you make your argument.

Dress for Success

John Molloy

John Molloy made his reputation in the late 1970s with the publication of his widely read and extraordinarily popular self-help book *Dress for Success,* first published in 1975. In it, Molloy claimed to have found a no-miss formula for dressing guaranteed to impress the corporate boss and to give the prospective job seeker the advantage over the competition. In the following selection from the book's introduction, Molloy describes his methods for studying the concept of dressing for success and presents some of his conclusions from that study. Molloy's study began with particular assumptions about dress and most people's response to dress. He assumed that dress was an important indicator of social and economic class. He further assumed that most white-collar employers judge potential employees by their dress. His experiments on dressing for success are built on those assumptions. Molloy was just as triumphant with his woman's guide to dressing for success, but the men's guide was one of the many self-help books that became a best-seller in the 1980s. Self-help books became a popular genre in the 1970s and 1980s. They addressed such problems as dieting, quitting smoking, changing personal relationships, and feeling less guilt. Like others in the genre, Molloy's book promotes a quick fix for a complex problem.

SUGGESTION FOR READING

Underline and annotate those passages in which Molloy develops his thesis about the importance of dress as a signal of class.

THE PROOF: WHAT WORKS AND WHAT DOESN'T

Since I had very early on discovered that the socioeconomic value of a man's clothing is important in determining his credibility with certain groups, his ability to attract certain kinds of women and his acceptance to the business community, one of the first elements I undertook to research was the socioeconomic level of all items of clothing.

Take the raincoat, for example. Most raincoats sold in this country are either beige or black; those are the two standard colors. Intuitively I felt that the beige raincoat was worn generally by the upper-middle class and black by the lower-middle class.

First I visited several Fifth Avenue stores that cater almost exclusively to upper-middle-class customers and attempted to ascertain the number of beige raincoats versus black raincoats being sold. The statistical breakdown was approximately four to one in favor of beige. I then checked stores on the lower-middle-class level and found that almost the reverse statistic applied. They sold four black raincoats to each beige raincoat.

This indicated that in all probability my feeling was correct, but recognizing that there were many variables that could discredit such preliminary research, I set the second stage in motion. On rainy days, I hired responsible college students to stand outside subway stations in determinable lower-middle-class neighborhoods and outside determinable upper-middle-class suburban commuter-stations, all in the New York area. The students merely counted the number of black and beige raincoats. My statistics held up at approximately four to one in either case, and I could now say that in the New York area, the upper-middle class generally wore beige raincoats and the lower-middle class generally wore black ones.

My next step was to take a rainy-day count in the two different socioeconomic areas in Chicago, Los Angeles, Dallas, Atlanta and six equally widespread small towns. The research again held up; statistics came back from the cities at about four to one and from the small towns at about two-and-a-half to three to one. (The statistics were not quite that clear cut, but averaged out into those ranges.)

From these statistics I was able to state that in the United States, the beige raincoat is generally worn by members of the upper-middle class and the black raincoat generally worn by members of the lower-middle class. From this, I was able to hypothesize that since these raincoats were an intrinsic part of the American environment, they had in all probability conditioned people by their predominance in certain classes, and automatic (Pavlovian) reactions could be expected.

In short, when someone met a man in a beige raincoat, he was likely to think of him as a member of the upper-middle class, and when he met a man in a black raincoat, he was likely to think of him as a member of the lower-middle class. I then had to see if my hypothesis would hold up under testing.

My first test was conducted with 1362 people—a cross section of the general public. They were given an "extrasensory perception" test in which they were asked to guess the answers to a number of problems to which the solutions (they were told) could only be known through ESP. The percentage of correct answers would indicate their ESP quotient. Naturally, a participant in this type of test attempts to get the right answer every time and has no reason to lie, since he wants to score high.

In this test, among a group of other problems and questions, I inserted a set of almost identical "twin pictures." There was only one variable. The twin pictures showed the same man in the same pose dressed in the same suit, the same shirt, the same tie, the same shoes. The only difference was the raincoat—one black, one beige. Participants were told that the pictures were of twin brothers, and were asked to identify the most prestigious of the two. Over 87 percent, or 1118 people, chose the man in the beige raincoat.

I next ran a field test. Two friends and I wore beige raincoats for one month, then switched to black raincoats the following month. We attempted to duplicate our other clothing during both months. At the end of each month, we recorded the general attitude of people toward us—waiters, store clerks, business associates, etc. All three of us agreed that the beige raincoat created a distinctly better impression upon the people we met.

Finally, I conducted one additional experiment alone. Picking a group of business offices at random, I went into each office with a *Wall Street Journal* in a manila envelope and asked the receptionist or secretary to allow me to deliver it personally to the man in charge. When wearing a black raincoat, it took me a day and a half to deliver twenty-five papers. In a beige raincoat, I was able to deliver the same number in a single morning.

The impression transmitted to receptionists and secretaries by my black raincoat and a nondescript suit, shirt and tie clearly was that I was a glorified delivery boy, and so I had to wait or was never admitted. But their opinion of me was substantially altered by the beige raincoat worn with the same other clothes. They thought I might be an associate or friend of the boss because that is what I implied, and they had better let me in. In short, they reacted to years of preconditioning and accepted the beige raincoat as a symbol of authority and status while they rejected the black raincoat as such.

This study was conducted in 1971. And although more and more lower-middle-class men are wearing beige raincoats each year (basically because of improved wash-and-wear methods that make them much less expensive to keep clean), the results of the study remain valid and will continue to be for years to come. You cannot wear a black raincoat, and you must wear a beige raincoat—if you wish to be accepted as a member of the upper-middle class and treated accordingly (among all other raincoat colors, only dark blue tests as acceptable).

I continue to test the beige raincoat each year in my multiple-item studies. In the field of clothing, multiple-item studies are those that incorporate an entire look: the upper-middle-class look, the lower-middle-class look, etc. These studies usually are not geared to test people's responses to specific items, but if a particular item is not consistent with the rest, it will destroy the effectiveness of the study because the incongruous item spoils the total look.

In one multiple-item study, I sent a twenty-five-year-old male college graduate from an upper-middle-class midwestern background to 100 offices. To fifty of them he wore an outfit made up entirely of garments that had been previously tested as having lower-middle-class characteristics; to the remaining fifty he wore an outfit of garments that had been previously tested as having upper-middle-class characteristics. Prior to his arrival at each office, I had arranged for the man in charge to tell his secretary that he had hired an assistant, and to instruct her to show the young man around. The executive also made sure that his secretary would not be going to lunch, would not be going home, and would not be overworked at the time of my man's arrival.

After being shown through the offices, which took anywhere from fifteen minutes to an hour, depending on the secretary and the office, the young man made a series of requests. He first asked for something simple like letterhead stationery or a pencil and pad. The responses of the secretaries to these requests had no statistical significance, although the young man did note that there was a substantial difference in attitude. In upper-middle-class garb, he received the requested item with no comment, but pejorative comments or quizzical looks were directed toward him at least one-third of the time when he wore lower-middle-class clothing.

Once the first request sequence was completed, the young man gave each secretary a standardized order. Before going to each office, he had been given the names of three people in the files of the office. These names were written on a card, and his procedure was always the same. Putting the card on the secretary's desk, he would say, "Miss (always using her name) Jones, please get these files for me; I will be at Mr. Smith's desk." He would then walk away, trying not to give the secretary a chance to answer him verbally. The results were quite significant.

In upper-middle-class garb, he received the files within ten minutes forty-two times. In lower-middle-class garb, he received the files only twelve times. Pejorative comments were directed at him twelve times while wearing upper-middle-class clothes, and eight times while wearing lower-middle-class clothes. This means that he received positive responses only four times out of fifty while wearing lower-middle-class garb; but he received positive responses thirty times out of fifty when he was wearing upper-middle-class garb.

From this experiment and many others like it, I was able to conclude that in upper-middle-class clothes, a young man will be more successful in giving orders to secretaries.

The experiment will give you an idea of why I have spent so many years and so much of my clients' money in determining what constitutes upper-middle-class dress. It is obvious from the experiment that secretaries, who generally were not members of the upper-middle-class, did in fact recognize upper-middle-class clothing, if not consciously then at least subconsciously, and they did react to it. The reactions of the secretaries indicate that dress is neither trivial nor frivolous, but an essential element in helping a man to function in the business world with maximum effectiveness.

But does everyone react as the secretaries did?

For years some companies have been attempting to increase the efficiency of employees by prescribing dress and establishing dress codes. Most of these schemes have proved ineffective because they have been created by amateurs who don't understand the effect clothing has on the work environment. Dress codes can work, as I will show later, but the assumption that clothing has a major, continuing impact on the wearer is erroneous. True, you may feel shabby when you wear shabby clothes, and your morale may perk up a bit when you splurge on an expensive tie. But clothing most significantly affects the people whom the wearer meets and, in the long run, affects the wearer only indirectly because it controls the reaction of the world to him. My research shows that in most business situations the wearer is not directly affected by his clothing, and that the effect of clothing on other people is mainly controlled by the socioeconomic level of the clothing.

Let me say it straight out: We all wear uniforms and our uniforms are clear and distinct signs of class. We react to them accordingly. In almost any situation where two men meet, one man's clothing is saying to the other man: "I am more important than you are, please show respect"; or "I am your equal and expect to be treated as such"; or "I am not your equal and I do not expect to be treated as such."

HOW 100 TOP EXECUTIVES DESCRIBED SUCCESSFUL DRESS

Over the years I have conducted literally thousands of studies, experiments and tests to aid my corporate and individual clients in using clothing better and as an indispensable tool of business life. Immediately prior to beginning this book, and specifically for this book, I asked several series of questions of 100 top executives in either medium-sized or major American corporations. The first series was to establish the most up-to-date attitudes on corporate dress.

I showed the executives five pictures of men, each of them wearing expensive, well-tailored, but high-fashion clothing. I asked if this was a proper look for the junior business executive. Ninety-two of the men said no, eight said yes.

I showed them five pictures of men neatly dressed in obvious lower-middle-class attire and asked if these men were dressed in proper attire for a young executive. Forty-six said yes, fifty-four said no.

I next showed them five pictures of men dressed in conservative upper-middle-class clothing and asked if they were dressed in proper attire for the young executive. All one hundred said yes.

I asked them whether they thought the men in the upper-middle-class garb would succeed better in corporate life than the men in the lower-middle-class uniform. Eighty-eight said yes, twelve said no.

I asked if they would choose one of the men in the lower-middle-class dress as their assistant. Ninety-two said no, eight said yes.

I next showed them pictures of four young men. The first had a very short haircut; the second had a moderate haircut with moderate sideburns; the third had a moderate haircut, but with fairly long sideburns; and the fourth had very long hair. I asked which haircut was the most profitable for a young man to wear. Eighty-two of them picked the moderate haircut with moderate sideburns; three picked the very short cut; and fifteen picked the moderate cut with long sideburns. No one picked the long hair.

I next asked if they would hire the man with long hair. Seventy-four said no.

To 100 other top executives of major corporations, I submitted the following written questions:

1. *Does your company have a written or an unwritten dress code?* Ninety-seven said yes. Three said no. Only two had a written dress code.

2. *Would a number of men at your firm have a much better chance of getting ahead if they knew how to dress?* Ninety-six said yes, four said no.

3. *If there were a course in how to dress for business, would you send your son?* All 100 said yes.

4. *Do you think employee dress affects the general tone of the office?* All 100 said yes.

5. *Do you think employee dress affects efficiency?* Fifty-two said yes, forty-eight said no.

6. *Would you hold up the promotion of a man who didn't dress properly?* Seventy-two said yes, twenty-eight said no.

7. *Would you tell a young man if his dress was holding him back?* Eighty said no, twenty said yes.

8. *Does your company at present turn down people who show up at job interviews improperly dressed on that basis alone?* Eighty-four said yes, sixteen said no.

9. *Would you take a young man who didn't know how to dress as your assistant?* Ninety-two said no, eight said yes.

10. *Do you think there is a need for a book that would explain to a young man how to dress?* Ninety-four said yes, six said no.

11. *Do you think there is a need for a book to tell people in business how to dress?* One hundred said yes.

Keep reading, fellows, you got it.

SUGGESTIONS FOR DISCUSSION

1. Although he uses the terms frequently, Molloy doesn't give readers many specific details of upper-middle-class and lower-middle-class dress. What examples of dress (besides Molloy's raincoats) can you think of that signal class? Do you think class is easily spotted by dress?

2. Review Molloy's description of his raincoat experiment. He calls the results of this experiment "the proof [of] what works and what doesn't." Do you find the results to be convincing? What, if anything, do they leave out?

3. John Molloy equates success in this culture with upward movement in corporations. What assumptions is he making about the nature of success in contemporary America?

SUGGESTIONS FOR WRITING

1. Write an essay in which you consider whether, as Molloy claims, dress is a marker of social class. Use examples from your own experience and from your observations of others.

2. Molloy's work suggests that we think about the clothes we own in terms of the effect those clothes have on the people around us. Write an essay in which you describe what you wear (or would want to wear) when you are trying to impress someone. Give examples of how or if your style changes depending on who it is you want to impress.

3. Spend some time in the local mall, the campus cafeteria, or any other public space that offers opportunities for people watching. Pay attention to the way the people around you dress and how they wear their hair. From your observations, what would you say clothing or hairstyles tell you about the people who wear them? Write an essay that explains how you identify people by their clothes and hairstyles. What details do you use in your judgments?

Style in Revolt: Revolting Style

Dick Hebdige

> Dick Hebdige is a lecturer in Communication at Goldsmith College, University
> of London. His research in such articles as "Reggae, Rastas and Rudies" has pri-
> marily focused on subcultures, those men and women who create their own cul-
> ture of speaking, acting, and dressing outside and against mainstream society's
> more accepted ways. The following selection is excerpted from Hebdige's 1979
> book-length study *Subculture: The Meaning of Style,* in which he examines the
> political and cultural importance of the British punk movement. In this short seg-
> ment from his study of style in subcultures, Hebdige examines the punk move-
> ment's use of style as a tool of disruption and revolt. The punk movement,
> originally a British subculture, made style a primary means of rebellion, threat-
> ening the stability of mainstream culture with images of violence and with a pro-
> found disrespect for all things conventional.

SUGGESTION FOR READING

As you read, notice the range of evidence Hebdige produces to develop his
characterization of punk culture. Underline passages in which he makes general points about that culture.

Nothing was holy to us. Our movement was neither mystical, communistic nor anarchistic. All
of these movements had some sort of programme, but ours was completely nihilistic. We spat
on everything, including ourselves. Our symbol was nothingness, a vacuum, a void.
> *George Grosz on Dada*

We're so pretty, oh so pretty…vac-unt.
> *The Sex Pistols*

Although it was often directly offensive (T-shirts covered in swear words) and threatening
(terrorist/guerilla outfits) punk style was defined principally through the violence of its
"cut ups." Like Duchamp's "ready mades"—manufactured objects which qualified as art
because he chose to call them such, the most unremarkable and inappropriate items—a pin,
a plastic clothes peg, a television component, a razor blade, a tampon—could be brought
within the province of punk (un)fashion. Anything within or without reason could be turned
into part of what Vivien Westwood called "confrontation dressing" so long as the rupture
between "natural" and constructed context was clearly visible (i.e., the rule would seem to
be: if the cap doesn't fit, wear it).

Objects borrowed from the most sordid of contexts found a place in the punks' ensem-
bles: lavatory chains were draped in graceful arcs across chests encased in plastic bin-liners.
Safety pins were taken out of their domestic "utility" context and worn as gruesome ornaments through the cheek, ear or lip. "Cheap" trashy fabrics (PVC, plastic, lurex, etc.) in vulgar designs (e.g., mock leopard skin) and "nasty" colours, long discarded by the quality end
of the fashion industry as obsolete kitsch, were salvaged by the punks and turned into garments (fly boy drainpipes, "common" mini-skirts) which offered self-conscious commentaries
on the notions of modernity and taste. Conventional ideas of prettiness were jettisoned along

with the traditional feminine lore of cosmetics. Contrary to the advice of every woman's magazine, make-up for both boys and girls was worn to be seen. Faces became abstract portraits: sharply observed and meticulously executed studies in alienation. Hair was obviously dyed (hay yellow, jet black, or bright orange with tufts of green or bleached in question marks), and T-shirts and trousers told the story of their own construction with multiple zips and outside seams clearly displayed. Similarly, fragments of school uniform (white brinylon shirts, school ties) were symbolically defiled (the shirts covered in graffiti, or fake blood; the ties left undone) and juxtaposed against leather drains or shocking pink mohair tops. The perverse and the abnormal were valued intrinsically. In particular, the illicit iconography of sexual fetishism was used to predictable effect. Rapist masks and rubber wear, leather bodices and fishnet stockings, implausibly pointed stiletto heeled shoes, the whole paraphernalia of bondage—the belts, straps and chains—were exhumed from the boudoir, closet and the pornographic film and placed on the street where they retained their forbidden connotations. Some young punks even donned the dirty raincoat—that most prosaic symbol of sexual "kinkiness"—and hence expressed their deviance in suitably proletarian terms.

Of course, punk did more than upset the wardrobe. It undermined every relevant discourse. Thus dancing, usually an involving and expressive medium in British rock and mainstream pop cultures, was turned into a dumbshow of blank robotics. Punk dances bore absolutely no relation to the desultory frugs and clinches which Geoff Mungham describes as intrinsic to the respectable working-class ritual of Saturday night at the Top Rank or Mecca.[1] Indeed, overt displays of heterosexual interest were generally regarded with contempt and suspicion (who let the BOF/wimp[2] in?) and conventional courtship patterns found no place on the floor in dances like the pogo, the pose and the robot. Though the pose did allow for a minimum sociability (i.e., it could involve two people) the "couple" were generally of the same sex and physical contact was ruled out of court as the relationship depicted in the dance was a "professional" one. One participant would strike a suitable cliché fashion pose while the other would fall into a classic "Bailey" crouch to snap an imaginary picture. The pogo forebade even this much interaction, though admittedly there was always a good deal of masculine jostling in front of the stage. In fact the pogo was a caricature—a reductio ad absurdum of all the solo dance styles associated with rock music. It resembled the "anti dancing" of the "Leapniks" which Melly describes in connection with the trad boom (Melly, 1972). The same abbreviated gestures—leaping into the air, hands clenched to the sides, to head an imaginary ball—were repeated without variation in time to the strict mechanical rhythms of the music. In contrast to the hippies' languid, free-form dancing, and the "idiot dancing" of the heavy metal rockers, the pogo made improvisation redundant: the only variations were imposed by changes in the tempo of the music—fast numbers being "interpreted" with manic abandon in the form of frantic on-the-spots, while the slower ones were pogoed with a detachment bordering on the catatonic.

The robot, a refinement witnessed only at the most exclusive punk gatherings, was both more "expressive" and less "spontaneous" within the very narrow range such terms acquired in punk usage. It consisted of barely perceptible twitches of the head and hands or more extravagant lurches (Frankenstein's first steps?) which were abruptly halted at random points. The resulting pose was held for several moments, even minutes, and the whole sequence was as suddenly, as unaccountably, resumed and re-enacted. Some zealous punks carried things one step further and choreographed whole evenings, turning themselves for a matter of hours, like Gilbert and George,[3] into automata, living sculptures.

The music was similarly distinguished from mainstream rock and pop. It was uniformly basic and direct in its appeal, whether through intention or lack of expertise. If the latter, then the punks certainly made a virtue of necessity ("We want to be amateurs"—Johnny Rotten). Typically, a barrage of guitars with the volume and treble turned to maximum accompanied by the occasional saxophone would pursue relentless (un)melodic lines against a turbulent background of cacophonous drumming and screamed vocals. Johnny Rotten succinctly defined punk's position on harmonics: "We're into chaos not music."

The names of the groups (the Unwanted, the Rejects, the Sex Pistols, the Clash, the Worst, etc.) and the titles of the songs: "Belsen was a Gas," "If You Don't Want to Fuck Me, Fuck Off," "I Wanna Be Sick on You," reflected the tendency towards willful desecration and the voluntary assumption of outcast status which characterized the whole punk movement. Such tactics were, to adapt Levi-Strauss's famous phrase, "things to whiten mother's hair with." In the early days at least, these "garage bands" could dispense with musical pretensions and substitute, in the traditional romantic terminology, "passion" for "technique," the language of the common man for the arcane posturings of the existing élite, the now familiar armoury of frontal attacks for the bourgeois notion of entertainment or the classical concept of "high art."

It was in the performance arena that punk groups posed the clearest threat to law and order. Certainly, they succeeded in subverting the conventions of concert and nightclub entertainment. Most significantly, they attempted both physically and in terms of lyrics and life-style to move closer to their audiences. This in itself is by no means unique: the boundary between artist and audience has often stood as a metaphor in revolutionary aesthetics (Brecht, the surrealists, Dada, Marcuse, etc.) for that larger and more intransigent barrier which separates art and the dream from reality and life under capitalism.[4] The stages of those venues secure enough to host "new wave" acts were regularly invaded by hordes of punks, and if the management refused to tolerate such blatant disregard for ballroom etiquette, then the groups and their followers could be drawn closer together in a communion of spittle and mutual abuse. At the Rainbow Theatre in May 1977 as the Clash played "White Riot," chairs were ripped out and thrown at the stage. Meanwhile, every performance, however apocalyptic, offered palpable evidence that things could change, indeed were changing: that performance itself was a possibility no authentic punk should discount. Examples abounded in the music press of "ordinary fans" (Siouxsie of Siouxsie and the Banshees, Sid Vicious of the Sex Pistols, Mark P of *Sniffin Glue,* Jordan of the Ants) who had made the symbolic crossing from the dance floor to the stage. Even the humbler positions in the rock hierarchy could provide an attractive alternative to the drudgery of manual labour, office work or a youth on the dole. The Finchley Boys, for instance, were reputedly taken off the football terraces by the Stranglers and employed as roadies.

If these "success stories" were, as we have seen, subject to a certain amount of "skewed" interpretation in the press, then there were innovations in other areas which made opposition to dominant definitions possible. Most notably, there was an attempt, the first by a predominantly working-class youth culture, to provide an alternative critical space within the subculture itself to counteract the hostile or at least ideologically inflected coverage which punk was receiving in the media. The existence of an alternative punk press demonstrated that it was not only clothes or music that could be immediately and cheaply produced from the limited resources at hand. The fanzines (*Sniffin Glue, Ripped and Torn,* etc.) were journals edited by an individual or a group, consisting of reviews, editorials and interviews with prominent punks, produced on a small scale as cheaply as possible, stapled together and distributed through a small number of sympathetic retail outlets.

The language in which the various manifestoes were framed was determinedly "working class" (i.e., it was liberally peppered with swear words) and typing errors and grammatical mistakes, misspellings and jumbled pagination were left uncorrected in the final proof. Those corrections and crossings out that were made before publication were left to be deciphered by the reader. The overwhelming impression was one of urgency and immediacy, of a paper produced in indecent haste, of memos from the front line.

This inevitably made for a strident buttonholing type of prose which, like the music it described, was difficult to "take in" in any quantity. Occasionally a written, more abstract item—what Harvey Garfinkel (the American ethnomethodologist) might call an "aid to sluggish imaginations"—might creep in. For instance, *Sniffin Glue,* the first fanzine and the one which achieved the highest circulation, contained perhaps the single most inspired item of propaganda produced by the subculture—the definitive statement of punk's do-it-yourself philosophy—a diagram showing three finger positions on the neck of a guitar over the caption: "Here's one chord, here's two more, now form your own band."

Even the graphics and typography used on record covers and fanzines were homologous with punk's subterranean and anarchic style. The two typographic models were graffiti which was translated into a flowing "spray can" script, and the ransom note in which individual letters cut up from a variety of sources (newspapers, etc.) in different type faces were pasted together to form an anonymous message. The Sex Pistols' "God Save the Queen" sleeve (later turned into T-shirts, posters, etc.) for instance incorporated both styles: the roughly assembled legend was pasted across the Queen's eyes and mouth which were further disfigured by those black bars used in pulp detective magazines to conceal identity (i.e., they connote crime or scandal). Finally, the process of ironic self abasement which characterized the subculture was extended to the name "punk" itself which, with its derisory connotations of "mean and petty villainy," "rotten," "worthless," etc. was generally preferred by hardcore members of the subculture to the more neutral "new wave."[5]

Notes

1. In his P.O. account of the Saturday night dance in an industrial town, Mungham (1976) shows how the constricted quality of working-class life is carried over into the ballroom in the form of courtship rituals, masculine paranoia and an atmosphere of sullenly repressed sexuality. He paints a gloomy picture of joyless evenings spent in the desperate pursuit of "booze and birds" (or "blokes and a romantic bus-ride home") in a controlled setting where "spontaneity is regarded by managers and their staff—principally the bouncers—as the potential hand-maiden of rebellion".

2. BOF = Boring Old Fart.
   Wimp = "wet."

3. Gilbert and George mounted their first exhibition in 1970 when, clad in identical conservative suits, with metallized hands and faces, a glove, a stick and a tape recorder, they won critical acclaim by performing a series of carefully controlled and endlessly repeated movements on a dais while miming to Flanagan and Allen's "Underneath the Arches." Other pieces with titles like "Lost Day" and "Normal Boredom" have since been performed at a variety of major art galleries throughout the world.

4. Of course, rock music had always threatened to dissolve these categories, and rock performances were popularly associated with all forms of riot and disorder—from the slashing of cinema seats by teddy boys through Beatlemania to the hippy happenings and festivals where freedom was expressed less aggressively in nudity, drug taking and general "spontaneity." However, punk represented a new departure.

5. The word "punk," like the black American "funk" and "superbad" would seem to form part of that "special language of fantasy and alienation" which Charles Winick describes (1959), "in which values are reversed and in which 'terrible' is a description of excellence." See also Wolfe (1969) where he describes the "cruising" scene in Los Angeles in the mid-60s—a subculture of custom-built cars, sweatshirts and "high-piled, perfect coiffure" where "rank" was a term of approval:

   > Rank! Rank is just the natural outgrowth of Rotten...Roth and Schorsch grew up in the Rotten Era of Los Angeles teenagers. The idea was to have a completely rotten attitude towards the adult world, meaning, in the long run, the whole established status structure, the whole system of people organising their lives around a job, fitting into the social structure embracing the whole community. The idea in Rotten was to drop out of conventional status competition into the smaller netherworld of Rotten Teenagers and start one's own league.

Works Cited

Melly, G. (1972), *Revolt into Style,* Penguin.

Mungham, G. (1976), "Youth in Pursuit of Itself," in G. Mungham and G. Pearson (eds.), *Working Class Youth Culture,* Routledge & Kegan Paul.

Winick, C. (1959), "The Uses of Drugs by Jazz Musicians," *Social Problems,* vol. 7, no. 3, Winter.

Wolfe, T. (1969), *The Pump House Gang,* Bantam.

SUGGESTIONS FOR DISCUSSION

1. What would you say is Hebdige's attitude toward the punk movement? Point to passages that best convey that attitude.

2. Hebdige's work is primarily about British styles. Is there a mainstream culture, a minority culture, a subculture, or several variations of those in your own community? How do you recognize each? What of Hebdige's discussion might seem to apply to the way these different groups express themselves?

3. Notice that Hebdige quite often compares punk fashion and punk actions to art movements and the artists in those movements. These artists, and the movements like Dada which he mentions, all rejected mainstream art values in order to create an art of their own which would surprise and shock a mass audience. What point is Hebdige attempting to make by comparing punks with such movements in the art world?

SUGGESTIONS FOR WRITING

1. Hebdige explains how punks use common objects or forms of dress in new ways. Write an essay on how a group that you know about uses objects or styles in ways that depart from their originally intended uses. What new meanings are invested in the style they create?

2. Write an essay that compares Hebdige's and Molloy's analyses of style. What do you think they might agree on? In what ways do their perspectives differ?

3. Write an essay that describes how a group or an individual in your school or local community uses style of dress as part of its group identity. What would you say are the key markers of this group's style? Explain how the group uses style to distinguish itself from other groups.

VISUAL CULTURE *PUMPED UP*

Although much attention has been given to the current demand in women's fashion for women to achieve what has been called a "painful thinness," men do not escape the idealizing vision that is often associated with stylishness or perfection. In the following excerpt, "The Male Nude," Richard Leppert examines the function that the "pumped up" look plays in idealizing the male body, especially as it is displayed in ads for body building equipment. Through pumping iron, men's bodies "become object-sights," Leppert tells us. "The 'strength' that they possess is literally for show only."

The Male Nude

Richard Leppert

Richard Leppert is professor and chair of the Department of Cultural Studies and Comparative Literature at the University of Minnesota. He has written extensively on the cultural dimensions of painting and music in such works as *The Sight of Sound: Music, Representation, and the History of the Body* (1993) and *Music and Image* (1988). The excerpt that follows is taken from *Art and the Committed Eye: The Cultural Functions of Imagery* (1996).

SUGGESTION FOR READING

You might discover that some of what is written below seems to be about more than just body building ads. This is because Leppert's discussion is set in the larger context of a more complete analysis of the appearance of the male nude in Western art. Don't let yourself be distracted by references that aren't immediately familiar to you. It might help you focus on what is being said here if you take some time after a first reading to review the excerpt and then write a brief summary.

All people learn by looking: Establishing identity depends on looking at one's own gender, at others like oneself. That is, "the stability of masculinity depends upon the visibility of the male body; to be learnt or consolidated, masculinity requires a visual exchange between men."[1] Furthermore, looking engenders not only "education" but also desires, which by their very nature inevitably involve the body and commonly—though not always—the erotic, narrowly conceived. Yet because of powerful proscriptions against homoeroticism, the male looking at the self through the same-sex Other is at best problematic. In no small part this explains why men organize their looking at other men in specifically sanctioned venues, those of professional sports especially, which, after all, exist to be viewed.[2]

Nor is it an accidental by-product that in sport we have located a terrain where a kind of physical contact between men is acceptable that would elsewhere be regarded as intolerable: the embracing and butt-slapping that occur when points are scored. Likewise, cable-television ads for body building equipment devise their appeal to men by negotiating a very thin line that separates the purportedly straight from the gay. To appeal to men, the ads mark themselves as straight; but to sell the product the beautiful male body must be made an object of desire to men who, since childhood, have been cautioned against looking at men. Moreover, the body that is the object of the gaze is itself objectified in ways very similar to the objectification of female nudes—with the crucial exception that the male body is made active, always on the move. Nonetheless, the body is principally made an object for display, hence looking. Its pumped-up muscles are not presented as necessary to any sort of physical labor (apart from body "sculpting"), save for the identity of masculinity that they presumably produce. Muscle-machine muscles are in essence designer muscles: They operate as pure and simple aesthetics, and aesthetics is a geography in our culture principally labeled as feminine. Moreover, the male body of the ads is not only deeply tanned but oiled. It is made into a reflective surface, the more eye-catching on that account, though functionally the oiled body is utterly illogical—except as spectacle (it makes a mess on the body building machine itself, stains gym shorts, etc.). The male bodies in the ads are *cosmetically* adjusted by the oiling—and makeup has long been culturally designated feminine....[These advertisements] operate by highlighting as desirable a body that few men possess, *and* by carefully and indirectly acknowledging culturally suppressed desires and practices.

Notes

1. Michael Hatt, "Muscles, Morals, Mind: The Male Body in Thomas Eakins' Salutat," in *The Body Imaged: The Human Form and Visual Culture Since the Renaissance,* eds. Kathleen Adler and Marcia Pointon (Cambridge: Cambridge University Press, 1993), p. 63.

2. See the valuable study by Whitney Davis, "Erotic Revision in Thomas Eakins's Narratives of Male Nudity," *Art History* 17 (1994), pp. 301–341.

©1995 Callard & Bowser-Suchard Inc.

SUGGESTIONS FOR DISCUSSION

1. Leppert's discussion of body building suggests that body building is more about men wanting to look good for other men than it is about their desire to impress women. Looking at the images reprinted here, how much would you say these ads conform to that analysis? Where do they depart from it?

2. Often when critics write about the female image in advertising, they note how the woman's body has been made into an object. She is often posed looking away from the camera so that the viewer seems to be looking in on her without her knowing. Do these images of pumped up male bodies

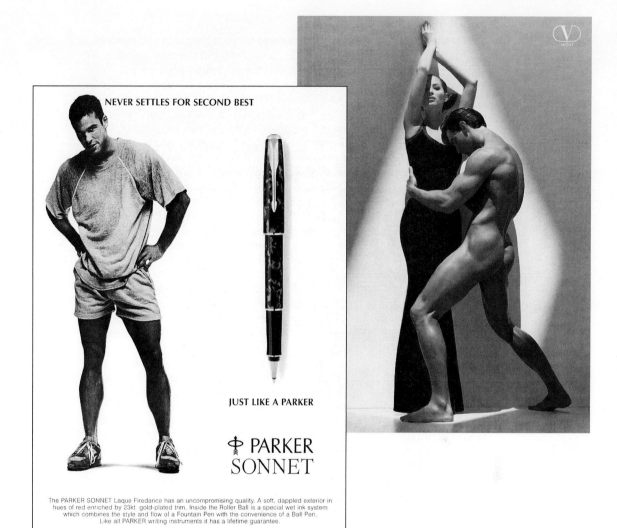

do the same? Pay attention to how the men are photographed. What seems to be emphasized in the ad? How are they posed? Do they look at the viewer, which may suggest that they have some control over their space, or do they look away? To what extent does physical activity depicted in these images give the models more or less control over the way we look at them? If they are pictured with female models, what is the relationship between the two?

3. Leppert writes that body building is more about "sculpting" the body than building any kind of real strength. What's more, this sculpted body is meant more to appeal to other men than to attract women. In what ways does this hold true (or not) for the 1953 He-Man ad?

SUGGESTED ASSIGNMENT

Although all advertising promises something to the potential buyer, many of those promises are implicit. The ads for Parker Pens and Valentino fashions, for example, link the product to an image that the advertisers hope we will find appealing. It isn't clear what the athlete has to do with the pen, for example, but most readers will make some connection (durability? attractiveness? a winner?). Whatever the connection, the ad copy tells us that this man "Never settles for second best," so if the model impresses us, perhaps the pen will, too. The Valentino ad's promise is entirely implicit but, in some respects, is easier to understand. The woman wearing Valentino fashions is the object of desire. The man, represented in a pose that recalls a Rodin sculpture, embraces this goddess-like figure. Apparently, Valentino fashions have quite the impact.

Typical body building ads are much more explicit in the promises they make. The 1953 He-Man ad is packed with promises: Success. Envy. New friends. Women. That ad may seem old-fashioned and even silly today, but a 1996 ad for Fitness King workout instruction makes very similar claims: "a body that has the look of success," one that undoubtedly drives a "Porsche, Jaguar, Mercedes." Likewise, Nordic Track's ad for NordicFlex™ UltraLift promised that you will "Finally, get the body you've always wanted!"

For this project, collect a series of body building ads (as many as fifteen to twenty). You can find these ads in a number of body building and fitness magazines, but they also run in more general publications such as *Esquire, Sports Illustrated,* and *Ebony.*

Use these ads as the basis for a paper in which you examine the promises made both explicitly (in what the ad copy says) and implicitly (in the images used) to men who "pump up," and how those promises convey a vision of what constitutes masculinity and how it is attained in this culture.

You might wish to review Richard Leppert's piece on body building ads and read or review Jean Kilbourne's "Beauty…and the Beast of Advertising" (see Images) to see how she talks of ideal feminine beauty in advertising. Both selections can suggest ways that you might write about the image hyped in most body building ads and what that image promises the consumer. On the other hand, you might wish to review selections in this chapter that discuss success and rebellion and how they are signaled by clothing and personal appearance, to help you read the vision of success hyped in the body building ads that you find.

FIELD WORK | *WRITING A QUESTIONNAIRE*

As John Molloy notes in his study, one of the best ways to find out what people are thinking about is to ask them. That is why you periodically find yourself being asked to fill in a questionnaire. You can't get the depth of information from a questionnaire that you can get from an interview, but you are likely to reach more people. Therefore, the kinds of questions you ask in a questionnaire must be as focused and specific as possible. You will notice, for example, that the questions listed at the end of the Molloy selection ask for only yes or no answers because he wanted to be able to quantify the results easily.

For this assignment, design and distribute a questionnaire that focuses on a topic that has come from your readings, your group and class discussions, or your own investigations. For example, like Molloy or Chapkis or Hebdige, you might be interested in finding out how people respond to mainstream and subculture "looks." Or hooks and Gates might have prompted you to be curious about how African Americans today feel about hairstyles and the concerns that arose in the 1960s over more "natural" looks. You might want to find out the current stereotypes for athletes or female beauty or subculture looks. There are certainly many other topics or questions raised by the writers in this chapter. There probably also were questions raised in class discussion for which you would like answers.

The examples below demonstrate the types of questions you can ask and the kind of answer you are likely to get depending on how you limit the response.

For very specific information about those filling out your survey, ask closed questions like these:

1. Gender (check one): ❏ male ❏ female

2. Age (check one): ❏ 16–25 ❏ 25–35 ❏ 35+

Questions like the following will provide information on specific styles that you can list and then quantify.

3. Which of the following best characterizes the clothing most popular among you and your friends (check one only):

❏ very baggy clothes   ❏ pro-sports logos   ❏ jeans and T-shirts

Questions, like the one below, that offer more than a yes/no response can reveal a range of attitudes:

4. Rate the following statement using the five-point scale below where 5 represents Strongly Agree and 1 represents Strongly Disagree. Circle the number that best represents your response: (You can write several statements in a row like the one in our sample.)

Tattoos are a counterculture statement.   5 4 3 2 1

Open-ended questions, like those that follow, will give your informants more freedom to compose an answer, but such answers can make it difficult for you to form any general conclusions about the attitudes of an entire group because they provide little control over possible responses:

5. How would you describe the prevailing style that you and your friends follow?

6. How would you describe counterculture styles in your school or home town?

You can, of course, design a questionnaire with more than one type of question, but since the questionnaire you will be designing for this project should be brief, you will probably want to limit the types of questions to those you can quantify. You can always include an open-ended question at the very end of your questionnaire if you want more information than your other questions are likely to give you.

The questionnaire you design will come from your interests, but it must be limited. You can't learn very much if you ask too much. If the questionnaire is too long and complicated, you will have trouble getting people to respond. Remember, for example, the work of Molloy. He used two pictures of the same person dressed in two different raincoats. His question was direct: Which one would you hire? His audience was specific: Potential employers.

You can design this questionnaire on your own, with a small group of classmates, or as an entire class. If you do it on your own, you will probably want to get fifteen to twenty-five responses. If you work with a small group, you can each get ten responses and have a fairly large sampling to compile. If the entire class uses the same questionnaire, each person can get ten responses and have a substantial amount of information to sort through. Of course, if you design your questionnaire with others, there's a good chance your own interests will not be addressed.

Even if you have only twenty-five responses to your questionnaire, you will have more than your own and your classmates' impressions from which to draw. That is the kind of information that can help you broaden your own response and begin to account for the differences as well as the similarities that you see around you.

SUGGESTIONS FOR DESIGNING A QUESTIONNAIRE

- *Make it brief and readable.* For this project, it is best to put your questionnaire on one side of a page. The simpler it seems to your audience, the more likely they will be able to take the time for it. Be sure to make it readable, as well. Don't try to crowd too many questions on the page or make instructions complicated. There should be plenty of white space, and the language should be simple and direct.

- *Write different kinds of questions to get different kinds of answers.* The kind of questions that you ask will determine the kind of information that you receive.

- *Decide who will answer your questionnaire.* If you want a response about youth styles from young people, limit your questionnaire to that group. You might, however, want an older audience's response to youth styles. Other kinds of issues might not be as limited to one group or another, but when you tally results, you will probably want to know the thoughts of people in different age brackets or of different genders.

REPORT ON YOUR FINDINGS

Once you have completed your questionnaire, plan to report your findings to the rest of the class. You can write a report, give a presentation, or design a graph that charts the information you received, as in the accompanying graph from a survey on what teenagers thought was hip in 1996.

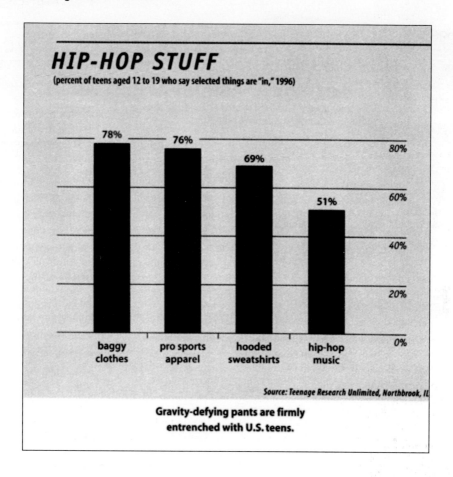

HIP-HOP STUFF

(percent of teens aged 12 to 19 who say selected things are "in," 1996)

Source: Teenage Research Unlimited, Northbrook, IL

Gravity-defying pants are firmly entrenched with U.S. teens.

Soirée de Paris
Yves St-Laurent's first creation for
Christian Dior, 1955.

Mining the Archive

FASHION IN HISTORY

Although you could go to old magazines for this work (*Vogue*, *Harper's Bazaar*, or *Mademoiselle*, for example), many museums throughout this country contain large, comprehensive collections of costumes, everyday clothing, work clothes, uniforms, and high fashion. Two of the best that also offer online research options are Kent State University Museum (http://www.kent.edu/museum/), and the Costume institute at the Metropolitan Museum of Art (http://www.metmuseum.org). There are others, or course, including a site devoted to how rationing affected fashion during World War II. You can find many of these other sites simply by entering "fashion history" into your search engine or by narrowing the search to fashion in a particular historical period.

For this assignment, locate a source for the history of clothing styles. This can be an online source like those we have already noted or a large or small museum or gallery near you that has a collection of clothing styles through the ages.

Most of these sites house women's fashions primarily, though some men's fashions are also included. As well, most museum collections—though not all—focus on high fashion rather than daily clothing or work clothes. After you have examined the collection, write a report on style in history. You can focus, for example, on how the ideal shape of women has changed through the ages or how fashion reflects the times (the freedom of the "Roaring Twenties," for example, or the focus on family in the 1950s). Your focus will be determined partially by the collection you find, so make your decision about your report after you have spent considerable time examining the collection and the support materials—histories, commentary, further recommended resources—available in the collection.

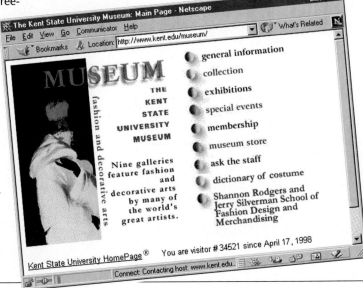

CHAPTER 6

Public Space

In wildness, is the preservation of the world.
Henry David Thoreau

When you go up to the city, you better have some cash,
'cause the people in the city don't mess around with trash.
Traditional blues lyric

O ne way of examining how a culture lives and what it values is to look at its public spaces—its streets, parks, sports arenas, shopping malls, museums—all those places where people gather to do business and play and loiter. Such spaces are abundant in countrysides and suburbs as well as in cities. Megamalls and fast food restaurants line the highway system as a result of urban sprawl, and in small towns and rural areas, the fairgrounds, town halls, county arenas, and churches still function as public gathering spots. In fact, even America's wilderness areas have become places where the public gathers, where tourists travel to catch a glimpse of the Grand Canyon, to picnic in Yellowstone, and to hike in the Adirondacks.

Most public spaces are designed to be simply functional, which is why much of

what you see every day is remarkable only for its similarity to nearly everything else you see. Office buildings that seem to pop up from the pavement overnight look like every other office building in the city. The new wing of a local hospital looks tacked on to the old wing—a high-rise box of rooms and corridors. One grocery store looks like all the others, schools look like schools, and doctors' offices look like doctors' offices. A popular motel chain even tried for a while to capitalize on its across-the-continent sameness. Holiday Inn ads promised "no surprises," apparently assuming that most Americans are uncomfortable with anything too flashy or too different. Perhaps that is why it is so easy to take most public spaces for granted. It is only when a place looks different—newer, flashier, stranger—that most visitors stop to look. In a world

271

crowded with so much to look at, it takes an effort, a real spectacle, to get people's attention.

It is very easy to think of the most famous or infamous public spaces in contemporary America as constituting spectacle above all else. From the Mall of America to Epcot Center, each new public space seems vying to be the biggest and most expensive. Such spaces compete for attention, inviting visitors to look, to linger, and to buy. These public spaces turned spectacle characterize at least one impulse in a consumer economy—the impulse to sell.

In America, perhaps the purest example of public space as spectacle is the Las Vegas casino strip. Writer Tom Wolfe once described Vegas as "the only town in the world whose skyline is made up of neither buildings, like New York, nor of trees, like Wilbraham, Massachusetts, but of signs....But such signs! They tower. They revolve, they oscillate, they soar in shapes before which the existing vocabulary of art history is helpless." As a place of spectacle, Las Vegas is pure flash, pure appearance—spectacle for its own sake.

Even that characterization is misleading, however, for the spectacle that is Las Vegas hardly exists for its own sake; it is there for the sake of the sale. In an era in which advertising is one of the most prolific forms of communication, spectacle emerges as a natural manifestation of the sales pitch. In this age of the automobile and the highway system, spectacle caters to a moving public, a public that hasn't time for a lengthy meal or a complex ad. Bright lights, motion, glitter, surprise—this is the landscape that modern Americans drive past in their motor homes.

Of course, our interest in public space has to do with more than just appearance. To say a space is public is to suggest it is there for the use of the population at large—a space for a community, not simply for private use. Yet more and more spaces that at first seem to be public aren't public in the strictest sense. Malls, for example, are often credited with becoming the new "town square," but a town square is clearly a public space where people in the community do have certain rights, like the right to free speech. Malls are private property. You cannot distribute campaign literature or any other kinds of materials without the permission of mall owners, and those owners are probably going to be very careful about letting anyone into their space

who seems to threaten business. So even though a mall might invite a Senior Mall Walker's Club to come and exercise before stores open for business, that is not the same as walking out your door and taking your morning jog through the neighborhood. The mall owners can rescind the invitation at any time and bar from the property anyone they feel interferes with business.

Even public streets are not so free to the public as we might imagine. Demonstrators at the 1996 Democratic National Convention in Chicago found themselves segregated into small groups, some very far from the convention site through the use of a "lottery system," as the city attempted to keep control of any potential disturbance. Officials of the St. Patrick's Day Parade in New York City have fought for years to ban gays from having a visible presence in that event. Throughout U.S. cities, town squares and shop fronts are purposely designed to keep people from being able to sit and chat or rest comfortably, so that loiterers, street people, groups of teenagers, and anyone without a "purpose" to be there won't be tempted to hang around.

What's more, the tension between public use of public space and private land ownership is a serious one, especially when it comes to wilderness land holdings. In the West, cattle ranchers fight all attempts to limit their access to or increase use fees on grazing land within national parks. The debate over whether or not to open the Black Hills to more gold mining is ongoing. Throughout the country, the national park system has continued privatizing many of its services. Consequently, parks have been changing in response to revenue generated by those new businesses. In other words, we live with contradiction: Americans want public spaces but value private use. It is a conflict that is not easily resolved.

The very design of our cities, towns, subdivisions, and planned communities can reflect the concerns and struggles of the culture at large. For example, the gap between rich and poor is apparent not only in people's income (or lack of income) but also in the breakdown of public services and the disrepair of buildings and roads in poorer parts of town. Whether you live in the city, the suburbs, or the country; if you have visited historical monuments; spent time in New York or Los Angeles; attended a ball game; watched a parade; shopped in a mall; eaten in a fast food restaurant; or simply attended a church bazaar or school dance, you already know a good deal about how public space is organized in contemporary America, and you probably make more judgments about public spaces than you think.

READING THE CULTURE OF PUBLIC SPACE

As you read and talk about the public spaces that constitute the "look" of the United States today, you will be asked to write your own impressions of and draw your own meanings from those spaces. The selections and assignments in this chapter move from consideration of wilderness areas to the malls of the suburbs to the world of the city. One way to look at public space is to recall the first impressions you have had of places you have seen. As you explore these memories, you may begin to understand how you form your own judgments of places. For many people across the United States, public space means open land, wilderness holdings, national parks, and other lands held by the government in the public trust. Edward Abbey's description of Arches National Monument offers one view of the importance of wilderness. What Abbey's selection might also suggest for you as a writer and thinker is that writing about place need not merely be a matter of describing what is there, as if it were natural or normal or inevitable. You can, instead, take a position on the meaning and value of place and how it ought to be treated. We follow that selection with an essay by Barry Lopez, whose own experience trying to locate an invisible border between the United States and Canada off the eastern Arctic coast of Alaska leads him both to lyric description and to the realization that land is never simply ours to enjoy. It comes with responsibility, especially as we use our votes in zoning referendums or the annexation of rural lands.

John Fiske's analysis of mall culture raises questions about how we design space, who needs it, and how it is used. Fiske's work suggests that you look at these spaces as emerging from the meanings and values of the culture in which they were created. Fiske is insistent that, though malls might exert a powerful pull on the senses, most consumers are not duped by the hype. Instead, most of us are able to use these spaces to meet our own needs, even when those uses directly contradict the carefully planned-for use of the developers. Thus, teenagers become mall rats, hanging out but rarely shopping in those megamalls that seem so seductive. That may be one reason, as Robyn Meredith reports, that the Mall of America has imposed a curfew on unescorted teens who want to hang out there on weekend nights. Meredith's article will give you the opportunity to talk about who should have control of public spaces, and which spaces are actually controlled by private interests and thus not subject to the same regulations truly *public* spaces must follow.

Our final selections—Mike Davis's "Fortress Los Angeles," Eva Cockroft and Holly Barnet-Sánchez's introduction to the Chicano mural movement ("Signs from the Heart"), and Eric Liu's commentary on the branding of public space—offer ways to examine how space is ordered, controlled, and claimed in major cities.

Though the work in this chapter begins with observation and memory, you will have the opportunity to do fieldwork, collect and examine images of public space, and offer your own assessments of the way we use the spaces we inhabit. What you write depends very much on what you have already experienced and what you already think about the topic. Take time, then, at the beginning of your reading to mine your memory about public spaces.

The First Morning

Edward Abbey

Edward Abbey was a novelist, naturalist, activist, and iconoclast. Throughout his life he fought the predominant notion in this country that "progress" means building something new. In response to an interviewer's question, Abbey once said that the Southwest's biggest enemy was "expansion, development, commercial greed, industrial growth. That kind of growth which has become a pathological condition in our society. That insatiable demand for more and more; the urge to dominate and consume and destroy." This excerpt and the one that follows are from *Desert Solitaire,* which Abbey wrote in 1968 as "not a travel guide but an elegy. A memorial." For two years in the mid-1950s, Abbey was a park ranger in Arches National Monument, at that time an undeveloped national park in southeastern Utah. For those two years, he kept a journal from which *Desert Solitaire* was written. In the two selections reprinted here, Abbey writes of why he treasures the park and what he sees as the foremost threat to its beauty.

SUGGESTION FOR READING

As you read, underline those passages that seem best to convey Abbey's attitude toward growth and expansion.

This is the most beautiful place on earth.

There are many such places. Every man, every woman, carries in heart and mind the image of the ideal place, the right place, the one true home, known or unknown, actual or visionary. A houseboat in Kashmir, a view down Atlantic Avenue in Brooklyn, a gray gothic farmhouse two stories high at the end of a red dog road in the Allegheny Mountains, a cabin on the shore of a blue lake in spruce and fir country, a greasy alley near the Hoboken waterfront, or even, possibly, for those of a less demanding sensibility, the world to be seen from a comfortable apartment high in the tender, velvety smog of Manhattan, Chicago, Paris, Tokyo, Rio or Rome—there's no limit to the human capacity for the homing sentiment. Theologians, sky pilots, astronauts have even felt the appeal of home calling to them from up above, in the cold black outback of interstellar space.

For myself I'll take Moab, Utah. I don't mean the town itself, of course, but the country which surrounds it—the canyonlands. The slickrock desert. The red dust and the burnt cliffs and the lonely sky—all that which lies beyond the end of the roads.

The choice became apparent to me this morning when I stepped out of a Park Service housetrailer—my caravan—to watch for the first time in my life the sun come up over the hoodoo stone of Arches National Monument.

I wasn't able to see much of it last night. After driving all day from Albuquerque—450 miles—I reached Moab after dark in cold, windy, clouded weather. At park headquarters north of town I met the superintendent and the chief ranger, the only permanent employees, except for one maintenance man, in this particular unit of America's national park system. After coffee they gave me a key to the housetrailer and directions on how to reach it; I am required to live and work not at headquarters but at this one-man station some twenty miles back in the interior, on my own. The way I wanted it, naturally, or I'd never have asked for the job.

Leaving the headquarters area and the lights of Moab, I drove twelve miles farther north on the highway until I came to a dirt road on the right, where a small wooden sign pointed the way: Arches National Monument Eight Miles. I left the pavement, turned east into the howling wilderness. Wind roaring out of the northwest, black clouds across the stars—all I could see were clumps of brush and scattered junipers along the roadside. Then another modest signboard:

WARNING: QUICKSAND

DO NOT CROSS WASH

WHEN WATER IS RUNNING

The wash looked perfectly dry in my headlights. I drove down, across, up the other side and on into the night. Glimpses of weird humps of pale rock on either side, like petrified elephants, dinosaurs, stone-age hobgoblins. Now and then something alive scurried across the road: kangaroo mice, a jackrabbit, an animal that looked like a cross between a raccoon and a squirrel—the ringtail cat. Farther on a pair of mule deer started from the brush and bounded obliquely through the beams of my lights, raising puffs of dust which the wind, moving faster than my pickup truck, caught and carried ahead of me out of sight into the dark. The road, narrow and rocky, twisted sharply left and right, dipped in and out of tight ravines, climbing by degrees toward a summit which I would see only in the light of the coming day.

Snow was swirling through the air when I crossed the unfenced line and passed the boundary marker of the park. A quarter-mile beyond I found the ranger station—a wide place in the road, an informational display under a lean-to shelter, and fifty yards away the little tin government housetrailer where I would be living for the next six months.

A cold night, a cold wind, the snow falling like confetti. In the lights of the truck I unlocked the housetrailer, got out bedroll and baggage and moved in. By flashlight I found the bed, unrolled my sleeping bag, pulled off my boots and crawled in and went to sleep at once. The last I knew was the shaking of the trailer in the wind and the sound, from inside, of hungry mice scampering around with the good news that their long lean lonesome winter was over—their friend and provider had finally arrived.

This morning I awake before sunrise, stick my head out of the sack, peer through a frosty window at a scene dim and vague with flowing mists, dark fantastic shapes looming beyond. An unlikely landscape.

I get up, moving about in long underwear and socks, stooping carefully under the low ceiling and the lower doorways of the housetrailer, a machine for living built so efficiently and compactly there's hardly room for a man to breathe. An iron lung it is, with windows and venetian blinds.

The mice are silent, watching me from their hiding places, but the wind is still blowing and outside the ground is covered with snow. Cold as a tomb, a jail, a cave; I lie down on the dusty floor, on the cold linoleum sprinkled with mouse turds, and light the pilot on the butane heater. Once this thing gets going the place warms up fast, in a dense unhealthy way, with a layer of heat under the ceiling where my head is and nothing but frigid air from the knees down. But we've got all the indispensable conveniences: gas cookstove, gas refrigerator, hot water heater, sink with running water (if the pipes aren't frozen), storage cabinets and shelves, everything within arm's reach of everything else. The gas comes from two steel bottles in a shed outside; the water comes by gravity flow from a tank buried in a hill close by. Quite luxurious for the wilds. There's even a shower stall and a flush toilet with a dead rat in the bowl. Pretty soft. My poor mother raised five children without any of these luxuries and might be doing without them yet if it hadn't been for Hitler, war and general prosperity.

Time to get dressed, get out and have a look at the lay of the land, fix a breakfast. I try to pull on my boots but they're stiff as iron from the cold. I light a burner on the stove and hold the boots upside down above the flame until they are malleable enough to force my feet into. I put on a coat and step outside. In the center of the world, God's navel, Abbey's country, the red wasteland.

The sun is not yet in sight but signs of the advent are plain to see. Lavender clouds sail like a fleet of ships across the pale green dawn; each cloud, planed flat on the wind, has a base of fiery gold. Southeast, twenty miles by line of sight, stand the peaks of the Sierra La Sal, twelve to thirteen thousand feet above sea level, all covered with snow and rosy in the morning sunlight. The air is dry and clear as well as cold; the last fogbanks left over from last night's storm are scudding away like ghosts, fading into nothing before the wind and the sunrise.

The view is open and perfect in all directions except to the west where the ground rises and the skyline is only a few hundred yards away. Looking toward the mountains I can see the dark gorge of the Colorado River five or six miles away, carved through the sandstone mesa, though nothing of the river itself down inside the gorge. Southward, on the far side of the river, lies the Moab valley between thousand-foot walls of rock, with the town of Moab somewhere on the valley floor, too small to be seen from here. Beyond the Moab valley is more canyon and tableland stretching away to the Blue Mountains fifty miles south. On the north and northwest I see the Roan Cliffs and the Book Cliffs, the two-level face of the Uinta Plateau. Along the foot of those cliffs, maybe thirty miles off, invisible from where I stand, runs U.S. 6–50, a major east-west artery of commerce, traffic and rubbish, and the main line of the Denver-Rio Grande Railroad. To the east, under the spreading sunrise, are more mesas, more canyons, league on league of red cliff and arid tablelands, extending through purple haze over the bulging curve of the planet to the ranges of Colorado—a sea of desert.

Within this vast perimeter, in the middle ground and foreground of the picture, a rather personal demesne, are the 33,000 acres of Arches National Monument of which I am now sole inhabitant, usufructuary, observer and custodian.

What are the Arches? From my place in front of the housetrailer I can see several of the hundred or more of them which have been discovered in the park. These are natural arches, holes in the rock, windows in stone, no two alike, as varied in form as in dimension. They range in size from holes just big enough to walk through to openings large enough to contain the dome of the Capitol building in Washington, D.C. Some resemble jug handles or flying buttresses, others natural bridges but with this technical distinction: a natural bridge spans a watercourse—a natural arch does not. The arches were formed through hundreds of thousands of years by the weathering of the huge sandstone walls, or fins, in which they are found. Not the work of a cosmic hand, nor sculptured by sand-bearing winds, as many people prefer to believe, the arches came into being and continue to come into being through the modest wedging action of rainwater, melting snow, frost, and ice, aided by gravity. In color they shade from off-white through buff, pink, brown and red, tones which also change with the time of day and the moods of the light, the weather, the sky.

Standing there, gaping at this monstrous and inhuman spectacle of rock and cloud and sky and space, I feel a ridiculous greed and possessiveness come over me. I want to know it all, possess it all, embrace the entire scene intimately, deeply, totally, as a man desires a beautiful woman. An insane wish? Perhaps not—at least there's nothing else, no one human, to dispute possession with me.

The snow-covered ground glimmers with a dull blue light, reflecting the sky and the approaching sunrise. Leading away from me the narrow dirt road, an alluring and primitive track into nowhere, meanders down the slope and toward the heart of the labyrinth of naked stone. Near the first group of arches, looming over a bend in the road, is a balanced rock about fifty feet high, mounted on a pedestal of equal height; it looks like a head from Easter Island, a stone god or a petrified ogre.

Like a god, like an ogre? The personification of the natural is exactly the tendency I wish to suppress in myself, to eliminate for good. I am here not only to evade for a while the clamor and filth and confusion of the cultural apparatus but also to confront, immediately and directly if it's possible, the bare bones of existence, the elemental and fundamental, the bedrock which sustains us. I want to be able to look at and into a juniper tree, a piece of quartz, a vulture, a spider, and see it as it is in itself, devoid of all humanly ascribed qualities, anti-Kantian, even the categories of scientific description. To meet God or Medusa face to face, even if it means risking everything human in myself. I dream of a hard and brutal mysticism in which the naked self merges with a nonhuman world and yet somehow survives still intact, individual, separate. Paradox and bedrock.

Well—the sun will be up in a few minutes and I haven't even begun to make coffee. I take more baggage from my pickup, the grub box and cooking gear, go back in the trailer and start breakfast. Simply breathing, in a place like this, arouses the appetite. The orange juice is frozen, the milk slushy with ice. Still chilly enough inside the trailer to turn my breath to vapor. When the first rays of the sun strike the cliffs I fill a mug with steaming coffee and sit in the doorway facing the sunrise, hungry for the warmth.

Suddenly it comes, the flaming globe, blazing on the pinnacles and minarets and balanced rocks, on the canyon walls and through the windows in the sandstone fins. We greet each other, sun and I, across the black void of ninety-three million miles. The snow glitters between us, acres of diamonds almost painful to look at. Within an hour all the snow exposed to the sunlight will be gone and the rock will be damp and steaming. Within minutes, even as I watch, melting snow begins to drip from the branches of a juniper nearby; drops of water streak slowly down the side of the trailerhouse.

I am not alone after all. Three ravens are wheeling near the balanced rock, squawking at each other and at the dawn. I'm sure they're as delighted by the return of the sun as I am and I wish I knew the language. I'd sooner exchange ideas with the birds on earth than learn to carry on intergalactic communications with some obscure race of humanoids on a satellite planet from the world of Betelgeuse. First things first. The ravens cry out in husky voices, blue-black wings flapping against the golden sky. Over my shoulder comes the sizzle and smell of frying bacon.

That's the way it was this morning.

Labor Day

Edward Abbey

Now here comes another clown with a scheme for the utopian national park: Central Park National Park, Disneyland National Park. Look here, he says, what's the matter with you fellows?—let's get cracking with this dump. Your road is bad; pave it. Better yet, build a paved road to every corner of the park; better yet, pave the whole damned place so any damn fool can drive anything anywhere—is this a democracy or ain't it? Next, charge a good stiff admission fee; you can't let people in free; that leads to socialism and regimentation. Next, get rid of all these homely rangers in their Smokey the Bear suits. Hire a crew of pretty girls, call them rangerettes, let them sell the tickets and give the campfire talks. And advertise, for godsake, advertise! How do you expect to get people in here if you don't advertise? Next, these here Arches—light them up. Floodlight them, turn on colored, revolving lights—jazz it up, man, it's dead. Light up the whole place, all night long, get on a 24-hour shift, keep them coming, keep them moving, you got two hundred million people out there waiting to see your product—is this a free country or what the hell is it? Next your campgrounds, you gotta do something about your campgrounds, they're a mess. People can't tell where to park their cars or which spot is whose—you gotta paint lines, numbers, mark out the campsites nice and neat. And they're still building fires on the ground, with wood! Very messy, filthy, waste-ful. Set up little grills on stilts, sell charcoal briquettes, better yet hook up with the gas line, install jets and burners. Better yet do away with the campgrounds altogether, they only cause delay and congestion and administrative problems—these people want to see America, they're not going to see it sitting around a goddamned campfire; take their money, give them the show, send them on their way—that's the way to run a business....

I exaggerate. Slightly. Was he real or only a bad dream? Am I awake or sleeping? Will Tuesday never come? No wonder they call it Labor Day.

SUGGESTIONS FOR DISCUSSION

1. Much of Edward Abbey's anger toward developers was aimed at those developers who wanted to "improve" places like Arches National Monu-ment by putting in roads and running water and convenience stores. What does Abbey see are the issues raised by development, growth, expansion, and "progress"? How does his position compare to your own?

2. Abbey calls the Arches "this monstrous and inhuman spectacle of rock and cloud and sky and space." How does Abbey's use of the term specta-cle differ from other uses of the term that you are familiar with?

3. What would you say are the assumptions about how human beings ought to live (or their relation to the natural world) that underlie Abbey's thinking? What are your own assumptions about how we ought to live?

SUGGESTIONS FOR WRITING

1. The two selections we have chosen from *Desert Solitaire* are written in first person, but the person who seems to be speaking "sounds" differ-ent in "The First Morning" from the person speaking in "Labor Day." Write an analysis of these two selections and explain how the tone of the writing changes from one passage to the next. In your analysis, you will want to suggest what Abbey accomplishes with the change in tone. What does he want his readers to understand about Arches National Park and tourism with these two descriptions? Abbey ends "Labor Day" by admitting that he exaggerates. Why would he admit that? What assumptions does he make about his reader that are perhaps signaled by that admission?

2. Some people object to Abbey's position on progress and development because they say he is being selfish: He wants places to be left alone because that is how he lives best; that is what he prefers. Write an essay and address that issue of selfishness and land conservation or preservation. From what you have read here, to what extent does Abbey's writing leave him open to such charges? If he had taken care to avoid those charges, what would be lost or changed in what he has written?

3. Write an essay about a place you know well that you have seen change. Describe the change. Use the nature of that change (good or bad, healthy or unhealthy, beautiful or garish, etc.) to explain your own posi-tion on progress or development—at least as it has worked in the case of the place that you are discussing.

Borders

Barry Lopez

Barry Lopez is a contributing editor for *Harper's* and a regular writer for such publications as the *New York Times, Paris Review,* and *North American Review*. He has been the recipient of such honors as the National Book Award (for *Arctic Dreams*), a Guggenheim Fellowship, and the Pushcart prize. The following essay from *Crossing Open Ground* (1989) originally appeared in 1981 in the magazine *Country Journal*. It was written during one of Lopez's trips to the Arctic north. Throughout his career, Lopez's essays and fiction have drawn readers' attention to the kinds of spaces most of us never see or even think much about— from the desert landscapes of the Southwest to the wilderness areas of Alaska and the Arctic.

SUGGESTION FOR READING

Lopez's story of his trip to locate the international line that separates Alaska and the Yukon Territory offers him an opportunity to write about the artificial nature of such borders discernible only by the markers set in place to claim territory. As you read, note in the margins where Lopez shifts from his story of the border excursion to his commentary on borders.

In early September, the eastern Arctic coast of Alaska shows several faces, most of them harsh. But there are days when the wind drops and the sky is clear, and for reasons too fragile to explain—the overflight of thousands of migrating ducks, the bright, silent austerity of the Romanzof Mountains under fresh snow, the glassy stillness of the ocean—these days have an edge like no others. The dawn of such a clear and windless day is cherished against memories of late August snow squalls and days of work in rough water under leaden skies.

One such morning, a few of us on a biological survey in the Beaufort Sea set that work aside with hardly a word and headed east over the water for the international border, where the state of Alaska abuts the Yukon Territory. The fine weather encouraged this bit of adventure.

There are no settlements along this part of the arctic coast. We did not in fact know if the border we were headed to was even marked. A northeast wind that had been driving loose pack ice close to the shore for several days forced us to run near the beach in a narrow band of open water. In the lee of larger pieces of sea ice, the ocean had begun to freeze, in spite of the strong sunlight and a benign feeling in the air. Signs of winter.

As we drove toward Canada, banking the open, twenty-foot boat in graceful arcs to avoid pieces of drift ice, we hung our heads far back to watch migrating Canada geese and black brant pass over. Rifling past us and headed west at fifty miles an hour a foot off the water were flocks of oldsquaw, twenty and thirty ducks at a time. Occasionally, at the edge of the seaward ice, the charcoal-gray snout of a ringed seal would break the calm surface of the ocean for breath.

We drew nearer the border, wondering aloud how we would know it. I remembered a conversation of years before, with a man who had escaped from Czechoslovakia to come to America and had later paddled a canoe the length of the Yukon. He described the border where the river crossed into Alaska as marked by a great swath cut through the spruce forest. In the middle of nowhere, I said ruefully; what a waste of trees, how ugly it must have seemed.

He looked silently across the restaurant table at me and said it was the easiest border crossing of his life.

I thought, as we drove on east, the ice closing in more now, forcing us to run yet closer to the beach, of the geographer Carl Sauer and his concept of biologically distinct regions. The idea of bioregionalism, as it has been developed by his followers, is a political concept that would reshape human life. It would decentralize residents of an area into smaller, more self-sufficient, environmentally responsible units, occupying lands the borders of which would be identical with the borders of natural regions—watersheds, for example. I thought of Sauer because we were headed that day for a great, invisible political dividing line: 141 degrees western longitude. Unlike the border between Utah and Colorado, this one is arbitrary. If it were not actually marked—staked—it would not be discernible. Sauer's borders are noticeable. Even the birds find them.

On the shore to our right, as we neared the mouth of Demarcation Bay, we saw the fallen remains of an Eskimo sod house, its meat-drying racks, made of driftwood, leaning askew. Someone who had once come this far to hunt had built the house. The house eventually became a dot on U.S. Coast and Geodetic Survey maps. Now its location is vital to the Inuit, for it establishes a politically important right of prior use, predating the establishment of the Arctic National Wildlife Refuge, within whose borders it has been included. I recall all this as we pass, from poring over our detailed maps the night before. Now, with the warmth of sunlight on the side of my face, with boyhood thoughts of the Yukon Territory welling up inside, the nearness of friends, with whom work has been such keen satisfaction these past few weeks, I have no desire to see maps.

Ahead, it is becoming clear that the closing ice is going to force us right up on the beach before long. The wedge of open water is narrowing. What there is is very still, skimmed with fresh slush ice. I think suddenly of my brother, who lives in a house on Block Island, off the coast of Rhode Island. When I visit we walk and drive around the island. Each time I mean to ask him, does he feel any more ordered in his life for being able to see so clearly the boundary between the ocean and the land in every direction? But I am never able to phrase the question right. And the old and dour faces of the resident islanders discourage it.

Far ahead, through a pair of ten-power binoculars, I finally see what appears to be a rampart of logs, weathered gray-white and standing on a bluff where the tundra falls off fifteen or twenty feet to the beach. Is this the border?

We are breaking ice now with the boat. At five miles an hour, the bow wave skitters across the frozen surface of the ocean to either side in a hundred broken fragments. The rumbling that accompanies this shattering of solid ice is like the low-throttled voice of the outboard engines. Three or four hundred yards of this and we stop. The pack ice is within twenty feet of the beach. We cannot go any farther. That we are only a hundred feet from our destination seems a part of the day, divinely fortuitous.

We climb up the bluff. Arctic-fox tracks in the patchy snow are fresh. Here and there on the tundra are bird feathers, remnants of the summer molt of hundreds of thousands of birds that have come this far north to nest, whose feathers blow inland and out to sea for weeks. Although we see no animals but a flock of snow geese in the distance, evidence of their residence and passage is everywhere. Within a few hundred feet I find caribou droppings. On a mossy tundra mound, like one a jaeger might use, I find two small bones that I know to be a ptarmigan's.

We examine the upright, weathered logs and decide on the basis of these and several pieces of carved wood that this is, indeed, the border. No one, we reason, would erect something like this on a coast so unfrequented by humans if it were not. (This coast is ice-free only eight or ten weeks in the year.) Yet we are not sure. The bluff has a certain natural prominence, though the marker's placement seems arbitrary. But the romance of it—this foot in Canada, that one in Alaska—is fetching. The delightful weather and the presence of undisturbed animals has made us almost euphoric. It is, after days of bottom trawls in thirty-one-degree water, of cold hours of patient searching for seals, so clearly a holiday for us.

I will fly over this same spot a week later, under a heavy overcast, forced down to two hundred feet above the water in a search for migrating bowhead whales. That trip, from the small settlement of Inuvik on the East Channel of the Mackenzie River in the Northwest Territories to Deadhorse, Alaska, will make this border both more real and more peculiar than it now appears. We will delay our arrival by circling over Inuvik until a Canadian customs officer can get there from the village of Tuktoyaktuk on the coast, though all we intend to do is to drop off an American scientist and buy gas. On our return trip we are required by law to land at the tiny village of Kaktovik to check through U.S. Customs. The entry through Kaktovik is so tenuous as to not exist at all. One might land, walk the mile to town, and find or not find the customs officer around. Should he not be there, the law requires we fly 250 miles south to Fort Yukon. If no one is there we are to fly on to Fairbanks before returning to Deadhorse on the coast, in order to reenter the country legally. These distances are immense. We could hardly carry the fuel for such a trip. And to fly inland would mean not flying the coast to look for whales, the very purpose of being airborne. We fly straight to Deadhorse, looking for whales. When we land we fill out forms to explain our actions and file them with the government.

Here, standing on the ground, the border seems nearly whimsical. The view over tens of square miles of white, frozen ocean and a vast expanse of tundra which rolls to the foot of snow-covered mountains is unimpeded. Such open space, on such a calm and innocent day as this, gives extraordinary release to the imagination. At such a remove—from horrible images of human death on borders ten thousand miles away, form the press of human anxiety one feels in a crowded city—at such a remove one is lulled nearly to foundering by the simple peace engendered, even at the border between two nations, by a single day of good weather.

As we turn to leave the monument, we see two swans coming toward us. They are immature tundra swans, in steel-gray plumage. Something odd is in their shape. Primary feathers. They have no primary feathers yet. Too young. And their parents, who should be with them, are nowhere to be seen. They are coming from the east, from Canada, paddling in a strip of water a few inches deep right at the edge of the beach. They show no fear of us, although they slow and are cautious. They extend their necks and open their pink bills to make gentle, rattling sounds. As they near the boat they stand up in the water and step ashore. They walk past us and on up the beach. Against the gritty coarseness of beach sand and the tundra-stained ice, their smooth gray feathers and the deep lucidity of their eyes vibrate with beauty. I watch them until they disappear from view. The chance they will be alive in two weeks is very slim. Perhaps it doesn't exist at all.

In two weeks I am thousands of miles south. In among the letters and magazines in six weeks of mail sitting on the table is a thick voter-registration pamphlet. One afternoon I sit down and read it. I try to read it with the conscientiousness of one who wishes to vote wisely. I think of Carl Sauer, whose ideas I admire. And of Wendell Berry, whose integrity and sense of land come to mind when I ponder any vote and the effect it might have. I think of the invisible borders of rural landscapes. Of Frost pondering the value of fences. I read in the pamphlet of referendums on statewide zoning and of the annexation of rural lands, on which I am expected to vote. I read of federal legislative reapportionment and the realignment of my county's border with that of an Indian reservation, though these will not require my vote. I must review, again, how the districts of my state representative and state senator overlap and determine if I am included now within the bounds of a newly created county commissioner's territory.

These lines blur and I feel a choking coming up in my neck and my face flushing. I set the pamphlet on the arm of the chair and get up and walk outside. It is going to take weeks, again, to get home.

SUGGESTIONS FOR DISCUSSION

1. Early in his essay, Lopez relates the story of a conversation with a refugee from Czechoslovakia who tells him that he remembers the border Lopez is looking for because, when he crossed it, it was marked by "a great swath cut through the spruce forest." Lopez, the naturalist, is appalled by the clear-cut, while the Czech man tells him it was "the easiest border crossing of his life." Later, Lopez directs his readers' attention to a sod house that once served as a makeshift fishing and hunting shack but now serves another more far-reaching function both for map makers and for the Inuit of the area. Why does Lopez tell these stories? How do the stories position Lopez for his readers?

2. Lopez recalls for the reader the work of Carl Sauer, who argues that borders should not be defined by politics or nationalism but by the natural biological regions of the earth. Lopez writes, "Sauer's borders are noticeable. Even the birds find them." Recount Lopez's brief description of Sauer's argument. Discuss with a group of your classmates your response to Sauer's proposal as Lopez explains it. How does your position compare to the position of your classmates? How do individual experiences contribute to the ways we might respond to a proposal like Sauer's?

3. At the end of this essay, Lopez returns home to a pile of mail and, particularly, to a voter registration packet. He writes here of his own role, as a voter, in creating borders and feels himself choking at the thoughts of zoning and reapportionment and more. To what extent would you compare Lopez's response to the choices voters make regarding land use to Abbey's response toward those who would "improve" Arches National Monument?

SUGGESTIONS FOR WRITING

1. Write an exploratory response to the Lopez essay in which you work out your own reactions to Lopez's comments on borders. An exploratory response (see Chapter 1) should allow you to find your voice and bring your thoughts on the essay into focus. This is an informal kind of writing in that it represents the beginnings of your thinking on the topic. However, it isn't exactly private writing. You should be able to share what you have written with others as you and your classmates discuss Lopez. Your explanatory writing should also allow you to begin to shape your own, more formal position on this topic.

2. Near the end of his essay, Lopez tells his readers that he is reminded of "the invisible borders of rural landscapes. Of Frost pondering the value of fences." Locate Robert Frost's poem "Mending Wall." You will find it in most college or public libraries in a volume of Frost's collected works. (You can even find it on the Internet simply by entering the poem's title into a search engine like Yahoo.) The poem opens with the line, "Something there is that doesn't love a wall," and ends "Good fences make

good neighbors." After rereading Lopez and Frost, write a brief explanation of Lopez's reference to the Frost poem.

3. Like Abbey, Lopez sets his deliberations within narrative (in this case, the story of a side trip to locate an invisible border) and description (images of the land—its textures, its animals, and its expanse of sea and frozen shoreline). In setting his discussion up this way, Lopez attempts to carry his reader with him. In essence, Lopez is giving the reader a reason to question the nature of borders in places where they seem to make little sense. As well, both writers are knowledgeable about the geographical features of the land, the weather patterns of the place, and the animals and plants that thrive there. You might say that Abbey and Lopez establish their authority through the use of such detail. Still, while the two writers might agree on much, they do not seem to respond in the same way to their experiences in wilderness areas. Write an essay in which you compare the responses Abbey and Lopez have to the ways we mark and use public lands.

Shopping for Pleasure: Malls, Power, and Resistance

John Fiske

John Fiske is a professor of Communication at the University of Wisconsin–Madison. He is among the many scholars today who make use of the artifacts of daily life to interpret modern culture. For Fiske, as well as others engaging in cultural studies, the analysis of popular culture can help reveal how a society produces meaning from its social experience. The following selection, taken from *Reading the Popular* and written in 1989, demonstrates how phenomena we take for granted in our everyday lives, such as shopping malls, are a part of that cultural production of meaning.

SUGGESTION FOR READING

You will notice, as you read, that Fiske makes reference to other studies from which he has drawn ideas, interpretations, and information. He uses those references to give scholarly weight to his argument and to acknowledge his use of others' work in building his own interpretation. If you are not familiar with the names (he nearly always uses last names only), don't let that stop your reading. The context in which the name is used can usually give you enough information to allow you to continue. As you read, underline passages in which Fiske distinguishes his own view from that of those other scholars.

Shopping malls are cathedrals of consumption—a glib phrase that I regret the instant it slides off my pen. The metaphor of consumerism as a religion, in which commodities become the icons of worship and the rituals of exchanging money for goods become a secular equivalent of holy communion, is simply too glib to be helpful, and too attractive to those whose intentions, whether they be moral or political, are to expose the evils and limitations of bourgeois materialism. And yet the metaphor is both attractive and common precisely because it does convey and construct a knowledge of consumerism; it does point to one set of "truths," however carefully selected a set.

Truths compete in a political arena, and the truths that the consumerism-as-contemporary-religion strives to suppress are those that deny the difference between the tenor and vehicle of the metaphor. Metaphor always works within that tense area within which the forces of similarity and difference collide, and aligns itself with those of similarity. Metaphor constructs similarity out of difference, and when a metaphor becomes a cliché, as the shopping mall-cathedral one has, then a resisting reading must align itself with the differences rather than the similarities, for clichés become clichés only because of their centrality to common sense: the cliché helps to construct the commonality of common sense.

So, the differences: the religious congregation is powerless, led like sheep through the rituals and meanings, forced to "buy" the truth on offer, all the truth, not selective bits of it. Where the interests of the Authority on High differ from those of the Congregation down Low, the congregation has no power to negotiate, to discriminate: all accommodations are made by the powerless, subjugated to the great truth. In the U.S. marketplace, 90 percent of new products fail to find sufficient buyers to survive (Schudson 1984), despite advertising, promotions, and all the persuasive techniques of the priests of consumption. In Australia, Sinclair (1987) puts the new product failure rate at 80 percent—such statistics are obviously best-guesstimates: what matters is that the failure rate is high. The power of consumer discrimination evidenced here has no equivalent in the congregation: no religion could tolerate a rejection rate of 80 or 90 percent of what it has to offer.

Religion may act as a helpful metaphor when our aim is to investigate the power of consumerism; when, however, our focus shifts to the power of the consumer, it is counterproductive....Shopping is the crisis of consumerism: it is where the art and tricks of the weak can inflict most damage on, and exert most power over, the strategic interests of the powerful. The shopping mall that is seen as the terrain of guerrilla warfare looks quite different from the one constructed by the metaphor of religion.

Pressdee (1986), in his study of unemployed youth in the South Australian town of Elizabeth, paints a clear picture of both sides in this war. The ideological practices that serve the interests of the powerful are exposed in his analysis of the local mall's promotional slogan, which appears in the form of a free ticket: "Your ticket to a better shopping world: ADMITS EVERYONE." He comments:

> The words "your" and "everyone" are working to socially level out class distinction and, in doing so, overlook the city's two working class groups, those who have work and those who do not. The word "admits" with a connotation of having to have or be someone to gain admittance is cancelled out by the word "everyone"—there are no conditions of admittance; everyone is equal and can come in.

This pseudoticket to consumerism denies the basic function of a ticket—to discriminate between those who possess one and those who do not—in a precise moment of the ideological work of bourgeois capitalism with its denial of class difference, and therefore of the inevitability of class struggle. The equality of "everyone" is, of course, an equality attainable only by those with purchasing power: those without are defined out of existence, as working-class interests (derived from class *difference*) are defined out of existence by bourgeois ideology. "The ticket to a better shopping world does not say 'Admits everyone with at least some money to spend'...; money and the problems associated with getting it conveniently disappear in the official discourse" (Pressdee 1986:10–11).

Pressdee then uses a variation of the religious metaphor to sum up the "official" messages of the mall:

The images presented in the personal invitation to all in Elizabeth is then that of the cargo cult. Before us a lightshaft beams down from space, which contains the signs of the "future"; "Target", "Venture"—gifts wrapped; a table set for two. But beamed down from space they may as well be, because…this imagery can be viewed as reinforcing denial of the production process—goods are merely beamed to earth. The politics of their production and consumption disappear.

Yet his study showed that 80 percent of unemployed young people visited the mall at least once a week, and nearly 100 percent of young unemployed women were regular visitors. He comments on these uninvited guests:

> For young people, especially the unemployed, there has been a congregating within these cathedrals of capitalism, where desires are created and fulfilled and the production of commodities, the very activity that they are barred from, is itself celebrated on the altar of consumerism. Young people, cut off from normal consumer power, are invading the space of those with consumer power. (p. 13)

Pressdee's shift from the religious metaphor to one of warfare signals his shift of focus from the powerful to the disempowered.

Thursday nights, which in Australia are the only ones on which stores stay open late, have become the high points of shopping, when the malls are at their most crowded and the cash registers ring up their profits most busily, and it is on Thursday nights that the youth "invasion" of consumer territory is most aggressive. Pressdee (1986) describes this invasion vividly:

> Thursday nights vibrate with youth, eager to show themselves:—it belongs to them, they have possessed it. This cultural response is neither spectacular nor based upon consumerism itself. Nor does it revolve around artifacts or dress, but rather around the possession of space, or to be more precise the possession of consumer space where their very presence challenges, offends and resists.
>
> Hundreds of young people pour into the centre every Thursday night, with three or four hundred being present at any one time. They parade for several hours, not buying, but presenting, visually, all the contradictions of employment and unemployment, taking up their natural public space that brings both life and yet confronts the market place. Security men patrol all night aided by several police patrols, hip guns visible and radios in use, bringing a new understanding to law and order.
>
> Groups of young people are continually evicted from this opulent and warm environment, fights appear, drugs seem plentiful, alcohol is brought in, in various guises and packages. The police close in on a group of young women, their drink is tested. Satisfied that it is only coca-cola they are moved on and out. Not wanted. Shopkeepers and shoppers complain. The security guards become agitated and begin to question all those seen drinking out of cans or bottles who are under 20, in the belief that they must contain alcohol. They appear frightened, totally outnumbered by young people as they continue their job in keeping the tills ringing and the passage to the altar both free and safe. (p. 14)

Pressdee coins the term "proletarian shopping" (p. 16) to describe this window shopping with no intention to buy. The youths consumed images and space instead of commodities, a kind of sensuous consumption that did not create profits. The positive pleasure of parading up and down, of offending "real" consumers and the agents of law and order, of asserting their difference within, and different use of, the cathedral of consumerism became an oppositional cultural practice.

The youths were "tricksters" in de Certeau's terms—they pleasurably exploited their knowledge of the official "rules of the game" in order to identify where these rules could be mocked, inverted, and thus used to free those they were designed to discipline. De Certeau (1984) points to the central importance of the "trickster" and the "guileful ruse" throughout peasant and folk cultures. Tricks and ruses are the art of the weak that enables them to exploit their understanding of the rules of the system, and to turn it to their advantage. They are a refusal to be subjugated:

> The actual order of things is precisely what "popular" tactics turn to their own ends, without any illusion that it will change any time soon. Though elsewhere it is exploited by a dominant power…here order is tricked by an art. (de Certeau 1984: 26)

This trickery is evidence of "an ethics of tenacity (countless ways of refusing to accord the established order the status of a law, a meaning or a fatality)" (p. 26).

Shopping malls are open invitations to trickery and tenacity. The youths who turn them into their meeting places, or who trick the security guards by putting alcohol into some, but only some, soda cans, are not actually behaving any differently from lunch hour window shoppers who browse through the stores, trying on goods, consuming and playing with images, with no intention to buy. In extreme weather people exploit the controlled climate of the malls for their own pleasure—mothers take children to play in their air-conditioned comfort in hot summers, and in winter older people use their concourses for daily walks. Indeed, some malls now have notices welcoming "mall walkers," and a few have even provided exercise areas set up with equipment and instructions so that the walkers can exercise more than their legs.

Of course, the mall owners are not entirely disinterested or altruistic here—they hope that some of the "tricky" users of the mall will become real economic consumers, but they have no control over who will, how many will, how often, or how profitably. One boutique owner told me that she estimated that 1 in 30 browsers actually bought something. Shopping malls are where the strategy of the powerful is most vulnerable to the tactical raids of the weak.

References

De Certeau, M. (1984). *The Practice of Everyday Life*. Berkeley: University of California Press.

Pressdee, M. (1986). "Agony or Ecstasy: Broken Transitions and the New Social State of Working-Class Youth in Australia." Occasional Papers, S. Australian Centre for Youth Studies, S.A. College of A.E., Magill, S. Australia.

Schudson, M. (1984). *Advertising: The Uneasy Persuasion*. New York: Basic Books.

Sinclair, J. (1987). *Images Incorporated: Advertising as Industry and Ideology*. London: Croom Helm.

SUGGESTIONS FOR DISCUSSION

1. Why does Fiske challenge the cathedral metaphor as a useful one for analyzing the place of malls in our culture? How is the mall of today like the great cathedrals of the past? How does the metaphor of the mall as a place of warfare work in Fiske's analysis?

2. What do you think Fiske means when he says, "The equality of 'everyone' is, of course, an equality attainable only by those with purchasing power; those without are defined out of existence"?

3. Fiske has based most of what he says on his observations of malls in Australia. How would you describe mall culture in America?

SUGGESTIONS FOR WRITING

1. As we mentioned in our Suggestion for Reading in this selection, the Fiske essay is a difficult one for some to follow because he relies heavily on others' writing as well as his own observations. You'll want to begin your

When most of us think about shopping malls, we naturally think of the kind of place of which John Fiske writes—an enclosed space containing department stores and several smaller stores where we go to shop or hang out or to get out of the weather. However, with increased use of Internet technology, virtual malls are now being created. Explore the Web for one of those virtual malls and consider how the entire concept of "mall" changes when the space it occupies is electronic. You can do that by using a search engine like Yahoo or Lycos. When we used Yahoo and simply entered the words virtual + mall, we found 538 sites, so there are many sites that at least consider themselves virtual malls. What would you say constitutes a "mall" space, virtual or not?

work with Fiske by making sure that you know what he is arguing. To get at his argument, write a one-page summary of Fiske's interpretation of mall culture. Share the summary you have written with a group of your classmates. As you read others' summaries, take note of ideas or details they noticed that you did not notice. Once you have finished your discussion, come to a consensus on what your group considers Fiske's most important assertions.

2. Review the opening two paragraphs of Fiske's essay. In that passage, he offers his readers a metaphor and then suggests that there are always problems with any metaphor. It can be a tough passage because it takes in more than just the metaphor of the mall, but it also suggests the problem with that metaphor and the problems with metaphors in general. Still, these early paragraphs contain important information for a reader to understand. Write a one-paragraph paraphrase of those opening paragraphs. (In a paraphrase, you restate using your own words from a portion of a text. This kind of exercise can be useful in helping you to make sure that you understand what you are reading and can apply it to other things, like examining the usefulness of the metaphors that Fiske offers. If you were to use your paraphrase in an essay, you would have to make sure that you acknowledge your source and give information about where you found the material. However, you would not use quotation marks around a paraphrase because you are using your language, not the language of the writer.)

3. Fiske's analysis of mall culture focuses attention away from the store owners and mall managers who make the rules and hope to profit from their investments. Instead, Fiske asks us to pay attention to how people use the mall. He writes, "Shopping malls are open invitations to trickery and tenacity. The youths who turn them into their meeting places, or who trick the security guards by putting alcohol into some, but only some, soda cans, are not actually behaving any differently from lunch hour shoppers who browse through the stores, trying on goods, consuming and playing with images, with no intention to buy." Choose another public space that people use for their own purposes rather than or in addition to the purpose for which it was designed, and write an essay that explains what it is about the place you have chosen that lends itself

to "trickery and tenacity," as Fiske says malls do. For this essay, you can rely on your own recollection of and experience with the place for your analysis. Remember to bring in events you have witnessed or things you and your friends or family have done in that place. You can also draw on Fiske's analysis of the way the public uses mall space to help you understand and explain the way the public uses the place you have chosen. If you wrote summaries and the paraphrase suggested above, you will find those helpful as resources for your own use of Fiske.

Big Mall's Curfew Raises Questions of Rights and Bias

Robyn Meredith

Robyn Meredith is a reporter for the *New York Times*. In the following article that ran in the *Times* September 4, 1996, Meredith reports on the decision by owners of Minnesota's Mall of America to place a curfew on teenagers who want to shop there. The curfew banned teenagers under age sixteen from the Mall on Friday and Saturday nights, unless they are accompanied by a parent or other adult over the age of twenty-one. In the article reprinted below, Meredith explores the implications of such a curfew, including charges that the ban has racist overtones. At the center of the controversy over the Mall of America's decision is the question of whether malls should be treated as public rather than private spaces.

SUGGESTION FOR READING

Meredith's article is what journalists call a feature story. In it, she not only reports on a particular newsworthy event but examines issues surrounding that event. As you read, make a list of arguments for and against the decision to ban unescorted teenagers from the Mall of America on weekend nights.

BLOOMINGTON, Minn, Aug. 29—Marcus D. Wilson, 18, has been coming to the Mall of America here once or twice a week since it opened four years ago. He buys tapes, plays video games and sees his friends, especially his girlfriend.

But starting Sept. 20, his habits will be disrupted by the mall's new chaperon policy. People under 16—including his 15-year-old girlfriend, Stephanie E. Jones—will be barred from the mall on Friday and Saturday nights unless they bring a parent or other grown-up over 21. Teenage shoppers who were interviewed recently said they would not be caught dead with their parents at the Mall of America, the biggest mall in the country and the coolest spot in town.

The Mall of America is one of the nation's first shopping centers to impose curfews on unchaperoned teenagers. Malls from New Jersey to California are watching the effort as they, too, struggle to control rowdy teen-agers.

The new policy here touches on many serious social issues: safety, race relations, parental responsibility and civil liberties. Malls have always been magnets for teen-agers, but rising levels of juvenile violence have put pressure on shopping centers to limit who walks in the door.

Although the rule means that his girlfriend will be excluded on Fridays and Saturdays after 6 P.M., Mr. Wilson favors the rules because he thinks they will make the mall safer. But

Ms. Jones, who works at a shoe store, said, "If I can work in the mall, I know how to handle myself." But she added, "I understand what they're trying to get at."

Every weekend night, at least 2,000 teen-agers gather at the Mall of America. On wintry Minnesota Saturday nights, 3,000 teen-agers swarm the shopping mall, disturbing other shoppers with chases, practical jokes and fistfights, said Teresa A. McFarland, a mall spokeswoman.

Still, Mr. Wilson called the policy "a little racist" because weekend nights are the only time large groups of black teen-agers, like him, show up at the suburban mall, which is near the Minneapolis airport. Mall workers already tend to hand him a copy of the mall's rules for behavior as he walks in the door, not bothering to give copies to the white teen-agers nearby, he said. Ms. McFarland bristled at that suggestion, saying the mall's policy was to hand all young people a copy of the rules.

That sentiment is one reason some local community groups are concerned about the mall's policy and how it will be enforced. Yusef Mgeni, president of the Minneapolis chapter of the Urban Coalition, a public policy research and advocacy group, said, "This policy has been drawn up in reaction to and in large part because of the large number of young people of color who congregate in the mall in the evening."

"The policy itself is neutral," said Mr. Mgeni (pronounced em-JANE-ey). "How they implement it will determine whether it is unfair."

Virgil H. Heatwole, a mall manager, denied that the policy was directed at children of color. "It is fair; it is across the board," he said. "We are not targeting any individual, any group, any ethnic group."

Under the policy, security officers posted at each of the mall's 23 entrances will ask unchaperoned youths to prove that they are at least 16 before letting them inside. Other workers will sweep the halls, ejecting those who are under 16.

Mr. Heatwole said he hoped the policy would result in children bringing their parents to the mall. "I think society itself, we need to look at where parents are today," he said.

The mall's policy is opposed by the American Civil Liberties Union. "It infringes on the rights of young people," said Chris Hansen, a senior staff counsel at the A.C.L.U. in Manhattan. "It ought to be the parents, not the mall or the government" who decide whether unchaperoned children can come to mall, he said.

"We don't object at all to the mall setting up rules of behavior," Mr. Hansen said. "But we do object to punishing the good kids for the behavior of kids that aren't behaving."

Federal courts have ruled in past cases that shopping malls are not considered public spaces and that First Amendment rights may be restricted inside them, Mr. Hansen said. But state courts are nearly evenly divided on the issue. New York holds that malls are private property, while California courts have ruled that shopping centers "now occupy the civic role that downtown used to," Mr. Hansen said.

Minnesota does not apply First Amendment principles to shopping malls, said Kathleen M. Milner, legal counsel for the Minnesota Civil Liberties Union, part of the A.C.L.U. For that reason, her group does not plan to sue over the chaperon rules.

While many shopping centers draw customers from only their immediate communities, the Mall of America draws people of differing generations and cultures. Families from across the country, here on two-day shopping binges, mix with local teen-agers, who include rebellious suburbanites with spiked hairdos as well as poorer children from nearby Minneapolis and St. Paul. It is an uneasy combination.

Of course, security concerns at the mall pale compared with those in cities like New York. "This is not like walking into the Port Authority at 3 o'clock in the morning," said Billy Ellis, a Manhattan native who manages the mall's Rainforest Cafe, where there has never been a drunk at the bar. Many people here leave their cars unlocked in the mall's parking lot, he said.

While the mall has more than 400 stores and is so big that its indoor amusement park sports a roller coaster and log ride, teen-agers congregate on the weekends along the railings on the mall's four floors, where they can peer at one another. Parents are nowhere to be seen, and mall workers have found children as young as 12 caring for 2-year-old siblings as they wander the mall.

Young people and adults agree that the teen-agers can be obnoxious. They race down the halls in groups, scattering shoppers in their paths. They use foul language when shouting to their friends two floors above. Some even drop food or spit over the railings, aiming at shoppers below.

Recently, the fun and games have taken an alarming turn. Security officers broke up a fight between two 15-year-old boys who were quarreling about a pair of red tennis shoes, Mr. Heatwole said. One boy had lifted the other's feet off the ground as if he intended to throw him over the railing, which "could have killed him," Mr. Heatwole said.

Perhaps the worst incident came one Saturday in June. Nancy A. Bordeaux and her family came to the Mall of America from Portland, Ore. They were eating hot dogs when a gang of Asian-American teen-agers chased a group of black teen-agers through a food court. One boy pointed a gun at her 16-year-old son, Felix, who is black, apparently mistaking him briefly for one of those being chased, Mrs. Bordeaux said.

Although no one was seriously hurt, "it was really pretty frightening," said Mrs. Bordeaux, who praised the mall's chaperon policy.

While the problems seem magnified here because of the mall's sheer size, they are common on a smaller scale at shopping centers around the country, mall managers and others in the industry said.

"It is a subject that was probably hardly ever discussed 15 years ago, and now it is at the top of the agenda for a lot of management companies, and that reflects societal changes," said Mark J. Schoifet, a spokesman for the industry trade group, the International Council of Shopping Centers, based in New York.

"Malls are put in the position of being baby sitters," Mr. Schoifet said. "These are mall managers, not social workers."

The Mall of America said it had partly patterned its policy after a shopping center in Asheville, N.C., that three years ago began requiring teen-agers to have chaperons on Saturday nights. Sunrise Mall in Corpus Christi, Tex., requires children under 14 to be accompanied by an adult at all times. But the mall's general manager, Brian K. Giffin, said the rule was enforced only when unaccompanied children caused trouble.

Few malls restricted teen-agers' access, Mr. Schoifet said, because their spending power tops $90 billion a year. "Nobody in our business wants to alienate this group in any way," he said. "It is a quandary."

Malls around the country will watch to see if the Mall of America's approach works, and some might follow its example, he added.

Some stores at the Mall of America have had their business hurt by the teen-age crowd. One is the Security Store, which sells personal security items on the first floor, near a stage where families, most of them white, gather by day to hear storytellers or children's songs.

But on Friday and Saturday nights, that part of the mall seems transformed, said the store's manager, Paul T. Barnes. One evening, as he stood outside his store, someone poured a chocolate shake on his head from the floor above.

On weekend nights, Mr. Barnes said, the crowds are younger. Thousands of teen-agers swarm near his store, "70 percent of them under the age of 20 and minority and wearing gang-related apparel," Mr. Barnes said. Many of his older customers are scared away. "A lot of people are not used to seeing large numbers of kids and large numbers of minority kids," he said.

Some young black shoppers said the new chaperon policy would only add to their sense that they were under added scrutiny at the Mall of America. Martino M. Landrum, 15, said, "Every time we go to a store, we've got the owner following us, and they let the white people alone." Mr. Landrum said he knew that black gang members came to the mall, but he said white skinheads did as well. He opposes the mall's policy and said it was aimed at blacks.

Most teen-agers interviewed in the mall last week said they thought the policy was unfair because it would punish all young people, not just the ones who cause trouble.

Jackie M. Soucek, 14, one of three girls outside the mall waiting for a bus to her suburban home one night, said, "They just took away the best shopping days." She and her friends had already visited the mall twice that week, and they vowed never to be seen there with their parents.

SUGGESTIONS FOR DISCUSSION

1. With a group of your classmates, share the list of arguments you made as you read this selection. Which arguments are most convincing? Why?

2. Under what conditions do you think a curfew might be justifiable in a shopping center?

3. Review John Fiske's article on mall culture. In what ways might his analysis help to explain what mall owners are trying to address with their curfew policy?

SUGGESTIONS FOR WRITING

1. A news feature like this one often elicits Letters to the Editor, where readers voice their opinions about the topic reported on in an article. Such a letter must be brief but clear to be at all effective. Your case must be stated quickly and yet be convincing. Sometimes, letter writers rely on their own experience to make their argument. Other times, they rely on research. (For example, someone writing in response to Meredith's article might find out more about the incidence of serious crime in the Mall that involves unaccompanied teenagers and use that information to state a position.) While you won't likely write a letter to the editor on an article published this long ago, you can use the letter-to-the-editor model to write a brief position paper in response to the Mall of America's curfew policy.

2. Present your position paper to a group of your classmates, fielding comments and questions on the position you have taken. Once you have presented your paper and received feedback, rewrite your paper, expand it, and take into account those questions or concerns you consider to be the most crucial to address to make your position more complex. The feedback you got on your original paper might even have convinced you to change your thinking about the topic entirely.

3. Review both Fiske's analysis of mall culture and Meredith's feature story about the curfew policy at the Mall of America. According to Fiske, teenagers are one of the groups who typically use malls for their own purposes, sometimes as "tricksters." At the end of his essay Fiske writes, "Of course, the mall owners are not entirely disinterested or altruistic here—they hope that some of the 'tricky' users of the mall will become

real economic consumers, but they have no control over who will, how
many will, how often, or how profitably." The Mall of America's decision
to place a curfew on unescorted teenagers is clearly an attempt by business owners to take back some control of that space. Using Fiske's analysis of mall culture and Meredith's report on the mall owners' solution,
write an essay in which you speculate how effective the curfew will be in
actually controlling the ways teens use the Mall of America in the future.

Fortress Los Angeles
The Militarization of Urban Space

Mike Davis

Mike Davis teaches urban planning and political economy at the Southern California Institute of Architecture and at UCLA. He is the author of the 1992 book
City of Quartz, nominated for the National Book Critics Circle Award, and of *Prisoners of the American Dream.* The selection that follows, from *City of Quartz,* is
an analysis of the way urban planning reflects cultural change and cultural
biases. In it, Davis argues that downtown Los Angeles has become a kind of
domestic militarized zone and a place where races and classes are separated visibly and purposefully.

SUGGESTION FOR READING

Mike Davis opens this selection with the following statement: "In Los Angeles—once a paradise of free beaches, luxurious parks, and 'cruising strips'—
genuinely democratic space is virtually extinct." As you read, underline and
annotate those parts of this selection where Davis explains specifically what he
means in that opening statement.

In Los Angeles—once a paradise of free beaches, luxurious parks, and "cruising strips"—genuinely democratic space is virtually extinct. The pleasure domes of the elite Westside rely
upon the social imprisonment of a third-world service proletariat in increasingly repressive
ghettos and barrios. In a city of several million aspiring immigrants (where Spanish-surname
children are now almost two-thirds of the school-age population), public amenities are
shrinking radically, libraries and playgrounds are closing, parks are falling derelict, and streets
are growing ever more desolate and dangerous.

Here, as in other American cities, municipal policy has taken its lead from the security
offensive and the middle-class demand for increased spatial and social insulation. Taxes previously targeted for traditional public spaces and recreational facilities have been redirected
to support corporate redevelopment projects. A pliant city government—in the case of Los
Angeles, one ironically professing to represent a liberal biracial coalition—has collaborated in
privatizing public space and subsidizing new exclusive enclaves (benignly called "urban villages"). The celebratory language used to describe contemporary Los Angeles—"urban renaissance," "city of the future," and so on—is only a triumphal gloss laid over the brutalization
of its inner-city neighborhoods and the stark divisions of class and race represented in its
built environment. Urban form obediently follows repressive function. Los Angeles, as always

in the vanguard, offers an especially disturbing guide to the emerging liaisons between urban architecture and the police state.

FORBIDDEN CITY

Los Angeles's first spatial militarist was the legendary General Harrison Gray Otis, proprietor of the *Times* and implacable foe of organized labor. In the 1890s, after locking out his union printers and announcing a crusade for "industrial freedom," Otis retreated into a new *Times* building designed as a fortress with grim turrets and battlements crowned by a bellicose bronze eagle. To emphasize his truculence, he later had a small, functional cannon installed on the hood of his Packard touring car. Not surprisingly, this display of aggression produced a response in kind. On October 1, 1910, the heavily fortified *Times* headquarters—the command-post of the open shop on the West Coast—was destroyed in a catastrophic explosion, blamed on union saboteurs.

Eighty years later, the martial spirit of General Otis pervades the design of Los Angeles's new Downtown, whose skyscrapers march from Bunker Hill down the Figueroa corridor. Two billion dollars of public tax subsidies have enticed big banks and corporate headquarters back to a central city they almost abandoned in the 1960s. Into a waiting grid, cleared of tenement housing by the city's powerful and largely unaccountable redevelopment agency, local developers and offshore investors (increasingly Japanese) have planted a series of block-square complexes: Crocker Center, the Bonaventure Hotel and Shopping Mall, the World Trade Center, California Plaza, Arco Center, and so on. With an increasingly dense and self-contained circulation system linking these superblocks, the new financial district is best conceived as a single, self-referential hyperstructure, a Miesian skyscape of fantastic proportions.

Like similar megalomaniacal complexes tethered to fragmented and desolate downtowns—such as the Renaissance Center in Detroit and the Peachtree and Omni centers in Atlanta—Bunker Hill and the Figueroa corridor have provoked a storm of objections to their abuse of scale and composition, their denigration of street life, and their confiscation of the vital energy of the center, now sequestered within their subterranean concourses or privatized plazas. Sam Hall Kaplan, the former design critic of the *Times*, has vociferously denounced the antistreet bias of redevelopment; in his view, the superimposition of "hermetically sealed fortresses" and random "pieces of suburbia" onto Downtown has "killed the street" and "dammed the rivers of life."[1]

Yet Kaplan's vigorous defense of pedestrian democracy remains grounded in liberal complaints about "bland design" and "elitist planning practices." Like most architectural critics, he rails against the oversights of urban design without conceding a dimension of foresight, and even of deliberate repressive intent. For when Downtown's new "Gold Coast" is seen in relation to other social landscapes in the central city, the "fortress effect" emerges, not as an inadvertent failure of design, but as an explicit—and, in its own terms, successful—socio-spatial strategy.

The goals of this strategy may be summarized as a double repression: to obliterate all connection with Downtown's past and to prevent any dynamic association with the non-Anglo urbanism of its future. Los Angeles is unusual among major urban centers in having preserved, however negligently, most of its Beaux Arts commercial core. Yet the city chose to transplant—at immense public cost—the entire corporate and financial district from around Broadway and Spring Street to Bunker Hill, a half-dozen blocks further west.

Photographs of the old Downtown in its 1940s prime show crowds of Anglo, black, and Mexican shoppers of all ages and classes. The contemporary Downtown "renaissance" renders such heterogeneity virtually impossible. It is intended not just to "kill the street" as Kaplan feared, but to "kill the crowd," to eliminate that democratic mixture that Olmsted believed was America's antidote to European class polarization. The new Downtown is designed to ensure a seamless continuum of middle-class work, consumption, and recreation, insulated from the city's "unsavory" streets. Ramparts and battlements, reflective glass and elevated pedways, are tropes in an architectural language warning off the underclass Other. Although architectural critics are usually blind to this militarized syntax, urban pariah groups—whether young black men, poor Latino immigrants, or elderly homeless white females—read the signs immediately.

MEAN STREETS

This strategic armoring of the city against the poor is especially obvious at street level. In his famous study of the "social life of small urban spaces," William Whyte points out that the quality of any urban environment can be measured, first of all, by whether there are convenient, comfortable places for pedestrians to sit. This maxim has been warmly taken to heart by designers of the high corporate precincts of Bunker Hill and its adjacent "urban villages." As part of the city's policy of subsidizing the white-collar residential colonization of Downtown, tens of millions of dollars of tax revenue have been invested in the creation of attractive, "soft" environments in favored areas. Planners envision a succession of opulent piazzas, fountains, public art, exotic shrubbery, and comfortable street furniture along a ten-block pedestrian corridor from Bunker Hill to South Park. Brochures sell Downtown's "livability" with idyllic representations of office workers and affluent tourists sipping cappuccino and listening to free jazz concerts in the terraced gardens of California Plaza and Grand Hope Park.

In stark contrast, a few blocks away, the city is engaged in a relentless struggle to make the streets as unlivable as possible for the homeless and the poor. The persistence of thousands of street people on the fringes of Bunker Hill and the Civic Center tarnishes the image of designer living Downtown and betrays the laboriously constructed illusion of an urban "renaissance." City Hall has retaliated with its own version of low-intensity warfare.

Although city leaders periodically propose schemes for removing indigents *en masse*—deporting them to a poor farm on the edge of the desert, confining them in camps in the mountains, or interning them on derelict ferries in the harbor—such "final solutions" have been blocked by council members' fears of the displacement of the homeless into their districts. Instead the city, self-consciously adopting the idiom of cold war, has promoted the "containment" (the official term) of the homeless in Skid Row, along Fifth Street, systematically transforming the neighborhood into an outdoor poorhouse. But this containment strategy breeds its own vicious cycle of contradiction. By condensing the mass of the desperate and helpless together in such a small space, and denying adequate housing, official policy has transformed Skid Row into probably the most dangerous ten square blocks in the world. Every night on Skid Row is Friday the 13th, and, unsurprisingly, many of the homeless seek to escape the area during the night at all costs, searching safer niches in other parts of Downtown. The city in turn tightens the noose with increased police harassment and ingenious design deterrents.

One of the simplest but most mean-spirited of these deterrents is the Rapid Transit District's new barrel-shaped bus bench, which offers a minimal surface for uncomfortable sitting while making sleeping impossible. Such "bumproof" benches are being widely introduced on the periphery of Skid Row. Another invention is the aggressive deployment of outdoor sprinklers. Several years ago the city opened a Skid Row Park; to ensure that the park could not be used for overnight camping, overhead sprinklers were programmed to drench unsuspecting sleepers at random times during the night. The system was immediately copied by local merchants to drive the homeless away from (public) storefront sidewalks. Meanwhile Downtown restaurants and markets have built baroque enclosures to protect their refuse from the homeless. Although no one in Los Angeles has yet proposed adding cyanide to the garbage, as was suggested in Phoenix a few years back, one popular seafood restaurant has spent $12,000 to build the ultimate bag-lady-proof trash cage: three-quarter-inch steel rod with alloy locks and vicious out-turned spikes to safeguard moldering fishheads and stale french fries.

Public toilets, however, have become the real frontline of the city's war on the homeless. Los Angeles, as a matter of deliberate policy, has fewer public lavatories than any other major North American city. On the advice of the Los Angeles police, who now sit on the "design board" of at least one major Downtown project, the redevelopment agency bulldozed the few remaining public toilets on Skid Row. Agency planners then considered whether to include a "free-standing public toilet" in their design for the upscale South Park residential development; agency chairman Jim Wood later admitted that the decision not to build the toilet was a "policy decision and not a design decision." The agency preferred the alternative of "quasi-public restrooms"—toilets in restaurants, art galleries, and office buildings—which can be made available selectively to tourists and white-collar workers while being denied to vagrants and other unsuitables. The same logic has inspired the city's transportation planners to exclude toilets from their designs for Los Angeles's new subway system.[2]

Bereft of toilets, the Downtown badlands east of Hill Street also lack outside water sources for drinking or washing. A common and troubling sight these days is the homeless men—many of them young refugees from El Salvador—washing, swimming, even drinking from the sewer effluent that flows down the concrete channel of the Los Angeles River on the eastern edge of Downtown. The city's public health department has made no effort to post warning signs in Spanish or to mobilize alternative clean-water sources.

In those areas where Downtown professionals must cross paths with the homeless or the working poor—such as the zone of gentrification along Broadway just south of the Civic Center—extraordinary precautions have been taken to ensure the physical separation of the different classes. The redevelopment agency, for example, again brought in the police to help design "twenty-four-hour, state-of-the-art security" for the two new parking structures that serve the *Los Angeles Times* headquarters and the Ronald Reagan State Office Building. In contrast to the mean streets outside, both parking structures incorporate beautifully landscaped microparks, and one even boasts a food court, picnic area, and historical exhibit. Both structures are intended to function as "confidence-building" circulation systems that allow white-collar workers to walk from car to office, or from car to boutique, with minimum exposure to the public street. The Broadway-Spring Center, in particular, which links the two local hubs of gentrification (the Reagan Building and the proposed Grand Central Square) has been warmly praised by architectural critics for adding greenery and art to parking. It also adds a considerable dose of menace—armed guards, locked gates, and ubiquitous security cameras—to scare away the homeless and the poor.

The cold war on the streets of Downtown is ever escalating. The police, lobbied by Downtown merchants and developers, have broken up every attempt by the homeless and their allies to create safe havens or self-governed encampments. "Justiceville," founded by homeless activist Ted Hayes, was roughly dispersed; when its inhabitants attempted to find refuge at Venice Beach, they were arrested at the behest of the local council member (a renowned environmentalist) and sent back to Skid Row. The city's own brief experiment with legalized camping—a grudging response to a series of deaths from exposure during the cold winter of 1987—was abruptly terminated after only four months to make way for the construction of a transit maintenance yard. Current policy seems to involve perverse play upon the famous irony about the equal rights of the rich and poor to sleep in the rough. As the former head of the city planning commission explained, in the City of the Angels it is not against the law to sleep on the street per se—"only to erect any sort of protective shelter."[3] To enforce this proscription against "cardboard condos," the police periodically sweep the Nickel, tearing down shelters, confiscating possessions, and arresting resisters. Such cynical repression has turned the majority of the homeless into urban bedouins. They are visible all over Downtown, pushing their few pathetic possessions in stolen shopping carts, always fugitive, always in motion, pressed between the official policy of containment and the inhumanity of Downtown streets.

SEQUESTERING THE POOR

An insidious spatial logic also regulates the lives of Los Angeles's working poor. Just across the moat of the Harbor Freeway, west of Bunker Hill, lies the MacArthur Park district—once upon a time the city's wealthiest neighborhood. Although frequently characterized as a no-man's-land awaiting resurrection by developers, the district is, in fact, home to the largest Central American community in the United States. In the congested streets bordering the park, a hundred thousand Salvadorans and Guatemalans, including a large community of Mayan-speakers, crowd into tenements and boarding houses barely adequate for a fourth as many people. Every morning at 6 A.M. this Latino Bantustan dispatches armies of sewing *operadoras*, dishwashers, and janitors to turn the wheels of the Downtown economy. But because MacArthur Park is midway between Downtown and the famous Miracle Mile, it too will soon fall to redevelopment's bulldozers.

Hungry to exploit the lower land prices in the district, a powerful coterie of developers, represented by a famous ex-councilman and the former president of the planning commission, has won official approval for their vision of "Central City West": literally, a second Downtown comprising 25 million square feet of new office and retail space. Although local politicians have insisted upon a significant quota of low-income replacement housing, such a palliative will hardly compensate for the large-scale population displacement sure to follow the construction of the new skyscrapers and yuppified "urban villages." In the meantime, Korean capital, seeking *lebensraum* for Los Angeles's burgeoning Koreatown, is also pushing into the MacArthur Park area, uprooting tenements to construct heavily fortified condominiums and office complexes. Other Asian and European speculators are counting on the new Metrorail station, across from the park, to become a magnet for new investment in the district.

The recent intrusion of so many powerful interests into the area has put increasing pressure upon the police to "take back the streets" from what is usually represented as an occupying army of drug-dealers, illegal immigrants, and homicidal homeboys. Thus in the summer of 1990 the LAPD announced a massive operation to "retake crime-plagued MacArthur Park" and surrounding neighborhoods "street by street, alley by alley." While the area is undoubtedly a major drug market, principally for drive-in Anglo commuters, the police have focused not only on addict-dealers and gang members, but also on the industrious sidewalk vendors who have made the circumference of the park an exuberant swap meet. Thus Mayan women selling such local staples as tropical fruit, baby clothes, and roach spray have been rounded up in the same sweeps as alleged "narcoterrorists."[4] (Similar dragnets in other Southern California communities have focused on Latino day-laborers congregated at street-corner "slave markets.")

By criminalizing every attempt by the poor—whether the Skid Row homeless or MacArthur Park venders—to use public space for survival purposes, law-enforcement agencies have abolished the last informal safety-net separating misery from catastrophe. (Few third-world cities are so pitiless.) At the same time, the police, encouraged by local businessmen and property owners, are taking the first, tentative steps toward criminalizing entire inner-city communities. The "war" on drugs and gangs again has been the pretext for the

LAPD's novel, and disturbing, experiments with community blockades. A large section of the Pico-Union neighborhood, just south of MacArthur Park, has been quarantined since the summer of 1989; "Narcotics Enforcement Area" barriers restrict entry to residents "on legitimate business only." Inspired by the positive response of older residents and local politicians, the police have subsequently franchised "Operation Cul-de-Sac" to other low-income Latino and black neighborhoods.

Thus in November 1989 (as the Berlin Wall was being demolished), the Devonshire Division of the LAPD closed off a "drug-ridden" twelve-block section of the northern San Fernando Valley. To control circulation within this largely Latino neighborhood, the police convinced apartment owners to finance the construction of a permanent guard station. Twenty miles to the south, a square mile of the mixed black and Latino Central-Avalon community has also been converted into Narcotic Enforcement turf with concrete roadblocks. Given the popularity of these quarantines—save amongst the ghetto youth against whom they are directed—it is possible that a majority of the inner city may eventually be partitioned into police-regulated "no-go" areas.

The official rhetoric of the contemporary war against the urban underclasses resounds with comparisons to the War in Vietnam a generation ago. The LAPD's community blockades evoke the infamous policy of quarantining suspect populations in "strategic hamlets." But an even more ominous emulation is the reconstruction of Los Angeles's public housing projects as "defensible spaces." Deep in the Mekong Delta of the Watts-Willowbrook ghetto, for example, the Imperial Courts Housing Project has been fortified with chain-link fencing, restricted entry signs, obligatory identity passes—and a substation of the LAPD. Visitors are stopped and frisked, the police routinely order residents back into their apartments at night, and domestic life is subjected to constant police scrutiny. For public-housing tenants and inhabitants of narcotic-enforcement zones, the loss of freedom is the price of "security."

Notes

1. *Los Angeles Times,* Nov. 4, 1978.
2. Tom Chorneau, "Quandary Over a Park Restroom," *Downtown News,* Aug. 25, 1986.
3. See "Cold Snap's Toll at 5 as Its Iciest Night Arrives," *Los Angeles Times,* Dec. 29, 1988.
4. *Los Angeles Times,* June 17, 1990.

SUGGESTIONS FOR DISCUSSION

1. From what you have read, what does Davis mean by "genuinely democratic space"?

2. Mike Davis makes it clear that one of the defining features of Los Angeles is the city planners' attempts to destroy public spaces, those places where people can congregate freely or just hang out. What problems do you see with the destruction or the preservation of public space?

3. Davis writes in his essay, "The American city is being systematically turned inward. The 'public' spaces of the new megastructures and supermalls have supplanted traditional streets and disciplined their spontaneity." This statement represents a judgment about what American cities once were and what they should be. With a group of your classmates, examine what that judgment is and respond with your own understanding of what American cities should be like and what they are like currently.

SUGGESTIONS FOR WRITING

1. Read over your annotations for this selection in preparation for writing a summary of Davis's argument. What are Davis's primary reasons for arguing that "The pleasure domes of the elite Westside rely upon the social imprisonment of a third-world service proletariat in increasingly repressive ghettos and barrios"?

2. Davis makes strong charges against city planners, corporate interests, the city council, and other official agencies that have anything to do with how Los Angeles is divided, how public services are distributed and repaired, and where "urban renewal" programs will be sited. His analysis is based partially but not solely on his familiarity with this place. He also has spent time finding out the history of Los Angeles's urban developments, where funding is directed, what areas of the city are in most serious disrepair, and what the ethnic and racial demographics are in each section of the city. You likely will not be able to do all of that, but you can map out the areas you think ought to be of most concern in the place where you grew up or the place with which you are most familiar or in which you are most interested. Choose a place (small town, city, subdivision, etc.). Sketch a map of that place and explain what you consider the most important issues to emerge from examining how the place is planned and where most funding or development seems to be occurring. Is there a "genuinely democratic space" available in this place? Does one section of the place seem to be segregated economically from other sections? What else do you notice?

3. Earlier in *City of Quartz,* Davis mentions several films that show the modern city as a dystopia—a place exactly the opposite of a utopia. Watch one of the films he mentions (*Bladerunner, Die Hard, Escape from New York*) and write an essay in which you compare the dystopian setting of that film with your own experience of or impression of large U.S. cities like Los Angeles, Chicago, or New York. This is the kind of essay you can write whether or not you live in or have visited large cities. Your focus in this essay should be on images that you see in popular culture and how they compare to the overall impression that you have of cities. That impression can come from firsthand experience, of course. But it also comes through news programs, magazine articles and ads, and television shows like *COPS* or *Law & Order* or even *Seinfeld.*

Signs from the Heart
California Chicano Murals

Eva Sperling Cockcroft and Holly Barnet-Sánchez

In his full-length work on Chicano culture in Los Angeles (*Anything but Mexican: Chicanos in Contemporary Los Angeles*), Rodolfo Acuña writes that "no space in East Lost Angeles is left unused or unmarked." For Acuña, Chicano or Latino culture has claimed, if not always the physical space that Mike Davis writes of, at least interpretive space—signs and images that mark a place as belonging to a certain group or person. Primarily among the ways interpretive space is claimed in East Los Angeles has been through the Los Angeles mural movement, which was begun in the 1960s, carried on today under the direction of the Social and Public Arts Resource Center (SPARC) and headed by artist and activist Judy Baca. In the following selection, artists Eva Cockcroft and Holly Barnet-Sánchez write of the origins of the mural movement in Los Angeles. Their essay appeared in 1993 in the book *Signs from the Heart: California Chicano Murals*.

SUGGESTION FOR READING

The selection we have reprinted consists of portions of an introduction to a collection of essays about California Chicano murals. The authors set the mural movement in the larger context of public art throughout history as a way of explaining what murals have meant in the past and what they have come to mean today. After you read this selection, write a brief outline that traces the rise and fall of murals from high art to popular statement as it is described in what Cockcroft and Barnet-Sánchez have written.

A truly "public" art provides society with the symbolic representation of collective beliefs as well as a continuing re-affirmation of the collective sense of self. Paintings on walls, or "murals" as they are commonly called, are perhaps the quintessential public art in this regard. Since before the cave paintings at Altamira some 15,000 years before Christ, wall paintings have served as a way of communicating collective visions within a community of people. During the Renaissance in Italy, considered by many to be the golden age of Western Art, murals were regarded as the highest form in the hierarchy of painting. They served to illustrate the religious lessons of the church and to embody the new Humanism of the period through artistic innovations like perspective and naturalistic anatomy.

After the Mexican Revolution of 1910–1917, murals again served as the artistic vehicle for educating a largely illiterate populace about the ideals of the new society and the virtues and evils of the past. As part of a re-evaluation of their cultural identity by Mexican-Americans during the Chicano movement for civil rights and social justice that began in the mid–1960s, murals again provided an important organizing tool and a means for the reclamation of their specific cultural heritage.

The desire by people for beauty and meaning in their lives is fundamental to their identity as human beings. Some form of art, therefore, has existed in every society throughout history. Before the development of a significant private picture market in Seventeenth Century Holland, most art was public, commissioned by royalty, clergy, or powerful citizens for the greater glory of their country, church, or city and placed in public spaces. However, after the Industrial Revolution and the development of modern capitalism with its stress on financial rather than social values, the art world system as we know it today with galleries, critics, and museums gradually developed. More and more, art became a luxury object to be enjoyed and traded like any other commodity. The break-up of the stable structures of feudal society and the fluidity and dynamism of post-Industrial society was reflected symbolically in art by the disruption of naturalistic space and the experimentation characteristic of Modernism.

Modernism has been a mixed blessing for art and artists. Along with a new freedom for innovation and the opportunity to express an individual vision that resulted from the loss of direct control by patrons of artistic production, artists experienced a sense of alienation from the materialistic values of capitalism, loss of a feeling of clearly defined social utility, and the freedom to starve. This unstable class situation and perception of isolation from society was expressed in the attitude of the bohemian *avant garde* artist who scorns both the crass commercialism of the bourgeoisie and the unsophisticated tastes of the working class, creating work exclusively for the appreciation of a new aristocracy of taste. Especially in the United States of the 1960s, for most people art had become an irrelevant and mysterious thing enjoyed only by a small educated elite.

When muralism emerged again as an important art movement in Mexico during the 1920s, the murals served as a way of creating a new national consciousness—a role quite similar to that of the religious murals of the Renaissance although directed toward a different form of social cohesion. Unlike the murals of the Italian Renaissance which expressed the commonly held beliefs of both rulers and masses, the Mexican murals portrayed the ideology of a worker, peasant and middle class revolution against the former ruling class: capitalists, clergy, and foreign interests. Since that time in the eyes of many, contemporary muralism has been identified with poor people, revolution, and communism. This association has been a major factor in changing muralism's rank within the hierarchy of the "fine arts" from the highest to the lowest. Once the favored art of popes and potentates, murals, especially Mexican-style narrative murals, now considered a "poor people's art," have fallen to a level of only marginal acceptance within the art world.

The three great Mexican artists whose names have become almost synonymous with that mural renaissance, Diego Rivera, Jose Clemente Orozco, and David Alfaro Siqueiros, were all influenced by stylistic currents in European modernism—Cubism, Expressionism, and Futurism—but they used these stylistic innovations to create a new socially motivated realism. Rather than continuing to use the naturalistic pictorial space of Renaissance murals, the Mex-

"La Familia" from *Chicago Time Trip*, 1977, East Los Streetscapers (Wayne Alaniz Healy and David Rivas Botello), Lincoln Heights, East Los Angeles. Total mural 18′ × 26′. A citywide mural project.

icans explored new forms of composition. Rivera used a collage-like discontinuous space which juxtaposed elements of different sizes; Orozco employed non-naturalistic brushwork, distorted forms, and exaggerated light and dark, while Siqueiros added expressive uses of perspective with extreme foreshortening that made forms burst right out of the wall. The stylistic innovations of the Mexicans have provided the basis for a modern mural language and most contemporary muralism is based to some extent or another on the Mexican model. The Mexican precedent has been especially important in the United States for the social realist muralists of the Works Progress Administration (WPA) and Treasury Section programs of the New Deal period and the contemporary mural movement that began in the late 1960s.

More than 2500 murals were painted with government sponsorship during the New Deal period in the United States. By the beginning of World War II however, support for social realist painting and muralism in general, had ended. During the Cold War period that followed, realistic painting became identified with totalitarian systems like that of the Soviet Union, while abstraction, especially New York-style Abstract Expressionism, was seen as symbolizing individual freedom in *avant garde* art circles. By the early 1960s, only the various kinds of abstract art from the geometric to the bio-morphic were even considered to really be art. Endorsed by critics and the New York museums, abstraction was promulgated abroad as the International Style and considered to be "universal"—in much the same way as straight-nosed, straight-haired, blondes were considered to be the "universal" ideal of beauty. Those who differed or complained were dismissed as ignorant, uncultured, or anti-American.

The concept of a "universal" ideal of beauty was closely related to the "melting pot" theory, then taught in schools, which held that all the different immigrants, races and national groups which composed the population of the United States could be assimilated into a single homogeneous "American." This theory ignored the existence of separate cultural enclaves within the United States as well as blatant discrimination and racism. It also ignored the complex dialectic between isolation and assimilation and the problem of identity for people like the Mexican-Americans of California who were neither wholly "American" nor "Mexican" but a new, unique, and constantly changing composite variously called "American of Mexican descent," "Mexican-American," Latino or Hispanic. In the 1960s the term "Chicano" with its populist origins was adopted by socially-conscious youth as a form of positive self-identification for Mexican-Americans. Its use became a form of political statement in and of itself.[1]

The dialectic between assimilation and separatism can be seen in the history of Los Angeles, for example, first founded in 1781 as a part of New Spain. In spite of constant pressure for assimilation including job discrimination and compulsory use of English in the schools, the Mexican-American population was able to maintain a culture sufficiently distinct so that, as historian Juan Gómez-Quiñones has frequently argued, a city within a city can be defined. This separate culture continues to exist as a distinct entity within the dominant culture, even though it is now approximately 150 years since Los Angeles was acquired by the United States. This situation, by itself, tends to discredit the melting pot concept.

The Civil Rights Movement, known among Mexican-Americans as the Chicano Movement or *el movimiento,* fought against the idea of a "universal" culture, a single ideal of beauty and order. It re-examined the common assumption that European or Western ideas represented the pinnacle of "civilization," while everything else, from the thought of Confucius to Peruvian portrait vases, was second-rate, too exotic, or "primitive." The emphasis placed by Civil Rights leaders on self-definition and cultural pride sparked a revision of standard histories to include the previously unrecognized accomplishments of women and minorities as well as a re-examination of the standard school curriculum. Along with the demonstrations, strikes, and marches of the political movement came an explosion of cultural expression.

"Pickers" from *Guadalupe Mural*, 1990, Judith F. Baca, Leroy Park, Guadalupe. Total mural (4 panels), 8' × 28'8", this panel 8' × 7'2".

As was the case after the Mexican Revolution, the Civil Rights Movement inspired a revival of muralism. However, this new mural movement differed in many important ways from the Mexican one. It was not sponsored by a successful revolutionary government, but came out of the struggle by the people themselves against the *status quo*. Instead of well-funded projects in government buildings, these new murals were located in the *barrios* and ghettos of the inner cities, where oppressed people lived. They served as an inspiration for struggle, a way of reclaiming a cultural heritage, or even as a means of developing self-pride. Perhaps most significantly, these murals were not the expression of an individual vision. Artists encouraged local residents to join them in discussing the content, and often, in doing the actual painting. For the first time, techniques were developed that would allow non-artists working with a professional to design and paint their own murals. This element of community participation, the placement of murals on exterior walls in the community itself, and the philosophy of community input, that is, the right of a community to decide on what kind of art it wants, characterized the new muralism.

Nowhere did the community-based mural movement take firmer root than in the Chicano communities of California. With the Mexican mural tradition as part of their heritage, murals were a particularly congenial form for Chicano artists to express the collective vision of their community. The mild climate and low, stuccoed buildings provided favorable physical conditions, and, within a few years, California had more murals than any other region of the country. As home to the largest concentration of Mexicans and people of Mexican ancestry anywhere outside of Mexico City, Los Angeles became the site of the largest concentration of Chicano murals in the United States. Estimates range from one thousand to fifteen hundred separate works painted between 1969 and the present. The Social and Public Art Resource Center's "California Chicano Mural Archive" compiled in 1984 documents close to 1000 mural projects throughout the state in slide form.

Because Chicano artists were consciously searching to identify the images that represented their shared experience they were continually led back to the *barrio*. It became the site for "finding" the symbols, forms, colors, and narratives that would assist them in the redefinition of their communities. Not interested in perpetuating the Hollywood notion that art was primarily an avenue of escape from reality, Chicano artists sought to use their art to create a dialogue of demystification through which the Chicano community could evolve toward cultural liberation. To this end, murals and posters became an ubiquitous element of the *barrioscape*. According to Ybarra-Frausto, they publicly represented the reclamation of individual Chicano minds and hearts through the acknowledgement and celebration of their community's identity through the creation of an art of resistance.

Uprising of the Mujeres, 1979, Judith F. Baca. Portable, acrylic on wood. 8' × 24'.

Prior to the Chicano movement, U.S. Mexicans were defined externally through a series of derogatory stereotypes with total assimilation as the only way to break out of the situation of social marginalization. Art that integrated elements of U.S. Mexican or *barrio* culture was also denigrated as "folk" art and not considered seriously. The explosion of Chicano culture and murals as a result of the political movement, provided new recognition and value for Chicano art which weakened the old barriers. According to Sánchez-Tranquilino, this experience allowed artists to figuratively break through the wall that confined artists either to the *barrio* or to unqualified assimilation. It gave them the confidence to explore new artistic forms and a new relationship to the dominant society.

Notes

1. Throughout this book several terms are used to identify Americans of Mexican descent: "Mexican-Americans," "U.S. Mexicans," and "Chicanos." Each carries specific meanings and they are not used interchangeably. "Mexican-American" is primarily a post World War II development in regular use until the politicization of *el movimiento,* the Chicano civil rights movement of the 1960s and 1970s. Its use acknowledges with pride the Mexican heritage which was hidden by an earlier, less appropriate term, "Spanish-American." However, it's hyphenated construction implies a level of equality in status between the Mexican and the American which in actuality belies the unequal treatment of Americans of Mexican descent within United States society.

   U.S. Mexican is a term developed by essayist Marcos Sánchez-Tranquilino to replace the term Mexican-American with one that represents both more generally and clearly all Mexicans within the United States whether their families were here prior to annexation in 1848, have been here for generations, or for only two days. In other words, it represents all Mexicans living within U.S. borders regardless of residence or citizenship status.

   The most basic definition of the term Chicano was made by journalist Ruben Salazar in 1970: "A Chicano is a Mexican-American who does not have an Anglo image of himself." It is a term of self-definition that denotes politicization.

SUGGESTIONS FOR DISCUSSION

1. Throughout this selection, Cockcroft and Barnet-Sánchez remind their readers that, though mural painting might have been considered high art in earlier periods when it was funded by church or state, by the time the Chicano mural movement had come to California, these highly realistic, working-class, public wall paintings were no longer valued by the art world. Instead, the mural movement became a part of the *barrioscape*—a sign of Chicano culture and a statement about Chicano politics. How do Cockcroft and Barnet-Sánchez explain the fall of murals from high to low in the art world? Why do you think artists or art collectors care whether or not such public art is considered "high culture" or not? How would you differentiate "art" from "wall paintings"?

2. One of the roles that the Chicano mural movement has played, according to this selection, has been to challenge universal standards of beauty. How do Cockcroft and Barnet-Sánchez define this "universal" standard? What do they see as its relation to the "melting pot"? Look over the murals reprinted in this selection with a group of your classmates, and explain how these paintings offer a challenge to that standard.

3. In our introduction to this selection, we note that Chicano murals have claimed an "interpretive space" in Los Angeles. That is, as Cockcroft and

Barnet-Sánchez write, these murals "publicly represented the reclamation of individual Chicano minds and hearts through the acknowledgment and celebration of their community's identity through the creation of an art of resistance." Why do you think it might be important for a group like the one described here to claim a space through art or signs or language or music (what we have been calling claiming "interpretive space")? In what ways do other groups or individuals that you know claim interpretive space?

SUGGESTIONS FOR WRITING

1. Write an essay in which you discuss how a knowledge of the mural movement, as it is described in the selection above, either changes or reinforces the impression that you got of Los Angeles from reading Mike Davis's analysis of that city.

2. Write an essay that examines why it might be important for marginalized groups to claim interpretive space through images or signs like the mural movement. Do you know of any similar strategies to the mural movement that other groups use to claim interpretive space? You can draw on your reading on Los Angeles and the mural movement to help you with this writing. You might also have experience in your own town or city or school that you can use to explain the need for those who feel like outsiders to claim interpretive space with images or signs.

3. Cockcroft and Barnet-Sánchez write, "Prior to the Chicano movement, U.S. Mexicans were defined externally through a series of derogatory stereotypes." Choose a film that includes or deals with Latinos in the United States (for example, *Selena, Mi Familia,* or *A Walk in the Clouds*). Watch the film and write an essay in which you address that question of Latino or Chicano stereotypes. In what ways do the characters and their situations break with the stereotypes with which you are familiar? In what ways do those stereotypes continue to be perpetuated? Before you begin your essay (and even before you begin watching one of these films), take time to make a list of familiar stereotypes. If you are unsure of the common Latino stereotypes, ask classmates, friends, and family to help you start on your exploration of this subject.

Remember When Public Space Didn't Carry Brand Names?

Eric Liu

Journalist Eric Liu is a regular contributor to MSNBC. A second-generation Chinese American, Liu has also written a memoir, *The Accidental Asian: Notes on a Native Speaker* (1998), that raises questions about the meaning of assimilation, ethnicity, and race. His commentary on brand names and public space appeared March 25, 1999, in *USA Today*.

SUGGESTIONS FOR READING

You can prepare yourself for this reading by making a casual survey of the spaces around you that carry some sort of brand name. Make a list of the brand names and logos you see in public spaces, including sports arenas, ice rinks, and public parks you see on television.

In a few weeks, when the world champion New York Yankees open their home season, will they take the field at Trump Stadium? Time Warner Park? Maybe AT&T Arena?

Chances are the park will still be called Yankee Stadium. But it won't be that way for long. Quietly, and with strikingly little protest, the Yankees have announced that they are planning to sell the "naming rights" to their Bronx homestead. By the time the 2000 season arrives, some lucky corporation may well have bought the sign outside the House that Ruth Built. And frankly, that turns my stomach.

It's not just that Yankee Stadium is a national treasure. It's not just that allowing the highest bidder to rename this 76-year-old icon feels like an insult—to New Yorkers, to tradition and to the memory of Yankees past, such as Joe DiMaggio. It's also that what is about to happen to Yankee Stadium is part of a deeper, accelerating trend in our society, the relentless branding of public spaces.

The sports world gives us piles of examples. San Francisco's fabled Candlestick Park is now 3Com Park. The selling of bowl game names has reached sublimely ridiculous levels. (Remember the Poulan/Weed Eater Independence Bowl?) And the trend is hardly confined to sports. Branding—the conspicuous marking of places and things with corporate names and logos—is now everywhere in the civic square.

Consider the public schools, some of which are flooded with advertising for merchandise and fast food. Districts around the country are raising money by making exclusive deals with Pepsi or Coke or with credit card companies or banks. In one Texas district, Dr. Pepper recently paid $3.45 million in part to plaster its logo on a high school roof to attract the attention of passengers flying in and out of Dallas.

Other efforts to turn public spaces into commercial vessels are no less corrosive. Rollerblade now hawks its wares in Central Park under the banner "The Official Skate of New York City Parks." Buses in Boston and other cities don't just carry ad placards anymore; some of them have been turned into rolling billboards.

How far can this go? Over in England, the legendary white cliffs of Dover now serve as the backdrop for a laser-projected Adidas ad. Here in America, we haven't draped Mount Rushmore with a Nike "swoosh." But things are heading in that general direction.

You might say at this point, "What's the big deal? America is commercialized—get over it!" And I admit my views may sound a bit old-fashioned. But this isn't a matter of priggishness or personal nostalgia.

Public spaces matter. They matter because they are the emblems, the physical embodiments, of a community's spirit and soul. A public space belongs to all who share in the life of a community. And it belongs to them in common, regardless of their differences in social station or political clout. Indeed, its very purpose is to preserve a realm where a person's worth or dignity doesn't depend on market valuations.

So when a shared public space, such as a park or a schoolhouse, becomes just another marketing opportunity for just another sponsor, something precious is undermined: the idea that we are equal as citizens even though we may be unequal as consumers.

What the commercialization of public spaces also does, gradually and subtly, is convert all forms of identity into brand identity.

We come to believe that without our brands, or without the right brands, we are literally and figuratively no-names. We question whether we belong in public, whether we are truly members.

We forget that there are other means, besides badges of corporate affiliation, to communicate with one another.

It could, of course, be said, with a place like Times Square in mind, that brands, logos, and slogans are now our most widely understood public language. It could be said that in this age of cultural fragmentation, the closest thing we have in common is commerce.

But is this the best vision of American life we can muster?

In the military, they worry about "mission creep." In civilian life, the problem is "market creep." And the question now is how to stem this creeping sickness. We know that there is some limit to what people will accept: A 1996 April Fools announcement that the Liberty Bell has been purchased and rechristened the "Taco Liberty Bell" provoked a storm of angry calls. Drawing the line there, though, isn't protecting an awful lot.

Maybe the renaming of Yankee Stadium will shame some legislators or zoning czars into action. Maybe the "corporatization" of our classrooms will spark some popular protest. Maybe the licensing away of Central Park will awaken us to the disappearance of public space—and to the erosion of the public idea.

Then again, maybe not. In which case, we'd better keep a close eye on Mount Rushmore.

SUGGESTIONS FOR DISCUSSION

1. Share the lists you made before your reading with a group of your classmates. To what extent do your lists confirm or fail to confirm Liu's fear of "the relentless branding of public spaces"?

2. Liu writes, "Public spaces matter. They matter because they are the emblems, the physical embodiments, of a community's spirit and soul." With a group of your classmates, make a list of public spaces—both famous ones like Times Square and those most available to you. In what ways do these spaces represent "a community's spirit and soul"? How might the introduction of brand names and logos to these spaces change or define them? What role do murals or graffiti play in those same spaces?

3. Liu mentions that England's white cliffs of Dover are now the site of a laser-projected Adidas ad. In fact, some of the billboards we see on television—behind the catcher in a baseball game, for example—are virtual rather than real signs. They are digitalized signs made to look like the older painted billboards we have come to expect on the walls of a baseball park or along the boards surrounding an ice rink. Some commentators fear that such easily placed and changeable signs are even more damaging than billboards or brand names in public spaces. What is your response to technology that makes it possible to place and change a sign in any spot at any time? Given what you have read, what would Liu say to this technology?

SUGGESTIONS FOR WRITING

1. On one level, Liu's commentary is a fairly simple and straightforward argument against the commercialization of public space. However, as you read, you should note that Liu moves beyond that to issues of commerce

in the classroom, what public space means, how our identity becomes entangled in consumerism, and more. Write a brief summary of Liu's commentary, taking care to detail Liu's full argument on brand names and public spaces.

2. Write a response to Liu's argument. You might decide that you agree with him or that he has overstated his case. Or you might decide that Liu's complaint is a good one but misses the point about how we use public space. Though it isn't necessary, you might find it useful to draw on other reading selections from this chapter. Lopez, Abbey, and Fiske all offer ways of thinking about how we use space or our responsibilities to space that you might be able to draw on in your response to Liu.

3. Images, writing, logos, graffiti, and other ways of marking public space take on different meanings depending on who is doing the marking and who the audience is. Choose a public space that you know well or can easily visit. Write a description of this space, focusing on how it is "marked," both commercially and culturally. Who has done the marking? Who is the audience for that marking? The audience very likely changes depending on whether the "mark" is commercial like a brand name or community like a mural—sanctioned or not—or private like graffiti. How do such markings characterize the space?

VISUAL CULTURE · *CLAIMING INTERPRETIVE SPACE*

Although the Chicano mural movement is one powerful way for a group to claim interpretive space with the use of signs or images, there are many other ways that such space is claimed. The ways that we decorate our office or dorm-room doors to make them look more like ours rather than the institution's, the signs officials put up to tell us how to use a space, subway art, graffiti—all of these signs and symbols make attempts to claim space.

The images reprinted here are some examples of the way signs and images can mark and even change a space entirely.

SUGGESTIONS FOR DISCUSSION

1. With a group of your classmates, examine the images reprinted here and discuss what each of these signs or images says about who is attempting to control the space and for what purpose.

2. Make a list of specific signs that claim interpretive space where you live. What do these signs say about the people who have put them up? What do they tell you about the space?

3. Although they are both public and populist forms, some people would argue that graffiti, unlike murals, is not an art form. Others would argue that murals are simply more graffiti. What do you think distinguishes what people call graffiti from what they consider art?

4. Collect several images or signs that mark or claim a public space for a group or an individual. Bring your images to class for a discussion of how signs claim interpretive space.

SUGGESTED ASSIGNMENT

Use the images you collected for class discussion to create a collage or poster illustrating how signs and images claim interpretive space.

FIELD WORK — COLLABORATING ON AN OBSERVATION OF PUBLIC SPACE

For this project, team up with one or two classmates and choose a space that offers some possibility for the kind of observation, description, and analysis that you have been reading about throughout this chapter. To some extent, all of the writers focus on how we use public space and on what certain spaces are designed for. John Fiske, for example, suggests that even though a mall might be designed to bring more people to stores to buy more goods, people go to malls for very different reasons. Some are not at all interested in buying, but they are interested in the space. Mike Davis suggests that urban planning (the design of public space) can reflect the extent to which race, class, and income level inform public policy decisions about urban space.

In order to find out more about how a space is used, spend time watching to see who goes there and what they do once they are there. You will have to make several visits to the same place and get as much input as possible, so this is a good project for collaboration.

MAPPING THE SPACE

When you begin your observation, take time to sketch a map of the space. Note the layout of the place. Where do groups of people gather? Do different groups (teens, senior citizens, serious shoppers, etc.) tend to congregate in certain places? Make a note of that on your map.

TAKING NOTES

As you begin a project like this one, you probably will not have a clear focus for your notes. You can look back at the notebook entry you wrote originally as a starting point for your observations, but your questions and concerns will likely change as you watch. Your notes may seem random at first. It takes practice to get used to noting down the kinds of things that happen around you daily that you don't notice or that you take for granted. That is why you'll need to make several visits and why a partner or two can help. Comparing your notes with others will help you to get distance on what you are recording. However, even at the beginning, you can focus on simple things: What does the space look like? Who uses it? What are they doing there?

Make sure you meet with your teammates throughout your project to compare notes, to get additional information, and to check your own observations.

WATCHING PEOPLE

Record who comes to the space. Note age, gender, ethnicity, appearance, and whether they are alone or with others.

Note how people seem to be using this space. In a mall, for example, are teens actually the "tricksters" who know the rules only to invert or mock them as Fiske claims? How else might their activity be described? Fast food restaurants are designed so that people get their food and, presumably, eat it quickly and get out. Is that how everyone uses this kind of space? In other words, how else might these spaces function for people in ways other than those for which they are designed by developers?

ASKING QUESTIONS

Although your primary job will be to watch and to take notes, you will find out even more if you stop to ask questions. Ask people that you see how often they come to the space, when, and why. Ask owners, business people, or caretakers what they think the space is meant for and how many of them actually use it for that purpose.

WRITING UP YOUR FINDINGS

When you have completed your observations, you will discover that what you write will depend very much on what you would like to emphasize from your findings. Basically, your paper might look more like an interpretation of space and the way it is used (in the way Fiske or Davis write), or it might look much more like a report on what you and your team have found.

Interpretive Essay

If you choose to write your findings as an interpretive essay, review several of the essays in this chapter. Each gives both a strong sense of place and a reflection on what the place means to the people who live there or use it. Many include first-person impressions or feelings but ground those impressions in information about the way the place is used, developed, or designed. It is easy, in this type of essay, to forget about the observation notes that you have taken and to fall back on your own impressions. But your impressions will be more convincing when they are tied to the fieldwork that you have done for this project. Furthermore, since you have worked with a partner or in a team, your interpretations will be informed by much of the team's conversation. Acknowledge the role your observation team played in the way that you now think of the place.

Report

If you are writing a report, you might be more likely to write collaboratively with your team-mates. Even if your teacher asks each of you to write your own report, you will need the cooperation of your team to make sure that you have all the information that you need for the report.

If your report is collaborative, this is a good opportunity to practice the kinds of negotiation that must take place when you must represent the findings of the entire team, not just your own findings or interpretations. Of course, whether the report is collaborative or not, it should fall into the typical report pattern: Introduction, Methods, Observations, Conclusions (see Fieldwork in Chapter 3, Schooling). To write collaboratively, you might choose to divide the work among team members—each of you writing a separate section—or to sit together and agree on the language of the report as you write. Even if you divide the work, all of you will need to go back over each others' sections, and add, change, or revise the report so that it doesn't look like it has been written by more than one person.

Mining the Archive

TAKE A WALKING TOUR

13 Finnish American Heritage Center

In 1990, Suomi College renovated the former St. Joseph's Catholic Church as a Finnish cultural center. The renovation reflects traditional Finnish architectural styles including the clipped gable roof, the stucco finish and the extensive use of trim moldings painted white. The fixed upper sash with mullions of the narrow casement windows form a cross. Vertical trim casing extends down past the horizontal apron. The blue roof and white walls not only reflect Finnish colors (the same as those in the flag of Finland), but also introduce bright colors to the mostly dark red block of the downtown.

The building currently houses a gallery, a performing arts center and the Finnish archives.

We normally think of an archive as a collection of papers or documents. Yet a city, town, or national park area can also function as a kind of archive—a place where you will find sites of historic, political, or cultural importance.

Certainly, one of the best ways to learn about a public space and its archival potential is to take a walking tour. Cities, towns, local and national parks, botanical gardens, museums, campuses, cemeteries, and historical buildings across this country have walking tours designed to show visitors the history of the place, the best places to shop, popular restaurants, homes of poets, artists, and politicians, little-known places of historic interest, and more. There tours usually include a step-by-step guide to the places on the tour, an easy-to-follow map, and a thumbnail description of the importance of each stop.

Begin this project by locating several sample walking tours. Most travel guides available in local bookstores and public libraries will include walking tours. For example, Frommer's guide to San Francisco includes a walking tour of Chinatown. *The Eyewitness Travel Guide to New York* includes walking tours of Greenwich Village, Lower Manhattan, and the Upper East Side. There are even alternative walking tours like Bruce Kayton's *Radical Walking Tours of New York City,* whose maps include the homes of leftists, anarchists, and radicals who are often left out of the commercial guides or chamber of commerce maps designed for most tourists.

Bring the walking tours you have located to class for a general discussion of what walking tours include, what they leave out, and how they identify public space.

A good walking tour should have

- A focus or theme
- A clear map
- A brief description of each stop on the tour
- Information about how to get there, how long the tour will take, and what difficulties a walker might encounter

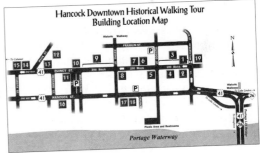

Hancock Downtown Historical Walking Tour
Building Location Map

Portage Waterway

We have reprinted portions of a walking tour of historic Hancock, Michigan. Study the map and entries we have selected from the guide's description of each stop. When you have a good sense of what a walking tour entails, make a walking tour of a place you know well. Be sure to draw a clear map and time the walk so that you know how long it will take. Give your tour a theme or focus. Michigan Tech's School of Forestry and Wood Products, for example, has published a botanical walking tour—Tech Tree Walk—which locates and identifies the different trees on campus. Your tour can focus on people, places, events, whatever ties the place together and might be of interest to visitors. You can even create an underground tour—of campus dorms or the library or the place where you grew up—that, like Bruce Kayton's *Radical Walking Tours of New York City,* highlights the people, places, and events not considered mainstream or not usually shown to visitors.

CHAPTER 7

Storytelling

Experience which is passed on from mouth to mouth is the source from which all storytellers have drawn. And among those who have written down the tales, it is the great ones whose written version differs least from the speech of the many nameless storytellers.

—Walter Benjamin, *The Storyteller*

One of the pleasures of listening to stories is suspending disbelief and entering into the imaginary world that storytelling creates. It doesn't matter so much whether the story is true or could have happened. What matters is that listeners know their feelings and their responses to a story are real. When people hear the words "Once upon a time..." at the beginning of a fairy tale (or Jason's footsteps in the *Friday the 13th* horror movies), they know they are entering a world that could never happen, yet this knowledge does not stop them from trying on, at least temporarily, the version of reality (or unreality) that the story offers.

Storytelling is a persistent form of popular entertainment, whether people tell ghost stories around a campfire or watch the electronic glow of a television set. Every culture has its own storytelling tradition of myths, legends, epics, fables, animal stories, fairy tales, and romances. Listeners take delight in the mythic powers of their heroes, laugh at the comic predicaments clowns and tricksters get themselves into, and feel awe—and sometimes terror—when they hear stories of unseen worlds and the supernatural. In every storytelling tradition, there is a repertoire of stock characters and plots that listeners recognize immediately—and know how to respond to through laughter, tears, excitement, fear, and grief—as if the events in the story were actually taking place.

But the fact that people everywhere, in all known cultures, tell stories only raises a series of questions we will ask you to explore in this chapter. We will be asking you to recall stories from the past and present in order to think about the functions storytelling performs, the occasions on which stories are told, and the people who tell stories. The reading and writing assignments in this chapter will ask you to look at some of the stories circulating in contemporary America. We will be asking you to explore the familiar stories that you hear from family and friends or watch on television and at the movies, to see what these stories can tell you about the culture that you are living in and the kinds of knowledge the imaginary worlds of storytelling transmit.

One of the key functions of storytelling, aside from entertaining listeners, is a pedagogical one. Storytelling is one of the oldest forms of human communication, and stories are important ways young people learn about the world and what their culture values. In traditional societies, before the advent of the mass media and the entertainment industry, stories were passed along orally, from generation to generation by word of mouth. The elders were responsible for initiating young people into the lore of the tribe. In many respects, the same is true today, in the mass-mediated world of contemporary America. To be an adult and a full member of society means knowing the stories a particular culture tells about the world and about itself. The familiar stories everyone knows make up a charter of cultural belief about the world and why people do the things they do.

We will be asking you to recall the stories that you tell in the course of casual conversation, when you explain what happened over the weekend or pass along the latest gossip, political controversy, or scandal. People love to tell and listen to stories about politicians, celebrities, and professional athletes—who is dating whom, who is getting divorced, who is checking into a drug or alcohol abuse clinic, who is under investigation for what. These kinds of stories—personal anecdotes, gossip, bits and pieces of the evening news—may seem so trivial that they don't really merit the title of storytelling. But while telling and listening to these stories may appear to be no more than a way to pass the time with family, neighbors, coworkers, and friends, in fact storytelling performs a very useful

social function within local communities. As people tell and listen to stories, perhaps without fully recognizing it, they are working out their own attitudes and evaluations of a wide range of social realities, from relations between the sexes to politics.

We will ask you to think about the stories that appear on television and in the movies—popular genres such as family sitcoms, hospital dramas, soap operas, action adventure, science fiction, mysteries, westerns, horrors, and so on. The cast of characters is a familiar one: interracial cop teams, super-heroes, cyberpunks, urban vigilantes, gangsters, android terminators, martial arts masters, hard-boiled private eyes, cowboys, swinging singles, career women, men behaving badly, parents and kids. These popular figures inhabit fictional worlds—the western frontier, the criminal underworld, interstellar space, the mean streets of the city, the middle-class homes of the suburbs—where they perpetually are working out the aspirations and anxieties of average people.

READING THE CULTURE OF STORYTELLING

Reading and writing about stories and storytelling will require you to listen again to the stories that surround you and to look for patterns in their familiar plots and characters. As Maxine Hong Kingston does in the opening selection, you might begin by recalling stories you heard when you were growing up. In "No Name Woman," Kingston retells a story from the Cantonese "talk story" tradition she heard from her mother in the Chinese American community in Stockton, California. Her retelling offers a good example of how writers use familiar stories told within the family and the local community and what happens when they add their own voices to an ongoing tradition of storytelling.

The next two selections explore "horror" stories—and why people like to be scared. The first is the folklorist Jan Harold Brunvand's "'The Hook' and Other Teenage Horrors," a part of Brunvand's larger work of collecting what he calls "urban legends." These are stories people tell that are plausible and have realistic settings but are bizarre and sometimes horrifying—the baby-sitter on LSD who put an infant in the oven because she thought it was a chicken, the spiders who laid eggs in the scalp of a woman with a beehive hairdo, the mouse's head in the Dr. Pepper bottle. Our suspicion is that Brunvand is correct when he claims that such stories are widespread and adapted to local conditions. It will be interesting to see how many comparable tales you can recall from your own experience. Then the well-known horror fiction writer Stephen King extends Brunvand's analysis of why people like a "good scare" by investigating "Why We Crave Horror Movies." For King, horror films owe their popularity to the way that they offer viewers an experience of violating the normal boundaries of everyday life, while at the same time reestablishing a need for normality.

Robert Warshow's essay "The Gangster as Tragic Hero" looks at one of the most familiar characters in American film. Warshow is interested in why the story of the American gangster turns out inevitably to be a tragic one—and what this tragedy says about American culture.

A cluster of readings follow, devoted in general to storytelling on television and in particular to the changing representations of women in sitcoms. The opening pair of readings offers different perspectives on *Ally McBeal* and the image of working women in TV shows. In the selection "In Praise of Roseanne," Elayne Rapping provides an unabashedly enthusiastic appreciation of the *Roseanne* show. The final reading, Ella Taylor's "TV Families: Three Generations of Packaged Dreams," offers a historical overview of TV families in domestic sitcoms since the 1950s.

Throughout this chapter you will be asked to recall and to retell stories that you have heard or read in the past. One of the pleasures in such research is that of simply remembering, not just the story but the occasion on which you heard it and the people you were with at the time. Remembering the stories you learned growing up—bringing them back into view to think and write about—can help you reconstruct the imaginary worlds that they created and the versions of reality that they transmitted. By the same token, looking for patterns in the familiar stories you hear in songs and see on television and at the movies can help you give shape to the larger popular culture and the fears and aspirations it represents.

No Name Woman

Maxine Hong Kingston

Maxine Hong Kingston is a Chinese American writer who grew up in Stockton, California, and now lives in Hawaii. In two remarkable award-winning books, *The Woman Warrior* and *China Men,* Kingston combines autobiography, history, myth, folklore, and legend to tell and retell stories about her family and her girlhood in the Chinese American community in Stockton. We have chosen the opening section of *The Woman Warrior* (1976), "No Name Woman," because it presents a striking example of how Kingston has recreated the mood of the "talk story," a Chinese tradition of storytelling she learned from her mother.

SUGGESTION FOR READING

Maxine Hong Kingston begins her story with her mother saying, "You must not tell anyone…what I am about to tell you." As you read, notice how this opening establishes a certain mood and announces certain purposes for her mother's "talk story."

"Y ou must not tell anyone," my mother said, "what I am about to tell you. In China your father had a sister who killed herself. She jumped into the family well. We say that your father had all brothers because it is as if she had never been born.

"In 1924 just a few days after our village celebrated seventeen hurry-up weddings—to make sure that every young man who went 'out on the road' would responsibly come home—

your father and his brothers and your grandfather and his brothers and your aunt's new husband sailed for America, the Gold Mountain. It was your grandfather's last trip. Those lucky enough to get contracts waved good-bye from the decks. They fed and guarded the stowaways and helped them off in Cuba, New York, Bali, Hawaii. 'We'll meet in California next year,' they said. All of them sent money home.

"I remember looking at your aunt one day when she and I were dressing; I had not noticed before that she had such a protruding melon of a stomach. But I did not think, 'She's pregnant,' until she began to look like other pregnant women, her shirt pulling and the white tops of her black pants showing. She could not have been pregnant, you see, because her husband had been gone for years. No one said anything. We did not discuss it. In early summer she was ready to have the child, long after the time when it could have been possible.

"The village had also been counting. On the night the baby was to be born the villagers raided our house. Some were crying. Like a great saw, teeth strung with lights, files of people walked zigzag across our land, tearing the rice. Their lanterns doubled in the disturbed black water, which drained away through the broken bunds. As the villagers closed in, we could see that some of them, probably men and women we knew well, wore white masks. The people with long hair hung it over their faces. Women with short hair made it stand up on end. Some had tied white bands around their foreheads, arms, and legs.

"At first they threw mud and rocks at the house. Then they threw eggs and began slaughtering our stock. We could hear the animals scream their deaths—the roosters, the pigs, a last great roar from the ox. Familiar wild heads flared in our night windows; the villagers encircled us. Some of the faces stopped to peer at us, their eyes rushing like searchlights. The hands flattened against the panes, framed heads, and left red prints.

"The villagers broke in the front and the back doors at the same time, even though we had not locked the doors against them. Their knives dripped with the blood of our animals. They smeared blood on the doors and walls. One woman swung a chicken, whose throat she had slit, splattering blood in red arcs about her. We stood together in the middle of our house, in the family hall with the pictures and tables of the ancestors around us, and looked straight ahead.

"At that time the house had only two wings. When the men came back, we would build two more to enclose our courtyard and a third one to begin a second courtyard. The villagers pushed through both wings, even your grandparents' rooms, to find your aunt's, which was also mine until the men returned. From this room a new wing for one of the younger families would grow. They ripped up her clothes and shoes and broke her combs, grinding them underfoot. They tore her work from the loom. They scattered the cooking fire and rolled the new weaving in it. We could hear them in the kitchen breaking our bowls and banging the pots. They overturned the great waist-high earthenware jugs; duck eggs, pickled fruits, vegetables burst out and mixed in acrid torrents. The old woman from the next field swept a broom through the air and loosed the spirits-of-the-broom over our heads. 'Pig.' 'Ghost.' 'Pig.' they sobbed and scolded while they ruined our house.

"When they left, they took sugar and oranges to bless themselves. They cut pieces from the dead animals. Some of them took bowls that were not broken and clothes that were not torn. Afterward we swept up the rice and sewed it back up into sacks. But the smells from the spilled preserves lasted. Your aunt gave birth in the pigsty that night. The next morning when I went for the water, I found her and the baby plugging up the family well.

"Don't let your father know that I told you. He denies her. Now that you have started to menstruate, what happened to her could happen to you. Don't humiliate us. You wouldn't like to be forgotten as if you had never been born. The villagers are watchful."

Whenever she had to warn us about life, my mother told stories that ran like this one, a story to grow up on. She tested our strength to establish realities. Those in the emigrant generations who could not reassert brute survival died young and far from home. Those of us in the first American generations have had to figure out how the invisible world the emigrants built around our childhoods fit in solid America.

The emigrants confused the gods by diverting their curses, misleading them with crooked streets and false names. They must try to confuse their offspring as well, who, I suppose, threaten them in similar ways—always trying to get things straight, always trying to name the unspeakable. The Chinese I know hide their names; sojourners take new names when their lives change and guard their real names with silence.

Chinese-Americans, when you try to understand what things in you are Chinese, how do you separate what is peculiar to childhood, to poverty, insanities, one family, your mother who marked your growing with stories, from what is Chinese? What is Chinese tradition and what is the movies?

If I want to learn what clothes my aunt wore, whether flashy or ordinary, I would have to begin, "Remember Father's drowned-in-the-well sister?" I cannot ask that. My mother has told me once and for all the useful parts. She will add nothing unless powered by Necessity, a riverbank that guides her life. She plants vegetable gardens rather than lawns; she carries the odd-shaped tomatoes home from the fields and eats food left for the gods.

Whenever we did frivolous things, we used up energy; we flew high kites. We children came up off the ground over the melting cones our parents brought home from work and the American movie on New Year's Day—*Oh, You Beautiful Doll* with Betty Grable one year, and *She Wore a Yellow Ribbon* with John Wayne another year. After the one carnival ride each, we paid in guilt; our tired father counted his change on the dark walk home.

Adultery is extravagance. Could people who hatch their own chicks and eat the embryos and the heads for delicacies and boil the feet in vinegar for party food, leaving only the gravel, eating even the gizzard lining—could such people engender a prodigal aunt? To be a woman, to have a daughter in starvation time was a waste enough. My aunt could not have been the lone romantic who gave up everything for sex. Women in the old China did not choose. Some man had commanded her to lie with him and be his secret evil. I wonder whether he masked himself when he joined the raid on her family.

Perhaps she encountered him in the fields or on the mountain where the daughters-in-law collected fuel. Or perhaps he first noticed her in the marketplace. He was not a stranger because the village housed no strangers. She had to have dealings with him other than sex. Perhaps he worked an adjoining field, or he sold her the cloth for the dress she sewed and wore. His demand must have surprised, then terrified her. She obeyed him; she always did as she was told.

When the family found a young man in the next village to be her husband, she stood tractably beside the best rooster, his proxy, and promised before they met that she would be his forever. She was lucky that he was her age and she would be the first wife, an advantage secure now. The night she first saw him, he had sex with her. Then he left for America. She had almost forgotten what he looked like. When she tried to envision him, she only saw the black and white face in the group photograph the men had had taken before leaving.

The other man was not, after all, much different from her husband. They both gave orders: she followed. "If you tell your family, I'll beat you. I'll kill you. Be here again next week." No one talked sex, ever. And she might have separated the rapes from the rest of living if only she did not have to buy her oil from him or gather wood in the same forest. I want her fear to have lasted just as long as rape lasted so that the fear could have been contained. No drawn-out fear. But women at sex hazarded birth and hence lifetimes. The fear did not stop but permeated everywhere. She told the man, "I think I'm pregnant." He organized the raid against her.

On nights when my mother and father talked about their life back home, sometimes they mentioned an "outcast table" whose business they still seemed to be settling, their voices tight. In a commensal tradition, where food is precious, the powerful older people made wrongdoers eat alone. Instead of letting them start separate new lives like the Japanese, who could become samurais and geishas, the Chinese family, faces averted but eyes glowering sideways, hung on to the offenders and fed them leftovers. My aunt must have lived in the same house as my parents and eaten at an outcast table. My mother spoke about the raid as if she had seen it, when she and my aunt, a daughter-in-law to a different household, should not have been living together at all. Daughters-in-law lived with their husbands' parents, not their own; a synonym for marriage in Chinese is "taking a daughter-in-law." Her husband's parents could have sold her, mortgaged her, stoned her. But they had sent her back to her own mother and father, a mysterious act hinting at disgraces not told me. Perhaps they had thrown her out to deflect the avengers.

She was the only daughter; her four brothers went with her father, husband, and uncles "out on the road" and for some years became western men. When the goods were divided among the family, three of the brothers took land, and the youngest, my father, chose an education. After my grandparents gave their daughter away to her husband's family, they had dispensed all the adventure and all the property. They expected her alone to keep the traditional ways, which her brothers, now among the barbarians, could fumble without detection. The heavy, deep-rooted women were to maintain the past against the flood, safe for returning. But the rare urge west had fixed upon our family, and so my aunt crossed boundaries not delineated in space.

The work of preservation demands that the feelings playing about in one's guts not be turned into action. Just watch their passing like cherry blossoms. But perhaps my aunt, my forerunner, caught in a slow life, let dreams grow and fade and after some months or years went toward what persisted. Fear at the enormities of the forbidden kept her desires delicate, wire and bone. She looked at a man because she liked the way the hair was tucked behind his ears, or she liked the question-mark line of a long torso curving at the shoulder and straight at the hip. For warm eyes or a soft voice or a slow walk—that's all—a few hairs, a line, a brightness, a sound, a pace, she gave up family. She offered us up for a charm that vanished with tiredness, a pigtail that didn't toss when the wind died. Why, the wrong lighting could erase the dearest thing about him.

It could very well have been, however, that my aunt did not take subtle enjoyment of her friend, but, a wild woman, kept rollicking company. Imagining her free with sex doesn't fit, though. I don't know any women like that, or men either. Unless I see her life branching into mine, she gives me no ancestral help.

To sustain her being in love, she often worked at herself in the mirror, guessing at the colors and shapes that would interest him, changing them frequently in order to hit on the right combination. She wanted him to look back.

On a farm near the sea, a woman who tended her appearance reaped a reputation for eccentricity. All the married women blunt-cut their hair in flaps about their ears or pulled it back in tight buns. No nonsense. Neither style blew easily into heart-catching tangles. And at their weddings they displayed themselves in their long hair for the last time. "It brushed the backs of my knees," my mother tells me. "It was braided, and even so, it brushed the backs of my knees."

At the mirror my aunt combed individuality into her bob. A bun could have been contrived to escape into black streamers blowing in the wind or in quiet wisps about her face, but only the older women in our picture album wear buns. She brushed her hair back from her forehead, tucking the flaps behind her ears. She looped a piece of thread, knotted into a circle between her index fingers and thumbs, and ran the double strand across her forehead. When she closed her fingers as if she were making a pair of shadow geese bite, the string twisted together catching the little hairs. Then she pulled the thread away from her skin, ripping the hairs out neatly, her eyes watering from the needles of pain. Opening her fingers, she cleaned the thread, then rolled it along her hairline and the tops of her eyebrows. My mother did the same to me and my sisters and herself. I used to believe that the expression "caught by the short hairs" meant a captive held with a depilatory string. It especially hurt at the temples, but my mother said we were lucky we didn't have to have our feet bound when we were seven. Sisters used to sit on their beds and cry together, she said, as their mothers or their slave removed the bandages for a few minutes each night and let the blood gush back into their veins. I hope that the man my aunt loved appreciated a smooth brow, that he wasn't just a tits-and-ass man.

Once my aunt found a freckle on her chin, at a spot that the almanac said predestined her for unhappiness. She dug it out with a hot needle and washed the wound with peroxide.

More attention to her looks than these pullings of hairs and pickings at spots would have caused gossip among the villagers. They owned work clothes and good clothes, and they wore good clothes for feasting the new seasons. But since a woman combing her hair hexes beginnings, my aunt rarely found an occasion to look her best. Women looked like great sea snails—the corded wood, babies, and laundry they carried were the whorls on their backs. The Chinese did not admire a bent back; goddesses and warriors stood straight. Still there must have been a marvelous freeing of beauty when a worker laid down her burden and stretched and arched.

Such commonplace loveliness, however, was not enough for my aunt. She dreamed of a lover for the fifteen days of New Year's, the time for families to exchange visits, money, and food. She plied her secret comb. And sure enough she cursed the year, the family, the village, and herself.

Even as her hair lured her imminent lover, many other men looked at her. Uncles, cousins, nephews, brothers would have looked, too, had they been home between journeys. Perhaps they had already been restraining their curiosity, and they left, fearful that their glances, like a field of nesting birds, might be startled and caught. Poverty hurt, and that was their first reason for leaving. But another, final reason for leaving the crowded house was the never-said.

She may have been unusually beloved, the precious only daughter, spoiled and mirror gazing because of the affection the family lavished on her. When her husband left, they welcomed the chance to take her back from the in-laws; she could live like the little daughter for just a while longer. There are stories that my grandfather was different from other people, "crazy ever since the little Jap bayoneted him in the head." He used to put his naked penis on the dinner table, laughing. And one day he brought home a baby girl, wrapped up inside his brown western-style greatcoat. He had traded one of his sons, probably my father, the youngest, for her. My grandmother made him trade back. When he finally got a daughter of his own, he doted on her. They must have all loved her, except perhaps my father, the only brother who never went back to China, having once been traded for a girl.

Brothers and sisters, newly men and women, had to efface their sexual color and present plain miens. Disturbing hair and eyes, a smile like no other, threatened the ideal of five generations living under one roof. To focus blurs, people shouted face to face and yelled from room to room. The immigrants I know have loud voices, unmodulated to American tones even after years away from the village where they called their friendships out across the fields. I have not been able to stop my mother's screams in public libraries or over telephones. Walking erect (knees straight, toes pointed forward, not pigeon-toed, which is Chinese-feminine) and speaking in an inaudible voice, I have tried to turn myself American-feminine. Chinese communication was loud, public. Only sick people had to whisper. But at the dinner table, where the family members came nearest one another, no one could talk, not the outcasts nor any eaters. Every word that falls from the mouth is a coin lost. Silently they gave and accepted food with both hands. A preoccupied child who took his bowl with one hand got a sideways glare. A complete moment of total attention is due everyone alike. Children and lovers have no singularity here, but my aunt used a secret voice, a separate attentiveness.

She kept the man's name to herself throughout her labor and dying; she did not accuse him that he be punished with her. To save her inseminator's name she gave silent birth.

He may have been somebody in her own household, but intercourse with a man outside the family would have been no less abhorrent. All the village were kinsmen, and the titles shouted in loud country voices never let kinship be forgotten. Any man within visiting distance would have been neutralized as a lover—"brother," "younger brother," "older brother"—one hundred and fifteen relationship titles. Parents researched birth charts probably not so much to assure good fortune as to circumvent incest in a population that has but one hundred surnames. Everybody has eight million relatives. How useless then sexual mannerisms, how dangerous.

As if it came from an atavism deeper than fear, I used to add "brother" silently to boys' names. It hexed the boys, who would or would not ask me to dance, and made them less scary and as familiar and deserving of benevolence as girls.

But, of course, I hexed myself also—no dates. I should have stood up, both arms waving, and shouted out across libraries, "Hey, you! Love me back." I had no idea, though, how to make attraction selective, how to control its direction and magnitude. If I made myself American-pretty so that the five or six Chinese boys in the class fell in love with me, everyone else—the Caucasian, Negro, and Japanese boys—would too. Sisterliness, dignified and honorable, made much more sense.

Attraction eludes control so stubbornly that whole societies designed to organize relationships among people cannot keep order, not even when they bind people to one another from childhood and raise them together. Among the very poor and the wealthy, brothers married their adopted sisters, like doves. Our family allowed some romance, paying adult brides' prices and providing dowries so that their sons and daughters could marry strangers. Marriage promises to turn strangers into friendly relatives—a nation of siblings.

In the village structure, spirits shimmered among the live creatures, balanced and held in equilibrium by time and land. But one human being flaring up into violence could open up a black hole, a maelstrom that pulled in the sky. The frightened villagers, who depended on one another to maintain the real, went to my aunt to show her a personal, physical representation of the break she had made in the "roundness." Misallying couples snapped off the future, which was to be embodied in true offspring. The villagers punished her for acting as if she could have a private life, secret and apart from them.

If my aunt had betrayed the family at a time of large grain yields and peace, when many boys were born, and wings were being built on many houses, perhaps she might have escaped such severe punishment. But the men—hungry, greedy, tired of planting in dry soil, cuckolded—had to leave the village in order to send food-money home. There were ghost plagues, bandit plagues, wars with the Japanese, floods. My Chinese brother and sister had died of an unknown sickness. Adultery, perhaps only a mistake during good times, became a crime when the village needed food.

The round moon cakes and round doorways, the round tables of graduated size that fit one roundness inside another, round windows and rice bowls—these talismans had lost their power to warn this family of the law: a family must be whole, faithfully keeping the descent line by having sons to feed the old and the dead, who in turn look after the family. The villagers came to show my aunt and her lover-in-hiding a broken house. The villagers were speeding up the circling of events because she was too short-sighted to see that her infidelity had already harmed the village, that waves of consequences would return unpredictably, sometimes in disguise, as now, to hurt her. This roundness had to be made coin-sized so that she would see its circumference: punish her at the birth of her baby. Awaken her to the inexorable. People who refused fatalism because they could invent small resources insisted on culpability. Deny accidents and wrest fault from the stars.

After the villagers left, their lanterns now scattering in various directions toward home, the family broke their silence and cursed her. "Aiaa, we're going to die. Death is coming. Death is coming. Look what you've done. You've killed us. Ghost! Dead ghost! Ghost! You've never been born." She ran out into the fields, far enough from the house so that she could no longer hear their voices, and pressed herself against the earth, her own land no more. When she felt the birth coming, she thought that she had been hurt. Her body seized together. "They've hurt me too much," she thought. "This is gall, and it will kill me." With forehead and knees against the earth, her body convulsed and then relaxed. She turned on her back, lay on the ground. The black well of sky and stars went out and out and out forever; her body and her complexity seemed to disappear. She was one of the stars, a bright dot in blackness, without home, without a companion, in eternal cold and silence. An agoraphobia rose in her, speeding higher and higher, bigger and bigger; she would not be able to contain it; there would be no end to fear.

Flayed, unprotected against space, she felt pain return, focusing her body. This pain chilled her—a cold, steady kind of surface pain. Inside, spasmodically, the other pain, the pain of the child, heated her. For hours she lay on the ground, alternately body and space. Sometimes a vision of normal comfort obliterated reality: she saw the family in the evening gambling at the dinner table, the young people massaging their elders' backs. She saw them congratulating one another, high joy on the mornings the rice shoots came up. When these pictures burst, the stars drew yet further apart. Black space opened.

She got to her feet to fight better and remembered that old-fashioned women gave birth in their pigsties to fool the jealous, pain-dealing gods, who do not snatch piglets. Before the next spasms could stop her, she ran to the pigsty, each step a rushing out into emptiness. She climbed over the fence and knelt in the dirt. It was good to have a fence enclosing her, a tribal person alone.

Laboring, this woman who had carried her child as a foreign growth that sickened her every day, expelled it at last. She reached down to touch the hot, wet, moving mass, surely smaller than anything human, and could feel that it was human after all—fingers, toes, nails, nose. She pulled it up on to her belly, and it lay curled there, butt in the air, feet precisely tucked one under the other. She opened her loose shirt and buttoned the child inside. After resting, it squirmed and thrashed and she pushed it up to her breast. It turned its head this way and that until it found her nipple. There, it made little snuffling noises. She clenched her teeth at its preciousness, lovely as a young calf, a piglet, a little dog.

She may have gone to the pigsty as a last act of responsibility: she would protect this child as she had protected its father. It would look after her soul, leaving supplies on her grave. But how would this tiny child without family find her grave when there would be no marker for her anywhere, neither in the earth nor the family hall? No one would give her a family hall name. She had taken the child with her into the wastes. At its birth the two of them had felt the same raw pain of separation, a wound that only the family pressing tight could close. A child with no descent line would not soften her life but only trail after her, ghost-like, begging her to give it purpose. At dawn the villagers on their way to the fields would stand around the fence and look.

Full of milk, the little ghost slept. When it awoke, she hardened her breasts against the milk that crying loosens. Toward morning she picked up the baby and walked to the well.

Carrying the baby to the well shows loving. Otherwise abandon it. Turn its face into the mud. Mothers who love their children take them along. It was probably a girl; there is some hope of forgiveness for boys.

"Don't tell anyone you had an aunt. Your father does not want to hear her name. She has never been born." I have believed that sex was unspeakable and words so strong and fathers so frail that "aunt" would do my father mysterious harm. I have thought that my family, having settled among immigrants who had also been their neighbors in the ancestral land, needed to clean their name, and a wrong word would incite the kinspeople even here. But there is more to this silence: they want me to participate in her punishment. And I have.

In the twenty years since I heard this story I have not asked for details nor said my aunt's name; I do not know it. People who can comfort the dead can also chase after them to hurt them further—a reverse ancestor worship. The real punishment was not the raid swiftly inflicted by the villagers, but the family's deliberately forgetting her. Her betrayal so maddened them, they saw to it that she would suffer forever, even after death. Always hungry, always needing, she would have to beg food from other ghosts, snatch and steal it from those whose living descendants give them gifts. She would have to fight the ghosts massed at crossroads for the buns a few thoughtful citizens leave to decoy her away from village and home so that the ancestral spirits could feast unharassed. At peace, they could act like gods, not ghosts, their descent lines providing them with paper suits and dresses, spirit money, paper houses, paper automobiles, chicken, meat, and rice into eternity—essences delivered up in smoke and flames, steam and incense rising from each rice bowl. In an attempt to make the Chinese care for people outside the family, Chairman Mao encourages us now to give our paper replicas to the spirits of outstanding soldiers and workers, no matter whose ancestors they may be. My aunt remains forever hungry. Goods are not distributed evenly among the dead.

My aunt haunts me—her ghost drawn to me because now, after fifty years of neglect, I alone devote pages of paper to her, though not origamied into houses and clothes. I do not think she always means me well. I am telling on her, and she was a spite suicide, drowning herself in the drinking water. The Chinese are always very frightened of the drowned one, whose weeping ghost, wet hair hanging and skin bloated, waits silently by the water to pull down a substitute.

SUGGESTIONS FOR DISCUSSION

1. Maxine Hong Kingston first gives her mother's version of her aunt's suicide, and then she devotes the rest of this selection to her own reflections on it. Why do you think Kingston has organized "No Name Woman" this way? What effect does it have on you as a reader?

2. How would you describe the relationship between Kingston and her mother—as mother and daughter and as "story talkers"?

3. Kingston says of her aunt, "Unless I see her life branching into mine, she gives me no ancestral help." Explain the significance of this statement.

SUGGESTIONS FOR WRITING

1. Write an essay about the way Maxine Hong Kingston tells the story "No Name Woman." You might consider why Kingston makes the first voice

that of her mother ("You must not tell anyone…what I am about to tell you") and why she breaks her mother's admonition to silence in order to retell the story of her aunt's suicide.

2. The story Maxine Hong Kingston's mother tells in "No Name Woman" might be considered a cautionary tale about the perils of growing up. Write an essay about a story you were told that transmitted some point about growing up or some lesson about life. You will want to take into account who told the story to you, the occasion on which the story was told, what gave the speaker the authority to tell you the story, and the point or lesson of the story. Re-create the setting and mood in order to retell the story through the voice of the person who told it to you. Also follow Kingston's example in "No Name Woman," and explore the effects on you of the story and the person telling it.

3. In "No Name Woman" (and throughout much of her writing), Kingston makes family stories into tales of ancestral spirits and ghosts that haunt her imagination. Are there such figures in your family tradition? In your own imagination? Write an essay that tells a story about one of your ancestors and explains what he or she represents in your imagination.

"The Hook" and Other Teenage Horrors

Jan Harold Brunvand

Jan Harold Brunvand is a folklorist and professor of English at the University of Utah. "'The Hook' and Other Teenage Horrors" is a chapter from Brunvand's book *The Vanishing Hitchhiker: American Urban Legends and Their Meaning* (1981). In *The Vanishing Hitchhiker* and its two sequels, *The Choking Doberman* and *The Mexican Pet,* Brunvand has gathered examples of contemporary story-telling—strange, scary, funny, macabre, and embarrassing tales storytellers relate as true accounts of real-life experience. Brunvand calls these stories "urban legends" because they are, by and large, set in contemporary America and, like all legends, are alleged to be about real people and real events. These legends, often about someone that the narrator knows or the "friend of a friend," are passed on by word of mouth, forming an oral tradition in the midst of America's print and media culture. As Brunvand says, urban legends "survive by being as lively and 'factual' as the television evening news, and, like the daily news-casts, they tend to concern deaths, injuries, kidnappings, tragedies, and scandals." Stories like "The Hook" are told and believed—or at least believable—as "human interest" stories that capture some of the fears and anxieties of contemporary America.

SUGGESTION FOR READING

As a folklorist, Brunvand is interested in interpreting urban legends as well as in gathering them. As you read through "'The Hook' and Other Teenage Horrors," underline and annotate the passages where Brunvand offers his own interpretations or those of other folklore scholars.

GROWING UP SCARED

People of all ages love a good scare. Early childlore is full of semiserious spooky stories and ghastly threats, while the more sophisticated black humor of Little Willies, Bloody Marys, Dead Babies, and other cycles of sick jokes enters a bit later. Among the favorite readings at school are Edgar Allan Poe's blood-soaked tales, and favorite stories at summer camp tell of maniacal ax-murderers and deformed giants lurking in the dark forest to ambush unwary Scouts. Halloween spook houses and Hollywood horror films cater to the same wish to push the level of tolerable fright as far as possible.

The ingredients of horror fiction change little through time, but the style of such stories does develop, even in oral tradition. In their early teens young Americans apparently reject the overdramatic and unbelievable juvenile "scaries" and adopt a new lore of more plausible tales with realistic settings. That is, they begin to enjoy urban legends, especially those dealing with "folks" like themselves—dating couples, students, and baby-sitters—who are subjected to grueling ordeals and horrible threats.

One consistent theme in these teenage horrors is that as the adolescent moves out from home into the larger world, the world's dangers may close in on him or her. Therefore, although the immediate purpose of many of these legends is to produce a good scare, they also serve to deliver a warning: Watch out! This could happen to you! Furthermore, the horror tales often contain thinly-disguised sexual themes which are, perhaps, implicit in the nature of such plot situations as parking in a lovers' lane or baby-sitting (playing house) in a strange home. These sexual elements furnish both a measure of further entertainment and definite cautionary notices about the world's actual dangers. Thus, from the teenagers' own major fears, concerns, and experiences, spring their favorite "true" oral stories.

The chief current example of this genre of urban legend—one that is even older, more popular, and more widespread than "The Boyfriend's Death"—is the one usually called "The Hook."

"THE HOOK"

On Tuesday, November 8, 1960, the day when Americans went to the polls to elect John F. Kennedy as their thirty-fifth president, thousands of people must have read the following letter from a teenager in the popular newspaper column written by Abigail Van Buren:

> Dear Abby: If you are interested in teenagers, you will print this story. I don't know whether it's true or not, but it doesn't matter because it served its purpose for me:
>
> A fellow and his date pulled into their favorite "lovers' lane" to listen to the radio and do a little necking. The music was interrupted by an announcer who said there was an escaped convict in the area who had served time for rape and robbery. He was described as having a hook instead of a right hand. The couple became frightened and drove away. When the boy took his girl home, he went around to open the car door for her. Then he saw—a hook on the door handle! I don't think I will ever park to make out as long as I live. I hope this does the same for other kids.
>
> *Jeanette*

This juicy story seems to have emerged in the late 1950s, sharing some common themes with "The Death Car" and "The Vanishing Hitchhiker" and then…influencing "The Boyfriend's Death" as that legend developed in the early 1960s. The story of "The Hook" (or "The Hookman") really needed no national press report to give it life or credibility, because the teenage oral-tradition underground had done the job well enough long before the election day of 1960. Teenagers all over the country knew about "The Hook" by 1959, and like other modern legends the basic plot was elaborated with details and became highly localized.

One of my own students, originally from Kansas, provided this specific account of where the event supposedly occurred:

> Outside of "Mac" [McPherson, Kansas], about seven miles out towards Lindsborg, north on old highway 81 is an old road called "Hookman's Road." It's a curved road, a traditional parking spot for the kids. When I was growing up it [the legend] was popular, and that was back in the '60's, and it was old then.

Another student told a version of the story that she had heard from her baby-sitter in Albuquerque in 1960:

> over the radio came an announcement that a crazed killer with a hook in place of a hand had escaped from the local insane asylum. The girl got scared and begged the boy to take her home. He got mad and stepped on the gas and roared off. When they got to her house, he got out and went around to the other side of the car to let her out. There on the door handle was a bloody hook.

But these two students were told, after arriving in Salt Lake City, that it had actually occurred *here* in Memory Grove, a well-wooded city park. "Oh, no," a local student in the class insisted. "This couple was parked outside of Salt Lake City *in a mountain canyon* one night, and…" It turned out that virtually every student in the class knew the story as adapted in some way to their hometowns.

Other folklorists have reported collecting "The Hook" in Maryland, Wisconsin, Indiana, Illinois, Kansas, Texas, Arkansas, Oregon, and Canada. Some of the informants' comments echo Dear Abby's correspondent in testifying to the story's effect (to discourage parking) even when its truth was suspect. The student said, "I believe that it *could* happen, and this makes it seem real," or "I don't really [believe it], but it's pretty scary; I sort of hope it didn't happen."

Part of the great appeal of "The Hook"—one of the most popular adolescent scare stories—must lie in the tidiness of the plot. Everything fits. On the other hand, the lack of loose ends would seem to be excellent testimony to the story's near impossibility. After all, what are the odds that a convicted criminal or crazed maniac would be fitted with a hook for a missing hand, that this same threatening figure would show up precisely when a radio warning had been broadcast of his escape, and that the couple would drive away rapidly just at the instant the hookman put his hook through the door handle? Besides, why wouldn't he try to open the door with his good hand, and how is it that the boy—furious at the interruption of their lovemaking—is still willing to go around politely to open the girl's door when they get home? Too much, too much—but it makes a great story.

In an adolescent novel titled *Dinky Hocker Shoots Smack!,* M. E. Kerr captured the way teenagers often react to such legends—with cool acceptance that it might have happened, and that's good enough:

> She told Tucker this long story about a one-armed man who was hanging around a lovers' lane in Prospect Park [Brooklyn]. There were rumors that he tried to get in the cars and carry off the girls. He banged on the windshields with his hooked wooden arm and frothed at the mouth. He only said two words: *bloody murder;* and his voice was high and hoarse.
>
> Dinky claimed this girl who went to St. Marie's was up in Prospect Park one night with a boyfriend. The girl and her boyfriend began discussing the one-armed man while they were parked. They both got frightened and decided to leave. The boy dropped the girl off at her house, and drove home. When he got out of his car, he found this hook attached to his door handle.
>
> Dinky said, "They must have driven off just as he was about to open the door."
>
> "I thought you weren't interested in the bizarre, anymore," Tucker said.
>
> "It's a true story."
>
> "It's still bizarre."

A key detail lacking in the *Dinky Hocker* version, however, is the boyfriend's frustrated anger resulting in their leaving the scene in a great hurry. Almost invariably the boy guns the motor and roars away: "...so he revs up the car and he goes torquing out of there." Or, "The boy floored the gas pedal and zoomed away," or "Her boyfriend was annoyed and the car screeched off...." While this behavior is essential to explain the sudden sharp force that tears loose the maniac's hook, it is also a reminder of the original sexual purpose of the parking, at least on the boy's part. While Linda Dégh saw "the natural dread of the handicapped," and "the boy's disappointment and suddenly recognized fear as an adequate explanation for the jump start of the car," folklorist Alan Dundes disagreed, mainly because of the curtailed sex quest in the plot.

Dundes, taking a Freudian line, interpreted the hook itself as a phallic symbol which penetrates the girl's door handle (or bumps seductively against her window) but which is torn off (symbolic of castration) when the car starts abruptly. Girls who tell the story, Dundes suggests, "are not afraid of what a man lacks, but of what he has"; a date who is "all hands" may really want to "get his hooks into her." Only the girl's winding up the window or insisting upon going home at once saves her, and the date has to "pull out fast" before he begins to act like a sex maniac himself. The radio—turned on originally for soft, romantic background music—introduces instead "the consciencelike voice from society," a warning that the girl heeds and the boy usually scorns. Dundes concluded that this popular legend "reflects a very real dating practice, one which produces anxiety...particularly for girls."

"THE KILLER IN THE BACKSEAT"

A similar urban legend also involves cars and an unseen potential assailant; this time a man threatens a woman who is driving alone at night. The following version of "The Killer in the Backseat" was contributed in 1967 by a University of Utah student who had heard other versions set in Denver and Aurora, Colorado:

> A woman living in the city [i.e., Salt Lake City] was visiting some friends in Ogden. When she got into her car in front of this friend's house, she noticed that a car started up right behind her car. It was about 2:00 in the morning, and there weren't any other cars on the road. After she had driven to the highway, she began to think that this car was following her. Some of the time he would drive up real close to her car, but he wouldn't ever pass. She was really scared to death and kept speeding to try to get away from him.
>
> When she got to Salt Lake, she started running stop lights to get away from him, but he would run right through them too. So when she got to her driveway she pulled in really fast, and this guy pulled in right behind her. She just laid on the horn, and her husband came running out. Just then, the guy jumped out of the car, and her husband ran over and said, "What the hell's goin' on here?" So he grabbed the guy, and his wife said, "This man's followed me all the way from Ogden." The man said, "I followed your wife because I was going to work, and as I got into my car, I noticed when I turned my lights on, a man's head bob down in her back seat." So the husband went over to her backseat, opened the door, and pulled this guy from out of the backseat.

This legend first appeared in print in 1968 in another version, also—coincidentally—set in Ogden, Utah, but collected at Indiana University, Bloomington. (This shows how the presence of folklorists in a locality will influence the apparent distribution patterns of folk material.) Twenty further texts have surfaced at Indiana University with, as usual, plenty of variations and localizations. In many instances the pursuing driver keeps flashing his headlights between the high and low beam in order to restrain the assailant who is popping up and threatening to attack the driver. Sometimes the pursuer is a burly truck driver or other tough-looking character, and in several of the stories the supposed would-be attacker (the pursuing rescuer) is specifically said to be a black man. (Both motifs clearly show white middle class fears of minorities or of groups believed to be socially inferior.)

In a more imaginative set of these legends the person who spots the dangerous man in back is a gas station attendant who pretends that a ten dollar bill offered by the woman driver in payment for gas is counterfeit. With this ruse he gets her safely away from her car before calling the police. In another version of the story, a passing motorist sharply warns the woman driver to roll up her window and follow him, driving in exactly the same manner he does. She obeys, speeding and weaving along the highway, until a suspected assailant—usually carrying an ax—is thrown from his perch on the roof of her car.

"THE BABY-SITTER AND THE MAN UPSTAIRS"

Just as a lone woman may unwittingly be endangered by a hidden man while she is driving at night, a younger one may face the same hazard in a strange home. The horror legend of "The Baby-sitter and the Man Upstairs," similar in structure to "The Killer in the Backseat," is possibly a later variation of the same story relocated to fit teenagers' other direct experiences. This standard version is from a fourteen-year-old Canadian boy (1973):

> There was this baby-sitter that was in Montreal baby-sitting for three children in a big house. She was watching TV when suddenly the phone rang. The children were all in bed. She picked up the phone and heard this guy on the other end laughing hysterically. She asked him what it was that he wanted, but he wouldn't answer and then hung up. She worried about it for a while, but then thought nothing more of it and went back to watching the movie.
>
> Everything was fine until about fifteen minutes later when the phone rang again. She picked it up and heard the same voice laughing hysterically at her, and then hung up. At this point she became really worried and phoned the operator to tell her what had been happening. The operator told her to calm down and that if he called again to try and keep him on the line as long as possible and she would try to trace the call.
>
> Again about fifteen minutes later the guy called back and laughed hysterically at her. She asked him why he was doing this, but he just kept laughing at her. He hung up and about five seconds later the operator called. She told the girl to get out of the house at once because the person who was calling was calling from the upstairs extension. She slammed down the phone and just as she was turning to leave she saw the man coming down the stairs laughing hysterically with a bloody butcher knife in his hand and meaning to kill her. She ran out onto the street but he didn't follow. She called the police and they came and caught the man, and discovered that he had murdered all the children.

The storyteller added that he had heard the story from a friend whose brother's girlfriend was the baby-sitter involved.

By now it should come as no surprise to learn that the same story had been collected two years earlier (1971) some 1500 miles southwest of Montreal, in Austin, Texas, and also in Bloomington, Indiana, in 1973 in a college dormitory. These three published versions are only samples from the wide distribution of the story in folk tradition. Their similarities and differences provide another classic case of folklore's variation within traditional boundaries. In all three legend texts the hour is late and the baby-sitter is watching television. Two of the callers make threatening statements, while one merely laughs. In all versions the man calls three times at regular intervals before the girl calls the operator, then once more afterwards. In both American texts the operator herself calls the police, and in the Indiana story she commands "Get out of the house immediately; don't go upstairs; don't do anything; just leave the house. When you get out there, there will be policemen outside and they'll take care of it." (One is reminded of the rescuers' orders not to look back at the car in "The

Boyfriend's Death.") The Texas telephone operator in common with the Canadian one gives the situation away by adding, "The phone call traces to the upstairs." The murder of the child or children (one, two, or three of them—no pattern) is specified in the American versions: in Texas they are "chopped into little bitty pieces"; in Indiana, "torn to bits." All of the storytellers played up the spookiness of the situation—details that would be familiar to anyone who has every baby-sat—a strange house, a television show, an unexpected phone call, frightening sounds or threats, the abrupt orders from the operator, and finally the shocking realization at the end that (as in "The Killer in the Backseat") the caller had been there in the house (or behind her) all the time. The technical problems of calling another telephone from an extension of the same number, or the actual procedures of call-tracing, do not seem to worry the storytellers.

Folklorist Sue Samuelson, who examined hundreds of unpublished "Man Upstairs" stories filed in American folklore archives, concluded that the telephone is the most important and emotionally-loaded item in the plot: the assailant is harassing his victim through the device that is her own favorite means of communication. Baby-sitting, Samuelson points out, is an important socializing experience for young women, allowing them to practice their future roles, imposed on them in a male-dominated society, as homemakers and mothers. Significantly, the threatening male figure is upstairs—on top of and in control of the girl—as men have traditionally been in the sexual relationship. In killing the children who were in her care, the man brings on the most catastrophic failure any mother can suffer. Another contributing factor in the story is that the baby-sitter herself is too intent on watching television to realize that the children are being murdered upstairs. Thus, the tale is not just another scary story, but conveys a stern admonition to young women to adhere to society's traditional values.

Occasionally these firmly believed horror legends are transformed from ghastly mysteries to almost comical adventures. The following Arizona version of "The Baby-sitter and the Man Upstairs," collected in 1976, is a good example:

> It was August 8, 1969. She was going to baby-sit at the Smiths who had two children, ages five and seven. She had just put the children to bed and went back to the living room to watch TV.
>
> The phone began to ring; she went to answer it; the man on the other end said, "I'm upstairs with the children; you'd better come up."
>
> She hung the phone up immediately, scared to death. She decided that it must be a prank phone call; again she went to watch TV. The phone rang again; she went to answer it, this time more scared than last.
>
> The man said, "I'm upstairs with the children," and described them in detail. So she hung up the phone, not knowing what to do. Should I call the police? Instead she decided, "I'll call the operator. They can trace these phone calls." She called the operator, and the operator said that she would try and do what she could. Approximately ten minutes later the phone rang again; this time she was shaking.
>
> She answered the phone and the man again said, "I'm upstairs with the children; you'd better come quick!" She tried to stay on the phone as long as she could so that the operator could trace the call; this time the man hung up.
>
> She called back, and the operator said, "Run out of the house; the man is on the extension."
>
> She didn't quite know what to do; should she go and get the children? "No," she said, "he's up there; if I go and get the children, I'll be killed too!!"
>
> She ran next door to the neighbor's house and called the police. The sirens came—there must have been at least ten police cars. They went inside the house, ran upstairs, and found not a man, but a seven-year-old child who was sitting next to the phone with a tape recorder. Later they found that a boy down the street had told this young boy to do this next time he had a baby-sitter. You see the boy didn't like his parents going out, and he didn't like having baby-sitters. So he felt this was the only way he could get rid of them. The boys [sic] don't have baby-sitters anymore; now they go to the nursery school.

"THE ROOMMATE'S DEATH"

Another especially popular example of the American adolescent shocker story is the widely known legend of "The Roommate's Death." It shares several themes with other urban legends. As in "The Killer in the Backseat" and "The Baby-sitter and the Man Upstairs," it is usually a lone woman in the story who is threatened—or thinks she is—by a strange man. As in "The Hook" and "The Boyfriend's Death," the assailant is often said to be an escaped criminal or a maniac. Finally, as in the latter legend, the actual commission of the crime is never described; only the resulting mutilated corpse is. The scratching sounds outside the girl's place of refuge are an additional element of suspense. Here is a version told by a University of Kansas student in 1965 set in Corbin Hall, a freshman women's dormitory there:

> These two girls in Corbin had stayed late over Christmas vacation. One of them had to wait for a later train, and the other wanted to go to a fraternity party given that night of vacation. The dorm assistant was in her room—sacked out. They waited and waited for the intercom, and then they heard this knocking and knocking outside in front of the dorm. So the girl thought it was her date and she went down. But she didn't come back and she didn't come back. So real late that night this other girl heard a scratching and gasping down the hall. She couldn't lock the door, so she locked herself in the closet. In the morning she let herself out and her roommate had had her throat cut, and if the other girl had opened the door earlier, she [the dead roommate] would have been saved.

At all the campuses where the story is told the reasons for the girls' remaining alone in the dorm vary, but they are always realistic and plausible. The girls' homes may be too far away for them to visit during vacation, such as in Hawaii or a foreign country. In some cases they wanted to avoid a campus meeting or other obligation. What separates the two roommates may be either that one goes out for food, or to answer the door, or to use the rest room. The girl who is left behind may hear the scratching noise either at her room door or at the closet door, if she hides there. Sometimes her hair turns white or gray overnight from the shock of the experience (an old folk motif). The implication in the story is that some maniac is after her (as is suspected about the pursuer in "The Killer in the Backseat"); but the truth is that her own roommate needs help, and she might have supplied it had she only acted more decisively when the noises were first heard. Usually some special emphasis is put on the victim's fingernails, scratched to bloody stumps by her desperate efforts to signal for help.

A story told by a California teenager, remembered from about 1964, seems to combine motifs of "The Baby-sitter and the Man Upstairs" with "The Roommate's Death." The text is unusually detailed with names and the circumstances of the crime:

> Linda accepted a baby-sitting job for a wealthy family who lived in a two-storey home up in the hills for whom she had never baby-sat for before. Linda was rather hesitant as the house was rather isolated and so she asked a girlfriend, Sharon, to go along with her, promising Sharon half of the baby-sitting fee she would earn. Sharon accepted Linda's offer and the two girls went up to the big two-storey house.
>
> The night was an especially dark and windy one and rain was threatening. All went well for the girls as they read stories aloud to the three little boys they were sitting for and they had no problem putting the boys to bed in the upstairs part of the house. When this was done, the girls settled down to watching television.
>
> It was not long before the telephone rang. Linda answered the telephone, only to hear the heavy breathing of the caller on the other end. She attempted to elicit a response from the caller but he merely hung up. Thinking little of it and not wanting to panic Sharon, Linda went back to watching her television program, remarking that the caller had dialed a wrong number. Upon receiving the second call at which time the caller first engaged in a bit of heavy breathing and then instructed them to check on the children, the two girls became frightened and decided to call the operator for assistance. The operator instructed the girls to keep the caller

on the line as long as possible should he call again so that she might be able to trace the call. The operator would check back with them.

The two girls then decided between themselves that one should stay downstairs to answer the phone. It was Sharon who volunteered to go upstairs. Shortly, the telephone rang again and Linda did as the operator had instructed her. Within a few minutes, the operator called back telling Linda to leave the house immediately with her friend because she had traced the calls to the upstairs phone.

Linda immediately hung up the telephone and proceeded to run to the stairway to call Sharon. She then heard a thumping sound coming from the stairway and when she approached the stairs she saw her friend dragging herself down the stairs by her chin, all of her limbs severed from her body. The three boys also lay dead upstairs in their beds.

Once again, the Indiana University Folklore Archive has provided the best published report on variants of "The Roommate's Death," Linda Dégh's summary of thirty-one texts and several subtypes and related plots collected since 1961. The most significant feature, according to her report, is the frequent appearance of a male rescuer at the end of the story. In one version, for example, two girls are left behind alone in the dorm by their roommate when she goes downstairs for food; they hear noises, and so stay in their room all night without opening the door. Finally the mailman comes around the next morning, and they call him from the window:

The mailman came in the front door and went up the stairs, and told the girls to stay in their room, that everything was all right but that they were to stay in their rooms [sic]. But the girls didn't listen to him cause he had said it was all right, so they came out into the hall. When they opened the door, they saw the girlfriend on the floor with a hatchet in her head.

In other Indiana texts the helpful male is a handyman, a milkman, or the brother of one of the roommates.

According to folklorist Beverly Crane, the male-female characters are only one pair of a series of significant opposites, which also includes home and away, intellectual versus emotional behavior, life and death, and several others. A male is needed to resolve the female's uncertainty—motivated by her emotional fear—about how to act in a new situation. Another male has mutilated and killed her roommate with a blow to her head, "the one part of the body with which women are not supposed to compete." The girls, Crane suggested, are doubly out of place in the beginning, having left the haven of home to engage in intellectual pursuits, and having remained alone in the campus dormitory instead of rejoining the family on a holiday. Ironically, the injured girl must use her fingernails, intended to be long, lovely, feminine adornments, in order to scratch for help. But because her roommate fails to investigate the sound, the victim dies, her once pretty nails now bloody stumps. Crane concluded this ingenious interpretation with these generalizations:

The points of value implicit in this narrative are then twofold. If women wish to depend on traditional attitudes and responses they had best stay in a place where these attitudes and responses are best able to protect them. If, however, women do choose to venture into the realm of equality with men, they must become less dependent, more self-sufficient, more confident in their own abilities, and, above all, more willing to assume responsibility for themselves and others.

One might not expect to find women's liberation messages embedded in the spooky stories told by teenagers, but Beverly Crane's case is plausible and well argued. Furthermore, it is not at all unusual to find up-to-date social commentary in other modern folklore—witness the many religious and sexual jokes and legends circulated by people who would not openly criticize a church or the traditional social mores. Folklore does not just purvey the old codes of morality and behavior; it can also absorb newer ideas. What needs to be done to analyze

Urban legends are no longer simply a matter of word of mouth. New technologies—cellular phones, fax machines, and the World Wide Web—are providing people with new means to circulate stories. In his book *The Baby Train* (1993), Jan Harold Brunvand traces the added twists via the new technologies to an urban legend about someone waking up in a hotel room only to discover that one of his or her kidneys has been carved out to be sold on the black market for transplant. The setting and characters change in the various accounts. In one version, a female tourist wakes up in a tub of ice in a third-rate hotel in Mexico to find one kidney missing. In another, a fraternity boy vacationing in Manhattan awakens from a night of debauchery with a fresh surgical wound on his back. In still another, a salesman is drugged in a New Orleans bar and wakes up minus one kidney. The "Urban Legends Reference Page" at http://www.snopes.com has become a prime source of such tales. Check it out. You'll see not only urban legends such as the kidney-snatching one but also testimonials to their validity, which claim the story really happened to a friend or friend of a friend. When you visit the "Urban Legends Reference Page," see how many stories you recognize and how they've been modified in the telling.

this is to collect what Alan Dundes calls "oral-literary criticism," the informants' own comments about their lore. How clearly would the girls who tell these stories perceive—or even accept—the messages extrapolated by scholars? And a related question: Have any stories with clear liberationist themes replaced older ones cautioning young women to stay home, be good, and—next best—be careful, and call a man if they need help?

SUGGESTIONS FOR DISCUSSION

1. Brunvand suggests that teenagers tell horror stories not only "to produce a good scare" but also "to deliver a warning" about the "world's actual dangers." To what extent do you think the stories in "The Hook" serve as cautionary tales? Do you think they would be heard and understood in different ways by male and female listeners?

2. Do you find Beverly Crane's interpretation of "The Roommate's Death" persuasive? How would you answer the question Brunvand poses at the end of this selection?

3. Work together with classmates to create your own collection of urban legends. Which of the stories in this selection or similar types of stories have you heard before? Where, when, and from whom did you hear a particular story? How were the details of the story adapted to local conditions? Did the narrator and the listeners seem to believe the story? What did the narrator and the listeners seem to feel were the most important meanings of the story? What fears, concerns, or experiences does the story seem to reflect?

SUGGESTIONS FOR WRITING

1. Jan Harold Brunvand begins this selection with the statement, "People of all ages love a good scare." Write an essay that explains why people enjoy being scared by ghost stories, horror films, and thrillers. To do this,

you may want to compare the horror story with another kind of story-telling, such as fairy tales or adventure stories.

2. Reread "'The Hook' and Other Teenage Horrors," and notice the interpretations of the stories you have marked. Pick one of the interpretations that you find particularly interesting or striking. Write an essay in which you summarize the interpretation and explain why it seems adequate or inadequate. Are there alternative interpretations that you would offer?

3. Use the individual stories and commentaries in this selection ("The Hook," "The Killer in the Backseat," "The Baby-Sitter and the Man Upstairs," and "The Roommate's Death") as a model to recreate and comment on an urban legend that you have heard. Be sure to set the scene of the storytelling—where, when, and who told it—and then give an account of the story. Follow this with a commentary of your own that interprets the dominant theme of the story.

Why We Crave Horror Movies

Stephen King

Stephen King is a writer whose best-selling novels and short stories have taken the genre of horror fiction to new heights of popularity. A number of his fictions have been turned into successful Hollywood films, such as *Carrie* and *The Shining*. In the following essay, originally published in *Playboy* (December 1981), King seeks to identify the reasons horror films have such a grip on the popular imagination. Before you read the essay, you might think about your own experience as a movie-goer and television viewer. Are there particular forms of storytelling—thrillers, soap operas, romances, science fiction, action-adventure, cops and robbers, westerns, and so on—to which you are particularly drawn? The question he asks—Why do we crave horror movies?—could, of course, be applied as well to other forms of popular storytelling.

SUGGESTION FOR READING

Notice how Stephen King presents his assumptions about people in the opening paragraph. As you read, follow King's argument by underlining the reasons he gives. Consider how his initial assumptions have shaped the reasons he offers as answers to the question: Why do we crave horror movies?

I think that we're all mentally ill; those of us outside the asylums only hide it a little better—and maybe not all that much better, after all. We've all known people who talk to themselves, people who sometimes squinch their faces into horrible grimaces when they believe no one is watching, people who have some hysterical fear—of snakes, the dark, the tight place, the long drop...and, of course, those final worms and grubs that are waiting so patiently underground.

When we pay our four or five bucks and seat ourselves at tenth-row center in a theater showing a horror movie, we are daring the nightmare.

Why? Some of the reasons are simple and obvious. To show that we can, that we are not afraid, that we can ride this roller coaster. Which is not to say that a really good horror movie may not surprise a scream out of us at some point, the way we may scream when the roller coaster twists through a complete 360 or plows through a lake at the bottom of the drop. And horror movies, like roller coasters, have always been the special province of the young; by the time one turns 40 or 50, one's appetite for double twists or 360-degree loops may be considerably depleted.

We also go to re-establish our feelings of essential normality; the horror movie is innately conservative, even reactionary. Freda Jackson as the horrible melting woman in *Die, Monster, Die!* confirms for us that no matter how far we may be removed from the beauty of a Robert Redford or a Diana Ross, we are still light-years from true ugliness.

And we go to have fun.

Ah, but this is where the ground starts to slope away, isn't it? Because this is a very peculiar sort of fun, indeed. The fun comes from seeing others menaced—sometimes killed. One critic has suggested that if pro football has become the voyeur's version of combat, then the horror film has become the modern version of the public lynching.

It is true that the mythic, "fairy-tale" horror film intends to take away the shades of gray....It urges us to put away our more civilized and adult penchant for analysis and to become children again, seeing things in pure blacks and whites. It may be that horror movies provide psychic relief on this level because this invitation to lapse into simplicity, irrationality and even outright madness is extended so rarely. We are told we may allow our emotions a free rein...or no rein at all.

If we are all insane, then sanity becomes a matter of degree. If your insanity leads you to carve up women like Jack the Ripper or the Cleveland Torso Murderer, we clap you away in the funny farm (but neither of those two amateur-night surgeons was ever caught, heh-heh-heh); if, on the other hand, your insanity leads you only to talk yourself when you're under stress or to pick your nose on your morning bus, then you are left alone to go about your business...though it is doubtful that you will ever be invited to the best parties.

The potential lyncher is in almost all of us (excluding saints, past and present; but then, most saints have been crazy in their own ways), and every now and then, he has to be let loose to scream and roll around in the grass. Our emotions and our fears form their own body, and we recognize that it demands its own exercise to maintain proper muscle tone. Certain of these emotional muscles are accepted—even exalted—in civilized society; they are, of course, the emotions that tend to maintain the status quo of civilization itself. Love, friendship, loyalty, kindness—these are all the emotions that we applaud, emotions that have been immortalized in the couplets of Hallmark cards and in the verses (I don't dare call it poetry) of Leonard Nimoy.

When we exhibit these emotions, society showers us with positive reinforcement; we learn this even before we get out of diapers. When, as children, we hug our rotten little puke of a sister and give her a kiss, all the aunts and uncles smile and twit and cry "Isn't he the sweetest little thing?" Such coveted treats as chocolate-covered graham crackers often follow. But if we deliberately slam the rotten little puke of a sister's fingers in the door, sanctions follow—angry remonstrance from parents, aunts and uncles; instead of a chocolate-covered graham cracker, a spanking.

But anticivilization emotions don't go away, and they demand periodic exercise. We have such "sick" jokes as, "What's the difference between a truckload of bowling balls and a truckload of dead babies?" (You can't unload a truckload of bowling balls with a pitchfork...a joke, by the way, that I heard originally from a ten-year-old). Such a joke may surprise a laugh or a grin out of us even as we recoil, a possibility that confirms the thesis: If we share a brotherhood of man, then we also share an insanity of man. None of which is intended as a defense of either the sick joke or insanity but merely as an explanation of why the best horror films like the best fairy tales, manage to be reactionary, anarchistic, and revolutionary all at the same time.

The mythic horror movie, like the sick joke, has a dirty job to do. It deliberately appeals to all that is worst in us. It is morbidity unchained, our most base instincts let free, our nastiest fantasies realized...and it all happens, fittingly enough, in the dark. For those reasons, good liberals often shy away from horror films. For myself, I like to see the most aggressive of them—*Dawn of the Dead,* for instance—as lifting a trap door in the civilized forebrain and throwing a basket of raw meat to the hungry alligators swimming around in that subterranean river beneath.

Why bother? Because it keeps them from getting out, man. It keeps them down there and me up here. It was Lennon and McCartney who said that all you need is love, and I would agree with that.

As long as you keep the gators fed.

SUGGESTIONS FOR DISCUSSION

1. Look over the reasons that you have underlined. Do you find some of the reasons King offers to explain why people "crave" horror movies more persuasive than others? Explain why his reasons are or are not persuasive to you. Are there reasons you can think of that King leaves out?

2. King begins his essay with a powerful assertion: "I think that we're all mentally ill." How does this assumption guide the development of the rest of the essay? What other assumptions might you begin with to explain the appeal of horror movies?

3. King suggests that horror movies perform a social function that is "innately conservative." To what extent do horror movies allow readers, in King's words, "to re-establish our feelings of essential normality"? Give specific examples of how particular horror movies do this. Can you make a similar argument about other kinds of movies, such as thrillers, romances, action-adventure, Westerns, and so on?

SUGGESTIONS FOR WRITING

1. Begin with King's suggestion that one of the social functions of the horror movie is first to violate and then to "re-establish our feelings of essential normality." Write an essay on a particular book, movie, or television show that uses this notion of violating and reestablishing social norms to analyze the story it tells and the appeal it has for readers or viewers.

2. Pick another genre of popular fiction, movies, or television shows with which you are familiar (such as soap operas, situation comedies, police shows, science fiction, fantasy, Westerns, and so on). Use King's essay as a model to write your own explanation of why we crave the form of storytelling that you have chosen.

3. Choose a genre of storytelling with which you are not familiar or do not care for. Find someone—a friend, classmate, relative, or acquaintance— who really likes that particular form of storytelling, whether in the novels they read or in the movies and television shows they watch. Write an essay to explain the person's attraction to the genre and also to generalize about the larger popular appeal of the genre.

The Gangster as Tragic Hero

Robert Warshow

Robert Warshow was a film critic and one of the first American intellectuals to write seriously about popular culture. The following essay "The Gangster as Tragic Hero" is taken from his book *The Immediate Experience*, published posthumously in 1962. (Warshow died in 1955.) The essay, though brief, is considered by many to be a classic example of film criticism and cultural analysis. Since the 1950s when Warshow was writing, any number of gangster films have appeared—*Bonnie and Clyde*, the famous *Godfather* trilogy, *Goodfellas*, a remake of *Scarface* (starring Al Pacino this time), a film version of the TV show *The Untouchables*, black gangster films such as *New Jack City*, gangsters in therapy in HBO's new hit *The Sopranos* as well as in the Robert DeNiro and Billy Crystal film *Analyze This*.

SUGGESTION FOR READING

As you read, keep the title of the essay "The Gangster as Tragic Hero" in mind. Underline and annotate passages in the essay where Warshow explains what makes gangsters tragic figures.

America, as a social and political organization, is committed to a cheerful view of life. It could not be otherwise. The sense of tragedy is a luxury of aristocratic societies, where the fate of the individual is not conceived of as having a direct and legitimate political importance, being determined by a fixed and supra-political—that is, non-controversial—moral order or fate. Modern equalitarian societies, however, whether democratic or authoritarian in their political forms, always base themselves on the claim that they are making life happier; the avowed function of the modern state, at least in its ultimate terms, is not only to regulate social relations, but also to determine the quality and the possibilities of human life in general. Happiness thus becomes the chief political issue—in a sense, the only political issue—and for that reason it can never be treated as an issue at all. If an American or a Russian is unhappy, it implies a certain reprobation of his society, and therefore, by a logic of which we can all recognize the necessity, it becomes an obligation of citizenship to be cheerful; if the authorities find it necessary, the citizen may even be compelled to make a public display of his cheerfulness on important occasions, just as he may be conscripted into the army in time of war.

Naturally, this civic responsibility rests more strongly upon the organs of mass culture. The individual citizen may still be permitted his private unhappiness so long as it does not take on political significance, the extent of this tolerance being determined by how large an area of private life the society can accommodate. But every production of mass culture is a public act and must conform with accepted notions of the public good. Nobody seriously questions the principle that it is the function of mass culture to maintain public morale, and certainly nobody in the mass audience objects to having his morale maintained.[1] At a time when the normal condition of the citizen is a state of anxiety, euphoria spreads over our culture like the broad smile of an idiot. In terms of attitudes towards life, there is very little difference between a "happy" movie like *Good News*, which ignores death and suffering, and a "sad" movie like *A Tree Grows in Brooklyn*, which uses death and suffering as incidents in the service of a higher optimism.

But, whatever its effectiveness as a source of consolation and a means of pressure for maintaining "positive" social attitudes, this optimism is fundamentally satisfying to no one, not even to those who would be most disoriented without its support. Even within the area of mass culture, there always exists a current of opposition, seeking to express by whatever means are available to it that sense of desperation and inevitable failure which optimism itself helps to create. Most often, this opposition is confined to rudimentary or semiliterate forms: in mob politics and journalism, for example, or in certain kinds of religious enthusiasm. When it does enter the field of art, it is likely to be disguised or attenuated: in an unspecific form of expression like jazz, in the basically harmless nihilism of the Marx Brothers, in the continually reasserted strain of hopelessness that often seems to be the real meaning of the soap opera. The gangster film is remarkable in that it fills the need for disguise (though not sufficiently to avoid arousing uneasiness) without requiring any serious distortion. From its beginnings, it has been a consistent and astonishingly complete presentation of the modern sense of tragedy.[2]

In its initial character, the gangster film is simply one example of the movies' constant tendency to create fixed dramatic patterns that can be repeated indefinitely with a reasonable expectation of profit. One gangster film follows another as one musical or one Western follows another. But this rigidity is not necessarily opposed to the requirements of art. There have been very successful types of art in the past which developed such specific and detailed conventions as almost to make individual examples of the type interchangeable. This is true, for example, of Elizabethan revenge tragedy and Restoration comedy.

For such a type to be successful means that its conventions have imposed themselves upon the general consciousness and become the accepted vehicles of a particular set of attitudes and a particular aesthetic effect. One goes to any individual example of the type with very definite expectations, and originality is to be welcomed only in the degree that it intensifies the expected experience without fundamentally altering it. Moreover, the relationship between the conventions which go to make up such a type and the real experience of its audience or the real facts of whatever situation it pretends to describe is of only secondary importance and does not determine its aesthetic force. It is only in an ultimate sense that the type appeals to its audience's experience of reality; much more immediately, it appeals to previous experience of the type itself: it creates its own field of reference.

Thus the importance of the gangster film, and the nature and intensity of its emotional and aesthetic impact, cannot be measured in terms of the place of the gangster himself or the importance of the problem of crime in American life. Those European movie-goers who think there is a gangster on every corner in New York are certainly deceived, but defenders of the "positive" side of American culture are equally deceived if they think it relevant to point out that most Americans have never seen a gangster. What matters is that the experience of the gangster *as an experience of art* is universal to Americans. There is almost nothing we understand better or react to more readily or with quicker intelligence. The Western film, though it seems never to diminish in popularity, is for most of us no more than the folklore of the past, familiar and understandable only because it has been repeated so often. The gangster film comes much closer. In ways that we do not easily or willingly define, the gangster speaks for us, expressing that part of the American psyche which rejects the qualities and the demands of modern life, which rejects "Americanism" itself.

The gangster is the man of the city, with the city's language and knowledge, with its queer and dishonest skills and its terrible daring, carrying his life in his hands like a placard, like a club. For everyone else, there is at least the theoretical possibility of another world—in that happier American culture which the gangster denies, the city does not really exist; it is only a more crowded and more brightly lit country—but for the gangster there is only the city; he must inhabit it in order to personify it: not the real city, but that dangerous and sad city of the imagination which is so much more important, which is the modern world. And the gangster—though there are real gangsters—is also, and primarily, a creature of the imagination.

The real city, one might say, produces only criminals; the imaginary city produces the gangster: he is what we want to be and what we are afraid we may become.

Thrown into the crowd without background or advantages, with only those ambiguous skills which the rest of us—the real people of the real city—can only pretend to have, the gangster is required to make his way, to make his life and impose it on others. Usually, when we come upon him, he has already made his choice or the choice has already been made for him, it doesn't matter which: we are not permitted to ask whether at some point he could have chosen to be something else than what he is.

The gangster's activity is actually a form of rational enterprise, involving fairly definite goals and various techniques for achieving them. But this rationality is usually no more than a vague background; we know, perhaps, that the gangster sells liquor or that he operates a numbers racket; often we are not given even that much information. So his activity becomes a kind of pure criminality: he hurts people. Certainly our response to the gangster film is most consistently and most universally a response to sadism; we gain the double satisfaction of participating vicariously in the gangster's sadism and then seeing it turned against the gangster himself.

But on another level the quality of irrational brutality and the quality of rational enterprise become one. Since we do not see the rational and routine aspects of the gangster's behavior, the practice of brutality—the quality of unmixed criminality—becomes the totality of his career. At the same time, we are always conscious that the whole meaning of this career is a drive for success: the typical gangster film presents a steady upward progress followed by a very precipitate fall. Thus brutality itself becomes at once the means to success and the content of success—a success that is defined in its most general terms, not as accomplishment or specific gain, but simply as the unlimited possibility of aggression. (In the same way, film presentations of businessmen tend to make it appear that they achieve their success by talking on the telephone and holding conferences and that success *is* talking on the telephone and holding conferences.)

From this point of view, the initial contact between the film and its audience is an agreed conception of human life: that man is a being with the possibilities of success or failure. This principal, too, belongs to the city; one must emerge from the crowd or else one is nothing. On that basis, the necessity of the action is established, and it progresses by inalterable paths to the point where the gangster lies dead and the principal has been modified: there is really only one possibility—failure. The final meaning of the city is anonymity and death.

In the opening scene of *Scarface*, we are shown a successful man; we know he is successful because he has just given a party of opulent proportions and because he is called Big Louie. Through some monstrous lack of caution, he permits himself to be alone for a few moments. We understand from this immediately that he is about to be killed. No convention of the gangster film is more strongly established than this: it is dangerous to be alone. And yet the very conditions of success make it impossible not to be alone, for success is always the establishment of an *individual* preeminence that must be imposed on others, in whom it automatically arouses hatred; the successful man is an outlaw. The gangster's whole life is an effort to assert himself as an individual, to draw himself out of the crowd, and he always dies *because* he is an individual; the final bullet thrusts him back, makes him, after all, a failure. "Mother of God," says the dying Little Caesar, "Is this the end of Rico?"—speaking of himself thus in the third person because what has been brought low is not the undifferentiated *man,* but the individual with a name, the gangster, the success; even to himself he is a creature of the imagination. (T. S. Eliot has pointed out that a number of Shakespeare's tragic heroes have this trick of looking at themselves dramatically; their true identify, the thing that is destroyed when they die, is something outside themselves—not a man, but a style of life, a kind of meaning.)

At bottom, the gangster is doomed because he is under the obligation to succeed, not because the means he employs are unlawful. In the deeper layers of the modern consciousness, *all* means are unlawful, every attempt to succeed is an act of aggression, leaving one alone and guilty and defenseless among enemies: one is *punished* for success. This is our intolerable dilemma: that failure is a kind of death and success is evil and dangerous, is—ultimately—impossible. The effect of the gangster film is to embody this dilemma in the person of the gangster and resolve it by his death. The dilemma is resolved because it is *his* death, not ours. We are safe; for the moment, we can acquiesce in our failure, we can choose to fail.

Notes

1. In her testimony before the House Committee on Un-American Activities, Ms. Leila Rogers said that the movie *None But the Lonely Heart* was un-American because it was gloomy. Like so much else that was said during the unhappy investigation of Hollywood, this statement was at once stupid and illuminating. One knew immediately what Mrs. Rogers was talking about; she had simply been insensitive enough to carry her philistinism to its conclusion.

2. Efforts have been made from time to time to bring the gangster film into line with the prevailing optimism and social constructiveness of our culture; *Kiss of Death* is a recent example. These efforts are usually unsuccessful; the reasons for their lack of success are interesting in themselves, but I shall not be able to discuss them here.

SUGGESTIONS FOR DISCUSSION

1. Warshow says that the gangster film is "a consistent and astonishingly complete presentation of the modern sense of tragedy." What does Warshow mean by tragedy here? In what sense are gangster films tragic? Pick a gangster film or two that you are familiar with and see if they fit Warshow's definition of tragedy. Does Warshow's definition hold? What update, if any, might it use?

2. Warshow says that for the gangster "the whole meaning of [his] career is a drive for success." What does he mean by this statement? What does "success" mean in this context? What do gangster films have to tell us about the American dream of success?

3. Warshow begins the essay by saying that "it is the function of mass culture to maintain public morale" and to "conform with accepted notions of public good." Think about some of the movies you have seen recently. To what extent does Warshow's statement seem valid? Consider the benefits and limits of America's commitment to what Warshow calls "a cheerful view of life."

SUGGESTIONS FOR WRITING

1. According to Warshow, gangsters are more attractive figures than the "good guys." Why is this so? Write an essay that explains why the gangster—or any other hero who lives outside the law—is such a popular figure in the American imagination.

2. Use Warshow's definition of tragedy to analyze a film or TV show featuring the gangster as a tragic hero.

3. Think of other films besides gangster movies that have a tragic ending for the main character or characters (such as *Titanic*, *Thelma and Louise*, *American Beauty*, *Ice Storm*, *American History X*, and *Snow Falling on Cedars*). Pick one whose tragic end represents something interesting and important about the limits of American culture. Write an essay that explains the tragedy in the film. What was the main character or characters striving to do? Why was their tragic end inevitable? What does this tragic end tell us about American culture?

PERSPECTIVES: ALLY MCBEAL

Ally McBeal first appeared on the Fox network in the 1997–98 television year and quickly became the source of much discussion about how the show represented young career women and whether these representations amounted to a betrayal of feminist ideals. The cover of *Time* magazine, for example, featured a picture of Calista Flockhart (the actress who plays Ally McBeal), along with Susan B. Anthony, Betty Friedan, and Gloria Steinem, to ask the question "Is Feminism Dead?" And since then, feminists, media critics, and cultural commentators have all weighed in with their views of *Ally McBeal* and what it signifies for the future of the women's movement for equal rights.

Ally McBeal is what Ellen Taylor (in "TV Families: Three Generations of Packaged Dreams," included later in this chapter) calls a "workplace" show—typical of current series such as *ER*, *Chicago Hope*, *LA Law*, and others where women are pictured doing professional work and pursuing careers. As Taylor notes, such series began in the 1970s and 1980s as a generation of career-oriented women entered the workplace. In a sense, these shows registered the cultural shift in women's lives from the domestic setting of the family to relationships at work.

Accordingly, TV series such as *Ally McBeal* have been analyzed in terms of what they can tell us about the pressures and conflicts facing career women and the way gender identities play themselves out in the workplace. As you will see, the two following readers take quite different perspectives on *Ally McBeal*.

Razor Thin, But Larger Than Life

Karen Durbin

Karen Durbin is the film critic for *Mirabella* magazine. The following essay appeared in the Arts and Leisure section of the Sunday *New York Times* in December 1998, halfway through the second season of *Ally McBeal*. Durbin identifies herself unapologetically as a "confirmed *Ally McBeal* fan," though she admits her "passion" for the show and its main character "is not boundless."

SUGGESTION FOR READING

Notice how Karen Durbin sets up her essay. First, she identifies four reasons Ally is seen by some as the antithesis of true feminism. Then, she presents reasons that seem to be intended to meet such objections. As you read, note how she responds to charges that *Ally McBeal* is part of an anti-feminist backlash.

The CBS sitcom *Everybody Loves Raymond* now regularly beats Fox's *Ally McBeal* in the Monday night Nielsens. Recently, an executive producer of *Raymond*, Philip Rosenthal, expressed his delight to *Entertainment Weekly* with a notable shortage of grace, semantic and otherwise. Asked how he accounted for the superior ratings, Mr. Rosenthal said, "Everyone on our show has no problem eating." Sore winners are bad enough; boorish ones should guffaw to themselves in private.

Mr. Rosenthal wasn't even being original; he's just the latest to jump on the Ally-bashing bandwagon, a vehicle that rolls with some regularity over the slender bones of the show's lawyer heroine and Calista Flockhart, the gifted young stage actress who plays her. The hysteria over Ms. Flockhart's putative anorexia reached such a pitch of meanness a couple of months ago that the actress took to eating large meals in public as self-defense.

Ms. Flockhart is hardly the only young woman on television these days who looks like a line drawing. In the print ads for HBO's *Sex and the City*, Sarah Jessica Parker's hips are no wider than the laptop she's typing on. According to my laptop, that's 11.5 inches, and she's sitting down. But nobody's rushing to stitch an "A" for anorexia on the skimpy little dresses Ms. Parker wears in the show. Nor, for that matter, has she been attacked for wearing them. *Sex and the City*, like the autobiographical sketches by Candace Bushnell that the show is based on, is a not-quite-tongue-in-cheek portrait of the educated young urban woman as a man-hungry gold digger. Nevertheless, when the editors of *Time* magazine felt moved last summer to ask the question "Is Feminism Dead?" they didn't make Ms. Parker or Ms. Bushnell the punch line of what must surely be the silliest cover of the year. Instead, their hilarious array of disembodied female heads floating in a funereal black sea proceeded from Susan B. Anthony through Betty Friedan and Gloria Steinem to—who else?—Ally McBeal.

The death of feminism tends to be greatly exaggerated, but journalists have been writing its obituary since 1975, when *Harper's* magazine did its own cover article. "Requiem for the Women's Movement," just in time to ride the antifeminist backlash while criticizing the movement for not being radical enough. *Time* does something similar, only the movement's problem now is that it's not serious enough. Ally is the antithesis of true feminism because (1) she gets upset when the supermarket doesn't have enough of her favorite snack, (2) her skirts are too short, and (3) she's a ditz who (4) thinks too much about her lousy love life.

I'm a confirmed *Ally McBeal* fan who first took to the streets with knees knocking and feminist fist upraised not quite 30 years ago, when my dress size was considerably smaller than it is now, and what dresses I owned seldom extended more than 12 inches down from the waist. I've never thought that her skirt length or eating habits were a threat to my political health. On the contrary, I identify. As for points (3) and (4), I come from a family of opinionated motormouths, but when I feel rattled or shy, heredity deserts me and my brain shifts into park. So when Ally gets that slightly wild deer-in-the-headlights look in her eye (it generally has to do with sex) and blurts something embarrassing, I identify with that too. It's a comfort to know that there's another woman out there, even an imaginary one, for whom the dance of desire begins with a foot in the mouth.

None of that would matter if Ally were just an airhead, but she isn't. She wins her cases with ingenious, sometimes inspired arguments that have less to do with the law than with an attempt to discern some rules to live by in the blur of a rapidly changing world.

At its uneven best, *Ally McBeal* is neither yuppie sitcom nor courtroom drama but an absurdist morality play that gives off sparks of screwball comedy. Its heroine is basically smart and thoughtful, with a prissy streak that's the downside of her penchant for worrying about what is right. If she's also confused and conflicted, that's because she exists in a state of uncomfortable dissent from the world around her. With her somewhat nutty integrity, Ally McBeal has always struck me as the weird little sister of Mary Richards, although she's not nearly so nice. Alone among her newsroom colleagues on *The Mary Tyler Moore Show,* Mary submissively called her boss Mr. Grant. When a judge tells Ally he will bar her from his courtroom unless she wears longer skirts, she calls him a pig. This is David E. Kelley, the show's creator, talking back to his critics, but it works within the terms of the character. It's not one of Ally's better moves, but to her own self she's certainly being true (not that she seems to have a choice).

And like most eccentrics, she harbors a fugitive longing to be normal. How else to explain her attachment to her terminally bland ex-boyfriend? Handsome Billy and his pretty wife, Georgia, are the show's only true yupsters, a totally conventional couple who resent and make a perfect foil for Ally's stubborn singularity. They gripe at her for making waves, for getting out of line, for being larger than life, for, in other words, not knowing her place. She's that quintessential feminist emblem, the inconvenient woman.

The *Time* magazine article lumped *Ally McBeal* together with *Bridget Jones's Diary.* But the heroine of Helen Fielding's comic British novel is consumed with the search for Mr. Right, while Ally spends much of her time turning eligible men away. (A little too much time, it seems to me; will she ever get to have sex again or was that cute nude model it?) *Bridget Jones* reads like something from a 50's time capsule. Candace Bushnell's money-grubbing hard-bodies are more believable (so that's how Donald Trump keeps getting dates), but they don't represent much besides themselves.

What rings both timely and true is Ally's mix of doubt, assertiveness and self-mocking humor, the last best expressed in her dissing contests with her roommate, Renee. If Ally is kin to Mary Richards, then Renee descends from Murphy Brown. Pugnacious and competitive, Renee copes with her vulnerability by putting on a tough front. Ally does it by putting on no front at all. Maybe that's why she creates such a disturbance both on and off the show. Her short skirts are a metaphor; she's all but walking naked through the world.

My passion for *Ally McBeal* is not boundless. Most of the new episodes lack the emotional heft that gives the show its real payoff. Without that, the absurdism seems unfocused (the whole subplot involving a colleague's pet frog) or worse, unfunny. I've always thought the pristine unisex bathroom was one of the show's more resonant absurdities, another metaphor for that rude and ridiculous place where men and women eventually meet and things happen that nobody can control. But the missing frog pops out of the toilet where Ally is sitting so that she can go eek? Somebody leaves the toilet seat up so that she can fall in? If this is what Ally gets instead of a lover or even a fling, maybe Mr. Kelley should take his subconscious in for a tuneup, before he becomes the worst Ally-basher of all.

What's the Deal, McBeal?

Andi Zeisler

> Andi Zeisler is a feminist media critic who edits the magazine *Bitch: Feminist Response to Pop Culture.* Her essay on *Ally McBeal* appeared in *Ms.* in the August/September 1999 issue, just before the third season of the show was about to begin. As you will see, Zeisler believes that after a promising first season, "something changed" and "women were hit hardest by these changes."

SUGGESTION FOR READING

Notice how Zeisler first explains why in her view *Ally McBeal* "worked" in its first season but then changed in a way she finds distressing. As you read, pay attention to Zeisler's analysis of these changes and what they signify for her initial hope that the show would take women's issues seriously.

Early in *Ally McBeal's* second season, our Chihuahua-like hero mused, "I once had a dream they put my face on the cover of *Time* magazine as the face of feminism." The line was a sly nudge to anyone who saw Ally on that now-famous cover alongside Betty Friedan, Gloria Steinem, an Susan B. Anthony. More importantly, though, it acknowledged the magazine's mistake in positing Ally as feminism's Angel of Death. This is, after all, a TV character who made clear where she stands on the issues when she said, "I plan to change [society]. But I'd just like to get married first." The subtext of Ally's *Time* comment was this: "You *know* me. For an entire season you've witnessed my stammering and dancing-baby hallucinations and deer-in-the-headlights pathos, so why, *why* are you asking for more?"

Why indeed? Women are far better served by any one of a handful of strong female characters represented in the prime-time hours, but millions of us, myself included, can't stop watching *Ally*. When it debuted in 1997, the show aimed to speak to young female professionals through a character whose spunky sensitivity reflected their own. That this character was a human matchstick whose peevishness and pratfalls were more Chevy Chase than Mary Richards wasn't supposed to matter; in fact, it was supposed to make us like her more, to make us embrace our own peevishness, our own pratfalls.

And it worked. Unlike TV's impenetrable Dana Scully types, Ally's appeal was that she wasn't completely formed and her contradictions were always front and center. She could be ferociously smart in court, then turn around and seem unable to string two words together when faced with her ex-boyfriend/coworker, Billy. While some of her workday concerns were as insubstantial as her skirts, others—the desire to be taken seriously, to make her voice heard, to get over a broken heart with some dignity—resonated deeply.

Still, a slice of professional life *Ally* wasn't. The characters spent work hours mulling over their love lives in the co-ed bathroom. And despite office tension and early court times, everyone's day always ended with a Kodak moment in the bar downstairs.

While the show's attempts at legal drama didn't fool anyone who had a passing familiarity with the law (or even a passing familiarity with *Law & Order*), its first season consistently offered up fresh, well-written, and compelling takes on issues like job discrimination, sexual harassment, and self-defense. At the same time, its refusal to kowtow to party-line, politically correct tropes, manifested in characters like Ally's smarmy boss, Richard Fish (who argued in one episode that women should qualify under the federal disabilities act: "They are less able....They cannot contend with having to do a job and have a man smile at them"), fomented passionate dialogues on the uses of gender, sex, and power. *Ally* could have its cake and demean it, too, and this made for some interesting television.

But when the show moved into its second season, sporting an armful of Golden Globe awards and 1998 Emmy nominations, something changed. Maybe it was due to the fact that Ally was so quickly made a feminist scapegoat, but the sophomore year seemed hell-bent on shrugging off any of the real-world comedy the first season offered, and serving up self-conscious legal slapstick in its place. And since *Ally* is basically a women's show, with female-centric plotlines, women were hit hardest by these changes.

In the first season, Ally and her colleagues—supposedly happily married Georgia, outspoken Renee, self-described slut Elaine—represented the loosening of the superwoman myth that allegedly puts women's happiness (read: chances for marriage) in jeopardy. They embodied a giddy, You-Go-Girl! Brand of feminism, in which equal-opportunity ogling counts as progress—when the men in the firm drooled over the delivery girl in one episode, the women retaliated a few episodes later by taking a life-drawing class and panting over the well-endowed male model.

The second season added two female characters: controlled, remote Nelle and furious, lawsuit-happy Ling. Instead of a broadened representation of women, we got stereotypes on parade: Ally, the unhinged neurotic, and Georgia, the clingy, jealous wife, were joined by Ling, a man-eating Dragon Lady, and Nelle, whose composure and—imagine!—refusal to fling her personal life around the office had earned her the nickname Subzero.

It's not that the female lawyers were portrayed as less intelligent than the men in the firm. The plotlines simply used every opportunity to take potshots at women, feminism, and the basic human capabilities of the female characters. Admittedly, this is no new trend in television. But since this limited version of professional womanhood is written and produced by David E. Kelly—a man who has written excellent, complex female characters for *Picket Fences, Chicago Hope,* and *The Practice*—*Ally* is worth examining as it enters its third season, even if common sense dictates that we just sigh and change the channel.

By now it's clear that the show has abandoned all hope of being taken seriously. The ongoing quirks, initially entertaining, have become an onslaught of self-congratulatory wackiness. And the once-compelling sex and power issues tackled in the courtroom have devolved into little more than mean-spirited attacks on women's issues.

The catalyst for much of the latter has been Ling, whose unpleasantness (like Ally's insecurity) was played for huge laughs. She sued the nurse of the doctor who performed her sister's breast implant surgery for false advertising; she sued a radio shock-jock for creating a hostile environment; she sued one of her employees for having sexual thoughts about her. Ling's rampant litigiousness framed harassment suits as the ridiculous, malicious revenge of a woman who hates men. But the show neatly dodged taking responsibility for this message. The surreal humor in which the cases were dressed was *Ally's* own defense—that highly sophisticated one known as "Can't you take a joke?"

Ally resisted all attempts to read feminist issues into its over-the-top content, yet constantly introduced characters and plot points that invited that reading. The result has been a disingenuous tease of a show, both intoxicated with its own cleverness and fearful that someone might actually take it seriously. (Kelley's public relations agency turned me down when I asked to interview him about the show's evolution.)

Sadly, the new approach seems to be working—last season *Ally's* audience increased by 21 percent among women ages 18–49, according to the Fox network, which airs the show. The most-watched episode ever was the Ally-Billy forbidden kiss—a record 17 million viewers (the average is 13.7 million per episode) tuned in last February to catch them whining at each other. For all the provocative courtroom action and baiting dialogue, the search for love is ultimately what *Ally* is about. Maybe surrounding this central theme with slapstick and stereotypes is a way to draw attention away from the courtroom and onto the kissing. Maybe. But more likely the show wants to remind viewers that it's as featherweight as its lead character—and that we've got no business making either of them into an icon of wasted potential.

SUGGESTIONS FOR DISCUSSION

1. Both Karen Durbin and Andi Zeisler identify themselves as feminist media critics. Nonetheless, their evaluations of *Ally McBeal* differ in important respects. In each of the essays, identify the central claim each writer

makes about the show. What do the criteria of judgment seem to be in each case? Though they differ, is there some sense in which each writer is using feminist principles in her response to *Ally McBeal*? How, then, would you account for their differences?

2. Imagine you are overhearing a conversation between Durbin and Zeisler concerning *Ally McBeal*. What do you think each would say to the other? You might turn this into a role-playing exercise in which you (or a group of students in your class) assume the role of Durbin and another student (or group of students) assumes Zeisler's role. Stage a dialogue between the two writers. Try to stay in character and keep to the views and assumptions of each. How would they respond to each other? Given their differences in evaluation, is there any common ground on which they might meet?

3. Durbin characterizes *Ally McBeal* as "neither yuppie sitcom nor courtroom drama but an absurdist morality play." Zeisler, on the other hand, calls it a "disingenuous tease of a show, both intoxicated with its own cleverness and fearful that someone might take it seriously." How adequate are these descriptions? How would you describe *Ally McBeal*? What descriptive labels can you invent to describe the show?

SUGGESTIONS FOR WRITING

1. Write an essay that considers the claims Durbin and Zeisler make about how *Ally McBeal* represents professional women. First, identify how each writer describes the show's representation of Ally and her female coworkers. Then, evaluate these descriptions. Do they seem to capture what you think the show is about and how it represents professional women? Explain your views and propose your own description of how the show represents professional women.

2. The June 29, 1998 issue of *Time* magazine featured on its cover the question "Is Feminism Dead?" Read Gina Bellafante's article "Feminism: It's All About Me" and Katha Pollitt's response "Dead Again?" in the *Nation* on July 13, 1998. Write an essay that explains how the show *Ally McBeal* fits into the debate about the future of feminism.

3. Write your own review of *Ally McBeal*. Set up your review by explaining the current debate about the show. Locate your own view of the show in relation to what others have said about it.

In Praise of Roseanne

Elayne Rapping

Elayne Rapping writes a regular column on television and popular culture for the *Progressive*, where "In Praise of Roseanne" appeared in 1994. Her most recent book is *Media-tions: Forays into the Culture and Gender Wars*. As you will see, Rapping's article focuses on one particular TV show, *Roseanne*, rather than tracing the history of the family sitcom genre. Rapping, as the article's title indicates, is unabashedly enthusiastic about Roseanne—as are her female and working-class students. Identifying herself as a fan (as well as a media critic), Rapping brings a perspective to the study of family sitcoms that differs considerably from Ella Taylor's in the subsequent essay "TV Families: Three Generations of Packaged Dreams."

SUGGESTION FOR READING

Rapping announces early on that she is a "big fan of Roseanne" and notes that there has been little serious analysis of the program *Roseanne* by academics and journalists. As you read, notice how Rapping explains the neglect of *Roseanne* and the reasons she offers to explain what attracts her to the program.

The other night, while flipping among the three nightly network news broadcasts, I stopped—as I often do—to check out the *Roseanne* rerun Fox cleverly schedules during that time slot in New York. And, as often happens, I found myself sticking around longer than I intended, watching the Conners wiggle their way through whatever crisis had hit their Kmart window fan that day.

On the three more respectable networks, the Dow Jones averages rise and fall; Congress and the courts hand down weighty decisions in lofty prose; the official weapons of state are deployed, around the globe and in the inner cities, to preserve democracy and the American way. But in the Conner residence, where most things are either in disrepair or not yet paid for, it is possible to glimpse—as it rarely is on the newscasts themselves—how the fallout from such headlines might actually affect those who are relatively low in the pecking order.

On CBS, NBC, ABC, and CNN, the problems of the women who make headlines are not likely to sound familiar to most of us. Zoë Baird may be struggling with the servant issue. Hillary may have misplaced her capital-gains records. The Queen of England may be embroiled in royal-family dysfunction. But Roseanne, matriarch of the shabby Conner household, will be coping with less glamorous trauma—unemployment, foreclosure, job stress, marital power struggles, unruly and unmotivated kids—in a less dignified but more realistic style.

I am a big fan of Roseanne—Barr, Arnold, Conner, whatever. So are my female and working-class students, who invariably claim her as their own and hang on to her for dear life as they climb the ladder of class and professional achievement—an effort in which their parents have so hopefully invested everything they own. But it recently occurred to me that I have never—in the many years I've regularly analyzed and commented on American popular culture—written a single word about her. Nor have I read many, outside the trashy tabloids, where her personal life and public persona are regularly recorded and described.

In the last year, I've read dozens of academic and popular articles, and two whole books, about *The Cosby Show*. Archie Bunker and *All in the Family* have been praised and analyzed endlessly. Even *Murphy Brown* and *The Mary Tyler Moore Show* are taken seriously in ever-broadening academic and journalistic circles. Not to mention the well-structured, post-structural Madonna, long the darling of feminist critics and academics.

What is it about these other media icons that makes them somehow more "respectable" subjects of intellectual analysis, more suitable to "serious" discourse? What is it about Roseanne that makes her so easy to ignore or write off, despite her (to me) obvious talent, originality, political *chutzpah,* and power? Gender and appearance are surely part of it; but I suspect that class—position as well as attitude—is the major factor. Bill Cosby's Cliff Huxtable, Mary Tyler Moore's Mary Richards, Candice Bergen's Murphy Brown are all well-turned out, well-educated liberal professionals. And the grungy, working-class Archie Bunker, far from scoring points for his class, is always beaten down by the liberal, professional mentality of everyone else on the show. As for Madonna, while she is certainly not respectable, she makes up for it by being blond, chic, and gorgeous, which, in our culture, covers a multitude of social sins.

But Roseanne is a different story, far more unassimilable into mainstream-media iconography than any of these others. Fat, sloppy, foul-mouthed, and bossy, she is just a bit too unrepentantly, combatively proud of her gender and class position and style to be easily molded into the "movin' on up" mode of American mass media. She isn't "movin' up" to anywhere. She is standing pat, week after week on her show—and a lot of the rest of the time in a lot of other places—speaking out for the dignity and the rights of those the media have set out to shame into invisibility or seduce into endless, self-hating efforts at personal transformation. With her bad hair and baggy pants and oversized shirts from the lower level of the mall, with her burned meat loaf and tuna casseroles and Malomars, with her rough language and politically incorrect child-rearing methods, with her dead-end minimum-wage jobs, Roseanne has gone further than Madonna or almost anyone else I can think of at turning the hegemonic norms of the corporate media on their heads. But few of the intellectual writing classes have seen fit to credit, much less celebrate, her for it. So I will.

To appreciate Roseanne's unlikely ascent into prime-time stardom, it's useful to place her within the generic traditions of the family sitcom. Roseanne is not a descendant of the pristine line of virginal wife/mothers who have set the norms for such characters from the days of June Cleaver to the present. No sweetly submissive smiles or politely helpful suggestions to hubby and kids for her. She is one of a rarer breed, the one invented and defined by Lucille Ball in *I Love Lucy,* in which the female protagonist is more Helpmeet from Hell than from Heaven.

The parallels between these two women are interesting, and reveal a lot about what has and hasn't changed for the women—white, working-class, and poor—who make up the female majority in this country (although you'd never know it from watching TV). Both were, and are, popular and powerful beyond the dreams of almost any woman performer of their times. And yet both eschewed the traditional feminine, white, middle-class persona dictated by the norms of their days, preferring to present themselves as wild women, out of bounds, loud, funny, and noisy—all attributes which sexist culture beats out of most of us very early on. In a world in which females are enjoined not to take up too much space, not to make "spectacles" of ourselves, not to "disturb" but to contain "the peace," women like Roseanne and Lucy have always been frightening, repulsive, even indecent. That's why they so appall us even as, consciously or subconsciously, we are drawn to them.

I used to cringe when I watched *I Love Lucy* as a child. She filled me with embarrassment because she was so stereotypically "hysterical," so much a failure in her endless efforts to move out of the confines of traditional femininity and its many indignities (indignities otherwise kept hidden by the Stepford-like types of Donna Reed and June Cleaver).

I was far more comfortable, as a middle-class girl, with the persona created by Mary Tyler Moore—first as the frustrated dancer/wife in *The Dick Van Dyke Show* and later as the first real career woman in her own show. Unlike Lucy, Mary Richards was perfectly groomed and mannered. She was sweetly deferential in her apologetic efforts at assertiveness; embarrassingly grateful for every nod of respect or responsibility from her boss, "Mr. Grant." Ambitious, yes, but never forgetful of the "ladylike" way of moving up the corporate ladder, one dainty, unthreatening step at a time. Where Lucy embarrassed, Mary was soothing. No pratfalls or dumb disguises for her.

But through Roseanne, I've come to see the very improper Lucy differently. For her time, after all, she was a real fighter against those feminine constraints. She tried to *do* things and she tried to do them with other women, against the resistance of every man on the show. She was not well groomed, did not live in tasteful elegance, did not support and help her husband at business and social affairs—far from it. She was full of energy and rebelliousness and, yes, independence—to a point.

But of course she always failed, and lost, and made a fool of herself. Her show was pure slapstick fantasy, because, back then, the things she was trying to achieve were so far from imaginable that someone like her could only exist in a farcical mode. But, as Roseanne's very different way of playing this kind of woman shows, that is no longer true.

Like Lucy, Roseanne is loud, aggressive, messy, and ambitiously bossy. Roseanne, too, has close relationships with other women. And Roseanne, too, is larger than life, excessive, to many frightening and repulsive. But her show is no fantasy. It is the most realistic picture of gender, class, and family relations on television today. And that's because Roseanne herself is so consciously political, so gender- and class-conscious, in every detail of her show.

No more the harried husband rolling his eyes at his wife's antics. Where other sitcoms either ignore feminism and reproduce traditional relations or, perhaps worse, present perfectly harmonious couples—like the Huxtables—for whom gender equity comes as naturally as their good looks. Roseanne and Dan duke it out over gender and power issues as equals who seem really to love, respect, and—not least—get angry at each other.

Nor does Roseanne need to think up crazy schemes for achieving the impossible—a project outside the home. Roseanne, like most of us, needs to work. The jobs she is forced to take—sweeping in a hair salon, waiting tables in malls and diners, working on an assembly line—are very like the ones Lucy nabbed and then messed up, to the wild laughter of the audience. But for Roseanne the humor is different. Roseanne fights with sexist, overbearing bosses, lashes out at her kids because she's stressed out at work, moonlights to get them through the rough days when Dan is out of work. And if these things are funny to watch, they are also deeply revealing of social and emotional truths in the lives of women and working-class families today.

The most touching and impressive thing about this series—and the main reason for its popularity—is its subtle presentation of progressive "messages" in a way that is neither preachy nor condescending to audiences. Much was made of the famous episode in which Roseanne was kissed by a lesbian character. (And it is surely a tribute to Roseanne's integrity and clout that this first lesbian kiss got past Standards and Practices because of her.) But the kiss itself was really no big deal. Lots of shows will be doing this kind of one minute/one scene "Wow, did you see that?" thing soon enough.

Sitcoms are, indeed, informed by liberal values, and they do, indeed, tend to preach to us about tolerance and personal freedom. Lesbianism, as an idea, an abstraction, a new entry on the now very long list of liberal tolerances to which the professional middle classes must pay lip service, was bound to hit prime time soon anyway. What made the Roseanne "lesbian episode" remarkable and radically different from the usual liberal sitcom style of tackling such issues was not the kiss itself but the startlingly honest discussions about homosexuality that followed the kiss, between Dan and his young son D.J.; and then between Dan and Roseanne, in bed.

This segment was politically audacious because it did not lecture the vast majority of Americans who are, yes, queasy about homosexuality. It presented them with a mirror image of their own confusion and anxiety, and led them to a position of relative comfort about it all, by sympathizing with their very real concern about radical social and sexual change.

This is how the show attacks all its difficult issues, sensational and mundane. Much has been made of Roseanne's way of yelling at her kids, even hitting them on at least one occasion. Clearly, this is not how parents, since Dr. Spock, have been told to behave, and for obvious and good reason. Nonetheless, we all do these things on occasion. (And those who don't, ever, probably have other serious parenting problems.) To pretend that parents don't do that—as most sitcoms do—is to condescend to viewers who know that this goes on everywhere, and who have, themselves, done it or at least fought the urge.

On *Roseanne,* such behavior is neither denied nor condemned; it is talked about and analyzed. After hitting her son, for example, Roseanne apologizes and confesses, heartbreakingly, that she was herself beaten as a child and that it was wrong then and wrong now. It is this kind of honesty about negative feelings—especially when they are placed in the kind of social and economic context this show never slights—that makes the positive feelings of love and mutual respect within this battered, battling family so very believable.

Which brings me, unavoidably, to the issue of Roseanne Arnold herself, as a public persona—surely the major factor in the public unease about her. There are two "Roseannes"—both media images constructed cleverly and carefully by Arnold herself. "Roseanne Conner" is, as Arnold herself says, "much nicer." She is the sitcom version of how someone overcomes personal and economic difficulty and not only survives but thrives. She comes from a long line of show-business satirists whose humor was based on social and political truth. Like the Marx Brothers and Charlie Chaplin, she is the lovable outsider sneaking into the polite world to expose its hypocrisy and phoniness.

That is the fictional "Roseanne" of sitcom fame. The other persona, "Roseanne Barr Arnold"—the woman who appears in tabloids, talk shows, news shows, and comedy clubs—is far more outrageous, more dangerous. She is the ultimate bad girl, the woman who shouts out to the entire world every angry, nasty, shameful truth and emotion she feels about the lives of women, especially poor women, in America today.

Much of what Roseanne confesses to—about incest, wife abuse, mental illness, obesity, prostitution, lesbianism—makes people uncomfortable. It's tacky, embarrassing, improper, déclassé to discuss these issues in public. But so was much of what we Second Wave feminists and student activists and antiwar protesters and others insisted upon talking about and confessing to and doing in the 1960s. So is what Anita Hill insisted—in much classier style but to no less shock and outrage—on throwing at us from the Senate hearing rooms. So is almost every political statement and action that rocks the reactionary boats of institutionalized power and authority.

And like those other actions and statements, Roseanne's antics are inherently political, radical, salutary. For in speaking out about her hidden demons and ghosts and scars—as a woman, a working-class person, a victim of family and institutional abuse—she speaks *for* the myriad damaged and disempowered souls, mostly still silent and invisible, who also bear the scars of such class, gender, and age abuse.

My timing, as I write this, couldn't be worse, of course. The tabloids are currently ablaze with the latest, and most unfortunate, of Arnold brouhahas. Roseanne, having loudly accused her husband of infidelity and spousal abuse, filed for divorce, then almost immediately rescinded the statements and reconciled with her husband, only to file for divorce again a few weeks later.

I am neither shocked nor disillusioned by this. Every abused woman I have ever known has attempted, unsuccessfully, to leave her destructive relationship many times, before finally finding the strength and support to make the break. This, after all, is the very essence of the abuse syndrome. Only Roseanne, as usual, has chosen to play it out, in all its gory details, in the spotlight.

I'm a Roseanne fan. I like her show and marvel at her compassion and intelligence, at what she manages to get away with. I like her style—even when she offends me and makes me nervous (which she often does)—because the world needs loudmouthed unattractive women with brains, guts, a social conscience, and a sense of humor. There are few enough of them who make it through puberty with their spirits and energies intact.

SUGGESTIONS FOR DISCUSSION

1. Rapping argues that "Roseanne has gone further than Madonna or almost anyone else I can think of at turning the hegemonic norms of the corporate media on its head." In Rapping's view, what "corporate norms" does Roseanne overturn? What evidence does Rapping provide to support this statement? Do you find it a persuasive interpretation of the program? Why or why not?

2. Rapping makes an extended comparison between Roseanne and Lucille Ball of *I Love Lucy*. What is the point of this comparison? How does it advance Rapping's explanation of why she is a fan of Roseanne?

3. Toward the end of the article, Rapping says that there are two "Roseannes"—one the fictional character in a TV show and the other a public personality. (Notice that she calls both of them "personas." From Rapping's perspective, both are "media images.") What does Rapping see as the relationship between the two "Roseannes"?

SUGGESTIONS FOR WRITING

1. Write a letter to Elayne Rapping that describes and explains your response to her column on Roseanne. Do you find her praise for Roseanne justified? Why or why not? Has she caused you to change or confirm your opinion of Roseanne? What points does she make that you find particularly insightful? What points does she make that you find questionable or confusing? Are there issues that you feel she has overlooked? Are there questions that you want to ask about her column? Imagine you are writing directly to Rapping. You need to be respectful—after all, you don't know Rapping personally. Use the letter as an occasion to think about the whole Roseanne phenomenon and its meanings.

2. For Rapping, part of Roseanne's appeal is that she is too "unrepentantly, combatively proud of her gender and class position and style to be easily molded into the 'movin' on up' mode of American mass media." In Rapping's view, sitcoms prefer characters who are "well-turned out, well-educated liberal professionals" like Bill Cosby's Cliff Huxtable or Calista Flockhart's Ally McBeal. Write an essay about the class position of the leading characters in a sitcom or two that you are familiar with. Take into account how viewers identify class position from verbal and visual clues about the character's occupation, style of dress, where they live, and how they talk to one another. Consider the messages conveyed about what it means to be working class or professional in contemporary America.

3. Use Elayne Rapping's "In Praise of Roseanne" as a model to write an essay that explains why you are a fan of a particular show or character. It is not necessary to restrict yourself to family sitcoms for this assignment. But you do need to go beyond assertions about what you like or dislike. The task here is to give reasons for your admiring the program or character that can be shared by other people.

TV Families: Three Generations of Packaged Dreams

Ella Taylor

> Ella Taylor is a scholar of popular culture and mass communication on the faculty at the University of Washington. In the following article from the *Boston Review,* Taylor traces the social and cultural history of television sitcom families. The representations of the American family that come to us on television, Taylor argues, are not mirror versions of the "normal" family but instead "are filtered" through market research and shifting cultural trends.

SUGGESTION FOR READING

To keep track of Taylor's history of TV families, make notes in the margin of the text on what Taylor sees as the characteristic features of each generation of TV families.

Few contemporary forms of storytelling offer territory as fertile as television for unearthing changing public ideas about family. The tube is at once the most truly popular and the most relentlessly familial entertainment medium we have. And our national culture is so thoroughly suffused with its images that you needn't ever have seen *The Cosby Show* or *All in the Family* or *Ozzie and Harriet* to know the outlines of what these TV institutions are about. Your kids, your parents, your friends and coworkers, or, failing these, other media will tell you even if you belong to that tiny group of perverse social isolates who proudly declare they don't own a television or that they watch only *Masterpiece Theatre* and wildlife documentaries. The shared experience of tele-history has become one of the major ways in which we locate ourselves in time, place, and generation, and at the heart of that history lies television's obsession—the family.

Domesticity was from the beginning built into the forms and structures of television, primarily for the sound business reasons that have always guided programming policy. An early alliance between broadcasters and advertising sponsors installed television, as it had radio, in private homes as a domestic appliance, used to sell other appliances to audiences conceived as family units. With its small screen, "talking heads" format, and interior settings, television combines the looming proximity of film with the constraining space of the theater. It lends itself to the intimacy of character and relationship rather than to action, the routinized intimacy of domestic life rather than the melodramatic intensity of live theater or film. In all its genres—whether comedy or dramatic series, day or nighttime soaps, TV movies, even news—the language and imagery of family break obsessively through its surface forms. Still, it is the episodic series, which fosters a gradual buildup of audience attachment to individual characters and primary relationships, that generates the fullest possibilities for a meditation on domestic themes. The situation comedy that TV inherited from radio and from vaudeville has evolved into a character comedy, more a continuous family chronicle than a conventionally plotted narrative, though it still provides the satisfaction of a weekly resolution that the soaps lack.

Of course, television is no more a mirror of (or an escape from) the social world than any other fiction. True, television's naturalism feeds our expectations of verisimilitude. Its mimetic visual form persuades us that Ozzie Nelson lives on, schmoozing the day away with his neighbor across the yard; that the Bunkers really live in Queens; that the Huxtables really frolic day

[margin note: Purpose of T.V. is to make $.]

after day in a well-appointed Manhattan town house. But family life never resembled that of the Nelsons, the Bunkers, or the Huxtables, at least not in any narrowly sociological sense. Like all storytelling, TV speaks to our collective worries and to our yearnings to improve, redeem, or repair our individual and collective lives, to complete what is incomplete, as well as to our desire to know what's going on out there in that elusive "reality." And if reality, as Lily Tomlin's bag lady Trudy has astutely observed, is anyway just a collective hunch, then television has in its time served up an array of hunches about what family means, or might mean.

Over the years, television's changing commentary on family life has been by turns reflective, utopian, dystopic, its mood now anxious, now euphoric, now redemptive. It articulates prevailing cultural attitudes—but these come filtered through the changing world views and daily routines of producers, network executives, and advertisers, and are filtered again through the varied perceptions of viewers. *Gets away from reality*

To some degree the stance TV adopts toward social trends has been determined by ad hoc changes in the strategies used by the TV industry to attract audiences. The powers that be who decided, in the early fifties, to phase out ethnic sitcoms like *Amos and Andy, Life with Luigi,* and *The Goldbergs* and replace them with the upper-middle-class white coziness of *Leave It to Beaver* and *Ozzie and Harriet* may well have thought they were reproducing the typical American family, if not of the present, then certainly of the near future—just the people their advertisers wanted to reach. What they reproduced, in fact, was not the reality of most family lives, but a postwar ideology breezily forecasting [a] steady rate of economic growth that would produce sufficient abundance to eliminate the basis for class and ethnic conflict. The "end of ideology" would produce a vast middle-class consensus, with the family as the essential building block integrating the individual into a fundamentally benign social order. So the Nelsons and the Cleavers were both advertising—and embodying—the American Dream.

It's unlikely that such grand visions circulated at programming conferences in the network entertainment divisions, or if they did they percolated through the more immediate, perceived imperatives of the market. From the beginning, producers and networks made their programming decisions with advertisers in mind. In the fifties that meant casting nets as wide as possible to deliver a "mass audience" of potential buyers for the explosion of consumer goods and services that poured off production lines. Fashioning a mass out of an enormous, heterogeneous, and highly mobile population meant, in practice, producing entertainment so bland that it would offend no one.

Out of this climate grew the motto of the successful network careerist, "least objectionable programming," and it produced those least objectionable families, the Cleavers, the Nelsons, and the Andersons of *Father Knows Best.* The magically spotless kitchens of those least objectionable wives and mothers, June Cleaver, Harriet Nelson, and Margaret Anderson, came amply stocked with all the latest consumer durables. Harriet promoted Listerine and other products on her own show, exhorting her viewers to become model consumers and, by extension, model families.

Taken together, these shows proposed family life as a zany, conflict-free adventure. Past and future merged into an eternal present in which parents would love and respect each other and their children forever. The children would grow up, go to college, and take up lives identical in most essentials to those of their parents, only wealthier. (The sad fate of that dream is well expressed in an early 1980s TV movie in which the Beaver returns, a true child of his generation, jobless, divorced, and confused.) Even the working-class families, the Kramdens and the Rileys, and the upwardly mobile ones like Lucy and Ricky, embraced the rags-to-riches mythology and labored ceaselessly, through their get-rich-quick schemes, to attain the rewards and the lifestyles of the middle class.

As British cultural historian Raymond Williams has pointed out, there are no masses, only ways of seeing masses. By the mid-sixties, the dream of a great harmonious middle-class America was fraying at the edges, and the latent schisms of class, race, gender, and age erupted into open conflict. But programming executives, for all their declared sensitivity to changes in public mood, stubbornly went on seeing—and producing for—the masses they needed to draw advertising dollars. Throughout the sixties the industry continued to consolidate around blandly consensual family comedies like *The Donna Reed Show* and *My Three Sons*, or loony clans like *The Munsters* and *The Addams Family*. *The Beverly Hillbillies*, one of the most popular (and populist) shows of the decade, plonked a preindustrial extended family down in big bad Los Angeles, extolling the virtues of unpretentious rural innocence at the same time as it poked fun at the double standards and snobbery of the urban *nouveaux riches*. *The Dick Van Dyke Show* extended the fifties dream of middle-class prosperity and harmony into the more sophisticated, urban/suburban style of John F. Kennedy's America. If TV news was preoccupied with urban unrest, an unstable economy, the escalating Vietnam War, and a generation of college kids rebelling against the values of their parents—the world of TV entertainment blithely pretended nothing was happening.

60's

Until 1970, that is, when a decisive shift in network ratings policy reshaped the industry's perception of its audience and created conditions more hospitable to the emergence of new kinds of family-oriented shows. Bob Wood, the incoming president of "top network" CBS, quickly realized that the network's most successful shows (*Gunsmoke, The Beverly Hillbillies,* and *Hee Haw*) appealed primarily to older, rural viewers and did less well in the big cities. Wood also saw that from the advertising sponsors' point of view, what mattered was less how many people turned in than how much they earned and spent. So he turned his attention to the political attitudes of the younger, better educated, and more affluent urban viewers between the ages of eighteen and thirty-four who, at least in the eyes of the media, were fast becoming cultural leaders. The new ratings game of "demographics" would break down the mass audience by age, gender, income, and other variables to isolate the most profitable markets for TV entertainment. Accordingly, scheduling became an elaborate strategic exercise whose purpose was no longer merely to reach the widest possible audience with any given show, but to group programs and commercials in time slots by the type of audience most likely to watch—and spend. The mass audience became a collection of specific "target" audiences.

70's

It was, then, largely as a marketing device that the turbulence of the middle to late sixties, and the lively adversarial spirit and liberal politics of the generation coming of age during this period, found their way into television entertainment. The "age of relevance," as it's often called in TV histories, was ushered in by Norman Lear's *All in the Family,* which after a rocky start on CBS shot to number one in the ratings and reigned over the top three positions for much of the decade, spawning spinoffs and clones on all three networks as it went. The Bunkers (and in their wake, the George Jeffersons and Maude Findlays and the Ann Romanos of *One Day at a Time*) quarrelled and stormed and suffered their way through the 1970s, blazing a trail for the vast array of social problems that have since become the standard fare of television families.

In their early years the Bunkers remained resolutely intact as a family unit, confining their squabbles to highly formalized public issues of race, class, gender, and government corruption. But as the decade went on, the problems that plagued those close to them—menopause, infidelity, divorce, alcoholism, impotence, depression—became steadily more private in nature and drew closer to the Bunkers themselves. Family-show comedy was mixed more and more with drama as the issue became the painful fragility of marriage and the family unit; many episodes were barely identifiable as comedies. Finally Gloria and Meathead, true to their generation, moved to California and divorced, and with Edith's death both Archie and Gloria were left free to negotiate the vicissitudes of life after the nuclear family, on their own spinoff shows.

For the first half of the 1970s, *All in the Family* set the tone for the TV series; the vast majority of series with domestic settings offered their viewers troubled or fractured or "reconstituted" families. (Two striking exceptions were *The Waltons* and *Little House on the Prairie*, both intact-family dramas but set in a rural past sodden with romantic nostalgia.) These early seventies domestic dramas echoed an anxiety about the erosion of domestic life that was beginning to punctuate the rhetoric of politicians and policymakers, social scientists and therapists. From the more visible problems like wife or child abuse, divorce, or teenage pregnancy, to the less tangible areas of marital and generational conflict, social trouble was increasingly being defined as family trouble. The women's movement was raising bracing questions about the compatibility of traditional family forms with women's emancipation, and since women (because they buy things and stay home more than men) are television's most prized viewers, a "prime time feminism" of sorts developed with heart-warming rapidity. It was television's new single women—Mary Richards, Rhoda Morgenstern, Maude Findlay, Ann Romano—who cobbled together all kinds of interesting new family forms from the remnants of old families.

There were striking parallels between the anxiety about family that streamed out of TV comedy during this period and the concerns of prominent intellectuals and cultural critics. Archie Bunker, whose blustery authority was eroded week after week by the hip liberal pluralism of his daughter and son-in-law, was precisely the disenfranchised patriarch whose demise Christopher Lasch was to lament in *The Culture of Narcissism* while feminists rejoiced. Archie's fulminations against "hebes" and "coons" and "fags" amounted to a long bellow of pain from a man whose most cherished guidelines for living—family, country, authority— were being pried loose by the relentless rush of modernity. It's fitting that his worn chair, icon not only of an outmoded patriarchy but of a whole working-class way of life, has ended up as a museum piece at the Smithsonian.

If TV's domestic hearth was becoming a repository for family anxiety, other, more benign images of family and community were surfacing in a subgenre also designed for the younger, upscale markets, the television workplace series. The success of *The Mary Tyler Moore Show* and *M*A*S*H* in CBS's Saturday night lineup early in the seventies led to a wave of shows with occupational settings like *Lou Grant, Taxi, Barney Miller, The Bob Newhart Show*. The emotional center of these shows was not work, not even the star, but the relationships between colleagues whose own family attachments were either severely attenuated or nonexistent. *M*A*S*H*'s medical team, the television producers of WJM in *The Mary Tyler Moore Show*, the detectives of *Barney Miller*, all these groups had the claustrophobic testiness and warm solidarity of the families we carry around as ideals in our heads. "You've been a family to me," cried tearful Mary Richards when WJM was shut down at the end of its seventh successful season. If the television workplace was offering a community that compensated for the ravaged instability of the domestic shows, it may also have been suggesting to a career-oriented generation that the opportunities for emotional engagement and support no longer lay in the family, but in the workplace.

American television is by nature faddish. The sheer volume of its ephemeral output; the fierce competition between the networks; their collective fear of the commercial threat from cable and pay TV, and of the power of home video and other new technologies to restructure viewing habits—all these constraints press into the routines of programming a demand for constant novelty with relatively little innovation. Even the most successful series usually last no longer than seven years, which, some critics argue, suggests that changes in genre or style have little significance as indices of social trends. Fads, however, are more than whims; they're the staple diet of our culture, and fads with staying power can tell us much about the ways people respond to social change. As advertisers and broadcasters try to second-guess the public mood (a daunting project, even if a unitary Zeitgeist existed), they pay earnest attention to what they consider to be the mirrors of public concern, namely the media themselves. Television feeds off itself and other media, and in this way its images both echo and participate in the shaping of cultural trends. Buzz words like "the sixties," "the me-decade," "yuppies," are casually threaded through the rhetoric of television and become enshrined in programming knowledge and routines. That makes them important, however short-lived.

By the 1980s, the craze for domestic comedies seemed to be tapering off and, in the wake of Reagan's massive victory at the polls, cultural diagnosticians at the networks were announcing a "shift to the right." Initially, as Todd Gitlin has shown in his ethnography of the Hollywood production scene *Inside Prime Time,* they guessed that what the vote had meant was an interest in cold-war-ish action-adventure and so produced series like *The CIA* and *Today's FBI.* All flopped by the end of the 1981 season.

In fact, the "shift to the right" was expressing itself with greatest force on the American domestic front. If in the seventies the *family* had been acknowledged as the primary arena for the expression of social conflict, by the early 1980s it had become the focus of a fierce backlash, led by the religious right. The failure of many states to ratify the Equal Rights Amendment, the struggles over abortion rights and contraception for teenagers, the call for a "return to basic values" (less government intervention in family matters and a reassertion of parental authority over the young), all became major issues of public concern. Television leaped onto the ideological bandwagon not just in news and talk shows, but also in its entertainment themes. The made-for-TV movie in particular, with its solemn, sociological-therapeutic format, framed the "official" social problems of our day—rape, anorexia, mental illness, drug abuse, incest, divorce, homosexuality—and resolved them within the family.

But it is the sitcom, where the routines of everyday "normal" life are rehearsed weekly, that works over and redefines the *meaning* of family. The character of family comedy was already changing in 1975 when, responding to one of the frequent bouts of pressure that came from lobbying groups to clean up TV sex and violence, the National Association of Broadcasters chose to censor itself by designating the nightly 8–9 P.M. slot "Family Hour," to be filled with programming allegedly purged of material deemed harmful to "children and other vulnerable groups." Although it didn't remove violent content from the small screen, the ruling succeeded in banishing from peak viewing time many of the "relevant" sitcoms, severely damaging their ratings potential. The Norman Lear series were quickly edged out by nostalgic, consensual comedies like *Happy Days* and *Laverne and Shirley,* and by the wave of nighttime soaps that began to colonize the top twenty.

The top ten shows for the 1982–3 season featured only two comedies (*M*A*S*H* and *Three's Company*), and the 1983–4 season only one (*Kate and Allie*), and critics began writing columns declaring the sitcom, for years the centerpiece of television entertainment, dead or dying. In fact, the glittering partnership of *The Cosby Show* and *Family Ties* in 1984 rapidly guaranteed that it was neither; both have topped the Nielsens for the last two years and produced imitators like *Growing Pains, Valerie,* and others.

Once again, the formula changed in the first instance as a response to change in industrial practice. The format of these series, with their discrete themes for teenagers, small children, and adults as well as for the family unit as a whole, suggests a new "demographics," in which several markets are laced together to create a new kind of mass audience (and a renewed need to avoid offending viewers). In the exquisite refinement of "demographic" ratings policies, whole evenings of prime time are now designed with particular aggregates of markets in mind, and scheduling becomes a key craft in the networks' race for supremacy. The extraordinarily successful Thursday night lineup that catapulted NBC to the head of the network race begins in Family Hour with *Cosby* and *Family Ties,* which secure the mass audience, and, after children's bedtime, moves smoothly into the adult markets with the work-families of *Cheers, Night Court,* and *Hill Street Blues,* now bounced in favor of the glossier *L.A. Law*: In short, an advertiser's paradise.

Like *All in the Family, The Cosby Show* has attracted an enormous amount of attention from critics and public interest groups, as well as a huge and devoted audience, but there the similarity ends. The robustly working-class Bunker household was never a model of consumer vitality, nor did it aspire to be. If Archie was dragged, kicking and screaming, into the seventies, the Huxtables embrace modernity with gusto. From grandparents to the disarmingly cute Rudy, this family is sexy and glamorous. Surrounded by the material evidence of their success, the Huxtables radiate wealth, health, energy, and up-to-the-minute style. *The Cosby Show* offers the same pleasures as a commercial, a parade of gleaming commodities and expensive designer clothing, unabashedly enjoyed by successful people. And Cosby himself is a talented promoter of the goods and services, from Jell-O to E. F. Hutton, that finance his series.

Given the troubled condition of many American families in the eighties, *Cosby* must be palpably compensatory for many of its fans. Week after week, the show offers what family comedy in the fifties offered, and what most of us don't have, the continuity of orderly lives lived without major trauma or disturbance, stretching back into an identical past and reaching confidently forward into an identical future. Two generations of Huxtable men attended "Hillman College" and met their wives there, and although Cliff's eldest daughter chooses Princeton, the next goes for Hillman too.

But where the TV families of the fifties casually took harmony and order for granted, the Huxtables work strenuously and self-consciously at showing us how well they get along. Not that much happens on *Cosby*. It's a virtually plotless chronicle of the small, quotidian details of family life, at the heart of which lies a moral etiquette of parenting and a developmental psychology of growing up. Every week provides family members, and us, with a Learning Experience and a lesson in social adjustment. Rudy's terrified playmate learns to love going to the dentist. Rudy learns to stop bossing her friends around. Theo learns not to embark on expensive projects he won't complete. Sondra and her boyfriend learn to arbitrate their bickering over sex roles. Denise learns to cope with bad grades in college. Even Cliff and Clair, who despite high-powered careers as physician and lawyer respectively, have all the leisure in the world to spend "quality time" with their kids, teach each other parenting by discussion as well as by example. The show's endless rehearsal of mild domestic disorder and its resolution suggests a perfect discussion as well as by example. The show's endless rehearsal of mild domestic disorder and its resolution suggests a perfect family that works. The family that plays, sings, dances, and, above all, communicates together, stays together.

Didacticism is nothing new in television entertainment. *All in the Family* was stuffed with messages of all kinds, but on *Cosby,* moral and psychological instruction are rendered monolithic and indisputable. Unlike the Bunkers, for whom every problem became the occasion for an all-out war of ideas, no one ever screams at Huxtable Manor. True, beneath their beguiling mildness there lurks a casual hostility, in which everyone, Clair and Cliff included, trades insults and makes fun of everyone else. But there's no dissent, no real difference of opinion or belief, only vaguely malicious banter that quickly dissolves into sweet agreement, all part of the busy daily manufacture of consensus.

Undercutting the warm color and light, the jokey good humor and the impeccable salutes of feminism, is a persistent authoritarianism. The tone is set by Cosby himself, whose prodigious charm overlays a subtle menace. If the pint-sized Rudy gets her laughs by aping the speech and manners of adults, Cliff gets his laughs—and his way—by turning into a giant child, and then slipping his kids or his wife their moral or psychological pills with a wordless, grimacing comic caper. A captivating child, undoubtedly, with his little vanities and his competitiveness, but he's also quietly coercive: Father knows best, or else. The cuddly, overgrown schoolboy becomes the amused onlooker and then the oracle, master of the strategic silence or the innocent question that lets one of his kids know they've said or done something dumb, or gives his wife to understand that her independence is slipping into bossiness. In Huxtable-speak, this is called "communicating." Cliff practices a thoroughly contemporary politics of strong leadership, managing potential conflicts with all the skill of a well-socialized corporate executive.

There's none of the generational warfare that rocked the Bunker household every week. And this family doesn't need the openly authoritarian "tough love" that's cropping up more and more in recent TV movies, because parental authority has already been internalized. The kids put up a token display of playful resistance, then surrender happily to the divine right of parents whose easy knowledge of the difference between right and wrong irons out the inconvenient ambiguities of contemporary life. Indeed, since the Huxtables are a supremely "intact" nuclear family, those ambiguities rarely come up, or if they do, they occur outside the charmed circle and stay outside it. A teenage pregnancy, a drug problem, a worker laid off; occasionally one of the problems that bedevil most families hovers near, casts a brief shadow on the bright domestic light, and then slinks away, intimidated by the fortress of Huxtable togetherness. Unlike the sitcoms of the fifties, whose vision of the social terrain outside the family was as benign as that inside it, the "world outside" *Cosby* is downright perilous, to the limited degree that it exists at all.

The Huxtables have friends but no discernible neighborhood community, indeed no public life to speak of aside from their jobs, which seem to run on automatic pilot. They inhabit a visibly black world, whose blackness is hardly ever alluded to. "I'm not going to talk about social justice or racial harmony or peace, because you all know how I feel about them," intones the retiring president of Cliff's alma mater, and delivers a limp homily exhorting old alumnae to invite young alumnae to dinner, which earns him a standing ovation from old and young alike—all black. No wonder *The Cosby Show* is number one in the South African ratings. It is, as a Johannesburg television executive remarked complacently on the nightly Hollywood chat show *Entertainment Tonight* last year, not a show about race, but about "family values."

Even *Family Ties* (the white obverse of *Cosby*), whose premise of ex-hippie parents with a precorporate, neoconservative son promises some refreshing friction, flattens genuine argument into the stifling warmth of domestic affection. The mild-mannered Keaton father, Steven, is persuaded by an old friend from the campus Left to start a radical magazine. A difference of opinion leads to Steven's being accused of copping out, but his wife, Elyse, assures him that "you're making a statement by the way you live your life and raise your children," suggesting not only that family integrity transcends politics, but that political affiliation is reducible to being nice to other people—especially your family.

This is not to say that the articulation of family trouble so central to seventies television has disappeared from the small screen. Other sitcoms retain the preoccupation with "reconstituted" families, if in watered-down form. "Do I have to be a relative to be family?" a small boy asks his mother on *Who's the Boss?* a role reversal comedy about two single parents (she the breadwinner, he the housekeeper) living together. "Not necessarily," his mother smiles down at him, "a family means people who share each other's lives and care about each other." An unexceptionable definition, and also virtually meaningless; with the sting of divorce and family poverty removed, single parenthood and stepparenting turn into a romp, a permanent pajama party. Even *Kate and Allie,* which began as a witty comedy of divorce manners and a chronicle of the single life encountered second time around, has slipped into the parenting psychology mold, focusing more on the kids and teenagers' rites of passage than on the adults. Here we see television hedging its bets by nodding in the direction of radical changes in family form and structure, without really taking them on. And the "single woman" comedy so wildly popular in the seventies seems to have little resonance for the eighties; several new shows of this kind, including a new *Mary Tyler Moore Show,* were cancelled in short order. Christine Cagney of *Cagney and Lacey* alone survives as a prototype of the mature single woman, and even she must be balanced with her partner, Marybeth Lacey, the harried working mother.

If anything, the locus of family disharmony on TV these days seems to be the nighttime soaps, and nothing else on prime time matches the seething ambiguities and flaring passions of these clans. On *Dynasty* this season, Blake Carrington struggles to contain his wife and his former wife (who collects younger men with a studied casualness only Joan Collins could bring off with a straight face); his son Steven, whose sexual identity oscillates between gay and straight as the plot requires; his son Adam, who turns out not to be his son at all (so he adopts him); his niece Leslie, who has just discovered her lover is her brother; and, in a grand but wildly implausible burst of televisual affirmative action, his sister Dominique, who's black. Season after season, the soaps' elastic tribal boundaries expand and contract to admit or expel undiscovered relatives, bogus and genuine. But I suspect that soap audiences appropriate these shows in the high camp spirit in which they're offered. This is not "reality," which may be why soap stars invariably collapse into disclaiming giggles when interviewed about the characters they play.

Bill Cosby, in his rare interviews, never *giggles.* The actor takes his responsibilities as an educator very seriously. *Newsweek* reported in 1984 that Cosby had commissioned a well-known black psychiatrist to review every *Cosby Show* script for authenticity. And the actor told the *Los Angeles Times* in 1985 that viewers loved the series because it showed that "the people in this house respect the parents and the parents respect the children and that there is a l-o-v-e generated in this house." Norman Lear in his heyday felt convinced that viewers loved *All in the Family* because it exposed bigotry and addressed "real life" problems. No one really knows much about audience responses to television, but there's probably always an asymmetry between producers' intentions and viewers' readings. It's equally plausible that Bunker fans were as engaged by the rage that imprinted itself on almost every episode of *All in the Family* as by its liberal politics.

Similarly, the Huxtable brand of patriarchal dominance may strike as resonant a chord as the l-o-v-e Cosby cites—testified to by the success of his recent book *Fatherhood,* which topped the bestseller list in 1986. And if Cosby's childlike charm works, it may also be catering to what is most childlike in us, his audience; namely the yearning for a perfectly synchronized family, or community, that provides for the needs of all its members and regulates itself through a benevolent dictatorship, a family that always was as perfect as it is now, and always will be. That isn't merely infantile; it also signals the political retrenchment that comes from a cultural exhaustion, a weary inability to imagine new forms of community, new ways of living.

In each successive television era, a particular congruence of marketing exigencies and cultural trends has produced different portraits of the American family. In television, genre is always about 80 percent commerce. But in the 1970s, commerce made room for lively, innovative programming that interrupted the hitherto bland conventions of the TV family, giving us programming that above all didn't condescend to its audiences. The Bunkers were never a restful or reassuring family, but their battles, however strident, raised the possibility that there might be, might have to be more ways than one to conduct family life, that blood ties are not the only bonds of community, that divorce is a feature of modern life to be confronted, that women and men must find new ways of living together and raising children.

Today, the generous space that was opened up then for public discussion is once again being narrowed. With their eyes firmly fixed on the new mass audience, *The Cosby Show* and its clones are short-circuiting the quarrelsome gutsiness of seventies TV by burying their heads in the nostalgic sands of "traditional values" that never were. Public interest groups may be all smiles at the jolly harmony of these shows. But their obsession with engineering a spurious consensus returns us to the dullest kind of television, with its twin besetting sins, sentimentality and a profound horror of argument.

SUGGESTIONS FOR DISCUSSION

1. Taylor says that "our national culture is so suffused with...images [of TV families] that you needn't ever have seen *The Cosby Show* or *All in the Family* or *Ozzie and Harriet* to know the outlines of what these TV institutions are about." What exactly does she mean? Draw on your own experience here. What do you know about TV families, past and present, whether or not you have watched their shows? What kinds of associations, values, and meanings do these shows carry for you?

2. Taylor sees a "decisive shift" in the early 1970s that led to the "emergence of new kinds of family-oriented shows." What is the shift to which she refers? What cultural, political, and economic factors contribute to the shift? What have been the results?

3. Taylor notes the "anxiety about family that streamed out of TV comedy" in the 1970s. What anxiety does she have in mind? Have these anxieties passed or do you find them—or new ones—on current family sitcoms?

SUGGESTIONS FOR WRITING

1. Watch two or three episodes of one of the older family sitcoms that Taylor mentions, such as *I Love Lucy, The Honeymooners, Leave It to Beaver, Ozzie and Harriet, The Beverly Hillbillies,* or *All in the Family*. Notice the roles family members play and the kinds of conflicts that emerge. What values and cultural beliefs do you see reflected? What do you think made the show successful with viewers? Write an essay that analyzes the representation of family life on the show and its appeal to viewers.

2. Choose a TV sitcom centered on single adults, such as *Seinfeld, Friends, Will and Grace, Dharma and Greg, Murphy Brown*, and *Ellen*. Watch two or three episodes. How does the show represent domestic life? What attractions does the single life appear to offer? What relation does this depiction of single life have to depictions of domestic life you find in family sitcoms? Write an essay that analyzes the representation of domestic life and what it tells us about alternatives to the family in contemporary culture.

3. Extend Ella Taylor's history of family sitcoms to account for the new shows of the 1990s. Begin by summarizing Taylor's characterizations of earlier TV families. Then bring the history up to present, noting whether current representations of TV families continue older traditions or depart from them. Following Taylor's line of analysis, consider the social, cultural, political, and economic circumstances that have come together to produce the contemporary TV family. Take into account recent sitcoms such as the Fox network TV families, *The Simpsons* and *Married...with Children*.

VISUAL CULTURE · *TELEVISION SITCOMS*

Part of the appeal of family sitcoms is that the camera brings us in to the home of the Kramdens, the Nelsons, the Bunkers, and the Huxtables. As viewers, we enter an intimate, domestic space, much as if we were visiting actual neighbors. But what we see, of course, is not someone's real home but a TV set, which is designed in particular ways to fit the show. The same is true of the wardrobes worn by family members and other characters. These visual features are a key part of television storytelling.

Write an analysis of the set and wardrobe on a family sitcom (or you could compare the sets on two different programs. Your task is to determine what meanings the look of the set and the wardrobe convey to viewers and how they contribute to the story. Follow these steps:

- *Pick a family sitcom or sitcoms that interest you.* You don't have to limit yourself to what appears on current prime time. Check listings for reruns on Fox and Nickelodeon of older sitcoms. (This way you could compare, say, *The Honeymooners* and *The Cosby Show* or *I Love Lucy* and *Roseanne*.)

- *Take notes on what you see.* What room or rooms does the camera bring you into? List the features of the room—the furniture, the arrangement, what is on the walls, the appliances, sporting goods, toys, and so on. Sketch the layout for future reference. Is the room tidy or messy? Are its furnishings expensive or cheap? What class status do they mark? Notice what people do in the room. Where do they sit? How do they move through the space? Is the set mostly for talking or do people conduct other activities?

- *What do the characters wear in the show?* Describe their wardrobes. What style or category would you fit it into? What does the physical appearance of each character signify about his or her identity on the show?

- *Now turn to analyzing your notes.* The key point here is to remember that what you see is not an actual room in someone's real house but a set constructed to send a message to viewers. What messages does the set send? What does it say about the class and social status of the family? Is it affluent, middle class, working class? What clues does the set give you about the relationships among family members? Does the father, say, have his own chair? Does the set routinely picture a mother working in the kitchen? How do the children use the space on the set? What messages do the characters' wardrobes send to viewers? How does the style of the characters create their identities on the show?

- *Based on your notes and analysis, write an essay that explains how the set and wardrobe define the characters in a TV family.* You will need to describe the look of the show that you see on the TV screen and the information that televisual images convey to viewers about the social status of the TV family, the identities of its members, and the relationships among them. Finally, you need to consider how these visual images shape viewers' attitudes and their emotional investments in the characters.

THE ACTIVE AUDIENCE

One of the familiar criticisms of television (and popular culture in general) is that it makes viewers passive bystanders, hypnotized by the visual medium. This view of the television audience as brainwashed zombies has been challenged recently, however, by ethnographic accounts of how people watch television, their reasons for doing so, the level of attentiveness they devote to viewing, and the uses and sense they make of their experience as viewers.

This new focus sees television viewers, as well as consumers of other forms of popular culture, as members of an active audience—not the cultural dupes of the mass media but individuals who use such cultural products as cult TV shows (*Star Trek, Dallas, Twilight Zone,* and so on), Elvis memorabilia, romance novels ("bodice-rippers"), cyberpunk fiction, and heavy metal music for their own purposes.

People become fans by fitting the products of popular culture into their social worlds, often detaching a television show, a book, or a musical performer from their intended meanings and remaking them to suit the fan's desires. Science-fiction fan P. L. Caruthers-Montgomery captures her own entrance into the world of *Star Trek* fandom, with its emotional investments and ritualized social interactions:

> I met one girl who liked some of the TV shows I liked….But I was otherwise a bookworm, no friends, working in the school library. Then my friend and I met some other girls a grade ahead of us but gaga over ST [*Star Trek*]. From the beginning, we met each Friday night at one of the two homes that had a color TV to watch *Star Trek* together. I had a reel-to-reel tape recorder. Silence was mandatory except during commercials, and, afterwards, we "discussed" each episode. We re-wrote each story and corrected the wrongs done to "Our Guys" by the writers. We memorized bits of dialog. We even started to write our own adventures. One of us liked Spock, one liked Kirk, one liked Scotty, and two of us were enamored of McCoy (Yes, I was a McCoy fan). To this day, I can identify each episode by name within the first few seconds of the teaser. I amaze my husband by reciting lines along with the characters. (I had listened to those tapes again and again, visualizing the episodes.)

Fans are not casual viewers, listeners, or spectators. As Caruthers-Montgomery reveals, they are committed to the point of re-writing the show, if necessary, to "correct wrongs." This section looks at ways to study fans—to look at the sense of identity they derive from their passionate attachment and to see how they use popular culture for their own purposes.

Television Fans

Henry Jenkins

Henry Jenkins directs the Film and Media studies program at MIT. The following excerpts come from his book *Textual Poachers: Television Fans and Participatory Culture.* Jenkins begins by recounting a *Saturday Night Live* skit that satirizes *Star Trek.* He does so, however, not to poke fun at these fans or to make them out to be "kooks" or "fanatics" (the root of "fan"), as media experts sometimes do. Instead, he wants to ask why such stereotypical representations of fans are widespread and what is at stake.

SUGGESTION FOR READING

Notice as you read that the opening section, where Jenkins recounts the *Saturday Night Live* skit, sets up the problem he goes on to explore in the following four paragraphs. These paragraphs may strike you as dense and academic, but stick with them. Keep in mind that Jenkins is seeking to explain why fans are viewed in such a negative light.

When *Star Trek* star William Shatner (Captain James T. Kirk) appeared as a guest host of *Saturday Night Live,* the program chose this opportunity to satirize the fans of his 1960s television series. The "Trekkies" were depicted as nerdy guys with glasses and rubber Vulcan ears, "I Grok Spock" T-shirts stretched over their bulging stomachs. One man laughs maliciously about a young fan he has just met who doesn't know Yeoman Rand's cabin number, while his friend mumbles about the great buy he got on a DeForest Kelly album. When Shatner arrives, he is bombarded with questions from fans who want to know about minor characters in individual episodes (which they cite by both title and sequence number), who seem to know more about his private life than he does, and who demand such trivial information as the combination to Kirk's safe. Finally, in incredulity and frustration, Shatner turns on the crowd: "Get a life, will you people? I mean, I mean, for crying out loud, it's just a TV show!" Shatner urges the fans to move out of their parent's basements and to proceed with adult experiences ("you, there, have you ever kissed a girl?"), to put their fannish interests behind them. The fans look confused at first, then, progressively more hurt and embarrassed. Finally, one desperate fan asks, "Are you saying we should pay more attention to the movies?" Enraged, Shatner storms off the stage, only to be confronted by an equally angry convention organizer. After a shoving match and a forced rereading of his contract, an embarrassed Shatner takes the stage again and tells the much-relieved fans that they have just watched a "recreation of the evil Captain Kirk from episode 27, 'The Enemy Within.'"

This much-discussed sketch distills many popular stereotypes about fans. Its "Trekkies":

a. are brainless consumers who will buy anything associated with the program or its cast (DeForest Kelly albums);

b. devote their lives to the cultivation of worthless knowledge (the combination to Kirk's safe, the number of Yeoman Rand's cabin, the numerical order of the program episodes);

c. place inappropriate importance on devalued cultural material ("It's just a television show");

d. are social misfits who have become so obsessed with the show that it forecloses other types of social experience ("Get a life");

e. are feminized and/or desexualized through their intimate engagement with mass culture ("Have you ever kissed a girl?");

f. are infantile, emotionally and intellectually immature (the suggestion that they should move out of their parents' basement, their pouting and befuddled responses to Shatner's criticism, the mixture of small children and overweight adults);

g. are unable to separate fantasy from reality ("Are you saying we should pay more attention to the movies?").

A SCANDALOUS CATEGORY

To understand the logic behind these particular discursive constructions of fans, we must reconsider what we mean by taste. Concepts of "good taste," appropriate conduct, or aesthetic merit are not natural or universal; rather, they are rooted in social experience and reflect particular class interests. As Pierre Bourdieu notes, these tastes often seem "natural" to those who share them precisely because they are shaped by our earliest experiences as members of a particular cultural group, reinforced by social exchanges, and rationalized through encounters with higher education and other basic institutions that reward appropriate conduct and proper tastes. Taste becomes one of the important means by which social distinctions are maintained and class identities are forged. Those who "naturally" possess appropriate tastes "deserve" a privileged position within the institutional hierarchy and reap the greatest benefits from the educational system, while the tastes of others are seen as "uncouth" and underdeveloped. Taste distinctions determine not only desirable and undesirable forms of culture but also desirable and undesirable ways of relating to cultural objects, desirable and undesirable strategies of interpretation and styles of consumption. Witness, for example, the ways that Shakespeare's plays have provoked alternative responses, demanded different levels of intellectual investment as they have moved from popular to elite culture.

Though the enculturation of particular tastes is so powerful that we are often inclined to describe our cultural preferences not simply as natural but as universal and eternal, taste is always in crisis; taste can never remain stable, because it is challenged by the existence of other tastes that often seem just as "natural" to their proponents. The boundaries of "good taste," then, must constantly be policed; proper tastes must be separated from improper tastes; those who possess the wrong tastes must be distinguished from those whose tastes conform more closely to our own expectations. Because one's taste is so interwoven with all other aspects of social and cultural experience, aesthetic distaste brings with it the full force of moral excommunication and social rejection. "Bad taste" is not simply undesirable; it is unacceptable. Debates about aesthetic choices or interpretive practices, then, necessarily have an important social dimension and often draw upon social or psychological categories as a source of justification. Materials viewed as undesirable within a particular aesthetic are often accused of harmful social effects or negative influences upon their consumers. Aesthetic preferences are imposed through legislation and public pressure; for example, in the cause of protecting children from the "corrupting" influence of undesired cultural materials. Those who enjoy such texts are seen as intellectually debased, psychologically suspect, or emotionally immature.

The stereotypical conception of the fan, while not without a limited factual basis, amounts to a projection of anxieties about the violation of dominant cultural hierarchies. The fans' transgression of bourgeois taste and disruption of dominant cultural hierarchies insures that their preferences are seen as abnormal and threatening by those who have a vested interest in the maintenance of these standards (even by those who may share similar tastes but express them in fundamentally different ways). As Bourdieu suggests, "The most intolerable thing for those who regard themselves as the possessors of legitimate culture is the sacrilegious reuniting of tastes which taste dictates shall be separated" (253). Fan culture muddies those boundaries, treating popular texts as if they merited the same degree of attention and appreciation as canonical texts. Reading practices (close scrutiny, elaborate exegesis, repeated and prolonged rereading, etc.) acceptable in confronting a work of "serious merit" seem perversely misapplied to the more "disposable" texts of mass culture. Fans speak of "artists" where others can see only commercial hacks, of transcendent meanings where others find only banalities, of "quality and innovation" where others see only formula and convention. One *Beauty and the Beast fan*, for example, constructed a historical account of American broadcasting, echoing the traditional narrative of a '50s golden age followed by a '60s wasteland, yet, using it to point toward certain fan favorites (*Twilight Zone, Outer Limits, Star Trek, The Avengers, The Prisoner*) as representing turning points or landmarks. These series stand apart from the bulk of broadcast material because of their appeal to the intelligence and discrimination of their viewers, contrasting sharply with "mediocre series," such as *Lost in Space, Land of the Giants, The Invaders,* or *The Greatest American Hero,* which were characterized by their "poor writing, ridiculous conflicts offering no moral or ethical choices, predictable and cardboard characterizations, and a general lack of attention to creativity and chance-taking". His historical narrative ends, naturally enough, with the appearance of his favorite series, *Beauty and the Beast,* which achieves the perfect melding of fantasy, science fiction, and classical literature that had been the goal of this "great tradition" of pop "masterpieces." Such an account requires not simply an acknowledgement of the superior qualities of a desired text but also a public rejection of the low standards of the "silly and childish offerings" that fall outside of the fan canon. The fan's claims for a favored text stand as the most direct and vocal affront to the legitimacy of traditional cultural hierarchies.

Yet the fans' resistance to the cultural hierarchy goes beyond simply the inappropriateness of their textual selections and often cuts to the very logic by which fans make sense of cultural experiences. Fan interpretive practice differs from that fostered by the educational system and preferred by bourgeois culture not simply in its object choices or in the degree of its intensity, but often in the types of reading skills it employs, in the ways that fans approach texts. From the perspective of dominant taste, fans appear to be frighteningly out of control, undisciplined and unrepentant, rogue readers. Rejecting the aesthetic distance Bourdieu suggests is a cornerstone of bourgeois aesthetics, fans enthusiastically embrace favored texts and attempt to integrate media representations into their own social experience. Unimpressed by institutional authority and expertise, the fans assert their own right to form interpretations, to offer evaluations, and to construct cultural canons. Undaunted by traditional conceptions of literary and intellectual property, fans raid mass culture, claiming its materials for their own use, reworking them as the basis for their own cultural creations and social interactions. Fans seemingly blur the boundaries between fact and fiction, speaking of characters as if they had an existence apart from their textual manifestations, entering into the realm of the fiction as if it were a tangible place they can inhabit and explore. Fan culture stands as an open challenge to the "naturalness" and desirability of dominant cultural hierarchies, a refusal of authorial authority and a violation of intellectual property. What may make all of this particularly damning is that fans cannot as a group be dismissed as intellectually inferior, they often are highly educated, articulate people who come from the middle classes, people who "should know better" than to spend their time constructing elaborate interpretations of television programs. The popular embrace of television can thus be read as a conscious repudiation of high culture or at least of the traditional boundaries between high culture and popular culture. What cannot easily be dismissed as ignorance must be read as aesthetic perversion. It is telling, of course, that sports fans (who are mostly male and who attach great significance to "real" events rather than fictions) enjoy very different status than media fans (who are mostly female and who attach great interest in debased forms of fiction); the authority to sanction taste, then, does not rest exclusively on issues of class but also encompasses issues of gender, which may account for why popular publications like Newsweek or programs like *Saturday Night Live* find themselves aligned with the academy in their distaste for media fans as well as why stereotypes portray fans either as overweight women (see Misery) or nerdy, degendered men (*see Fade to Black*).

SUGGESTIONS FOR DISCUSSION

1. Describe in your own words the characterization of *Star Trek* fans that comes across in the *Saturday Night Live* skit. Have you encountered such representations of fans, Trekkies or otherwise, before? If so, in what context? Do you think you would fall into the category of fan? If so, explain.

2. In the analytical section following the account of the Trekkie skit, Jenkins draws heavily on Pierre Bourdieu's understanding of "good taste" and its relation to social distinction and "legitimate" culture. Jenkins gives few

examples, however, and the passage may therefore seem somewhat abstract. Try filling it in by providing your own examples of "good" and "bad" taste. Explain how you acquired your sense of what constitutes "good" and "bad" taste.

3. Jenkins says that the reading skills used by fans differ from those fostered by educational institutions. To what extent is this true of your own experience? Do you read fiction, listen to music, or watch movies or television differently when you are doing it for school as opposed to when you are doing it for your own purposes? Explain how you have been taught to approach a story in school. How does this compare to the way you approach a story outside of school, in a novel, film, or television show? If you see important differences, how would you account for them?

FIELDWORK PROJECT

This project focuses on the way fans—people who are not academics, critics, or journalists—write about popular culture. Following are a number of ways you can find material written for and by fans:

- *Contact the fan club of a media celebrity, movie, or television show that interests you.* (Album covers often include information on fan clubs, or consult the *Encyclopedia of Associations* in your library and look for "fan clubs.")
- *Find copies of a newsletter or fanzine devoted to a particular celebrity.* (Music stores and alternative bookstores often carry fanzines.)
- *Log on to one of the many newsgroups or Web sites devoted to a movie, TV show, or media figure.*

Once you have assembled your materials and read through them, plan an essay that analyzes the kind of writing that makes up the particular fan culture that you have investigated. Here are some questions to take into account:

- *What information does the material contain about the person, movie, or show?* Who is likely to be interested in such information? Who writes it?
- *Are readers encouraged to write?* Is there interchange among fans? If so, about what?
- *What relationship to the person, movie, or show do the written materials seem to promote?* What sense of belongingness or collective identity does the writing project? Are there opportunities offered to meet other fans?
- *Finally, how does the writing differ from "legitimate" media criticism?* (Elayne Rapping identifies herself as a "fan," but does her approach differ from the fans that you have investigated?)

Mining the Archive

COMIC STRIPS AND COMIC BOOKS

Comic strips started to appear in daily newspapers and the Sunday papers in the late 1890s and early 1900s, establishing a new medium of story-telling that brings together three key ingredients: a narrative sequence of pictures, speech balloons and a regular cast of characters. The Yellow Kid (1895)—a bald, gap-toothed street urchin dressed in a yellow nightshirt—became the first comic-strip celebrity, followed by the Katzenjammer Kids (1897), Happy Hooligan (1900), Mutt and Jeff (1907), and Krazy Kat (1910).

You can find examples of these early joke-a-day gag strips that anticipate Pogo (1949), Peanuts (1950), Doonesbury (1970), Cathy (1976), and Dilbert (1989) in Robert C. Harvey's books, *The Art of the Funnies: An Aesthetic History* (1994) and *Children of the Yellow Kid: The Evolution of the American Comic Strip* (1998). The website Krazy Kat Daily Strips at rrnet.com/-nakamura/soba/kat/day/ contains 30 enlargements of Krazy Kat strips. As you look at old comic strips, consider how the narrative sequencing from panel to panel sets up the humor and how cartooning styles give the characters their particular identities.

You can also find examples in Harvey's two books of detective and adventure themes in comic strips such as Dick Tracy (1931), Terry and the Pirates (1934), Prince Valiant (1937), and Steve Canyon (1947), as well as domestic sitcoms such as Bringing Up Father (1913), Gasoline Alley (1918), Little Orphan Annie (1924), and Blondie (1930).

In the 1930s, the narrative techniques of the comic strip found a new outlet in comic books. In 1938, Superman—the first of the great comic-book heroes—made his appearance, followed quickly by Batman, Green Lantern, Wonder Woman, Captain America, and Plastic Man. You can find examples of these superheroes in Jules Feiffer's *The Great Comic Book Heroes* (1965) and Robert C. Harvey's *The Art of the Comic Book: An Aesthetic History* (1996). Comic books offer opportunities to think about how the integration of the visual and the verbal has created new narrative possibilities in graphic storytelling.

CHAPTER 8

Work

Never leave that to tomorrow, which you can do today.
—*Benjamin Franklin*, Poor Richard's Almanac

McJob: A low-pay, low-prestige, low-benefit, no-future job in the service sector. Frequently considered a satisfying career choice by people who have never held one.
—*Douglas Coupland*, Generation X

Men and women in the United States historically have had a love/hate relationship with their jobs. That may be due partially to something typically called the Protestant work ethic, a philosophy of living that has formed a part of the character of this nation from the first European settlements. According to this ethic, "Idle hands are the devil's workshop." The contrast between fruitful labor and wasteful leisure is one the Puritans brought with them as they traveled to the New World to explore and to settle in this country. Its message is a simple (and simplistic) one: Success is the reward for diligence. Failure is the consequence of idleness.

Of course, success and failure are never so easily explained away, but a cul-tural myth—even one as readily dispelled as this one—is very difficult to ignore. Workers who lose their jobs might well have been fired through no fault of their own, but the suspicion often remains that those let go somehow deserved dismissal. For many American workers, getting a good job and keeping it is a measure of success. Losing it, for whatever reason, seems to signal failure.

Our identities are formed, in many respects, by the jobs that we hold or want to hold. From the time children start school, parents and teachers ask them what they want to be when they grow up. By adulthood, we are expected to have a "career"—a job that will support a family, provide opportunities for professional advancement, buy leisure time, perhaps contribute to community well-being, signal status, and be fulfilling all at once. Influenced by such expectations, many workers consider losing a job of any type to be a threat not only to the promise of financial security but to self-respect as well.

Most recently, the threat to many workers is a practice called *downsizing*. Downsizing is a word made popular in the 1990s as companies laid workers off in response to marketplace demands, technological changes, and the relocation of industries either to countries outside the United States or to areas in this country that provided tax incentives for new businesses. Obviously, downsizing is not simply about the individual worker and self-esteem. Downsizing erodes the belief in an unspoken social contract between labor and corporations. No matter the economic conditions, many workers feel betrayed when companies downsize or move to new locations and leave a large, unemployed workforce behind. Workers want loyalty from the companies that they give their lives to and companies want loyalty in return. When Michael Moore produced his satirical documentary *Roger and Me* detailing GM's pull-out from Flint, Michigan, many critics argued that the company had every right to do what it needed to do to stay profitable. That is how capitalism works. Moore disagreed. From his point of view, GM had brought prosperity and promises to Flint. When the company left, it turned its back on the people who had helped make that prosperity possible, leaving the city to survive (or not) on its own.

Perhaps because many workers in this country suffer from stress-related illnesses, complain of having little time outside their jobs, and fear the loss of those jobs to economic whims, the old work ethic is now more frequently being called into question. In an era of downsizing, studies show that more and more workers do not believe that their jobs are secure. They know that factories have closed or moved and that technology often displaces manual labor. A 1997 study at Brown University, for example, found that 68 percent of those surveyed believed that companies are less loyal to employees and 59 percent believed employees are less loyal to companies today than they were only ten years earlier. That atmosphere of distrust has led some to question the role of labor unions, to challenge the appropriateness of affirmative action legislation, and

to call attention to the growing disparity between the salaries of CEOs and their employees.

Even with workers' growing suspicion that their jobs are always subject to the whims of the marketplace, researchers also are finding that the workplace has become, for many, a sanctuary from the tensions of home life or a second neighborhood where friendships are forged, jokes are traded, and identities are formed. Work as a home away from home continues to be popular for television series that place sitcoms and dramas—shows like *ER*, *NYPD Blue*, or *Third Watch*, for example—in something that has been called the "work-family" setting. On television, the work-family is a group of people in the workplace who substitute for the home family. That substitute family has become popular in television drama as well as situation comedies. When, for example, *NYPD Blue*'s perpetually cranky cop Sippowitz lost his original partner because the actor playing the role wanted to move from television to film, audiences were much more concerned than when Sippowitz's on-screen wife suddenly disappeared from the storyline. At least in part, that reaction likely had something to do with the fact that, while Sippowitz's work-family involves intense drama and ongoing action, his home life is pretty boring. The work-family setting is a formula that began with the old *Mary Tyler Moore Show* and has grown in popularity ever since. That these work-family shows are so popular might indicate some of our fascination with and our hopes for the world of work.

READING THE CULTURE OF WORK

As you read, talk, and write about work, you will be asked to pay attention to how the writers in this chapter voice their concerns about the state of their own workplace or the fairness of wages, working conditions, and advancement. The selections in this chapter represent the good and bad experiences of working, the arguments over downsizing, and the ongoing battles for a living wage for all workers. These writers can help you to explore your own expectations and disappointments in the work you do or the situations in which you often find yourself, or they might just as well suggest areas for further research.

We open with Sandra Cisneros's "The First Job," a story about a young woman experiencing the work world for the first time. Cisneros's story might prompt you to think about your own first expectations of the workplace and the times that you did not understand interactions with others or even the basic routine of the job you had been assigned.

In Robert J. Samuelson's "Downsizing Isn't All That Heartless," Manning Marable's "Fighting for a Decent Wage," and Barbara Ehrenreich's "Nickel-and-Dimed: On (Not) Getting By in America," we move away from individual stories and back to broader discussions of economic politics. The first two selections offer an opportunity to consider the issue of downsizing from very different positions, reminding readers that a phenomenon like downsizing has wide-ranging significance. Ehrenreich's experiment in working minimum-wage jobs and trying to make it on the income she made in those jobs throws into question the reported success of welfare reform policies.

The next selections ask you to reconsider what work and the workplace have come to mean in a high-technology, work-oriented culture. Juliet B. Schor's introduction to her book-length study, *The Overworked American: The Unexpected Decline of Leisure*, raises questions about what technology accomplishes if it does not provide workers with more leisure time. In fact, many workers choose to spend more and more time at work, not because they are being forced to but because they simply feel more "at home" in the workplace than in their own homes. At least that is what Arlie Russell Hochschild discovered when she interviewed workers for her article "Work: The Great Escape."

For others, however, the office might be the place where most of their time is spent, but it isn't so much a home away from home as it is a daily encounter with the absurd world of corporate decision making. In his article "The Dilbert Principle," Scott Adams explains how he creates the cartoon character Dilbert—perhaps the 1990s most popular and insightful commentator on the bureaucracy of office life.

To read the culture of work, you will need to think about your own work experiences, about how work has been represented in this culture, about how workers have interpreted their own work environments, and about what can be learned by researching current labor and marketplace issues. Throughout this chapter, you will be asked to think and write about the role that work plays in this culture.

Work, as you will see, is rarely just as simple as a place to go to earn a paycheck. Workers' identities are often tied to the work that they do or the work that they would like to do. We may not continue to believe in the simple logic of the Protestant work ethic, but this is a culture concerned at some level with the dignity of work. It is that concern for dignity and fair play that comes into nearly every discussion about work.

The First Job

Sandra Cisneros

Sanda Cisneros was born in Chicago, the daughter of a Mexican father and a Mexican American mother. She has been a poet in the schools, a teacher for high school dropouts, and an arts administrator. Cisneros is the author of *My Wicked Ways* (1987), a volume of poetry, *The House on Mango Street* (1985), a collection of stories from which the following selection has been excerpted, and *Woman Hollering Creek* (1991), a more recent collection of short stories.

SUGGESTION FOR READING

Write a brief description of a time when you found yourself in a situation that was uncomfortable—something that you did not expect. After you have read Cisneros's story, use your own memory piece to help you focus on what the event that she writes of means to you.

It wasn't as if I didn't want to work. I did. I had even gone to the social security office the month before to get my social security number. I needed money. The Catholic high school cost a lot, and Papa said nobody went to public school unless you wanted to turn out bad. I thought I'd find an easy job, the kind other kids had, working in the dime store or maybe a hotdog stand. And though I hadn't started looking yet, I thought I might the week after next. But when I came home that afternoon, all wet because Tito had pushed me into the open water hydrant—only I had sort of let him—Mama called me in the kitchen before I could even go and change, and Aunt Lala was sitting there drinking her coffee with a spoon. Aunt Lala said she had found a job for me at the Peter Pan Photo Finishers on North Broadway where she worked and how old was I and to show up tomorrow saying I was one year older and that was that.

So the next morning I put on the navy blue dress that made me look older and borrowed money for lunch and bus fare because Aunt Lala said I wouldn't get paid 'til the next Friday and I went in and saw the boss of the Peter Pan Photo Finishers on North Broadway where Aunt Lala worked and lied about my age like she told me to and sure enough I started that same day.

In my job I had to wear white gloves. I was supposed to match negatives with their prints, just look at the picture and look for the same one on the negative strip, put it in the envelope, and do the next one. That's all. I didn't know where these envelopes were coming from or where they were going. I just did what I was told.

It was real easy and I guess I wouldn't have minded it except that you got tired after a while and I didn't know if I could sit down or not, and then I started sitting down only when the two ladies next to me did. After a while they started to laugh and came up to me and said I could sit when I wanted to and I said I knew.

When lunch time came I was scared to eat alone in the company lunchroom with all those men and ladies looking, so I ate real fast standing in one of the washroom stalls and had lots of time left over so I went back to work early. But then break time came and not knowing where else to go I went into the coatroom because there was a bench there.

I guess it was time for the night shift or middle shift to arrive because a few people came in and punched the time clock and an older Oriental man said hello and we talked for a while about my just starting and he said we could be friends and next time to go in the lunchroom and sit with him and I felt better. He had nice eyes and I didn't feel so nervous anymore. Then he asked if I knew what day it was and when I said I didn't he said it was his birthday and would I please give him a birthday kiss. I thought I would because he was so old and just as I was about to put my lips on his cheek, he grabs my face with both hands and kisses me hard on the mouth and doesn't let go.

SUGGESTIONS FOR DISCUSSION

1. Why does the narrator tell us "It wasn't as if I didn't want to work"? How would you describe her motivations for getting a job, and how would you explain the situation in which she finds herself?

2. Compare the event that you wrote about before you read this story with the events that your classmates wrote about. Do any of them have anything in common with what Cisneros's narrator experienced? How common do you think an experience like hers is?

3. Why do you think the older man thought he could get away with his actions? Would anything comparable to this have happened to her had she been a young man?

SUGGESTIONS FOR WRITING

1. As readers, we often understand or relate to stories because they touch upon something that we already have experienced or an emotion that we have felt. Cisneros has written a story of a young woman's first day on a new job. Hers is a brief and confusing encounter with an adult world of which she had no prior knowledge. In an exploratory piece of writing, examine the narrator's response to this world of work and human interaction. What you write here will no doubt depend very much on your own experiences in the working world or in situations that seemed out of your control, so you may want to touch on the connection that you see between the narrator's experience and your own. It isn't necessary, though, to try to make this writing correspond to your own experiences. Even if you have experienced nothing like this, you probably have a reaction to or an understanding of how the young woman in this story felt. Use this writing to explain that reaction and how you think it is evoked in the story.

2. Reread Cisneros and notice how abruptly her story ends and especially how the attitude of the narrator shifts so suddenly in that last paragraph. Write an explanation of how that sudden shift changes the story. How does that ending affect the way that you understand what this story is about?

3. Tell a story about one of the first jobs you ever held (whether it was a paying job or just some new responsibility that you were asked to take on in the family, the community, your peer group, an organization, or for school or church). In your story, try to convey what the job meant to you and how you did or didn't fit into this new world. Like Cisneros, you will want to choose a moment that sticks with you for some reason, probably because it seemed to capsulize your entire experience with the world of work or the world of adults. In preparation for this writing, you might want to spend some time just listing jobs you found yourself doing and jotting memories of people, places, and events connected to those jobs. Notice how Cisneros manages to tell us a great deal about why she began working, about the workplace, and about the event that concludes this story in a very short piece of writing. Before you actually begin composing your story, reread Cisneros to see how the form of her narrative might help you to plan your own.

PERSPECTIVES: DOWNSIZING THE WORKFORCE

Throughout the 1990s the trend to downsize led to plant closings, large-scale layoffs, and what some have called exporting labor outside the United States to take advantage of lower wages and fewer environmental restrictions. Others, however, see downsizing as a necessary economic move in what has come to be called the Global Economy. In the two commentaries that follow, Robert Samuelson and Manning Marable argue from very different positions. Samuelson asks his readers to look at downsizing as a part of the larger picture of reshaping an economy. Marable asks readers to pay attention to the plight of the lowest paid labor—a group some have called "the working poor."

> This discussion, as you will see, actually centers on the question of whether or not, in the push for maximum profits, corporations can or should be held accountable for individuals workers' economic well-being.

Downsizing Isn't All That Heartless

Robert J. Samuelson

Robert J. Samuelson writes about the economy for the *Washington Post*. The editorial reprinted below appeared in a 1996 *Providence-Journal Bulletin,* where it was reprinted from *Newsweek*. Samuelson argues that, far from destroying the American workforce, downsizing might actually be good for the economy. His editorial is a response to a *New York Times* series *The Downsizing of America,* which appeared March 3–9, 1996, and was later published in a book-length edition.

SUGGESTION FOR READING

Samuelson purposefully offers an argument that contradicts much of the discussion on downsizing, especially the version offered by the *New York Times* series. Very quickly in the opening paragraph, Samuelson establishes his position: "I want to extend the discussion by suggesting that, in some respects, downsizing may improve the economy." As you read, keep that argument in mind and note in the margins the reasons that Samuelson gives for believing that downsizing could improve the economy.

Many labor market observers have asserted that the link between workers and employers has become more tenuous…labor market statistics, however, call into question the extent of any move toward less job stability.

Report on the American Work Force, U.S. Department of Labor, 1995

As the Labor Department report shows, the hysteria over downsizing—whipped up in part by Labor Secretary Robert Reich and a massive series in the *New York Times,* and reprinted this week in the *Journal-Bulletin*'s news pages—is just that. Companies are turning more often to layoffs, but there never was a time of total job security, and downsizing doesn't destroy most stable jobs. I have written about all this before, but now I want to extend the discussion by suggesting that, in some respects, downsizing may improve the economy.

It seems counterintuitive. We are uneasy with the possibility that what's bad for individuals may be good for society. But this may be, and the argument is not simply that downsizing enables some companies to survive. The notion is broader: It is that the anxieties that unsettle people may make them more prudent and productive in ways that strengthen the economy.

Though little noted, the present economic expansion recently became the third longest since World War II. It has lasted almost 60 months and is exceeded only by the expansions of the 1960s (106 months) and of the 1980s (92 months). But in some ways, it is superior to these because it hasn't yet spawned higher inflation. Since 1990, inflation has dropped from 6.1 percent to 2.5 percent. By contrast, it rose in the 1960s, from 1.4 percent in 1960 to 6.2 percent in 1969.

The 1960s boom is often viewed as a "golden age," when it actually set the stage for the most turbulent economic period since 1945. The severity of the two worst postwar recessions (those of 1973–75 and 1981–82, with peak monthly unemployment rates of 9 percent and

10.8 percent, respectively) stemmed directly from double-digit inflation (12.3 percent in 1974 and 13.3 percent in 1979).

We are much better off today in most respects. What happened? The answer, I think, is that there has been a profound shift in economic ideas. From the 1960s to the early 1980s, government officials and corporate managers consciously strove to expand employment, eliminate recessions and enhance job security.

The experiment failed: We got higher unemployment as well as higher inflation. In the 1980s, economic ideas changed. The Federal Reserve moved ruthlessly against inflation. Meanwhile, companies grew less concerned with saving jobs and focused more on raising market share and profits.

The result is that, since then, average unemployment has dropped and the one subsequent recession in 1990–91 was fairly mild (peak monthly unemployment—7.8 percent). One reason for improvement is that we finally recognized that the promises of economic stability and job security were self-defeating; they perversely inspired behavior that made both goals harder to achieve.

Quelling inflationary behavior has aided economic growth. Job fears have also reduced inflationary pressures by lowering wage demands. What economists call the "natural rate" of unemployment—the rate at which labor shortages trigger wage inflation—may have dropped. A crude consensus had put it around 6 percent; but in 1995, unemployment averaged 5.6 percent with (as yet) no sharp rise of inflation.

None of this means that there won't be future recessions (there will), that all downsizing is justified (it isn't) or that some workers don't suffer terribly (they do). But in a market economy, job loss is unavoidable, and the social harm may be muted if layoffs are spread out and not concentrated—as in the past—in slumps or periods of industry crisis. Fired workers can be rehired more quickly in a growing economy. The *Times* visits Dayton, Ohio, where "everything, seemingly, is in upheaval," in part because NCR (absorbed into AT&T) is downsizing. Belatedly, we learn that the county unemployment rate is only 4.8 percent. Contrast that with Flint, Mich., in the early 1980s, when auto layoffs sent the jobless rate to 20 percent.

What's missing in this debate is a sense of how jobs are created. Companies hire workers to make a profit; workers take jobs to make a living. If profitable hiring becomes too hard, firms won't do it; if being unemployed becomes too easy, people won't look for jobs. Europeans increasingly admire our flexibility, because their system—though outwardly more compassionate—stifles job creation. They have more generous jobless benefits, steeper payroll taxes (to pay for the benefits), more restrictions on firing and higher unemployment. In Germany, the jobless rate is 10.3 percent.

What Europe teaches is that societies can't outlaw job insecurity but they can inadvertently outlaw job creation. Our system isn't perfect, but we shouldn't trash it unless we know how to improve it. We don't.

Fighting for a Decent Wage

Manning Marable

> Manning Marable is director of the Institute for Research in African American Studies at Columbia University. The editorial below appeared in a 1996 issue of *The Witness* devoted specifically to the need for a new American labor movement. *The Witness* is a small magazine owned and published by the Episcopal Church Publishing Company. In its masthead, it describes itself as an "indepen-

dent journal with an ecumenical readership." Typically, the magazine is devoted to social issues, especially as U.S. churches have had a role in those issues.

SUGGESTION FOR READING

Marable's argument includes statistics about wages, the percentage of workers who are women, the growing number of working poor, and more. Those numbers are important to his discussion, but they can get lost by a reader if they seem to go by too quickly. As you read, make notes next to these statistics and pay particular attention to what information each set of numbers contributes to the evidence Marable is building for his claim that downsizing has been much worse for the economy than one may think. In other words, how is Marable using these statistics?

In the summer of 1969, my first real job was working in a large warehouse, unloading box cars and cleaning toilets. I earned the minimum wage, which at that time was $1.60 an hour. In today's wages, that was equal to $6.45. By working all summer, I earned enough to cover most of my first year's college tuition.

Today, millions of Americans work over 40 hours each week, and never take home enough money to feed and clothe their families. Minimum wage workers have been making $4.25 an hour, or approximately $170 for a 40-hour week. Almost 60 percent of these workers are women. Nearly two-thirds are adults who are trying to support their families.

In the 1980s, millions of new jobs were created in the U.S. economy, but relatively few were at wage levels that could support families. Eighty-five percent of all new jobs were located in low-pay or part-time service work. Nearly two out of ten workers had no health insurance, and two out of five had no pension. Economist Lester Thurow observes that "median household incomes have fallen more than 7 percent after correcting for inflation and family size, to $31,241 in 1993, from $33,585."

What is most significant about this decline is that the country's per capita Gross Domestic Product (GDP) was rising. Moreover, the share of wealth held by the top 1 percent of the U.S. population *doubled* in the last 20 years. As Thurow states: "In effect, we are conducting an enormous social and political experiment—something like putting a pressure cooker on the stove over a full flame and waiting to see how long it takes to explode."

Not only have American workers witnessed a decline in their standards of living, but they also face an increasingly uncertain future. In 1995, a study about employment trends in the metropolitan Chicago area was completed as part of the MacArthur Foundations' Working Poor Project. The study indicated that during the next 10 years, about 140,000 new jobs will be created in Chicago. One half of these jobs will be available to workers with a high school education—but none will pay more than an annual wage of $23,000, which is hardly enough to maintain a family. And the competition for skilled blue-collar jobs will be higher than ever before.

LOSING WHITE PRIVILEGE?

Another factor is the racial dimension of the class struggle. In unprecedented numbers, millions of white people are confronting what many African Americans and Latinos have known for years—unemployment, poverty and hunger. A recent study by Isaac Shapiro, of the Center on Budget and Policy Priorities, documents the growing crisis of non-Hispanic whites. One-half of all Americans living in poverty, nearly 18 million people, are white. For white female-headed households, more than one in three are poor. Between 1979 and 1991, the poverty rate for white families headed by an individual between 25 to 34 years old nearly doubled.

For millions of white Americans, "whiteness" used to mean a relatively privileged lifestyle, a standard of living superior to that of most racial minorities. Now as they are losing ground, they are desperately trying to understand why their "whiteness" no longer protects them. Alienated, angry white workers are finding the "American Dream" has become a nightmare. Politicians like Pat Buchanan offer them easy scapegoats—immigrants, blacks, Latinos, welfare recipients, the homeless—to explain their misery. But the empty rhetoric of Buchanan won't reverse the class warfare that is destroying millions of American households.

THE UNIONS

A half century ago, at the end of World War II, American unions and capital reached an agreement about the future of labor relations. The union movement essentially agreed to expel radicals and Communists from its ranks, and to limit strikes and militant actions. In return, the corporations shared their profits in the form of higher wages and benefits. By the early 1970s, American workers enjoyed the highest living standard in the world. As AFL-CIO president George Meany declared, "We believe in the American profit system."

But as global competition increased, capitalists cut costs, lowered wages and fired workers. Millions of jobs were shipped abroad to exploit low-wage, non-unionized labor. In many factories, occupational safety standards deteriorated, and employees lost many of their health benefits and pensions. But most unions had collaborated with the bosses for so long, they were unable to mount a counteroffensive against the corporations.

When President Reagan smashed the air traffic controllers' union during its 1981 strike, it sent a clear message to the corporations that union busting was on the immediate agenda. By 1987, nearly three-fourths of all contracts that covered 1,000 or more workers included wage concessions. Approximately 200,000 workers became non-union due to decertification elections in the 1980s. By the end of the decade, union membership declined to 16 percent of the American labor force. Workers lacked an effective, progressive labor movement which could fight for higher living standards.

Another reason that millions of American workers feel betrayed is the widespread wave of corporate layoffs. In the 1990s, as Wall Street stocks reached all-time highs and corporate profits soared, millions of workers were thrown out of work. In December, 1991, General Motors announced that it was firing 74,000 workers.

Barely one year later, Sears, Roebuck and Company fired 50,000 employees. Soon other corporations began to fire thousands of workers to improve their profitability. In 1993, Boeing dismissed 28,000 workers, Philip Morris cut 14,000, and IBM slashed 60,000 jobs. The next year, Delta Air Lines announced 15,000 layoffs, NYNEX cut 16,800 jobs, and Scott Paper fired more than one-third of its total work force, over 11,000 people. This January, AT&T Chief Executive Officer Robert Allen announced that his corporation was firing 40,000 employees. Coincidentally, Allen's annual salary at AT&T was $3.3 million.

Who can expect American workers to feel any loyalty to companies that only are concerned about profits and not people? Corporate executives pay themselves millions of dollars in salaries, fringe benefits, bonuses and stock options, while millions are losing their jobs. In 1975 the average chief executive officer of a corporation received about 40 times the salary of an average worker. Today that ratio has jumped to *190 times as much*. The typical CEO of America's 100 largest corporations receives about $900,000 in annual salary, and $3.5 million in overall compensation.

A LIVING WAGE

We need governmental policies which create jobs and promote income growth for working people. One essential step toward that goal is the reallocation of government expenditures from wasteful military spending into the social and economic infrastructure that makes productivity possible.

We urgently need to make massive public investments in housing, streets, highways, railroads, bridges, hospitals and clinics, public schools and universities to create new jobs.

One national organization that is leading the fight for decent wages is ACORN—the Association of Community Organizations for Reform Now. Last year, ACORN participated in the Chicago Jobs and Living Wage Campaign, a coalition of over 40 community groups, labor unions and religious leaders. The Campaign has called for a city ordinance requiring businesses that receive subsidies or hold city contracts to pay their workers at least $7.60 an hour. The majority of Chicago's City Council now supports the living wage ordinance, but it is opposed by Mayor Richard Daley. ACORN is also pushing for a living wage in St. Louis, Mo., and Houston, Tex.

However, the effort to achieve decent wages for working people will not be won without a struggle. In St. Paul, Minn., last year, a local initiative that would have required any company that received over $25,000 in public subsidies to pay their employees at least $7.21 an hour was defeated. Activists from ACORN, the New Party, religious and labor groups were viciously attacked by politicians and the press. A sophisticated campaign was orchestrated by one of St. Paul's largest public relations firms to mobilize opposition. Advocates for a living wage were smeared as "Stalinesque" and "job killers."

We cannot wait for Congress or Clinton to "do the right thing." Labor unions and civil rights organizations must lead a national campaign for a significant hike in the minimum wage, as well as for full employment legislation.

SUGGESTIONS FOR DISCUSSION

1. With a group of your classmates, begin your discussion by summarizing the evidence Samuelson gives to support his claim that downsizing might be a good thing for the economy. What of his evidence do you find compelling? What doesn't convince you? Why? Do the same with Marable's argument. Discuss, in particular, what Marable's statistics tell us about jobs and wages in the United States today. After you have completed your discussion, report your conclusions to the entire class.

2. Based on what you have read here, what do you think Marable would say to Samuelson's contention that "the anxieties that unsettle people may make them more prudent and productive in ways that strengthen the economy"?

3. Marable is making an argument that begins with a history of wages and jobs starting in the late 1960s and ends with a call to action. In his last paragraph he writes, "We cannot wait for Congress or Clinton to 'do the right thing.' Labor unions and civil rights organizations must lead a national campaign for a significant hike in the minimum wage, as well as for full employment legislation." How has Marable led his readers to this conclusion? To what extent are you persuaded by this argument? What would Samuelson's response be to that argument?

SUGGESTIONS FOR WRITING

1. Write a summary of Marable's and Samuelson's arguments. Be sure to include some representation of both the history they trace and the statistics they use in their arguments.

2. Marable and Samuelson offer very different ways of thinking about workers' rights and corporate responsibility. Reread these two articles and write a comparison in which you explain where the two essays seem to be making much the same argument and where they depart from each other.

3. Samuelson writes, "We are uneasy with the possibility that what's bad for individuals may be good for society. But this may be, and the argument is not simply that downsizing enables some companies to survive. The notion is broader: It is that the anxieties that unsettle people may make them more prudent and productive in ways that strengthen the economy." Reread Marable and then write and essay in which you suggest how he might respond to Samuelson's challenge. As you write your own essay, you will want to go back to Marable and point to specific passages from his commentary that already seem to counter or support or give a different dimension to Samuelson's claim.

Nickel-and-Dimed
On (Not) Getting By in America

Barbara Ehrenreich

Barbara Ehrenreich is a contributing editor of *Harper's Magazine,* a regular contributor to *The Nation,* and the author of a dozen books including *Fear of Falling: The Inner Life of the Middle Class* (1989), which was nominated for a National Book Critics Award. The following excerpts, taken from a longer essay detailing Ehrenreich's experiment with the life of minimum-wage labor, originally appeared in *Harper's* (January 1999).

SUGGESTION FOR READING

Throughout her narrative, Ehrenreich uses figures from such sources as the Department of Housing and Urban Development, the Economic Policy Institute, and the National Coalition for the Homeless to support her discussion of how difficult it is for anyone to live on the wages paid in most service jobs. It will help you keep track of Ehrenreich's argument if you keep those reports in mind as you read.

At the beginning of June 1998 I leave behind everything that normally soothes the ego and sustains the body—home, career, companion, reputation, ATM card—for a plunge into the low-wage workforce. There, I become another, occupationally much diminished "Barbara Ehrenreich"—depicted on job-application forms as a divorced homemaker whole sole work experience consists of housekeeping in a few private homes. I am terrified, at the beginning, of being unmasked for what I am: a middle-class journalist setting out to explore the world that welfare mothers are entering, at the rate of approximately 50,000 a month, as welfare reform kicks in. Happily, though, my fears turn out to be entirely unwarranted: during a month of poverty and toil, my name goes unnoticed and for the most part unuttered. In this parallel universe where my father never got out of the mines and I never got through college, I am "baby," "honey," "blondie," and, most commonly, "girl."

My first task is to find a place to live. I figure that if I can earn $7 an hour—which, from the want ads, seems doable—I can afford to spend $500 on rent, or maybe, with severe economies, $600. In the Key West area, where I live, this pretty much confines me to flop-houses and trailer homes—like the one, a pleasing fifteen-minute drive from town, that has no air-conditioning, no screens, no fans, no television, and, by way of diversion, only the challenge of evading the landlord's Doberman pinscher. The big problem with this place, though, is the rent, which at $675 a month is well beyond my reach. All right, Key West is expensive. But so is New York City, or the Bay Area, or Jackson Hole, or Telluride, or Boston, or any other place where tourists and the wealthy compete for living space with the people who clean their toilets and fry their hash browns.[1] Still, it is a shock to realize that "trailer trash" has become, for me, a demographic category to aspire to.

So I decide to make the common trade-off between affordability and convenience, and go for a $500-a-month efficiency thirty miles up a two-lane highway from the employment opportunities of Key West, meaning forty-five minutes if there's no road construction and I don't get caught behind some sun-dazed Canadian tourists. I hate the drive, along a roadside studded with white crosses commemorating the more effective head-on collisions, but it's a sweet little place—a cabin, more or less, set in the swampy back yard of the converted mobile home where my landlord, an affable TV repairman, lives with his bartender girlfriend. Anthropologically speaking, a bustling trailer park would be preferable, but here I have a gleaming white floor and a firm mattress, and the few resident bugs are easily vanquished.

Besides, I am not doing this for the anthropology. My aim is nothing so mistily subjective as to "experience poverty" or find out how it "really feels" to be a long-term low-wage worker. I've had enough unchosen encounters with poverty and the world of low-wage work to know it's not a place you want to visit for touristic purposes; it just smells too much like fear. And with all my real-life assets—bank account, IRA, health insurance, multiroom home—waiting indulgently in the background, I am, of course, thoroughly insulated from the terrors that afflict the genuinely poor.

No, this is a purely objective, scientific sort of mission. The humanitarian rationale for welfare reform—as opposed to the more punitive and stingy impulses that may actually have motivated it—is that work will lift poor women out of poverty while simultaneously inflating their self-esteem and hence their future value in the labor market. Thus, whatever the hassles involved in finding child care, transportation, etc., the transition from welfare to work will end happily, in greater prosperity for all. Now there are many problems with this comforting prediction, such as the fact that the economy will inevitably undergo a downturn, eliminating many jobs. Even without a downturn, the influx of a million former welfare recipients into the low-wage labor market could depress wages by as much as 11.9 percent, according to the Economic Policy Institute (EPI) in Washington, D.C.

But is it really possible to make a living on the kinds of jobs currently available to unskilled people? Mathematically, the answer is no, as can be shown by taking $6 to $7 an hour, perhaps subtracting a dollar or two an hour for child care, multiplying by 160 hours a month, and comparing the result to the prevailing rents. According to the National Coalition for the Homeless, for example, in 1998 it took, on average nationwide, an hourly wage of $8.89 to afford a one-bedroom apartment, and the Preamble Center for Public Policy estimates that the odds against a typical welfare recipient's landing a job at such a "living wage" are about 97 to 1. If these numbers are right, low-wage work is not a solution to poverty and possibly not even to homelessness.

It may seem excessive to put this proposition to an experimental test. As certain family members keep unhelpfully reminding me, the viability of low-wage work could be tested, after a fashion, without ever leaving my study. I could just pay myself $7 an hour for eight hours a day, charge myself for room and board, and total up the numbers after a month. Why leave the people and work that I love? But I am an experimental scientist by training. In that business, you don't just sit at a desk and theorize; you plunge into the everyday chaos of nature, where surprises lurk in the most mundane measurements. Maybe, when I got into it, I would discover some hidden economies in the world of the low-wage worker. After all, if 30 percent of the workforce toils for less than $8 an hour, according to the EPI, they may have found some tricks as yet unknown to me. Maybe—who knows?—I would even be able to detect in myself the bracing psychological effects of getting out of the house, as promised by the welfare wonks at places like the Heritage Foundation. Or, on the other hand, maybe there would be unexpected costs—physical, mental, or financial—to throw off all my calculations. Ideally, I should do this with two small children in tow, that being the welfare average, but mine are grown and no one is willing to lend me theirs for a month-long vacation in penury. So this is not the perfect experiment, just a test of the best possible case: an unencumbered woman, smart and even strong, attempting to live more or less off the land.

On the morning of my first full day of job searching, I take a red pen to the want ads, which are auspiciously numerous. Everyone in Key West's booming "hospitality industry" seems to be looking for someone like me—trainable, flexible, and with suitably humble expectations as to pay. I know I possess certain traits that might be advantageous—I'm white and, I like to think, well-spoken and poised—but I decide on two rules: One, I cannot use any skills derived from my education or usual work—not that there are a lot of want ads for satirical essayists anyway. Two, I have to take the best-paid job that is offered me and of course do my best to hold it; no Marxist rants or sneaking off to read novels in the ladies' room. In addition, I rule out various occupations for one reason or another: Hotel front-desk clerk, for example, which to my surprise is regarded as unskilled and pays around $7 an hour, gets eliminated because it involves standing in one spot for eight hours a day . Waitressing is similarly something I'd like to avoid, because I remember it leaving me bone tired when I was eighteen, and I'm decades of varicosities and back pain beyond that now. Telemarketing, one of the first refuges of the suddenly indigent, can be dismissed on grounds of personality. This leaves certain supermarket jobs, such as deli clerk, or housekeeping in Key West's thousands of hotel and guest rooms. Housekeeping is especially appealing, for reasons both atavistic and practical: it's what my mother did before I came along, and it can't be too different from what I've been doing part-time, in my own home, all my life.

So I put on what I take to be a respectful-looking outfit of ironed Bermuda shorts and scooped-neck T-shirt and set out for a tour of the local hotels and supermarkets. Best Western, Econo Lodge, and Ho Jo's all let me fill out application forms, and these are, to my relief, interested in little more than whether I am a legal resident of the United States and have committed any felonies. My next stop is Winn-Dixie, the supermarket, which turns out to have a particularly onerous application process, featuring a fifteen-minute "interview" by computer since, apparently, no human on the premises is deemed capable of representing the corporate point of view. I am conducted to a large room decorated with posters illustrating how to look "professional" (it helps to be white and, if female, permed) and warning of the slick promises that union organizers might try to tempt me with. The interview is multiple choice: Do I have anything, such as child-care problems, that might make it hard for me to get to work on time? Do I think safety on the job is the responsibility of management? Then, popping up cunningly out of the blue: How many dollars' worth of stolen goods have I purchased in the last year? Would I turn in a fellow employee if I caught him stealing? Finally, "Are you an honest person?"

Apparently, I ace the interview, because I am told that all I have to do is show up in some doctor's office tomorrow for a urine test. This seems to be a fairly general rule: if you want to stack Cheerio boxes or vacuum hotel rooms in chemically fascist America, you have to be willing to squat down and pee in front of some health worker (who has no doubt had to do the same thing herself). The wages Winn-Dixie is offering—$6 and a couple of dimes to start with—are not enough, I decide, to compensate for this indignity.[2]

I lunch at Wendy's, where $4.99 gets you unlimited refills at the Mexican part of the Superbar, a comforting surfeit of refried beans and "cheese sauce." A teenage employee, seeing me studying the want ads, kindly offers me an application form, which I fill out, though here, too, the pay is just $6 and change an hour. Then it's off for a round of the locally owned inns and guesthouses. At "The Palms," let's call it, a bouncy manager actually takes me around to see the rooms and meet the existing housekeepers, who, I note with satisfaction, look pretty much like me—faded ex-hippie types in shorts with long hair pulled back in braids. Mostly, though, no one speaks to me or even looks at me except to proffer an application form. At my last stop, a palatial B&B, I wait twenty minutes to meet "Max," only to be told that there are no jobs now but there should be one soon, since "nobody lasts more than a couple of week." (Because none of the people I talked to knew I was a reporter, I have changed their names to protect their privacy and, in some cases perhaps, their jobs.)

Three days go by like this, and, to my chagrin, no one out of the approximately twenty places I've applied calls me for an interview. I had been vain enough to worry about coming across as too educated for the jobs I sought, but no one even seems interested in finding out how overqualified I am. Only later will I realize that the want ads are not a reliable measure of the actual jobs available at any particular time. They are, as I should have guessed from Max's comment, the employers' insurance policy against the relentless turnover of the low-wage workforce. Most of the big hotels run ads almost continually, just to build a supply of applicants to replace the current workers as they drift away or are fired, so finding a job is just a matter of being at the right place at the right time and flexible enough to take whatever is being offered that day. This finally happens to me at one of the big discount hotel chains, where I go, as usual, for housekeeping and am sent, instead, to try out as a waitress at the attached "family restaurant," a dismal spot with a counter and about thirty tables that looks out on a parking garage and features such tempting fare as "Pollish [sic] sausage and BBQ sauce" on 95-degree days. Philip, the dapper young West Indian who introduces himself as the manager, interviews me with about as much enthusiasm as if he were a clerk processing me for Medicare, the principal questions being what shifts can I work and when can I start. I mutter something about being woefully out of practice as a waitress, but he's already on to the uniform: I'm to show up tomorrow wearing black slacks and black shoes; he'll provide the rust-colored polo shirt with HEARTHSIDE embroidered on it, though I might want to wear my own shirt to get to work, ha ha. At the word "tomorrow," something between fear and indignation rises in my chest. I want to say, "Thank you for your time, sir, but this is just an experiment, you know, not my actual life."

So begins my career at the Hearthside, I shall call it, one small profit center within a global discount hotel chain, where for two weeks I work from 2:00 till 10:00 P.M. for $2.43 an hour plus tips.[3] In some futile bid for gentility, the management has barred employees from using the front door, so my first day I enter through the kitchen, where a red-faced man with shoulder-length blond hair is throwing frozen steaks against the wall and yelling, "Fuck this shit!" "That's just Jack," explains Gail, the wiry middle-aged waitress who is assigned to train me. "He's on the rag again"—a condition occasioned, in this instance, by the fact that the cook on the morning shift had forgotten to thaw out the steaks. For the next eight hours, I run after the agile Gail, absorbing bits of instruction along with fragments of personal tragedy. All food must be trayed, and the reason she's so tired today is that she woke up in a cold sweat thinking of her boyfriend, who killed himself recently in an upstate prison. No refills on lemonade. And the reason he was in prison is that a few DUIs caught up with him, that's all, could have happened to anyone. Carry the creamers to the table in a monkey bowl, never in your hand. And after he was gone she spent several months living in her truck, peeing in a plastic pee bottle and reading by candlelight at night, but you can't live in a truck in the summer, since you need to have the windows down, which means anything can get in, from mosquitoes on up.

At least Gail put to rest any fears I had of appearing overqualified. From the first day on, I find that of all the things I have left behind, such as home and identity, what I miss the most is competence. Not that I have ever felt utterly competent in the writing business, in which one day's success augurs nothing at all for the next. But in my writing life, I at least have some notion of procedure: do the research, make the outline, rough out a draft, etc. As a server, though, I am beset by requests like bees: more iced tea here, ketchup over there, a to-go box for table fourteen, and where are the high chairs, anyway? Of the twenty-seven tables, up to six are usually mine at any time, though on slow afternoons or if Gail is off, I sometimes have the whole place to myself. There is the touch-screen computer-ordering system to master, which is, I suppose, meant to minimize server-cook contact, but in practice requires constant verbal fine-tuning: "That's gravy on the mashed, okay? None on the meatloaf," and so forth—while the cook scowls as if I were inventing these refinements just to torment him. Plus, something I had forgotten in the years since I was eighteen: about a third of a server's job is "side work" that's invisible to customers—sweeping, scrubbing, slicing, refilling, and restocking. If it isn't all done, every little bit of it, you're going to face the 6:00 P.M. dinner rush defenseless and probably go down in flames. I screw up dozens of times at the beginning, sustained in my shame entirely by Gail's support—"It's okay, baby, everyone does that sometime"—because, to my total surprise and despite the scientific detachment I am doing my best to maintain, I care.

You might imagine, from a comfortable distance, that people who live, year in and year out, on $6 to $10 an hour have discovered some survival stratagems unknown to the middle class. But no. It's not hard to get my co-workers to talk about their living situations, because housing, in almost every case, is the principal source of disruption in their lives, the first thing they fill you in on when they arrive for their shifts. After a week, I have compiled the following survey:

- Gail is sharing a room in a well-known downtown flophouse for which she and a roommate pay about $250 a week. Her roommate, a male friend, has begun hitting on her, driving her nuts, but the rent would be impossible alone.

- Claude, the Haitian cook, is desperate to get out of the two-room apartment he shares with his girlfriend and two other, unrelated, people. As far as I can determine, the other Haitian men (most of whom only speak Creole) live in similarly crowded situations.

- Annette, a twenty-year-old server who is six months pregnant and has been abandoned by her boyfriend, lives with her mother, a postal clerk.

- Marianne and her boyfriend are paying $170 a week for a one-person trailer.

- Jack, who is, at $10 an hour, the wealthiest of us, lives in the trailer he owns, paying only the $400-a-month lot fee.

- The other white cook, Andy, lives on his dry-docked boat, which, as far as I can tell from his loving descriptions, can't be more than twenty feet long. He offers to take me out on it, once it's repaired, but the offer comes with inquiries as to my marital status, so I do not follow up on it.

- Tina and her husband are paying $60 a night for a double room in a Days Inn. This is because they have no car and the Days Inn is within walking distance of the Hearthside. When Marianne, one of the breakfast servers, is tossed out of her trailer for subletting (which is against the trailer-park rules), she leaves her boyfriend and moves in with Tina and her husband.

- Joan, who had fooled me with her numerous and tasteful outfits (hostesses wear their own clothes), lives in a van she parks behind a shopping center at night and showers in Tina's motel room. The clothes are from thrift shops.[4]

When I moved out of the trailer park, I gave the key to number 46 to Gail and arranged for my deposit to be transferred to her. She told me that Joan is still living in her van and that Stu had been fired from the Hearthside. I never found out what happened to George.

In one month, I had earned approximately $1,040 and spent $517 on food, gas, toiletries, laundry, phone, and utilities. If I had remained in my $500 efficiency, I would have been able to pay the rent and have $22 left over (which is $78 less than the cash I had in my pocket at the start of one month). During this time I bought no clothing except for the required slacks and no prescription drugs or medical care (I did finally buy some vitamin B to compensate for the lack of vegetables in my diet). Perhaps I could have saved a little on food if I had gotten to a supermarket more often, instead of convenience stores, but it should be noted that I lost almost four pounds in four weeks, on a diet weighted heavily toward burgers and fries.

How former welfare recipients and single mothers will (and do) survive in the low-wage workforce, I cannot imagine. Maybe they will figure out how to condense their lives—including child-raising, laundry, romance, and meals—into the couple of hours between full-time jobs. Maybe they will take up residence in their vehicles, if they have one. All I know is that I couldn't hold two jobs and I couldn't make enough money to live on with one. And I had advantages unthinkable to many of the long-term poor—health, stamina, a working car, and no children to care for and support. Certainly nothing in my experience contradicts the conclusion of Kathryn Edin and Laura Lein, in their recent book *Making Ends Meet: How Single Mothers Survive Welfare and Low-Wage Work*, that low-wage work actually involves more hardship and deprivation than life at the mercy of the welfare state. In the coming months and years, economic conditions for the working poor are bound to worsen, even without the almost inevitable recession. As mentioned earlier, the influx of former welfare recipients into the low-skilled workforce will have a depressing effect on both wages and the number of jobs available. A general economic downturn will only enhance these effects, and the working poor will of course be facing it without the slight, but nonetheless often saving, protection of welfare as a backup.

The thinking behind welfare reform was that even the humblest jobs are morally uplifting and psychologically buoying. In reality they are likely to be fraught with insult and stress. But I did discover one redeeming feature of the most abject low-wage work—the camaraderie of people who are, in almost all cases, far too smart and funny and caring for the work they do and the wages they're paid. The hope, of course, is that someday these people will come to know what they're worth, and take appropriate action.

Notes

1. According to the Department of Housing and Urban Development, the "fair-market rent" for an efficiency is $551 here in Monroe County, Florida. A comparable rent in the five boroughs of New York City is $704; in San Francisco, $713; and in the heart of Silicon Valley, $808. The fair-market

rent for an area is defined as the amount that would be needed to pay rent plus utilities for "privately owned, decent, safe, and sanitary rental housing of a modest (non-luxury) nature with suitable amenities."

2. According to the *Monthly Labor Review* (November 1996), 28 percent of work sites surveyed in the service industry conduct drug tests (corporate workplaces have much higher rates), and the incidence of testing has risen markedly since the Eighties. The rate of testing is highest in the South (56 percent of work sites polled), with the Midwest in second place (50 percent). The drug most likely to be detected—marijuana, which can be detected in urine for weeks—is also the most innocuous, while heroin and cocaine are generally undetectable three days after use. Prospective employees sometimes try to cheat the tests by consuming excessive amounts of liquids and taking diuretics and even masking substances available through the Internet.

3. According to the Fair Labor Standards Act, employers are not required to pay "tipped employees," such as restaurant servers, more than $2.13 an hour in direct wages. However, if the sum of tips plus $2.13 an hour falls below the minimum wage, or $5.15 an hour, the employer is required to make up the difference. This fact was not mentioned by managers or otherwise publicized at either of the restaurants where I worked.

4. I could find no statistics on the number of employed people living in cars or vans, but according to the National Coalition for the Homeless's 1997 report, "Myths and Facts About Homelessness," nearly one in five homeless people (in twenty-nine cities across the nation) is employed in a full- or part-time job.

SUGGESTIONS FOR DISCUSSION

1. Ehrenreich tells the story of her own experience and of the lives of people she encountered during her experiment. She also makes an argument using both her story and the studies and reports she cites. With a group of your classmates, summarize Ehrenreich's argument. What in the argument depends on her stories of individuals and what depends on the broader reports and studies?

2. Currently one fast food chain is running advertisements in which they depict jobs at their restaurants as "starter jobs." In these commercials, employees are shown making shakes or handing food out the drive-up window, or ringing up an order while the voice-over tells us that one is a future aerospace engineer, and another is a future CEO of a multi-million-dollar corporation. Why might a successful fast food chain bother to make what is clearly an image-building advertisement? Why focus on the future of its employees?

3. How does Ehrenreich's discussion of minimum-wage work touch on Marable's discussion of downsizing and corporate responsibility? Given his position on the economy, what might Samuelson say of Ehrenreich's conclusions?

SUGGESTIONS FOR WRITING

1. Make a list of service-sector jobs that you are familiar with—because you have held them or have frequented a business that depends on them (fast food restaurants, motels, bars, for example). Write an essay in which you examine to what extent Ehrenreich's experience working in the service sector rings true for you. How does your own experience (or lack of experience) with these kinds of jobs influence your reading?

2. Ehrenreich writes that she does not expect to "experience poverty" because she is aware that she can always go back to her middle-class lifestyle when things get tough or when she tires of this life. In addition, she admits that friends have pointed out that if she just wants to prove that it is extremely difficult to live on minimum-wage work, she can do that easily enough on paper. Given that Ehrenreich knows she does not have to do the experiment, write an assessment of what she accomplished by posing as an out-of-work, down-on-her-luck single woman.

3. Write an essay in which you examine Ehrenreich's argument about the life of minimum-wage workers in light of what Samuelson and Marable say are the realities of the economy and of labor. What does Ehrenreich add to this discussion? What does she leave out?

The Overworked American

Juliet B. Schor

Economist Juliet Schor argues in the following excerpt from *The Overworked American: The Unexpected Decline of Leisure* that, although we can now produce as much in four hours as it once took eight hours to produce, Americans work longer, less productive hours than ever before. Her analysis of contemporary working conditions raises questions about how our work and leisure time are spent and what it is that we call leisure. At the time of this book's publication, Juliet Schor was associate professor of economics at Harvard University.

SUGGESTION FOR READING

Although Schor's analysis is about work, it is more specifically about the loss of leisure time. As you read, pay particular attention to and annotate those passages in which Schor makes her argument about how the decline of leisure in America today affects our lives.

In the last twenty years the amount of time Americans have spent at their jobs has risen steadily. Each year the change is small, amounting to about nine hours, or slightly more than one additional day of work. In any given year such a small increment has probably been imperceptible. But the accumulated increase over two decades is substantial. When surveyed, Americans report that they have only sixteen and a half hours of leisure a week, after the obligations of job and household are taken care of. Working hours are already longer than they were forty years ago. If present trends continue, by the end of the century Americans will be spending as much time at their jobs as they did back in the nineteen twenties.

The rise of worktime was unexpected. For nearly a hundred years, hours had been declining. When this decline abruptly ended in the late 1940s, it marked the beginning of a new era in worktime. But the change was barely noticed. Equally surprising, but also hardly recognized, has been the deviation from Western Europe. After progressing in tandem for nearly a century, the United States veered off into a trajectory of declining leisure, while in Europe work has been disappearing. Forty years later, the differences are large. U.S. manufacturing employees currently work 320 more hours—the equivalent of over two months—than their counterparts in West Germany or France.

The decline in Americans' leisure time is in sharp contrast to the potential provided by the growth of productivity. Productivity measures the goods and services that result from each hour worked. When productivity rises, a worker can either produce the current output in less time, or remain at work the same number of hours and produce more. Every time productivity increases, we are presented with the possibility of either more free time or more money. That's the productivity dividend.

Since 1948, productivity has failed to rise in only five years. The level of productivity of the U.S. worker has more than doubled. In other words, we could now produce our 1948 standard of living (measured in terms of marketed goods and services) in less than half the time it took in that year. We actually could have chosen the four-hour day. Or a working year of six months. Or, *every worker in the United States could now be taking every other year off from work—with pay.* Incredible as it may sound, this is just the simple arithmetic of productivity growth in operation.

But between 1948 and the present we did not use any of the productivity dividend to reduce hours. In the first two decades after 1948, productivity grew rapidly, at about 3 percent a year. During that period, worktime did not fall appreciably. Annual hours per labor force participant fell only slightly. And on a per-capita (rather than a labor force) basis, they even rose a bit. Since then, productivity growth has been lower, but still positive, averaging just over 1 percent a year. Yet hours have risen steadily for two decades. In 1990, the average American owns and consumes more than twice as much as he or she did in 1948, but also has less free time.

How did this happen? Why has leisure been such a conspicuous casualty of prosperity? In part, the answer lies in the difference between the markets for consumer products and free time. Consider the former, the legendary American market. It is a veritable consumer's paradise, offering a dazzling array of products varying in style, design, quality, price, and country of origin. The consumer is treated to GM versus Toyota, Kenmore versus GE, Sony, or Magnavox, the Apple versus the IBM. We've got Calvin Klein, Anne Klein, Liz Claiborne, and Levi-Strauss; McDonald's, Burger King, and Colonel Sanders. Marketing experts and advertisers spend vast sums of money to make these choices appealing—even irresistible. And they have been successful. In cross-country comparisons, Americans have been found to spend more time shopping than anyone else. They also spend a higher fraction of the money they earn. And with the explosion of consumer debt, many are now spending what they haven't earned.

After four decades of this shopping spree, the American standard of living embodies a level of material comfort unprecedented in human history. The American home is more spacious and luxurious than the dwellings of any other nation. Food is cheap and abundant. The typical family owns a fantastic array of household and consumer appliances: we have machines to wash our clothes and dishes, mow our lawns, and blow away our snow. On a per-person basis, yearly income is nearly $22,000 a year—or sixty-five times the average income of half the world's population.

On the other hand, the "market" for free time hardly even exists in America. With few exceptions, employers (the sellers) don't offer the chance to trade off income gains for a shorter work day or the occasional sabbatical. They just pass on income, in the form of annual pay raises or bonuses, or, if granting increased vacation or personal days, usually do so unilaterally. Employees rarely have the chance to exercise an actual choice about how they will spend their productivity dividend. The closest substitute for a "market in leisure" is the travel and other leisure industries that advertise products to occupy our free time. But this indirect effect has been weak, as consumers crowd increasingly expensive leisure spending into smaller periods of time.

Nor has society provided a forum for deliberate choice. The growth of worktime did not occur as a result of public debate. There has been little attention from government, academia, or civic organizations. For the most part, the issue has been off the agenda, a nonchoice, a hidden trade off. It was not always so. As early as 1791, when Philadelphia carpenters went on strike for the ten-hour day, there was public awareness about hours of work. Throughout the nineteenth century, and well into the twentieth, the reduction of worktime was one of the nation's most pressing social issue. Employers and workers fought about the length of the working day, social activists delivered lectures, academics wrote treatises, courts handed down decisions, and government legislated hours of work. Through the Depression, hours remained a major social preoccupation. Today these debates and conflicts are long forgotten. Since the 1930s, the choice between work and leisure has hardly been a choice at all, at least in any conscious sense.

In its starkest terms, my argument is this: Key incentive structures of capitalist economies contain biases toward long working hours. As a result of these incentives, the development of capitalism led to the growth of what I call "long hour jobs." The eventual recovery of leisure came about because trade unions and social reformers waged a protracted struggle for shorter hours. Some time between the Depression and the end of the Second World War, that struggle collapsed. As the inevitable pressures toward long hours reasserted themselves, U.S. workers experienced a new decline that now, at the century's end, has created a crisis of leisure time. I am aware that these are strong claims which overturn most of what we have been taught to believe about the way our economy works....

Ironically, the tendency of capitalism to expand work is often associated with a growth in joblessness. In recent years, as a majority have taken on the extra month of work, nearly one-fifth of all participants in the labor force are unable to secure as many hours as they want or need to make ends meet. While many employees are subjected to mandatory overtime and are suffering from overwork, their co-workers are put on involuntary part-time. In the context of my story, these irrationalities seem to make sense. The rational, and humane, solution—reducing hours to spread the work—has practically been ruled out of court.

In speaking of "long hour jobs" exclusively in terms of the capitalist marketplace, I do not mean to overlook those women who perform their labor in the privacy of their own homes. Until the late nineteenth century, large numbers of single and married women did participate in the market economy, either in farm labor or through various entrepreneurial activities (taking in boarders, sewing at home, and so on). By the twentieth century, however, a significant percentage of married women, particularly white women, spent all their time outside the market nexus, as full-time "domestic laborers," providing goods and, increasingly, services for their families. And they, too, have worked at "long hour jobs."

Studies of household labor beginning in the 1910s and continuing through to the 1970s show that the amount of time a full-time housewife devoted to her work remained virtually unchanged for over fifty years—despite dramatic changes in household technology. As homes, like factories, were "industrialized," refrigerators, laundry machines, vacuum cleaners, and microwaves took up residence in the American domicile. Ready-made clothes and processed food supplanted the home-produced variety. Yet with all these labor-saving innovations, no labor has been saved. Instead, housework expanded to fill the available time. Norms of cleanliness rose. Standards of mothering grew more rigorous. Cooking and baking became more complicated. At the same time, a variety of cheaper and more efficient ways of providing household services failed in the market, and housewives continued to do their own.

The stability of housewives' hours was due to a particular bias in the incentives of what we may term the "labor market for housewives." Just as the capitalist labor market contains structural biases toward long hours, so too has the housewife's situation....And in neither case has technology automatically saved labor. It has taken women's exodus from the home itself to reduce their household labor. As women entered paid employment, they cut back their hours of domestic work significantly—but not by enough to keep their total working time unchanged. According to my estimates, when a woman takes a paying job, her schedule expands by at least twenty hours a week. The overwork that plagues many Americans, especially married women, springs from a combination of full-time male jobs, the expansion of housework to fill the available hours, and the growth of employment among married women.

However scarce academic research on the rising workload may be, what we do know suggests it has contributed to a variety of social problems. For example, work is implicated in the dramatic rise of "stress." Thirty percent of adults say that they experience high stress nearly every day; even higher numbers report high stress once or twice a week. A third of the population says that they are rushed to do the things they have to do—up from a quarter in 1965. Stress-related diseases have exploded, especially among women, and jobs are a major factor. Workers' compensation claims related to stress tripled during just the first half of the 1980s. Other evidence also suggests a rise in the demands placed on employees on the job. According to a recent review of existing findings, Americans are literally working themselves to death—as jobs contribute to heart disease, hypertension, gastric problems, depression, exhaustion, and a variety of other ailments. Surprisingly, the high-powered jobs are not the most dangerous. The most stressful workplaces are the "electronic sweatshops" and assembly lines where a demanding pace is coupled with virtually no individual discretion.

Sleep has become another casualty of modern life. According to sleep researchers, studies point to a "sleep deficit" among Americans, a majority of whom are currently getting between 60 and 90 minutes less a night than they should for optimum health and performance. The number of people showing up at sleep disorder clinics with serious problems has skyrocketed in the last decade. Shiftwork, long working hours, the growth of a global economy (with its attendant continent-hopping and twenty-four-hour business culture), and the accelerating pace of life have all contributed to sleep deprivation. If you need an alarm clock, the experts warn, you're probably sleeping too little.

The juggling act between job and family is another problem area. Half the population now says they have too little time for their families. The problem is particularly acute for women: in one study, half of all employed mothers reported it caused either "a lot" or an "extreme" level of stress. The same proportion feel that "when I'm at home I try to make up to my family for being away at work, and as a result I rarely have any time for myself." This stress has placed tremendous burdens on marriages. Two-earner couples have less time together, which researchers have found reduces the happiness and satisfaction of a marriage. These couples often just don't have enough time to talk to each other. And growing numbers of husbands and wives are like ships passing in the night, working sequential schedules to manage their child care. Among young parents the prevalence of at least one partner working outside regular daytime hours is now close to one half. But this "solution" is hardly a happy one. According to one parent: "I work 11–7 to accommodate my family—to eliminate the need for babysitters. However, the stress on myself is tremendous."

A decade of research by Berkeley sociologist Arlie Hochschild suggests that many marriages where women are doing the "second shift" are close to the breaking point. When job, children, and marriage have to be attended to, it's often the marriage that is neglected. The failure of many men to do their share at home creates further problems. A twenty-six-year-old legal secretary in California reports that her husband "does no cooking, no washing, no anything else. How do I feel? Furious. If our marriage ends, it will be on this issue. And it just might."

Serious as these problems are, the most alarming development may be the effect of the work explosion on the care of children. According to economist Sylvia Hewlett, "child neglect has become endemic to our society." A major problem is that children are increasingly left alone, to fend for themselves while their parents are at work. Nationwide, estimates of children in "self"—or, more accurately, "no"—care range up to seven million. Local studies have found figures of up to one-third of children caring for themselves. At least half a million preschoolers are thought to be left at home part of each day. One 911 operator reports large numbers of frightened callers: "It's not uncommon to hear from a child of six or seven who has been left in charge of even younger siblings."

Even when parents are at home, overwork may leave them with limited time, attention, or energy for their children. One working parent noted, "My child has severe emotional problems because I am too tired to listen to him. It is not quality time; it's bad quantity time that's destroying my family." Economist Victor Fuchs has found that between 1960 and 1986, the time parents actually had available to be with children fell ten hours a week for whites and twelve for blacks. Hewlett links the "parenting deficit" to a variety of problems plaguing the country's youth: poor performance in school, mental problems, drug and alcohol use, and teen suicide. According to another expert, kids are being "cheated out of childhood....There is a sense that adults don't care about them."

Of course, there's more going on here than lack of time. Child neglect, marital distress, sleep deprivation and stress-related illnesses all have other causes. But the growth of work has exacerbated each of these social ailments. Only by understanding why we work as much as we do, and how the demands of work affect family life, can we hope to solve these problems.

The past forty years should provide a warning. They have brought us nothing in the way of leisure time and a saner pace of life. The bias of the system is strongly toward the status quo. But time poverty is straining the social fabric. Continued growth threatens environmental balance, and gender equality requires new work patterns. Despite these obstacles, I am hopeful. By understanding how we came to be caught up in the cycle of work-and-spend, perhaps we can regain a reasonable balance between work and leisure.

SUGGESTIONS FOR DISCUSSION

1. Make a list of some of the people that you know well who hold jobs outside the home. How much leisure time would you estimate that most of them have? Do you think that any of them would identify a lack of leisure time as a particular problem for them?

2. Explain the connection that Schor makes between the loss of leisure time and the rise of conspicuous consumption.

3. With a group of classmates, discuss why or why not the loss of leisure time should be a serious concern for anyone about to enter the job market or for others who have been working for many years.

SUGGESTIONS FOR WRITING

1. Summarize Shor's arguments for the reevaluation of workloads. Make sure you include her historical argument as well as her discussion of the problems connected with diminished leisure time.

2. As others have, Schor argues that labor-saving technology may end up increasing rather than decreasing our workload. Write an essay in which you identify specific labor-saving technology that has actually increased your own work. (Some would argue, for example, that word processors make us work more rather than less on our writing.)

3. Write an essay in which you spell out your own position on the value of, loss of, or usefulness of leisure time. Write from your reading, from your experience, and from your observations of others.

Work: The Great Escape

Arlie Russell Hochschild

> Arlie Russell Hochschild is a professor of sociology at the University of California at Berkeley. For over three years, Hochschild interviewed workers about their jobs and their daily routines in preparation for her book *The Time Bind: When Work Becomes Home and Home Becomes Work*. The selection reprinted here has been adapted from that book and originally appeared in the *New York Times Magazine* (April 20, 1997). In it, Hochschild describes the workplace as a haven from the tensions of home. Hers is a departure from more recent discussions of Americans who spend too much time at work with no time left in their lives for leisure or family activities. According to Hochschild's research, Americans are spending more time at work not because they must but because they want to.

SUGGESTION FOR READING

> Hochschild alternates her argument about work as refuge with stories of workers who choose to spend more time at work than they might have to. As you read, pay attention to each of these stories as individual examples of the larger argument that Hochschild wants to make.

Over three years, I interviewed 130 respondents for a book. They spoke freely and allowed me to follow them through "typical" days, on the understanding that I would protect their anonymity. I have changed the names of the company and of those I interviewed, and altered certain identifying details. Their words appear here as they were spoken.—A. R. H.

It's 7:40 A.M. when Cassie Bell, 4, arrives at the Spotted Deer Child-Care Center, her hair half-combed, a blanket in one hand, a fudge bar in the other. "I'm late," her mother, Gwen, a sturdy young woman whose short-cropped hair frames a pleasant face, explains to the child-care worker in charge. "Cassie wanted the fudge bar so bad, I gave it to her," she adds apologetically.

"*Pleeese*, can't you take me with you?" Cassie pleads.

"You know I can't take you to work," Gwen replies in a tone that suggests that she has been expecting this request. Cassie's shoulders droop. But she has struck a hard bargain—the morning fudge bar—aware of her mother's anxiety about the long day that lies ahead at the center. As Gwen explains later, she continually feels that she owes Cassie more time than she gives her—she has a "time debt."

Arriving at her office just before 8, Gwen finds on her desk a cup of coffee in her personal mug, milk no sugar (exactly as she likes it), prepared by a co-worker who managed to get in ahead of her. As the assistant to the head of public relations at a company I will call Amerco, Gwen has to handle responses to any reports that may appear about the company in the press—a challenging job, but one that gives her satisfaction. As she prepares for her first meeting of the day, she misses her daughter, but she also feels relief; there's a lot to get done at Amerco.

Gwen used to work a straight eight-hour day. But over the last three years, her workday has gradually stretched to eight and a half or nine hours, not counting the E-mail messages and faxes she answers from home. She complains about her hours to her co-workers and listens to their complaints—but she loves her job. Gwen picks up Cassie at 5:45 and gives her a long, affectionate hug.

At home, Gwen's husband, John, a computer programmer, plays with their daughter while Gwen prepares dinner. To protect the dinner "hour"—8:00–8:30—Gwen checks that the phone machine is on, hears the phone ring during dinner but resists the urge to answer. After Cassie's bath, Gwen and Cassie have "quality time," or "Q.T.," as John affectionately calls it. Half an hour later, at 9:30, Gwen tucks Cassie into bed.

There are, in a sense, two Bell households: the rushed family they actually are and the relaxed family they imagine they might be if only they had time. Gwen and John complain that they are in a time bind. What they say they want seems so modest—time to throw a ball, to read to Cassie, to witness the small dramas of her development, not to speak of having a little fun and romance themselves. Yet even these modest wishes seem strangely out of reach. Before going to bed, Gwen has to E-mail messages to her colleagues in preparation for the next day's meeting; John goes to bed early, exhausted—he's out the door by 7 every morning.

Nationwide, many working parents are in the same boat. More mothers of small children than ever now work outside the home. In 1993, 56 percent of women with children between 6 and 17 worked outside the home full time year round; 43 percent of women with children 6 and under did the same. Meanwhile, fathers of small children are not cutting back hours of work to help out at home. If anything, they have increased their hours at work. According to a 1993 national survey conducted by the Families and Work Institute in New York, American men average 48.8 hours of work a week, and women 41.7 hours, including overtime and commuting. All in all, more women are on the economic train, and for many—men and women alike—that train is going faster.

But Amerco has "family friendly" policies. If your division head and supervisor agree, you can work part time, share a job with another worker, work some hours at home, take parental leave or use "flex time." But hardly anyone uses these policies. In seven years, only two Amerco fathers have taken formal parental leave. Fewer than 1 percent have taken advantage of the opportunity to work part time. Of all such policies, only flex time—which rearranges but does not shorten work time—has had a significant number of takers (perhaps a third of working parents at Amerco).

Forgoing family-friendly policies is not exclusive to Amerco workers. A 1991 study of 188 companies conducted by the Families and Work Institute found that while a majority offered part-time shifts, fewer than 5 percent of employees made use of them. Thirty-five percent offered "flex place"—work from home—and fewer than 3 percent of their employees took advantage of it. And an earlier Bureau of Labor Statistics survey asked workers whether they preferred a shorter workweek, a longer one or their present schedule. About 62 percent preferred their present schedule; 28 percent would have preferred longer hours. Fewer than 10 percent said they wanted a cut in hours.

Still, I found it hard to believe that people didn't protest their long hours at work. So I contacted Bright Horizons, a company that runs 136 company-based child-care centers associated with corporations, hospitals and Federal agencies in 25 states. Bright Horizons allowed me to add questions to a questionnaire they sent out to 3,000 parents whose children attended the centers. The respondents, mainly middle-class parents in their early 30's, largely confirmed the picture I'd found at Amerco. A third of fathers and a fifth of mothers described themselves as "workaholic," and 1 out of 3 said their partners were.

To be sure, some parents have tried to shorten their hours. Twenty-one percent of the nation's women voluntarily work part time, as do 7 percent of men. A number of others make under-the-table arrangements that don't show up on surveys. But while working parents say they need more time at home, the main story of their lives does not center on a struggle to get it. Why? Given the hours parents are working these days, why aren't they taking advantage of an opportunity to reduce their time at work?

The most widely held explanation is that Working Parents cannot afford to work shorter hours. Certainly this is true for many. But if money is the whole explanation, why would it be that at places like Amerco, the best-paid employees—upper-level managers and professionals—were the least interested in part-time work or job sharing, while clerical workers who earned less were more interested?

Similarly, if money were the answer, we would expect poorer new mothers to return to work more quickly after giving birth than rich mothers. But among working women nationwide, well-to-do new mothers are not much more likely to stay home after 13 weeks with a new baby than low-income new mothers. When asked what they look for in a job, only a third of respondents in a recent study said salary came first. Money is important, but by itself, money does not explain why many people don't want to cut back hours at work.

A second explanation goes that workers don't dare ask for time off because they are afraid it would make them vulnerable to layoffs. With recent downsizings at many large corporations, and with well-paying, secure jobs being replaced by lower-paying, insecure ones, it occurred to me that perhaps employees are "working scared." But when I asked Amerco employees whether they worked long hours for fear of getting on a layoff list, virtually everyone said no. Even among a particularly vulnerable group—factory workers who were laid off in the downturn of the early 1980's and were later rehired—most did not cite fear for their jobs as the only, or main, reason they worked overtime. For unionized workers, layoffs are assigned by seniority, and for nonunionized workers, layoffs are usually related to the profitability of the division a person works in, not to an individual work schedule.

Were workers uninformed about the company's family-friendly policies? No. Some even mentioned that they were proud to work for a company that offered such enlightened policies. Were rigid middle managers standing in the way of workers using these policies? Sometimes. But when I compared Amerco employees who worked for flexible managers with those who worked for rigid managers, I found that the flexible managers reported only a few more applicants than the rigid ones. The evidence, however counterintuitive, pointed to a paradox: workers at the company I studied weren't protesting the time bind. They were accommodating to it.

Why? I did not anticipate the conclusion I found myself coming to: namely, that work has become a form of "home" and home has become "work." The worlds of home and work have not begun to blur, as the conventional wisdom goes, but to reverse places. We are used to thinking that home is where most people feel the most appreciated, the most truly "themselves," the most secure, the most relaxed. We are used to thinking that work is where most people feel like "just a number" or "a cog in a machine." It is where they have to be "on," have to "act," where they are least secure and most harried.

But new management techniques so pervasive in corporate life have helped transform the workplace into a more appreciative, personal sort of social world. Meanwhile, at home the divorce rate has risen, and the emotional demands have become more baffling and complex. In addition to teething, tantrums and the normal developments of growing children, the needs of elderly parents are creating more tasks for the modern family—as are the blending, unblending, reblending of new stepparents, stepchildren, exes and former in-laws.

This idea began to dawn on me during one of my first interviews with an Amerco worker. Linda Avery, a friendly, 38-year-old mother, is a shift supervisor at an Amerco plant. When I meet her in the factory's coffee-break room over a couple of Cokes, she is wearing blue jeans and a pink jersey, her hair pulled back in a long, blond ponytail. Linda's husband, Bill, is a technician in the same plant. By working different shifts, they manage to share the care of their 2-year-old son and Linda's 16-year-old daughter from a previous marriage. "Bill works the 7 A.M. to 3 P.M. shift while I watch the baby," she explains. "Then I work the 3 P.M. to 11 P.M. shift and he watches the baby. My daughter works at Walgreen's after school."

Linda is working overtime, and so I begin by asking whether Amerco required the overtime, or whether she volunteered for it. "Oh, I put in for it," she replies. I ask her whether, if finances and company policy permitted, she'd be interested in cutting back on the overtime. She takes off her safety glasses, rubs her face and, without answering my question, explains: "I get home, and the minute I turn the key, my daughter is right there. Granted, she needs somebody to talk to about her day....The baby is still up. He should have been in bed two hours ago, and that upsets me. The dishes are piled in the sink. My daughter comes right up to the door and complains about anything her stepfather said or did, and she wants to talk about her job. My husband is in the other room hollering to my daughter, 'Tracy, I don't ever get any time to talk to your mother, because you're always monopolizing her time before I even get a chance!' They all come at me at once."

Linda's description of the urgency of demands and the unarbitrated quarrels that await her homecoming contrast with her account of arriving at her job as a shift supervisor: "I usually come to work early, just to get away from the house. When I arrive, people are there waiting. We sit, we talk, we joke. I let them know what's going on, who has to be where, what changes I've made for the shift that day. We sit and chitchat for 5 or 10 minutes. There's laughing, joking, fun."

For Linda, home has come to feel like work and work has come to feel a bit like home. Indeed, she feels she can get relief from the "work" of being at home only by going to the "home" of work. Why has her life at home come to seem like this? Linda explains it this way: "My husband's a great help watching our baby. But as far as doing housework or even taking the baby when I'm at home, no. He figures he works five days a week; he's not going to come home and clean. But he doesn't stop to think that I work seven days a week. Why should I have to come home and do the housework without help from anybody else? My husband and I have been through this over and over again. Even if he would just pick up from the kitchen table and stack the dishes for me, that would make a big difference. He does nothing. On his weekends off, he goes fishing. If I want any time off, I have to get a sitter. He'll help out if I'm not here, but the minute I am, all the work at home is mine."

With a light laugh, she continues: "So I take a lot of overtime. The more I get out of the house, the better I am. It's a terrible thing to say, but that's the way I feel."

When Bill feels the need for time off, to relax, to have fun, to feel free, he climbs in his truck and takes his free time without his family. Largely in response, Linda grabs what she also calls "free time"—at work. Neither Linda nor Bill Avery wants more time together at home, not as things are arranged now.

How do Linda and Bill Avery fit into the broader picture of American family and work life? Current research suggests that however hectic their lives, women who do paid work feel less depressed, think better of themselves and are more satisfied than women who stay at home. One study reported that women who work outside the home feel more valued at home than housewives do. Meanwhile, work is where many women feel like "good mothers." As Linda reflects: "I'm a good mom at home, but I'm a better mom at work. At home, I get into fights with Tracy. I want her to apply to a junior college, but she's not interested. At work, I think I'm better at seeing the other person's point of view."

Many workers feel more confident they could "get the job done" at work than at home. One study found that only 59 percent of workers feel their "performance" in the family is "good or unusually good," while 86 percent rank their performance on the job this way.

Forces at work and at home are simultaneously reinforcing this "reversal." The lure of work has been enhanced in recent years by the rise of company cultural engineering—in particular, the shift from Frederick Taylor's principles of scientific management to the Total Quality principles originally set out by W. Edwards Deming. Under the influence of a Taylorist world view, the manager's job was to coerce the worker's mind and body, not to appeal to the worker's heart. The Taylorized worker was de-skilled, replaceable and cheap, and as a consequence felt bored, demeaned and unappreciated.

Using modern participative management techniques, many companies now train workers to make their own work decisions, and then set before their newly "empowered" employees moral as well as financial incentives. At Amerco, the Total Quality worker is invited to feel recognized for job accomplishments. Amerco regularly strengthens the familylike ties of co-workers by holding "recognition ceremonies" honoring particular workers or self-managed production teams. Amerco employees speak of "belonging to the Amerco family," and proudly wear their "Total Quality" pins or "High Performance Team" T-shirts, symbols of their loyalty to the company and of its loyalty to them.

The company occasionally decorates a section of the factory and serves refreshments. The production teams, too, have regular get-togethers. In a New Age recasting of an old business slogan—"The Customer Is Always Right"—Amerco proposes that its workers "Value the Internal Customer." This means: Be as polite and considerate to co-workers inside the company as you would be to customers outside it. How many recognition ceremonies for competent performance are being offered at home? Who is valuing the internal customer there?

Amerco also tries to take on the role of a helpful relative with regard to employee problems at work and at home. The education-and-training division offers employees free courses (on company time) in "Dealing With Anger," "How to Give and Accept Criticism," "How to Cope With Difficult People."

At home, of course, people seldom receive anything like this much help on issues basic to family life. There, no courses are being offered on "Dealing With Your Child's Disappointment in You" or "How to Treat Your Spouse Like an Internal Customer."

If Total Quality calls for "re-skilling" the worker in an "enriched" job environment, technological developments have long been de-skilling parents at home. Over the centuries, store-bought goods have replaced homespun cloth, homemade soap and home-baked foods. Day care for children, retirement homes for the elderly, even psychotherapy are, in a way, commercial substitutes for jobs that a mother once did at home. Even family-generated entertainment has, to some extent, been replaced by television, video games and the VCR. I sometimes watched Amerco families sitting together after their dinners, mute but cozy, watching sitcoms in which television mothers, fathers and children related in an animated way to one another while the viewing family engaged in relational loafing.

The one "skill" still required of family members is the hardest one of all—the emotional work of forging, deepening or repairing family relationships. It takes time to develop this skill, and even then things can go awry. Family ties are complicated. People get hurt. Yet as broken homes become more common—and as the sense of belonging to a geographical community grows less and less secure in an age of mobility—the corporate world has created a sense of "neighborhood," of "feminine culture," of family at work. Life at work can be insecure; the company can fire workers. But workers aren't so secure at home, either. Many employees have been working for Amerco for 20 years but are on their second or third marriages or relationships. The shifting balance between these two "divorce rates" may be the most powerful reason why tired parents flee a world of unresolved quarrels and unwashed laundry harmony and managed cheer of work. People are getting their "pink slips" at home.

Amerco workers have not only turned their offices into "home" and their homes into work-places; many have also begun to "Taylorize" time at home, where families are succumbing to a cult of efficiency previously associated mainly with the office and factory. Meanwhile, work time, with its ever longer hours, has become more hospitable to sociability—periods of talk-ing with friends on E-mail, patching up quarrels, gossiping. Within the long workday of many Amerco employees are great hidden pockets of inefficiency while, in the far smaller number of waking weekday hours at home, they are, despite themselves, forced to act increasingly time-conscious and efficient.

The Averys respond to their time bind at home by trying to value and protect "quality time." A concept unknown to their parents and grandparents, "quality time" has become a powerful symbol of the struggle against the growing pressures at home. It reflects the extent to which modern parents feel the flow of time to be running against them. The premise behind "quality time" is that the time we devote to relationships can somehow be separated from ordinary time. Relationships go on during quantity time, of course, but then we are only passively, not actively, wholeheartedly, specializing in our emotional ties. We aren't "on." Quality time at home becomes like an office appointment. You don't want to be caught "goof-ing off around the water cooler" when you are "at work."

Quality time holds out the hope that scheduling intense periods of togetherness can compensate for an overall loss of time in such a way that a relationship will suffer no loss of quality. But this is just another way of transferring the cult of efficiency from office to home. We must now get our relationships in good repair in less time. Instead of nine hours a day with a child, we declare ourselves capable of getting "the same result" with one intensely focused hour.

Parents now more commonly speak of time as if it is a threatened form of personal cap-ital they have no choice but to manage and invest. What's new here is the spread into the home of a financial manager's attitude toward time. Working parents at Amerco owe what they think of as time debts at home. This is because they are, in a sense, inadvertently "Tay-lorizing" the house—speeding up the pace of home life as Taylor once tried to "scientifically" speed up the pace of factory life.

Advertisers of products aimed at women have recognized that this new reality provides an opportunity to sell products, and have turned the very pressure that threatens to explode the home into a positive attribute. Take, for example, an ad promoting Instant Quaker Oatmeal: it shows a smiling mother ready for the office in her square-shouldered suit, hugging her happy son. A caption reads: "Nicky is a very picky eater. With Instant Quaker Oatmeal, I can give him a terrific hot breakfast in just 90 seconds. And I don't have to spend any time coax-ing him to eat it!" Here, the modern mother seems to have absorbed the lessons of Frederick Taylor as she presses for efficiency at home because she is in a hurry to get to work.

Part of modern parenthood seems to include coping with the resistance of real children who are not so eager to get their cereal so fast. Some parents try desperately not to appease their children with special gifts or smooth-talking promises about the future. But when time is scarce, even the best parents find themselves passing a system-wide familial speed-up along to the most vulnerable workers on the line. Parents are then obliged to try to control the dam-age done by a reversal of worlds. They monitor mealtime, homework time, bedtime, trying to cut out "wasted" time.

In response, children often protest the pace, the deadlines, the grand irrationality of "effi-cient" family life. Children dawdle. They refuse to leave places when it's time to leave. They insist on leaving places when it's not time to leave. Surely, this is part of the usual stop-and-go of childhood itself, but perhaps, too, it is the plea of children for more family time, and more control over what time there is. This only adds to the feeling that life at home has become hard work.

Instead of trying to arrange shorter or more flexible work schedules, Amerco parents often avoid confronting the reality of the time bind. Some minimize their ideas about how much care a child, a partner or they themselves "really need." They make do with less time, less attention, less understanding and less support at home than they once imagined possible. They *emotionally downsize* life. In essence, they deny the needs of family members, and they themselves become emotional ascetics. If they once "needed" time with each other, they are now increasingly "fine" without it.

Another way that working parents try to evade the time bind is to buy themselves out of it—an approach that puts women in particular at the heart of a contradiction. Like men, women absorb the work-family speed-up far more than they resist it; but unlike men, they still shoulder most of the workload at home. And women still represent in people's minds the heart and soul of family life. They're the ones—especially women of the urban middle and upper-middle classes—who feel most acutely the need to save time, who are the most tempted by the new "time saving" goods and services—and who wind up feeling the most guilty about it. For example, Playgroup Connections, a Washington-area business started by a former executive recruiter, matches playmates to one another. One mother hired the service to find her child a French-speaking playmate.

In several cities, children home alone can call a number for "Grandma, Please!" and reach an adult who has the time to talk with them, sing to them or help them with their homework. An ad for Kindercare Learning Centers, a for profit child-care chain, pitches its appeal this way: "You want your child to be active, tolerant, smart, loved, emotionally stable, self-aware, artistic and get a two-hour nap. Anything else?" It goes on to note that Kindercare accepts children 6 weeks to 12 years old and provides a number to call for the Kindercare nearest you. Another typical service organizes children's birthday parties, making out invitations ("sure hope you can come") and providing party favors, entertainment, a decorated cake and balloons. Creative Memories is a service that puts ancestral photos into family albums for you.

An overwhelming majority of the working mothers I spoke with recoiled from the idea of buying themselves out of parental duties. A bought birthday party was "too impersonal," a 90-second breakfast "too fast." Yet a surprising amount of lunchtime conversation between female friends at Amerco was devoted to expressing complex, conflicting feelings about the lure of trading time for one service or another. The temptation to order flash-frozen dinners or to call a local number for a homework helper did not come up because such services had not yet appeared at Spotted Deer Child-Care Center. But many women dwelled on the question of how to decide where a mother's job began and ended, especially with regard to baby sitters and television. One mother said to another in the breakroom of an Amerco plant: "Damon doesn't settle down until 10 at night, so he hates me to wake him up in the morning and I hate to do it. He's cranky. He pulls the covers up. I put on cartoons. That way, I can dress him and he doesn't object. I don't like to use TV that way. It's like a drug. But I do it."

The other mother countered: "Well, Todd is up before we are, so that's not a problem. It's after dinner, when I feel like watching a little television, that I feel guilty, because he gets too much TV at the sitter's."

As task after task falls into the realm of time-saving goods and services, questions arise about the moral meanings attached to doing or not doing such tasks. Is it being a good mother to bake a child's birthday cake (alone or together with one's partner)? Or can we gratefully save time by ordering it, and be good mothers by planning the party? Can we save more time by hiring a planning service, and be good mothers simply by watching our children have a good time? "Wouldn't that be nice!" one Amerco mother exclaimed. As the idea of the "good mother" retreats before the pressures of work and the expansion of motherly services, mothers are in fact continually reinventing themselves.

The final way working parents tried to evade the time bind was to develop what I call "potential selves." The potential selves that I discovered in my Amerco interviews were fantasy creations of time-poor parents who dreamed of living as time millionaires.

One man, a gifted 55-year-old engineer in research and development at Amerco, told how he had dreamed of taking his daughters on a camping trip in the Sierra Mountains: "I bought all the gear three years ago when they were 5 and 7, the tent, the sleeping bags, the air mattresses, the backpacks, the ponchos. I got a map of the area. I even got the freeze-dried food. Since then the kids and I have talked about it a lot, and gone over what we're going to do. They've been on me to do it for a long time. I feel bad about it. I keep putting it off, but we'll do it, I just don't know when."

Banished to garages and attics of many Amerco workers were expensive electric saws, cameras, skis and musical instruments, all bought with wages it took time to earn. These items were to their owners what Cassie's fudge bar was to her—a substitute for time, a talisman, a reminder of the potential self.

Obviously, not everyone, not even a majority of Americans, is making a home out of work and a work-place out of home. But in the working world, it is a growing reality, and one we need to face. Increasing numbers of women are discovering a great male secret—that work can be an escape from the pressures of home, pressures that the changing nature of work itself are only intensifying. Neither men nor women are going to take up "family friendly" policies, whether corporate or governmental, as long as the current realities of work and home remain as they are. For a substantial number of time-bound parents, the stripped-down home and the neighborhood devoid of community are simply losing out to the pull of the workplace.

There are several broader, historical causes of this reversal of realms. The last 30 years have witnessed the rapid rise of women in the workplace. At the same time, job mobility has taken families farther from relatives who might lend a hand, and made it harder to make close friends of neighbors who could help out. Moreover, as women have acquired more education and have joined men at work, they have absorbed the views of an older, male-oriented work world, its views of a "real career," far more than men have taken up their share of the work at home. One reason women have changed more than men is that the world of "male" work seems more honorable and valuable than the "female" world of home and children.

So where do we go from here? There is surely no going back to the mythical 1950's family that confined women to the home. Most women don't wish to return to a full-time role at home—and couldn't afford it even if they did. But equally troubling is a workaholic culture that strands both men and women outside the home.

For a while now, scholars on work-family issues have pointed to Sweden, Norway and Denmark as better models of work-family balance. Today, for example, almost all Swedish fathers take two paid weeks off from work at the birth of their children, and about half of fathers and most mothers take additional "parental leave" during the child's first or second year. Research shows that men who take family leave when their children are very young are more likely to be involved with their children as they grow older. When I mentioned this Swedish record of paternity leave to a focus group of American male managers, one of them replied, "Right, we've already heard about Sweden." To this executive, paternity leave was a good idea not for the U.S. today, but for some "potential society" in another place and time.

Meanwhile, children are paying the price. In her book *When the Bough Breaks: The Cost of Neglecting Our Children,* the economist Sylvia Hewlett claims that "compared with the previous generation, young people today are more likely to "underperform at school; commit suicide; need psychiatric help; suffer a severe eating disorder; bear a child out of wedlock; take drugs, be the victim of a violent crime." But we needn't dwell on sledgehammer problems like heroin or suicide to realize that children like those at Spotted Deer need more of our time. If other advanced nations with two-job families can give children the time they need, why can't we?

SUGGESTIONS FOR DISCUSSION

1. Although Hochschild says she is writing about all workers, most of her information seems to focus on women in the workplace. Identify the main argument of her article and explain why women's stories of finding a haven at work might be more useful for that argument than would men's stories.

2. What are the overall impressions of work vs. home that Hochschild leaves us with? To what extent do you accept her representation of home and work? What of that representation does not seem convincing entirely to you?

3. Hochschild writes that salary is not the most important reason for working long hours because, according to her research, some of the best-paid employees are least willing to cut back their hours while the lower paid workers seem to be willing to choose time away from work for home. Are there other reasons, besides finding more pleasure at work than at home, that you can think of for employees to make these choices?

SUGGESTIONS FOR WRITING

1. Write an exploratory essay that addresses Hochschild's discussion of women in the workplace. To begin planning your writing, consider asking questions like the following: How representative are Hochschild's descriptions of working women's lives? Do you know any woman who holds a job and is raising a family at the same time? Is her story like the stories in Hochschild's article, or do you find something different in the choices she makes? What is your overall impression of what Hochschild expects from women in the workplace?

2. Hochschild writes that even though many companies have "family friendly" policies that offer flex-time or part-time work to give parents a chance to spend more time at home, very few employees take advantage of those benefits. We might guess that part of the reason some employees don't take advantage of these policies could be in the way that the company presents them to its employees. Imagine that you have to write a memo convincing employees to take advantage of "family friendly" policies. To write this memo, you will have to address many different kinds of employees, all with the same memo. You cannot assume they are all in the same situation. You will have to make the policy seem attractive, but you can't promise too much because, after all, the company does need its employees on the job—it is a rare company that would be willing to lose money on such a benefit. You will also have to convey the sense that, as a manager, you value both the work and the home environments. Because it is a memo, and you'll want everyone to read it, it should be direct and brief—no more than one single-spaced page.

3. In our introduction to this chapter, we suggested that television dramas and sitcoms often use the work-family as a setting for their stories. Choose a current television show with a workplace environment and write an essay in which you examine the characters and setting as the work-family. In what ways does this setting take precedence over any home setting for the characters? In what ways does the work-family spill over into the home setting in the program that you have chosen? How might Hochschild's analysis of the ways people feel about their jobs, as opposed to their obligations at home, help you to explain the appeal or popularity of the work-family on television?

The Dilbert Principle

Scott Adams

Scott Adams received his MBA from Berkeley and worked for several years in a cubicle in the offices of Pacific Bell in Northern California before he quit to devote all of his time to the Dilbert cartoon strip. The article included here originally appeared in the *Wall Street Journal* on May 22, 1995. It got a huge response and led to the creation of Adams's book with the same title. In August 1996, *Newsweek* published a cover story on Adams and his book *The Dilbert Principle,* reporting that the cartoon character had moved "from cult status to mass phenomenon" as *The Dilbert Principle* moved to number one on the New York Times bestseller list shortly after it was published. Office workers all over the United States were clipping Dilbert strips because Dilbert's office life seemed so much like their own. That closeness to reality is partially due to the fact that Adams gets many of his ideas from readers who send him stories of the workplace over e-mail.

SUGGESTION FOR READING

When you read this article, you will have to remind yourself that, though there is much in *The Dilbert Principle* that strikes office workers as real, the purpose of the piece is humor. Some might call it serious humor, but it is humor nonetheless. Of course, humor (especially satire) historically has been one way to comment on the shortcomings of modern society. As you read, take note of places that strike you as funny but painfully true.

I use a lot of "bad boss" themes in my syndicated cartoon strip "Dilbert." I'll never run out of material. I get at least two hundred e-mail messages a day, mostly from people who are complaining about their own clueless managers. Here are some of my favorite stories, all allegedly true:

- A vice president insists that the company's new battery-powered product be equipped with a light that comes on to tell you when the power is off.

- An employee suggests setting priorities so the company will know how to apply its limited resources. The manager's response: "Why can't we concentrate our resources across the board?"

- A manager wants to find and fix software bugs more quickly. He offers an incentive plan: $20 for each bug the Quality Assurance people find and $20 for each bug the programmers fix. (These are the same programmers who create the bugs.) Result: An underground economy in "bugs" springs up instantly. The plan is rethought after one employee nets $1,700 the first week.

Stories like these prompted me to do the first annual Dilbert Survey to find out what management practices were most annoying to employees. The choices included the usual suspects: Quality, Empowerment, Reengineering, and the like. But the number-one vote-getter in this highly unscientific survey was "Idiots Promoted to Management."

This seemed like a subtle change from the old concept by which capable workers were promoted until they reached their level of incompetence—best described as the "Peter Principle." Now, apparently, the incompetent workers are promoted directly to management without ever passing through the temporary competence stage.

When I entered the workforce in 1979, the Peter Principle described management pretty well. Now I think we'd all like to return to those Golden Years when you had a boss who was once good at something.

I get all nostalgic when I think about it. Back then, we all had hopes of being promoted beyond our levels of competence. Every worker had a shot at someday personally navigating the company into the tar pits while reaping large bonuses and stock options. It was a time when inflation meant everybody got an annual raise; a time when we freely admitted that the customers didn't matter. It was a time of joy.

We didn't appreciate it then, but the much underrated Peter Principle always provided us with a boss who understood what we did for a living. Granted, he made consistently bad decisions—after all he had no management skills. But at least they were the informed decisions of a seasoned veteran from the trenches.

EXAMPLE

Boss: "When I had your job I could drive a three-inch rod through a metal casing with one motion. If you're late again I'll do the same thing to your head."

Nitpickers found lots of problems with the Peter Principle, but on the whole it worked. Lately, however, the Peter Principle has given way to the "Dilbert Principle." The basic concept of the Dilbert Principle is that the most ineffective workers are systematically moved to the place where they can do the least damage: management.

This has not proved to be the winning strategy that you might think.

Maybe we should learn something from nature. In the wild, the weakest moose is hunted down and killed by dingo dogs, thus ensuring survival of the fittest. This is a harsh system—especially for the dingo dogs who have to fly all the way from Australia. But nature's process is a good one; everybody agrees, except perhaps for the dingo dogs and the moose in question...and the flight attendants. But the point is that we'd all be better off if the least competent managers were being eaten by dingo dogs instead of writing Mission Statements.

It seems as if we've turned nature's rules upside down. We systematically identify and promote the people who have the least skills. The usual business rationalization for promoting idiots (the Dilbert Principle in a nutshell) is something along the lines of "Well, he can't

write code, he can't design a network, and he doesn't have any sales skill. But he has very good hair..."

If nature started organizing itself like a modern business, you'd see, for example, a band of mountain gorillas led by an "alpha" squirrel. And it wouldn't be the most skilled squirrel; it would be the squirrel nobody wanted to hang around with.

I can see the other squirrels gathered around an old stump saying stuff like "If I hear him say, 'I like nuts' one more time, I'm going to kill him." The gorillas, overhearing this conversation, lumber down from the mist and promote the unpopular squirrel. The remaining squirrels are assigned to Quality Teams as punishment.

You may be wondering if you fit the description of a Dilbert Principle manager. Here's a little test:

1. Do you believe that anything you don't understand must be easy to do?
2. Do you feel the need to explain in great detail why "profit" is the difference between income and expense?
3. Do you think employees should schedule funerals only during holidays?
4. Are the following words a form of communication or gibberish:
   The Business Services Leadership Team will enhance the organization in order to continue on the journey toward a Market Facing Organization (MFO) model. To that end, we are consolidating the Object Management for Business Services into a cross strata team.
5. When people stare at you in disbelief do you repeat what you just said, only louder and more slowly?

Now give yourself one point for each question you answered with the letter "B." If your score is greater than zero, congratulations—there are stock options in your future.
(The language in question four is from an actual company memo.)

SUGGESTIONS FOR DISCUSSION

1. How would you explain Dilbert's popularity? What do you recognize (the setting, the interactions, the people) in this world, whether you have done office work or not?

2. Scott Adams's humor is much like the humor you might find in Matt Groening (his Hell series) or Gary Larson's *Far Side*. Bring to class a comic strip that uses satire or dark humor to make us laugh. What is it about these strips that makes you laugh even when they make you cringe?

Besides the e-mail address, included in most of the Dilbert strips, Scott Adams with United Feature Syndicate, Inc., maintains an official website called The Dilbert Zone. Find the website and look for unofficial sites to see what difference it makes when fans represent or use this cartoon character and the situational humor of Dilbert. You will also find other sites on "job humor" on the Web. How does the humor in these compare to Dilbert?

3. As we mentioned above, Scott Adams gets many of his ideas from office workers who send him real situations and real memos over e-mail or the Internet. With two or three of your classmates, make a list of absurdities from your own experience with bureaucracy that you would send Adams.

SUGGESTIONS FOR WRITING

1. Write about a time when you found yourself caught up in bureaucracy—in a situation where no one quite knew what the job they were assigned was supposed to be. How did you handle it? In what ways was it typical of that workplace or organization?

2. Although Adams probably doesn't expect anyone to take the potential manager's test at the end of this article, he does expect his readers to understand what he is saying about management by asking these questions. Write a brief essay that characterizes the manager who might emerge from a test like this one.

3. In a *Newsweek* cover story on *The Dilbert Principle, Newsweek* reporters write of "the suppressed rage of workers who tolerate abuses and absurdities in a marketplace leaned-and-meaned to Wall Street's specifications. Reading Dilbert allows them, in some small way, to strike back, or at least to experience a pleasant catharsis by identifying the nature of the beast: a general yet pervasive sense of idiocy in corporate America that is seldom dealt with by the captains of industry who have great hair and offices with doors." Write an essay in which you offer a possible explanation for how reading Dilbert helps abused workers strike back or how humor, graffiti, or any underground type of activity can help individuals in what seems like a repressive system feel as if they have some control.

LEWIS HINE AND THE SOCIAL USES OF PHOTOGRAPHY

American photographer Lewis Hine did most of his work, especially his child labor series represented in part by the following images, between 1907 and 1917. Hine believed that photography had an educational and social role to play, and he used images like these to educate Americans about the conditions of working life in the United States at the time. For many years, Hine did work for the National Child Labor Committee. It was for that committee that he designed the poster reprinted below. Historian Alan Trachtenberg says of Hine that for him "social photography meant that the photography itself performed a social act, made a particular communication." That is very clear, not only in Hine's poster work, but in his individual photographs as well.

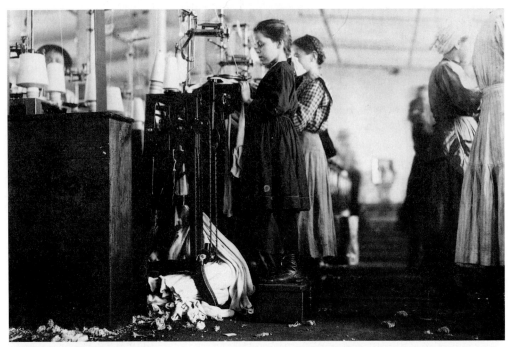

"Mill Girls," Lewis Hine.

"Glass Factory Workers," Lewis Hine.

"Child Labor Committee Poster," Lewis Hine.

Gap parody ad from *Adbusters Magazine.*

SUGGESTIONS FOR DISCUSSION

1. Often when we think of images that make a social statement, we think of extremely sensational scenes. The images you are likely to see in a World Hunger campaign, for example, show the most extreme cases of starvation. Photographers make that choice because they want the image to have the most powerful impact quickly. As we mentioned in our introduction to these photos, Lewis Hine believed that his photography could be instructional and that it could make a difference in people's lives. However, some of his most famous photographs of children at work could not be called sensational in the most obvious sense of the term. They are, instead, matter-of-fact. The girl at the cotton mill is shown simply standing before the machinery, doing her work. If Hine thought these images would make a difference in child labor laws, what assumptions would you say he was making about his audience's attitudes toward children or labor or the ability of such images to make a statement?

2. How do Hine's images change when they are placed in the posters he made for the National Child Labor Committee?

3. The following is an image produced for the magazine *Adbusters,* a publication advocating writing over ads or satirizing ad campaigns to make a political statement. How does the Hine image change for you when it is placed in a more contemporary context like the satirical Gap ad above?

SUGGESTED ASSIGNMENT

For this project, gather a series of images that help you visually represent a labor issue that is relevant today. You can draw this issue from any of the readings in this chapter or from your own experience with or concerns about labor. For example, how might you visually represent Juliet Schor's "overworked American" or Arlie Hochschild's work family? Or you might want to represent "McJob" or the dilemmas of the downsized worker. You should notice that Hine took his own pictures and often combined those pictures with language to make poster arguments against child labor. You can take your own pictures as Hine does, or find pictures in magazines or photocopy pictures from books. Then combine those images with language to create a statement about work.

FIELD WORK · *RECONSTRUCTING THE NETWORK OF A WORKPLACE*

In any job you hold you are likely to discover that, besides the obvious work tasks that have to be done, negotiating the workplace involves understanding the people and how they do their jobs, how they relate to each other and to you, how they have established unspoken rules for daily routines and interactions, and where you fit into all of that. As the narrator in Sandra Cisneros's story "The First Job" discovered, the people who have been in a workplace for some period of time seem to know almost automatically how to act, when to speak, when to sit, and when to make sure they are working diligently.

That sort of knowledge is the knowledge of the "social network" established in any job that involves more than one or two people. If you have ever stood in front of a secretary's desk and felt frustrated or confused when the person behind the desk seemed to ignore you, only to discover that the receptionist is at the next desk, you have probably stumbled onto one of the unspoken rules that has evolved from the social network in that office. Customers often are confused by such networks and, for example, might call the wrong waitress to their table or ask the stocker at a discount store to help them decide on an item that they are trying to buy. Workers, on the other hand, must learn these social networks quickly or they are likely to make mistakes in front of the supervisor that veterans in that workplace would never make.

One way that anthropologists have studied the culture of the workplace is to try to understand the social networks established on the job. To do that, they have relied on interviews and on participant-observation studies, like the one described in the next selection by James Spradley and Brenda Mann.

The Cocktail Waitress

James P. Spradley and Brenda J. Mann

James Spradley, a professor of anthropology at MacAlaster College in St. Paul, Minnesota, and Brenda Mann, who has worked as a senior product analyst at Dialog Information Services, spent a year studying the culture of the workplace from the point of view of "cocktail waitresses," as waitresses in bars were still called in 1975 when this study was completed. The selection reprinted below is from *The Cocktail Waitress* and illustrates how workers daily and almost automatically interpret their own workplace. It is the kind of interpretation necessary for workers to know who to go to for information or who to avoid or what tasks will hang them up.

SUGGESTION FOR READING

Spradley and Mann make a clear distinction between the "social structure" that has been established in Brady's bar and the "social network." Underline and annotate those places in the selection where Spradley and Mann provide examples or explanations for each. After you have completed your reading, review your annotations and use them to write a short explanation of the difference between the two.

Denise moves efficiently through her section, stopping at a few of her tables. "Another round here?" she asks at the first table. They nod their assent and she moves on. "Would you like to order now?" "Two more of the usual here?" She takes orders from four of the tables and heads back to the bar to give them to the bartender. The work is not difficult for her now, but when she first started at Brady's, every night on the job was confusing, frustrating, embarrassing, and exhausting. Now it is just exhausting.

Her first night was chaos. When introduced to the bartender, Mark Brady, he responded with: "Haven't I seen you somewhere before?" Flustered, she shook her head. "He's not going to be one of those kind, is he?" she thought. Then later, following previous instruction, she asked two obviously underaged girls for identification, which they didn't have. As she was asking them to leave Mark called Denise over and told her not to card those two particular girls. Embarrassed, Denise returned to their table, explained they could stay, and took their order. A customer at the bar kept grabbing her every time she came to her station, and tried to engage her in conversation. Not knowing what to do, she just smiled and tried to look busy. She asked one customer what he wanted to drink and he said, "the usual" and she had to ask him what that was. An older man seated at the bar smiled and said, "Hello, Denise," as he put a dollar bill on her tray. Again, she didn't know what to say or do so she just smiled and walked away, wondering what she had done or was supposed to do to make her worth the dollar. Another customer at a table grabbed her by the waist each time she walked past his table and persistently questioned her: "Are you new here?" "What nights do you work?" "What are you doing after work?" And so went the rest of the evening. It wasn't until several nights later and following similar encounters that she began to sort out and make sense of all this. She began to learn who these people were, what special identities they had in the bar culture, and where each one was located in the social structure of Brady's Bar.

The bartender's initial question, albeit a rather standard come-on, had been a sincere and friendly inquiry. The two girls she carded were *friends of the Brady family* and often drank there despite their young age. The grabby and talkative customer at the bar was Jerry, a *regular customer* and harmless drinker. The dollar tip came from *Mr. Brady,* the patriarch of the business. The man with the hands and persistent questions was a *regular* from the University who had a reputation with the other waitresses as a *hustler* to be avoided. These people were more than just customers, as Denise had initially categorized them. Nor could she personalize them and treat each one as a unique individual. They were different *kinds* of people who came into Brady's, and all required different kinds of services and responses from her.

SOCIAL STRUCTURE

Social structure is a universal feature of culture. It consists of an organized set of social identities and the expected behavior associated with them. Given the infinite possibilities for organizing people, anthropologists have found it crucial to discover the particular social structure in each society they study. It is often necessary to begin by asking informants for the social identity of specific individuals. "He is a *big man*." "That's my *mother*." "She is my *co-wife*." "He is my *uncle*." "She is my *sister*." Then one can go on to examine these categories being used to classify people. A fundamental feature of every social structure is a set of such categories, usually named, for dividing up the social world. In the area of kinship, for example, some societies utilize nearly 100 categories, organizing them in systematic ways for social interaction.

When we began our research at Brady's Bar, the various categories of the social structure were not easy to discern. Of course the different activities of waitresses, bartenders, and customers suggested these three groupings, but finer distinctions were often impossible to make without the assistance of informants. At first we thought it would be possible to arrange all the terms for different kinds of people into a single folk taxonomy, much like an anthropologist might do for a set of kinship terms. With this in mind, we began listening, for example, to the way informants talked about customers and asked them specifically, "What are all the different kinds of customers?" This procedure led to a long list of terms, including the following:

girl	regular	cougar
jock	real regular	sweetie
animal	person off street	waitress
bartender	policeman	loner
greaser	party	female
businessman	zoo	drunk
redneck	bore	Johnny
bitch	pig	hands
creep	slob	couple
bastard	hustler	king and his court
obnoxo	Annie	

This list was even more confusing as we checked out the various terms. For example, we asked, "Would a waitress say that a bartender is a kind of customer?" Much to our surprise, the answer was affirmative. Then we discovered that a *regular* could be an *obnoxo* or a *bore,* a *party* could be a *zoo,* a *cougar* was always a *jock,* but a *jock* could also be a *regular* or *person off the street*. Even though it seemed confusing, we knew it was important to the waitresses to make such fine distinctions among types of customers and that they organized all these categories in some way. As our research progressed it became clear that waitresses operated with several different sets of categories. One appeared to be the basis for the formal social structure of the bar, the others could only be understood in terms of the specific social networks of the waitresses. Let us examine each briefly.

The formal social structure included three major categories of people *customers, employees,* and *managers*. When someone first enters the bar and the waitresses look to see who it is, they quickly identify an individual in terms of one or another category in this formal social structure. The terms used form a folk taxonomy shown in Figure 8.1. Waitresses use these categories to identify who people are, anticipate their behavior, and plan strategies for performing their role.

Although waitresses often learn names and individual identities, it is not necessary. What every girl must know is the category to which people belong. It is essential, for example, to distinguish between a real regular and a person off the street. Both are customers, but both do not receive identical service from her. For example, a waitress should not have to ask a real regular what he's drinking, she should expect some friendly bantering as she waits on him, and she won't be offended if he puts his arm around her waist. A person off the street, however, receives only minimal attention from the waitress. Denise will have to inquire what he

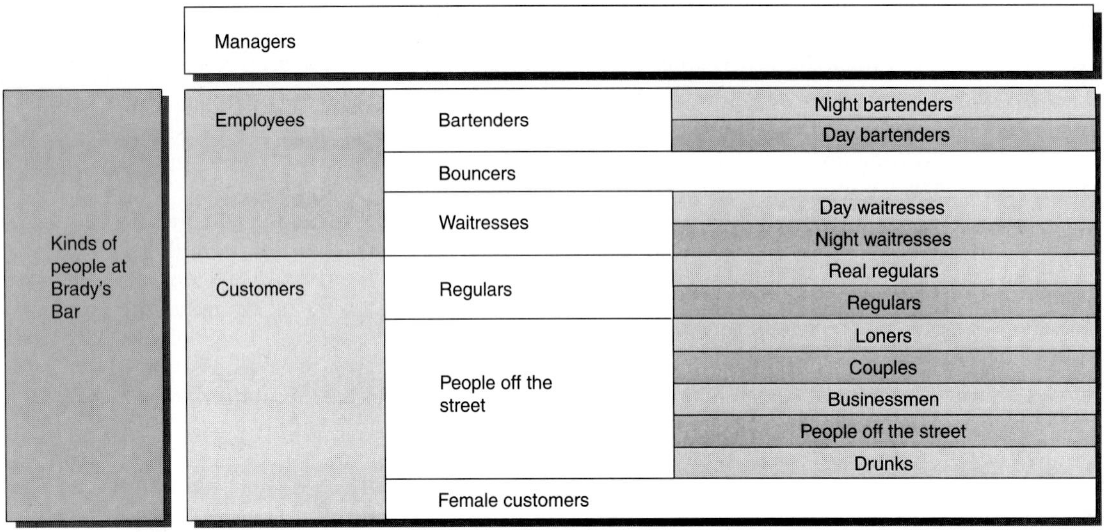

Kinds of people at Brady's Bar	Managers		
	Employees	Bartenders	Night bartenders
			Day bartenders
		Bouncers	
		Waitresses	Day waitresses
			Night waitresses
	Customers	Regulars	Real regulars
			Regulars
		People off the street	Loners
			Couples
			Businessmen
			People off the street
			Drunks
		Female customers	

FIGURE 8.1

Formal social structure of Brady's Bar.

or she wants to drink, she won't be interested in spending her time talking with him, and she will be offended if he makes physical advances. It is important that Denise recognize these differences and not confuse the two kinds of customers. Being a good waitress means she can make such important distinctions. Although a knowledge of this formal social structure is essential to waitresses, it is not sufficient for the complexities of social interaction in Brady's Bar. In order to understand the other categories for identifying people and also to see how waitresses use the social structure, we need to examine the nature of *social networks*.

SOCIAL NETWORK

Social network analysis shifts our attention from the social structure as a formal system to the way it is seen through the eyes of individual members, in this case, the cocktail waitresses. Each waitress is at the center of several social networks. [See Figure 8.2] Some link her to specific individuals in the bar; other networks have strands that run outside the bar to college professors, roommates, friends, and parents. In addition to the formal social structure, we discovered at least three different sets of identities that make up distinct social networks. Only through an awareness of these networks is it possible to understand the way waitresses view their social world.

The first is a social network determined by the behavioral attributes of people. As the girls make their way between the bar and tables each night, identities such as *customer, waitress,* and *bartender* become less significant than ones like *bitch,* and *obnoxo* based on specific actions of individuals. Sue returns to a table of four men as she balances a tray of drinks. No sooner has she started placing them on the table than she feels a hand on her leg. In the semidarkness no one knows of this encounter but the customer and the waitress. Should she ignore it or call attention to this violation of her personal space? She quietly steps back and the hand disappears, yet every time she serves the table this regular makes a similar advance. By the middle of the evening Sue is saying repeatedly, "Watch the hands." When Sandy takes over

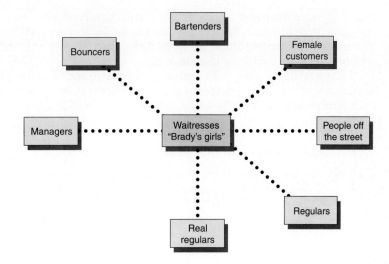

FIGURE 8.2
Social network of
waitresses.

for her break, Sue will point out *hands,* a man who has taken on a special social identity in the waitresses' network. The real regular, businessman, loner, person off the street, or almost any kind of male customer can fall into the same network category if his behavior warrants it. A customer who peels paper off the beer bottles and spills wax from the candle becomes a *pig.* The person who slows down the waitress by always engaging her in conversation, perhaps insisting that she sit at his table and talk, becomes a *bore.* As drinking continues during an evening, the behavior of some individuals moves so far outside the bounds of propriety that they become *obnoxos. Hustlers* gain their reputation by seeking to engage the waitress in some after-work rendezvous. The bartender who is impatient or rude becomes someone for the waitress to avoid, a real *bastard.* Even another waitress can be a *bitch* by her lack of consideration for the other girls. When a new waitress begins work, she doesn't know what kind of actions to expect nor how to evaluate them. Part of her socialization involves learning the categories and rules for operating within this network.

A second social network is based on social identities from outside the bar itself. Holly's roommate from college often visits the bar and one or another waitress serves her. Although she is a *customer,* they treat her as one of the other girl's *roommates* who has a special place in this social network. Each waitress will reciprocate when the close friends of other waitresses come to the bar, offering special attention to these customers. The colleges attended by customers and employees provide another basis for identifying people. "That's a table of Annie's," Joyce will say about the girls from St. Anne's College. *Cougars* are customers who also play on the university football team. Even *bartenders* and *waitresses* can be terms for kinds of customers when they have these identities from other bars where they work.

Finally, there is a special network of insiders that crosscuts the formal social structure. This is *the Brady family,* made up of managers, employees, and customers—especially real regulars. The new waitress does not know about this select group of people when she first starts work. Sooner or later she will end up hanging around after work to have a drink on the house and talk. In this inner circle she will no longer think of the others as waitresses, bartenders, or customers, but now they are part of the Brady family. This network overarches all the specific categories of people in a dualistic kind of organization, a system not uncommon in non-Western societies. For example, a Nuer tribesman in Africa organizes people primarily on the basis of kinship. He has dozens of kinship terms to sort people into various identities and to anticipate their behavior. But every fellow tribesman, in a general sense, is either *both* or *mar,* distinctions that are important for social interaction. For the waitress, everyone in the bar is either in the Brady family or outside of it.

The social life of Brady's Bar derives its substance and form from the formal social structure as well as the various networks that waitresses and others activate for special purposes. Each waitress finds herself linked in some way to others in the bar with varying degrees of involvement.

SUGGESTIONS FOR DISCUSSION

1. Although this selection opens with a scene of a particular waitress working Brady's Bar, Spradley and Mann are not writing a story of the bar or a description of the shift of one waitress. Why give us this opening scene? How does it help readers to understand the information and analysis provided in the rest of the selection?

2. Recall a place where you have worked or think about the place where you currently work. What are some of the types of people who make up that workplace? Make a "single folk taxonomy" list the way Spradley and Mann do for Brady's Bar. In what way might your list be divided into a more formal social structure as the researchers divided their list of types at Brady's?

3. From what you have read here, explain how the social network at Brady's functions to help waitresses do their job and, at the same time, creates what Spradley and Mann call the "social life" of the bar.

FIELDWORK PROJECT

For this assignment, you should, much like Spradley and Mann, reconstruct the social network in a workplace. You can do this assignment whether or not you are currently holding a job. If you currently are holding a job (even if it is volunteer work, campus work, or work for an organization that is paid or unpaid), then you should spend some time taking field notes (see Participant Observation Fieldwork in Chapter 3, Schooling) and keep the questions below in mind. If you currently are not holding a job, write about a job that you have done before and use the questions below to help you recall details of that workplace. Divide your report into three sections: Background, Analysis, and Conclusion.

Background

Begin your report by giving your audience a general background summary of the workplace. The questions below can help you to prepare that summary:

1. What is the nature of this business or organization?

2. When did you begin working there? What was/is your job? What difficulties did you encounter during the initial stages of the job?

3. Who are the people in this workplace, and how many employees typically are on the job at one time?

4. Who supervises the workplace? Is that person always present or only occasionally present?

5. What is the pay, or how many volunteer hours are expected of those who work there?

6. What do people expect from employees in this workplace? (For example, do customers expect to be waited on or left to themselves to browse?)

7. What is the work space like? Describe it. How large is it? Is there enough room here for workers to do a job comfortably? Is there anything in particular that is important to mention about the space? (For example, is it exceptionally dark or open or crowded?)

Analysis: Reconstructing the Social Network of the Workplace

Your aim in this central section of your report is to reconstruct the social network of the workplace that you have chosen. Spradley and Mann use both visual diagrams and descriptive analysis to explain how workers and customers interact in the bar to form the social network at Brady's. You can do the same. Begin by visually mapping out relationships and follow that diagram with a description of the social network that you have reconstructed. The following questions can help you with your analysis:

1. Who is in charge (either by actually having a position above others or by virtue of less formal or unstated determinations)? Is the boss or supervisor always in control, or do subordinates have their own ways of doing what they want?

2. How do workers spend their time while on the job?

3. How do workers know what to do and when to do it?

4. What kinds of things happen that help or impede the work done in this place? Are there certain people you would identify as interfering with work and others you would say facilitate the work being done?

5. What seems to be the attitude of those working as they are doing their job?

6. How do workers interact with each other? Do they interact with customers or outside people coming into the work space? (For example, what are the typical informal as well as formal interactions among employees, employees and customers, staff and supervisors, etc.?)

7. Is there a person (supervisor or not) who must be pleased or not crossed? How do workers know that?

8. What are some things that go on in the job that you only learned on your own after working there for a time?

9. What are the unspoken rules of this workplace, and how does the social network that has evolved here seem to convey and sustain those rules?

Conclusion

The concluding paragraph of the Spradley and Mann selection offers a quick summary of their descriptive analysis:

> The social life of Brady's Bar derives its form from the formal social structure as well as the various networks that waitresses and others activate for special purposes. Each waitress finds herself linked in some way to others in the bar with varying degrees of involvement.

Your conclusion ought to do the same. Summarize your analysis quickly in this concluding portion of the report.

Sewing Girl, from Harper's Bazaar, February 18, 1971

Courtesy New York Library

Impoverished seamstresses were familiar figures in early-19th-century American cities, filling the needs of an expanding garment industry. Working at home, they stitched bundles of pre-cut fabric into clothing worn by Southern slaves, Western miners, and New England gentlemen. Dressmakers were responsible for producing an entire garment and could earn a decent wage. Seamstresses, however, were poorly compensated for work that was both physically demanding and unpredictable. Paid by the piece, seamstresses worked 16 hours a day during the busiest seasons, but their income rarely exceeded bare subsistence. Making matters worse, shop owners were notorious for finding fault with the finished garments and withholding payment. Consequently, seamstresses often relied on charity for their own and their families' survival.

Mining the Archive

SWEATSHOP FASHION

Sweater: employer who underpays and overworks his employees, especially a contractor for piecework in the tailoring trade.

Standard Dictionary of the English Language, *1895*

Although Lewis Hine's images of child labor that appear in our discussion of visual culture were taken at the start of this century, concern over child labor has returned to the news as a serious social matter. Much of the discussion has to do with working conditions outside the United States, but little attention has been given to sweatshops that investigators continue to find in this country.

Some of the most interesting and innovative reporting and activism connected with this issue is available through Internet sources. By far the most thorough and interactive site for sweatshop history is the Smithsonian Institute's site devoted to its exhibit *Between a Rock and a Hard Place: A History of American Sweatshops 1820–Present* (http://americanhistory.si.edu/sweatshops/). Begin your work by visiting this site and following the many links that trace sweatshop history from the early part of the nineteenth century to the El Monte, California, sweatshop raid on August 2, 1995. After you have visited this site, you may wish to extend your searches to sites such as the Cornell WorkNet page.

The information you find in your research can serve as a resource for any of the following projects:

- Design your own Web page that provides both background to the issue and other sites for research to explore.
- Write a letter to a corporation that uses child labor or other unfair labor practices in which you attempt to persuade the company to change its working conditions.
- Write a report on this issue in which you detail the difficulties corporations have experienced when they try to change labor policies in other countries.
- Create a public service announcement (video, audio, or print) using the information you have found in your investigations to make consumers aware of this issue.

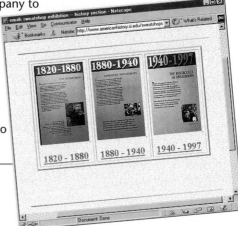

CHAPTER 9

History

One of the marks of a good professional historian is the consistency with which he reminds his readers of the purely provisional nature of his characterization of events, agents, and agencies found in the always incomplete historical record.

—*Hayden White*, Tropics of Discourse

If you would ask what history is, most people would probably say that it is the story of what has happened in the past, and they might think of the dates they memorized and the events they learned in school. Most Americans encounter history in school as a set of facts about the Louisiana Purchase, the Mexican-American War, or the Homestead Act. Accounts of these events can be verified by records and evidence from the past, and we take them to be true—to be based on the facts.

But it is precisely because history claims an authority based on fact that we need to ask a further question, namely, where do the facts come from in the writing of history? It is true, of course, that in one sense the facts are simply there—in historical records, newspapers, government documents, archives, and so forth. The facts, however, cannot come forward on their own to speak for themselves. So while it seems incontestable that Columbus did indeed sail from Spain to the West Indies in 1492, the meanings of the event that people have brought forward can vary considerably. Among our concerns in this chapter are the perspectives from which historians and other writers look at the past and how these ways of looking bring certain facts into view while ignoring or suppressing others.

The purpose of this chapter, in other words, is to investigate the writing of history—and why individuals and groups might tell different versions of the past. In this chapter you will be asked to read, think, and write about the version of American history that you learned in school. You will be asked to recall not only what you learned but also what lessons you were led to draw from the study of the past. You will be asked to think about whose version of the American past you learned, and whose perspectives are included and whose are excluded in the story. You will be asked to consider whether American history needs to be rewritten in order to embody those perspectives that are absent—the voices from the past that have been silent in the history Americans learn in school.

There are some things in school that students have to learn by heart. The alphabet. The multiplication tables. The names of the continents and oceans. But students also learn history by heart—and it is worth examining for a moment just what that phrase "to learn by heart" might mean. On the one hand, it means memorizing dates, names, and events—and probably getting tested on them. On the other hand, learning something by heart also suggests an emotional investment. To learn the history of the American revolution or the Civil War by heart is not just to acquire the facts. It also means acquiring judgments and attitudes and forming social allegiances and loyalties. History, most students understand, despite the ostensibly objective tone of their textbooks, is a moral drama that contains lessons to teach them about which side they belong to in the unfolding story of the American nation.

The story Americans learn through school and history textbooks is a tale of national destiny—of how hard-working Americans developed a democratic society in the New World and how America prospered and grew bigger and stronger to become an industrial and geopolitical power in the twentieth century. According to this story, the expansion of America's borders and productivity is simply the natural growth and development of the nation, the inevitable unfolding of the country's role in history. This sense of destiny and national purpose is linked closely to Americans' image of themselves and their mission as a people. For many Americans, history is a form of collective memory that joins the country together in a national identity and explains how America became what it is today. American history, in this regard, is not just a mat-

ter of the facts. It takes on a mythic dimension by telling of the founding events, heroic acts, and tragic sacrifices that have made this country a powerful nation.

Until fairly recently there existed a broad consensus about the meaning of American history and its principles of development. Nowadays, however, the version of American history that has prevailed in schools and textbooks has been called into question. Historians have started to reread the historical record, to see what voices have been silenced or ignored in the story of America's national development. New perspectives—from women, African Americans, Hispanics, American Indians, Asian Americans, and working-class people—are being added to America's collective history; these alternative accounts complicate the picture of the American past considerably. The westward expansion, for example, from the perspective of Native Americans, looks less like the progressive development of the land and its agricultural and mineral resources and more like the military conquest and occupation of traditional tribal holdings.

One of the things you will be asked to do in this chapter is to read for the plot in historians' and other writers' accounts of the past—to describe what their perspectives bring into view about the past and how they have selected and arranged the events to tell a story. By looking at how historians and writers construct versions of the past (always from their particular perspective in the present), you can identify not only the techniques that they use to tell a story but also the different versions of the past that they make available to us today. In contemporary America, to think about history is to think about competing versions of the past, and you will want to consider how the plots differ—and what is thereby at stake—in the various accounts of the past that you read in the following selections. We have chosen the readings in this chapter to include contrasting examples of historical writing—official versions of American history taken from textbooks, as well as efforts of revisionist historians and writers to retell the story of the American past. What you will see is that the differences in plots and perspectives raise profound questions about who is entitled to write American history and whose voices are heard.

The answers you get to these and to other questions that you will discover in the following readings are concerned finally not just with the study of the past but also with how you as a reader and writer align yourself in the present—how you know what the sides are in American history and where your sympathies reside. The purpose of this chapter, therefore, is to think about the role that history plays in your own and other people's lives and how it defines (or challenges) our sense of identity as a people and as a nation.

READING HISTORY

One way to think about the role history plays in people's lives is to think about how you have learned about the past. The opening two selections offer perspectives on how learning about history is not simply a matter of learning what happened in the past. As Mary Gordon suggests in "More Than Just a Shrine: Paying Homage to the Ghosts of Ellis Island," visiting historical sites can be more than a history lesson. It can also offer an occasion to honor ancestors, in this case the Irish, Italians, and Lithuanian Jews in Gordon's family who immigrated to the United States around the turn of the century and whose lives show up only as statistics in the official historical record. By the same token, in "Columbus in Chains," a chapter selected from the novel *Annie John,* Jamaica Kincaid reveals how a young West Indian schoolgirl learns which "side" she is on by studying the history of Columbus's voyages to the New World. Taken together, these selections indicate how writers have constructed their own histories against the grain of the familiar stories of immigration or Christopher Columbus, by retelling these stories for their own purposes. These readings suggest that the meaning of the past can never be complete. We can never exhaust fully the meaning of the past because reasons and urgencies in the present seem to compel new versions of history, new plots, and new interpretations.

In "'Indians': Textualism, Morality, and the Problem of History," Jane Tompkins takes up the question of how historians' differing points of view and underlying assumptions result in conflicting interpretations of the past. Tompkins provides a personal account of her research on the Puritans' relations with Native Americans and how she dealt with the differences that she found in historians' accounts of the past.

The next cluster of readings concern the Vietnam War and make up a case study of how the history of this traumatic time is told and interpreted, not only by professional historians but also by participants and by Hollywood. "The Tragedy of Vietnam," from George B. Tindall and David E. Shi's textbook *America: A Narrative History,* is paired with a number of passages, grouped under the title "God's Country and American Know-How," from Loren Baritz's book-length study of the cultural causes of the Vietnam War, *Backfire: A History of How American Culture Led Us Into the Vietnam War.* Each selection, as you will see, offers an explanation of American military involvement in Vietnam but differs considerably in scope and emphasis.

The next three readings offer personal accounts of the Vietnam War, giving us voices from the war of ordinary people who are not always heard in the official record. In the first, "When Heaven and Earth Changed Places," Le Ly Hayslip explains the war from the perspective of Vietnamese peasants in the countryside, while "Private First Class Reginald 'Malik' Edwards," an oral history from Wallace Terry's book *Bloods,* offers the recollections of an American soldier. The final reading, Kristin Ann Hass's "Making a Memory of War: Building the Vietnam Veterans Memorial," explores the way memorials, monuments, statues, and other commemorations seek to make sense of war, thereby raising questions about how Americans have come to terms with painful memories and the still unsettled experience of the Vietnam War.

As you read, think, talk, and write about how American history has been constructed, you will be asked to consider where the meanings Americans ascribe to their history come from and how the meanings we give to the past position people in relation to the social, cultural, and political realities of the present. What do Americans as a people choose to remember and commemorate about their past? How does historical memory influence life in contemporary America?

More Than Just a Shrine
Paying Homage to the Ghosts of Ellis Island

Mary Gordon

> Mary Gordon is an acclaimed novelist and short-story writer who teaches at
> Barnard College. Her novels *Final Payments, The Company of Women,* and *The
> Other Side* explore the history and culture of Irish Catholics in America. In the
> following selection, an essay originally published in the *New York Times* (1987),
> Gordon offers her personal reflections on the history of immigration that
> brought her ancestors—Irish, Italian, and Lithuanian Jews—to the United States
> by way of Ellis Island, the point of entry in New York Harbor for over 16 million
> immigrants between 1892 and 1924. In her essay, Gordon suggests that history
> is a living relationship to the past, in this case to the "ghosts of Ellis Island" that
> she wants to honor.

SUGGESTION FOR READING

> As you read, notice that Mary Gordon provides a good deal of historical infor-
> mation about Ellis Island, and yet her main point is to establish her own per-
> sonal connection to this American landmark. Mark passages where Gordon
> locates herself in relation to what took place in the past.

I once sat in a hotel in Bloomsbury trying to have breakfast alone. A Russian with a habit of
compulsively licking his lips asked if he could join me. I was afraid to say no; I thought it
might be bad for détente. He explained to me that he was a linguist and that he always
liked to talk to Americans to see if he could make any connection between their speech and
their ethnic background. When I told him about my mixed ancestry—my mother is Irish
and Italian, my father was a Lithuanian Jew—he began jumping up and down in his seat,
rubbing his hands together and licking his lips even more frantically.

"Ah," he said, "so you are really somebody who comes from what is called the boiling
pot of America." Yes, I told him; yes, I was; but I quickly rose to leave. I thought it would be
too hard to explain to him the relation of the boiling potters to the main course, and I wanted
to get to the British Museum. I told him that the only thing I could think of that united people whose backgrounds, histories, and points of view were utterly diverse was that their
people had landed at a place called Ellis Island.

I didn't tell him that Ellis Island was the only American landmark I'd ever visited. How
could I describe to him the estrangement I'd always felt from the kind of traveler who visits
shrines to America's past greatness, those rebuilt forts with muskets behind glass and sabers
mounted on the walls and gift shops selling maple sugar candy in the shape of Indian head-
dresses, those reconstructed villages with tables set for fifty and the Paul Revere silver gleaming? All that Americana—Plymouth Rock, Gettysburg, Mount Vernon, Valley Forge—it all
inhabits for me a zone of blurred abstraction with far less hold on my imagination than the
Bastille or Hampton Court. I suppose I've always known that my uninterest in it contains a
large component of the willed: I am American, and those places purport to be my history.
But they are not mine.

Ellis Island is, though; it's the one place I can be sure my people are connected to. And
so I made a journey there to find my history, like any Rotarian traveling in his Winnebago

to Antietam to find his. I had become part of that humbling democracy of people looking in some site for a past that has grown unreal. The monument I traveled to was not, however, a tribute to some old glory. The minute I set foot upon the island I could feel all that it stood for: insecurity, obedience, anxiety, dehumanization, the terrified and careful deference of the displaced. I hadn't traveled to the Battery and boarded a ferry across from the Statue of Liberty to raise flags or breathe a richer, more triumphant air. I wanted to do homage to the ghosts.

I felt them everywhere, from the moment I disembarked and saw the building with its high-minded brick, its hopeful little lawn, its ornamental cornices. The place was derelict when I arrived; it had not functioned for more than thirty years—almost as long as the time it had operated at full capacity as a major immigration center. I was surprised to learn what a small part of history Ellis Island had occupied. The main building was constructed in 1892, then rebuilt between 1898 and 1900 after a fire. Most of the immigrants who arrived during the latter half of the nineteenth century, mainly northern and western Europeans, landed not at Ellis Island but on the western tip of the Battery, at Castle Garden, which had opened as a receiving center for immigrants in 1855.

By the 1880s, the facilities at Castle Garden had grown scandalously inadequate. Officials looked for an island on which to build a new immigration center, because they thought that on an island immigrants could be more easily protected from swindlers and quickly transported to railroad terminals in New Jersey. Bedloe's Island was considered, but New Yorkers were aghast at the idea of a "Babel" ruining their beautiful new treasure, "Liberty Enlightening the World." The statue's sculptor, Frédéric-Auguste Bartholdi, reacted to the prospect of immigrants landing near his masterpiece in horror; he called it a "monstrous plan." So much for Emma Lazarus.

Ellis Island was finally chosen because the citizens of New Jersey petitioned the federal government to remove from the island an old naval powder magazine that they thought dangerously close to the Jersey shore. The explosives were removed; no one wanted the island for anything. It was the perfect place to build an immigration center.

I thought about the island's history as I walked into the building and made my way to the room that was the center in my imagination of the Ellis Island experience: the Great Hall. It had been made real for me in the stark, accusing photographs of Louis Hine and others, who took those pictures to make a point. It was in the Great Hall that everyone had waited—waiting, always, the great vocation of the dispossessed. The room was empty, except for me and a handful of other visitors and the park ranger who showed us around. I felt myself grow insignificant in that room, with its huge semicircular windows, its air, even in dereliction, of solid and official probity.

I walked in the deathlike expansiveness of the room's disuse and tried to think of what it might have been like, filled and swarming. More than sixteen million immigrants came through that room; approximately 250,000 were rejected. Not really a large proportion, but the implications for the rejected were dreadful. For some, there was nothing to go back to, or there was certain death; for others, who left as adventurers, to return would be to adopt in local memory the fool's role, and the failure's. No wonder that the island's history includes reports of three thousand suicides.

Sometimes immigrants could pass through Ellis Island in mere hours, though for some the process took days. The particulars of the experience in the Great Hall were often influenced by the political events and attitudes on the mainland. In the 1890s and the first years of the new century, when cheap labor was needed, the newly built receiving center took in its immigrants with comparatively little question. But as the century progressed, the economy worsened, eugenics became both scientifically respectable and popular, and World War I made American xenophobia seem rooted in fact.

Immigration acts were passed; newcomers had to prove, besides moral correctness and financial solvency, their ability to read. Quota laws came into effect, limiting the number of immigrants from southern and eastern Europe to less than 14 percent of the total quota. Intelligence tests were biased against all non-English-speaking persons, and medical examinations became increasingly strict, until the machinery of immigration nearly collapsed under its own weight. The Second Quota Law of 1924 provided that all immigrants be inspected and issued visas at American consular offices in Europe, rendering the center almost obsolete.

On the day of my visit, my mind fastened upon the medical inspections, which had always seemed to me most emblematic of the ignominy and terror the immigrants ensured. The medical inspectors, sometimes dressed in uniforms like soldiers, were particularly obsessed with a disease of the eyes called trachoma, which they checked for by flipping back the immigrants' top eyelids with a hook used for buttoning gloves—a method that sometimes resulted in the transmission of the disease to healthy people. Mothers feared that if their children cried too much, their red eyes would be mistaken for a symptom of the disease and the whole family would be sent home. Those immigrants suspected of some physical disability had initials chalked on their coats. I remembered the photographs I'd seen of people standing, dumbstruck and innocent as cattle, with their manifest numbers hung around their necks and initials marked in chalk upon their coats: "E" for eye trouble, "K" for hernia, "L" for lameness, "X" for mental defects, "H" for heart disease.

I thought of my grandparents as I stood in the room: my seventeen-year-old grandmother, coming alone from Ireland in 1896, vouched for by a stranger who had found her a place as a domestic servant to some Irish who had done well. I tried to imagine the assault it all must have been for her; I've been to her hometown, a collection of farms with a main street—smaller than the athletic field of my local public school. She must have watched the New York skyline as the first- and second-class passengers were whisked off the gangplank with the most cursory of inspections while she was made to board a ferry to the new immigration center.

What could she have made of it—this buff-painted wooden structure with its towers and its blue slate roof, a place *Harper's Weekly* described as "a latter-day watering place hotel"? It would have been the first time she had heard people speaking something other than English. She would have mingled with people carrying baskets on their heads and eating foods unlike any she had ever seen—dark-eyed people, like the Sicilian she would marry ten years later, who came over with his family at thirteen, the man of the family, responsible even then for his mother and sister. I don't know what they thought, my grandparents, for they were not expansive people, nor romantic; they didn't like to think of what they called "the hard times," and their trip across the ocean was the single adventurous act of lives devoted after landing to security, respectability, and fitting in.

What is the potency of Ellis Island for someone like me—an American, obviously, but one who has always felt that the country really belonged to the early settlers, that, as J. F. Powers wrote in *Morte D'Urban,* it had been "handed down to them by the Pilgrims, George Washington and others, and that they were taking a risk in letting you live in it." I have never been the victim of overt discrimination; nothing I have wanted has been denied me because of the accidents of blood. But I suppose it is part of being an American to be engaged in a somewhat tiresome but always self-absorbing process of national definition. And in this process, I have found in traveling to Ellis Island an important piece of evidence that could remind me I was right to feel my differentness. Something had happened to my people on that island, a result of the eternal wrongheadedness of American protectionism and the predictabilities of simple greed. I came to the island, too, so I could tell the ghosts that I was one of them, and that I honored them—their stoicism, and their innocence, the fear that turned them inward, and their pride. I wanted to tell them that I liked them better than I did the Americans who made them pass through the Great Hall and stole their names and chalked their weaknesses in public on their clothing. And to tell the ghosts what I have always thought: that American history was a very classy party that was not much fun until they arrived, brought the good food, turned up the music, and taught everyone to dance.

SUGGESTIONS FOR DISCUSSION

1. Mary Gordon describes the "estrangement I'd always felt from the kind of traveler who visits shrines to America's past greatness" and goes on to say that "those places purport to be my history. But they are not mine." Why does Gordon feel this way? What is she suggesting about the way that we experience the history of America? Do some parts belong to you but not others?

2. What historical landmarks have you visited with your family or on class trips in elementary or high school? What were your feelings about those trips? Compare your experience to Gordon's. Did you experience these historical sites as part of your history? Explain.

3. Gordon says that Ellis Island is "the one place I can be sure my people are connected to." Name a place to which your people are connected, where you could, as Gordon puts it, "do homage to the ghosts." To what extent is the place you have named alike or different from the places that your classmates have named?

SUGGESTIONS FOR WRITING

1. Mary Gordon says the one thing that unifies her ancestors—Irish, Italian, and Lithuanian Jews "whose backgrounds, histories, and points of view were utterly diverse"—is that they all landed at Ellis Island. Write an essay that explores the diversity among your ancestors and considers whether there is something—a place such as Ellis Island or a historical event such as immigration—that unites them.

2. Use Gordon's account of her visit to Ellis Island as a model to write an essay that explains your response to visiting a historical site. Make sure you explain the historical importance of the place you visited, but also follow Gordon's example to explain your own relation to that history. Did you experience the place as part of a history to which you felt connected, or did you, for some reason, feel estranged?

3. Gordon's essay suggests that history is as much a matter of paying "homage to the ghosts" as it is learning a chronology of events. Pick a historical figure, place, or event in American history with which you feel a strong personal identification. Describe the person, place, or event and then explain the reasons for your identification. Use the essay as an occasion to pay homage—to explain your personal allegiances and why the person, place, or event seems important to you.

Columbus in Chains

Jamaica Kincaid

Jamaica Kincaid is an award-winning novelist, short-story writer, and essayist who grew up on the West Indian island of Antigua and now lives in Vermont. Her fiction, *At the Bottom of the River, Annie John,* and *Lucy,* concerns the coming of age of a young West Indian woman, the intense emotional bonds between mothers and daughters, and the struggles of Kincaid's main character to assert her independence and individuality. The following selection, "Columbus in Chains," was originally published as a short story in the *New Yorker* and then became a chapter in *Annie John* (1985). Here, Annie John, Kincaid's precocious heroine, offers readers an alternative perspective on Columbus's voyages to the New World.

SUGGESTION FOR READING

The following reading explores, among other things, the interaction of two cultures in the West Indies—the British culture of the schools and the local Antiguan culture. As you read, annotate passages where the narrator Annie John gives us clues to the two cultures and to their relationship.

Outside, as usual, the sun shone, the trade winds blew; on her way to put some starched clothes on the line, my mother shooed some hens out of her garden; Miss Dewberry baked the buns, some of which my mother would buy for my father and me to eat with our afternoon tea; Miss Henry brought the milk, a glass of which I would drink with my lunch, and another glass of which I would drink with the bun from Miss Dewberry; my mother prepared our lunch; my father noted some perfectly idiotic thing his partner in housebuilding, Mr. Oatie, had done, so that over lunch he and my mother could have a good laugh.

The Anglican church bell struck eleven o'clock—one hour to go before lunch. I was then sitting at my desk in my classroom. We were having a history lesson—the last lesson of the morning. For taking first place over all the other girls, I had been given a prize, a copy of a book called *Roman Britain,* and I was made prefect of my class. What a mistake the prefect part had been, for I was among the worst-behaved in my class and did not at all believe in setting myself up as a good example, the way a prefect was supposed to do. Now I had to sit in the prefect's seat—the first seat in the front row, the seat from which I could stand up and survey quite easily my classmates. From where I sat I could see out the window. Sometimes when I looked out, I could see the sexton going over to the minister's house. The sexton's daughter, Hilarene, a disgusting model of good behavior and keen attention to scholarship, sat next to me, since she took second place. The minister's daughter, Ruth, sat in the last row, the row reserved for all the dunce girls. Hilarene, of course, I could not stand. A girl that good would never do for me. I would probably not have cared so much for first place if I could be sure it would not go to her. Ruth I liked, because she was such a dunce and came from England and had yellow hair. When I first met her, I used to walk her home and sing bad songs to her just to see her turn pink, as if I had spilled hot water all over her.

Our books, *A History of the West Indies,* were open in front of us. Our day had begun with morning prayers, then a geometry lesson, then it was over to the science building for a lesson in "Introductory Physics" (not a subject we cared much for) taught by the most dingy-toothed Mr. Slacks, a teacher from Canada, then precious recess, and now this, our history lesson. Recess had the usual drama: this time, I coaxed Gwen out of her disappointment at not being allowed to join the junior choir. Her father—how many times had I wished he would become a leper and so be banished to a leper colony for the rest of my long and happy life with Gwen—had forbidden it, giving as his reason that she lived too far away from church, where choir rehearsals were conducted, and that it would be dangerous for her, a young girl, to walk home alone at night in the dark. Of course, all the streets had lamplight, but it was useless to point that out to him. Oh, how it would have pleased us to press and rub our knees together as we sat in our pew while pretending to pay close attention to Mr. Simmons, our choirmaster, as he waved his baton up and down and across, and how it would have pleased us even more to walk home together, alone in the "early dusk" (the way Gwen had phrased it, a ready phrase always on her tongue), stopping, if there was a full moon, to lie down in a pasture and expose our bosoms in the moonlight. We had heard that full moonlight would make our breasts grow to a size we would like. Poor Gwen! When I first heard from her that she was one of ten children, right on the spot I told her that I would love only her, since her mother already had so many other people to love.

Our teacher, Miss Edward, paced up and down in front of the class in her usual way. In front of her desk stood a small table, and on it stood the dunce cap. The dunce cap was in the shape of a coronet, with an adjustable opening in the back, so that it could fit any head. It was made of cardboard with a shiny gold paper covering and the word "DUNCE" in shiny red paper on the front. When the sun shone on it, the dunce cap was all aglitter, almost as if you were being tricked into thinking it a desirable thing to wear. As Miss Edward paced up and down, she would pass between us and the dunce cap like an eclipse. Each Friday morning, we were given a small test to see how well we had learned the things taught to us all week. The girl who scored lowest was made to wear the dunce cap all day the following Monday. On many Mondays, Ruth wore it—only, with her short yellow hair, when the dunce cap was sitting on her head she looked like a girl attending a birthday party in *The Schoolgirl's Own Annual*.

It was Miss Edward's way to ask one of us a question the answer to which she was sure the girl would not know and then put the same question to another girl who she was sure would know the answer. The girl who did not answer correctly would then have to repeat the correct answer in the exact words of the other girl. Many times, I had heard my exact words repeated over and over again, and I liked it especially when the girl doing the repeating was one I didn't care about very much. Pointing a finger at Ruth, Miss Edward asked a question the answer to which was "On the third of November 1493, a Sunday morning, Christopher Columbus discovered Dominica." Ruth, of course, did not know the answer, as she did not know the answer to many questions about the West Indies. I could hardly blame her. Ruth had come all the way from England. Perhaps she did not want to be in the West Indies at all. Perhaps she wanted to be in England, where no one would remind her constantly of the terrible things her ancestors had done; perhaps she had felt even worse when her father was a missionary in Africa. I could see how Ruth felt from looking at her face. Her ancestors had been the masters, while ours had been the slaves. She had such a lot to be ashamed of, and by being with us every day she was always being reminded. We could look everybody in the eye, for our ancestors had done nothing wrong except just sit somewhere, defenseless. Of course, sometimes, what with our teachers and our books, it was hard for us to tell on which side we really now belonged—with the masters or the slaves—for it was all history, it was all in the past, and everybody behaved differently now; all of us celebrated Queen Victoria's birthday, even though she had been dead a long time. But we, the descendants of the slaves, knew quite well what had really happened, and I was sure that if the tables had been turned we would have acted differently; I was sure that if our ancestors had gone from Africa to Europe and come upon the people living there, they would have taken a proper interest in the Europeans on first seeing them, and said, "How nice," and then gone home to tell their friends about it.

I was sitting at my desk, having these thoughts to myself. I don't know how long it had been since I lost track of what was going on around me. I had not noticed that the girl who was asked the question after Ruth failed—a girl named Hyacinth—had only got a part of the answer correct. I had not noticed that after these two attempts Miss Edward had launched into a harangue about what a worthless bunch we were compared to girls of the past. In fact, I was no longer on the same chapter we were studying. I was way ahead, at the end of the chapter about Columbus's third voyage. In this chapter, there was a picture of Columbus that took up a whole page and it was in color—one of only five color pictures in the book. In this picture Columbus was seated in the bottom of a ship. He was wearing the usual three-quarter trousers and a shirt with enormous sleeves, both the trousers and shirt made of maroon-colored velvet. His hat, which was cocked up on one side of his head, had a gold feather in it, and his black shoes had huge gold buckles. His hands and feet were bound up in chains, and he was sitting there staring off into space, looking quite dejected and miserable. The picture had as a title "Columbus in Chains," printed at the bottom of the page. What had happened was that the usually quarrelsome Columbus had got into a disagreement with people who were even more quarrelsome, and a man named Bobadilla, representing King Ferdinand and Queen Isabella, had sent him back to Spain fettered in chains attached to the bottom of a ship. What just desserts, I thought, for I did not like Columbus. How I loved this picture— to see the usually triumphant Columbus, brought so low, seated at the bottom of a boat just watching things go by. Shortly after I first discovered it in my history book, I heard my mother read out loud to my father a letter she had received from her sister, who still lived with her mother and father in the very same Dominica, which is where my mother came from. Ma Chess was fine, wrote my aunt, but Pa Chess was not well. Pa Chess was having a bit of trouble with his limbs; he was not able to go about as he pleased; often he had to depend on someone else to do one thing or another for him. My mother read the letter in quite a state, her voice rising to a higher pitch with each sentence. After she read the part about Pa Chess's stiff limbs, she turned to my father and laughed as she said, "So the great man can no longer just get up and go. How I would love to see his face now!" When I next saw the picture of Columbus sitting there all locked up in his chains, I wrote under it the words "The Great Man Can No Longer Just Get Up and Go." I had written this out with my fountain pen, and in Old English lettering—a script I had recently mastered. As I sat there looking at the picture, I traced the words with my pen over and over, so that the letters grew big and you could read what I had written from not very far away. I don't know how long it was before I heard that my name, Annie John, was being said by this bellowing dragon in the form of Miss Edward bearing down on me.

I had never been a favorite of hers. Her favorite was Hilarene. It must have pained Miss Edward that I so often beat out Hilarene. Not that I liked Miss Edward and wanted her to like me back, but as the other teachers regarded me with much affection they would always tell my mother that I was the most charming student they had ever had, beamed at me when they saw me coming, and were very sorry when they had to write some version of this on my report card: "Annie is an unusually bright girl. She is well behaved in class, at least in the presence of her masters and mistresses, but behind their backs and outside the classroom quite the opposite is true." When my mother read this or something like it, she would burst into tears. She had hoped to display, with a great flourish, my report card to her friends, along with whatever prize I had won. Instead, the report card would have to take a place at the bottom of the old trunk in which she kept any important thing that had to do with me. I became not a favorite of Miss Edward's in the following way: Each Friday afternoon, the girls in the lower forms were given, instead of a last lesson period, an extra-long recess. We were to use this in lady-like recreation—walks, chats about the novels and poems we were reading, showing each other the new embroidery stitches we had learned to master in home class, or something just as seemly. Instead, some of the girls would play a game of cricket or rounders or stones, but most of us would go to the far end of the school grounds and play band. In this game, of which teachers and parents disapproved and which was sometimes absolutely forbidden, we would place our arms around each other's waist or shoulders, forming lines of ten or so girls, and then we would dance from one end of the school grounds to the other. As we danced, we would sometimes chant these words: "Tee la la la, come go. Tee la la la, come go." At other times we would sing a popular calypso song which usually had lots of unladylike words to it. Up and down the schoolyard, away from our teachers, we would dance and sing. At the end of recess—forty-five minutes—we were missing ribbons and other ornaments from our hair, the pleats of our linen tunics became unset, the collars of our blouses were pulled out, and we were soaking wet all the way down to our bloomers. When the school bell rang, we would make a whooping sound, as if in a great panic, and then we would throw ourselves on top of each other as we laughed and shrieked. We would then run back to our classes, where we prepared to file into the auditorium for evening prayers. After that, it was home for the weekend. But how could we go straight home after all that excitement? No sooner were we on the street than we would form little groups, depending on the direction we were headed in. I was never keen on joining them on the way home, because I was sure I would run into my mother. Instead, my friends and I would go to our usual place near the back of the churchyard and sit on the tombstones of people who had been buried there way before slavery was abolished, in 1833. We would sit and sing bad songs, use forbidden words, and, of course, show each other various parts of our bodies. While some of us watched, the others would walk up and down on the large tombstones showing off their legs. It was immediately a popular idea; everybody soon wanted to do it. It wasn't long before many girls—the ones whose mothers didn't pay strict attention to what they were doing—started to come to school on Fridays wearing not bloomers under their uniforms but underpants trimmed with lace and satin frills. It also wasn't long before an end came to all that. One Friday afternoon, Miss Edward, on her way home from school, took a shortcut through the churchyard. She must have heard the commotion we were making, because there she suddenly was, saying, "What is the meaning of this?"—just the very thing someone like her would say if she came unexpectedly on something like us. It was obvious that I was the ringleader. Oh, how I wished the ground would open up and take her in, but it did not. We all, shamefacedly, slunk home, I with Miss Edward at my side. Tears came to my mother's eyes when she heard what I had done. It was apparently such a bad thing that my mother couldn't bring herself to repeat my misdeed to my father in my presence. I got the usual punishment of dinner alone, outside under the breadfruit tree, but added on to that, I was not allowed to go to the library on Saturday, and on Sunday, after Sunday school and dinner, I was not allowed to take a stroll in the botanical gardens, where Gwen was waiting for me in the bamboo grove.

That happened when I was in the first form. Now here Miss Edward stood. Her whole face was on fire. Her eyes were bulging out of her head. I was sure that at any minute they would land at my feet and roll away. The small pimples on her face, already looking as if they were constantly irritated, now ballooned into huge, on-the-verge-of-exploding boils. Her head shook from side to side. Her strange bottom, which she carried high in the air, seemed to rise up so high that it almost touched the ceiling. Why did I not pay attention, she said. My impertinence was beyond endurance. She then found a hundred words for the different forms my impertinence took. On she went. I was just getting used to this amazing bellowing when suddenly she was speechless. In fact, everything stopped. Her eyes stopped, her bottom stopped, her pimples stopped. Yes she had got close enough so that her eyes caught a glimpse of what I had done to my textbook. The glimpse soon led to closer inspection. It was bad enough that I had defaced my schoolbook by writing in it. That I should write under the picture of Columbus "The Great Man..." etc. was just too much. I had gone too far this time, defaming one of the great men in history, Christopher Columbus, discoverer of the island that was my home. And now look at me. I was not even hanging my head in remorse. Had my peers ever seen anyone so arrogant, so blasphemous?

I was sent to the headmistress, Miss Moore. As punishment, I was removed from my position as prefect, and my place was taken by the odious Hilarene. As an added punishment, I was ordered to copy Books I and II of *Paradise Lost,* by John Milton, and to have it done a week from that day. I then couldn't wait to get home to lunch and the comfort of my mother's kisses and arms. I had nothing to worry about there yet; it would be a while before my mother and father heard of my bad deeds. What a terrible morning! Seeing my mother would be such a tonic—something to pick me up.

When I got home, my mother kissed me absentmindedly. My father had got home ahead of me, and they were already deep in conversation, my father regaling her with some unusually outlandish thing the oaf Mr. Oatie had done. I washed my hands and took my place at table. My mother brought me my lunch. I took one smell of it, and I could tell that it was the much hated breadfruit. My mother said not at all, it was a new kind of rice imported from Belgium, and not breadfruit, mashed and forced through a ricer, as I thought. She went back to talking to my father. My father could hardly get a few words out of his mouth before she was a jelly-fish of laughter. I sat there, putting my food in my mouth. I could not believe that she couldn't see how miserable I was and so reach out a hand to comfort me and caress my cheek, the way she usually did when she sensed that something was amiss with me. I could not believe how she laughed at everything he said, and how bitter it made me feel to see how much she liked him. I ate my meal. The more I ate of it, the more I was sure that it was breadfruit. When I finished, my mother got up to remove my plate. As she started out the door, I said, "Tell me, really, the name of the thing I just ate."

My mother said, "You just ate some breadfruit. I made it look like rice so that you would eat it. It's very good for you, filled with lots of vitamins." As she said this, she laughed. She was standing half inside the door, half outside. Her body was in the shade of our house, but her head was in the sun. When she laughed, her mouth opened to show off big, shiny, sharp white teeth. It was as if my mother had suddenly turned into a crocodile.

SUGGESTIONS FOR DISCUSSION

1. Describe the perspective of the narrator in *Annie John*. Identify passages where Annie John locates herself in relation to the history of her people. In what sense is Annie's "defacing" her textbook a rewriting of history? What is Annie's version of the story of Columbus, and what is its relation to the official version in the schools and textbooks?

2. The key event in the chapter "Columbus in Chains" involves an act of writing—when Annie John letters "The Great Man Can No Longer Just Get Up and Go" under the picture of Columbus in chains—but there are also a number of other references to reading and writing and to written materials throughout the chapter. Identify passages where reading and writing take place or where Annie John mentions written material of one

kind or another. What role, literally and symbolically, do reading and writing play in this chapter?

3. Describe your own experience learning history in school. How does it compare to Annie's? Take into account how teachers and textbooks represented the history of your people.

SUGGESTIONS FOR WRITING

1. In the following passage, Annie John records Miss Edwards's reaction to writing in her textbook:

> It was bad enough that I had defaced my textbook by writing in it. That I should write under the picture of Columbus "The Great Man..." etc. was just too much. I had gone too far this time, defaming one of the great men in history, Christopher Columbus, discoverer of the island that was my home.

Write an essay that explains why Annie John has "gone too far" and what makes her act of writing (in Miss Edwards's words) "arrogant" and "blasphemous." Begin by analyzing Miss Edwards's reaction, but use this analysis to explore the versions of history that are presented in this chapter. Provide your own evaluation of what makes Annie's act appear to be such a transgression.

2. Speaking of the history of her ancestors, Annie John says, "Of course, sometimes what with our teachers and our books, it was hard for us to tell on which side we really now belonged—with the masters or the slaves—for it was all history, it was all in the past, everybody behaved differently then." A line or two later, however, Annie John says that "we, the descendants of the slaves, knew quite well what had really happened." Write an essay that explains how learning history in school has taught you to which side you belong. How does the history you learned in school present "sides"? You might want to consider whether the history of your ancestors and their side of things have been presented in history textbooks or whether you, like Annie John, have learned the history of your people elsewhere.

"Indians"
Textualism, Morality, and the Problem of History

Jane Tompkins

Jane Tompkins currently is a professor of English at Duke University. She is well known for her literary criticism, including the two books *Sensational Designs: The Cultural Work of American Fiction, 1790–1860* (1985) and *West of Everything: The Inner Life of Westerns* (1992). The following essay was written for the journal of literary criticism *Critical Inquiry* and originally appeared in 1986. As you will see, the essay reports on how Tompkins dealt with the conflicting historical interpretations that she encountered in her research on the Puritans' relation with Native Americans.

SUGGESTION FOR READING

Notice that Tompkins's essay can be divided into three parts. The first part raises the problem of conflicting interpretations. The second part—the longest part of the essay—reports on her research and the differing assumptions, per-spectives, and interpretations that she has found. In the final part, Tompkins explains how she found a "way out" of the difficulties that these "irreconcilable points of view" posed for her. As you read, annotate the essay to help you keep track of what Tompkins is doing.

When I was growing up in New York City, my parents used to take me to an event in Inwood Park at which Indians—real American Indians dressed in feathers and blankets—could be seen and touched by children like me. This event was always a disappointment. It was more fun to imagine that you were an Indian in one of the caves in Inwood Park than to shake the hand of an old man in a headdress who was not overwhelmed at the opportu-nity of meeting you. After staring at the Indians for a while, we would take a walk in the woods where the caves were, and once I asked my mother if the remains of a fire I had seen in one of them might have been left by the original inhabitants. After that, wandering up some stone steps cut into the side of the hill, I imagined I was a princess in a rude castle. My Indians, like my princesses, were creatures totally of the imagination, and I did not care to have any real exemplars interfering with what I already knew.

I already knew about Indians from having read about them in school. Over and over we were told the story of how Peter Minuit had bought Manhattan Island from the Indians for twenty-four dollars' worth of glass beads. And it was a story we didn't mind hearing because it gave us the rare pleasure of having someone to feel superior to, since the poor Indians had not known (as we eight-year-olds did) how valuable a piece of property Manhattan Island would become. Generally, much was made of the Indian presence in Manhattan; a poem in one of our readers began: "Where we walk to school today / Indian children used to play," and we were encouraged to write poetry on this topic ourselves. So I had a fairly rich rela-tionship with Indians before I ever met the unprepossessing people in Inwood Park. I felt that I had a lot in common with them. They, too, liked animals (they were often named after ani-mals); they, too, made mistakes—they liked the brightly colored trinkets of little value that the white men were always offering them; they were handsome, warlike, and brave and had led an exciting, romantic life in the forest long ago, a life such as I dreamed of leading myself. I felt lucky to be living in one of the places where they had definitely been. Never mind where they were or what they were doing now.

My story stands for the relationship most non-Indians have to the people who first pop-ulated this continent, a relationship characterized by narcissistic fantasies of freedom and adventure, of a life lived closer to nature and to spirit than the life we lead now. As Vine Delo-ria Jr. has pointed out, the American Indian Movement in the early seventies couldn't get people to pay attention to what was happening to Indians who were alive in the present, so powerful was this country's infatuation with people who wore loincloths, lived in tepees, and roamed the plains and forests long ago.[1] The present essay, like these fantasies, doesn't have much to do with actual Indians, though its subject matter is the histories of European-Indian relations in seventeenth-century New England. In a sense, my encounter with Indians as an adult doing "research" replicates the childhood one, for while I started out to learn about Indians, I ended up preoccupied with a problem of my own.

This essay enacts a particular instance of the challenge poststructuralism poses to the study of history. In simpler language, it concerns the difference that point of view makes when people are giving accounts of events, whether at first or second hand. The problem is that if all accounts of events are determined through and through by the observer's frame of reference, then one will never know, in any given case, what really happened.

I encountered this problem in concrete terms while preparing to teach a course in colonial American literature. I'd set out to learn what I could about the Puritans' relations with American Indians. All I wanted was a general idea of what had happened between the English settlers and the natives in seventeenth-century New England; poststructuralism and its dilemmas were the furthest thing from my mind. I began, more or less automatically, with Perry Miller, who hardly mentions the Indians at all, then proceeded to the work of historians who had dealt exclusively with the European-Indian encounter. At first, it was a question of deciding which of these authors to believe, for it quickly became apparent that there was no unanimity on the subject. As I read on, however, I discovered that the problem was more complicated than deciding whose version of events was correct. Some of the conflicting accounts were not simply contradictory, they were completely incommensurable, in that their assumptions about what counted as a valid approach to the subject, and what the subject itself was, diverged in fundamental ways. Faced with an array of mutually irreconcilable points of view, points of view which determined what was being discussed as well as the terms of the discussion, I decided to turn to primary sources for clarification, only to discover that the primary sources reproduced the problem all over again. I found myself, in other words, in an epistemological quandary, not only unable to decide among conflicting versions of events but also unable to believe that any such decision could, in principle, be made. It was a moral quandary as well. Knowledge of what really happened when the Europeans and the Indians first met seemed particularly important, since the result of that encounter was virtual genocide. This was the kind of past "mistake" which, presumably, we studied history in order to avoid repeating. If studying history couldn't put us in touch with actual events and their causes, then what was to prevent such atrocities from happening again?

For a while, I remained at this impasse. But through analyzing the process by which I had reached it, I eventually arrived at an understanding which seemed to offer a way out. This essay records the concrete experience of meeting and solving the difficulty I have just described (as an abstract problem, I thought I had solved it long ago). My purpose is not to throw new light on antifoundationalist epistemology—the solution I reached is not a new one—but to dramatize and expose the troubles antifoundationalism gets you into when you meet it, so to speak, in the road.

My research began with Perry Miller. Early in the preface to *Errand into the Wilderness,* while explaining how he came to write his history of the New England mind, Miller writes a sentence that stopped me dead. He says that what fascinated him as a young man about his country's history was "the massive narrative of the movement of European culture into the vacant wilderness of America."[2] "Vacant?" Miller, writing in 1956, doesn't pause over the word "vacant," but to people who read his preface thirty years later, the word is shocking. In what circumstances could someone proposing to write a history of colonial New England not take account of the Indian presence there?

The rest of Miller's preface supplies an answer to this question, if one takes the trouble to piece together its details. Miller explains that as a young man, jealous of older compatriots who had had the luck to fight in World War I, he had gone to Africa in search of adventure. "The adventures that Africa afforded," he writes, "were tawdry enough, but it became the setting for a sudden epiphany" (p. vii). "It was given to me," he writes, "disconsolate on the edge of a jungle of central Africa, to have thrust upon me the mission of expounding what I took to be the innermost propulsion of the United States, while supervising, in that barbaric tropic, the unloading of drums of case oil flowing out of the inexhaustible wilderness of

America" (p. viii). Miller's picture of himself on the banks of the Congo furnishes a key to the kind of history he will write and to his mental image of a vacant wilderness; it explains why it was just there, under precisely these conditions, that he should have had his epiphany.

The fuel drums stand, in Miller's mind, for the popular misconception of what this country is about. They are "tangible symbols of [America's] appalling power," a power that everyone but Miller takes for the ultimate reality (p. ix). To Miller, "the mind of man is the basic factor in human history," and he will plead, all unaccommodated as he is among the fuel drums, for the intellect—the intellect for which his fellow historians, with their chapters on "stoves or bathtubs, or tax laws," "the Wilmot Proviso" and "the chain store," "have so little respect" (p. viii, ix). His preface seethes with a hatred of the merely physical and mechanical, and this hatred, which is really a form of moral outrage, explains not only the contempt with which he mentions the stoves and bathtubs but also the nature of his experience in Africa and its relationship to the "massive narrative" he will write.

Miller's experiences in Africa are "tawdry," his tropic is barbaric because the jungle he stands on the edge of means nothing to him, no more, indeed something less, than the case oil. It is the nothingness of Africa that precipitates his vision. It is the barbarity of the "dark continent," the obvious (but superficial) parallelism between the jungle at Matadi and America's "vacant wilderness" that releases in Miller the desire to define and vindicate his country's cultural identity. To the young Miller, colonial Africa and colonial America are—but for the history he will bring to light—mirror images of one another. And what he fails to see in the one landscape is the same thing he overlooks in the other: the human beings who people it. As Miller stood with his back to the jungle, thinking about the role of mind in human history, his failure to see that the land into which European culture had moved was not vacant but already occupied by a varied and numerous population, is of a piece with his failure, in his portrait of himself at Matadi, to notice who was carrying the fuel drums he was supervising the unloading of.

The point is crucial because it suggests that what is invisible to the historian in his own historical moment remains invisible when he turns his gaze to the past. It isn't that Miller didn't "see" the black men, in a literal sense, any more than it's the case that when he looked back he didn't "see" the Indians, in the sense of not realizing they were there. Rather, it's that neither the Indians nor the blacks *counted* for him, in a fundamental way. The way in which Indians can be seen but not counted is illustrated by an entry in Governor John Winthrop's journal, three hundred years before, when he recorded that there had been a great storm with high winds "yet through God's great mercy it did no hurt, but only killed one Indian with the fall of a tree."[3] The juxtaposition suggests that Miller shared with Winthrop a certain colonial point of view, a point of view from which Indians, though present, do not finally matter.

A book entitled *New England Frontier: Puritans and Indians, 1620–1675,* written by Alden Vaughan and published in 1965, promised to rectify Miller's omission. In the outpouring of work on the European-Indian encounter that began in the early sixties, this book is the first major landmark, and to a neophyte it seems definitive. Vaughan acknowledges the absence of Indian sources and emphasizes his use of materials which catch the Puritans "off guard."[4] His announced conclusion that "the New England Puritans followed a remarkably humane, considerate, and just policy in their dealings with the Indians" seems supported by the scope, documentation, and methodicalness of his project (NEF, p. vii). The author's fair-mindedness and equanimity seem everywhere apparent, so that when he asserts "the history of interracial relations from the arrival of the Pilgrims to the outbreak of King Philip's War is a credit to the integrity of both peoples," one is positively reassured (NEF, p. viii).

But these impressions do not survive an admission that comes late in the book, when, in the course of explaining why works like Helen Hunt Jackson's *Century of Dishonor* had spread misconceptions about Puritan treatment of the Indians, Vaughan finally lays his own cards on the table.

> The root of the misunderstanding [about Puritans and Indians]...lie[s] in a failure to recognize the nature of the two societies that met in seventeenth century New England. One was unified, visionary, disciplined, and dynamic. The other was divided, self-satisfied, undisciplined, and static. It would be unreasonable to expect that such societies could live side by side indefinitely with no penetration of the more fragmented and passive by the more consolidated and active. What resulted, then, was not—as many have held—a clash of dissimilar ways of life, but rather the expansion of one into the areas in which the other was lacking. (NEF, p. 323)

From our present vantage point, these remarks seem culturally biased to an incredible degree, not to mention inaccurate: was Puritan society unified? If so, how does one account for its internal dissensions and obsessive need to cast out deviants? Is "unity" necessarily a positive culture trait? From what standpoint can one say that American Indians were neither disciplined nor visionary, when both these characteristics loom so large in the ethnographies? Is it an accident that ways of describing cultural strength and weakness coincide with gender stereotypes—active/passive, and so on? Why is one culture said to "penetrate" the other? Why is the "other" described in terms of "lack"?

Vaughan's fundamental categories of apprehension and judgment will not withstand even the most cursory inspection. For what looked like evenhandedness when he was writing *New England Frontier* does not look that way anymore. In his introduction to *New Directions in American Intellectual History,* John Higham writes that by the end of the sixties

> the entire conceptual foundation on which [this sort of work] rested [had] crumbled away....Simultaneously, in sociology, anthropology, and history, two working assumptions...came under withering attack: first, the assumption that societies tend to be integrated, and second, that a shared culture maintains that integration....By the late 1960s all claims issued in the name of an "American mind"...were subject to drastic skepticism.[5]

"Clearly," Higham continues, "the sociocultural upheaval of the sixties created the occasion" for this reaction.[6] Vaughan's book, it seemed, could only have been written before the events of the sixties had sensitized scholars to questions of race and ethnicity. It came as no surprise, therefore, that ten years later there appeared a study of European-Indian relations which reflected the new awareness of social issues the sixties had engendered. And it offered an entirely different picture of the European-Indian encounter.

Francis Jennings's *The Invasion of America* (1975) rips wide open the idea that the Puritans were humane and considerate in their dealings with the Indians. In Jennings's account, even more massively documented than Vaughan's, the early settlers lied to the Indians, stole from them, murdered them, scalped them, captured them, tortured them, raped them, sold them into slavery, confiscated their land, destroyed their crops, burned their homes, scattered their possessions, gave them alcohol, undermined their systems of belief, and infected them with diseases that wiped out ninety percent of their numbers within the first hundred years after contact.[7]

Jennings mounts an all-out attack on the essential decency of the Puritan leadership and their apologists in the twentieth century. The Pequot War, which previous historians had described as an attempt on the part of Massachusetts Bay to protect itself from the fiercest of the New England tribes, becomes, in Jennings's painstakingly researched account, a deliberate war of extermination, waged by whites against Indians. It starts with trumped-up charges, is carried on through a series of increasingly bloody reprisals, and ends in the massacre of scores of Indian men, women, and children, all so that Massachusetts Bay could gain political and economic control of the southern Connecticut Valley. When one reads this and then turns over the page and sees a reproduction of the Bay Colony seal, which depicts an Indian from whose mouth issue the words "Come over and help us," the effect is shattering.[8]

But even so powerful an argument as Jennings's did not remain unshaken by subsequent work. Reading on, I discovered that if the events of the sixties had revolutionized the study of European-Indian relations, the events of the seventies produced yet another transformation. The American Indian Movement, and in particular the founding of the Native American Rights Fund in 1971 to finance Indian litigation, and a court decision in 1975 which gave the tribes the right to seek redress for past injustices in federal court, created a climate within which historians began to focus on the Indians themselves. "Almost simultaneously," writes James Axtell, "frontier and colonial historians began to discover the necessity of considering the American natives as real determinants of history and the utility of ethnohistory as a way of ensuring parity of focus and impartiality of judgment."[9] In Miller, Indians had been simply beneath notice; in Vaughan, they belonged to an inferior culture; and in Jennings, they were the more or less innocent prey of power-hungry whites. But in the most original and provocative of the ethnohistories, Calvin Martin's *Keepers of the Game,* Indians became complicated, purposeful human beings, whose lives were spiritually motivated to a high degree.[10] Their relationship to the animals they hunted, to the natural environment, and to the whites with whom they traded became intelligible within a system of beliefs that formed the basis for an entirely new perspective on the European-Indian encounter.

Within the broader question of why European contact had such a devastating effect on the Indians, Martin's specific aim is to determine why Indians participated in the fur trade which ultimately led them to the brink of annihilation. The standard answer to this question had always been that once the Indian was introduced to European guns, copper kettles, woolen blankets, and the like, he literally couldn't keep his hands off them. In order to acquire these coveted items, he decimated the animal populations on which his survival depended. In short, the Indian's motivation in participating in the fur trade was assumed to be the same as the white European's—a desire to accumulate material goods. In direct opposition to this thesis, Martin argues that the reason why Indians ruthlessly exploited their own resources had nothing to do with supply and demand, but stemmed rather from a breakdown of the cosmic worldview that tied them to the game they killed in a spiritual relationship of parity and mutual obligation.

The hunt, according to Martin, was conceived not primarily as a physical activity but as a spiritual quest, in which the spirit of the hunter must overmaster the spirit of the game animal before the kill can take place. The animal, in effect, *allows* itself to be found and killed, once the hunter has mastered its spirit. The hunter prepared himself through rituals of fasting, sweating, or dreaming which revealed the identity of his prey and where he can find it. The physical act of killing is the least important element in the process. Once the animal is killed, eaten, and its parts used for clothing or implements, its remains must be disposed of in ritually prescribed fashion, or the game boss, the "keeper" of that species, will not permit more animals to be killed. The relationship between Indians and animals, then, is contractual; each side must hold up its end of the bargain, or no further transactions can occur.

What happened, according to Martin, was that as a result of diseases introduced into the animal population by Europeans, the game suddenly disappeared, began to act in inexplicable ways, or sickened and died in plain view, and communicated their diseases to the Indians. The Indians, consequently, believed that their compact with the animals had been broken and that the keepers of the game, the tutelary spirits of each animal species whom they had been so careful to propitiate, had betrayed them. And when missionization, wars with the Europeans, and displacement from their tribal lands had further weakened Indian society and its belief structure, the Indians, no longer restrained by religious sanctions, in effect, turned on the animals in a holy war of revenge.

Whether or not Martin's specific claim about the "holy war" was correct, his analysis made it clear to me that, given the Indians' understanding of economic, religious, and physical processes, an Indian account of what transpired when the European settlers arrived here would look nothing like our own. Their (potential, unwritten) history of the conflict could bear only a marginal resemblance to Eurocentric views. I began to think that the key to understanding European-Indian relations was to see them as an encounter between wholly disparate cultures, and that therefore either defending or attacking the colonists was beside the point since, given the cultural disparity between the two groups, conflict was inevitable and in large part a product of mutual misunderstanding.

But three years after Martin's book appeared, Shepard Krech III edited a collection of seven essays called *Indians, Animals, and the Fur Trade,* attacking Martin's entire project. Here the authors argued that we don't need an ideological or religious explanation for the fur trade. As Charles Hudson writes,

> The Southeastern Indians slaughtered deer (and were prompted to enslave and kill each other) because of their position on the outer fringes of an expanding modern world-system....In the modern world-system there is a core region which establishes *economic* relations with its colonial periphery....If the Indians could not produce commodities, they were on the road to cultural extinction....To maximize his chances for survival, an eighteenth-century Southeastern Indian had to...live in the interior, out of range of European cattle, forestry, and agriculture....He had to produce a commodity which was valuable enough to earn him some protection from English slavers.[11]

Though we are talking here about Southeastern Indians, rather than the subarctic and Northeastern tribes Martin studied, what really accounts for these divergent explanations of why Indians slaughtered the game are the assumptions that underlie them. Martin believes that the Indians acted on the basis of perceptions made available to them by their own cosmology; that is, he explains their behavior as the Indians themselves would have explained it (insofar as he can), using a logic and a set of values that are not Eurocentric but derived from within Amerindian culture. Hudson, on the other hand, insists that the Indians' own beliefs are irrelevant to an explanation of how they acted, which can only be understood, as far as he is concerned, in the terms of a Western materialist economic and political analysis. Martin and Hudson, in short, don't agree on what counts as an explanation, and this disagreement sheds light on the preceding accounts as well. From this standpoint, we can see that Vaughan, who thought that the Puritans were superior to the Indians, and Jennings, who thought the reverse, are both, like Hudson, using Eurocentric criteria of description and evaluation. While all three critics (Vaughan, Jennings, and Hudson) acknowledge that Indians and Europeans behave differently from one another, the behavior differs, as it were, within the order of the same: all three assume, though only Hudson makes the assumption explicit, that an understanding of relations between the Europeans and the Indians must be elaborated in European terms. In Martin's analysis, however, what we have are not only two different sets of behavior but two incommensurable ways of describing and assigning meaning to events. This difference at the level of explanation calls into question the possibility of obtaining any theory-independent account of interaction between Indians and Europeans.

At this point, dismayed and confused by the wildly divergent views of colonial history the twentieth-century historians had provided, I decided to look at some primary materials. I thought, perhaps, if I looked at some firsthand accounts and at some scholars looking at those accounts, it would be possible to decide which experts were right and which were wrong by comparing their views with the evidence. Captivity narratives seemed a good place to begin, since it was logical to suppose that the records left by whites who had been captured by Indians would furnish the sort of firsthand information I wanted.

I began with two fascinating essays based on these materials written by the ethnohistorian James Axtell, "The White Indians of Colonial America" and "The Scholastic Philosophy of the Wilderness."[12] These essays suggest that it would have been a privilege to be captured by North American Indians and taken off to Canada to dwell in a wigwam for the rest of one's life. Axtell's reconstruction of the process by which Indians taught European captives to feel comfortable in the wilderness, first taking their shoes away and giving them moccasins, carrying the children on their backs, sharing the scanty food supply equally, ceremonially cleansing them of their old identities, giving them Indian clothes and jewelry, assiduously teaching them the Indian language, finally adopting them into their families, and even visiting them after many years if, as sometimes happened, they were restored to white society—all of this creates a compelling portrait of Indian culture and helps to explain the extraordinary attraction that Indian culture apparently exercised over Europeans.

But, as I had by now come to expect, this beguiling portrait of the Indians' superior humanity is called into question by other writings on Indian captivity—for example, Norman Heard's *White into Red,* whose summation of the comparative treatment of captive children east and west of the Mississippi seems to contradict some of Axtell's conclusions:

> The treatment of captive children seems to have been similar in initial stages....Most children were treated brutally at the time of capture. Babies and toddlers usually were killed immediately and other small children would be dispatched during the rapid retreat to the Indian villages if they cried, failed to keep the pace, or otherwise indicated a lack of fortitude needed to become a worthy member of the tribe. Upon reaching the village, the child might face such ordeals as running the gauntlet or dancing in the center of a throng of threatening Indians. The prisoner might be so seriously injured at this time that he would no longer be acceptable for adoption.[13]

One account which Heard reprints is particularly arresting. A young girl captured by the Comanches who had not been adopted into a family but used as a slave had been peculiarly mistreated. When they wanted to wake her up the family she belonged to would take a burning brand from the fire and touch it to her nose. When she was returned to her parents, the flesh of her nose was completely burned away, exposing the bone.[14]

Since the pictures drawn by Heard and Axtell were in certain respects irreconcilable, it made sense to turn to a firsthand account to see how the Indians treated their captives in a particular instance. Mary Rowlandson's "The Sovraignty and Goodness of God," published in Boston around 1680, suggested itself because it was so widely read and had set the pattern for later narratives. Rowlandson interprets her captivity as God's punishment on her for failing to keep the Sabbath properly on several occasions. She sees everything that happens to her as a sign from God. When the Indians are kind to her, she attributes her good fortune to divine Providence; when they are cruel, she blames her captors. But beyond the question of how Rowlandson interprets events is the question of what she saw in the first place and what she considered worth reporting. The following passage, with its abrupt shifts of focus and peculiar emphases, makes it hard to see her testimony as evidence of anything other than the Puritan point of view:

> Then my heart began to fail: and I fell weeping, which was the first time to my remembrance, that I wept before them. Although I had met with so much Affliction, and my heart was many times ready to break, yet could I not shed one tear in their sight: but rather had been all this while in a maze, and like one astonished: but not I may say as, Psal. 137.1. *By the Rivers of Babylon, there we sate down; yea, we wept when we remembered Zion.* There one of them asked me, why I wept, I could hardly tell what to say: yet I answered, they would kill me: No, said he, none will hurt you. Then came one of them and gave me two spoon-fulls of Meal to comfort me, and another gave me half a pint of Pease; which was more worth than many Bushels

at another time. Then I went to see King Philip, he bade me come in and sit down, and asked me whether I woold smoke it (a usual Complement nowadayes among Saints and Sinners) but this no way suited me. For though I had formerly used Tobacco, yet I had left it ever since I was first taken. It seems to be a Bait, the Devil layes to make men loose their precious time: I remember with shame, how formerly, when I had taken two or three pipes, I was presently ready for another, such a bewitching thing it is: But I thank God, he has now given me power over it; surely there are many who may be better imployed than to ly sucking a stinking Tobacco-pipe.[15]

Anyone who has ever tried to give up smoking has to sympathize with Rowlandson, but it is nonetheless remarkable, first, that a passage which begins with her weeping openly in front of her captors, and comparing herself to Israel in Babylon, should end with her railing against the vice of tobacco; and, second, that it has not a word to say about King Philip, the leader of the Indians who captured her and mastermind of the campaign that devastated the white population of the English colonies. The fact that Rowlandson has just been introduced to the chief of chiefs makes hardly any impression on her at all. What excites her is a moral issue which was being hotly debated in the seventeenth century: to smoke or not to smoke (Puritans frowned on it, apparently, because it wasted time and presented a fire hazard). What seem to us the peculiar emphases in Rowlandson's relation are not the result of her having screened out evidence she couldn't handle, but of her way of constructing the world. She saw what her seventeenth-century English Separatist background made visible. It is when one realizes that the biases of twentieth-century historians like Vaughan or Axtell cannot be corrected for simply by consulting the primary materials, since the primary materials are constructed according to *their* authors' biases, that one begins to envy Miller his vision at Matadi. Not for what he didn't see—the Indian and the black—but for his epistemological confidence.

Since captivity narratives made a poor source of evidence for the nature of European-Indian relations in early New England because they were so relentlessly pietistic, my hope was that a better source of evidence might be writings designed simply to tell Englishmen what the American natives were like. These authors could be presumed to be less severely biased, since they hadn't seen their loved ones killed by Indians or been made to endure the hardships of captivity, and because they weren't writing propaganda calculated to prove that God had delivered his chosen people from the hands of Satan's emissaries.

The problem was that these texts were written with aims no less specific than those of the captivity narratives, though the aims were of a different sort. Here is a passage from William Wood's *New England's Prospect,* published in London in 1634.

To enter into a serious discourse concerning the natural conditions of these Indians might procure admiration from the people of any civilized nations, in regard of their civility and good natures....These Indians are of affable, courteous and well disposed natures, ready to communicate the best of their wealth to the mutual good of one another;...so...perspicuous is their love...that they are as willing to part with a mite in poverty as treasure in plenty....If it were possible to recount the courtesies they have showed the English, since their first arrival in those parts, it would not only steady belief, that they are a loving people, but also win the love of those that never saw them, and wipe off that needless fear that is too deeply rooted in the conceits of many who think them envious and of such rancorous and inhumane dispositions, that they will one day make an end of their English inmates.[16]

However, in a pamphlet published twenty-one years earlier, Alexander Whitaker of Virginia has this to say of the natives:

These naked slaves...serve the divell for feare, after a most base manner, sacrificing sometimes (as I have heere heard) their own Children to him....They live naked in bodie, as if their shame of their sinne deserved no covering: Their names are as naked as their bodie: They esteem it a virtue to lie, deceive and steale as their master the divell teacheth to them.[17]

According to Robert Berkhofer in *The White Man's Indian,* these divergent reports can be explained by looking at the authors' motives. A favorable report like Wood's, intended to encourage new emigrants to America, naturally represented Indians as loving and courteous, civilized and generous, in order to allay the fears of prospective colonists. Whitaker, on the other hand, a minister who wishes to convince his readers that the Indians are in need of conversion, paints them as benighted agents of the devil. Berkhofer's commentary constantly implies that white men were to blame for having represented the Indians in the image of their own desires and needs.[18] But the evidence supplied by Rowlandson's narrative, and by the accounts left by early reporters such as Wood and Whitaker, suggests something rather different. Though it is probably true that in certain cases Europeans did consciously tamper with the evidence, in most cases there is no reason to suppose that they did not record faithfully what they saw. And what they saw was not an illusion, was not determined by selfish motives in any narrow sense, but was there by virtue of a way of seeing which they could no more consciously manipulate than they could choose not to have been born. At this point, it seemed to me, the ethnocentric bias of the firsthand observers invited an investigation of the cultural situation they spoke from. Karen Kupperman's *Settling with the Indians* (1980) supplied just such an analysis.

Kupperman argues that Englishmen inevitably looked at Indians in exactly the same way that they looked at other Englishmen. For instance, if they looked down on Indians and saw them as people to be exploited, it was not because of racial prejudice or antique notions about savagery, it was because they looked down on ordinary English men and women and saw them as subjects for exploitation as well.[19] According to Kupperman, what concerned these writers most when they described the Indians were the insignia of social class, of rank, and of prestige. Indian faces are virtually never described in the earliest accounts, but clothes and hairstyles, tattoos and jewelry, posture and skin color are. "Early modern Englishmen believed that people can create their own identity, and that therefore one communicates to the world through signals such as dress and other forms of decoration who one is, what group or category one belongs to."[20]

Kupperman's book marks a watershed in writings on European-Indian relations, for it reverses the strategy employed by Martin two years before. Whereas Martin had performed an ethnographic analysis of Indian cosmology in order to explain, from within, the Indians' motives for engaging in the fur trade, Kupperman performs an ethnographic study of seventeenth-century England in order to explain, from within, what motivated Englishmen's behavior. The sympathy and understanding that Martin, Axtell, and others extend to the Indians are extended in Kupperman's work to the English themselves. Rather than giving an account of "what happened" between Indians and Europeans, like Martin, she reconstructs the worldview that gave the experience of one group its content. With her study, scholarship on European-Indian relations comes full circle.

It may well seem to you at this point that, given the tremendous variation among the historical accounts, I had no choice but to end in relativism. If the experience of encountering conflicting versions of the "same" events suggests anything certain it is that the attitude a historian takes up in relation to a given event, the way in which he or she judges and even describes "it"—and the "it" has to go in quotation marks because depending on the perspective, that event either did or did not occur—this stance, these judgments and descriptions are a function of the historian's position in relation to the subject. Miller, standing on the banks of the Congo, couldn't see the black men he was supervising because of his background, his assumptions, values, experiences, goals. Jennings, intent on exposing the distortions introduced into the historical record by Vaughan and his predecessors stretching all the way back to Winthrop, couldn't see that Winthrop and his peers were not racists but only Englishmen who looked at other cultures in the way their own culture had taught them to see one another. The historian can never escape the limitations of his or her own position in history and so inevitably gives an account that is an extension of the circumstances from which it springs. But it seems to me that when one is confronted with this particular succession of stories, cultural and historical relativism is not a position that one can comfortably assume. The phenomena to which these histories testify—conquest, massacre, and genocide, on the one hand; torture, slavery, and murder on the other—cry out for judgment. When faced with claims and counterclaims of this magnitude one feels obligated to reach an understanding of what actually did occur. The dilemma posed by the study of European-Indian relations in early America is that the highly charged nature of the materials demands a moral decisiveness which the succession of conflicting accounts effectively precludes. That is the dilemma I found myself in at the end of this course of reading, and which I eventually came to resolve as follows.

After a while it began to seem to me that there was something wrong with the way I had formulated the problem. The statement that the materials on European-Indian relations were so highly charged that they demanded moral judgment, but that the judgment couldn't be made because all possible descriptions of what happened were biased, seemed to contain an internal contradiction. The statement implied that in order to make a moral judgment about something, you have to know something else first—namely, the facts of the case you're being called upon to judge. My complaint was that their perspectival nature would disqualify any facts I might encounter and that therefore I couldn't judge. But to say as I did that the materials I had read were "highly charged" and therefore demanded judgment suggests both that I was reacting to something real—to some facts—*and* that I had judged them. Perhaps I wasn't so much in the lurch morally or epistemologically as I had thought. If you—or I—react with horror to the story of the girl captured and enslaved by Comanches who touched a firebrand to her nose every time they wanted to wake her up, it's because we read this as a story about cruelty and suffering, and not as a story about the conventions of prisoner exchange or the economics of Comanche life. The *seeing* of the story as a cause for alarm rather than as a droll anecdote or a piece of curious information is evidence of values we already hold, of judgments already made, of facts already perceived as facts.

My problem presupposed that I couldn't judge because I didn't know what the facts were. All I had, or could have, was a series of different perspectives, and so nothing that would count as an authoritative source on which moral judgments could be based. But, as I have just shown, I did judge, and that is because, as I now think, I did have some facts. I seemed to accept as facts that ninety percent of the native American population of New England died after the first hundred years of contact, that tribes in eastern Canada and the northeastern United States had a compact with the game they killed, that Comanches had subjected a captive girl to casual cruelty, that King Philip smoked a pipe, and so on. It was only where different versions of the same event came into conflict that I doubted the text was a record of something real. And even then, there was no question about certain major catastrophes. I believed that four hundred Pequots were killed near Saybrook, that Winthrop was the Governor of the Massachusetts Bay Colony when it happened, and so on. My sense that certain events, such as the Pequot War, did occur in no way reflected the indecisiveness that overtook me when I tried to choose among the various historical versions. In fact, the need I felt to make up my mind was impelled by the conviction that certain things *had* happened that shouldn't have happened. Hence it was never the case that "what happened" was completely unknowable or unavailable. It's rather that in the process of reading so many different approaches to the same phenomenon I became aware of the difference in the attitudes that informed these approaches. This awareness of the interests motivating each version cast suspicion over everything, in retrospect, and I ended by claiming that there was nothing I could know. This, I now see, was never really the case. But how did it happen?

Someone else, confronted with the same materials, could have decided that one of these historical accounts was correct. Still another person might have decided that more evidence was needed in order to decide among them. Why did I conclude that none of the accounts was accurate because they were all produced from some particular angle of vision? Presumably there was something in my background that enabled me to see the problem in this way. That something, very likely, was poststructuralist theory. I let my discovery that Vaughan was a product of the fifties, Jennings of the sixties, Rowlandson of a Puritan worldview, and so on lead me to the conclusion that all facts are theory dependent because that conclusion was already a thinkable one for me. My inability to come up with a true account was not the product of being situated nowhere; it was the product of certitude that existed *somewhere else,* namely, in contemporary literary theory. Hence, the level at which my indecision came into play was a function of particular beliefs I held. I was never in a position of epistemological indeterminacy, I was never *en abyme*. The idea that all accounts are perspectival seemed to me a superior standpoint from which to view all the versions of "what happened," and to regard with sympathetic condescension any person so old-fashioned and benighted as to believe that there really was some way of arriving at the truth. But this skeptical standpoint was just as firm as any other. The fact that it was also seriously disabling—it prevented me from coming to any conclusion about what I had read—did not render it any less definite.

At this point something is beginning to show itself that has up to now been hidden. The notion that all facts are only facts within a perspective has the effect of emptying statements of their content. Once I had Miller and Vaughan and Jennings, Martin and Hudson, Axtell and Heard, Rowlandson and Wood and Whitaker, and Kupperman; I had Europeans and Indians, ships and canoes, wigwams and log cabins, bows and arrows and muskets, wigs and tattoos, whiskey and corn, rivers and forts, treaties and battles, fire and blood—and then suddenly all I had was a metastatement about perspectives. The effect of bringing perspectivism to bear on history was to wipe out completely the subject matter of history. And it follows that bringing perspectivism to bear in this way on any subject matter would have a similar effect; everything is wiped out and you are left with nothing but a single idea—perspectivism itself.

But—and it is a crucial but—all this is true only if you believe that there is an alternative. As long as you think that there are or should be facts that exist outside of any perspective, then the notion that facts are perspectival will have this disappearing effect on whatever it touches. But if you are convinced that the alternative does not exist, that there really are no facts except as they are embedded in some particular way of seeing the world, then the argument that a set of facts derives from some particular worldview is no longer an argument against that set of facts. If all facts share this characteristic, to say that any one fact is perspectival doesn't change its factual nature in the slightest. It merely reiterates it.

This doesn't mean that you have to accept just anybody's facts. You can show that what someone else asserts to be a fact is false. But it does mean that you can't argue that someone else's facts are not facts *because they are only the product of a perspective,* since this will be true of the facts that you perceive as well. What this means then is that arguments about "what happened" have to proceed much as they did before poststructuralism broke in with all its talk about language-based reality and culturally produced knowledge. Reasons must be given, evidence adduced, authorities cited, analogies drawn. Being aware that all facts are motivated, believing that people are always operating inside some particular interpretive framework or other is a pertinent argument when what is under discussion is the way beliefs are grounded. But it doesn't give one any leverage on the facts of a particular case.[21]

What this means for the problem I've been addressing is that I must piece together the story of European-Indian relations as best I can, believing this version up to a point, that version not at all, another almost entirely, according to what seems reasonable and plausible, given everything else that I know. And this, as I've shown, is what I was already doing in the back of my mind without realizing it, because there was nothing else I *could* do. If the accounts don't fit together neatly, that is not a reason for rejecting them all in favor of a metadiscourse about epistemology; on the contrary, one encounters contradictory facts and divergent points of view in practically every phase of life, from deciding whom to marry to choosing the right brand of cat food, and one decides as best one can given the evidence available. It is only the nature of the academic situation which makes it appear that one can linger on the threshold of decision in the name of an epistemological principle. What has really happened in such a case is that the subject of debate has changed from the question of what happened in a particular instance to the question of how knowledge is arrived at. The absence of pressure to decide what happened creates the possibility for this change of venue.

The change of venue, however, is itself an action taken. In diverting attention from the original problem and placing it where Miller did, on "the mind of man," it once again ignores what happened and still is happening to American Indians. The moral problem that confronts me now is not that I can never have any facts to go on, but that the work I do is not directed toward solving the kinds of problems that studying the history of European-Indian relations has awakened me to.

Notes

1. See Vine Deloria Jr., *God Is Red* (New York, 1973), pp. 39–56.

2. Perry Miller, *Errand into the Wilderness* (Cambridge, Mass., 1964), p. vii; all further references will be included in the text.

3. This passage from John Winthrop's *Journal* is excerpted by Perry Miller in his anthology *The American Puritans: Their Prose and Poetry* (Garden City, N.Y., 1956), p. 43. In his headnote to the selections from the *Journal,* Miller speaks of Winthrop's "characteristic objectivity" (p. 37).

4. Alden T. Vaughan, *New England Frontier: Puritans and Indians, 1620–1675* (Boston, 1965), pp. vi–vii; all further references to this work, abbreviated NEF, will be included in the text.

5. John Higham, intro. to *New Directions in American Intellectual History,* ed. Higham and Paul K. Conkin (Baltimore, 1979), p. xii.

6. Ibid.

7. See Francis Jennings, *The Invasion of America: Indians, Colonialism, and the Cant of Conquest* (New York, 1975), pp. 3–31. Jennings writes: "The so-called settlement of America was a resettlement, reoccupation of a land made waste by the diseases and demoralization introduced by the newcomers. Although the source data pertaining to populations have never been compiled, one careful scholar, Henry F. Dobyns, has provided a relatively conservative and meticulously reasoned estimate conforming to the known effects of conquest catastrophe. Dobyns has calculated a total aboriginal population for the western hemisphere within the range of 90 to 112 million, of which 10 to 12 million lived north of the Rio Grande" (p. 30).

8. Jennings, fig. 7, p. 229; and see pp. 186–229.

9. James Axtell, *The European and the Indian: Essays in the Ethnohistory of Colonial North America* (Oxford, 1981), p. viii.

10. See Calvin Martin, *Keepers of the Game: Indian-Animal Relationships and the Fur Trade* (Berkeley and Los Angeles, 1978).

11. See the essay by Charles Hudson in *Indians, Animals, and the Fur Trade: A Critique of "Keepers of the Game,"* ed. Shepard Krech III (Athens, Ga., 1981), pp. 167–69.

12. See Axtell, "The White Indians of Colonial America" and "The Scholastic Philosophy of the Wilderness," *The European and the Indian,* pp. 168–206 and 131–67.

13. J. Norman Heard, *White into Red: A Study of the Assimilation of White Persons Captured by Indians* (Metuchen, N.J., 1973), p. 97.

14. See ibid., p. 98.

15. Mary Rowlandson, "The Soveraignty and Goodness of God, Together with the Faithfulness of His Promises Displayed; Being a Narrative of the Captivity and Restauration of Mrs. Mary Rowlandson (1676)," in *Held Captive by Indians: Selected Narratives, 1642–1836,* ed. Richard VanDerBeets (Knoxville, Tenn., 1973), pp. 57–58.

16. William Wood, *New England's Prospect,* ed. Vaughan (Amherst, Mass., 1977), pp. 88–89.

17. Alexander Whitaker, *Goode Newes from Virginia* (1613), quoted in Robert F. Berkhofer Jr., *The White Man's Indian: Images of the American Indian from Columbus to the Present* (New York, 1978), p. 19.

18. See, for example, Berkhofer's discussion of the passages he quotes from Whitaker (*The White Man's Indian,* pp. 19, 20).

19. See Karen Ordahl Kupperman, *Settling with the Indians: The Meeting of English and Indian Cultures in America, 1580–1640* (Totowa, N.J., 1980), pp. 3, 4.

20. Ibid., p. 35.

21. The position I've been outlining is a version of neopragmatism. For an exposition, see *Against Theory: Literary Studies and the New Pragmatism,* ed. W. J. T. Mitchell (Chicago, 1985).

SUGGESTIONS FOR DISCUSSION

1. What exactly is the problem that Tompkins poses in the opening section of the essay? What does she mean when she says that conflicting historical interpretations posed an "epistemological" and a "moral quandary" for her? According to Tompkins, what is at stake when research turns up "an array of mutually irreconcilable points of view"?

2. Return to Tompkins's essay and notate each of the historians or first-person witnesses discussed in the long middle section. What interpretation of European-Indian relations in colonial New England does each offer? What differing assumptions does each make? It may help to create a chart that notes each historian or eyewitness and the interpretations and assumptions.

3. Think of an occasion or two when you encountered conflicting and irreconcilable interpretations of an event. The event could be one that you studied in a history class or one from personal experience. What differing perspectives and points of view produced the conflicting interpretations? How did you deal with these conflicting interpretations? Explain how Tompkins deals with conflicting interpretations in the final section of the essay. In what sense has she found the "way out" that she describes in the opening section? Compare her resolution of the issue to the way that you handled conflicting interpretations. What do you see as the main similarities and differences? How do you account for them?

SUGGESTIONS FOR WRITING

1. Write an essay that uses Jane Tompkins's account of her research as a model. Choose a research project that you did for a class in school—for example, a term paper, a report, or a history fair exhibit. Following Tompkins's style, explain the connections between the topic that you researched and your personal experience. Then take readers behind the scenes to explain how you did the research and how you dealt with any differing points of view or conflicting interpretations that you encountered. Use your account as a way to pose the problem of historical research and working with other people's accounts of the past.

2. Write a critical review of the historians' points of view and the interpretations that Tompkins presents in her essay. Provide an introduction that generally explains the problems and issues that the historians as a group are addressing. Assess the perspective that each historian brings to his or her research—what it helps us to see and what it obscures—and compare the strengths and weaknesses of the historians' various interpretations. As you review the historians' accounts, explain how you might piece them together and what view of Indian-settler relations in colonial New England ultimately emerges for you.

3. Consult American history textbooks that are used in high school and college and compare their treatment of European-Indian relations in seventeenth-century New England to the perspectives of the various historians in Tompkins's essay. (You can focus on just one textbook or extend your research to a number of texts.) What point of view and what assumptions seem to determine the treatment of Indians and Europeans in the textbook? How is this treatment similar to or different from the interpretations that you have read in Tompkins's essay? What perspectives seem to dominate? The textbook may well present this material as a factual account. If so, you'll need to read between the lines to identify the perspective that the textbook author or authors bring to Indian-settler relations in colonial New England.

PERSPECTIVES: INTERPRETING THE VIETNAM WAR

The Vietnam War was the longest and perhaps most controversial war in American history. From the mid-1950s when the Eisenhower administration sent CIA advisors and a military cadre to Vietnam through Lyndon Johnson's escalation of the war in the 1960s to the eventual withdrawal of American forces in 1972 and 1973 and the ultimate victory of Ho Chi Minh in 1975, the Vietnam War increasingly preoccupied American policy makers and divided the country. Of all the wars fought by the United States, the Vietnam War still seems in some fundamental sense unresolved, a bitter legacy that continues to trouble the nation.

The following two selections are the work of professional historians who have tried to come to grips with the meaning of the Vietnam War. As you will see, they offer very different perspectives and, in the process, raise important questions about how historians seek to explain the causes and significance of historical events. George B. Tindall and David E. Shi's "The Tragedy of Vietnam" may appear at first reading to be simply a historical narrative of U.S. involvement in Vietnam, while Loren Baritz's "God's Country and American Know-How" is clearly tied to Baritz's thesis that long-standing patterns in American culture led to military intervention in Vietnam. Your task as a reader is to make sense of these two treatments of the Vietnam War and to decide whether Tindall and Shi offer an interpretation as much as Baritz does.

The Tragedy of Vietnam

George B. Tindall and David E. Shi

George B. Tindall teaches history at the University of North Carolina, Chapel Hill, and David E. Shi at Davidson College. The following selection, "The Tragedy of Vietnam," appeared originally in their textbook *American: A Narrative History*.

As violence was escalating in America's inner cities, the war in Vietnam also reached new levels of intensity and destruction. At the time of President Kennedy's death there were 16,000 American military advisors in Vietnam. Lyndon Johnson inherited a commitment to prevent a Communist takeover in South Vietnam along with a reluctance to assume the military burden for fighting the war. One president after another had done just enough to avoid being charged with having "lost" Vietnam. Johnson did the same, fearing that any other course would undermine his influence and endanger his Great Society programs in Congress. But this path took him and the United States inexorably deeper into intervention in Asia.

ESCALATION

The official sanction for America's "escalation"—a Defense Department term coined in the Vietnam era—was the Tonkin Gulf Resolution, voted by Congress on August 7, 1964. Johnson reported in a national television address that two American destroyers had been attacked by North Vietnamese vessels on August 2 and 4 in the Gulf of Tonkin off the coast of North Vietnam. Although he described the attacks as unprovoked, in truth the destroyers had been monitoring South Vietnamese raids against two North Vietnamese islands—raids planned by American advisors. The Tonkin Gulf Resolution authorized the president to "take all necessary measures to repel any armed attack against the forces of the United States and to prevent further aggression."

Three months after Johnson's landslide victory over Goldwater, he and his advisors made the crucial decisions that shaped American policy in Vietnam for the next four years. On February 5, 1965, Vietcong guerrillas killed 8 and wounded 126 Americans at Pleiku. Further attacks on Americans later that week led Johnson to order operation "Rolling Thunder," the first sustained American bombings of North Vietnam, which were intended to stop the flow of soldiers and supplies into the south. Six months later a task force concluded that the bombing had little effect on the supplies pouring down the "Ho Chi Minh Trail" from North Vietnam through Laos. Still, the bombing continued.

In March 1965 the new American army commander in Vietnam, Gen. William C. Westmoreland, requested and got the first installment of combat troops, ostensibly to defend American airfields. By the end of 1965 there were 184,000 American troops in Vietnam; in 1966 the troop level reached 385,000. And as combat operations increased, so did the list of American casualties, announced each week on the nightly news along with the "body count" of alleged enemy dead. "Westy's War," although fought with helicopter gunships, chemical defoliants, and napalm, became like the trench warfare of World War I—a grinding war of attrition.

THE CONTEXT FOR POLICY

Johnson's decision to "Americanize" the war, so ill-starred in retrospect, was entirely consistent with the foreign policy principles pursued by all American presidents after World War II. The version of the containment theory articulated in the Truman Doctrine, endorsed by Eisenhower and Dulles throughout the 1950s, and reaffirmed by Kennedy, pledged United States opposition to the advance of communism anywhere in the world. "Why are we in Vietnam?" Johnson asked rhetorically at Johns Hopkins University in 1965. "We are there because we have a promise to keep....To leave Vietnam to its fate would shake the confidence of all these people in the value of American commitment." Secretary of State Dean Rusk repeated this rationale before countless congressional committees, warning that Thailand, Burma, and the rest of Southeast Asia would fall to communism if American forces withdrew. American military intervention in Vietnam was thus no aberration, but a logical culmination of the assumptions widely shared by the foreign policy establishment and leaders of both political parties since the early days of the Cold War.

Nor did the United States blindly "stumble into a quagmire" in Vietnam, as some commentators maintained. Johnson insisted from the start that American military involvement must not reach levels that would provoke the Chinese or Soviets into direct intervention. He therefore exercised a tight rein over the bombing campaign, once boasting that "they can't even bomb an outhouse without my approval." Such a restrictive policy meant, in effect, that military victory in any traditional sense of the term was never possible. "It was startling to me to find out," the new secretary of defense, Clark Clifford, recalled in 1968, "that we had no military plan to end the war." America's goal was not to win the war in a conventional sense by capturing enemy territory, but to prevent the North Vietnamese and Vietcong from winning. This meant that America would have to maintain a military presence as long as the enemy retained the will to fight.

As it turned out, American public support for the war eroded faster than the will of the North Vietnamese leaders to tolerate casualties. Opposition to the war broke out on college campuses with the escalation of 1965. And in January 1966 Sen. J. William Fulbright of Arkansas, chairman of the Senate Foreign Relations Committee, began congressional investigations into American policy. George Kennan, the founding father of the containment doctrine, told Fulbright's committee that the doctrine was appropriate for Europe, but not Southeast Asia. By 1967 opposition to the war had become so pronounced that antiwar demonstrations in New York and at the Pentagon attracted massive support. Nightly television accounts of the fighting—Vietnam was the first war to receive extended television coverage, and hence has been dubbed the "living room war"—brought the horrors of guerrilla warfare into American dens. As Secretary of Defense McNamara admitted, "The picture of the world's greatest superpower killing or injuring 1,000 noncombatants a week, while trying to pound a tiny backward nation into submission on an issue whose merits are hotly disputed, is not a pretty one."

In a war of political will, North Vietnam had the advantage. Johnson and his advisors never came to appreciate the tenacity of North Vietnam's commitment to unify Vietnam and expel the United States. Ho Chi Minh had warned the French in the 1940s that "You can kill ten of my men for every one I kill of yours, but even at those odds, you will lose and I will win." He knew that in a battle of attrition, the Vietnamese Communists had the advantage, for they were willing to sacrifice all for their cause. Indeed, just as General Westmoreland was assuring Johnson and the American public that his forces in early 1968 were on the verge of gaining the upper hand, the Communists again displayed their resilience.

THE TURNING POINT

On January 31, 1968, the first day of the Vietnamese New Year (Tet), the Vietcong and North Vietnamese defied a holiday truce to launch a wave of surprise assaults on American and South Vietnamese forces throughout South Vietnam. The old capital city of Hué fell to the Communists, and Vietcong units temporarily occupied the grounds of the American embassy in Saigon. But within a few days American and South Vietnamese forces organized a devastating counterattack. General Westmoreland justifiably proclaimed the Tet offensive a major defeat for the Vietcong. But while Vietcong casualties were enormous, the psychological impact of the offensive on the American public was more telling. *Time* and *Newsweek* soon ran antiwar editorials urging American withdrawal. Walter Cronkite, the dean of American television journalists, confided to his viewers that he no longer believed the war was winnable. "If I've lost Walter," Johnson was reported to say, "then it's over. I've lost Mr. Average Citizen." Polls showed that Johnson's popularity declined to 35 percent, lower than any president since Truman's darkest days. In 1968 the United States was spending $322,000 on every enemy killed in Vietnam; the poverty programs at home received only $53 per person.

During 1968 Johnson grew increasingly isolated. The secretary of defense reported that a task force of prominent soldiers and civilians saw no prospect for a military victory. Robert Kennedy was considering a run for the presidency in order to challenge Johnson's Vietnam policy. And Sen. Eugene McCarthy of Minnesota had already decided to oppose Johnson in the Democratic primaries. With antiwar students rallying to his candidacy, McCarthy polled 42 percent of the vote to Johnson's 48 percent in New Hampshire's March primary. Though voters had to write in Johnson's name to vote for the president, it was still a remarkable showing for a little-known senator, and each presidential primary now promised to become a referendum on Johnson's Vietnam policy.

Despite Johnson's troubles in the conduct of foreign policy, he remained a master at reading the political omens. On March 31 he announced a limited halt to the bombing of North Vietnam and fresh initiatives for a negotiated cease-fire. Then he added a dramatic postscript: "I have concluded that I should not permit the Presidency to become involved in the partisan divisions that are developing in this political year. Accordingly, I shall not seek, and I will not accept, the nomination of my party for another term as your President." Although American troops would remain in Vietnam for five more years and the casualties would mount, the quest for military victory had ended. Now the question was how the most powerful nation in the world could extricate itself from Vietnam with a minimum of damage to its prestige. It would not be easy. When direct negotiations with the North Vietnamese finally began in Paris in May 1968 they immediately bogged down over North Vietnam's demand for an American bombing halt as a precondition for further discussion.

God's Country and American Know-How

Loren Baritz

> Loren Baritz taught American Studies for many years at the University of Michigan and is now retired. The following selection, "God's Country and American Know-How," is taken from his book *Backfire: A History of How American Culture Led Us into Vietnam* (1985).

SUGGESTION FOR READING

As you read, notice how Loren Baritz develops his idea that America's quest for moral leadership led policymakers to involve the United States in Vietnam. Compare this perspective on American military intervention in Vietnam to the perspective offered by Tindall and Shi in "The Tragedy of Vietnam." When you finish reading, think about what these perspectives have in common and how they differ.

Americans were ignorant about the Vietnamese not because we were stupid, but because we believe certain things about ourselves. Those things necessarily distorted our vision and confused our minds in ways that made learning extraordinarily difficult. To understand our failure we must think about what it means to be an American.

The necessary test for understanding the condition of being an American is a single sentence written by Herman Melville in his novel *White Jacket:* "And we Americans are the peculiar, chosen people—the Israel of our time; we bear the ark of the liberties of the world." This was not the last time this idea was expressed by Americans. It was at the center of thought of the men who brought us the Vietnam War. It was at the center of the most characteristic American myth.

This oldest and most important myth about America has an unusually specific origin. More than 350 years ago, while in mid-passage between England and the American wilderness, John Winthrop told the band of Puritans he was leading to a new and dangerous life that they were engaged in a voyage that God Himself not only approved, but in which He participated. The precise way that Brother Winthrop expressed himself echoes throughout the history of American life. He explained to his fellow travelers, "We shall find that the God of Israel is among us, when ten of us shall be able to resist a thousand of our enemies, when he shall make us a praise and glory, that men shall say of succeeding plantations [settlements]: the Lord make it like that of New England: for we must Consider that we shall be as a City upon a Hill, the eyes of all people are upon us." The myth of America as a city on a hill implies that America is a moral example to the rest of the world, a world that will presumably keep its attention riveted on us. It means that we are a Chosen People, each of whom, because of God's favor and presence, can smite one hundred of our heathen enemies hip and thigh.

The society Winthrop meant to establish in New England would do God's work, insofar as sinners could. America would become God's country. The Puritans would have understood this to mean that they were creating a nation of, by, and for the Lord. About two centuries later, the pioneers and the farmers who followed the Puritans translated God's country from civilization to the grandeur and nobility of nature, to virgin land, to the purple mountains' majesty. Relocating the country of God from civilization to nature was significant in many ways, but the conclusion that this New World is specially favored by the Lord not only endured but spread.

In countless ways Americans know in their gut—the only place myths can live—that we have been Chosen to lead the world in public morality and to instruct it in political virtue. We believe that our own domestic goodness results in strength adequate to destroy our opponents who, by definition, are enemies of virtue, freedom, and God. Over and over, the founding Puritans described their new settlement as a beacon in the darkness, a light whose radiance could keep Christian voyagers from crashing on the rocks, a light that could brighten the world. In his inaugural address John Kennedy said, "The energy, the faith, the devotion which we bring to this endeavor [defending freedom] will light our country and all who serve it—and the glow from that fire can truly light the world." The city on a hill grew from its first tiny society to encompass the entire nation. As we will see, that is one of the reasons why we compelled ourselves to intervene in Vietnam.

An important part of the myth of America as the city on a hill has been lost as American power increased. John Winthrop intended that his tiny settlement should be only an example of rectitude to the cosmos. It could not have occurred to him that his small and weak band of saints should charge about the world to impose the One Right Way on others who were either too wicked, too stupid, or even too oppressed to follow his example. Because they also had domestic distractions, the early American Puritans could not even consider foreign adventures. In almost no time they had their hands full with a variety of local malefactors: Indians, witches, and, worst of all, shrewd Yankees who were more interested in catching fish than in catching the spirit of the Lord. Nathaniel Hawthorne, brooding about these Puritans, wrote that civilization begins by building a jail and a graveyard, but he was only two-thirds right. Within only two generations, the New England saints discovered that there was a brothel in Boston, the hub of the new and correct Christian order.

The New World settlement was puny, but the great ocean was a defensive moat that virtually prohibited an onslaught by foreign predators. The new Americans could therefore go about perfecting their society without distracting anxiety about alien and corrupting intrusions from Europe. This relative powerlessness coupled with defensive security meant that the city on a hill enjoyed a favorable "peculiar situation." It was peculiarly blessed because the decadent world could not come here, and we did not have to go there. The rest of the world, but especially Europe, with its frippery, pomp, and Catholicism, was thought to be morally leprous. This is what George Washington had in mind when he asked a series of rhetorical questions in his farewell address in 1796:

> Why forego the advantages of so peculiar a situation? Why quit our own to stand upon foreign ground? Why, by interweaving our destiny with that of any part of Europe, entangle our peace and prosperity in the toils of European ambition, rivalship, interest, humor, of caprice?

This is also what Thomas Jefferson told his countrymen when he was inaugurated five years later. This enlightened and skeptical philosopher-President announced that this was a "chosen country" which had been "kindly separated by nature and a wide ocean from the exterminating havoc of one quarter of the globe." He said that the young nation could exult in its many blessings if it would only keep clear of foreign evil. His prescription was that America should have "entangling alliances with none."

One final example of the unaggressive, unimperial interpretation of the myth is essential. The entire Adams family had a special affinity for old Winthrop. Perhaps it was that they grew up on the soil in which he was buried. On the Fourth of July, in 1821, John Quincy Adams gave a speech that captured every nuance of the already ancient myth. His speech could have been the text for the Vietnam War critics. He said that America's heart and prayers would always be extended to any free and independent part of the world. "But she goes not abroad in search of monsters to destroy." America, he said, hoped that freedom and independence would spread across the face of the earth. "She will recommend the general cause by the countenance of her voice, and by the benignant sympathy of her example." He said that the new nation understood that it should not actively intervene abroad even if such an adventure would be on the side of freedom because "she would involve herself beyond the power of extrication." It just might be possible for America to try to impose freedom elsewhere, to assist in the liberation of others. "She might," he said, "become the dictatress of the world. She would no longer be the ruler of her own spirit."

In 1966, this speech was quoted by George F. Kennan, the thoughtful analyst of Soviet foreign affairs, to the Senate Foreign Relations Committee which was conducting hearings on the Vietnam War. Perhaps not knowing the myth, Mr. Kennan said that he was not sure what Mr. Adams had in mind when he spoke almost a century and a half earlier. But whatever it was, Mr. Kennan told the senators who were then worrying about Vietnam, "He spoke very directly and very pertinently to us here today."

The myth of the city on a hill became the foundation for the ritualistic thinking of later generations of Americans. This myth helped to establish nationalistic orthodoxy in America. It began to set an American dogma, to fix the limits of thought for Americans about themselves and about the rest of the world, and offered a choice about the appropriate relationship between us and them.

The benevolence of our national motives, the absence of material gain in what we seek, the dedication to principle, and our impenetrable ignorance were all related to the original myth of America. It is temptingly easy to dismiss this as some quaint idea that perhaps once had some significance, but lost it in this more sophisticated, toughminded, modern America. Arthur Schlesinger, Jr., a close aide to President Kennedy, thought otherwise. He was concerned about President Johnson's vastly ambitious plans to create a "Great Society for Asia." Whatever the President meant, according to Professor Schlesinger, such an idea

> demands the confrontation of an issue deep in the historical consciousness of the United States: whether this country is a chosen people, uniquely righteous and wise, with a moral mission to all mankind...The ultimate choice is between messianism and maturity.

The city myth should have collapsed during the war. The war should have taught us that we could not continue to play the role of moral adviser and moral enforcer to the world. After the shock of the assassinations, after the shock of Tet, after President Johnson gave up the presidency, after the riots, demonstrations, burned neighborhoods, and the rebellion of the young, it should have been difficult to sustain John Winthrop's optimism. It was not difficult for Robert Kennedy who, after Senator Eugene McCarthy had demonstrated LBJ's vulnerability in New Hampshire, finally announced that he would run for the presidency himself. The language he used in his announcement speech proved that the myth was as alive and as virulent as it had ever been: "At stake," Senator Kennedy said, "is not simply the leadership of our party, and even our own country, it is our right to the moral leadership of this planet." Members of his staff were horrified that he could use such language because they correctly believed that it reflected just the mind-set that had propelled us into Vietnam in the first place. He ignored their protests. This myth could survive in even the toughest of the contemporary, sophisticated, hard-driving politicians. Of course, he may have used this language only to persuade his listeners, to convince the gullible. But, even so, it showed that he believed that the myth was what they wanted to hear. In either case, the city on a hill continued to work its way.

The myth of the city on a hill combined with solipsism in the assumptions about Vietnam made by the American war planners. In other words, we assumed that we had a superior moral claim to be in Vietnam, and because, despite their quite queer ways of doing things, the Vietnamese shared our values, they would applaud our intentions and embrace our physical presence. Thus, Vice President Humphrey later acknowledged that all along we had been ignorant of Vietnam. He said that "to LBJ, the Mekong and the Pedernales were not that far apart." Our claim to virtue was based on the often announced purity of our intentions. It was said, perhaps thousands of times, that all we wanted was freedom for other people, not land, not resources, and not domination.

Because we believed that our intentions were virtuous, we could learn nothing from the French experience in Vietnam. After all, they had fought only to maintain their Southeast Asian colonies and as imperialists deserved to lose. We assumed that this was why so mighty a European power lost the important battle of Dien Bien Phu to General Giap's ragged army.

America's moral authority was so clear to us that we assumed that it also had to be clear to the Vietnamese. This self-righteousness was the clincher in the debate to intensify the conflict in Vietnam, according to George W. Ball, an undersecretary of state for Presidents Kennedy and Johnson. Washington's war planners, Mr. Ball said in 1973, had been captives of their own myths. Another State Department official also hoped, after the fact, that Americans "will be knocked out of our grandiosity…[and] will see the self-righteous, illusory quality of that vision of ourselves offered by the high Washington official who said that while other nations have 'interests' the United States has 'a sense of responsibility.'" Our power, according to this mentality, gives us responsibility, even though we may be reluctant to bear the burden. Other peoples' greed or selfishness gives them interests, even though they may not be strong enough to grab all they want.

Our grandiosity will, however, not be diminished so easily. At least since World War II, America's foreign affairs have been the affairs of Pygmalion. We fall in love with what we create. We create a vision of the world made in what we think is our own image. We are proud of what we create because we are certain that our intentions are pure, our motives good, and our behavior virtuous. We know these things to be true because we believe that we are unique among the nations of the world in our collective idealism.

Although the nationalists of the world all share a peoples' pride in who they are, a loyalty to place and language and culture, there are delicate but important differences. Because of its Puritan roots, it is not surprising that America's nationalism is more Protestant than that of other countries. It is more missionary in its impulses, more evangelical. It typically seeks to correct the way other people think rather than to establish its own physical dominion over them. It is, as it were, more committed to the Word, as befits serious Protestants, than other nationalisms.

One of the peculiarities of American Protestant nationalism, especially in its most aggressive mood, is its passion about ideas. What we want is to convert others to the truth as we understand it. We went to war in Vietnam in the name of ideas, of principles, of abstractions. Thus, President Johnson said in his inaugural, "We aspire to nothing that belongs to others." And added in his important address at Johns Hopkins in April 1965: "Because we fight for values and we fight for principles, rather than territory or colonies, our patience and our determination are unending." This is what we mean when we think of ourselves as idealists, magnanimous and moral. It is what cold warriors mean when they say over and over that we are engaged with the Soviet Union "in a competition of ideas."

Tangled up in old myths, fearful of speaking plain English on the subject, the political conscience of many Americans must be troubled. There is bad faith in accepting the city myth of American uniqueness as if the myth can be freed from its integral Protestantism, almost always of a fundamentalist flavor. Conservatives have less need to launder the myth of its religion. Because liberals require a secular version of nationalism, and if they need or want to retain some sense of the unique republic, they are required to rest their case on a secular basis. Wilsonian idealism was the answer in the 1960s, as liberals argued that America was the only society capable of creating social justice and genuine democracy at home and abroad. These ideals merged with the cold war and persuaded the best of American liberals to bring us Vietnam.

In America, as elsewhere, elected officials are especially susceptible to the fundamental myths of nationalism because they must embody them to get elected and act on them to govern. The vision of the world that suffused Mr. Wilson's Fourteen Points and League of Nations was also the vision of John Kennedy and his circle. They were pained by the knowledge that a people anywhere in the world struggled toward freedom but was frustrated by the imposition of force. So it was that John F. Kennedy's inspired inaugural address carried the burden of Woodrow Wilson's idealism, and also carried the deadly implication that America was again ready for war in the name of goodness.

President Kennedy's language must be understood in the light of what was just around the corner in Vietnam. He announced to the world. "We shall pay any price, bear any burden, meet any hardship, support any friend, oppose any foe to assure the survival and the success of liberty." He said that it was the rare destiny of his generation to defend freedom when it was at its greatest risk. "I do not shrink from this responsibility—I welcome it."

The difference between the two sons of the Commonwealth of Massachusetts, John Quincy Adams and John Fitzgerald Kennedy, was the difference between good wishes and war, but also the difference between a tiny and isolated America and the world's most powerful nation. Presidents Wilson and Kennedy both fairly represented American liberalism at its most restless and energetic. This was a liberalism that wanted, as President Wilson put it, to make the world safe for democracy, or as President Kennedy said, to defend "those human rights to which this nation has always been committed, and to which we are committed today at home and around the world." JFK described this as "God's work."

An important part of the reason we marched into Vietnam with our eyes fixed was liberalism's irrepressible need to be helpful to those less fortunate. But the decency of the impulse, as was the case with President Wilson, cannot hide the bloody eagerness to kill in the name of virtue. In 1981, James C. Thomson, an aide in the State Department and a member of the National Security Council under President Johnson, finally concluded that our Vietnamese intervention had been motivated by a national missionary impulse, a "need to do good to others." In a phrase that cannot be improved, he and others called this "sentimental imperialism." The purity of intention and the horror of result is unfortunately the liberal's continuing burden.

American conservatives had it easier, largely because they believed in the actuality of evil. In his first public statement, President Eisenhower informed the American public, "The forces of good and evil are massed and armed and opposed as rarely before in history." For him the world struggle was not merely between conflicting ideologies. "Freedom is pitted against slavery; lightness against the dark."

Conservatives in America are closer than liberals to the myth of the city on a hill because they are not embarrassed by public professions of religion. They are therefore somewhat less likely to ascribe American values and behavior to other cultures. This is so because of the conservatives' conviction that America is so much better—more moral, godly, wise, and especially rich—than other nations that they could not possibly resemble us. Thus, President Eisenhower announced that one of America's fixed principles was the refusal to "use our strength to try to impress upon another people our own cherished political and economic institutions." The idea of uniqueness means, after all, that we are alone in the world.

Conservatives shared with liberals the conviction that America could act, and in Vietnam did act, with absolute altruism, as they believed only America could. Thinking of this war, President Nixon, another restless descendent of Mr. Wilson, declared that "never in history have men fought for less selfish motives—not for conquest, not for glory, but only for the right of a people far away to choose the kind of government they want." This was especially attractive because in this case the kind of government presumably sought by this faraway people was opposed to Communism, our own enemy. It was therefore an integral part of the universal struggle between freedom and slavery, lightness and dark. As a result it was relatively easy for conservatives to think of Vietnam as a laboratory to test ways to block the spreading stain of political atheism.

Power is sometimes a problem for liberals and a solution for conservatives. When Senator Goldwater rattled America's many sabers in his presidential campaign of 1964, and when

General Curtis LeMay wanted to bomb North Vietnam "back to the stone age," they both made liberals cringe, partly from embarrassment, and partly because the liberals were appalled at the apparent cruelty. In the 1950s, Dr. Kissinger cleverly argued that the liberal embarrassment over power made its use, when necessary, even worse than it had to be. "Our feeling of guilt with respect to power," he wrote, "has caused us to transform all wars into crusades, and then to apply our power in the most absolute ways." Later, when he ran America's foreign policy, his own unambivalent endorsement of the use in Vietnam of enormous power inevitably raised the question of whether bloody crusades are caused only by the squeamishness of liberals or also by the callousness of conservatives.

Implicit in John Winthrop's formulation of the city myth was the idea that the new Americans could, because of their godliness, vanquish their numerically superior enemies. The idea that warriors, because of their virtue, could beat stronger opponents, is very ancient. Pericles spoke of it in his funeral oration to the Athenians. The Christian crusaders counted on it. *Jihad,* Islam's conception of a holy war, is based on it. The Samurai believed it. So did the Nazis.

In time, the history of America proved to Americans that we were militarily invincible. The Vietnam War Presidents naturally cringed at the thought that they could be the first to lose a war. After all, we had already beaten Indians, French, British (twice), Mexicans, Spaniards, Germans (twice), Italians, Japanese, Koreans, and Chinese. Until World War II, the nation necessarily had to rely on the presumed virtue, not the power, of American soldiers to carry the day, and the war. This was also the case in the South during our Civil War.

Starting in the eighteenth century, the nation of farmers began to industrialize. As the outcome of war increasingly came to depend on the ability to inject various forms of flying hardware into the enemy's body, victory increasingly depended on technology. The acceleration of industrialization in the late nineteenth century inevitably quickened the pace of technological evolution. By then no other power could match the Americans' ability to get organized, to commit resources to development, and to invent the gadgets that efficiently produced money in the marketplace, and, when necessary, death on the battlefield. The idea of Yankee ingenuity, American know-how, stretches back beyond the nineteenth century. Our admiration for the tinkerer whose new widget forms the basis of new industry is nowhere better shown than in our national reverence of Thomas Edison.

Joining the American sense of its moral superiority with its technological superiority was a marriage made in heaven, at least for American nationalists. We told ourselves that each advantage explained the other, that the success of our standard of living was a result of our virtue, and our virtue was a result of our wealth. Our riches, our technology, provided the strength that had earlier been missing, that once had forced us to rely only on our virtue. Now, as Hiroshima demonstrated conclusively, we could think of ourselves not only as morally superior, but as the most powerful nation in history. The inevitable offspring of this marriage of an idea with a weapon was the conviction that the United States could not be beaten in war—not by any nation, and not by any combination of nations. For that moment we thought that we could fight where, when, and how we wished, without risking failure. For that moment we thought that we could impose our will on the recalcitrant of the earth.

A great many Americans, in the period just before the war in Vietnam got hot, shared a circular belief that for most was probably not very well formed: America's technological supremacy was a symptom of its uniqueness, and technology made the nation militarily invincible. In 1983, the playwright Arthur Miller said, "I'm an American. I believe in technology. Until the mid-60s I never believed we could lose because we had technology."

The memory of World War II concluding in a mushroom cloud was relatively fresh throughout the 1950s. It was unthinkable that America's military could ever fail to establish its supremacy on the battlefield, that the industrial, scientific, and technological strength of the nation would ever be insufficient for the purposes of war. It was almost as if Americans were technology. The American love affair with the automobile was at its most passionate in the 1950s, our well-equipped armies stopped the Chinese in Korea, for a moment our nuclear supremacy was taken for granted, and affluence for many white Americans seemed to be settling in as a way of life.

It is, of course, unfortunate that the forces of evil may be as strong as the forces of virtue. The Soviet Union exploded its first atomic bomb way ahead of what Americans thought was a likely schedule. This technology is not like others because even a weak bomb is devastating. Even if our bombs are better than theirs, they can still do us in. America's freedom of action after 1949 was not complete. President Eisenhower and John Foster Dulles, the Secretary of State, threatened "massive retaliation" against the Soviet Union if it stepped over the line. They knew, and we knew, that this threat was not entirely real, and that it freed the Soviets to engage in peripheral adventures because they correctly believed that we would not destroy the world over Korea, Berlin, Hungary, or Czechoslovakia.

Our policy had to become more flexible. We had to invent a theory that would allow us to fight on the edges without nuclear technology. This theory is called "limited war." Its premise is that we and the Soviets can wage little wars, and that each side will refrain from provoking the other to unlock the nuclear armory.

Ike threatened the Chinese, who at the time did not have the bomb, with nuclear war in Korea. JFK similarly threatened the Soviets, who had nuclear capability, over Cuba. But, although some military men thought about using nuclear weapons in Vietnam, the fundamental assumption of that war was to keep it limited, not to force either the Soviets or the Chinese, who now had their own sloppy bombs, to enter the war. Thus, we could impose our will on the recalcitrant of the earth if they did not have their own nuclear weapons, and if they could not compel the Soviets or the Chinese to force us to quit.

In Vietnam we had to find a technology to win without broadening the war. The nuclear stalemate reemphasized our need to find a more limited ground, to find, so to speak, a way to fight a domesticated war. We had to find a technology that would prevail locally, but not explode internationally. No assignment is too tough for the technological mentality. In fact, it was made to order for the technicians who were coming into their own throughout all of American life. This war gave them the opportunity to show what they could do. This was to be history's most technologically sophisticated war, most carefully analyzed and managed, using all of the latest wonders of managerial procedures and systems. It was made to order for bureaucracy.

James C. Thomson, who served both JFK and LBJ as an East Asia specialist, understood how the myths converged. He wrote of *"the rise of a new breed of American ideologues who see Vietnam as the ultimate test of their doctrine."* These new men were the new missionaries and had a trinitarian faith: in military power, technological superiority, and our altruistic idealism. They believed that the reality of American culture "provides us with the opportunity and obligation to ease the nations of the earth toward modernization and stability: toward a full-fledged *Pax Americana Technocratica*." For these parishioners in the church of the machine, Vietnam was the ideal laboratory.

SUGGESTIONS FOR DISCUSSION

1. How are these two accounts alike and different in the way they explain U.S. involvement in Vietnam? What do the titles that these historians have given to the selections—"The Tragedy of Vietnam" and "God's Country and American Know-How"—indicate about their respective points of view? What advantages and disadvantages do you see in each selection's attempt to explain the origins of the Vietnam War?

2. Recall how and what you have learned about the Vietnam War. What has shaped your understanding—school, friends, relatives, movies, books, television shows? How does your own sense of the Vietnam War compare to the perspectives presented by the two reading selections?

3. Baritz describes the "trinitarian faith" of American policymakers in "military power, technological superiority, and altruistic idealism" that he believes led the country into the Vietnam War. Is this "faith" still strongly held today? What, if any, relation do you see between this faith and post-Vietnam military interventions in Grenada, Panama, Iraq, Somalia, Kosovo, and Haiti? What problems or issues does such "faith" ignore or suppress?

SUGGESTIONS FOR WRITING

1. Write an essay that compares Tindall and Shi's and Baritz's accounts of the origins of the Vietnam War. Take into account both differences and similarities in their explanations of causes. End the essay with your own sense of the relative strengths and weaknesses of each way of doing and explaining history.

2. Write an essay on what Baritz calls America's "missionary impulse." What do you see as the problems, if any, with this "altruistic idealism"? Does it invariably lead, as Baritz suggests, to "purity of intention" on the one hand, and "the horror of result" on the other? It will help your essay to look at a particular instance with which you are familiar, where the desire to act "in that name of goodness" backfired on the benefactors. You needn't limit yourself here to matters of international or military policy. There may well be instances much closer to home in which someone or some group that seeks to do good actually produces the opposite effect. Your task here is to analyze why and how this is the case.

3. Write an essay that locates your own understanding of the Vietnam War in relation to the accounts of these professional historians. Agree and disagree with them as you see fit, but the main point is to use their versions of the Vietnam War to develop your own. Make sure you explain how you learned about the Vietnam War, through which sources—school, friends, relatives, popular media—and how these sources shaped your understanding.

CHECKING OUT THE WEB

There is abundant information on the Vietnam War on the Web. You can start your own search by using search engines such as Lycos or Yahoo and entering vietnam + war (or vietnam + conflict). The Vietnam War Internet Project at the University of Texas, www.lbjlib.utexas.edu/shwv/shwvhome.html, provides access to documents, an image library, articles, memoirs, military unit home pages, and a recommended reading list, as well as a USENET newsgroup, soc.history.war.vietnam. The Vietnam War Pictorial site at dspace.dial.pipex.com/nam/index.shtml contains hundreds of photos. Spend some time browsing through various websites related to the Vietnam War. What different types of information are available? How would you categorize them? Compare your findings to what others found. How might the results of these searches fit into a writing project you could imagine yourself doing on an aspect of the Vietnam War?

When Heaven and Earth Changed Places

Le Ly Hayslip

> Le Ly Hayslip was born into a peasant family in central Vietnam and, when she was a teenager, fought for the Viet Cong. The following selection is taken from the Prologue to her book *When Heaven and Earth Changed Places* (1989), which recounts her experiences with the Viet Cong and, after she fled from the fighting in the countryside, in the bars, brothels, and black markets of war-torn Saigon (now Ho Chi Minh City). Hayslip married an American civilian working in Vietnam and, in 1970, followed him to the United States, where she founded the East Meets West Foundation, a charitable relief organization dedicated to healing the wounds of the Vietnam War.

SUGGESTION FOR READING

> As you read, notice that Hayslip, like the authors of the two previous selections, attempts to explain the causes of the Vietnam War and why people took sides to fight. Consider how the perspective of Vietnamese peasants differs from those of professional historians.

Everything I knew about the war I learned as a teenaged girl from the North Vietnamese cadre leaders in the swamps outside Ky La. During these midnight meetings, we peasants assumed everything we heard was true because what the Viet Cong said matched, in one way or another, the beliefs we already had.

The first lesson we learned about the new "American" war was why the Viet Cong was formed and why we should support it. Because this lesson came on the heels of our war with the French (which began in 1946 and lasted, on and off, for eight years), what the cadre leaders told us seemed to be self-evident.

First, we were taught that Vietnam was *con rong chau tien*—a sovereign nation which had been held in thrall by Western imperialists for over a century. That all nations had a right to determine their own destiny also seemed beyond dispute, since we farmers subsisted by our own hands and felt we owed nothing to anyone but god and our ancestors for the right to live as we saw fit. Even the Chinese, who had made their own disastrous attempt to rule Vietnam in centuries past, had learned a painful lesson about our country's zeal for independence. "Vietnam," went the saying that summarized their experience, "is nobody's lapdog."

Second, the cadres told us that the division of Vietnam into North and South in 1954 was nothing more than a ploy by the defeated French and their Western allies, mainly the United States, to preserve what influence they could in our country.

"*Chia doi dat nuoc?*" the Viet Cong asked, "Why should outsiders divide the land and tell some people to go north and others south? If Vietnam were truly for the Vietnamese, wouldn't we choose for ourselves what kind of government our people wanted? A nation cannot have two governments," they said, "any more than a family can have two fathers."

Because those who favored America quickly occupied the seats of power formerly held by the French, and because the North remained pretty much on its own, the choice of which side best represented independence was, for us, a foregone conclusion. In fact, the Viet Cong usually ended our indoctrination sessions with a song that played on our worst fears:

Americans come to kill our people,

Follow America, and kill your relatives!

The smart bird flies before it's caught.

The smart person comes home before Tet.

Follow us, and you'll always have a family.

Follow America, and you'll always be alone!

After these initial "lessons," the cadre leaders introduced us to the two Vietnamese leaders who personified each view—the opposite poles of our tiny world. On the South pole was President Ngo Dinh Diem, America's staunch ally, who was Catholic like the French. Although he was idolized by many who said he was a great humanitarian and patriot, his religion alone was enough to make him suspicious to Buddhists on the Central Coast. The loyalty we showed him, consequently, was more duty to a landlord than love for a founding father. Here is a song the Republican schoolteachers made us learn to praise the Southern president:

In stormy seas, Vietnam's boat rolls and pitches.

Still we must row; our President's hand upon the helm.

The ship of state plows through heavy seas.

Holding fast its course to democracy.

Our President is celebrated from Europe to Asia.

He is the image of philanthropy and love.

He has sacrificed himself for our happiness.

He fights for liberty in the land of the Viet.

Everyone loves him earnestly, and behind him we will march

Down the street of freedom, lined with fresh flowers,

The flag of liberty crackling above our heads!

In the North, on the other pole, was Ho Chi Minh, whom we were encouraged to call *Bac Ho*—Uncle Ho—the way we would refer to a trusted family friend. We knew nothing of his past beyond stories of his compassion and his love for our troubled country—the independence of which, we were told, he had made the mission of his life.

Given the gulf between these leaders, the choice of whom we should support again seemed obvious. The cadre leaders encouraged our natural prejudices (fear of outsiders and love of our ancestors) with stirring songs and tender stories about Uncle Ho in which the Communist leader and our ancient heroes seemed to inhabit one congenial world. Like an unbroken thread, the path from our ancestors and legends seemed to lead inevitably to the Northern leader—then past him to a future of harmony and peace.

But to achieve that independence, Ho said, we must wage total war. His cadremen cried out "We must hold together and oppose the American empire. There is nothing better than freedom, independence, and happiness!"

To us, these ideas seemed as obvious as everything else we had heard. *Freedom* meant a Vietnam free of colonial domination. *Independence* meant one Vietnamese people—not two countries, North and South—determining its own destiny. *Happiness* meant plenty of food and an end to war—the ability, we assumed, to live our lives in accordance with our ancient ways. We wondered: how can the Southerners oppose these wonderful things? The answer the Viet Cong gave us was that the Republicans prized Yankee dollars more than the blood of their brothers and sisters. We did not think to question with our hearts what our minds told us must be true.

Although most of us thought we knew what the Viet Cong meant by freedom, independence, and happiness, a few of us dared to ask what life the Northerners promised when the war was over. The answer was always the same: "Uncle Ho promises that after our victory, the Communist state will look after your rights and interests. Your highest interest, of course, is the independence of our fatherland and the freedom of our people. Our greatest right is the right to determine our own future as a state." This always brought storms of applause from the villagers because most people remembered what life was like under the French.

Nonetheless, despite our vocal support, the Viet Cong never took our loyalty for granted. They rallied and rewarded and lectured us sternly, as the situation demanded, while the Republicans assumed we would be loyal because we lived south of a line some diplomats had drawn on a map. Even when things were at their worst—when the allied forces devastated the countryside and the Viet Cong themselves resorted to terror to make us act the way they wanted— the villagers clung to the vision the Communists had drummed into us. When the Republicans put us in jail, we had the image of "Communist freedom"—freedom from war—to see us through. When the Viet Cong executed a relative, we convinced ourselves that it was necessary to bring "Communist happiness"—peace in the village—a little closer. Because the Viet Cong encouraged us to voice our basic human feelings through patriotic songs, the tortured, self-imposed silence we endured around Republicans only made us hate the government more. Even on those occasions when the Republicans tried to help us, we saw their favors as a trick or sign of weakness. Thus, even as we accepted their kindness, we despised the Republicans for it.

As the war gathered steam in the 1960s, every villager found his or her little world expanded—usually for the worse. The steady parade of troops through Ky La meant new opportunities for us to fall victim to outsiders. Catholic Republicans spurned and mistreated Buddhists for worshiping their ancestors. City boys taunted and cheated the "country bumpkins" while Vietnamese servicemen from other provinces made fun of our funny accents and strange ways. When the tactics on both sides got so rough that people were in danger no matter which side they favored, our sisters fled to the cities where they learned about liquor, drugs, adultery, materialism, and disrespect for their ancestors. More than one village father died inside when a "stranger from Saigon" returned in place of the daughter he had raised.

In contrast to this, the Viet Cong were, for the most part, our neighbors. Even though our cadre leaders had been trained in Hanoi, they had all been born on the Central Coast. They did not insult us for our manners and speech because they had been raised exactly like us. Where the Republicans came into the village overburdened with American equipment designed for a different war, the Viet Cong made do with what they had and seldom wasted their best ammunition—the goodwill of the people. The cadremen pointed out to us that where the Republicans wore medals, the Viet Cong wore rags and never gave up the fight. "Where the Republicans pillage, rape, and plunder," they said, "we preserve your houses, crops, and family"; for they knew that it was only by these resources—our food for rations, our homes for hiding, our sons and brothers for recruits—that they were able to keep the field.

Of course, the Viet Cong cadremen, like the Republicans, had no desire (or ability, most of them) to paint a fairer picture. For them, there could be no larger reason for Americans fighting the war than imperialist aggression. Because we peasants knew nothing about the United States, we could not stop to think how absurd it would be for so large and wealthy a nation to covet our poor little country for its rice fields, swamps, and pagodas. Because our only exposure to politics had been through the French colonial government (and before that, the rule of Vietnamese kings), we had no concept of democracy. For us, "Western culture" meant bars, brothels, black markets, and *xa hoi van minh*—bewildering machines—most of them destructive. We couldn't imagine that life in the capitalist world was anything other than a frantic, alien terror. Because, as peasants, we defined "politics" as something other people did someplace else, it had no relevance to our daily lives—except as a source of endless trouble. As a consequence, we overlooked the power that lay in our hands: our power to achieve virtually anything we wanted if only we acted together. The Viet Cong and the North, on the other hand, always recognized and respected this strength.

We children also knew that our ancestral spirits demanded we resist the outsiders. Our parents told us of the misery they had suffered from the invading Japanese ("small death," our neighbors called them) in World War II, and from the French, who returned in 1946. These soldiers destroyed our crops, killed our livestock, burned our houses, raped our women, and tortured or put to death anyone who opposed them—as well as many who did not. Now, the souls of all those people who had been mercilessly killed had come back to haunt Ky La—demanding revenge against the invaders. This we children believed with all our hearts. After all, we had been taught from birth that ghosts were simply people we could not see.

There was only one way to remove this curse. Uncle Ho had urged the poor to take up arms so that everyone might be guaranteed a little land on which to cultivate some rice. Because nearly everyone in Central Vietnam was a farmer, and because farmers must have land, almost everyone went to war: with a rifle or a hoe; with vigilance to give the alarm; with food and shelter for our fighters; or, if one was too little for anything else, with flowers and songs to cheer them up. Everything we knew commanded us to fight. Our ancestors called us to war. Our myths and legends called us to war. Our parents' teachings called us to war. Uncle Ho's cadre called us to war. Even President Diem had called us to fight for the very thing we now believe he was betraying—an independent Vietnam. Should an obedient child be less than an ox and refuse to do her duty?

And so the war began and became an insatiable dragon that roared around Ky La. By the time I turned thirteen, that dragon had swallowed me up.

SUGGESTIONS FOR DISCUSSION

1. This selection closes with the lines, "And so the war began and became an insatiable dragon that roared around Ky La. By the time I turned thirteen, that dragon had swallowed me up." How does Hayslip explain the origins of the Vietnam War in the countryside and why Vietnamese peasants fought for the Viet Cong? How does Hayslip's account differ from the accounts offered by Tindall and Shi in "The Tragedy of Vietnam" and by Baritz in "God's Country and American Know-How"? What implications about the nature of the war do you draw from your answer?

2. The Vietnam War was not only an encounter between the American military and the Viet Cong and North Vietnamese forces. It was also a cross-cultural encounter between Americans and the Vietnamese. Hayslip offers the perspective of Vietnamese villagers on the arrival of "Western culture" in their country. What can you learn about the nature and meaning of the war by taking this perspective into account?

3. History is often presented in school and in popular opinion as the story of how the leaders of great nations shaped historical events. People, therefore, often think of history in terms of prominent figures such as George Washington, Napoleon, Abraham Lincoln, V. I. Lenin, Adolf Hitler, Mao Zedong, and Mohandas Gandhi. Hayslip, on the other hand, offers a view of history as it is lived at the local level, through the experience of ordinary people. What can you learn about the meaning of history from this local perspective? What does it bring to light that gets overlooked in other historical accounts?

SUGGESTIONS FOR WRITING

1. Write an essay that compares Hayslip's account of the origins of the Vietnam War to the accounts offered by Tindall and Shi in "The Tragedy of Vietnam" and by Baritz in "God's Country and American Know-How." The point here is not to decide which account is more accurate (they could all be accurate, from the perspectives they take) but to consider how the three quite different perspectives on the Vietnam War offer quite different representations of the nature and meaning of the war.

2. Hayslip says, "Our ancestors called us to war. Our myths and legends called us to war." She seems to suggest here that a people's willingness to wage a war of national liberation is not simply a matter of geopolitical conflicts but is deeply ingrained in their culture. Write an essay that considers whether Hayslip's statement, "Everything we knew commanded us to fight," can be applied to your "ancestors," to the "myths and legends" passed down to you. How you define ancestors, myths, and legends for this essay is up to you. Don't feel restricted to the perspective of American culture, its ancestors, myths, and legends. Depending on your own background, you might write, for example, about African American, Armenian, Irish, or Puerto Rican ancestors, myths, and legends. In any case, consider whether and how the desire for independence is expressed through your people's culture and what the consequences have been.

3. By representing the lived experience of Vietnamese villagers, Hayslip offers an account of the Vietnam War that differs dramatically from the two previous accounts, in which the Vietnamese are largely invisible. The Vietnam War, of course, is not the only encounter of Americans with another culture. Pick another instance where Americans have encountered another people and write an essay that develops the perspective of ordinary people in that culture to the arrival of Americans. Don't feel that you have to write only about military encounters. You might want to consider other cross-cultural encounters such as those between New England missionaries and American Indians or between slave traders and West Africans.

Private First Class Reginald "Malik" Edwards

Wallace Terry

The following selection is a chapter from *Bloods: An Oral History of the Vietnam War by Black Veterans* (1984) by the journalist and documentary film producer Wallace Terry. *Bloods* consists of twenty oral histories that Terry gathered from African Americans who served in Vietnam, enlisted men and officers from the U.S. Army, Navy, Marines, and Air Force—what Terry calls "a representative cross-section of the black combat force." As Terry says, these men's "stories are not to be found in the expanding body of Vietnam literature" but "deservedly belong in the forefront because of the unique experience of the black Vietnam veteran." We have chosen the story told by Malik Edwards, but all of the stories are equally eloquent, telling of life in combat, racism in the military, relations between Americans and Vietnamese, and the difficulties of returning to civilian life in a racially divided society.

SUGGESTION FOR READING

As you read, notice how Malik Edwards offers both anecdotal accounts of particular incidents in the war and his own commentary on the meaning of the war. Mark those passages where Edwards explains his feelings about the war.

Rifleman
9th Regiment
U.S. Marine Corps
Danang
June 1965–March 1966

I'm in the Amtrac with Morley Safer, right? The whole thing is getting ready to go down. At Cam Ne. The whole bit that all America will see on the *CBS Evening News,* right? Marines burning down some huts. Brought to you by Morley Safer. Your man on the scene. August 5, 1965.

When we were getting ready for Cam Ne, the helicopters flew in first and told them to get out of the village 'cause the Marines are looking for VC. If you're left there, you're considered VC.

They told us if you receive one round from the village, you level it. So we was coming into the village, crossing over the hedges. It's like a little ditch, then you go through these bushes and jump across, and start kickin' ass, right?

Not only did we receive one round, three Marines got wounded right off. Not only that, but one of the Marines was our favorite Marine, Sergeant Bradford. This brother that everybody loved got shot in the groin. So you know how we felt.

The first thing happened to me, I looked out and here's a bamboo snake. That little short snake, the one that bites you and you're through bookin'. What do you do when a bamboo snake comin' at you? You drop your rifle with one hand, and shoot his head off. You don't think you can do this, but you do it. So I'm so rough with this snake, everybody thinks, well, Edwards is shootin' his ass off today.

So then this old man runs by. This other sergeant says, "Get him, Edwards." But I missed the old man. Now I just shot the head off a snake. You dig what I'm sayin'? Damn near with one hand. M-14. But all of a sudden, I missed this old man. 'Cause I really couldn't shoot him.

So Brooks—he's got the grenade launcher—fired. Caught my man as he was comin' through the door. But what happened was it was a room full of children. Like a schoolroom. And he was runnin' back to warn the kids that the Marines were coming. And that's who got hurt. All those little kids and people.

Everybody wanted to see what had happened, 'cause it was so fucked up. But the officers wouldn't let us go up there and look at what shit they were in. I never got the count, but a lot of people got screwed up. I was telling Morley Safer and his crew what was happening, but they thought I was trippin', this Marine acting crazy, just talking shit. 'Cause they didn't want to know what was going on.

So I'm going on through the village. Like the way you go in, you sweep, right? You fire at the top of the hut in case somebody's hangin' in the rafters. And if they hit the ground, you immediately fire along the ground, waist high, to catch them on the run. That's the way I had it worked out, or the way the Marines taught me. That's the process.

All of a sudden, this Vietnamese came runnin' after me, telling me not to shoot: "Don't shoot. Don't shoot." See, we didn't go in the village and look. We would just shoot first. Like you didn't go into a room to see who was in there first. You fired and go in. So in case there was somebody there, you want to kill them first. And we was just gonna run in, shoot through the walls. 'Cause it was nothin' to shoot through the walls of a bamboo hut. You could actually set them on fire if you had tracers. That used to be a fun thing to do. Set hootches on fire with tracers.

So he ran out in front of me. I mean he's runnin' into my line of fire. I almost killed him. But I'm thinking, what the hell is wrong? So then we went into the hut, and it was all these women and children huddled together. I was gettin' ready to wipe them off the planet. In this one hut. I tell you, man, my knees got weak. I dropped down, and that's when I cried. First time I cried in the 'Nam. I realized what I would have done. I almost killed all them people. That was the first time I had actually had the experience of weak knees.

Safer didn't tell them to burn the huts down with they lighters. He just photographed it. He could have got a picture of me burning a hut, too. It was just the way they did it. When you say level a village, you don't use torches. It's not like in the 1800s. You use a Zippo. Now you would use a Bic. That's just the way we did it. You went in there with your Zippos. Everybody. That's why people bought Zippos. Everybody had a Zippo. It was for burnin' shit down.

I was a Hollywood Marine. I went to San Diego, but it was worse in Parris Island. Like you've heard the horror stories of Parris Island—people be marchin' into the swamps. So you were happy to be in San Diego. Of course, you're in a lot of sand, but it was always warm.

At San Diego, they had this way of driving you into this base. It's all dark. Back roads. All of a sudden you come to this little adobe-looking place. All of a sudden, the lights are on, and all you see are these guys with these Smokey the Bear hats and big hands on their hips. The light is behind them, shining through at you. You all happy to be with the Marines. And they say, "Better knock that shit off, boy. I don't want to hear a goddamn word out of your mouth." And everybody starts cursing and yelling and screaming at you.

My initial instinct was to laugh. But then they get right up in your face. That's when I started getting scared. When you're 117 pounds, 150 look like a monster. He would just come screaming down your back, "What the hell are you looking at, shit turd?" I remembered the time where you cursed, but you didn't let anybody adult hear it. You were usually doing it just to be funny or trying to be bold. But these people were actually serious about cursing your ass out.

Then here it is. Six o'clock in the morning. People come in bangin' on trash cans, hittin' my bed with night sticks. That's when you get really scared, 'cause you realize I'm not at home anymore. It doesn't look like you're in the Marine Corps either. It looks like you're in jail. It's like you woke up in a prison camp somewhere in the South. And the whole process was not to allow you to be yourself.

I grew up in a family that was fair. I was brought up on the Robin Hood ethic, and John Wayne came to save people. So I could not understand that if these guys were supposed to be the good guys, why were they treating each other like this?

I grew up in Plaquemines Parish. My folks were poor, but I was never hungry. My stepfather worked with steel on buildings. My mother worked wherever she could. In the fields, pickin' beans. In the factories, the shrimp factories, oyster factories. And she was a housekeeper.

I was the first person in my family to finish high school. This was 1963. I knew I couldn't go to college because my folks couldn't afford it. I only weighed 117 pounds, and nobody's gonna hire me to work for them. So the only thing left to do was go into the service. I didn't want to go into the Army, 'cause everybody went into the Army. Plus the Army didn't seem like it did anything. The Navy I did not like 'cause of the uniforms. The Air Force, too. But the Marines was bad. The Marine Corps built men. Plus just before I went in, they had all these John Wayne movies on every night. Plus the Marines went to the Orient.

Everybody laughed at me. Little, skinny boy can't work in the field going in the Marine Corps. So I passed the test. My mother, she signed for me 'cause I was seventeen.

There was only two black guys in my platoon in boot camp. So I hung with the Mexicans, too, because in them days we never hang with white people. You didn't have white friends. White people was the aliens to me. This is '63. You don't have integration really in the South. You expected them to treat you bad. But somehow in the Marine Corps you hoping all that's gonna change. Of course, I found out this was not true, because the Marine Corps was the last service to integrate. And I had an Indian for a platoon commander who hated Indians. He used to call Indians blanket ass. And then we had a Southerner from Arkansas that liked to call you chocolate bunny and Brillo head. That kind of shit.

I went to jail in boot camp. What happened was I was afraid to jump this ditch on the obstacle course. Every time I would hit my shin. So a white lieutenant called me a nigger. And, of course, I jumped the ditch farther than I'd ever jumped before. Now I can't run. My leg is really messed up. I'm hoppin'. So it's pretty clear I can't do this. So I tell the drill instructor, "Man, I can't fucking go on." He said, "You said what?" I said it again. He said, "Get out." I said, "Fuck you." This to a drill instructor in 1963. I mean you just don't say that. I did seven days for disrespect. When I got out of the brig, they put me in a recon. The toughest unit.

We trained in guerrilla warfare for two years at Camp Pendleton. When I first got there, they was doing Cuban stuff. Cuba was the aggressor. It was easy to do Cuba because you had a lot of Mexicans. You could always let them be Castro. We even had Cuban targets. Targets you shoot at. So then they changed the silhouettes to Vietnamese. Everything to Vietnam. Getting people ready for the little gooks. And, of course, if there were any Hawaiians and Asian-Americans in the unit, they played the roles of aggressors in the war games.

Then we are going over to Okinawa, thinking we're going on a regular cruise. But the rumors are that we're probably going to the 'Nam. In Okinawa we was trained as raiders. Serious, intense jungle-warfare training. I'm gonna tell you, it was some good training. The best thing about the Marine Corps, I can say for me, is that they teach you personal endurance, how much of it you can stand.

The only thing they told us about the Viet Cong was they were gooks. They were to be killed. Nobody sits around and gives you their historical and cultural background. They're the enemy. Kill, kill, kill. That's what we got in practice. Kill, kill, kill. I remember a survey they did in the mess hall where we had to say how we felt about the war. The thing was, get out of Vietnam or fight. What we were hearing was Vietnamese was killing Americans. I felt that if people were killing Americans, we should fight them. As a black person, there wasn't no problem fightin' the enemy. I knew Americans were prejudiced, were racist and all that, but basically, I believed in America 'cause I was an American.

I went over with the original 1st Battalion 9th Marines. When we got there, it was nothing like you expect a war to be. We had seen a little footage of the war on TV. But we was on the ship dreaming about landing on this beach like they did in World War II. Then we pulled into this area like a harbor almost and just walked off the ship.

And the first Vietnamese that spoke to me was a little kid up to my knee. He said, "You give me cigarette. You give me cigarette." That really freaked me out. This little bitty kid smokin' cigarettes. That is my first memory of Vietnam. I thought little kids smokin' was the most horrible thing that you could do. So the first Vietnamese words I learned was *Toi khong hut thuoc lo.* "I don't smoke cigarettes." And *Thuoc la co hai cho suc khoe.* "Cigarettes are bad for your health."

Remember, we were in the beginning of the war. We wasn't dealing with the regular army from the North. We was still fightin' the Viet Cong. The NVA was moving in, but they really hadn't made their super move yet. So we were basically runnin' patrols out of Danang. We were basically with the same orders that the Marines went into Lebanon with. I mean we couldn't even put rounds in the chambers at first.

It was weird. The first person that died in each battalion of the 9th Marines that landed was black. And they were killed by our own people. Comin' back into them lines was the most dangerous thing then. It was more fun sneakin' into Ho Chi Minh's house than comin' back into the lines of Danang. Suppose the idiot is sleeping on watch and he wake up. All of a sudden he sees people. That's all he sees. There was a runnin' joke around Vietnam that we was killing more of our people than the Vietnamese were. Like we were told to kill any Vietnamese in black. We didn't know that the ARVN had some black uniforms, too. And you could have a platoon commander calling the air strikes, and he's actually calling on your position. It was easy to get killed by an American.

They called me a shitbird, because I would stay in trouble. Minor shit, really. But they put me on point anyway. I spent most of my time in Vietnam runnin'. I ran through Vietnam 'cause I was always on point, and points got to run. They can't walk like everybody else. Specially when you hit them open areas. Nobody walked through an open area. After a while, you develop a way to handle it. You learned that the point usually survived. It was the people behind you who got killed.

And another thing. It's none of that shit, well, if they start shootin' at you, now all of a sudden we gonna run in there and outshoot them. The motherfuckers hit, you call in some air. Bring in some heavy artillery, whatever you need to cool them down. You wipe that area up. You soften it up. Then you lay to see if you receive any fire. And *then* you go on in.

I remember the first night we had went out on patrol. About 50 people shot this old guy. Everybody claimed they shot him. He got shot 'cause he started running. It was an old man running to tell his family. See, it wasn't s'posed to be nobody out at night but the Marines. Any Vietnamese out at night was the enemy. And we had guys who were frustrated from Korea with us. Guys who were real gung ho, wanted a name for themselves. So a lot of times they ain't tell us shit about who is who. People get out of line, you could basically kill them. So this old man was running like back towards his crib to warn his family. I think people said "Halt," but we didn't know no Vietnamese words.

It was like shootin' water buffaloes. Somebody didn't tell us to do this. We did it anyway. But they had to stop us from doing that. Well, the water buffaloes would actually attack Americans. I guess maybe we smelled different. You would see these little Vietnamese kids carrying around this huge water buffalo. That buffalo would see some Marines and start wantin' to run 'em down. You see the poor little kids tryin' to hold back the water buffalo, because these Marines will kill him. And Marines, man, was like, like we was always lookin' for shit to go wrong. Shit went wrong. That gave us the opportunity.

I remember we had went into this village and got pinned down with a Australian officer. When we finally went on through, we caught these two women. They smelled like they had weapons. These were all the people we found. So the Australian dude told us to take the women in. So me and my partner, we sittin' up in this Amtrac with these women. Then these guys who was driving the Amtrac come in there and start unzippin' their pants as if they gonna screw the women. So we say, "Man, get outta here. You can't do it to our prisoners." So they get mad with us. Like they gonna fight us. And we had to actually lock and load to protect the women. They said, "We do this all the time."

One time we had went into this place we had hit. We was takin' prisoners. So this one guy broke and ran. So I chased him. I ran behind him. Everybody say, "Shoot him. Shoot him." 'Cause they was pissed that I was chasin' him. So I hit him. You know I had to do something to him. I knew I couldn't just grab him and bring him back. And his face just crumbled. Then I brought him back, and they said, "You could have got a kill, Edwards."

The first time we thought we saw the enemy in big numbers was one of these operations by Marble Mountain. We had received fire. All of a sudden we could see people in front of us. Instead of waiting for air, we returned the fire, and you could see people fall. I went over to this dude and said, "Hey, man, I saw one fall." Then everyone started yelling, "We can see 'em fall. We can see 'em fall." And they were fallin'. Come to find out it was Bravo Company. What the VC had done was suck Bravo Company in front of us. 'Cause they attacked us and Bravo Company at the same time. They would move back as Bravo Company was in front of us. It was our own people. That's the bodies we saw falling. They figured out what was happening, and then they ceased fire. But the damage is done real fast. I think we shot up maybe 40 guys in Bravo Company. Like I said, it was easy to get killed by an American.

The first time I killed somebody up close was when we was tailing Charlie on a patrol somewhere around Danang. It was night. I was real tired. At that time you had worked so hard during the day, been on so many different details, you were just bombed out.

I thought I saw this dog running. Because that white pajama top they wore at night just blend into that funny-colored night they had over there. All of a sudden, I realized that somebody's runnin'. And before I could say anything to him, he's almost ran up on me. There's nothing I can do but shoot. Somebody get that close, you can't wait to check their ID. He's gonna run into you or stop to shoot you. It's got to be one or the other. I shot him a bunch of times. I had 20-round clip, and when he hit the ground, I had nothing. I had to reload. That's how many times he was shot.

Then the sergeant came over and took out the flashlight and said, "Goddamn. This is fucking beautiful. This is fucking beautiful."

This guy was really out of it. He was like moanin'. I said, "Let me kill him." I couldn't stand the sound he was makin'. So I said, "Back off, man. Let me put this guy out of his misery." So I shot him again. In the head.

He had a grenade in his hand. I guess he was committing suicide. He was just runnin' up to us, pullin' a grenade kind of thing. I caught him just in time.

Everybody was comin' congratulatin' me, saying what a great thing it was. I'm tryin' to be cool, but I'm really freakin' out. So then I start walking away, and they told me I had to carry the body back to base camp. We had a real kill. We had one we could prove. We didn't have to make this one up.

So then I start draggin' this body by the feet. And his arm fell off. So I had to go back and get his arm. I had to stick it down his pants. It was a long haul.

And I started thinkin'. You think about how it feels, the weight. It was rainin'. You think about the mist and the smells the rain brings out. All of a sudden I realize this guy is a person, has got a family. All of a sudden it wasn't like I was carrying a gook. I was actually carrying a human being. I started feeling guilty. I just started feeling really badly.

I don't feel like we got beat in Vietnam. We never really fought the war. People saying that America couldn't have won that war is crazy.

The only way we could actually win the war was to fight every day. You couldn't fight only when you felt like it. Or change officers every month. Troops would learn the language, learn the people, learn the areas. If you're gonna be fighting in an area, you get to know everybody in the area and you stay there. You can't go rotate your troops every 12 months. You always got new people coming in. Plus they may not get to learn anything. They may die the first day. If you take a guy on patrol and he gets killed the first day, what good is he? See, if you have seasoned troops, you can move in and out of the bush at will. You get the smell of the country on you. You start to eat the food. You start to smell like it. You don't have that fresh smell so they can smell you when you're comin'. Then you can fight a war. Then you can just start from one tip of South Vietnam and work your way to the top. To China. Of course, if we had used the full might of the military, we'd be there now. We could never give the country back up. Plus we'd have to kill millions of Vietnamese. Do we want to do that? What had they done to us to deserve all that? So to do it would have been wrong. All we did was give our officers the first combat training they had since Korea. It was more like a big training ground. If it was a real war, you either would have come out in a body bag or you would have come out when the war was over.

Sometimes I think we would have done a lot better by getting them hooked on our life-style than by trying to do it with guns. Give them credit cards. Make them dependent on television and sugar. Blue jeans works better than bombs. You can take blue jeans and rock 'n' roll records and win over more countries than you can with soldiers.

When I went home, they put me in supply, probably the lowest job you can have in the Marines. But they saw me drawing one day and they said, "Edwards can draw." They sent me over to the training-aids library, and I became an illustrator. I reenlisted and made sergeant.

When I went to Quantico, my being black, they gave me the black squad, the squad with most of the blacks, especially the militant blacks. And they started hippin' me. I mean I was against racism. I didn't even call it racism. I called it prejudice. They hipped me to terms like "exploitation" and "oppression." And by becoming an illustrator, it gave you more time to think. And I was around people who thought. People who read books. I would read black history where the white guys were going off on novels or playing rock music. So then one day, I just told them I was black. I didn't call them *blanco,* they didn't have to call me Negro. That's what started to get me in trouble. I became a target. Somebody to watch.

Well, there was this riot on base, and I got busted. It started over some white guys using a bunch of profanity in front of some sisters. I was found guilty of attack on an unidenti-fied Marine. Five months in jail, five months without pay. And a suspended BCD. In jail they didn't want us to read our books, draw any pictures, or do anything intellectually stim-ulating or what they thought is black. They would come in my cell and harass me. So one day I was just tired of them, and I hit the duty warden. I ended up with a BCD in 1970. After six years, eight months, and eight days, I was kicked out of the Corps. I don't feel it was fair. If I had been white, I would never have went to jail for fighting. That would have been impossible.

With a BCD, nothing was happenin'. I took to dressin' like the Black Panthers, so even blacks wouldn't hire me. So I went to the Panther office in D.C. and joined. I felt the party was the only organization that was fighting the system.

I liked their independence. The fact that they had no fear of the police. Talking about self-determination. Trying to make Malcolm's message reality. This was the first time black people had stood up to the state since Nat Turner. I mean armed. It was obvious they wasn't gonna give us anything unless we stood up and were willing to die. They obviously didn't care anything about us, 'cause they had killed King.

For me the thought of being killed in the Black Panther Party by the police and the thought of being killed by Vietnamese was just a qualitative difference. I had left one war and came back and got into another one. Most of the Panthers then were veterans. We figured if we had been over in Vietnam fighting for our country, which at that point wasn't serving us properly, it was only proper that we had to go out and fight for our own cause. We had already fought for the white man in Vietnam. It was clearly his war. If it wasn't, you wouldn't have seen as many Confederate flags as you saw. And the Confederate flags was an insult to any person that's of color on this planet.

I rose up into the ranks. I was an artist immediately for the newspaper. Because of my background in the military, obviously I was able to deal with a lot of things of a security nature. And eventually I took over the D.C. chapter.

At this time, Huey Newton and Bobby Seale were in jail and people sort of idealized them. The party didn't actually fall apart until those two were released, and then the real leader, David Hilliard, was locked up. Spiro Agnew had a lot to do with the deterioration when he said take the Panthers out of the newspapers and then they will go away. And the FBI was harassing us, and we started turning on each other because of what they were spreading. And the power structure started to build up the poverty programs. Nobody was going to follow the Panthers if they could go down to the poverty program and get a check and say they are going to school.

We just didn't understand the times. All we wanted to do was kick whitey's ass. We didn't think about buying property or gaining economic independence. We were, in the end, just showing off.

I think the big trip America put us on was to convince us that having money was somehow harmful. That building businesses and securing our economic future, and buying and controlling areas for our group, our family, our friends like everybody else does, was wrong. Doing that doesn't make you antiwhite. I think white people would even like us better if we had more money. They like Richard Pryor. And Sammy Davis. And Jabbar.

Economically, black folks in America have more money than Canada or Mexico. It's obvious that we are doing something wrong. When people say we're illiterate, that doesn't bother me as much. Literacy means I can't read these books. Well neither does a Korean or a Vietnamese. But where they're not illiterate is in the area of economics. Sure, we're great artists, great singers, play great basketball. But we're not great managers yet. It's pretty obvious that you don't have to have guns to get power. People get things out of this country and they don't stick up America to do it. Look at the Vietnamese refugees running stores now in the black community where I live.

Right now, I'm an unemployed artist, drawing unemployment. I spent time at a community center helping kids, encouraging kids to draw.

I work for the nuclear-freeze movement, trying to convince people nuclear war is insane. Even when I was in the Marine Corps, I was against nuclear war. When I was a child, I was against nuclear weapons, because I thought what they did to Hiroshima and Nagasaki was totally cold. There's nothing any human being is doing on the planet that I could want to destroy the planet for future generations. I think we should confine war to our century and our times. Not to leave the residue around for future generations. The residue of hate is a horrible thing to leave behind. The residue of nuclear holocaust is far worse.

I went to see *Apocalypse Now,* because a friend paid my way. I don't like movies about Vietnam 'cause I don't think that they are prepared to tell the truth. *Apocalypse Now,* didn't tell the truth. It wasn't real. I guess it was a great thing for the country to get off on, but it didn't remind me of anything I saw. I can't understand how you would have a bridge lit up like a Christmas tree. A USO show at night? Guys attacking the women on stage. That made no sense. I never saw us reach the point where nobody is in charge in a unit. That's out of the question. If you don't know anything, you know the chain of command. And the helicopter attack on the village? Fuckin' ridiculous. You couldn't hear music comin' out of a helicopter. And attacking a beach in helicopters was just out of the question. The planes and the napalm would go in first. Then, the helicopters would have eased in after the fact. That was wild.

By making us look insane, the people who made that movie was somehow relieving themselves of what they asked us to do over there. But we were not insane. We were not insane. We were not ignorant. We knew what we were doing.

I mean we were crazy, but it's built into the culture. It's like institutionalized insanity. When you're in combat, you can do basically what you want as long as you don't get caught. You can get away with murder. And the beautiful thing about the military is there's always somebody that can serve up as a scapegoat. Like Calley. I wondered why they didn't get Delta Company 1–9 because of Cam Ne. We were real scared. But President Johnson came out and defended us. But like that was before My Lai. When they did My Lai, I got nervous again. I said my God, and they have us on film.

I was in Washington during the National Vietnam Veterans Memorial in 1982. But I didn't participate. I saw all these veterans runnin' around there with all these jungle boots on, all these uniforms. I didn't want to do that. It just gave me a bad feeling. Plus some of them were braggin' about the war. Like it was hip. See, I don't think the war was a good thing. And there's no memorial to Cam Ne, to My Lai. To all those children that was napalmed and villages that were burned unnecessarily.

I used to think that I wasn't affected by Vietnam, but I been livin' with Vietnam ever since I left. You just can't get rid of it. It's like that painting of what Dali did of melting clocks. It's a persistent memory.

I remember most how hard it was to just shoot people.

I remember one time when three of our people got killed by a sniper from this village. We went over to burn the village down. I was afraid that there was going to be shootin' people that day, so I just kind of dealt with the animals. You know, shoot the chickens. I mean I just couldn't shoot no people.

I don't know how many chickens I shot. But it was a little pig that freaked me out more than the chickens. You think you gonna be shootin' a little pig, it's just gonna fall over and die. Well, no. His little guts be hangin' out. He just be squiggling around and freakin' you out.

See, you got to shoot animals in the head. If we shoot you in your stomach, you may just fall over and die. But an animal, you got to shoot them in the head. They don't understand that they supposed to fall over and die.

SUGGESTIONS FOR DISCUSSION

1. Compare the passages that you marked with the passages that were marked by your classmates. See if you can decide what Edwards's feelings are about the Vietnam War. How would you characterize his understanding of why the war was fought and what it means? If you think his feelings are contradictory or inconsistent, how would you explain this?

2. Edwards says that the "only thing they told us about the Viet Cong was they were gooks. They were to be killed. Nobody sits around and gives you their historical and cultural background. They're the enemy. Kill, kill, kill." Explain the meaning of this passage. How, in wartime, is the "enemy" created? What might have happened if American soldiers knew the historical and cultural background of the Vietnamese people?

3. Edwards says that when he returned to the United States, he "had left one war and came back and got into another one." What does he mean? How are these two "wars" alike and different?

SUGGESTIONS FOR WRITING

1. Write an essay that develops your own personal response to reading the selection by Malik Edwards. How did it make you feel about the Vietnam

War? What changes, if any, occurred in your understanding of the war? Why do you think you reacted as you did?

2. Edwards says, "You can take blue jeans and rock 'n' roll records and win over more countries than you can with soldiers." Write an essay that explains what Edwards means by this statement. Use the essay to develop your own position on what it means for the United States to "hook" other countries "on our life-style." How does this (or does it not) differ from "trying to do it with guns"? What are the wider issues—ethical, cultural, and political—that you see involved here?

3. Write an essay that compares Edwards's experience of the Vietnam War to that of Le Ly Hayslip. What do you see as the significance of these two descriptions of the war?

Making a Memory of War
Building the Vietnam Veterans Memorial

Kristen Ann Hass

Kristen Ann Hass teaches in the program in American Culture at the University of Michigan, Ann Harbor. The selection "Making a Memory of War: Building the Vietnam Veterans Memorial" is taken from the first chapter of her book *Carried to the Wall: American Memory and the Vietnam Veterans Memorial*. Hass is interested in how the American public has grappled with the problem of memorializing the 58,000 soldiers killed in the long, unpopular, and controversial Vietnam War. As you will see, Americans' unresolved feelings about the war played a powerful role in debates about Maya Lin's design of the Vietnam Veterans Memorial and the subsequent addition of two other memorials, Frederick Hart's *The Three Fightingmen* and Glenna Goodacre's Vietnam Women's Memorial.

SUGGESTION FOR READING

At the end of Hass's introductory section, she asks why so many Americans have left letters, military medals, beer cans, teddy bears, and other offerings at the Vietnam Veterans Memorial. The purpose of her book *Carried to the Wall* is to provide analysis and interpretation to answer this question. As you read, notice how Hass's discussion of the memorial's design complicates her question and anticipates her answers.

American materialism is...The materialism of action and abstraction.
Gertrude Stein, in Gertrude Stein's America

In 1971 angry Vietnam veterans gathered outside the White House gates and on the steps of Capitol Hill. Chanting and jeering, they hurled their Purple Hearts, their Bronze Stars, their awards of valor and bravery, over the White House fence and against the limestone Capitol. In a radical breach of military and social decorum, these highly decorated military men spit back their honors. They had been betrayed, lied to, and abandoned. They had had no chance to be Hollywood heroes; instead they had fought an ugly war, survived, and lost.

In 1982, in the calm of the Constitution Gardens, these medals started to appear at the base of the Vietnam Veterans Memorial. They were set carefully under a name (or a group of names of soldiers who lost their lives together) by the owners of the medals and the fathers of the dead. Chances are good that there was no chanting or jeering as the medals were laid down; the Wall is a startlingly quiet place. And although the medals and ribbons were sometimes accompanied by a photograph or a note hastily written on stationery from a local hotel, the awards were left at the Wall one at a time. At first, they were set down without publicity or organized purpose. Thousands of Americans had the same unanticipated response to the memorial. They came and left their precious things. Why?

Hurling your Purple Heart at the powers that be and setting it at the foot of a memorial to your dead friends are very different acts. The veterans' throwing of their medals is not difficult to interpret as the rejection of an honor, a disdainful public protest against betrayal. However defiant, these veterans were still acting within commonly understood social codes. The things they threw had clearly defined social meanings.

The things offered at the memorial were given new meaning in a much less clear social context. Mainstream funerary and memorial traditions in American culture do not involve the offering of things. Flowers and flags are for memorials. Medals of valor and old cowboy boots are for mantels and attics. This new response to a veterans memorial, then, raises some fascinating questions. Why did so many people have the same unconventional, unanticipated response to the memorial? Where did it come from? What meaning do these things have? Are these offerings left for the dead or the living? Is the medal left as a show of respect? Or of anger?

More than 20 million visitors, about one in ten Americans, have visited the Wall, and every day for fifteen years some of these visitors have left offerings. The flowers and flags have been accompanied by long letters to the dead, poems, teddy bears, wedding rings, human remains, photographs, ravaged military uniforms, high school yearbooks, fishing lures, cans of beer, collections of stories, Bibles, and bullets. In November of 1990, eight years after the dedication of the monument, nearly six hundred objects were left, including seventy military medals, one urn containing human ashes, and a large sliding glass door. Why?

THE MEMORIAL

> Dear Smitty,
>
> Perhaps, now I can bury you; at least in my soul. Perhaps now I won't again see you night after night when the war reappears and we are once more amidst the myriad hells that Vietnam engulfed us in....I never cried. My chest becomes unbearably painful and my throat tightens so I can't even croak, but I haven't cried. I wanted to, just couldn't. I think I can today. Damm, I'm crying now. Bye Smitty. Get some rest.
>
> *Anonymous note left at the Wall*

The average age of the soldiers killed in Vietnam was nineteen; most of those who died had been drafted. The Vietnam Veterans Memorial was born out of a clear vision of what was to be represented: the dead, the veterans, and the sense of community that had made the war palatable to some Americans between 1957 and 1975. The problem, however, of what the death, the veterans, and the lost community suggested together and how they might be represented was the subject of many public and private battles. The work of any memorial is to construct the meaning of an event from fragments of experience and memory. A memorial gives shape to and consolidates public memory; it makes history. As historian James Mayo argues, "how the past is commemorated through a country's war memorials mirrors what people want to remember, and lack of attention reflects what they wish to forget." The veterans fighting to shape the meaning of the Vietnam War found that their efforts to commemorate this country's longest war were met with all of the conflicting emotions and ideologies expressed about the war itself. There was no consensus about what the names represented, about what to remember or what to forget.

The deeply controversial nature of the war, its unpopularity, and the reality that it was lost created an enormous void of meaning that compounded the difficult work of memorializing. What it meant to die in this war was as unclear as what it meant to fight in it. Moreover, the duration of the war, the military's system of rotation, and the defeat precluded the ticker-tape parades young boys going to war might have anticipated. Veterans came home to changing ideas about patriotism and heroism; they returned to a society riven by the civil rights movement, Watergate, and the assassinations of the men who had inspired many of them to fight. There was no clear ideology around which a community of grief could have formed. It was a muddled, lost war waiting to be forgotten even before it was over. People who lost their children, husbands, father, sisters, and their own hearts were without a public community for the expression of grief or rage or pride. This lack of community not only made them deeply crave a remembrance of the experience of Americans in Vietnam but also made the work of remembering especially difficult. Commemorating the war and the deaths required giving new shape to the broken meanings of the war. It required a reimagination of the nation.

In March of 1979 Jan Scruggs, a vet and the son of a rural milkman, went to see *The Deer Hunter*. He came home terrified and inspired. This Hollywood movie, about the horrors of the war, the impossibility of coming home, and the struggles of a small, working-class Pennsylvania community to come to terms with its losses, convinced Scruggs that it was time for the nation to publicly remember the war. In the movie a community shattered by the war regains its bearings in a tentative return to the patriotic ideals that had inspired its boys to fight. It is a troubling response, but it offered Scruggs some hope; the possibility of a community healing itself inspired in him the idea of building a memorial. So with a few of his veteran friends, Scruggs formed the Vietnam Veterans Memorial Fund (VVMF) in April of 1979.

The fund's first attempts to gain public support were not entirely successful. No more than a dozen reporters showed up for the first press conference, on May 28, 1979. Scruggs and his friends tried to launch a national fundraising campaign, but they received a handful of heart-wrenching letters and worn dollar bills instead of the generous checks for which they had hoped. The veterans fighting for a memorial were angry and determined, but they were not socially or politically powerful; and their cause was not easily or quickly embraced. They did, however, attract the attention of a few influential Vietnam veterans. Jack Wheeler, a Harvard- and Yale-educated West Pointer, joined the VVMF and began to draw in Vietnam veterans from high places throughout Washington. And although the founders of the VVMF had wanted to oppose the power structures whose work they were trying to memorialize, they learned that they could not raise public interest—let alone funds—without the aid of a few Washington power brokers. The fund's first major contributions came after a brunch for defense contractors organized by Senator John Warner.

The men and women who came to form the core of the VVMF were by no means politically or socially unified. Some had protested after serving in the war, and others continued to believe in the ideals of the conflict; nearly all, however, were white veterans who were keenly aware of their outcast social position as survivors of a deeply unpopular war. They wanted a national monument to help them reclaim a modicum of recognition and social standing.

As the money began to trickle in, the VVMF made several key decisions that determined a great deal about the character of the memorial and the kind of community that it rebuilt. The fund wanted a monument that listed all the names of those killed, missing in action, or still held as prisoners of war in Vietnam. Although the dead became the heart of the project because they were, in an important sense, all these veterans could agree upon, there was no easy agreement about how the memorial should remember the dead. The fund imagined a *veterans* memorial not a *war* memorial; the former would ensure a memory that emphasized the contributions of the soldiers rather than the federal government. The members of the fund did not ask for federal money because they did not want to be perceived as more Vietnam vets looking for a handout and because after Ronald Reagan cut $12 million from the Veterans Administrations budget in 1980, the vets did not trust his administration to give them the kind of memorial they hoped for. Building it with private contributions would also prove that a larger American public wanted to remember, and they wanted the memorial built on the Mall in Washington, D.C., to assure the memory of the veterans a place of national prominence.

The VVMF found itself in a complicated political position. The fund expected strong opposition from the antiwar movement and from the Washington bureaucracy; so it had to negotiate a public memory without either celebrating or explicitly renouncing the war, which would have been politically disastrous for any administration. As a result, strange alliances were formed at every step of the memorializing process. In 1980 the VVMF raised money through letters from Bob Hope calling for a reward for sacrifices made. Gerald Ford, Rosalynn Carter, Nancy Reagan, James Webb, Admiral James Stockdale, General William Westmoreland, and George McGovern made unlikely companions on the fund's letterhead. Few of the alliances were easily made, and not all of them held.

Early on the average donation to the $10 million project was $17.93 and envelopes were sent in with $2 change. Eventually, however, the campaign worked, and the success clearly demonstrated to the VVMF organizers that there was a population that wanted to publicly remember this war. Building this community of supportees and contributors, tenuous though it may have been, was an essential first step in the work of making a public meaning of the war. To memorialize the war, to solidify its shape and meaning, the fund had to bring together diverse experiences and ideologies. The seeming impossibility of the project was not only in facing the "myriad hells that Vietnam engulfed" the country in but also in repairing the social and political understandings that the war had fractured. In the end, the design of the memorial was a response to the problem of making memory in the wake of the Vietnam War; this is the history they made.

THE DESIGN

> I came down today to pay respects to the good friends of mine. Go down to visit them sometime. They are on panel 42E, lines 22 and 26. I think that you will like them.
>
> *Anonymous note left at the Wall*

Most war memorials in America—statues, schools, stadiums, bridges, parks—proudly salute American triumph. How do you memorialize a painfully mired, drawn-out defeat that called into question the most fundamental tenets of American patriotism?

The design of the Vietnam Memorial was bound to be controversial. Its promoters understood that it would be impossible to find a representation of the war that could satisfy a deeply polarized society. The leaders of the VVMF decided to hold an open juried contest because they knew that without the participation of some recognized bearers of cultural capital they would never get a design through Washington's notoriously difficult architectural gatekeepers—The National Planning Commission. Choosing the jury was difficult, though. Who should decide how the war would be represented? There was some noise made about including a Vietnam veteran, an African American, and a woman; but it was feared that jurors might defer too much to the opinions of a vet, and, oddly, they were unable to locate a qualified woman or a qualified African American. So the decision was turned over to the most traditional bearers of culture: early in 1981 a panel of distinguished architects, landscape architects, sculptors, and critics was organized by Washington architect Paul Spreiregen. The unpaid veterans who had worked long hours to bring the memorial to this point were impressed by the prestige of the jury but nervous about turning their project over to men "the same age as the people who sent [them] to 'Nam."

The jury and the contestants were given only a few simple, if wildly ambitious, instructions: the design should "(1) be reflective and contemplative in character; (2) harmonize with its surroundings; (3) contain the names of those who had died in the conflict or who were still missing; and (4) make no political statement about the war." The most important task of the design, however, was the creation of a memorial that would, as Scruggs wrote, "begin a healing process, a reconciliation of the grievous divisions wrought by the war." One of the great ironies of these guidelines is that Vietnam's death toll of fifty-eight thousand is, compared with that of most other American wars, so low that all of the names could actually be reproduced on one memorial. (The effect is overwhelming, of course, but possible only because so relatively few Americans died.)

By April 26, 1981, more than fourteen hundred designs had been entered. On May 1, 1981, the jurors, after remarkably little deliberation, unanimously selected a simple black granite V, set into a small hill in the Constitution Gardens, carved with the name of every man and woman who never came back from Vietnam. They were impressed with the eloquence and the simplicity of the design. The jurors, one of whom noted of the designer, "he knows what he's doing, all right," were no doubt startled to discover that their winner was a remarkable impossibility: a twenty-one-year-old art student at Yale University—young, intellectual, female, and Chinese American.

In imagining her design, Maya Ying Lin made a clear decision not to study the history of the war, or to enmesh herself in the controversies surrounding it. Her design lists the names of the men and women killed in Vietnam in the order in which they were killed. The names are carved into black granite panels that form a large V at a 125-degree angle and suggest the pages of an open book. The first panel cuts only a few inches into the gently sloping hillside, but each panel is longer than the last and cuts more deeply into the ground, so that you walk down-hill toward the apex, at which point the black panels tower three or four feet above your head. At the center you are half buried in a mass of names; pulled toward the black granite, you see yourself and the open lawns of the mall behind you reflected in the memorial. The center of the monument is a strangely private, buffered public space. Literally six feet into the hillside you are confronted simultaneously with the names and with yourself. The black granite is so highly reflective that even at night visitors see their own faces as they look at the Wall. The Wall manages to capture the unlikely simultaneous experiences of reflection and burial. This brilliant element of the design asks for a personal, thoughtful response. As you exit, the panels diminish in size, releasing you back into the daylight. Lin's design did not initially include the word "Vietnam"; she gave form not to the event that caused the deaths but to the names of the dead, to the fact of the deaths.

The names are carved out of polished granite from Bangalore, India. The carving invites tangible interaction. Each name has a physical presence. It asks to be touched. Lin wanted visitors to be able to feel the names in many different ways, and she wanted people to be able to take something of the Wall away with them—a rubbing of a name.

The Wall tries to make a somehow individuated memory of a war. The events in Vietnam are remembered through the names of the dead: these men and women—many of whom, even those drafted against their will, might have imagined, at least in part, that their experience would be like that portrayed in the movie *How I Won the War with John Wayne*—are each remembered as tragically fallen individuals. The power of the design lies in the overwhelming presence of individual names, which represent complicated human lives cut short. This attention to individual lives lost would not, however, be as potent if it were separated from the black expanse of all of the names together, the effect of which is so overwhelming that it both foregrounds the individual names and hides them. Lin's organization of the names also contributes to this tension between particular names and the whole formed by the names together. The dead appear on the Wall not alphabetically but rather in the order in which they died in Vietnam. Soldiers who died together are listed together on the Wall, so that on every line on every panel stories of particular times and places are inscribed with the names. This placement of the names, however, makes finding an individual name in the list impossible without the aid of the phone book–like alphabetical indexes at the entrances to the memorial. Although the index provides information about every name—including hometown, birth date, and death date—it requires a certain amount of participation on the part of any visitor interested in a particular name.

Maya Lin's design earned her a B in her funerary architecture class at Yale, but that was the least of her troubles. She was thrown into a noisy "firestorm of the national heart." Her design was dubbed the "black gash of shame." Its shape was considered an affront to veteran and conservative manhood especially when compared to the shape of the neighboring Washington Monument: the V shape hinted at the peace sign, or a reference to the Vietcong; the black stone was more mournful than heroic. It seemed to many too clear an admission of defeat. The public outcry reflected outrage with Lin's design and with the principles that the VVMF required of all designs: the Wall was too abstract, too intellectual, too reflective. It was, in the minds of many, high art, the art of the class that lost the least in the war. It was not celebratory, heroic, or manly. James Webb, a member of the VVMF's National Sponsoring Committee, called it a "wailing Wall for future anti-draft and anti-nuclear demonstrators." Tom Carhart, a veteran who had been awarded a Purple Heart and had submitted a design of his own, coined a key phrase for those who hated the design when he wrote in a *New York Times* op-ed piece that it was "pointedly insulting to the sacrifices made for their country by all Vietnam veterans…by this we will be remembered: a black gash of shame and sorrow, hacked into the national visage that is the mall."

The popular press offered some support for the design, but the conservative press was enraged by it. In the *Moral Majority Weekly* Phyllis Schlafly called it a "tribute to Jane Fonda." *National Review* described it as an "Orwellian glob." In an open letter to President Reagan, Republican Representative Henry Hyde complained that it was "a political statement of shame and dishonor." And in September of 1981 an editorial in *National Review* demanded that Reagan intervene, arguing: "Okay, we lost the Vietnam war, okay the thing was mismanaged from start to finish. But American soldiers who died in Vietnam fought for their country and for the freedom of others, and they deserve better than the outrage that has been approved as their memorial…the Reagan administration should throw the switch on the project."

Its implicit admission that the war was disastrous, of course, is precisely what others loved about the design. A great many Vietnam veterans reacted with cautious approval. The VVMF and all leading veterans organizations, including the Veterans of Foreign Wars and the American Legion, officially approved of the design. The best evidence of the reaction of the larger community of veterans was their continued effort to support the monument despite the barrage of bitter publicity about the design. Veterans held garage sales, bingo games, and "pass the helmet" campaigns to raise funds for construction. At one of these events in Matoon, Illinois, a vet remarked to Scruggs that "everything Vietnam touches seems to go sour….I may never have the money to get to D.C., but it would make me feel good to know that my buddies' names are up there."

Of course, since the official dedication of the Wall in 1982 volumes of praise have been written for the design and the reflection that it has inspired. The Wall's emphasis on the tragedy of each death has appealed to critics and supporters alike. Strong hopes that this monument will guard against future wars have been expressed: James Kilpatrick, a nationally syndicated columnist, wrote, "this will be the most moving memorial even erected…each of us may remember what he wishes to remember—the cause, the heroism, the blunders, or the waste." One vet carried a sign at the memorial's opening that expressed a commonly held sentiment: "I am a Vietnam Veteran / I like the memorial / And if it makes it difficult to send people to battle again / I like it even more." A *New York Times* editorial reprinted in the Gold Star Mothers Association newsletter argued, "Nowadays, patriotism is a complicated matter. Ideas about heroism, or art, for that matter, are no longer what they were before Vietnam….But perhaps the V-shaped, black granite lines merging gently with the sloping earth make the winning design seem a lasting and appropriate image of dignity and sadness."

Understanding the design as an attempt to represent a new, complicated patriotism may have appealed to many veterans and Gold Star Mothers, but to the newly elected leaders of the "Reagan revolution" it was an abomination. The design flew in the face of the recently revived strain of relentlessly nostalgic patriotism that had sent them to the capital. It is not surprising that in this political climate, the czars of American conservatism resented the abstraction and the ambiguity of the proposed war memorial, or that opposition to the design came from high places in Washington. James Watt, then secretary of the interior, was a key figure in the design controversy. It was Watt—with the support of irate VVMF contributor H. Ross Perot—who demanded that Lin's deign be supplemented, if not supplanted, by a more heroic, representational, figural memorial. Watt would not let the Wall be *the* Vietnam War memorial. Sculptor Frederick Hart made himself and his concrete bronze design, *The Three Fightingmen*, readily available to Watt, Perot, and the press. His intense lobbying efforts were well rewarded. Watt took to Hart's figures and threatened to hold up construction indefinitely unless the VVMF agreed to use the sculpture. With their backs against the wall, the VVMF decided that the memorial was worth the compromise.

Ultimately, this compromise reflects the impossibility of finding a single design that could represent the Vietnam War for all Americans. Hart's figural sculpture satisfied powerful voices that required concrete representation, but it did not solve the problem of representation presented by the war. His figures, a white man flanked by an African American man and a third man whose race is unclear, stand a hundred feet away facing the Wall, apparently transfixed by its power. They are strong, highly masculinized, and heroic. The white man holds his hands out slightly to his side as if to warn his companions, in a patrician gesture that mimics the imperial nature of the war, of some impending danger. Although frozen, they, like the human figures who walk the memorial's path, are drawn to the black granite that recedes into the earth and then delivers into the light. Hart had intended the figures to look warily into the distance for the ubiquitous, hidden Vietnamese enemy, but the negotiations involved in the addition of the sculpture turned their gaze on the Wall and opened up a broad range of interpretive possibilities. This ironic fate for Hart's symbolically stable, heroic figures is indicative of the difficulty he faced in trying to divert attention from Lin's design. The sculpture in the end dramatizes the difficulties of representation and the power of the names; the main attraction of the memorial continues to be the Wall.

Even after the addition of the figures in 1984, the official commemoration of the war was not yet finished. In 1993, nearly ten years later, another battle over the memory of the war took shape on the Mall. After years of struggling to raise money and interest, Vietnam veteran Diane Carlson Evans presided over the dedication of the Vietnam Women's Memorial. This memorial is the first national memorial to female veterans. Its four figures—a prone, blindfolded, injured male soldier, a white nurse who holds him in her arms, an African American woman comforting the nurse and looking to the sky, and a third woman kneeling over medical equipment—stand about three hundred feet from the Wall, sheltered in a grove of tall trees. It is a very straightforward figural memorial. And while the sculptor, Glenna Goodacre, was swiftly written off by art critics for whom her pietà is uninspiring, the principal argument against a memorial to the women who served in Vietnam was that it would set a precedent for a whole slew of other "special interest memorials." This complaint, as hollow as it might seem in light of the utter lack of memorials to the sacrifices made by American women at war, held considerable sway with the Park Service and the Fine Arts Commission; it is a reminder of the strength of the ideal that one symbolic gesture should be able to make a memory of this twenty-year war.

Evans wanted a women's memorial because the Wall did not heal the particular, complicated alienation of women veterans she had experienced, and it did not make women visible at the memorial. But her efforts to make the work of women in this war an obvious part of its official memory became a struggle against the firmly held ideal of a singular public memory. This struggle was particularly frustrating because the monument already included two sculptures and because women's war work in the United States has been invisible for so long despite the central role of women in the forging of public memory. The Mount Vernon Ladies' Association of the Union, the Daughters of the Confederacy, the Gold Star Mothers Association, and other women's volunteer associations have been essential to the history of memorializing in America. They have worked to ensure that national memories have been preserved and respected, but their contributions to the history of commemoration have not been recorded. Their roles in the work of making memory have been carefully prescribed—they have nurtured the memories of war as mothers, daughters, wives, and sisters but have not been seen as participants worth remembering. Women were undoubtedly a part of the life of the Vietnam Veterans Memorial in its first ten years, but they were principally visible as grievers, not as veterans. Diane Evans wanted to rewrite the history with the figure of a nurse.

Maya Lin sagely observed about the first statue, "In a funny sense, the compromise brings the memorial closer to the truth. What is also memorialized is that people still cannot resolve the war, nor can they separate the issues, the politics from it." This is true about both of the added statues. Hart's sculpture memorializes a need to remember these veterans as manly and heroic; Goodacre's sculpture, eight years later, memorializes a victory for women veterans over the perceived threat to patriotism posed by the idea of making any memory of war that is not singular and masculine. Hart's and Goodacre's additions to the Wall commemorate the difficulty of making memory in the midst of shifting cultural values. It is, in part, this sense of the impossibility of representation that pulls personal, individual memorials from visitors to the Wall; with their things people are bringing the monument "closer to the truth."

In the statement she submitted with her design proposal, Maya Lin wrote, "it is up to each individual to resolve or to come to terms with this loss. For death is in the end a personal and private matter and the area containing this within the memorial is a quiet place, meant for personal reflection and private reckoning." Lin was entirely right. She probably could not have anticipated the extent to which visitors to this memorial would take on the responsibility for the memory of the war, but she did appreciate the constantly unfinished, contested nature of the memory of this war. She understood that memorializing the war necessarily meant undoing the traditional idea of patriotic nationalism in the shape of a singular, heroic memorial. The multiplication of memorials, names, and objects at the Wall has, indeed, replaced the possibility of a singular memory of the war; the single figure of the male citizen embodying the nation has been supplanted by three official memorials and a steady stream of combat boots, bicycle parts, and St. Christophers. People come to this memorial and they make their own memorials.

SUGGESTIONS FOR DISCUSSION

1. In the final line of this selection, Kristen Ann Hass says, "People come to this memorial and they make their own memorials." Consider this statement in light of the questions Hass begins with, about why people leave offerings at the wall. Trace her line of reasoning through the two sections "The Memorial" and "The Design." How does her discussion in these middle sections provide the groundwork for the answer she offers? What evidence does she offer to link her closing answer to the opening question?

2. Hass notes that in 1984, two years after the wall was built, another memorial—Frederick Hart's heroic, representational *The Three Fightingmen*—was added. Then, nearly ten years later, in 1993, a third was completed, the Vietnam Women's Memorial. What does Hass see as the significance of these additions? Consider the designs of the three memorials. (You can find images of the three memorials in the Reading Culture website <www.awl.com/george> in the Visual Culture section of Chapter 9.) What does each seem to signify? What do they signify when taken together as a group? How do they compare to earlier war memorials, such as *The Flag-Raising at Iwo Jima* and its commemoration of World War II?

3. Locate memorials in the area around your college or hometown. You are likely to find a number of war memorials, but you need not limit yourself to just commemorations of the military dead. Americans have also memorialized Holocaust and AIDS victims, those killed or maimed in the Oklahoma City bombing, students who died or were wounded in the Littleton shootings. A wall was erected in South Central Los Angeles to memorialize those injured in the uprising following the Rodney King trial, and murals in Chicano communities commemorate those who died in gang violence. In other words, the memorials you choose could be, like the Vietnam memorials, official monuments, as well as schools, bridges, stadiums, parks, or plaques. But you can also consider more informal or popular memorials that exist outside established institutions. Work together in groups of three or four, with each group preparing a class presentation on one of the memorials. You will need to do research on who sponsored the memorial and why, as well as on public attitudes to the war or event. In your presentation, describe the memorial in detail, paying attention to its design and its location. It will help to bring photographs of the memorial to class and other print or visual information available. Use this description to explain how the memorial commemorates the dead and what cultural meanings it seems to project. What vision of the past does it bring to the present? What sense of national identity, patriotism, community does it seem to embody?

SUGGESTIONS FOR WRITING

1. Kristin Ann Hass sees the addition of the two memorials—*The Three Fightingmen* and the Vietnam Women's Memorial—as a compromise that reflects "the impossibility of finding a single design that could represent the Vietnam War for all Americans." Write an essay that focuses on the visual design of the three memorials and the lack of consensus they reveal in American memories of the Vietnam War. Consider what each memorial signifies and what they signify as a group. (To find images of the memorials, go to the Visual Culture section of Chapter 9 at the Reading Culture website <www.awl.com/george>.)

2. Hass talks about Americans' "restless memory of the Vietnam War," an apparent inability to reach emotional closure about the meaning of the war for individuals and for the country. In the previous reading, Malik Edwards says, "I used to think I wasn't affected by Vietnam, but I been livin' with Vietnam ever since I left. You just can't get rid of it." Interview someone who lived through the Vietnam years—someone who went to Vietnam, who was active in the antiwar movement, whose son or daughter was in the military. How does your subject remember those years? What lasting effects did the war have on the person? What memories does the person carry with him or her? Use the interview to write a character sketch of how history lives in the memory of ordinary people.

3. Monuments and statues are not the only forms of cultural expression that reflect and shape the way Americans remember the Vietnam War. Films are also important repositories of historical memory. Hollywood films have a long history of memorializing war—from the vision of the Civil War contained in *Gone with the Wind* (1939) to Stephen Spielberg's recent tribute to World War II, *Saving Private Ryan*. Some of the best known and readily available films that treat the Vietnam War are *Coming Home*, *The Deer Hunter*, *Platoon*, *Born on the Fourth of July*, *Full Metal Jacket*, and the *Rambo* series. Watch one or more of these films. Write an essay that explains the historical memory of the Vietnam War they offer viewers. Keep in mind the issue is not whether the film is historically accurate or not but the vision of the past it presents.

VISUAL CULTURE — *PHOTOGRAPHING HISTORY*

One of the ways that we remember the past is through photographs. Family scrapbooks, photo albums, wedding portraits, high school yearbooks, the school pictures exchanged with friends—all record the history of ordinary lives. The same is true of our collective memory of public history. Single photographic images have taken on the power to contain and represent whole historical events.

From Mathew Brady's photographs of the American Civil War to present-day photojournalism, photographs have created immediately recognizable images of complex historical forces that have been captured in the concrete details of a moment. Alfred Stieglitz's "The Steerage" (1907), for example, seems to distill the waves of immigration from Southern and Eastern Europe from 1880 to 1920 in a single frame depicting "huddled masses."

By the same token, the Depression of the 1930s has come to be known and remembered through the photographs of Dorothea Lange, Walker Evans, Arthur Rothstein, and others in the Farm Security Administration (see, for example, Dorothea Lange's famous photograph "Migrant Mother, Florence Thompson and Her Children"). We think of these photos as a reliable source, a

"A Harvest of Death," Gettysburg,
July 1863," T. H. O'Sullivan.

"The Steerage, 1907," Alfred Stieglitz.

"Migrant Mother, Florence Thompson and Her
Children, 1936," Dorothea Lange.

The flag-raising at Iwo Jima.

John Carlos and Tommy Smith at the 1968 Olympics.

documentary account of the life experience of workers, sharecroppers, Dust Bowl migrants, and the unemployed. These photos have taken on the authority to bring the past to life and to show how things really were.

Such photographs not only convey images that stand, in immediately recognizable ways, for larger historical events. They also carry attitudes toward these events. Grounded in the relationship that they have with their subjects, photographers' attitudes become visible in the way that they aim the viewfinder and frame the shot. Photographs convey visual images to viewers, not directly but mediated through a lens, from a perspective or way of seeing.

Photographs offer viewers identities as well as information. When people look at a photograph of the flag-raising at Iwo Jima, for example, they are likely to recall the story of World War II as one of national unity to fight the "good war." In a sense, the photo seeks to recruit viewers—to have them join the just cause and commemorate American victory. In other instances, such as the picture of John Carlos and Tommy Smith raising their fists on the victory stand at the 1968 Olympics in Mexico City while the American national anthem was playing, the insurgent force of a photograph can precipitate a crisis of identity, as viewers respond with fear, anxiety, outrage, pleasure, identification, or some combination of mixed feelings to this powerful image of black power and the freedom struggle of the 1960s.

This section investigates how photographs have become such a powerful means to document history and to shape historical memory.

Reading American Photographs

Alan Trachtenberg

> Alan Trachtenberg is a distinguished professor of English and American Studies at Yale and the author of many articles and books, including *The Incorporation of America: Culture and Society in the Gilded Age.* The following selection is an excerpt from the preface to his book *Reading American Photographs: Images as History Mathew Brady to Walker Evans* (1989). Trachtenberg holds that the historian and photographer share a similar task, namely "how to make the random, fragmentary, and accidental details of everyday existence meaningful without loss of the details themselves."

SUGGESTION FOR READING

> As you read, consider what Trachtenberg means when he says that " photographs are not simple depictions but constructions." When you are finished reading, summarize Trachtenberg's argument in three to four sentences.

My argument throughout is that American photographs are not simple depictions but constructions, that the history they show is inseparable from the history they enact: a history of photographers employing their medium to make sense of their society. It is also a history of photographers seeking to define themselves, to create a role for photography as an American art. How might the camera be used for social commentary and cultural interpretation? Consisting of images rather than words, photography places its own constraints on interpretation, requiring that photographers invent new forms of presentation, of collaboration between image and text, between artist and audience.

For the reader of photographs there is always the danger of overreading, of too facile a conversion of images into words. Speaking of "the camera's affinity for the indeterminate," Kracauer remarks that, "however selective," photographs are still "bound to record nature in the raw. Like the natural objects themselves, they will therefore be surrounded by a fringe of indistinct multiple meanings." All photographs have the effect of making their subjects seem at least momentarily strange, capable of meaning several things at once, or nothing at all. Estrangement allows us to see the subject in new and unexpected ways. Photographs entice viewers by their silence, the mysterious beckoning of another world. It is as enigmas, opaque and inexplicable as the living world itself, that they most resemble the data upon which history is based. Just as the meaning of the past is the prerogative of the present to invent and choose, the meaning of an image does not come intact and whole. Indeed, what empowers an image to represent history is not just what it shows but the struggle for meaning we undergo before it, a struggle analogous to the historian's effort to shape an intelligible and usable past. Representing the past, photographs serve the present's need to understand itself and measure its future. Their history lies finally in the political visions they may help us realize.

READING PHOTOGRAPHS FOR HISTORY

To understand the relation of photographs to historical events, we need to begin with the physical presence of the camera at some precisely datable moment in the past. Unlike writing or painting, which necessarily take place over time, shooting a picture occurs in an instant, and the events which the camera records are thereby non-repeatable. This technical ability to capture such unique and distinct moments gives photographs an authority in documenting the past that no other records or accounts can claim.

But the technical character of the photographic image also poses a problem in terms of historical meaning. The photographic image, after all, is visual. It sends a message but, as Roland Barthes says, an "uncoded message," one that cannot immediately and self-evidently be converted into words. The photographic image simultaneously is filled with information and opaque. The "meaning of the image," as Trachtenberg puts it, "does not come intact and whole." The reason a photograph can stand in for a larger historical event like the Civil War or the Depression is not just what it shows but how the image has been made memorable— the "struggle for meaning we undergo before it."

Visual ESSAY — *THE VIETNAM WAR*

The "struggle for meaning" that Trachtenberg refers to is strikingly evident in the photographs that are assembled here from the Vietnam War. Each captures not only a distinct moment but one that reveals a different aspect of the war. Taken together, the images stand in an uneasy relationship to each other, bound by a common event but divided by what they depict and the meanings that they make available. Just as the meaning of the Vietnam War remains volatile and contested in politics, historical interpretation, and popular culture, these images jostle against each other, and call us to different scenes and different ways of seeing the war.

SUGGESTIONS FOR DISCUSSION

1. Look closely at each of the photographs. What aspect of the Vietnam War does each call to the viewer's attention? How do these images shape our historical memory of the war? To what extent do they tell the same version or different versions of the war?

2. The images in this visual essay have been arranged in chronological order, but that is not the only way they could be organized. Photographers often create sequences of images so that individual photos interact with each other and enable meanings to emerge that are not available through use of a single photo. Work together in a group with two or three other students to create your own visual essay about the Vietnam War. You can use the Vietnam photos presented here or supplement them with photos from websites (see the Checking Out the Web box for helpful sites). As you assemble your visual essay, take into account what you want your viewers' experience of the photos to be and the story you want the photos to tell. Then compare the visual essay your group composed to those of other groups. Don't argue about whether one set of choices is right or wrong. The issue is how the various visual essays juxtapose photographs and shape the way we remember the Vietnam War.

American combat troops,
Larry Burrows, *Life.*

3. The written captions that sometimes accompany photographic images
can influence the way that viewers understand photos. Depending on the
circumstances, captions can be informative by identifying the date, place,
and people depicted in the photo. Other times, captions can be interpretive or argumentative by providing not just information but a point of
view. Work with a group of classmates, and find three photos of historical
events (use any of the photos in this chapter, if you wish). Write two captions for each photo—one that is informative, the second interpretive or
argumentative. Exchange the photos and captions on which your group
has worked with those from another group. Ask members of the other
group how the captions shape or slant their experience of the photo. In
turn, respond to the other group's captions in the same way.

Colonel Nguyen Ngoc Loan, South Vietnam's police chief, executing a Viet-cong suspect in Saigon, World Wide.

SUGGESTED ASSIGNMENT

Select one of the photographs in this chapter or another historical photo of your own choosing. Write a detailed analysis of how the photo brings to life an historical event and how its composition establishes a vantage point for viewers. To do this, you will need to look at the photograph closely and carefully. Here are some questions that you might take into account:

- *What is depicted in the photo?* How do the details create an impression on viewers? How is the image able to stand in for a larger historical event? What version of the event does it seem to tell?

- *Does the photo have vectors (or eye-lines) that establish relationships among the people (and perhaps things) in the photo?* What story do the vectors enable viewers to fill in? (See the discussion of vectors in the Visual Culture section in Chapter 3, "Picturing Schooldays.")

Antiwar demonstration in New York City, Black Star.

Americans and South Vietnamese fleeing from American embassy, 1975, United Press International.

- *What is the perspective of the camera shot—frontal, oblique, high, low?* How does the use of perspective shape the viewer's attitude toward the event depicted in the photo? (See the discussion of perspective in the Visual Culture section in Chapter 3, "Picturing Schooldays.")

- *How does the camera space frame the event that it records?* How close does the camera take viewers to its subject? Is the photo a wide shot, full shot, medium shot, or close up? How does camera space influence the viewer's experience of the photo? (See the discussion of camera space in Chapter 1, "The Case of Daytime Talk TV.")

FIELD WORK | ORAL HISTORY

As you have seen, oral histories, such as the chapter "Private First Class Reginald 'Malik' Edwards" from Wallace Terry's *Bloods: An Oral History of the Vietnam War by Black Veterans,* offer the personal perspectives of individuals who are caught up in the history of their time. Oral history is a branch of historical studies that draws on the experience and memories of ordinary people in order to give us new insight into the meaning and texture of historical events. Sometimes referred to as "history from the bottom up," oral history is an organized effort to record the stories of people like Malik Edwards, who traditionally have been ignored by historians. In this sense, oral histories are important correctives to older versions of history that focus on "great men," geopolitics, and institutions of power.

This does not mean, however, that oral histories are any more useful or authoritative than traditional historical work that is based on archives, government documents, or the correspondence of national leaders. The value of oral histories depends a great deal on the historian's craft.

CHOOSING A SUBJECT

Part of this craft is the selection of people to interview. Not everyone, after all, will have interesting things to say, even if they were intimately involved in an historical event. Moreover, everyone's memory will be selective in some sense. An oral historian can expect no more than to get a version of events, though one that may open up unforeseen perspectives.

INTERVIEWING

A second part of the oral historian's craft involves the interview itself. This is not just a matter of turning on the tape recorder and allowing the informant to speak. The informant needs to know the purpose for the interview and, in a general sense, for what the historian is looking.

In this regard, the oral historian needs to strike a fine balance. The historian needs to put the informant on track so that he or she feels free to recall the past in some detail. But if the historian is too directive, the informant may skip over what might be key information or simply tell the historian what the informant thinks that he or she wants to hear.

Once an interview begins, the oral historian may well face decisions along the way—about, say, whether a rambling account is going somewhere or that the historian should intervene to redirect the informant. Should the historian stop the informant and ask for clarification of points, or does this risk interrupting the speaker's train of thought?

WRITING THE ORAL HISTORY

The final aspect of the oral historian's craft is rendering the interview into a readable oral history. The transcript of an interview amounts to a kind of raw data that is likely to be filled with pauses, asides, fragmentary remarks, false starts, and undeveloped trains of thought. The oral historian's task is to fashion an account that is faithful to the informant and readable. There are a number of decisions which oral historians typically face at this point:

- *How much of the original transcript should be used?* Oral historians rarely use all of the material in the transcript. In the Introduction to *Portraits in Steel* (1993), a collection of photographs and oral histories of Buffalo steel workers, the oral historian Michael Frisch says he used as little as 20 percent of an original transcript and in no case more than 60 percent. When they decide to omit material from the transcript, oral historians are careful to make sure that their editing does not distort the informant's views or suppress important information.

- *How should the material in the transcript be arranged?* Oral historians often decide to rearrange some of the material in the original transcript, so that related points appear together and the final version has a coherence that may be missing from the taped interview. The oral historian is by no means obliged to follow the chronological order of the transcript but again needs to make sure that any restructuring is faithful to the informant.

- *Should the interviewer's questions appear?* In many cases, such as in Wallace Terry's *Bloods* and the many oral histories by Studs Terkel (*Working, The Good War, American Dreams*), the oral historian crafts the interview into a narrative that is told through the informant's voice. This is the usual approach to long oral histories: The oral historian stays out of the way, and we have the sense as readers that the informant is speaking directly to us. In other cases, however, the oral historian may decide to appear in the final text as an interviewer, and the question-and-answer format gives the oral history more of a conversational character, with a greater sense of dialogue and give-and-take.

- *How much editing should be done at the sentence level?* Oral historians face the task of turning the transcript into readable prose that retains the distinctive qualities of the informant's voice. Notice, for example, how Wallace Terry has edited Malik Edwards's oral history so that it appears in complete, grammatically correct sentences, but uses a few exceptions ("people be marchin' into swamps," "'cause it was nothin' to shoot through the walls"), along with slang and profanity, to suggest Edwards's particular way of speaking.

FIELDWORK PROJECT

Conduct your own interview to produce an oral history. Follow these steps:

1. *Choose a person and an event that will interest readers*—a Vietnam or Gulf War veteran; someone with experience in the antiwar movement or the counterculture of the Sixties; an older person who remembers the Great Depression, the bombing of Pearl Harbor, the end of World War II; a trade unionist involved in an important organizing drive or strike. The events listed here are largely on the national or international scene but you may also find informants to talk about an important and interesting local event.

2. *Prepare for the interview by familiarizing yourself with the event in question.* Do some background reading. Develop a list of leading questions that will elicit detailed and in-depth responses from your informant (but don't be tied rigidly to them in the interview if it takes another, potentially fruitful, direction). Set a time with your informant, bring a tape recorder, and conduct the interview.

3. *Type up a transcript from the interview that you can edit into an oral history.* Review the discussion above, "Writing the Oral History," for choices that you will need to take into account.

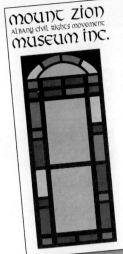

mount zion
ALBANY civil rights movement
museum inc.

Telling a story of change

The Mount Zion Albany Civil Rights Movement Museum will tell the story of the impact of the southwest Georgia movement on the rest of the world while focusing on the role of the African American church and the freedom music that emerged during this period.

The stories will be told through oral histories from those who were there—those who lived it, those who breathed it, those who walked it, those who went to jail and those who attended the mass meetings and sang about it.

The museum will restore much of Mount Zion Church as it was in the 1960s. The sanctuary will convey the sense of place as a church where visitors will be treated to stirring renditions of freedom songs and other public performances. Restored pews will seat 100.

A portion of the church will house the museum's artifacts. Educational exhibits will detail the civil rights struggle ranging from voter education and registration to nonviolent protest, song, economic boycott and legal action. The museum will also serve as a center for ongoing academic research and provide school tours and other programs and lectures. Through educational programming, the museum will preserve a part of the history of America and south Georgia and challenge today's and tomorrow's youth to learn more about themselves as citizens.

Promoters of the Mount Zion Albany Civil Rights Movement Museum have a vision beyond restoring the church into a museum. Long-range planning, in coordination with the Albany Dougherty Inner-City Authority and the Albany Convention and Visitors Bureau, includes a historic district and walking tours of restored buildings and residences in the Whitney Avenue neighborhood. These tours will depict life in the African American neighborhood before the end of segregation.

Mining the Archive

LOCAL MUSEUMS AND HISTORICAL SOCIETIES

Many towns and cities, as well as colleges and universities, have local museums or historical societies that collect and display historical materials, sponsor research, and put on public programs about local and regional history. There is likely to be one or more in the area near you. Your college library can help you find out where they are located and what kind of archival materials they hold.

Visit a local museum or historical society. Sometimes this will require making specific arrangements with its staff. Take as the purpose of your visit acquiring an overview of the archival materials and collections. How does the museum or historical society describe its function? What are the nature and scope of the holdings? How were they acquired? What historical periods are represented? Who uses the collection? What kind of research do they do? Does the archive publish books, pamphlets, or journals? Does it issue an annual report, newsletter, or other informative materials about its holdings and activities?

Use your answers to these questions—and other information you picked up during your visit—to prepare a report (either written or oral) on the kinds of historical questions you could attempt to answer by drawing on the archive's collection.

A celebration of courage and freedom

The Mount Zion Albany Civil Rights Movement Museum is a celebration of courage and freedom of ordinary people and their leaders in the Albany and southwest Georgia movements who bore witness to equal rights and helped to spark the national Civil Rights Movement and international struggles for freedom.

The eyes of the nation were on Albany in the early 1960s as thousands of people attended mass meetings and marched in the streets seeking freedom and justice. In December 1961, Dr. Martin Luther King Jr. joined local activists and further inspired overflowing crowds who gathered to hear him at Mount Zion and neighboring Shiloh Baptist Church.

The strength of the Albany Movement gave rise to campaigns in nearby communities:

"Woke up this morning with my mind stayed on freedom..."
Freedom Song

Americus, Moultrie, Dawson, Thomasville, Cordele, Leesburg, Cairo and Newton.

We have in Albany a symbol of that historic struggle in Mount Zion Church. Silent for decades, the boarded-up windows and dust-covered pews of this historic 1906 church, that once echoed with freedom songs and the call for nonviolent social change, soon will give voice to a key part of the 1960s history of Albany and southwest Georgia.

The Albany Movement sprang from the community's grass roots. Young and old, rich and poor—citizens of every class, color and occupation were involved in it.

Many of those who participated in the Movement are members of the community today—our neighbors, co-workers and family members. The museum offers us a chance to hear their stories.

Multicultural America

How does it happen that in the United States, where the inhabitants have only recently immigrated to the land which they now occupy, and brought neither customs nor traditions with them there; where they met one another for the first time with no previous acquaintances; where, in short, the instinctive love of country can scarcely exist; how does it happen that everyone takes as zealous an interest in the affairs of his township, his county, and the whole state as if they were his own?
—*Alexis de Tocqueville*

No, I'm not an American. I'm one of the 22 million black people who are the victims of Americanism.
—*Malcolm X*

America has always been a multicultural society. From Columbus's first contact with the Taino tribe in the West Indies, the exploration and settlement of America by Europeans has involved a series of encounters with peoples outside the dominant white, Protestant, middle-class culture—not only with American Indians but also with the West Africans who were brought forcibly to America through the slave trade; with Mexicans when the United States appropriated California, Texas, and the Southwest in the Mexican War; with Irish and Chinese laborers who were recruited to build the transcontinental railroad; and with the Italian Catholics and Eastern European Jews who immigrated to the United States between 1880 and 1920 to work in the mines, steel mills, garment trades, and other industries of an expanding capitalist economy.

The founding premise of the early American republic was that Americans would become one people with a common culture, by forging a new national identity. When the French writer Hector St. John de Crevecoeur visited America in the eighteenth century, he marveled at the diversity of the settlers—"[a] mixture of English, Scotch, Irish, Dutch, Germans, and Swedes...a promiscuous breed" intermarrying and giving birth to a new people rather than preserving the old ethnic cultures and traditions. "Here," de Crevecoeur said, "individuals of all nations are melted into a new race of men."

This vision of the assimilation of many diverse peoples into one common culture has become a fixture in American consciousness, expressed in the image of the melting pot and the national slogan *E pluribus unum*. But it has also remained just that—a vision of an imaginary unified America without cultural differences. The fact of the matter is that a lot of people did not melt in, as de Crevecoeur thought they would, but instead they have been marginalized and subordinated, rendered politically powerless and culturally invisible. The American experiment to form a new people has in actuality produced not a common culture and national identity but a multicultural society that is divided along racial and ethnic lines.

The issue Americans have always faced, then, is not whether they can establish a unified culture but whether they can learn to live and work together with their differences. The historical record is an uneven one, and for every instance of cooperation across cultural differences or racial lines, such as the Underground Railroad to assist runaway slaves before the Civil War or the unity of black and white workers during the union organizing drives in the 1930s, there have been far too many cases where the dominant culture has sanctioned the oppression of Americans who are different. The Jim Crow laws and lynchings of southern blacks that followed the end of Reconstruction, the genocidal military campaigns to dispossess American Indians, and the internment of Japanese Americans during World War II are only the most obvious examples of a nation turning to force instead of negotiating its cultural differences.

The point, though, is that Americans now live, as they always have, whether they have recognized it or not, in a multicultural society—and the skills of negotiating differences have become a matter of urgency, not to undo differences but to discover new ways to arrange our collective life. Despite what is often presented in the media and popular press, multiculturalism is neither a new phenomenon nor a plot by leftwing college professors to dismantle the Western tradition. Debates about multicultural education have been raging for a number of years now and are likely to continue. These are important debates, and they are touched on in some of the selections in this chapter. But in another sense, debates about whether or not the curriculum students study and teachers teach should be multicultural make it sound as if there were a choice to be made—for or against multiculturalism. The purpose of this chapter is not to offer a choice but to explore the consequences of a fact: Multiculturalism is, and always has been, deeply embedded in the lived experience of Americans.

Americans are living, as Mary Louise Pratt puts it, in a "contact zone," where encounters with cultural differences, whether they are based on race, class, gender, ethnicity, religion, or sexual orientation, simply are not optional. The United States is changing, and current demographic trends indicate that the country is becoming less white and less middle class. The recent wave of immigration from Southeast Asia and Latin America has been the largest since the turn of the nineteenth century. If anything, the future of America is going to be more multicultural than ever. For some, this is a troubling prospect, and there have been disturbing outbreaks of violence against recent immigrants, attempts to close the border, and initiatives to make English the official language. Old myths die hard, and the belief that America was once a unified nation with a common culture continues to hang on in the face of evidence to the contrary.

As the readings we have gathered here reveal, the contact zones of multicultural America are problematic places in which individuals and groups work out their identities and aspirations in relation both to the identities and aspirations of other groups of Americans and to the structures of power that organize and maintain the dominant culture. The purpose of this closing chapter, then, is to invite you to read America as a multicultural society, to locate yourself and your own heritage in relation to the various cultures and ethnic groups that now populate the country, and to consider the cultural meanings of multiculturalism for life in contemporary America.

READING MULTICULTURAL AMERICA

The readings that are presented here look at the realities of multicultural America from a variety of perspectives and propose a number of terms to describe contemporary American experience. The first two reading selections show America to be a multicultural society, but Ishmael Reed's "America: The Multinational Society" emphasizes the diversity and mix of cultures, while Alejandro Portes and Alex Stepick's "Miami: City on the Edge" emphasizes conflict.

The next two readings offer ways of understanding lives of individuals in multicultural America. In "How to Tame a Wild Tongue," Gloria Anzaldua uses the term "borderlands" to describe the experience of Chicanos in the Southwest, located between Anglo and Mexican cultures. Elaine H. Kim, in "Home Is Where the Han Is: A Korean American Perspective on the Los Angeles Upheavals," sees Korean Americans caught in the middle—in her word, "squeezed"—between the dominant white culture on one hand, and African American and Latino communities on the other.

In "Arts of the Contact Zone," Mary Louise Pratt proposes still another term—"contact zone"—to characterize the interactions of various cultures in the Americas and how these cultures represent themselves to each other. Two contrasting essays, Neil Strauss's "A Land with Rhythm and Beats for All" and Touré's "In the End, Black Men Must Lead," comment on the current state, boundaries, and membership of today's multiracial "hip-hop nation"—another instance of cultural borrowing and musical cross-fertilization.

As you read the selections in this chapter, think and write about the way that each writer characterizes the multicultural realities of contemporary America. Taken together, these writers challenge conventional views that American culture is coherent and unified and that there is a single national identity that binds together all Americans. Instead, these writers emphasize repeatedly the mix of cultures, the splits and conflicts of life in the "contact zone," at the "border," or "squeezed" between cultures. In this sense, the writers we have gathered not only raise important issues about multicultural America. They also complicate what it might mean to read culture—to picture American culture as a place where people negotiate their differences.

America
The Multinational Society

Ishmael Reed

Ishmael Reed is one of the foremost novelists in America today. In *Flight to Canada, Mumbo Jumbo, The Last Days of Louisiana Red,* and other novels, Reed uses the experimentalism of postmodernist fiction to create a body of African American fictions. Reed is also a critic and essayist, as you will see in the following selection. The essay "America: The Multinational Society" appeared in Reed's collection of essays and reviews, *Writin' Is Fightin'* (1988). Here Reed raises the perspective that despite textbook accounts of American history, America has always been a multinational culture—not exactly a melting pot so much as a stew of disparate peoples.

SUGGESTION FOR READING

As you read, you will notice that Ishmael Reed opens the essay with a series of examples, including the lead quote from the *New York Times*. Notice how this sets Reed up to step back and generalize. Underline and annotate the passage where Reed first announces the theme of the essay.

At the annual Lower East Side Jewish Festival yesterday, a Chinese woman ate a pizza slice in front of Ty Thuan Duc's Vietnamese grocery store. Beside her a Spanish-speaking family patronized a cart with two signs: "Italian Ices" and "Kosher by Rabbi Alper." And after the pastrami ran out, everybody ate knishes.

New York Times, 23 June 1983

On the day before Memorial Day, 1983, a poet called me to describe a city he had just visited. He said that one section included mosques, built by the Islamic people who dwelled there. Attending his reading, he said, were large numbers of Hispanic people, forty thousand of whom lived in the same city. He was not talking about a fabled city located in some mysterious region of the world. The city he'd visited was Detroit.

A few months before, as I was leaving Houston, Texas, I heard it announced on the radio that Texas's largest minority was Mexican American, and though a foundation recently issued a report critical of bilingual education, the taped voice used to guide the passengers on the air trams connecting terminals in Dallas Airport is in both Spanish and English. If the trend continues, a day will come when it will be difficult to travel through some sections of the country without hearing commands in both English and Spanish; after all, for some western states, Spanish was the first written language and the Spanish style lives on in the western way of life.

Shortly after my Texas trip, I sat in an auditorium located on the campus of the University of Wisconsin at Milwaukee as a Yale professor—whose original work on the influence of African cultures upon those of the Americas has led to his ostracism from some monocultural intellectual circles—walked up and down the aisle, like an old-time southern evangelist, dancing and drumming the top of the lectern, illustrating his points before some serious Afro-American intellectuals and artists who cheered and applauded his performance and his mastery of information. The professor was "white." After his lecture, he joined a group of Milwaukeeans in a conversation. All of the participants spoke Yoruban, though only the professor had ever traveled to Africa.

One of the artists told me that his paintings, which included African and Afro-American mythological symbols and imagery, were hanging in the local McDonald's restaurant. The next day I went to McDonald's and snapped pictures of smiling youngsters eating hamburgers below paintings that could grace the walls of any of the country's leading museums. The manager of the local McDonald's said, "I don't know what you boys are doing, but I like it," as he commissioned the local painters to exhibit in his restaurant.

Such blurring of cultural styles occurs in everyday life in the United States to a greater extent than anyone can imagine and is probably more prevalent than the sensational conflict between people of different backgrounds that is played up and often encouraged by the media. The result is what the Yale professor, Robert Thompson, referred to as a cultural bouillabaisse, yet members of the nation's present educational and cultural Elect still cling to the notion that the United States belongs to some vaguely defined entity they refer to as "Western civilization," by which they mean, presumably, a civilization created by the people of Europe, as if Europe can be viewed in monolithic terms. Is Beethoven's Ninth Symphony, which includes Turkish marches, a part of Western civilization, or the late nineteenth- and twentieth-century French paintings whose creators were influenced by Japanese art? And what of the cubists, through whom the influence of African art changed modern painting, or the surrealists, who were so impressed with the art of the Pacific Northwest Indians that, in their map of North America, Alaska dwarfs the lower forty-eight in size?

Are the Russians, who are often criticized for their adoption of "Western" ways by Tsarist dissidents in exile, members of Western civilization? And what of the millions of Europeans who have black African and Asian ancestry, black Africans having occupied several countries for hundreds of years? Are these "Europeans" members of Western civilization, or the Hungarians, who originated across the Urals in a place called Greater Hungary, or the Irish, who came from the Iberian Peninsula?

Even the notion that North America is part of Western civilization because our "system of government" is derived from Europe is being challenged by Native American historians who say that the founding fathers, Benjamin Franklin especially, were actually influenced by the system of government that had been adopted by the Iroquois hundreds of years prior to the arrival of large numbers of Europeans.

Western civilization, then, becomes another confusing category like Third World or Judeo-Christian culture, as man attempts to impose his small-screen view of political and cultural reality upon a complex world. Our most publicized novelist recently said that Western civilization was the greatest achievement of mankind, an attitude that flourishes on the street level as scribbles in public restrooms: "White Power," "Niggers and Spics Suck," or "Hitler was a prophet," the latter being the most telling, for wasn't Adolph Hitler the archetypal monoculturalist who, in his pigheaded arrogance, believed that one way and one blood was so pure that it had to be protected from alien strains at all costs? Where did such an attitude, which has caused so much misery and depression in our national life, which has tainted even our noblest achievements, begin? An attitude that caused the incarceration of Japanese American citizens during World War II, the persecution of Chicanos and Chinese Americans, the near-extermination of the Indians, and the murder and lynchings of thousands of Afro-Americans.

Virtuous, hardworking, pious, even though they occasionally would wander off after some fancy clothes, or rendezvous in the woods with the town prostitute, the Puritans are idealized in our schoolbooks as "a hardy band" of no-nonsense patriarchs whose discipline razed the forest and brought order to the New World (a term that annoys Native American historians). Industrious, responsible, it was their "Yankee ingenuity" and practicality that created the work ethic. They were simple folk who produced a number of good poets, and they set the tone for the American writing style, of lean and spare lines, long before Hemingway. They worshiped in churches whose colors blended in with the New England snow, churches with simple structures and ornate lecterns.

The Puritans were a daring lot, but they had a mean streak. They hated the theater and banned Christmas. They punished people in a cruel and inhuman manner. They killed children who disobeyed their parents. When they came in contact with those whom they considered heathens or aliens, they behaved in such a bizarre and irrational manner that this chapter in the American history comes down to us as a late-movie horror film. They exterminated the Indians, who taught them how to survive in a world unknown to them, and their encounter with the calypso culture of Barbados resulted in what the tourist guide in Salem's Witches' House refers to as the Witchcraft Hysteria.

The Puritan legacy of hard work and meticulous accounting led to the establishment of a great industrial society; it is no wonder that the American industrial revolution began in Lowell, Massachusetts, but there was the other side, the strange and paranoid attitudes toward those different from the Elect.

The cultural attitudes of that early Elect continue to be voiced in everyday life in the United States: the president of a distinguished university, writing a letter to the *Times,* belittling the study of African civilizations; the television network that promoted its show on the Vatican art with the boast that this art represented "the finest achievements of the human spirit." A modern up-tempo state of complex rhythms that depends upon contacts with an international community can no longer behave as if it dwelled in a "Zion Wilderness" surrounded by beasts and pagans.

When I heard a schoolteacher warn the other night about the invasion of the American educational system by foreign curriculums, I wanted to yell at the television set, "Lady, they're already here." It has already begun because the world is here. The world has been arriving at these shores for at least ten thousand years from Europe, Africa, and Asia. In the late nineteenth and early twentieth centuries, large numbers of Europeans arrived, adding their cultures to those of the European, African, and Asian settlers who were already here, and recently millions have been entering the country from South America and the Caribbean, making Yale Professor Bob Thompson's bouillabaisse richer and thicker.

One of our most visionary politicians said that he envisioned a time when the United States could become the brain of the world, by which he meant the repository of all of the latest advanced information systems. I thought of that remark when an enterprising poet friend of mine called to say that he had just sold a poem to a computer magazine and that the editors were delighted to get it because they didn't carry fiction or poetry. Is that the kind of world we desire? A humdrum homogeneous world of all brains and no heart, no fiction, no poetry; a world of robots with human attendants bereft of imagination, of culture? Or does North America deserve a more exciting destiny? To become a place where the cultures of the world crisscross. This is possible because the United States is unique in the world: The world is here.

SUGGESTIONS FOR DISCUSSION

1. Western civilization, in Reed's view, has become a "confusing category." What do you understand the term "Western civilization" to mean? Where did you learn the meaning of the term? Compare your sense of the term to those of your classmates. How would you account for similarities and differences? Do you agree with Reed that it is a "confusing category"? If so, what exactly makes it "confusing"?

2. Describe Reed's perspective on the Puritans. What about the Puritans is he trying to bring into view? How does his portrait differ from ones you have read in history textbooks? What does Reed see as the result of the "Puritan legacy"? Do you find his characterization of the Puritans and their legacy to be a useful one? What would you add or leave out?

3. The metaphor of the melting pot has been used widely by American historians and other writers to describe the intermingling of immigrants to form one people. Reed, on the other hand, draws on a different metaphor—that of a "cultural bouillabaisse." What do you see as the main differences between the two metaphors? What does each reveal and conceal? What, in your view, are the advantages and disadvantages of each?

SUGGESTIONS FOR WRITING

1. Use the opening section of Ishmael Reed's essay as a model to create your own scenes and examples of America as a "cultural bouillabaisse." Write three or four sketches of things that you have seen and experienced. Then, following Reed's example, step back and generalize about the significance of your sketches.

2. One of Reed's central points is that American culture has always been a "blurring of cultural styles." Pick an example of cultural expression with which you are familiar—whether in music, art, literature, everyday

speech, fashion, or whatever—and write an essay that explains and analyzes the components from different cultures that are combined and
"blurred" together.

3. Reed points to the "cultural attitudes of the early Elect," the Puritans, in
explaining the sources of resistance to recognizing America as a "multinational" instead of a "monocultural" society. Write an essay that extends
Reed's analysis of the sources of resistance to portraying America as a
multicultural society.

Miami
City on the Edge

Alejandro Portes and Alex Stepick

> Alejandro Portes is a professor of sociology and international relations at Johns
> Hopkins University. Alex Stepick teaches sociology and directs the Comparative
> Sociology Graduate Program at Florida International University. The following
> selection is taken from the preface and first chapter of their book *City on the
> Edge: The Transformation of Miami.*

SUGGESTION FOR READING

As you read, notice how Portes and Stepick first define three distinct perspectives on civic life in Miami—"Anglo cultural reaffirmation," "Cuban or pan-
Latin success story," and "Black double marginality"—then present interviews
to illustrate the perspectives.

Miami is not a microcosm of the American city. It never was. From its very beginnings a
century ago, the Biscayne Bay metropolis possessed an air of unreality, a playground
divorced from its natural habitat by the deeds of Yankee developers. For a while it seemed
that no fantasy, no matter how farfetched, could not be enacted here. The thin strip of land
between jungle and reef hence became less an American Riviera than a compendium of the
nation's foibles. During the last three decades or so Miami has evolved, shedding its light-
hearted past to become a serious, some say tragic, place. The Cuban Revolution marked the
beginning of this change, which was pushed along by new influxes of Caribbean migrants
and by native reactions to the presence of so many outsiders. Cubans, of course, played a pivotal role in the transformation, for their actions and dreams, while inspiring the Cuban community, also affected the character and identity of other groups. And thereby the entire
community changed.

Our interest in this city dates back to the early seventies when we began studying the
arrival and resettlement of new immigrant groups in the area. As sociologists, our principal
focus was the adaptation of foreign-born minorities to their new environment. As time
passed, however, it became clear that the environment itself was changing in ways that we
could not have anticipated. The immigrants were transforming not only themselves, but also
the city around them. Unwittingly, Miami had become the nation's first full-fledged experiment in bicultural living in the contemporary era.

Other U.S. cities, such as New York and Los Angeles, also have large Spanish-speaking
and immigrant populations, but nowhere has the social and economic weight of the new-

comers or their political significance been greater than in South Florida. In New York, new arrivals are promptly absorbed into the immense fabric of the city; the very diversity of nationalities in New York conspires against any single group becoming too prominent. In Miami, the regrouped Cuban bourgeoisie not only redefined the character of the city, but also prompted other ethnic communities—native Blacks and whites included—to cast their own identities in sharper relief.

Other bilingual and bicultural cities and regions have of course existed in the history of the nation. Milwaukee and St. Louis at the turn of the twentieth century were German towns; northern Wisconsin and Michigan were heavily Scandinavian; inhabitants of parishes in the Louisiana lowlands spoke Acadian French; and San Antonio, Santa Fe, and other towns in the vast territories taken from Mexico retained Spanish for a long while. But the passage of time and the growing hegemony of American culture diluted these experiences and accustomed us to the spectacle of immigrants who had been Americanized before reaching U.S. shores or who promptly shed their cultural trappings in quest of assimilation. Arising from a unique set of historical circumstances, the Miami experiment is unique and unlikely to be repeated. Yet the passions that it awoke and the social energies that it released may carry significant lessons as America becomes again, under the influence of growing immigration, a multiethnic society.

COMPETING DISCOURSES

Social facts are not self-intelligible. Their interpretation depends on the cognitive frames in which they are placed, and these in turn are products of prior social interactions. Common meanings are arrived at when relevant audiences agree to stress certain aspects of a given phenomenon and interpret them on the basis of shared past experience. Existing "frames" of what American urban life is like, including those elaborated in the sociological research literature, prove to be of limited utility for rendering events in South Florida understandable. These events represent social change without a blueprint; because they led precisely to the fragmentation of previously held consensual views, it is not surprising that several competing discourses emerged to explain them, each with its own distinct shades of meaning and moral tone. Only in such a context would it be conceivable for William Lozano, convicted felon, to solicit and obtain support from a wide segment of the very city where his alleged crime was committed.

To approach developments in Miami, we first make use of W. I. Thomas's concept of "definition of the situation," a term that highlights how subjective perceptions of reality can influence reality itself. In our view, definitions of the situation comprise (a) a frame of reference embodying one or more generalized ideas and (b) an "object" that is interpreted in terms of those ideas. Different objects are interrelated by reference to the common frame, giving rise to a perspective, or "discourse," in which apparently disparate aspects of reality are integrated into a meaningful interpretive whole. The difference between Miami and most communities studied by sociologists in the past is that in Miami even everyday events—not to mention more explosive conflicts between social classes and interest groups—are not necessarily assessed within a common frame of reference, but may be inserted into different, mutually unintelligible, interpretive frameworks.

At present, several perspectives sufficiently broad to provide a coherent account of life in this metropolitan area are identifiable. The most common ones may be labeled the "Anglo cultural reaffirmation," the "Cuban or pan-Latin success story," and the "Black double marginality" discourses. By way of illustration, the following excerpts of statements made by community leaders in interviews, addressing four frequent "objects" of debate in Miami, may be taken as typical of each discourse. The statements are drawn from interviews, conducted between 1983 and 1988, with approximately sixty of the most prominent business, political, and religious leaders in the city as a complement to a large survey of the recently arrived immigrant population in the area. Three of these "objects"—Miami's "major problem," language, and interethnic relations—were posed as questions to all respondents; the fourth—the *Miami Herald*—emerged spontaneously in several conversations.

Miami's Major Problem

Native white business executive, former chairman of a large local corporation (interviewed in 1987):
　　　　You have two levels, one is what is going to happen to the nation as a whole over the next fifty years when the Hispanic population may become over fifty percent of the population; and the other level is the short-term impact of Hispanics in a city like this one. You deal with perceptions because you don't really know what percentage of the population is making the noise, but you hear the noise, the major noise, the dominant noise, and you are beginning to hear more and more that the Cubans are not interested in integrating into American society, and if that is the case, then that has to be the number-one problem in Miami.
　　　　That is a problem because there isn't a great deal in Caribbean and Latin American cultures that's going to add anything to democracy at all. And I think there is a good chance that it will detract from it. Cubans really value economic freedom, but there are other freedoms they don't value.

Cuban businessman, owner of a local factory, emigrated in the early 1960s (1986):
　　　　Our most serious problem in Miami is the devaluation of South American currencies because in this city there has been created a large current of business with Central and South America; many properties were built, many apartments were sold, apart from the exports. The devaluations in Venezuela, Mexico, and Brazil paralyzed economic activity in Miami. At the same time, construction of apartments for all those South Americans who wanted to own something here stopped. This is our most serious problem today. Until currencies regain their value and economic tranquillity returns to those countries, Miami—which is the key link between the United States and Latin America—will continue to suffer.

Black community activist, director of a social service agency in Liberty City, the major Black area of South Florida (1987):
　　　　The real problem in 1987 is that the Blacks have not concluded that they must take control of their destiny. That's the real problem now. But that was not the real problem in 1964. Then, the problem was to remove the shackles of segregation. You had to go through that process in order to get to where we are in 1987....Now, having gone through that process, the final lap is to put everything in perspective, and to ask ourselves what are we going to do about it, because all they have done since 1619 has not been in our interest, but theirs. In order to take charge of its own destiny, this community must simply, selfishly become unabatedly pro-Black.
　　　　Case in point: there is something special about Blacks and Revlon beauty care products. We find out that Blacks buy over fifty-one percent of all the beauty care products made in the country....If we are the main consumers in that industry, then the appropriate response is for us to become major producers of that which we consume.

Language

Jewish lawyer, director of the regional branch of a major national Jewish organization (1986):
　　　　This is a community like a volcano....A major issue concerns the tensions between native Americans and Hispanics. The focal point is language. There is a very strong "English Only" movement or variations of it. In twenty-five years, close to three hundred thousand Cubans have come here, and many have done very well. The fact is that they have taken over the city both in terms of numbers and economic presence. This has created a lot of resentment and bitterness in some circles. I think the popularized statement that typified the tension was the

bumper sticker that read, "When the last American leaves Miami, please take the flag." That represents the middle- and lower-middle-class feeling about what happened here.

Native white business executive (quoted above with regard to Miami's major problem):
What happens is that in an open store there will be two or three women talking in an incomprehensible language, and people, I think, sometimes just get tired of being surrounded by Spanish. More importantly, there are many, many times when the Cubans know that the people in the room with them don't understand. Like my wife and her hairdresser: she speaks Spanish entirely while she is working on her hair. My son is an absolute linguist, he speaks Portuguese and Spanish fluently. He learned while he was in Rochester, New York, not while he lived in Miami, Florida. It is popular there to be bilingual; it isn't popular in Miami.

Cuban civic activist, head of a multiethnic community organization, emigrated in the early 1960s (1986):
Language has great importance because if an individual owns a store whose clients come from Latin America, he will need bilingual employees. During Christmastime, ninety percent of the stores advertise for bilingual employees. To a person who does not know the language, this situation represents an economic problem because he knows that, unless he knows Spanish, he would not compete successfully in the labor market. This problem is especially important in the Black community, which has the greatest number of unemployed. The young Black knows that it would be much more difficult to secure a job if he does not speak Spanish.

Black owner of a major business in Liberty City, active in the local chamber of commerce (1987):
There is also a growing number of Cuban-owned businesses in Black neighborhoods but they don't hire Blacks. For example, I was in a drugstore a couple of weeks ago and there was a black Cuban lady at one of the cash registers. I went to her and she didn't even want to talk to me. I thought to myself, "Talk to me, if I'm going to leave my money here, you ought to learn how to speak English." They come in our areas, they take our jobs, they take our dollars, and don't even have the decency to learn the language!

Interethnic Relations

Native white attorney, partner in a large local law firm (1987):
The problem of Blacks in Miami is very serious. But my feeling is that the Black population is so relatively small in number that I am not sure it's on anybody's agenda....The number of Hispanics is so overwhelming that the contest is over. I mean there is competition, there is tension, there is concern in the Black community. But Cubans are so well entrenched, so large in numbers, that it's not an issue anymore.

Now, there is another big problem worth investigating: the concept of giving in the Latin community. One of the problems that FIU [Florida International University] has had is that [former president] Wolfe couldn't raise any money. So what did we do? The power structure and the Cubans said, "Let's go get ourselves a good old Cuban boy." Let's see whether old Maidique [Cuban-born, U.S.-educated president of FIU], President Mitch, can demonstrate that he can raise dollars from the Latin community. If he can't raise dollars, in my book he's failed.

There is a lot of work that needs to be done in teaching the concept of philanthropy within the Latin community. The Cubans have been here over twenty years, they have made great economic strides, the kids play football and baseball, they go to the operas, they do all these things; why not give more to the community?

Cuban businessman (quoted above with regard to Miami's major problem):
Relations between the different ethnic communities in Miami are normal as in any democratic country. Ethnic differences do not interfere at all in commercial relations. As to community activities, each one works in the place he or she prefers. There are persons who like to work in the United Way; and there is the Liga contra el cancer [League Against Cancer, a charity founded in Havana], which everyone joins to work for a good cause.

Perhaps, the most affected relations could be those between Cubans and Blacks, in the sense that Blacks are less trained as entrepreneurs, but I do not believe that there is an extraordinary friction. Our chief accountant was Black, a great Black, but right now there are no American Blacks working in our company. When we arrived from Cuba and opened our small business, the situation was like this: when a shipment arrived in customs, we would go to a corner and there would be ten, fifteen, twenty Blacks standing waiting for work. We picked them up so that they would unload our boxes, paid them, and returned them to the same place. Today, you don't see anything like this. I sincerely believe that, in Miami, the person who doesn't work is because he or she does not want to. Proof: why are so many Haitians now sewing in our factory?

Black attorney, community activist (1987):
Initially, as the Cubans began to be very competitive, as the new banks tended to be Cuban, as the Cubans began to come into the insurance and traditional financial markets where the Jews had played an important role, the issue was no longer Jews against Anglos but one of the survival of the status quo....

Blacks were left behind. Miami is the only city I've ever seen where Blacks don't own a radio station, or a television station, or a car dealership, or a savings and loan, or an insurance company—anything! Blacks here have not only been manipulated out of the mainstream of the power structure, but, more importantly, they have been manipulated out of the economic mainstream of Miami, and when you're out of the economic mainstream, you're out of the political arena.

Black community activist (quoted above with regard to Miami's major problem):
In those days, I said to Cubans in a speech that there was going to be a time when white folks are going to try to treat you all like niggers. They're going to put you again in your place as they do with all minority groups. But unlike Black Americans, Cubans had no history of being kept in their place, and as a result, they responded differently. We Black folks were saying to white folks, "Let us in." Cubans were saying to white folks, "Let us in so that we can take over." Now, in 1987, you hear whites telling us that we should form an alliance with them to keep Cubans in their place. I say, "I've had my experience with you all. Don't tell me now that you and I can buddy-buddy because you're trying to keep Cubans from doing what is right for their own."

SUGGESTIONS FOR DISCUSSION

1. Use the table on the "Ethic Composition of Metropolitan Miami 1950–90" (Table 10.1) to summarize the demographic changes that have taken place during those years. How would you relate these changes to the perspectives that you see in the interviews?

2. Reread the interviews in the section on "Language." How would you characterize the range of perspectives that are represented here? Imagine that the speakers were sitting in a room together. What would they say to each other? Where do you see main points of difference? Where are there areas of agreement?

3. According to Portes and Stepick, what has taken place in Miami over the past fifty years amounts to "social change without a blueprint." What do they mean by that phrase? From what you have read and know from your own experience, how would you assess developments in Miami?

SUGGESTIONS FOR WRITING

1. In "America: The Multinational Society," Ishmael Reed proposes the metaphor of a "cultural bouillabaisse" to replace the older image of

TABLE 10.1

Ethnic composition of metropolitan Miami, 1950–90

	1950	*1960*	*1970*	*1980*	*1990*
Population total	495,000	935,000	1,268,000	1,626,000	1,937,000
U.S. rank[a]	—	19	17	12	11
Percent increase in preceding decade	—	88.9	35.6	28.2	19.1
White, non-Hispanic	410,000	748,000	779,000	776,000	586,000
Percent of total	82.8	80.0	61.4	47.7	30.3
Percent increase/decrease in preceding decade	—	82.4	4.1	-0.4	-24.5
Hispanic[b]	20,000	50,000	299,000	581,000	953,000
Percent of total	4.0	5.3	23.6	35.7	49.2
Percent increase in preceding decade	—	150.0	498.0	94.3	64.0
Black[c]	65,000	137,000	190,000	280,000	369,000
Percent of total	13.1	14.7	15.0	17.2	19.5
Percent increase in preceding decade	—	110.8	38.7	47.4	31.8

[a]Among standard metropolitan statistical areas.
[b]Hispanics can be of any race.
[c]There is some overlap between the Hispanic and Black categories owing to the presence of black Hispanics. In 1980, the Metro-Dade Research Division reported 11,000 blacks of Hispanic origin; in 1990, there were 28,372 such persons. The table includes them as "Black" for the sake of congruence with earlier figures where this separation was not made.

Sources: Metro-Dade Planning Department, Research Division, Dade County Facts (Miami: Metropolitan Dade County Government, 1990); idem, Persons of Hispanic Origin by Race, City, and Census Tract (Miami: Metropolitan Dade County Government, 1990).

America as a "melting pot." Does Reed's metaphor make sense for Miami as described by Portes and Stepick? Write an essay that begins by explaining what Reed has in mind and then use Miami as a test case to see if the metaphor "cultural bouillabaisse" is applicable.

2. Imagine that you are writing an American history textbook for high school students. You have come to the 1990s and the growing awareness that the United States is a multicultural society. Draw on this reading to write an account of the demographic and cultural changes in Miami to illustrate the point and to indicate what its consequences may be.

3. Use the notion of "definition of the situation" that Portes and Stepick have taken from W. I. Thomas to explain a situation which you have encountered where no common frame of reference seemed to exist and that the people involved had a hard time understanding each other. First, explain what the term "definition of the situation" means. Then identify the differing frameworks that people brought to the situation. Explain why this produced different interpretations and evaluations of what was taking place.

How to Tame a Wild Tongue

Gloria Anzaldua

Gloria Anzaldua writes in a language that grows out of the multiple cultures in the American Southwest—a mosaic of English (both standard and slang), Spanish (both Castilian and Mexican), northern Mexican and Chicano Spanish dialects, Tex-Mex, *Pachuco* (the vernacular of urban zoot suiters), and the Aztec language Nahuatl. The following selection is a chapter from her book, *Borderlands/La Frontera,* which was originally published in 1987. As the title of her book indicates, Anzaldua sees herself as a "border woman." "I grew up between two cultures," she says, "the Mexican (with a heavy Indian influence) and the Anglo (as a member of a colonized people in our own territory). I have been straddling that *tejas*-Mexican border, and others, all my life." Like Mary Louise Pratt's notion of the "contact zone," Anzaldua's "borderland" refers to those places "where two or more cultures edge each other, where people of different races occupy the same territory, where under, lower, middle, and upper classes touch, where the space between two individuals shrinks with intimacy."

SUGGESTION FOR READING

As you read, you will notice how Gloria Anzaldua combines English and Spanish in a sentence or a paragraph. Consider the effects of Anzaldua's prose and how it locates you as a reader on the border where two cultures and languages touch.

W e're going to have to control your tongue," the dentist says, pulling out all the metal from my mouth. Silver bits plop and tinkle into the basin. My mouth is a motherlode. The dentist is cleaning out my roots. I get a whiff of the stench when I gasp. "I can't cap that tooth yet, you're still draining," he says.

"We're going to have to do something about your tongue," I hear the anger rising in his voice. My tongue keeps pushing out the wads of cotton, pushing back the drills, the long thin needles. "I've never seen anything as strong or as stubborn," he says. And I think, how do you tame a wild tongue, train it to be quiet, how do you bridle and saddle it? How do you make it lie down?

Who is to say that robbing a people of its language is less violent than war?

Ray Gwyn Smith[1]

I remember being caught speaking Spanish at recess—that was good for three licks on the knuckles with a sharp ruler. I remember being sent to the corner of the classroom for "talking back" to the Anglo teacher when all I was trying to do was tell her how to pronounce my name. "If you want to be American, speak 'American.' If you don't like it, go back to Mexico where you belong."

"I want you to speak English. *Pa' hallar buen trabajo tienes que saber hablar el inglés bien. Qué vale toda tu educatión si todavía hablas inglés con un* 'accent,'" my mother would say, mortified that I spoke English like a Mexican. At Pan American University, I and all Chicano students were required to take two speech classes. Their purpose: to get rid of our accents.

Attacks on one's form of expression with the intent to censor are a violation of the First Amendment. *El Anglo con care de inocente nos arrancó la lengua.* Wild tongues can't be tamed, they can only be cut out.

OVERCOMING THE TRADITION OF SILENCE

Ahogadas, escupimos el oscuro. Peleando con nuestra propia sombra el silencio nos sepulta.

En boca cerrada no entran moscas. "Flies don't enter a closed mouth" is a saying I kept hearing when I was a child. *Ser habladora* was to be a gossip and a liar, to talk too much. *Muchachitas bien criadas,* well-bred girls don't answer back. *Es una falta de respeto* to talk back to one's mother or father. I remember one of the sins I'd recite to the priest in the confession box the few times I went to confession: talking back to my mother, *hablar pa' 'tras, repelar. Hocicona, repelona, chismosa,* having a big mouth, questioning, carrying tales are all signs of being *mal criada.* In my culture they are all words that are derogatory if applied to women—I've never heard them applied to men.

The first time I heard two women, a Puerto Rican and a Cuban, say the word *"nosotras,"* I was shocked. I had not known the word existed. Chicanas use *nosotros* whether we're male or female. We are robbed of our female being by the masculine plural. Language is a male discourse.

> And our tongues have become dry the wilderness has dried out our tongues and we have forgotten speech.
>
> *Irena Klepfisz[2]*

Even our own people, other Spanish speakers *nos quieren poner candados en la boca.* They would hold us back with their bag of *reglas de academia.*

OYÉ COMO LADRA: EL LENGUAJE DE LA FRONTERA

Quien tiene boca se equivoca.

Mexican saying

"Pocho, cultural traitor, you're speaking the oppressor's language by speaking English, you're ruining the Spanish language," I have been accused by various Latinos and Latinas. Chicano Spanish is considered by the purist and by most Latinos deficient, a mutilation of Spanish.

But Chicano Spanish is a border tongue which developed naturally. Change, *evolución, enriquecimiento de palabras nuevas por invención o adopción* have created variants of Chicano Spanish, *un nuevo lenguaje. Un lenguaje que corresponde a un modo de vivir.* Chicano Spanish is not incorrect, it is a living language.

For a people who are neither Spanish nor live in a country in which Spanish is the first language; for a people who live in a country in which English is the reigning tongue but who are not Anglo; for a people who cannot entirely identify with either standard (formal, Castilian) Spanish nor standard English, what recourse is left to them but to create their own language? A language which they can connect their identity to, one capable of communicating the realities and values true to themselves—a language with terms that are neither *español ni inglés,* but both. We speak a patois, a forked tongue, a variation of two languages.

Chicano Spanish sprang out of the Chicanos' need to identify ourselves as a distinct people. We need a language with which we could communicate with ourselves, a secret language. For some of us, language is a homeland closer than the Southwest—for many Chicanos today live in the Midwest and the East. And because we are a complex, heterogeneous people, we speak many languages. Some of the languages we speak are

1. Standard English
2. Working-class and slang English
3. Standard Spanish

4. Standard Mexican Spanish

5. North Mexican Spanish dialect

6. Chicano Spanish (Texas, New Mexico, Arizona, and California have regional variations)

7. Tex-Mex

8. *Pachuco* (called *caló*)

My "home" tongues are the languages I speak with my sister and brothers, with my friends. They are the last five listed, with 6 and 7 being closest to my heart. From school, the media, and job situations, I've picked up standard and working class English. From Mama-grande Locha and from reading Spanish and Mexican literature, I've picked up Standard Spanish and Standard Mexican Spanish. From *los recién llegados,* Mexican immigrants, and *braceros,* I learned the North Mexican dialect. With Mexicans I'll try to speak either Standard Mexican Spanish or the North Mexican dialect. From my parents and Chicanos living in the Valley, I picked up Chicano Texas Spanish, and I speak it with my mom, younger brother (who married a Mexican and who rarely mixes Spanish with English), aunts, and older relatives.

With Chicanas from *Nuevo México* or *Arizona* I will speak Chicano Spanish a little, but often they don't understand what I'm saying. With most California Chicanas I speak entirely in English (unless I forget). When I first moved to San Francisco, I'd rattle off something in Spanish, unintentionally embarrassing them. Often it is only with another Chicana *tejano* that I can talk freely.

Words distorted by English are known as anglicisms or *pochismos*. The *pocho* is an anglicized Mexican or American of Mexican origin who speaks Spanish with an accent characteristic of North Americans and who distorts and reconstructs the language according to the influence of English.[3] Tex-Mex, or Spanglish, comes most naturally to me. I may switch back and forth from English to Spanish in the same sentence or in the same word. With my sister and my brother Nune and with Chicano *tejano* contemporaries I speak in Tex-Mex.

From kids and people my own age I picked up *Pachuco. Pachuco* (the language of the zoot suiters) is a language of rebellion, both against Standard Spanish and Standard English. It is a secret language. Adults of the culture and outsiders cannot understand it. It is made up of slang words from both English and Spanish. *Ruca* means girl or woman, *vato* means guy or dude, *chale* means no, *simón* means yes, *churro* is sure, talk is *periquiar, pigionear* means petting, *que gacho* means how nerdy, *ponte águila* means watch out, death is called *la pelona*. Through lack of practice and not having others who can speak it, I've lost most of the *Pachuco* tongue.

CHICANO SPANISH

Chicanos, after 250 years of Spanish/Anglo colonization, have developed significant differences in the Spanish we speak. We collapse two adjacent vowels into a single syllable and sometimes shift the stress in certain words such as *maíz/maiz, cohete/cuete*. We leave out certain consonants when they appear between vowels: *lado/lao, mojado/mojao*. Chicanos from South Texas pronounce *f* as *j* as in *jue* (*fue*). Chicanos use "archaisms," words that are no longer in the Spanish language, words that have been evolved out. We say *semos, truje, haiga, ansina,* and *naiden*. We retain the "archaic" *j*, as in *jalar,* that derives from an earlier *h* (the French *halar* or the Germanic *halon* which was lost to standard Spanish in the sixteenth century), but which is still found in several regional dialects such as the one spoken in South Texas. (Due to geography, Chicanos from the Valley of South Texas were cut off linguistically from other Spanish speakers. We tend to use words that the Spaniards brought over from Medieval Spain. The majority of the Spanish colonizers in Mexico and the Southwest came from Extremadura—Hernán Cortés was one of them—and Andalucía. Andalucians pronounce *ll* like a *y*, and their *d*'s tend to be absorbed by adjacent vowels: *tirado* becomes *tirao*. They brought *el lenguaje popular, dialectos y regionalismos*.)[4]

Chicanos and other Spanish speakers also shift *ll* to *y* and *z* to *s*.[5] We leave out initial syllables, saying *tar* for *estar, toy* for *estoy, hora* for *ahora* (*cubanos* and *puertorriqueños* also leave out initial letters of some words). We also leave out the final syllable such as *pa* for *para*. The intervocalic *y*, the *ll* as in *tortilla, ella, botella*, gets replaced by *tortia* or *tortiya, ea, botea*. We add an additional syllable at the beginning of certain words: *atocar* for *tocar, agastar* for *gastar*. Sometimes we'll say *lavaste las vacijas*, other times *lavates* (substituting the *ates* verb endings for the *aste*).

We used anglicisms, words borrowed from English: *bola* from ball, *carpeta* from carpet, *máchina de lavar* (instead of *lavadora*) from washing machine. Tex-Mex argot, created by adding a Spanish sound at the beginning or end of an English word such as *cookiar* for cook, *watchar* for watch, *parkiar* for park, and *rapiar* for rape, is the result of the pressures on Spanish speakers to adapt to English.

We don't use the word *vosotros/as* or its accompanying verb form. We don't say *claro* (to mean yes), *imagínate*, or *me emociona*, unless we picked up Spanish from Latinas, out of a book, or in a classroom. Other Spanish-speaking groups are going through the same, or similar, development in their Spanish.

LINGUISTIC TERRORISM

> *Deslenguadas. Somos los del español deficiente.* We are your linguistic nightmare, your linguistic aberration, your linguistic *mestisaje,* the subject of your *burla.* Because we speak with tongues of fire we are culturally crucified. Racially, culturally, and linguistically *somos huérfanos*—we speak an orphan tongue.

Chicanas who grew up speaking Chicano Spanish have internalized the belief that we speak poor Spanish. It is illegitimate, a bastard language. And because we internalize how our language has been used against us by the dominant culture, we use our language differences against each other.

Chicana feminists often skirt around each other with suspicion and hesitation. For the longest time I couldn't figure it out. Then it dawned on me. To be close to another Chicana is like looking into the mirror. We are afraid of what we'll see there. *Pena.* Shame. Low estimation of self. In childhood we are told that our language is wrong. Repeated attacks on our native tongue diminish our sense of self. The attacks continue throughout our lives.

Chicanas feel uncomfortable talking in Spanish to Latinas, afraid of their censure. Their language was not outlawed in their countries. They had a whole lifetime of being immersed in their native tongue; generations, centuries in which Spanish was a first language, taught in school, heard on radio and TV, and read in the newspaper.

If a person, Chicana or Latina, has a low estimation of my native tongue, she also has a low estimation of me. Often with *mexicanas y latinas* we'll speak English as a neutral language. Even among Chicanas we tend to speak English at parties or conferences. Yet, at the same time, we're afraid the other will think we're *agringadas* because we don't speak Chicano Spanish. We oppress each other trying to out-Chicano each other, vying to be the "real" Chicanas, to speak like Chicanos. There is no one Chicano language just as there is no one Chicano experience. A monolingual Chicana whose first language is English or Spanish is just as much a Chicana as one who speaks several variants of Spanish. A Chicana from Michigan or Chicago or Detroit is just as much a Chicana as one from the Southwest. Chicano Spanish is as diverse linguistically as it is regionally.

By the end of this century, Spanish speakers will comprise the biggest minority group in the United States, a country where students in high schools and colleges are encouraged to take French classes because French is considered more "cultured." But for a language to remain alive it must be used.[6] By the end of this century English, and not Spanish, will be the mother tongue of most Chicanos and Latinos.

So, if you want to really hurt me, talk badly about my language. Ethnic identity is twin skin to linguistic identity—I am my language. Until I can take pride in my language, I cannot take pride in myself. Until I can accept as legitimate Chicano Texas Spanish, Tex-Mex, and all the other languages I speak, I cannot accept the legitimacy of myself. Until I am free to write bilingually and to switch codes without having always to translate, while I still have to speak English or Spanish when I would rather speak Spanglish, and as long as I have to accommodate the English speakers rather than having them accommodate me, my tongue will be illegitimate.

I will no longer be made to feel ashamed of existing. I will have my voice: Indian, Spanish, white. I will have my serpent's tongue—my woman's voice, my sexual voice, my poet's voice. I will overcome the tradition of silence.

My fingers

move sly against your palm

Like women everywhere, we speak in code....

Melanie Kaye/Kantrowitz[7]

"VISTAS," CORRIDOS, Y COMIDA: MY NATIVE TONGUE

In the 1960s, I read my first Chicano novel. It was *City of Night* by John Rechy, a gay Texan, son of a Scottish father and a Mexican mother. For days I walked around in stunned amazement that a Chicano could write and could get published. When I read *I Am Joaquín*[8] I was surprised to see a bilingual book by a Chicano in print. When I saw poetry written in Tex-Mex for the first time, a feeling of pure joy flashed through me. I felt like we really existed as a people. In 1971, when I started teaching High School English to Chicano students, I tried to supplement the required texts with works by Chicanos, only to be reprimanded and forbidden to do so by the principal. He claimed that I was supposed to teach "American" and English literature. At the risk of being fired, I swore my students to secrecy and slipped in Chicano short stories, poems, a play. In graduate school, while working toward a Ph.D., I had to "argue" with one adviser after the other, semester after semester, before I was allowed to make Chicano literature an area of focus.

Even before I read books by Chicanos or Mexicans, it was the Mexican movies I saw at the drive-in—the Thursday night special of $1.00 a carload—that gave me a sense of belonging. "*Vámonos a las vistas,*" my mother would call out and we'd all—grandmother, brothers, sister, and cousins—squeeze into the car. We'd wolf down cheese and bologna white bread sandwiches while watching Pedro Infante in melodramatic tearjerkers like *Nosotros los pobres,* the first "real" Mexican movie (that was not an imitation of European movies). I remember seeing *Cuando los hijos se van* and surmising that all Mexican movies played up the love a mother has for her children and what ungrateful sons and daughters suffer when they are not devoted to their mothers. I remember the singing-type "westerns" of Jorge Negrete and Miquel Aceves Mejía. When watching Mexican movies, I felt a sense of homecoming as well as alienation. People who were to amount to something didn't go to Mexican movies, or bailes, or tune their radios to *bolero, rancherita,* and *corrido* music.

The whole time I was growing up, there was *norteño* music sometimes called North Mexican border music, or Tex-Mex music, or Chicano music, or *cantina* (bar) music. I grew up listening to *conjuntos,* three- or four-piece bands made up of folk musicians playing guitar, *bajo sexto,* drums, and button accordion, which Chicanos had borrowed from the German immigrants who had come to Central Texas and Mexico to farm and build breweries. In the Rio Grande Valley, Steve Jordan and Little Joe Hernández were popular, and Flaco Jiménez was the accordion king. The rhythms of Tex-Mex music are those of the polka, also adapted from the Germans, who in turn had borrowed the polka from the Czechs and Bohemians.

I remember the hot, sultry evenings when *corridos*—songs of love and death on the Texas-Mexican borderlands—reverberated out of cheap amplifiers from the local *cantinas* and wafted in through my bedroom window.

Corridos first became widely used along the South Texas/Mexican border during the early conflict between Chicanos and Anglos. The *corridos* are usually about Mexican heroes who do valiant deeds against the Anglo oppressors. Pancho Villa's song, *"La cucaracha,"* is the most famous one. *Corridos* of John F. Kennedy and his death are still very popular in the Valley. Older Chicanos remember Lydia Mendoza, one of the great border *corrido* singers who was called *la Gloria de Tejas.* Her *"El tango negro,"* sung during the Great Depression, made her a singer of the people. The ever-present *corridos* narrated one hundred years of border history, bringing news of events as well as entertaining. These folk musicians and folk songs are our chief cultural mythmakers, and they made our hard lives seem bearable.

I grew up feeling ambivalent about our music. Country-western and rock-and-roll had more status. In the fifties and sixties, for the slightly educated and *agringado* Chicanos, there existed a sense of shame at being caught listening to our music. Yet I couldn't stop my feet from thumping to the music, could not stop humming the words, nor hide from myself the exhilaration I felt when I heard it.

There are more subtle ways that we internalize identification, especially in the forms of images and emotions. For me food and certain smells are tied to my identity, to my homeland. Woodsmoke curling up to an immense blue sky; woodsmoke perfuming my grandmother's clothes, her skin. The stench of cow manure and the yellow patches on the ground; the crack of a .22 rifle and the reek of cordite. Homemade white cheese sizzling in a pan, melting inside a folded *tortilla.* My sister Hilda's hot, spicy *menudo, chile colorado* making it deep red, pieces of *panza* and hominy floating on top. My brother Carito barbequing *fajitas* in the backyard. Even now and 3,000 miles away, I can see my mother spicing the ground beef, pork, and venison with chile. My mouth salivates at the thought of the hot steaming *tamales* I would be eating if I were home.

SI LE PREGUNTAS A MI MAMÁ, "¿QUÉ ERES?"

> Identity is the essential core of who we are as individuals, the conscious experience of the self inside.
>
> *Gershen Kaufman*[9]

Nosotros los Chicanos straddle the borderlands. On one side of us, we are constantly exposed to the Spanish of the Mexicans, on the other side we hear the Anglos' incessant clamoring so that we forget our language. Among ourselves we don't say *nosotros los americanos, o nosotros los españoles, o nosotros los hispanos.* We say *nosotros los mexicanos* (by *mexicanos* we do not mean citizens of Mexico; we do not mean a national identity, but a racial one). We distinguish between *mexicanos del otro lado* and *mexicanos de este lado.* Deep in our hearts we believe that being Mexican has nothing to do with which country one lives in. Being Mexican is a state of soul—not one of mind, not one of citizenship. Neither eagle nor serpent, but both. And like the ocean, neither animal respects borders.

> *Dime con quien andas y te diré quien eres.*
> (Tell me who your friends are and I'll tell you who you are.)
>
> *Mexican saying*

Si le preguntas a mi mamá, "¿Qué eres?" te dirá, "Soy mexicana." My brothers and sister say the same. I sometimes will answer *"soy mexicana"* and at others will say *"soy Chicana" o "soy tejana."* But I identified as *"Raza"* before I ever identified as *"mexicana"* or "Chicana."

As a culture, we call ourselves Spanish when referring to ourselves as a linguistic group and when copping out. It is then that we forget our predominant Indian genes. We are 70–80 percent Indian.[10] We call ourselves Hispanic[11] or Spanish American or Latin American or Latin when linking ourselves to other Spanish-speaking peoples of the Western hemisphere and when copping out. We call ourselves Mexican American[12] to signify we are neither Mexican nor American, but more the noun "American" than the adjective "Mexican" (and when copping out).

Chicanos and other people of color suffer economically for not acculturating. This voluntary (yet forced) alienation makes for psychological conflict, a kind of dual identity—we don't identify with the Anglo-American cultural values and we don't totally identify with the Mexican cultural values. We are a synergy of two cultures with various degrees of Mexicanness or Angloness. I have so internalized the borderland conflict that sometimes I feel like one cancels out the other and we are zero, nothing, no one. *A veces no soy nada ni nadie. Pero hasta cuando no lo soy, lo soy.*

When not copping out, when we know we are more than nothing, we call ourselves Mexican, referring to race and ancestry; *mestizo* when affirming both our Indian and Spanish (but we hardly ever own our Black) ancestry; Chicano when referring to a politically aware people born and/or raised in the United States; *Raza* when referring to Chicanos; *tejanos* when we are Chicanos from Texas.

Chicanos did not know we were a people until 1965 when Cesar Chavez and the farmworkers united and *I Am Joaquin* was published and *la Raza Unida* party was formed in Texas. With that recognition, we became a distinct people. Something momentous happened to the Chicano soul—we became aware of our reality and acquired a name and a language (Chicano Spanish) that reflected that reality. Now that we had a name, some of the fragmented pieces began to fall together—who we were, what we were, how we had evolved. We began to get glimpses of what we might eventually become.

Yet the struggle of identities continues, the struggle of borders is our reality still. One day the inner struggle will cease and a true integration take place. In the mean-time, *tenémos que hacer la lucha. ¿Quién está protegiendo los ranchos de mi gente? ¿Quién está tratando de cerrar la fisura entre la india y el blanco en nuestra sangre? El Chicano, si, el Chicano que anda como un ladrón en su propia casa.*

Los Chicanos, how patient we seem, how very patient. There is the quiet of the Indian about us.[13] We know how to survive. When other races have given up their tongue we've kept ours. We know what it is to live under the hammer blow of the dominant *norteamericano* culture. But more than we count the blows, we count the days the weeks the years the centuries the aeons until the white laws and commerce and customs will rot in the deserts they've created, lie bleached. *Humildes* yet proud, *quietos* yet wild, *nosotros los mexicanos-Chicanos* will walk by the crumbling ashes as we go about our business. Stubborn, persevering, impenetrable as stone, yet possessing a malleability that renders us unbreakable, we, the *mestizas* and *mestizos,* will remain.

Notes

1. Ray Gwyn Smith, *Moorland Is Cold Country,* unpublished book.

2. Irena Klepfisz, "*Di rayze aheym*/The Journey Home," in *The Tribe of Dina: A Jewish Women's Anthology,* Melanie Kaye/Kantrowitz and Irena Klepfisz, eds. (Montpelier, VT: Sinister Wisdom Books, 1986), 49.

3. R. C. Ortega, *Dialectologia Del Barrio,* trans. Hortencia S. Alwan (Los Angeles, CA: R. C. Ortega Publisher & Bookseller, 1977), 132.

4. Eduardo Hernandéz-Chávez, Andrew D. Cohen, and Anthony F. Beltramo, *El Lenguaje de los Chicanos: Regional and Social Characteristics of Language Used by Mexican Americans* (Arlington, VA: Center for Applied Linguistics, 1975), 39.

5. Hernandéz-Chávez, xvii.

6. Irena Klepfisz, "Secular Jewish Identity: Yidishkayt in America," in *The Tribe of Dina,* Kaye/Kantrowitz and Klepfisz, eds., 43.

7. Melanie Kaye/Kantrowitz, "Sign," in *We Speak in Code: Poems and Other Writings* (Pittsburgh, PA: Motheroot Publications, Inc., 1980), 85.

8. Rodolfo Gonzales, *I Am Joaquín/Yo Soy Joaquín* (New York, NY: Bantam Books, 1972). It was first published in 1967.

9. Gershen Kaufman, *Shame: The Power of Caring* (Cambridge, MA: Schenkman Books, Inc., 1980), 68.

10. John R. Chávez, *The Lost Land: The Chicano Images of the Southwest* (Albuquerque, NM: University of New Mexico Press, 1984), 88–90.

11. "Hispanic" is derived from *Hispanis* (*España,* a name given to the Iberian Peninsula in ancient times when it was a part of the Roman Empire) and is a term designated by the U.S. government to make it easier to handle us on paper.

12. The Treaty of Guadalupe Hidalgo created the Mexican American in 1848.

13. Anglos, in order to alleviate their guilt for dispossessing the Chicano, stressed the Spanish part of us and perpetrated the myth of the Spanish Southwest. We have accepted the fiction that we are Hispanic, that is Spanish, in order to accommodate ourselves to the dominant culture and its abhorrence of Indians. Chávez, 88–91.

SUGGESTIONS FOR DISCUSSION

1. Compare your experience of reading Gloria Anzaldua's polyglot prose with the experiences of others in your class. As we have suggested, the purpose of Anzaldua's mix of language is to recreate the conditions of the borderland, where the use of one language leaves out or excludes those who know only the other language. But what are readers to do with such prose? If you don't know Spanish, how did you try to make sense of the Spanish words and phrases Anzaldua uses? Even if you do know Spanish, are you familiar with the terms that she draws from regional dialects? What does your experience reading "How to Tame a Wild Tongue" reveal to you about the nature of cultural encounters at the borderlands?

2. Anzaldua has composed the chapter "How to Tame a Wild Tongue" like a mosaic, in which she juxtaposes seven separate sections without offering an overarching statement of purpose or meaning to unify the sections. At the same time, the sections do seem to go together in an associative, nonlinear way. Look back over the sections of the chapter to identify how (or whether) the separate parts work together to form a whole. What in your view is the principle of combination that links them together?

3. Anzaldua says that the "voluntary (yet forced) alienation [of Chicanos and other people of color] makes for psychological conflict, a kind of dual identity—we don't identify with the Anglo-American cultural values and we don't totally identify with the Mexican cultural values. We are a synergy of two cultures with various degrees of Mexicanness or Angloness. I have so internalized the borderland conflict that sometimes I feel like one cancels out the other and we are zero, nothing, no one." Yet she also says, a few lines later, "Stubborn, perserving, impenetrable as stone, yet possessing a malleability that renders us unbreakable, we, the *mestizas* and *mestizos,* will remain," What is the struggle of identities Anzaldua articulates here? How do you account for the abrupt shift from the pessimism of the first statement to the optimism of the second? How does Anzaldua's sense of dual identity compare to Adrienne Rich's notion of herself as "split at the root"?

SUGGESTIONS FOR WRITING

1. Write an essay describing and analyzing your experience reading "How to Tame a Wild Tongue." How do the mix of languages and the fragmentary character of the text put special demands on you as a reader? How and in what sense is this reading experience equivalent to what Anzaldua calls the "borderland"? What does your position as a reader on the border reveal to you about the nature of encounters across cultures in multicultural America?

2. Write an essay that compares Anzaldua's position as a *mestiza* of the borderlands to Adrienne Rich's portrayal of herself as a middle-class Jewish southerner "split at the root." To what extent are their experiences similar? In what respects do they differ? Don't settle in your essay for just describing differences and similarities. The issue is how you explain what they have in common and what makes them different. What, in your view, is the significance of these similarities and differences?

3. Use Anzaldua's chapter as a model to write your own essay about the contradictory and conflicting meanings of language use and cultural expression in your life. This assignment is meant to be an experiment in writing that asks you to emulate Anzaldua in incorporating multiple voices, dialects, slangs, and languages and in composing by way of a collage that juxtaposes fragments of thought and experience instead of developing a linear piece of writing with a main point and supporting evidence. To develop ideas for this essay, you might begin by thinking of the different voices, musics, foods, and other cultural forms that are part of your experience, the conflicting ways of life that you have lived, and the multiple identities that you inhabit.

Home Is Where the "Han" Is
A Korean American Perspective on the Los Angeles Upheavals

Elaine H. Kim

Elaine H. Kim teaches Asian American Studies at the University of California–Berkeley. She has written and edited a number of books on Asian American writers and artists, and she has been involved in the production of television documentaries on Asian women. The following selection originally appeared as a chapter in a collection of essays, *Reading Rodney King/Reading Urban Uprising* (1993). In her chapter, Kim suggests that the uprising that followed the acquittal of four police officers in the Rodney King beating case was a "baptism into what it really means for a Korean to 'become American' in the 1990s." The failure of the Los Angeles police to respond to the looting and burning of stores and homes in Koreatown revealed to the Korean community, Kim says, the contradiction between the American dream and American reality and what she calls the "interstitial position" of Korean Americans, caught in a racially divided society between "predominantly Anglo and mostly African American and Latino communities."

SUGGESTION FOR READING

As you read, notice how Elaine H. Kim combines commentary on the Los Angeles uprising with the history of the Korean people and an analysis of readers' responses to the "My Turn" column she wrote for *Newsweek* magazine. To help you follow Kim's line of thought, underline and annotate key passages that develop her central ideas. How do the various sections locate Korean Americans as caught in the middle—on the one hand, between the dominant Anglo and the minority African American and Latino communities, and on the other, between the United States and Korea?

About half of the estimated $850 million in estimated material losses incurred during the Los Angeles upheavals was sustained by a community no one seems to want to talk much about. Korean Americans in Los Angeles, suddenly at the front lines when violence came to the buffer zone they had been so precariously occupying, suffered profound damage to their means of livelihood.[1] But my concern here is the psychic damage which, unlike material damage, is impossible to quantify.

I want to explore the questions of whether or not recovery is possible for Korean Americans, and what will become of our attempts to "become American" without dying of *han. Han* is a Korean word that means, loosely translated, the sorrow and anger that grow from the accumulated experiences of oppression. Although the word is frequently and commonly used by Koreans, the condition it describes is taken quite seriously. When people die of *han,* it is called dying of *hwabyong,* a disease of frustration and rage following misfortune.

Situated as we are on the border between those who have and those who have not, between predominantly Anglo and mostly African American and Latino communities, from our current interstitial position in the American discourse of race, many Korean Americans have trouble calling what happened in Los Angeles an "uprising." At the same time, we cannot quite say it was a "riot." So some of us have taken to calling it *sa-i-ku,* April 29, after the manner of naming other events in Korean history—3.1 (*sam-il*) for March 1, 1919, when massive protests against Japanese colonial rule began in Korea; 6.25 (*yook-i-o*), or June 25, 1950, when the Korean War began; and 4.19 (*sa-il-ku*), or April 19, 1960, when the first student movement in the world to overthrow a government began in South Korea. The ironic similarity between 4.19 and 4.29 does not escape most Korean Americans.

Los Angeles Koreatown has been important to me, even though I visit only a dozen times a year. Before Koreatown sprang up during the last decade and a half, I used to hang around the fringes of Chinatown, although I knew that this habit was pure pretense. For me, knowing that Los Angeles Koreatown existed made a difference; one of my closest friends worked with the Black-Korean Alliance there, and I liked to think of it as a kind of "home"—however idealized and hypostatized—for the soul, an anchor, a potential refuge, a place in America where I could belong without ever being asked, "Who are you and what are you doing here? Where did you come from and when are you going back?"

Many of us watched in horror the destruction of Koreatown and the systematic targeting of Korean shops in South Central Los Angeles after the Rodney King verdict. Seeing those buildings in flames and those anguished Korean faces, I had the terrible thought that there would be no belonging and that we were, just as I had always suspected, a people destined to carry our *han* around with us wherever we went in the world. The destiny (*p'aljja*) that had spelled centuries of extreme suffering from invasion, colonization, war, and national division had smuggled itself into the U.S. with our baggage.

AFRICAN AMERICAN AND KOREAN AMERICAN CONFLICT

As someone whose social consciousness was shaped by the African American–led civil rights movement of the 1960s, I felt that I was watching our collective dreams for a just society disintegrating, cast aside as naive and irrelevant in the bitter and embattled 1990s. It was the courageous African American women and men of the 1960s who had redefined the meaning of "American," who had first suggested that a person like me could reject the false choice between being treated as a perpetual foreigner in my own birthplace, on the one hand, and relinquishing my identity for someone else's ill-fitting and impossible Anglo American one on the other. Thanks to them, I began to discern how institutional racism works and why Korea was never mentioned in my world-history textbooks. I was able to see how others besides Koreans had been swept aside by the dominant culture. My American education offered nothing about Chicanos or Latinos, and most of what I was taught about African and Native Americans was distorted to justify their oppression and vindicate their oppressors.

I could hardly believe my ears when, during the weeks immediately following *sa-i-ku,* I heard African American community leaders suggesting that Korean American merchants were foreign intruders deliberately trying to stifle African American economic development, when I knew that they had bought those liquor stores at five times gross receipts from African American owners, who had previously bought them at two times gross receipts from Jewish owners after Watts. I saw anti-Korean flyers that were being circulated by African American political candidates and read about South Central residents petitioning against the reestablishment of swap meets, groups of typically Korean immigrant-operated market stalls. I was disheartened with Latinos who related the pleasure they felt while looting Korean stores that they believed "had it coming" and who claimed that it was because of racism that more Latinos were arrested during *sa-i-ku* than Asian Americans. And I was filled with despair when I read about Chinese Americans wanting to dissociate themselves from us. According to one Chinese American reporter assigned to cover Asian American issues for a San Francisco daily, Chinese and Japanese American shopkeepers, unlike Koreans, always got along fine with African Americans in the past. "Suddenly," admitted another Chinese American, "I am scared to be Asian. More specifically, I am afraid to be mistaken for Korean." I was enraged when I overheard European Americans discussing the conflicts as if they were watching a dogfight or a boxing match. The situation reminded me of the Chinese film *Raise the Red Lantern,* in which we never see the husband's face. We only hear his mellifluous voice as he benignly admonishes his four wives not to fight among themselves. He can afford to be kind and pleasant because the structure that pits his wives against each other is so firmly in place that he need never sully his hands or even raise his voice.

BATTLEGROUND LEGACY

Korean Americans are squeezed between black and white and also between U.S. and South Korean political agendas. Opportunistic American and South Korean presidential candidates toured the burnt ruins, posing for the television cameras but delivering nothing of substance to the victims. Like their U.S. counterparts, South Korean news media seized upon *sa-i-ku,* featuring sensational stories that depicted the problem as that of savage African Americans attacking innocent Koreans for no reason. To give the appearance of authenticity, Seoul newspapers even published articles using the names of Korean Americans who did not in fact write them.

Those of us who chafe at being asked whether we are Chinese or Japanese as if there were no other possibilities or who were angered when the news media sought Chinese and Japanese but not Korean American views during *sa-i-ku* are sensitive to an invisibility that seems particular to us. To many Americans, Korea is but the gateway to or the bridge between China and Japan, or a crossroads of major Asian conflicts.

It can certainly be said that, although little known or cared about in the Western world, Korea has been a perennial battleground. Besides the Mongols and the Manchus, there were the *Yăjin* (Jurched), the *Koran* (Khitan), and the *Waega* (Wäkö) invaders. In relatively recent years, there was the war between China and Japan that ended in 1895 and the war between Japan and Russia in 1905; both of which were fought on Korean soil and resulted in extreme suffering for the Korean people. Japan's 36 years of brutal colonial rule ended with the U.S. and what was then the Soviet Union dividing the country in half at the 38th parallel. Thus, Korea was turned into a Cold War territory that ultimately became a battleground for world superpowers during the conflict of 1950–53.

BECOMING AMERICAN

One of the consequences of war, colonization, national division, and superpower economic and cultural domination has been the migration of Koreans to places like Los Angeles, where they believed their human rights would be protected by law. After all, they had received U.S.-influenced political educations. They started learning English in the seventh grade. They all knew the story of the poor boy from Illinois who became president. They all learned that the U.S. Constitution and Bill of Rights protected the common people from violence and injustice. But they who grew up in Korea watching *Gunsmoke, Night Rider,* and *McGyver* dubbed in Korean were not prepared for the black, brown, red, and yellow America they encountered when they disembarked at the Los Angeles International Airport. They hadn't heard that there is no equal justice in the U.S. They had to learn about American racial hierarchies. They did not realize that, as immigrants of color, they would never attain political voice or visibility but would instead be used to uphold the inequality and the racial hierarchy they had no part in creating.

Most of the newcomers had underestimated the communication barriers they would face. Like the Turkish workers in Germany described in John Berger and Jean Mohr's *A Seventh Man,* their toil amounted to only a pile of gestures and the English they tried to speak changed and turned against them as they spoke it. Working 14 hours a day, six or seven days a week, they rarely came into sustained contact with English-speaking Americans and almost never had time to study English. Not feeling at ease with English, they did not engage in informal conversations easily with non-Koreans and were hated for being curt and rude. They did not attend churches or do business in banks or other enterprises where English was required. Typically, the immigrant, small-business owners utilized unpaid family labor instead of hiring people from local communities. Thanks to Eurocentric American cultural practices, they knew little or nothing good about African Americans or Latinos, who in turn and for similar reasons knew little or nothing good about them. At the same time, Korean shopowners in South

Central and Koreatown were affluent compared with the impoverished residents, whom they often exploited as laborers or looked down upon as fools with an aversion to hard work. Most Korean immigrants did not even know that they were among the many direct beneficiaries of the African American–led civil rights movement, which helped pave the way for the 1965 immigration reforms that made their immigration possible.

Korean-immigrant views, shaped as they were by U.S. cultural influences and official, anticommunist, South Korean education, differed radically from those of many poor people in the communities Korean immigrants served: unaware of the shameful history of oppression of nonwhite immigrants and other people of color in the U.S., they regarded themselves as having arrived in a meritocratic "land of opportunity" where a person's chances for success are limited only by individual lack of ability or diligence. Having left a homeland where they foresaw their talents and hard work going unrecognized and unrewarded, they were desperate to believe that the "American dream" of social and economic mobility through hard work was within their reach.

SA-I-KU

What they experienced on 29 and 30 April was a baptism into what it really means for a Korean to "become American" in the 1990s. In South Korea, there is no 911, and no one really expects a fire engine or police car if there is trouble. Instead, people make arrangements with friends and family for emergencies. At the same time, guns are not part of Korean daily life. No civilian in South Korea can own a gun. Guns are the exclusive accoutrement of the military and police who enforce order for those who rule the society. When the Korean Americans in South Central and Koreatown dialed 911, nothing happened. When their stores and homes were being looted and burned to the ground, they were left completely alone for three horrifying days. How betrayed they must have felt by what they had believed was a democratic system that protects its people from violence. Those who trusted the government to protect them lost everything; those who took up arms after waiting for help for two days were able to defend themselves. It was as simple as that. What they had to learn was that, as in South Korea, protection in the U.S. is by and large for the rich and powerful. If there were a choice between Westwood and Koreatown, it is clear that Koreatown would have to be sacrificed. The familiar concept of privilege for the rich and powerful would have been easy for the Korean immigrant to grasp if only those exhortations about democracy and equality had not obfuscated the picture. Perhaps they should have relied even more on whatever they brought with them from Korea instead of fretting over trying to understand what was going on around them here. That Koreatown became a battleground does seem like the further playing out of a tragic legacy that has followed them across oceans and continents. The difference is that this was a battle between the poor and disenfranchised and the invisible rich, who were being protected by a layer of clearly visible Korean American human shields in a battle on the buffer zone.

This difference is crucial. Perhaps the legacy is not one carried across oceans and continents but one assumed immediately upon arrival, not the curse of being Korean but the initiation into becoming American, which requires that Korean Americans take on this country's legacy of five centuries of racial violence and inequality, of divide and rule, of privilege for the rich and oppression of the poor. Within this legacy, they have been assigned a place on the front lines. Silenced by those who possess the power to characterize and represent, they are permitted to speak only to reiterate their acceptance of this role.

SILENCING THE KOREAN AMERICAN VOICE

Twelve years ago, in Kwangju, South Korea, hundreds of civilians demonstrating for constitutional reform and free elections were murdered by U.S.-supported and -equipped South

Korean elite paratroopers. Because I recorded it and played it over and over again, searching for a sign or a clue, I remember clearly how what were to me heartrendingly tragic events were represented in the U.S. news media. For a few fleeting moments, images of unruly crowds of alien-looking Asians shouting unintelligible words and phrases and wearing white headbands inscribed with unintelligible characters flickered across the screen. The Koreans were made to seem like insane people from another planet. The voice in the background stated simply that there were massive demonstrations but did not explain what the protests were about. Nor was a single Korean ever given an opportunity to speak to the camera.

The next news story was about demonstrations for democracy in Poland. The camera settled on individuals' faces which one by one filled the screen as each man or woman was asked to explain how he or she felt. Each Polish person's words were translated in a voice-over or subtitle. Solidarity leader Lech Walesa, who was allowed to speak often, was characterized as a heroic human being with whom all Americans could surely identify personally. Polish Americans from New York and Chicago to San Francisco, asked in man-on-the-street interviews about their reactions, described the canned hams and blankets they were sending to Warsaw.

This was for me a lesson in media representation, race, and power politics. It is a given that Americans are encouraged by our ideological apparatuses to side with our allies (here, the Polish resisters and the anti-communist South Korean government) against our enemies (here, the communist Soviet Union and protesters against the South Korean government). But visual-media racism helps craft and reinforce our identification with Europeans and whites while distancing us from fearsome and alien Asiatic hordes.

In March of last year, when two delegates from North Korea visited the Bay Area to participate in community-sponsored talks on Korean reunification, about 800 people from the Korean American community attended. The meeting was consummately newsworthy, since it was the first time in history that anyone from North Korea had ever been in California for more than 24 hours just passing through. The event was discussed for months in the Korean-language media—television, radio, and newspapers. Almost every Korean-speaking person in California knew about it. Although we sent press releases to all the commercial and public radio and television stations and to all the Bay Area newspapers, not a single mainstream media outfit covered the event. However, whenever there was an African American boycott of a Korean store or whenever conflict surfaced between Korean and African Americans, community leaders found a dozen microphones from all the main news media shoved into their faces, as if they were the president's press secretary making an official public pronouncement. Fascination with interethnic conflicts is rooted in the desire to excuse or minimize white racism by buttressing the mistaken notion that all human beings are "naturally" racist, and when Korean and African Americans allow themselves to be distracted by these interests, their attention is deflected from the social hierarchies that give racism its destructive power.

Without a doubt, the U.S. news media played a major role in exacerbating the damage and ill will toward Korean Americans, first by spotlighting tensions between African Americans and Koreans above all efforts to work together and as opposed to many other newsworthy events in these two communities, and second by exploiting racist stereotypes of Koreans as unfathomable aliens, this time wielding guns on rooftops and allegedly firing wildly into crowds. In news programs and on talk shows, African and Korean American tensions were discussed by blacks and whites, who pointed to these tensions as the main cause of the uprising. I heard some European Americans railing against rude and exploitative Korean merchants for ruining peaceful race relations for everyone else. Thus, Korean Americans were used to deflect attention from the racism they inherited and the economic injustice and poverty that had been already well woven into the fabric of American life, as evidenced by a judicial system that could allow not only the Korean store owner who killed

Latasha Harlins but also the white men who killed Vincent Chin and the white police who beat Rodney King to go free, while Leonard Peltier still languishes in prison.

As far as I know, neither the commercial nor the public news media has mentioned the many Korean and African American attempts to improve relations, such as joint church services, joint musical performances and poetry readings, Korean merchant donations to African American community and youth programs, African American volunteer teachers in classes for Korean immigrants studying for citizenship examinations, or Korean translations of African American history materials.

While Korean immigrants were preoccupied with the mantra of day-to-day survival, Korean Americans had no voice, no political presence whatsoever in American life. When they became the targets of violence in Los Angeles, their opinions and views were hardly solicited except as they could be used in the already-constructed mainstream discourse on race relations, which is a sorry combination of blaming the African American and Latino victims for their poverty and scapegoating the Korean Americans as robotic aliens who have no "real" right to be here in the first place and therefore deserve whatever happens to them.

THE *NEWSWEEK* EXPERIENCE

In this situation, I felt compelled to respond when an editor from the "My Turn" section of *Newsweek* magazine asked for a 1000-word personal essay. Hesitant because I was given only a day and a half to write the piece, not enough time in light of the vastness of American ignorance about Koreans and Korean Americans, I decided to do it because I thought I could not be made into a sound bite or a quote contextualized for someone else's agenda.

I wrote an essay accusing the news media of using Korean Americans and tensions between African and Korean Americans to divert attention from the roots of racial violence in the U.S. I asserted that these lie not in the Korean-immigrant-owned corner store situated in a community ravaged by poverty and police violence, but reach far back into the corridors of corporate and government offices in Los Angeles, Sacramento, and Washington, D.C. I suggested that Koreans and African Americans were kept ignorant about each other by educational and media institutions that erase or distort their experiences and perspectives. I tried to explain how racism had kept my parents from ever really becoming Americans, but that having been born here, I considered myself American and wanted to believe in the possibility of an American dream.

The editor of "My Turn" did everything he could to frame my words with his own viewpoint. He faxed his own introductory and concluding paragraphs that equated Korean merchants with cowboys in the Wild West and alluded to Korean/African American hatred. When I objected, he told me that my writing style was not crisp enough and that as an experienced journalist, he could help me out. My confidence wavered, but ultimately I rejected his editing. Then he accused me of being overly sensitive, confiding that I had no need to be defensive—because his wife was a Chinese American. Only after I had decided to withdraw the piece did he agree to accept it as I wrote it.

Before I could finish congratulating myself on being able to resist silencing and the kind of decontextualization I was trying to describe in the piece, I started receiving hate mail. Some of it was addressed directly to me, since I had been identified as a University of California faculty member, but most of it arrived in bundles, forwarded by *Newsweek*. Hundreds of letters came from all over the country, from Florida to Washington state and from Massachusetts to Arizona. I was unprepared for the hostility expressed in most of the letters. Some people sent the article, torn from the magazine and covered with angry, red-inked obscenities scratched across my picture. "You should see a good doctor," wrote someone from Southern California, "you have severe problems in thinking, reasoning, and adjusting to your environment."

A significant proportion of the writers, especially those who identified themselves as descendants of immigrants from Eastern Europe, wrote *Newsweek* that they were outraged, sickened, disgusted, appalled, annoyed, and angry at the magazine for providing an arena for the paranoid, absurd, hypocritical, racist, and childish views of a spoiled, ungrateful, whining, bitching, un-American bogus faculty member who should be fired or die when the next California earthquake dumps all of the "so-called people of color" into the Pacific Ocean.

I was shocked by the profound ignorance of many writers' assumptions about the experiences and perspectives of American people of color in general and Korean and other Asian Americans in particular. Even though my essay revealed that I was born in the U.S. and that my parents had lived in the U.S. for more than six decades, I was viewed as a foreigner without the right to say anything except words of gratitude and praise about America. The letters also provided some evidence of the dilemma Korean Americans are placed in by those who assume that we are aliens who should "go back" and at the same time berate us for not rejecting "Korean American identity" for "American identity."

> How many Americans migrate to Korea? If you are so disenchanted, Korea is still there. Why did you ever leave it? Sayonara.
>
> Ms. Kim appears to have a personal axe to grind with this country that has given her so much freedom and opportunity....I should suggest that she move to Korea, where her children will learn all they ever wanted about that country's history.
>
> [Her] whining about the supposedly racist U.S. society is just a mask for her own acute inferiority complex. If she is so dissatisfied with the United States why doesn't she vote with her feet and leave? She can get the hell out and return to her beloved Korea—her tribal afinity [sic] where her true loyalty and consciousness lies [sic].
>
> You refer to yourself as a Korean American and yet you have lived all your life in the United States...you write about racism in this country and yet you are the biggest racist by your own written words. If you cannot accept the fact that you are an American, maybe you should be living your life in Korea.
>
> My stepfather and cousin risked their lives in the country where your father is buried to ensure the ideals of our country would remain. So don't expect to find a sympathetic ear for your pathetic whining.

Many of the letter writers assumed that my family had been the "scum" of Asia and that I was a college teacher only because of American justice and largesse. They were furious that I did not express gratitude for being saved from starvation in Asia and given the opportunity to flourish, no doubt beyond my wildest dreams, in America.

> Where would she be if her parents had not migrated to the United States? For a professor at Berkeley University [sic] to say the American dream is only an empty promise is ludicrous. Shame, shame, shame on Elaine!
>
> [Her father and his family] made enough money in the USA to ship his corpse home to Korea for burial. Ms. Kim herself no doubt has a guaranteed life income as a professor paid by California taxpayers. Wouldn't you think that she might say kind things about the USA instead of whining about racism?

At the same time some letters blamed me for expecting "freedom and opportunity":

> It is wondrous that folks such as you find truth in your paranoia. No one ever promised anything to you or your parents.

Besides providing indications of how Korean Americans are regarded, the letters revealed a great deal about how American identity is thought of. One California woman explained that although her grandparents were Irish immigrants, she was not an Irish American, because "if you are not with us, you are against us." A Missouri woman did not seem to realize that she was conflating race and nationality and confusing "nonethnic" and "nonracial," by which she seems to have meant "white," with "American." And, although she insists that it is impossible to be both "black" and "American," she identifies herself at the outset as a "white American."

> I am a white American. I am proud to be an American. You cannot be black, white, Korean, Chinese, Mexican, German, French, or English or any other and still be an American. Of course the culture taught in schools is strictly American. That's where we are and if you choose to learn another [culture] you have the freedom to settle there. You cannot be a Korean American which assumes you are not ready to be an AMERICAN. Do you get my gist?

The suggestion that more should be taught in U.S. schools about America's many immigrant groups and people of color prompted many letters in defense of Western civilization against non-Western barbarism:

> You are dissatisfied with current school curricula that excludes Korea. Could it possibly be because Korea and Asia for that matter has [sic] not had...a noticeable impact on the shaping of Western culture, and Korea has had unfortunately little culture of its own?
>
> Who cares about Korea, Ms. Kim?...And what enduring contributions has the Black culture, both here in the US and on the continent contributed to the world, and mankind? I'm from a culture, Ms. Kim, who put a man on the moon 23 years ago, who established medical schools to train doctors to perform open heart surgery, and...who created a language of music so that musicians, from Beethoven to the Beatles, could easily touch the world with their brilliance forever and ever and ever. Perhaps the dominant culture, whites obviously, "swept aside Chicanos...Latinos...African Americans...Koreans," because they haven't contributed anything that made—be mindful of the cliche—a world of difference?
>
> Koreans' favorite means of execution is decapitation...Ms. Kim, and others like her, came here to escape such injustice. Then they whine at riots to which they have contributed by their own fanning of flames of discontent....Yes! Let us all study more about Oriental culture! Let us put matters into proper perspective.
>
> Fanatical multiculturalists like you expect a country whose dominant culture has been formed and influenced by Europe..., nearly 80% of her population consisting of persons whose ancestry is European, to include the history of every ethnic group who has ever lived here. I truly feel sorry for you. You and your bunch need to realize that white Americans are not racists....We would love to get along, but not at the expense of our own culture and heritage.
>
> Kim's axe-to-grind confirms the utter futility of race-relations—the races were never meant to live together. We don't get along and never will....Whats [sic] needed is to divide the United States up along racial lines so that life here can finally become livable.

What seemed to anger some people the most was their idea that, although they worked hard, people of color were seeking handouts and privileges because of their race, and the thought of an ungrateful Asian American siding with African Americans, presumably against whites, was infuriating. How dare I "bite the hand that feeds" me by siding with the champion "whiners who cry 'racism'" because to do so is the last refuge of the "terminally incompetent"?

> The racial health in this country won't improve until minorities stop erecting "me first" barriers and strive to be Americans, not African Americans or Asian Americans expecting privileges.
>
> Ms. Kim wants preferential treatment that immigrants from Greece-to-Sweden have not enjoyed....Even the Chinese...have not created any special problems for themselves or other Americans. Soon those folk are going to express their own resentments to the insatiable demands of the Blacks and other colored peoples, including the wetbacks from Mexico who sneak into this country then pilfer it for all they can.
>
> The Afroderived citizens of Los Angeles and the Asiatic derivatives were not suffering a common imposition....The Asiatics are trying to build their success. The Africans are sucking at the teats of entitlement.

As is usual with racists, most of the writers of these hate letters saw only themselves in their notions about Korea, America, Korean Americans, African Americans. They felt that their own sense of American identity was being threatened and that they were being blamed as individuals for U.S. racism. One man, adept at manipulating various fonts on his word processor, imposed his preconceptions on my words:

> Let me read between the lines of your little hate message:
> ... "The roots...stretch far back into the corridors of corporate and government offices in Los Angeles, Sacramento, and Washington, D.C."
> All white America and all American institutions are to blame for racism.
> ... "I still want to believe the promise is real."
> I have the savvy to know that the American ideals of freedom and justice are a joke but if you want to give me what I want I'm willing to make concessions.
> Ms. Kim,...if you want to embody the ignorant, the insecure, and the emotionally immature, that's your right! Just stop preaching hate and please, please, quit whining.
> *Sincerely, A proud White American teaching my children not to be prejudicial*

Especially since my essay had been subdued and intensely personal, I had not anticipated the fury it would provoke. I never thought that readers would write over my words with their own. The very fact that I used words, and English words at that, particularly incensed some: one letter writer complained about my use of words and phrases like "mani-festation" and "zero-sum game," and "suzerain relationship," which is the only way to describe Korea's relationship with China during the T'ang Dynasty. "Not more than ten people in the USA know what [these words] mean," he wrote. "You are on an ego trip." I wondered if it made him particularly angry that an Asian American had used those English words, or if he would make such a comment to George Will or Jane Bryant Quinn.

Clearly I had encountered part of America's legacy, the legacy that insists on silencing certain voices and erasing certain presences, even if it means deportation, internment, and outright murder. I should not have been surprised by what happened in Koreatown or by the ignorance and hatred expressed in the letters to *Newsweek*, any more than African Americans should have been surprised by the Rodney King verdict. Perhaps the news media, which constituted *sa-i-ku* as news, as an extraordinary event in no way continuous with our everyday lives, made us forget for a moment that as people of color many of us simultaneously inhabit two Americas: the America of our dreams and the America of our experience.

Who among us does not cling stubbornly to the America of our dreams, the promise of a multicultural democracy where our cultures and our differences might be affirmed instead of distorted in an effort to destroy us?

After *sa-i-ku,* I was able to catch glimpses of this America of my dreams because I received other letters that expressed another American legacy. Some people identified themselves as Norwegian or Irish Americans interested in combating racism. Significantly, while most of the angry mail had been sent not to me but to *Newsweek*, almost all of the sympathetic mail, particularly the letters from African Americans, came directly to me. Many came from Korean Americans who were glad that one of their number had found a vehicle for self-expression. Others were from Chinese and Japanese Americans who wrote that they had had similar experiences and feelings. Several were written in shaky longhand by women fervently wishing for peace and understanding among people of all races. A Native American from Nashville wrote a long description of cases of racism against African, Asian, and Native Americans in the U.S. criminal-justice system. A large number of letters came from African Americans, all of them supportive and sympathetic—from judges and professors who wanted better understanding between Africans and Koreans to poets and laborers who scribbled their notes in pencil while on breaks at work. One man identified himself as a Los Angeles African American whose uncle had married a Korean woman. He stated that as a black man in America, he knew what other people feel when they face injustice. He ended his letter apologizing for his spelling and grammar mistakes and asking for materials to read on Asian Americans. The most touching letter I received was written by a prison inmate who had served twelve years of a 35-to-70-year sentence for armed robbery during which no physical injuries occurred. He wrote:

> I've been locked in these prisons going on 12 years now…and since being here I have studied fully the struggles of not just blacks, but all people of color. I am a true believer of helping "your" people "first," but also the helping of all people no matter where there at or the color of there skin. But I must be truthful, my struggle and assistance is truly on the side of people of color like ourselves. But just a few years ago I didn't think like this.
>
> I thought that if you wasn't black, then you was the enemy, but…many years of this prison madness and much study and research changed all of this….[I]t's not with each other, blacks against Koreans or Koreans against blacks. No, this is not what it's about. Our struggle(s) are truly one in the same. What happened in L.A. during the riot really hurt me, because it was no way that blacks was suppose to do the things to your people, my people (Koreans) that they did. You're my sister, our people are my people. Even though our culture may be somewhat different, and even though we may worship our God(s) different…white-Amerikkka [doesn't] separate us. They look at us all the same. Either you're white, or you're wrong….I'm just writing you to let you know that, you're my sister, your people's struggle are my people's struggle.

This is the ground I need to claim now for Korean American resistance and recovery, so that we can become American without dying of *han*.

Although the sentiments expressed in these letters seemed to break down roughly along racial lines—that is, all writers who were identifiably people of color wrote in support—and one might become alarmed at the depth of the divisions they imply, I like to think that I have experienced the desire of many Americans, especially Americans of color, to do as Rodney King pleaded on the second day of *sa-i-ku:* "We're all stuck here for awhile….Let's try to work it out."

In my view, it's important for us to think about *all* of what Rodney King said and not just the words "we all can get along," which have been depoliticized and transformed into a Disneyesque catchphrase for Pat Boone songs and roadside billboards in Los Angeles. It seems to me the emphasis is on the being "stuck here for awhile" together as we await "our day in court."

Like the African American man who wrote from prison, the African American man who had been brutally beaten by white police might have felt the desire to "love everybody," but he had to amend—or rectify—that wish. He had to speak last about loving "people of color." The impulse to "love everybody" was there, but the conditions were not right. For now, the most practical and progressive agenda may be people of color trying to "work it out."

FINDING COMMUNITY THROUGH NATIONAL CONSCIOUSNESS

The place where Korean and American legacies converge for Korean Americans is the exhortation to "go home to where you belong."

One of the letters I received was from a Korean American living in Chicago. He had read a translation of my essay in a Korean language newspaper. "Although you were born in the U.S.A.," he wrote, noticing what none of the white men who ordered me to go back to "my" country had, "your ethnical background and your complexion belong to Korea. It is time to give up your U.S. citizenship and go to Korea."

Some ruined merchants are claiming that they will pull up stakes and return to Korea, but I know that this is not possible for most of them. Even if their stores had not been destroyed, even if they were able to sell their businesses and take the proceeds to Korea, most of them would not have enough to buy a home or business there, since both require total cash up front. Neither would they be able to find work in the society they left behind because it is plagued by recession, repression, and fierce economic competition.

Going back to Korea. The dream of going back to Korea fed the spirit of my father, who came to Chicago in 1926 and lived in the United States for 63 years, during which time he never became a U.S. citizen, at first because the law did not allow it and later because he did not want to. He kept himself going by believing that he would return to Korea in triumph one day. Instead, he died in Oakland at 88. Only his remains returned to Korea, where we buried him in accordance with his wishes.

Hasn't the dream of going back home to where you belong sustained most of America's unwanted at one time or another, giving meaning to lives of toil and making it possible to endure other people's hatred and rejection? Isn't the attempt to find community through national consciousness natural for people refused an American identity because racism does not give them that choice?

Korean national consciousness, the resolve to resist and fight back when threatened with extermination, was all that could be called upon when the Korean Americans in Los Angeles found themselves abandoned. They joined together to guard each other's means of livelihood with guns, relying on Korean-language radio and newspapers to communicate with and help each other. On the third day after the outbreak of violence, more than 30,000 Korean Americans gathered for a peace march in downtown L.A. in what was perhaps the largest and most quickly organized mass mobilization in Asian American history. Musicians in white, the color of mourning, beat traditional Korean drums in sorrow, anger, and celebration of community, a call to arms like a collective heartbeat. I believe that the mother of Edward Song Lee, the Los Angeles–born college student mistaken for a looter and shot to death in the streets, has been able to persevere in great part because of the massive outpouring of sympathy expressed by the Korean American community that shared and understood her *han*.

I have been critical lately of cultural nationalism as detrimental to Korean Americans, especially Korean American women, because it operates on exclusions and fosters intolerance and uniformity of thought while stifling self-criticism and encouraging sacrifice, even to the point of suicide. But *sa-i-ku* makes me think again: what remains for those who are left to stand alone? If Korean Americans refuse to be victims or political pawns in the U.S. while rejecting the exhortation that we go back to Korea where we belong, what will be our weapons of choice?

In the darkest days of Japanese colonial rule, even after being stripped of land and of all economic means of survival, Koreans were threatened with total erasure when the colonizers rewrote Korean history, outlawed the Korean language, forced the subjugated people to worship the Japanese emperor, and demanded that they adopt Japanese names. One of the results of these cultural-annihilation policies was Koreans' fierce insistence on the sanctity of Korean national identity that persists to this day. In this context, it is not difficult to understand why nationalism has been the main refuge of Koreans and Korean Americans.

While recognizing the potential dangers of nationalism as a weapon, I for one am not ready to respond to the antiessentialists' call to relinquish my Korean American identity. It is easy enough for the French and Germans to call for a common European identity and an end to nationalisms, but what of the peoples suppressed and submerged while France and Germany exercised their national prerogatives? I am mindful of the argument that the resurgence of nationalism in Europe is rooted in historical and contemporary political and economic inequality among the nations of Europe. Likewise, I have noticed that many white Americans do not like to think of themselves as belonging to a race, even while thinking of people of color almost exclusively in terms of race. In the same way, many men think of themselves as "human beings" and of women as the ones having a gender. Thus crime, small businesses, and all Korean-African American interactions are seen and interpreted through the lens of race in the same dominant culture that angrily rejects the use of the racial lens for viewing yellow/white or black/white interactions and insists suddenly that we are all "American" whenever we attempt to assert our identity as people of color. It is far easier for Anglo Americans to call for an end to cultural nationalisms than for Korean Americans to give up national consciousness, which makes it possible to survive the vicious racism that would deny our existence as either Korean Americans or Americans.

Is there anything of use to us in Korean nationalism? During one thousand years of Chinese suzerainty, the Korean ruling elite developed a philosophy called *sadaejui,* or reliance of the weak on the strong. In direct opposition to this way of thought is what is called *jaju* or *juche sasang,* or self-determination. Both *sadaejui* and *juche sasang* are ways of dealing with unequal power relationships and resisting the transformation of one's homeland into a battlefield for others, but *sadaejui* has never worked any better for Koreans than it has for any minority group in America. *Juche sasang,* on the other hand, has the kind of oppositional potential needed in the struggle against silence and invisibility. From Korean national consciousness, we can recover this fierce refusal to accept subjugation, which is the first step in the effort to build community, so that we can work with others to challenge the forces that would have us annihilate each other instead of our mutual oppression.

What is clear is that we cannot "become American" without dying of *han* unless we think about community in new ways. Self-determination does not mean living alone. At least for now, that may mean mining the rich and haunted lode of Korean national consciousness while we struggle to understand how our fate is entwined with the fate of others lying prostrate before the triumphal procession of the winners of History. During the past fifteen years or so, many young Korean nationalists have been studying the legacies of colonialism and imperialism that they share with peoples in many Asian, African, and Latin American nations. At the same time that we take note of this work, we can also try to understand how nationalism and feminism can be worked together to demystify the limitations and reductiveness of each as a weapon of empowerment. If Korean national consciousness is ever to be such a weapon for us, we must use it to create a new kind of nationalism-in-internationalism to help us call forth a culture of survival and recovery, so that our *han* might be released and we might be freed to dream fiercely of different possibilities.

Notes

1. I am deeply indebted to the activists in the Los Angeles Korean American community, especially Bong Hwan Kim and Eui-Young Yu, whose courage and commitment to the empowerment of the disenfranchised, whether African American, Latino, or Korean American, during this crisis in Los Angeles has been a continuous source of inspiration for me. I would also like to thank Barry Maxwell for critically reading this manuscript and offering many insightful suggestions; my niece Sujin Kim, David Lloyd, and Caridad Souza for their encouragement; and Mia Chung for her general assistance.

SUGGESTIONS FOR DISCUSSION

1. Elaine H. Kim describes *han* as a Korean term for "the sorrow and anger that grow from the accumulated experiences of oppression." Why, do you think, has she titled her chapter "Home Is Where the *Han* Is"? How does the notion of *han* inform Kim's line of thought throughout the chapter?

2. Kim presents the Korean American community as one that is "squeezed between black and white and also between U.S. and South Korean political agendas." Explain what Kim means by this "squeeze." What are the

effects of this "interstitial position [of Korean Americans] in the American discourse of race"? In what sense have African American and Korean American conflicts been used to justify the racial divisions in contemporary America? How and by whom?

3. Kim compares the television coverage of South Korean demonstrations for constitutional reform and free elections to the coverage of the pro-democratic Solidarity movement in Poland. How does she explain the differences in coverage? How in a more general sense does the media represent minority communities of Asian Americans, African Americans, Latinos, and so on? What are the effects of these representations on social, cultural, and political life in contemporary America?

SUGGESTIONS FOR WRITING

1. Kim suggests that minority groups such as Korean Americans are silenced or incorporated into a drama of interethnic conflict (thereby showing how all humans are "naturally" racist) by the media. Write an essay that analyzes how a particular minority or ethnic group is represented by the media—on the news, in films, or in television shows. What are the social, cultural, and political effects of such representations?

2. Use the letters from *Newsweek* readers that Kim quotes to write an essay that analyzes the responses that she received to her "My Turn" column, which appeared in *Newsweek* on May 18, 1992. First of all, go to the library and read the column. Then reread the responses that she quotes in the essay, both positive and negative. The point of your essay is not simply to dismiss (or denounce) the responses that are racist or ethnocentric, though some of them certainly are. The point rather is to identify what the letters indicate about deeply entrenched beliefs and attitudes about the nature of American culture, the position of immigrants, the multicultural debates, and so on. Consider how readers are making sense of the multicultural realities of contemporary America and what they reveal about life today in the "contact zone."

3. The central metaphor Kim uses in this essay differs from those in earlier selections, whether Reed's "bouillabaise," Portes and Stepick's "City on the Edge," or Anzaldua's "borderland." For Kim, the lives of Korean Americans are "squeezed between black and white and also between U.S. and South Korean political agendas." Notice how Kim develops her own position of being "squeezed," caught between the lessons that she learned from the African American–led civil rights movement and her feelings of dismay and sorrow at anti-Korean sentiments expressed by African Americans in Los Angeles. Along the same lines, she is also caught between her desire to affirm her Korean identify and her anger that the South Korean media depicted the Los Angeles uprising as "savage African Americans attacking innocent Koreans for no reason." Kim's position in the "contact zone" is a complicated one, but in certain respects there are no doubt ways in which many other Americans also feel "squeezed," caught in the middle of contending cultural and political forces. Use Kim's essay as a model to write an essay where you describe and analyze how you are, or have been, in some sense "squeezed," caught in the

middle. In this essay, you will need to explain carefully how you were
caught in the middle, between which communities and contending
forces. You will need also to explain what conflicting loyalties that you
experienced and what you did (or did not do) to deal with the "squeeze"
that you felt.

Arts of the Contact Zone

Mary Louise Pratt

Mary Louise Pratt teaches in the departments of Comparative Literature and
Spanish and Portuguese at Stanford University, where she was involved in
designing a freshman culture program to replace the Western civilization course
that Stanford had traditionally required of its incoming students. As Pratt notes
toward the end of her essay, the course that she teaches in the new program,
"Europe and the Americas," focuses on the "multiple cultural histories (including European ones) that have intersected" in the Americas. The title of Pratt's
essay, "Arts of the Contact Zone," originally published in *Profession 91,* captures
her notion of America as a multicultural place where "peoples geographically
and historically separated come into contact with each other and establish ongoing relations, usually involving conditions of coercion, radical inequality, and
intractable conflict." The "arts" of the contact zone refer, then, to what Pratt
sees as the "interactive, improvisational dimensions of colonial encounters,"
whereby both colonizers and colonized come to an understanding of themselves
through their mutual if unequal relations.

SUGGESTION FOR READING

As you read, you will notice that Mary Louise Pratt's essay is a wide-ranging
one that makes considerable demands on readers to put its parts together.
She ranges from talking about her children to discussing the letter *New Chronicle and Good Government,* written in 1613 by the Incan Guaman Poma to
King Philip III of Spain, to recounting a brief history of European literacy to
describing the curriculum reform at Stanford. To help you follow the main line
of thought, notice where the essay divides into sections. Annotate passages
where Pratt develops her general argument across the various sections.

Whenever the subject of literacy comes up, what often pops first into my mind is a conversation I overheard eight years ago between my son Sam and his best friend, Willie,
aged six and seven, respectively: "Why don't you trade me Many Trails for Carl
Yats...Yesits...Yastrum-scrum." "That's not how you say it, dummy, it's Carl Yes...Yes...oh, I
don't know." Sam and Willie had just discovered baseball cards. Many Trails was their decod-
ing, with the help of first-grade English phonics, of the name Manny Trillo. The name they
were quite rightly stumped on was Carl Yastrzemski. That was the first time I remembered
seeing them put their incipient literacy to their own use, and I was of course thrilled.

Sam and Willie learned a lot about phonics that year by trying to decipher surnames on
baseball cards, and a lot about cities, states, heights, weights, places of birth, stages of life. In
the years that followed, I watched Sam apply his arithmetic skills to working out batting averages and subtracting retirement years from rookie years; I watched him develop senses of pat-

terning and order by arranging and rearranging his cards for hours on end, and aesthetic judgment by comparing different photos, different series, layouts, and color schemes. American geography and history took shape in his mind through baseball cards. Much of his social life revolved around trading them, and he learned about exchange, fairness, trust, the importance of processes as opposed to results, what it means to get cheated, taken advantage of, even robbed. Baseball cards were the medium of his economic life too. Nowhere better to learn the power and arbitrariness of money, the absolute divorce between use value and exchange value, notions of long- and short-term investment, the possibility of personal values that are independent of market values.

Baseball cards meant baseball card shows, where there was much to be learned about worlds as well. And baseball cards opened the door to baseball books, shelves and shelves of encyclopedias, magazines, histories, biographies, novels, books of jokes, anecdotes, cartoons, even poems. Sam learned the history of American racism and the struggle against it through baseball; he saw the depression and two world wars from behind home plate. He learned the meaning of commodified labor, what it means for one's body and talents to be owned and dispensed by another. He knows something about Japan, Taiwan, Cuba, and Central America and how men and boys do things there. Through the history and experience of baseball stadiums he thought about architecture, light, wind, topography, meteorology, the dynamics of public space. He learned the meaning of expertise, of knowing about something well enough that you can start a conversation with a stranger and feel sure of holding your own. Even with an adult—especially with an adult. Throughout his preadolescent years, baseball history was Sam's luminous point of contact with grown-ups, his lifeline to caring. And, of course, all this time he was also playing baseball, struggling his way through the stages of the local Little League system, lucky enough to be a pretty good player, loving the game and coming to know deeply his strengths and weaknesses.

Literacy began for Sam with the newly pronounceable names on the picture cards and brought him what has been easily the broadest, most varied, most enduring, and most integrated experience of his thirteen-year life. Like many parents, I was delighted to see schooling give Sam the tools with which to find and open all these doors. At the same time I found it unforgivable that schooling itself gave him nothing remotely as meaningful to do, let alone anything that would actually take him beyond the referential, masculinist ethos of baseball and its lore.

However, I was not invited here to speak as a parent, nor as an expert on literacy. I was asked to speak as an MLA member working in the elite academy. In that capacity my contribution is undoubtedly supposed to be abstract, irrelevant, and anchored outside the real world. I wouldn't dream of disappointing anyone. I propose immediately to head back several centuries to a text that has a few points in common with baseball cards and raises thoughts about what Tony Sarmienro, in his comments to the conference, called new visions of literacy. In 1908 a Peruvianist named Richard Pietschmann was exploring in the Danish Royal Archive in Copenhagen and came across a manuscript. It was dated in the city of Cuzco in Peru, in the year 1613, some forty years after the final fall of the Inca empire to the Spanish and signed with an unmistakably Andean indigenous name: Felipe Guaman Poma de Ayala. Written in a mixture of Quechua and ungrammatical, expressive Spanish, the manuscript was a letter addressed by an unknown but apparently literate Andean to King Philip III of Spain. What stunned Pietschmann was that the letter was twelve hundred pages long. There were almost eight hundred pages of written text and four hundred of captioned line drawings. It was titled *The First New Chronicle and Good Government*. No one knew (or knows) how the manuscript got to the library in Copenhagen or how long it had been there. No one, it appeared, had ever bothered to read it or figured out how. Quechua was not thought of as a written language in 1908, nor Andean culture as a literate culture.

Pietschmann prepared a paper on his find, which he presented in London in 1912, a year after the rediscovery of Machu Picchu by Hiram Bingham. Reception, by an international congress of Americanists, was apparently confused. It took twenty-five years for a facsimile edition of the work to appear, in Paris. It was not till the late 1970s, as positivist reading habits gave way to interpretive studies and colonial elitisms to postcolonial pluralisms, that Western scholars found ways of reading Guaman Poma's *New Chronicle and Good Government* as the extraordinary intercultural tour de force that it was. The letter got there, only 350 years too late, a miracle and a terrible tragedy.

I propose to say a few more words about this erstwhile unreadable text, in order to lay out some thoughts about writing and literacy in what I like to call the *contact zones*. I use this term to refer to social spaces where cultures meet, clash, and grapple with each other, often in contexts of highly asymmetrical relations of power, such as colonialism, slavery, or their aftermaths as they are lived out in many parts of the world today. Eventually I will use the term to reconsider the models of community that many of us rely on in teaching and theorizing and that are under challenge today. But first a little more about Guaman Poma's giant letter to Philip III.

Insofar as anything is known about him at all, Guaman Poma exemplified the sociocultural complexities produced by conquest and empire. He was an indigenous Andean who claimed noble Inca descent and who had adopted (at least in some sense) Christianity. He may have worked in the Spanish colonial administration as an interpreter, scribe, or assistant to a Spanish tax collector—as a mediator, in short. He says he learned to write from his half brother, a mestizo whose Spanish father had given him access to religious education.

Guaman Poma's letter to the king is written in two languages (Spanish and Quechua) and two parts. The first is called the *Nueva corónica* "New Chronicle." The title is important. The chronicle of course was the main writing apparatus through which the Spanish represented their American conquests to themselves. It constituted one of the main official discourses. In writing a "new chronicle," Guaman Poma took over the official Spanish genre for his own ends. Those ends were, roughly, to construct a new picture of the world, a picture of a Christian world with Andean rather than European peoples at the center of it—Cuzco, not Jerusalem. In the *New Chronicle* Guaman Poma begins by rewriting the Christian history of the world from Adam and Eve (Fig. 10.1), incorporating the Amerindians into it as offspring of one of the sons of Noah. He identifies five ages of Christian history that he links in parallel with the five ages of canonical Andean history—separate but equal trajectories that diverge with Noah and reintersect not with Columbus but with Saint Bartholomew, claimed to have preceded Columbus in the Americas. In a couple of hundred pages, Guaman Poma constructs a veritable encyclopedia of Inca and pre-Inca history, customs, laws, social forms, public offices, and dynastic leaders. The depictions resemble European manners and customs description, but also reproduce the meticulous detail with which knowledge in Inca society was stored on *quipus* and in the oral memories of elders.

Guaman Poma's *New Chronicle* is an instance of what I have proposed to call an *autoethnographic* text, by which I mean a text in which people undertake to describe themselves in ways that engage with representations others have made of them. Thus if ethnographic texts are those in which European metropolitan subjects represent to themselves their others (usually their conquered others), autoethnographic texts are representations that the so-defined others construct in *response to* or in dialogue with those texts. Autoethnographic texts are not, then, what are usually thought of as autochthonous forms of expression or self-representation (as the Andean *quipus* were). Rather they involve a selective collaboration with and appropriation of idioms of the metropolis or the conqueror. These are merged or infiltrated to varying degrees with indigenous idioms to create self-representations intended to intervene in metropolitan

FIGURE 10.1

Adam and Eve.

modes of understanding. Autoethnographic works are often addressed to both metropolitan audiences and the speaker's own community. Their reception is thus highly indeterminate. Such texts often constitute a marginalized group's point of entry into the dominant circuits of print culture. It is interesting to think, for example, of American slave autobiography in its autoethnographic dimensions, which in some respects distinguish it from Euramerican autobiographical tradition. The concept might help explain why some of the earliest published writing by Chicanas took the form of folkloric manners and customs sketches written in English and published in English-language newspapers or folklore magazines (see Treviño). Autoethnographic representation often involves concrete collaborations between people, as between literate ex-slaves and abolitionist intellectuals, or between Guaman Poma and the Inca elders who were his informants. Often, as in Guaman Poma, it involves more than one language. In recent decades autoethnography, critique, and resistance have reconnected with writing in a contemporary creation of the contact zone, the *testimonio*.

Guaman Poma's *New Chronicle* ends with a revisionist account of the Spanish conquest, which, he argues, should have been a peaceful encounter of equals with the potential for benefiting both, but for the mindless greed of the Spanish. He parodies Spanish history. Following contact with the Incas, he writes, "In all Castille, there was a great commotion. All day and at night in their dreams the Spaniards were saying 'Yndias, yndias, oro, plata, oro, plata del Piru'" ("Indies, Indies, gold, silver, gold, silver from Peru") (Fig. 10.2). The Spanish, he writes, brought nothing of value to share with the Andeans, nothing "but armor and guns con la codicia de oro, plata, oro y plata, yndias, a las Yndias, Piru" ("with the lust for gold, silver, gold and silver, Indies, the Indies, Peru") (372). I quote these words as an example of a conquered subject using the conqueror's language to construct a parodic, oppositional representation of the conqueror's

FIGURE 10.2
Conquista Meeting of Spaniard and Inca. The Inca says in Quechua, "You eat this gold?" Spaniard replies in Spanish, "We eat this gold."

own speech. Guaman Poma mirrors back to the Spanish (in their language, which is alien to him) an image of themselves that they often suppress and will therefore surely recognize. Such are the dynamics of language, writing, and representation in contact zones.

The second half of the epistle continues the critique. It is titled *Buen gobierno y justicia* "Good Government and Justice" and combines a description of colonial society in the Andean region with a passionate denunciation of Spanish exploitation and abuse. (These, at the time he was writing, were decimating the population of the Andes at a genocidal rate. In fact, the potential loss of the labor force became a main cause for reform of the system.) Guaman Poma's most implacable hostility is invoked by the clergy, followed by the dreaded *corregidores,* or colonial overseers (Fig. 10.3). He also praises good works, Christian habits, and just men where he finds them, and offers at length his views as to what constitutes "good government and justice." The Indies, he argues, should be administered through a collaboration of Inca and Spanish elites. The epistle ends with an imaginary question-and-answer session in which, in a reversal of hierarchy, the king is depicted asking Guaman Poma questions about how to reform the empire—a dialogue imagined across the many lines that divide the Andean scribe from the imperial monarch, and in which the subordinated subject single-handedly gives himself authority in the colonizer's language and verbal repertoire. In a way, it worked—this extraordinary text did get written—but in a way it did not, for the letter never reached its addressee.

To grasp the import of Guaman Poma's project, one needs to keep in mind that the Incas had no system of writing. Their huge empire is said to be the only known instance of a full-blown bureaucratic state society built and administered without writing. Guaman Poma constructs his text by appropriating and adapting pieces of the representational repertoire of the invaders. He does not simply imitate or reproduce it; he selects and adapts it along Andean lines to express (bilingually, mind you) Andean interests and aspirations. Ethnographers have used the term *transculturation* to describe processes whereby members of subordinated or marginal groups select and invent from materials transmitted by a dominant or metropolitan culture. The

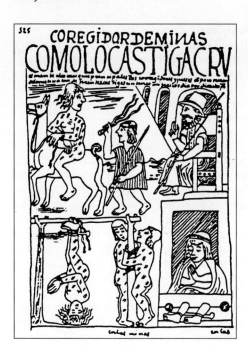

FIGURE 10.3

Corregidor de minas. Catalog of Spanish abuses of indigenous labor force.

term, originally coined by Cuban sociologist Fernando Ortiz in the 1940s, aimed to replace overly reductive concepts of acculturation and assimilation used to characterize culture under conquest. While subordinate peoples do not usually control what emanates from the dominant culture, they do determine to varying extents what gets absorbed into their own and what it gets used for. Transculturation, like autoethnography, is a phenomenon of the contact zone.

As scholars have realized only relatively recently, the transcultural character of Guaman Poma's text is intricately apparent in its visual as well as its written component. The genre of the four hundred line drawings is European—there seems to have been no tradition of representational drawing among the Incas—but in their execution they deploy specifically Andean systems of spatial symbolism that express Andean values and aspirations.[1]

In figure 10.1, for instance, Adam is depicted on the left-hand side below the sun, while Eve is on the right-hand side below the moon, and slightly lower than Adam. The two are divided by the diagonal of Adam's digging stick. In Andean spatial symbolism, the diagonal descending from the sun marks the basic line of power and authority dividing upper from lower, male from female, dominant from subordinate. In figure 10.2, the Inca appears in the same position as Adam, with the Spaniard opposite, and the two at the same height. In figure 10.3, depicting Spanish abuses of power, the symbolic pattern is reversed. The Spaniard is in a high position indicating dominance, but on the "wrong" (right-hand) side. The diagonals of his lance and that of the servant doing the flogging mark out a line of illegitimate, though real, power. The Andean figures continue to occupy the left-hand side of the picture, but clearly as victims. Guaman Poma wrote that the Spanish conquest had produced "un mundo al reves" "a world in reverse."

In sum, Guaman Poma's text is truly a product of the contact zone. If one thinks of cultures, or literatures, as discrete, coherently structured, monolingual edifices, Guaman Poma's text, and indeed any autoethnographic work, appears anomalous or chaotic—as it apparently did to the European scholars Pietschmann spoke to in 1912. If one does not think of cultures this way, then

Guaman Poma's text is simply heterogeneous, as the Andean region was itself and remains today. Such a text is heterogeneous on the reception end as well as the production end: it will read very differently to people in different positions in the contact zone. Because it deploys European and Andean systems of meaning making, the letter necessarily means differently to bilingual Spanish-Quechua speakers and to monolingual speakers in either language; the drawings mean differently to monocultural readers, Spanish or Andean, and to bicultural readers responding to the Andean symbolic structures embodied in European genres.

In the Andes in the early 1600s there existed a literate public with considerable intercultural competence and degrees of bilingualism. Unfortunately, such a community did not exist in the Spanish court with which Guaman Poma was trying to make contact. It is interesting to note that in the same year Guaman Poma sent off his letter, a text by another Peruvian was adopted in official circles in Spain as the canonical Christian mediation between the Spanish conquest and Inca history. It was another huge encyclopedic work, titled the *Royal Commentaries of the Incas,* written, tellingly, by a mestizo, Inca Garcilaso de la Vega. Like the mestizo half brother who taught Guaman Poma to read and write, Inca Garcilaso was the son of an Inca princess and a Spanish official, and had lived in Spain since he was seventeen. Though he too spoke Quechua, his book is written in eloquent, standard Spanish, without illustrations. While Guaman Poma's life's work sat somewhere unread, the *Royal Commentaries* was edited and reedited in Spain and the New World, a mediation that coded the Andean past and present in ways thought unthreatening to colonial hierarchy.[2] The textual hierarchy persists: the *Royal Commentaries* today remains a staple item on PhD reading lists in Spanish, while the *New Chronicle and Good Government,* despite the ready availability of several fine editions, is not. However, though Guaman Poma's text did not reach its destination, the transcultural currents of expression it exemplifies continued to evolve in the Andes, as they still do, less in writing than in storytelling, ritual, song, dance-drama, painting and sculpture, dress, textile art, forms of governance, religious belief, and many other vernacular art forms. All express the effects of long-term contact and intractable, unequal conflict.

Autoethnography, transculturation, critique, collaboration, bilingualism, mediation, parody, denunciation, imaginary dialogue, vernacular expression—these are some of the literate arts of the contact zone. Miscomprehension, incomprehension, dead letters, unread masterpieces, absolute heterogeneity of meaning—these are some of the perils of writing in the contact zone. They all live among us today in the transnationalized metropolis of the United States and are becoming more widely visible, more pressing, and, like Guaman Poma's text, more decipherable to those who once would have ignored them in defense of a stable, centered sense of knowledge and reality.

CONTACT AND COMMUNITY

The idea of the contact zone is intended in part to contrast with ideas of community that underlie much of the thinking about language, communication, and culture that gets done in the academy. A couple of years ago, thinking about the linguistic theories I knew, I tried to make sense of a utopian quality that often seemed to characterize social analyses of language by the academy. Languages were seen as living in "speech communities," and these tended to be theorized as discrete, self-defined, coherent entities, held together by a homogeneous competence or grammar shared identically and equally among all the members. This abstract idea of the speech community seemed to reflect, among other things, the utopian way modern nations conceive of themselves as what Benedict Anderson calls "imagined communities."[3] In a book of that title, Anderson observes that with the possible exception of what he calls "primordial villages," human communities exist as *imagined* entities in which people "will never know most of their fellow-members, meet them or even hear of them, yet in the minds of each lives the image of their communion." "Communities are distinguished," he goes on to say, "not by their falsity/genuineness, but by *the style in which they are imagined*" (15; emphasis mine). Anderson proposes three features that characterize the style in which the modern nation is imagined. First, it is imagined as *limited*, by "finite, if elastic, boundaries"; second, it is imagined as *sovereign*, and, third, it is imagined as *fraternal*, "a deep, horizontal comradeship" for which millions of people are prepared "not so much to kill as willingly to die" (15). As the image suggests, the nation-community is embodied metonymically in the finite, sovereign, fraternal figure of the citizen-soldier.

Anderson argues that European bourgeoisies were distinguished by their ability to "achieve solidarity on an essentially imagined basis" (74) on a scale far greater than that of elites of other times and places. Writing and literacy play a central role in this argument. Anderson maintains, as have others, that the main instrument that made bourgeois nation-building projects possible was print capitalism. The commercial circulation of books in the various European vernaculars, he argues, was what first created the invisible networks that would eventually constitute the literate elites and those they ruled as nations. (Estimates are that 180 million books were put into circulation in Europe between the years 1500 and 1600 alone.)

Now obviously this style of imagining of modern nations, as Anderson describes it, is strongly utopian, embodying values like equality, fraternity, liberty, which the societies often profess but systematically fail to realize. The prototype of the modern nation as imagined community was, it seemed to me, mirrored in ways people thought about language and the speech community. Many commentators have pointed out how modern views of language as code and competence assume a unified and homogeneous social world in which language exists as a shared patrimony—as a device, precisely, for imagining community. An image of a universally shared literacy is also part of the picture. The prototypical manifestation of language is generally taken to be the speech of individual adult native speakers face-to-face (as in Saussure's famous diagram) in monolingual, even monodialectal situations—in short, the most homogeneous case linguistically and socially. The same goes for written communication. Now one could certainly imagine a theory that assumed different things—that argued, for instance, that the most revealing speech situation for understanding language was one involving a gathering of people each of whom spoke two languages and understood a third and held only one language in common with any of the others. It depends on what workings of language you want to see or want to see first, on what you choose to define as normative.

In keeping with autonomous, fraternal models of community, analyses of language use commonly assume that principles of cooperation and shared understanding are normally in effect. Descriptions of interactions between people in conversation, classrooms, medical and bureaucratic settings, readily take it for granted that the situation is governed by a single set of rules or norms shared by all participants. The analysis focuses then on how those rules produce or fail to produce an orderly, coherent exchange. Models involving games and moves are often used to describe interactions. Despite whatever conflicts or systematic social differences might be in play, it is assumed that all participants are engaged in the same game and that the game is the same for all players. Often it is. But of course it often is not, as, for example, when speakers are from different classes or cultures, or one party is exercising authority and another is submitting to it or questioning it. Last year one of my children moved to a new elementary school that had more open classrooms and more flexible curricula than the conventional school he started out in. A few days into the term, we asked him what it was like at the new school. "Well," he said, "they're a lot nicer, and they have a lot less rules. But know why they're nicer?" "Why?" I asked. "So you'll obey all the rules they don't have," he replied. This is a very coherent analysis with considerable elegance and explanatory power, but probably not the one his teacher would have given.

When linguistic (or literate) interaction is described in terms of orderliness, games, moves, or scripts, usually only legitimate moves are actually named as part of the system, where legitimacy is defined from the point of view of the party in authority—regardless of what other parties might see themselves as doing. Teacher-pupil language, for example, tends to be described almost entirely from the point of view of the teacher and teaching, not from the point of view of pupils and pupiling (the word doesn't even exist, though the thing certainly does). If a classroom is analyzed as a social world unified and homogenized with respect to the teacher, whatever students do other than what the teacher specifies is invisible or anomalous to the analysis. This can be true in practice as well. On several occasions my fourth grader, the one busy obeying all the rules they didn't have, was given writing assignments that took the form of answering a series of questions to build up a paragraph. These questions often asked him to identify with the interests of those in power over him—parents, teachers, doctors, public authorities. He invariably sought ways to resist or subvert these assignments. One assignment, for instance, called for imagining "a helpful invention." The students were asked to write single-sentence responses to the following questions:

What kind of invention would help you?

How would it help you?

Why would you need it?

What would it look like?

Would other people be able to use it also?

What would be an invention to help your teacher?

What would be an invention to help your parents?

Manuel's reply read as follows:

A grate adventchin

Some inventchins are GRATE!!!!!!!!!!! My inventchin would be a shot that would put every thing you learn at school in your brain. It would help me by letting me graduate right now!! I would need it because it would let me play with my friends, go on vacachin and, do fun a lot more. It would look like a regular shot. Ather peaple would use to. This inventchin would help my teacher parents get away from a lot of work. I think a shot like this would be GRATE!

Despite the spelling, the assignment received the usual star to indicate the task had been fulfilled in an acceptable way. No recognition was available, however, of the humor, the attempt to be critical or contestatory, to parody the structures of authority. On that score, Manuel's luck was only slightly better than Guaman Poma's. What is the place of unsolicited oppositional discourse, parody, resistance, critique in the imagined classroom community? Are teachers supposed to feel that their teaching has been most successful when they have eliminated such things and unified the social world, probably in their own image? Who wins when we do that? Who loses?

Such questions may be hypothetical, because in the United States in the 1990s, many teachers find themselves less and less able to do that even if they want to. The composition of the national collectivity is changing and so are the styles, as Anderson put it, in which it is being imagined. In the 1980s in many nation-states, imagined national syntheses that had retained hegemonic force began to dissolve. Internal social groups with histories and lifeways different from the official ones began insisting on those histories and lifeways *as part of their citizenship,* as the very mode of their membership in the national collectivity. In their dialogues with dominant institutions, many groups began asserting a rhetoric of belonging that made demands beyond those of representation and basic rights granted from above. In universities we started to hear, "I don't just want you to let me be here, I want to belong here; this institution should belong to me as much as it does to anyone else." Institutions have responded with, among other things, rhetorics of diversity and multiculturalism whose import at this moment is up for grabs across the ideological spectrum.

These shifts are being lived out by everyone working in education today, and everyone is challenged by them in one way or another. Those of us committed to educational democracy are particularly challenged as that notion finds itself besieged on the public agenda. Many of those who govern us display, openly, their interest in a quiescent, ignorant, manipulable electorate. Even as an ideal, the concept of an enlightened citizenry seems to have disappeared from the national imagination. A couple of years ago the university where I work went through an intense and wrenching debate over a narrowly defined Western-culture requirement that had been instituted there in 1980. It kept boiling down to a debate over the ideas of national patrimony, cultural citizenship, and imagined community. In the end, the requirement was transformed into a much more broadly defined course called Cultures, Ideas, Values.[4] In the context of the change, a new course was designed that centered on the Americas and the multiple cultural histories (including European ones) that have intersected here. As you can imagine, the course attracted a very diverse student body. The classroom functioned not like a homogeneous community or a horizontal alliance but like a contact zone. Every single text we read stood in specific historical relationships to the students in the class, but the range and variety of historical relationships in play were enormous. Everybody had a stake in nearly everything we read, but the range and kind of stakes varied widely.

It was the most exciting teaching we had ever done, and also the hardest. We were struck, for example, at how anomalous the formal lecture became in a contact zone (who can forget Atahuallpa throwing down the Bible because it would not speak to him?). The lecturer's traditional (imagined) task—unifying the world in the class's eyes by means of a monologue that rings equally coherent, revealing, and true for all, forging an ad hoc community, homogeneous with respect to one's own words—this task became not only impossible but anomalous and unimaginable. Instead, one had to work in the knowledge that whatever one said was going to be systematically received in radically heterogeneous ways that we were neither able nor entitled to prescribe.

The very nature of the course put ideas and identities on the line. All the students in the class had the experience, for example, of hearing their culture discussed and objectified in ways that horrified them; all the students saw their roots traced back to legacies of both glory and shame; all the students experienced face-to-face the ignorance and incomprehension, and occasionally the hostility, of others. In the absence of community values and the hope of synthesis, it was easy to forget the positives; the fact, for instance, that kinds of marginalization once taken for granted were gone. Virtually every student was having the experience of seeing the world described with him or her in it. Along with rage, incomprehension, and pain, there were exhilarating moments of wonder and revelation, mutual understanding, and new wisdom—the joys of the contact zone. The sufferings and revelations were, at different moments to be sure, experienced by every student. No one was excluded, and no one was safe.

The fact that no one was safe made all of us involved in the course appreciate the importance of what we came to call "safe houses." We used the term to refer to social and intellectual spaces where groups can constitute themselves as horizontal, homogeneous, sovereign communities with high degrees of trust, shared understandings, temporary protection from legacies of oppression. This is why, as we realized, multicultural curricula should not seek to replace ethnic or women's studies, for example. Where there are legacies of subordination, groups need places for healing and mutual recognition, safe houses in which to construct shared understandings, knowledges, claims on the world that they can then bring into the contact zone.

Meanwhile, our job in the Americas course remains to figure out how to make that crossroads the best site for learning that it can be. We are looking for the pedagogical arts of the contact zone. These will include, we are sure, exercises in storytelling and in identifying with the ideas, interests, histories, and attitudes of others; experiments in transculturation and collaborative work and in the arts of critique, parody, and comparison (including unseemly comparisons between elite and vernacular cultural forms); the redemption of the oral; ways for people to engage with suppressed aspects of history (including their own histories), ways to move *into and out of* rhetorics of authenticity; ground rules for communication across lines of difference and hierarchy that go beyond politeness but maintain mutual respect; a systematic approach to the all-important concept of *cultural mediation*. These arts were in play in every room at the extraordinary Pittsburgh conference on literacy. I learned a lot about them there, and I am thankful.

Notes

1. For an introduction in English to these and other aspects of Guaman Poma's work, see Rolena Adorno. Adorno and Mercedes Lopez-Baralt pioneered the study of Andean symbolic systems in Guaman Poma.

2. It is far from clear that the *Royal Commentaries* was as benign as the Spanish seemed to assume. The book certainly played a role in maintaining the identity and aspirations of indigenous elites in the Andes. In the mid-eighteenth century, a new edition of the *Royal Commentaries* was suppressed by Spanish authorities because its preface included a prophecy by Sir Walter Raleigh that the English would invade Peru and restore the Inca monarchy.

3. The discussion of community here is summarized from my essay "Linguistic Utopias."

4. For information about this program and the contents of courses taught in it, write Program in Cultures, Ideas, Values (CIV), Stanford Univ., Stanford, CA 94305.

Works Cited

Adorno, Rolena. *Guaman Poma de Ayala: Writing and Resistance in Colonial Peru.* Austin: U of Texas P, 1986.
Anderson, Benedict. *Imagined Communities: Reflections on the Origins and Spread of Nationalism.* London: Verso, 1984.
Garcilaso de la Vega, El Inca. *Royal Commentaries of the Incas.* 1613. Austin: U of Texas P, 1966.
Guaman Poma de Ayala, Felipe. *El primer nueva corónica y buen gobierno.* Manuscript. Ed. John Murra and Rolena Adorno. Mexico: Siglo XXI, 1980.
Pratt, Mary Louise. "Linguistic Utopias." *The Linguistics of Writing.* Ed. Nigel Fabb et al. Manchester: Manchester UP, 1987. 48–46.
Treviño, Gloria. "Cultural Ambivalence in Early Chicano Prose Fiction." Diss. Stanford U, 1985.

SUGGESTIONS FOR DISCUSSION

1. Compare with other students how you have divided Mary Louise Pratt's essay into sections and how you have annotated it. The point here is not to decide whether one set of divisions and annotations is better than another but to use all those available to put together a reading of the essay by reconstructing its development and its general line of argument. Your task here is to explain how (or whether) the essay establishes a central perspective from its various parts.

2. Pratt's notion of the "arts of the contact zone" is not without its difficulties. At the end of her discussion of Guaman Poma's letter, she offers the following summary:

> Autoethnography, transculturation, critique, collaboration, bilingualism, mediation, parody, denunciation, imaginary dialogue, vernacular expression—these are some of the literate arts of the contact zone. Miscomprehension, incomprehension, dead letters, unread masterpieces, absolute heterogeneity of meaning—these are some of the perils of writing in the contact zone. They all live among us today in the transnationalized metropolis of the United States and are becoming more widely visible, …more decipherable to those who once would have ignored them in defense of a stable, centered sense of knowledge and reality.

Take your time deciphering this passage, for it is a complicated one. At the same time, it is a crucial passage in the essay where Pratt is summing up what she sees as the significance of Guaman Poma's letter and where she is preparing readers for the final sections of the essay. Work together with other students to clarify the meaning of this passage and how it represents Pratt's overall line of thought.

3. Each of the first three selections in this chapter relies on a central metaphor to describe the lived realities of multicultural America. Ishmael Reed uses "bouillabaise," in contrast to the conventional image of America as a melting pot while Portes and Stepick locate America "on the edge" and Anzaldua as a "borderland." By the same token, Pratt offers the metaphor of the "contact zone" to describe culture as a complicated intersection and interaction of various languages, cultural practices, knowledges, beliefs, and perspectives, in contrast to the representation of culture as "discrete, coherently structured, monolingual edifices." Compare these metaphors of cultural experience. What do they have in common? How do they differ? What changes do they ask readers to make in their understandings of American culture? What do you see as the benefits or liabilities of these changes?

SUGGESTIONS FOR WRITING

1. Write a letter to a friend at another college who has not read Mary Louise Pratt's "Arts of the Contact Zone." Assume that your friend is interested in thinking about new ways to describe and analyze American culture. In the letter, explain Pratt's main line of thought and what she is arguing about the nature of American culture. You will need to explain the meanings Pratt derives from Guaman Poma's letter, but it may help your friend, who has not read the essay, to use other examples of the "contact zone" as well. Since this is a letter to a friend, you will also want to describe your own experience working through Pratt's essay and to explain your own sense of the value of thinking about American culture as a "contact zone."

2. In many respects, Pratt's analysis of Guaman Poma's letter is the centerpiece of her essay, the occasion that she uses to develop her notion of the "literate arts of the contact zone." If her term is useful, then you should be able to apply it to other, more contemporary forms of cultural expression. Write an essay that works with the notion of the "contact zone," that uses it as a practical tool of analysis to discuss what you see as a form of cultural expression written, produced, or performed in the contact

zone. The choice of materials is up to you, but keep in mind how Guaman Poma's letter represents the experience of outsiders to the dominant
culture. You might think, for example, of how African Americans, Hispanics, Asians, Jews, Irish, Italians, or gays and lesbians represent themselves
to mainstream American culture, or how children and young people represent themselves to adult society.

3. Pratt is offering a view of American culture and the communities in which
   Americans live that contrasts dramatically with conventional ideas about a
   common, unified national culture and communities that share a common
   way of life. Think of the various communities in which you have lived—
   the particular neighborhood, town, or region of the country where you
   have grown up in, the community in which you participate at school or
   at work, in the military, in church, and so forth. Write an essay that uses
   Pratt's notion of the "contact zone" to contrast the view that particular
   community holds of itself as a unified body with Pratt's sense that communities are invariably based on the interactions of cultural differences as
   much as on the similarities of its members. Begin your essay by describing how the community of which you are writing represents itself in
   terms of common values and beliefs. Then use Pratt's notion of "contact
   zones" to redescribe that community as insiders and outsiders representing themselves and their differences to each other.

PERSPECTIVES: THE HIP-HOP NATION

Hip-hop culture emerged in black America in the late 1970s and early 1980s,
a young, largely male, urban style conveyed by rappers, graffiti artists, break
dancers, and the large crew who make up what the two music critics presented here call the "hip-hop nation." Many predicted in its early days that
hip-hop was just another musical and cultural fad, likely to disappear within a
few years. Of course, just the opposite occurred. Hip-hop styles and attitudes
spread as the audience for rap music grew and diversified, making rap a mass-
market cross-over phenomenon as well as a street-wise credential. The following two selections appeared together, as a pair, under the title "The Hip-Hop
Nation: Whose Is It?" in the *New York Times* in the summer of 1999, staging a
discussion of the current state of hip-hop culture, its meanings, boundaries,
and membership, and raising pointed questions about race relations in the
contemporary United States.

A Land with Rhythm and Beats for All

Neil Strauss

Neil Strauss is a music critic at the *New York Times*, where he reviews popular
music recordings and shows. As you will see, both he and Touré in the accompanying article begin with the problem of mapping the hip-hop nation. In

Strauss's version of mapmaking, the borders of the hip-hop nation cannot be drawn according to an oversimplified black-white dichotomy. Instead, as Strauss says, they are "more fluid and blurry than many people would like to believe."

SUGGESTION FOR READING

Notice that Strauss begins, in the first four paragraphs, by describing a hip-hop nation based on "White Imperialism" and "cultural theft." Then, in the fifth paragraph, he shifts to "another nation," which he goes on to characterize as "beyond racial boundaries and mythologies." As you read the rest of the selection, consider whether the evidence Strauss offers adequately supports this characterization.

I live in a country every map maker will respect. It is a place with many languages, cultural differences and alternate histories, as much a nation as ancient Rome or 19th-century England. A place my countrymen call White Imperialism, purposely invoking all of the bloody acquisition and manifest destiny that enabled nationalists throughout history to march to power. Our path to nationhood has been paved by many fathers: Alexander the Great, Napoleon, Cecil Rhodes, Hernando Cortés, General Custer and Pat Boone. And now we are coming for hip-hop.

Our army amassed at Woodstock '99. More than 200,000 troops strong. When DMX—who, more than most popular rappers before him, orients his music toward a strictly black audience—came on stage, the almost entirely white crowd pumped its collective fist in the air and sang along with every word, drowning out DMX himself as they shouted the lyrics to "My Niggas." Then our brave troops watched the most popular white rock bands of today—Kid Rock, Limp Bizkit, Insane Clown Posse, Everlast, Korn, Rage Against the Machine—shamelessly plunder every trick in the hip-hop book without every trying to display (with the sole exception of Everlast) any hip-hop credentials. And then our army raped, pillaged and looted. That's what armies do.

And, yes, the revolution was televised.

And so it goes: rap—like most everything from the blues to alternative rock before it—has been officially embraced by those who originally ostracized it, avariciously consumed by those it was invented in part to declare independence from.

At least this is one way to see it, chalking up the immense popularity of rap among white musicians and fans to a tradition of cultural theft going back to the days of minstrelsy, when white entertainers would visit plantations to gather new songs and dances from slaves. This may be part of the picture, but it's not the whole picture.

Because I also live in another nation. It is a country no map maker, cultural critic, radio programmer or marketing consultant will ever respect. A place where the language, culture and history are always changing. A place many of my countrymen don't even know they are living in. It is a world beyond racial boundaries and mythologies. It has no name, but for now we can call it Gray, because it is neither black nor white. Map makers and radio programmers are people who need borders, but this world eludes them because it has no clear borders, and we don't want it to.

In this nation, the boundaries are more fluid and blurry than many people would like to believe: white people are listening to and using elements of rap not for theft but because they relate to it, because the music is a legitimate part of their cultural heritage. Black and white music fans are driving around flipping back and forth between the local rock and rap radio stations, simply looking for the best song.

In this nation, white rappers like Eminem are moving freely between urban and rock radio, between guest appearances on rap and rock records, between hard rock and gangsta rap concerts without changing a word or note. And in this nation black rappers are finding that it is now possible to serve both the black and the white audience without betraying either; they are finding that any adolescent who has ever felt victimized can relate to most rap lyrics because pop music has always communicated through metaphor, innuendo and fantasy; and they are finding that certain common denominators transcend race, as in the Jay Z and DMX song "Money, Cash, Hoes."

In 1999, not only is the most important and popular white music being made derived from rap, but hip-hop is easily the most important genre in America. It dominates popular music. Everything from Europop to teeny-bop incorporates some elements of hip-hop, even the genre's trailblazers, the Sugar Hill Gang, have transformed into a loveable oldies act that just recorded a kid's album and is currently touring with Britney Spears.

All of this makes the notion of race and rap an extremely complicated one, in which creating a black-white dichotomy is an over-simplification. The hip-hop nation, the imperialist nation and the gray nation exist simultaneously and overlap one another (as well as portions of many other nations, including Latin American and Asian American ones, that have taken hip-hop to heart), all of them muddled together in a society that remains on the whole a racist one.

In the suburbs, rap has been integral to youth life style since at least 1986, when for the first time a rap album (by the Beastie Boys) crossed over to No. 1 on the Billboard charts. Back then, when white kids—the Beastie Boys, Rick Rubin and hard-rock bands like Faith No More and Anthrax—were getting into rap, it was a genre they were just discovering. But today, rap (with 70 percent of its records sold to a white audience) is like the Beatles. It is a birth-right, something white kids grow up listening to, a standard by which they calibrate their lifetime notion of pop music. And as they grow older the music they want to make and hear is music that incorporates both genres (just as Kid Rock says today that he was weaned on both Lynyrd Skynrd and Big Daddy Kane).

White kids are also intrinsically attracted to hip-hop because it is the only popular music genre that their rockist baby-boomer parents just don't get. The great lie of hip-hop, what has enabled it to remain vital for some 20 years, is that it is a heavily coded dialogue made by and for the urban black community. But the more street and coded hip-hop becomes (as in the music of Juvenile, DMX, JT Money or Trick Daddy), the more attractive it is to a middle-class white audience. Not only do more insider rules and street signifiers make the club more exciting to join; they also increase rap's power as fuel for the escapist suburban dreams that were formerly the domain of heavy metal.

So, understandably, there is a lot of hand-wringing going on in the rap community, because the music's mission to spread across the land has succeeded all too well. White kids are walking around calling each other nigger, wearing T-shirts that say "pimpin' ain't easy" and flashing gang signs they don't understand. Judging by the movie *Bulworth,* even Warren Beatty seems possessed by a desire to be a young black man in America today. In the meantime, scores of white bands are incorporating hip-hop DJ's while just as many are rapping, but most without paying more than lip service to the culture the music came from. So is all of this easing the difficulty of being black in America or exacerbating it? The genre is slipping through the fingers of those who need it most, and they understandably don't want to let it go.

But rest assured, as hip-hop leaves its original context, it transmutes (just as gospel became rhythm-and-blues in a secular environment and rhythm-and-blues became rock-and-roll when Alan Freed didn't want it to seem as if his 1950's white radio audience was listening to black music). The best hip-hop performers will always be black, just as the best blues performers were. Eric Clapton plays the blues, he knows the blues, he feels the blues, he even releases whole albums of the blues, but nonetheless few people see him as a bluesman. What most white performers are doing with rap is hijacking it, using it to breathe new life into their music, not unlike what the Beatles and the Rolling Stones did with the blues (or what Jamaicans like Coxsone Dodd and the Skatalites did with American R-and-B). Who knows? Maybe it will even result in a genre as important as what we now fondly refer to as classic rock.

"I don't think it's a put-down to say that a white kid can't sing a black man's music," the former Rolling Stones bassist Bill Wyman said in a recent interview in *The Oxford American*. "If you really love the music, you can get pretty close and you can do it your way—you don't do it their way. You start off with their ideas, and you just slightly adapt them to suit you."

There are already at least five genres of white rap: the metal-rap of Limp Bizkit and Kid Rock; the post modern rap-rock collage of Beck and Beta Band; the lewd, sophomoric joke-rap of the Insane Clown Posse and Twiztid; the gentle, spoken kiddie rap of 1,000 Clowns and LFO, and the all-embracing, old-school-conscious rap, punk and electro fusion of the Beastie Boys and Len.

Since Vanilla Ice's spurious rap credentials were exposed, few white bands have tried to claim hip-hop credibility. The best way to gain acceptance is to show knowledge but admit outsider status, as Kid Rock and Eminem do, using rap to speak about growing up impoverished and white. In some cases, indulging in the same mythomania that gangsta rappers do.

"If you ain't never been to the ghetto, don't ever come to the ghetto, because you wouldn't understand the ghetto," Naughty by Nature warned off all pretenders in 1991. And for the most part they stayed away, with Kid Rock boasting in 1999, "I ain't straight outta Compton, I'm straight out the trailer." Eminem, despite naming himself after a candy that can be any color on the outside but is always dark on the inside, is quick to acknowledge his precedents. In songs, he describes himself as a "corny-looking white boy" and puts himself in the context of previous white rappers (including MC Serch of 3rd Bass and the former House of Pain member turned rocker Everlast) with the lyrics, "I'm on a Serch to crush a Milkbone/I'm Everlasting/I'll melt Vanilla Ice like silicone."

The new rap movie *Whiteboys* begins by depicting three teenagers from the cornfields of Iowa freestyle rapping and beat-boxing in their bedroom. But in the end, the movie's white, Jewish creator, Danny Hoch, imbues the film with the message that whitey just doesn't get it: you have to live it to rap it. It is a message that paradoxically gives him status as an insider (he gets to rap with Snoop Doggy Dogg on the soundtrack). Similarly, Everlast admits his lack of rock as well as rap credentials with the album title *Whitey Ford Sings the Blues,* and it was the predominantly white rap group 3rd Bass that condemned Vanilla Ice the most, creating a video that depicted the rapper getting beat up for faking the funk. But maybe the thesis that you have to live it to rap it is another fallacy, given the wide spectrum of class backgrounds that successful rappers come from. All you have to do is rap it as if you live it.

So who owns hip-hop? Is it the sub-section of fans that rolls blunts with Dutch Masters, uses up-to-date slang and knows what an MPC 2000 is? Is it members of the white lower class, one of the only minorities in America that it's still P.C. to denigrate, or is it all African Americans under 35? Is it bands like the Beastie Boys and DJ's like Craze, the X-ecutioners and Shadow, who keep alive the less mainstream aspects of the hip-hop arts? Is it corporations that use hip-hop to sell hamburgers, like McDonald's, or clothes, like Tommy Hilfiger? Is it Seagrams, Time Warner and Thorn-EMI, the multinational conglomerates that distribute most of the music?

Or is it the black Chicago businesswoman with the Lexus and the white kid flipping burgers, the Crip in Compton and the frat boy in Arizona, the French mama's boy in a track suit with one leg rolled up and the Kurdish teenager with a drawer full of every bootleg American cassette he can find? Because there is rap music that speaks to all these people. This, at the dawn of a new millennium, is the hip-hop empire: an aggregation of many nations, under God, very divisible, with rhymes and beats for all.

In the End, Black Men Must Lead

Touré

Touré is a contributing editor to *Rolling Stone*. While Strauss focuses on the reasons rap music has become so popular among white fans and musicians, Touré concentrates on the leadership of the hip-hop nation, what he calls "our senator-MC's." As you will see, in the discussion about who belongs to the hip-hop nation, Strauss and Touré share a number of points in common, especially concerning its multicultural composition. Their differences are not so much a matter of taking polarized positions but of emphasizing different angles and perspectives.

SUGGESTION FOR READING

As you read, note the examples Touré gives to show how the hip-hop nation is a multiracial one, "swelling to include whites, women and Southerners." Nonetheless, he argues in the closing paragraphs that "urban black men will remain our leading speakers." Keep track of the reasons he offers to support this view.

I live in a country no map maker will every respect. A place with its own language, culture and history. It is as much a nation as Italy or Zambia. A place my countrymen call the Hip-Hop Nation, purposefully invoking all of the jingoistic pride that nationalists throughout history have leaned on. Our path to nationhood has been paved by a handful of fathers: Muhammad Ali with his ceaseless bravado, Bob Marley with his truth-telling rebel music, Huey Newton with his bodacious political style, James Brown with his obsession with funk.

We are a nation with no precise date or origin, no physical land, no single chief. But if you live in the Hip-Hop Nation, if you are not merely a fan of the music but a daily imbiber of the culture, if you sprinkle your conversation with phrases like off the meter (for something that's great) or got me open (for something that gives an explosive positive emotional release), if you know why Dutch Masters make better blunts than Phillies (they're thinner), if you know at a glance why Allen Iverson is hip-hop and Grant Hill is not, if you feel the murders of Tupac Shakur and the Notorious B.I.G. in the1997–98 civil war were assassinations (no other word fits), if you can say yes to all of these questions (and a yes to some doesn't count), then you know the Hip-Hop Nation is a place as real as America on a pre-Columbus atlas. It's there even though the rest of you ain't been there yet.

The Nation exists in any place where hip-hop music is being played or hip-hop attitude is being exuded. Once I went shopping for a Macintosh. The salesman, a wiry 20-something white guy, rattled on about Macs, then, looking at the rapper, or what we call an MC, on my

T-shirt, said: "You like Nas? Did you hear him rhyme last night on the 'Stretch and Bobbito' show? I felt as if my jaw had dropped. He had invoked a legendary hip-hop radio show broadcast once a week on college radio at 2 in the morning. It was as if we were secret agents, and he had uttered the code phrase that revealed him to be my contact. We stood for an hour talking MC's and DJ's, beats and flows, turning that staid computer store into an outpost of the Hip-Hop Nation.

The Nation's pioneers were a multiracial bunch—whites were among the early elite graffiti artists and Latinos were integral to the shaping of DJing and MCing, b-boying (break dancing) and general hip-hop style. Today's Nation makes brothers of men black, brown, yellow and white. But this world was built to worship urban black maleness: the way we speak, walk, dance, dress, think. We are revered by others, but our leadership is and will remain black. As it should.

We are a nation with our own gods and devils, traditions and laws (one of them is to not share them with outsiders), but there has never been and never will be a president of the Hip-Hop Nation. Like black America, we're close-knit yet still too fractious for one leader. Instead, a powerful senate charts our future. That senate is made up of our leading MC's, their every album and single a bill or referendum proposing linguistic, musical and topical directions for the culture. Is Compton a cool spot? Can Edie Brickell, an embodiment of American female whiteness, be the source for a sample? Is a thick countrified Southern accent something we want to hear? Is police brutality still a rallying point? Like a politician with polls and focus groups, an MC must carefully calibrate his musical message because once the music is released, the people vote with their dollars in the store and their butts in the club, ignoring certain MC's and returning them to private life while anointing others, granting them time on our giant national microphone.

Unlike rhythm-and-blues, hip-hop has a strong memoristic impulse, meaning our senator-MC's speak about themselves, their neighborhoods, the people around them, playing autobiographer, reporter and oral historian. Telling the stories as they actually happened is what is meant by the catch phrase keeping it real. Outsiders laugh when that hallowed phrase is seemingly made hollow by obvious self-mythologizing—materialistic boasts that would be beyond even the Donald or tales of crimes that would be envied by a Gotti. But this bragging is merely people speaking of the people they dream of being, which, of course, is a reflection of the people they are.

How do you get into this senate? The answer is complex, involving both rhyming technique and force of personality. To be a great MC you must have a hypnotizing flow—a cadence and delivery that get inside the drum and bass patterns and create their own rhythm line. You must have a magnetic voice—it can be deliciously nasal like Q-Tip's, or delicate and sing-songy like Snoop Doggy Dogg's, or deep-toned like that of Rakim, who sounds as commanding as Moses—but it must be a compelling sound. And you must say rhymes with writerly details, up-to-the-minute slang, bold punch lines, witty metaphors and original political or sociological insights.

But, again like a politician, to be a great MC you must seem like an extension of the masses and, simultaneously, an extraordinary individual. There must be a certain down-homeness about you, a way of carrying yourself that replicates the way people in your home base feel about life. You must be the embodiment of your audience.

At the same time, you must seem greater than your audience. You must come across as supercool—an attitude based on toughness or sex appeal or intellect or bravado that inspires your listeners to say, I'd like to be you.

In the first decade and a half after the first hip-hop record was released in 1979, hip-hop was a national conversation—about urban poverty and police brutality, the proliferation of guns and the importance of safe sex, as well as the joy of a good party—in which the only speakers were black men.

In recent years that conversation has opened up. Hip-hop has become more democratic, cracking the monopoly that black men from New York and L.A. have long held over the Hip-Hop Nation senate.

Traditionally, hip-hop has been hypermodern, disdaining the surreal for gritty images of urban life. But Missy Elliott and her producer, Timbaland, have constructed a post-modern esthetic that manifests itself, on her latest album, *Da Real World,* in references to the sci-fi film *The Matrix* and videos in which Missy dresses as if she were in a scene from the 1982 movie *Blade Runner*. Her music also has a futuristic feel, from Timbaland's spare, propulsive beats filled with quirky sounds that evoke science-fiction to Missy's experiments with singing and rhyming, as well as using onomatopoeias in her rhymes. The duo have become part of the Nation's sonic vanguard, as well as door-openers for a new genre: hip-hop scifi.

Groups from the South Coast like GooDie Mob, Eightball and MJG and Outkast have also brought new perspectives. (The Hip-Hop Nation reconfigures American geography with a Saul Steinberg-like eye, maximizing cities where the most important hip-hop has come from, microscoping other places. When we speak of the East Coast, we mean the five boroughs of New York, Long Island, Westchester County, New Jersey and Philadelphia; by West Coast we mean Los Angeles, Compton, Long Beach, Vallejo and Oakland; and the region made up of Atlanta, New Orleans, Virginia, Miami and Memphis is called the South Coast.)

Outkast is a pair of Atlanta MC's, Dre (Andre Benjamin) and Big Boi (Antwan Patton), who are not new to many in the Hip-Hop Nation. But with the success of *Aquemini,* their third album, and months of touring as the opening act for Lauryn Hill, they are new to power within hip-hop. Their hip-hop mixes the cerebraness of New York rappers and the George Clinton–drenched funk favored out West with a particularly Southern musicality, soulfulness, twang-drenched rhymes and Baptist churchlike euphoric joy.

But the most polarizing and revolutionary new entry to the hip-hop senate is Eminem (born Marshall Mathers). There have been white MC's before him, but none have been as complex. Either they were clearly talentless (like Vanilla Ice) or they worshipped blackness (like MC Serch of 3rd Bass). Eminem is different. The fervency of fans, black and white, marveling at his skill and laughing at his jokes, has kept him in office, despite those offended by his whiny white-boy shock-jock shtick.

He is an original voice in the national conversation that is hip-hop because he speaks of the dysfunctionality of his white-trash world—his absentee father, his drugged-out mom, his daughter's hateful mother, his own morally bankrupt conscience. With Eminem the discussion turns to problems in the white community, or at least—because he is from a black neighborhood in Detroit—to the problems of whites in the black community. On a recent song (called "Busa Rhyme" from Missy's new album *Da Real World*) Eminem rhymes darkly: "I'm homicidal/ and suicidal/ with no friends/ holdin' a gun with no handle / just a barrel at both ends." Finally someone has arrived to represent the Dylan Klebolds and Eric Harrises of America.

A rash of overprotectiveness within our nation keeps many fans from enjoying the hip-hop of a sneering white MC, but why shouldn't we welcome a frank discussion of white maladies into our homes when millions of white people allow our MC's into their homes to talk about our disorders every day?

The Hip-Hop Nation senate is swelling to include whites, women and Southerners, but don't expect that senate to become a true melting pot anytime soon. As long as upper-class white men stay in charge of the United States Senate, urban black men will remain our leading speakers. Hip-hop's history is long enough to grant us the maturity to open our world, but America is still white enough that we know we need our own oasis.

It all began with a few parties. Jams in New York city parks thrown by DJ's like Kool Herc, Grandmaster Flash and Afrika Bambaataa. To your eyes it would've appeared to be a rapper in a public park, a DJ behind him, his cables plugged into the street lamp, the police not far away, waiting for just the right moment to shut it all down. But to us those parks were the center of a universe. The cops—or rather, five-oh (from the television series *Hawaii Five-O*)—were Satan. The music—James Brown, Sly Stone, Funkadelic and anything with a stone cold bass and drum rhythm you could rhyme over—breathed meaning and substance and soul into our bodies. It gave life. It was God.

From behind the turntables in his roped-off pulpit in the park, the DJ gave a rousing sermon sonically praising God's glory. Then up stepped the High Priest, the conduit between God and you—the MC. How crucial was he? In 1979, in its seminal song, "Rapper's Delight," the Sugar Hill Gang explained that even Superman was useless if he couldn't flow: "He may be able to fly all through the night / But can he rock a party til the early light?"

A few years later, in the early 80's, a trickle of cassettes began appearing in urban mom-and-pop record stores like Skippy White's on Blue Hill Avenue in Mattapan Square in Boston. As a 12-year-old I would walk there from my father's office. Every other month or so a new hip-hop tape would arrive, direct from New York City: Run-DMC…MC Shan…the Fat Boys. A kid on an allowance could own all the hip-hop albums ever made. For all the force of the music, the culture was so small and precious you held it in your hands as delicately as a wounded bird.

In the mid-80's hip-hop won the nation's attention and was branded a fad that would soon die like disco. Hip-hoppers closed ranks, constructed a wall and instituted a siege mentality. We became like Jews, a tribe that knew how close extinction was and responded to every attack and affront, no matter how small, as if it were a potential death blow. Where Jews battle anti-Semitic attitudes and actions, we fought fans who are not orthodox and music not purely concerned with art. Where Jews hold holidays that celebrate specific legends, ancestors and miracles, hip-hoppers spoke of the old school with a holy reverence and urged new jacks to know their history. Our Zionism was the Hip-Hop Nation.

By the late 80's and early 90's mainstreaming had arrived bringing powerful gifts, as the devil always does. Now our music was broadcast on prime-time MTV and our political views, via Chuck D and KRS-One, were heard on CNN and *Nightline* Hip-hop, like jazz and rock-and-roll before it, had become the defining force of a generation. It was not going to die. The siege mentality subsided.

The guards at the gate were retired. The fan base grew, and the music diversified, which caused the fan base to grow larger still and the music to diversify further. But we continue to live in America, to suffer the daily assaults of racism. And our sanity continues to rely on having a place where the heroes look like us and play by our rules. As long as being a black man is a cross to bear and not a benediction, you can find me and my comrades locked inside one of those mass therapy sessions called a party, inside that tri-coastal support group called the Hip-Hop Nation.

SUGGESTIONS FOR DISCUSSION

1. How do Neil Strauss and Touré answer the question "The Hip-Hop Nation: Whose Is It?" To what extent do their answers overlap? To what extent do they offer different perspectives? Notice that in a number of instances they draw on the same examples, such as Vanilla Ice and Eminem, as evidence. What points do they want to make with these examples—the same or different ones? In the end, are there points of disagreement that divide them?

2. While some forms of popular music are largely limited to particular sub-cultures, rap music can be heard everywhere from boom boxes on city streets to television advertising. It is hard to imagine someone who has never encountered it. Work in a group with three or four other students. Describe each of your experiences with rap music and hip-hop culture. When did you become aware of it? Would you describe yourself as a casual listener, fan, or participant? What role, if any, does it play in your life or the lives of people you know? What meanings do you associate with rap and the people who listen to it? After you have answered these questions individually, consider what patterns you can identify in the responses. How do these patterns compare to points Strauss and Touré make in their articles on the hip-hop nation?

3. Both Strauss and Touré want to avoid simplistic black-white dichotomies and to acknowledge hip-hop's multiracial and multicultural character. At the same time, each writer also holds that U.S. society remains on the whole a racist one. What issues concerning racial equality does rap seem to raise? In what ways is its popularity in the white suburbs a matter of "cultural theft"? How would you answer the question Strauss raises about hip-hop culture, "So is all of this easing the difficulty of being black in America or exacerbating it?"

SUGGESTIONS FOR WRITING

1. The two articles appeared in the weekly Arts and Leisure section of *The New York Times* in its Sunday edition. Write a response to Strauss and Touré for the letters section of Arts and Leisure. Take as your main purpose an assessment of the significance of their discussion and how they answer the question "The Hip-Hop Nation: Whose Is It?" Make sure you refer to specific points and perspectives each offers. You may align yourself with one of the writers and distance yourself from the other. Or you may want to provide commentary that does not depend on agreeing or disagreeing with the articles.

2. Imaging that the discussion "The Hip-Hop Nation: Whose Is It?" consisted of three articles. Write the third essay. Begin as both Strauss and Touré do with the phrase "I live in a country…" but complete the sentence with your own meaning. Follow Strauss's and Touré's example. Map what you see as the terrain, borders, and membership of the hip-hop nation. Then explain the significance and consequence of your perspective. Notice that neither Strauss nor Touré replies directly to the other but each covers similar ground in his own way.

3. In many respects, both Strauss and Touré are grappling with one of the main issues in this chapter, namely how can we effectively characterize multicultural America. Consider their articles in light of the analyses and metaphors you find in the other selections in this chapter—especially the use of terms such as "melting pot," "cultural bouillabaisse," "border-land," and "contact zone." In what sense do the articles on hip-hop culture fit into or resist these characterizations of U.S. culture? How do they illustrate or illuminate the realities of multicultural America?

ENGLISH ONLY LEGISLATION

Case STUDY

In 1986, California was the first state to pass by ballot initiative an amendment to the state constitution declaring English as the official language. Since then, voters in three other states—Arizona, Colorado, and Florida—passed similar amendments, and nearly forty state legislatures have considered English Only laws, though such measures passed in only a handful of cases. Much of what you have read in this chapter—and elsewhere in the book—can help explain why the English Only movement has drawn such attention.

The issues posed by English Only legislation are serious ones, and are closely related to the multicultural practices and realities that you have been exploring in this chapter. Is it a matter of the common good for the state to make English the official language? Would it be better to encourage bilingualism in all spheres of life? Whose interests does English Only serve? What values does it affirm? What does it oppose? On whose behalf does it speak? Who becomes excluded? What relations of power come into play?

You can begin to formulate some answers to these and questions of your own by examining the primary documents concerning Proposition 63, the 1986 California initiative that became the first English language amendment to a state constitution in U.S. history. Included here is the original text of the amendment and arguments and rebuttals in favor of or against Proposition 63. All of these documents appeared on the state ballot at the time of the 1986 general election.

SUGGESTION FOR READING

Notice that two pairs of supporting and opposing statements appeared on the ballot—first an argument for Proposition 63, followed by rebuttal, and then an argument against Proposition 63, followed by its rebuttal. At first glance this may seem redundant. After all, there are only two sides—for or against. But the ballot follows the conventions of formal debate, which gives each side an opportunity to make its own presentation as well as to reply to its opponent's case.

Proposition 63, California State Ballot, 1986

TEXT OF PROPOSED LAW

This initiative measure is submitted to the people in accordance with the provisions of Article II, Section 8 of the Constitution.

This initiative measure amends the Constitution by adding sections thereto; therefore, new provisions proposed to be added are printed in *italic type* to indicate that they are new.

Proposed Amendment to Article III

Section 1. Section 6 is added to Article III of the Constitution to read as follows:

SEC. 6. (a) Purpose.

English is the common language of the people of the United States of America and the State of California. This section is intended to preserve, protect and strengthen the English language, and not to supersede any of the rights guaranteed to the people by this Constitution.

(b) English as the Official Language of California.

English is the official language of the State of California.

(c) Enforcement.

The Legislature shall enforce this section by appropriate legislation. The Legislature and officials of the State of California shall take all steps necessary to insure that the role of English as the common language of the State of California is preserved and enhanced. The Legislature shall make no law which diminishes or ignores the role of English as the common language of the State of California.

(d) Personal Right of Action and Jurisdiction of Courts.

Any person who is a resident of or doing business in the State of California shall have standing to sue the State of California to enforce this section, and the Courts of record of the State of California shall have jurisdiction to hear cases brought to enforce this section. The Legislature may provide reasonable and appropriate limitations on the time and manner of suits brought under this section.

Section 2. *Severability*

If any provision of this section, or the application of any such provision to any person or circumstance, shall be held invalid, the remainder of this section to the extent it can be given effect shall not be affected thereby, and to this end the provisions of this section are severable.

ARGUMENT* IN FAVOR OF PROPOSITION 63

The State of California stands at a crossroads. It can move toward fears and tensions of language rivalries and ethnic distrust. Or it can reverse that trend and strengthen our common bond, the English language.

Our immigrants learned English if they arrived not knowing the language. Millions of immigrants now living have learned English or are learning it in order to participate in our culture. With one *shared* language we learn to respect other people, other cultures, with sympathy and understanding.

Our American heritage is now threatened by language conflicts and ethnic separatism. Today, there is a serious erosion of English as our common bond. This amendment reaffirms California's oneness as a state, and as one of fifty states united by a common tongue.

This amendment establishes a broad principle: English is the official language of California. It is entitled to legal recognition and protection as such. No other language can have a similar status. This amendment recognizes in law what has long been a political and social reality.

Nothing in the amendment prohibits the use of languages other than English in unofficial situations, such as family communications, religious ceremonies or private business. Nothing in this amendment forbids teaching foreign languages. Nothing in this amendment removes or reduces any Californian's constitutional rights.

The amendment gives guidance to the Legislature, the Governor and the courts. Government must protect English:

- by passing no law that ignores or diminishes English;
- by issuing voting ballots and materials in English only (except where required by federal law);

*Arguments printed on this page are the opinions of the authors and have not been checked for accuracy by any official agency.

- by ensuring that immigrants are taught English as quickly as possible (except as required by federal law);
- by functioning in English, except where public health, safety and justice require the use of other languages;
- by weighing the effect of proposed legislation on the role of English; and
- by preserving and enhancing the role of English our common language.

Californians have already expressed themselves decisively. More than a million Californians asked to place this measure on the ballot, the third largest number of petition signatures in California history. In 1984, 70+ percent California voters, 6,300,000, approved Proposition "Voting Materials in English *ONLY*."

This amendment sends a clear message: English is the official language of California. To function, to participate in our society, we must know English. English is the language of opportunity, of government, of unity. English, a fundamental sense, is *US*.

Every year California's government makes decisions which ignore the role of English in our state; some may cause irreversible harm. Government's bilingual activities cost millions of taxpayers' dollars each year. This amendment will force government officials to stop and think before taking action.

The future of California hangs in the balance—a state divided or a state united—a true part of the Union. *YES* is for unity—for what is right and best for our state, for our country, and for all of us.

PLEASE VOTE *YES* ON PROPOSITION 63—FOR ENGLISH AS THE OFFICIAL LANGUAGE OF CALIFORNIA.

S. I. HAYAKAWA, Ph.D.
United States Senator, 1977–1982
J. WILLIAM OROZCO
Businessman
STANLEY DIAMOND
Chairman, California English Campaign

REBUTTAL TO ARGUMENT IN FAVOR OF PROPOSITION 63

Proposition 63 doesn't simply make English our "official" language; it seeks to make it California's *only* language. It does *nothing positive* to increase English proficiency. It only punishes those who haven't had a fair opportunity to learn it.

Proposition 63 threatens to isolate those who haven't yet mastered English from essential government services such as 911 emergency operators, public service announcements, schools, and courts. By preventing them from becoming better, more involved citizens while making the transition into American society, Proposition 63 will *discourage* rather than encourage the assimilation of new citizens.

Worse yet, because Proposition 63 amends the *Constitution,* its harmful effects will be virtually *permanent* and *unchangeable.* All governmental bodies, from the State Legislature to local school boards, police and hospitals will be powerless to meet the changing and varying needs of the public.

Proposition 63 is inflexible. It does not contain the exceptions the proponents claim. It has *no* exception for use of foreign languages where public health, safety and justice require.

Inevitable disputes over the meaning of Proposition 63 sweeping language will mean our government will be dragged into countless, costly lawsuits at taxpayers' expense.

America's greatness and uniqueness lie in the fact that we are a nation of diverse people with a shared commitment to democracy, freedom and fairness. *That* is the common bond which holds our nation and state together It runs much deeper than the English language.

Proposition 63 breeds intolerance and divisiveness. It betrays our democratic ideals.

Vote NO on Proposition 63!

THE HONORABLE DIANNE FEINSTEIN
Mayor, San Francisco
ART TORRES
State Senator, 24th District
STATE COUNCIL OF SERVICE EMPLOYEES

ARGUMENT AGAINST PROPOSITION 63

This summer we celebrated the 100th anniversary of the Statue of Liberty. That glorious 4th of July brought all Americans together. Now, four months later, Proposition 63 threatens to divide us and tarnish our proud heritage of tolerance and diversity.

This proposition, despite its title, does not preserve English as our common language. Instead, it undermines the efforts of new citizens of our state to contribute to and enter the mainstream of American life.

English is and will remain the language of California. Proposition 63 won't change that. What it *will* do is produce a nightmare of expensive litigation and needless resentment.

Proposition 63 could mean that state and local government must eliminate multilingual police, fire, and emergency services such as 911 telephone operators, thereby jeopardizing the lives and safety of potential victims.

It could mean that court interpreters for witnesses, crime victims, and defendants have to be eliminated.

It could outlaw essential multilingual public service information such as pamphlets informing non-English-speaking parents how to enroll their children in public schools.

Even foreign street signs and the teaching of languages in public schools could be in jeopardy.

We can hope that sensible court decisions will prevent these consequences. But Proposition 63 openly invites costly legal attempts to seek such results. It is certain to set Californian against Californian with tragic consequences.

What makes this especially troubling is that the overwhelming majority of immigrants *want* to learn English. In fact, a recent study shows that 98% of Latin parents say it is essential for their children to read and write English well.

Asians, Latinos and other recent immigrants fill long waiting lists for English courses at community colleges an adult schools. But this initiative does nothing *positive* to help. For instance, it provides for no increase in desperately needed night and weekend English classes.

The Los Angeles County Board of Supervisors, when faced with a negative local measure like this one, firmly and wisely rejected it by a unanimous, bipartisan vote. On April 21, 1986, they said in part:

"English as the official language resolutions will not help anyone learn English. They will not improve human relations, and they will not lead to a better community They will create greater intergroup tension and ill will, encourage resentment and bigotry, pit neighbor against neighbor and group against group. They reflect our worst fears, not our best values.

"In many areas...non-English-speaking persons have sometimes represented a problem for schoolteachers, service providers, law enforcement officers, who are unable to understand them. The problem will be solved over time as newcomers learn English. It has happened many times before in our history. In the meanwhile...common sense...good will, sensitivity, and humor will help us through this challenging period."

Well said by public officials representing both sides of the political spectrum.

Proposition 63 is unnecessary. It is negative and counterproductive. It is, in the most fundamental sense, un-American. Vote NO on Proposition 63!

JOHN VAN DE KAMP
Attorney General
WILLIE L. BROWN JR.
Speaker, California State Assembly
DARYL F. GATES
Police Chief, Los Angeles Police Department

REBUTTAL TO ARGUMENT AGAINST PROPOSITION 63

When this country was founded, immigrants from all over the world streamed to our shores with one hope—a chance at success. People with divergent backgrounds were forced into close contact, yet the assimilation of these cultures was remarkably constructive. This assimilation into one nation gave us a diversity, a strength and a uniqueness that today we treasure. Every schoolchild learns to marvel at the miracle of the American melting pot.

But the melting pot was not an accident. There was a common thread that tied society together. The common thread in early America and current California was the English language. Proposition 63 will strengthen the English language and invigorate our melting pot. It will not eliminate bilingual police and fire services. It will not prohibit the teaching of foreign languages in our schools. Instead, Proposition 63 will serve as a directional marker towards which we as society can point our new immigrants.

The official language proposition is not an attempt to isolate anyone. Indeed, it is the opposite. We want all immigrants to assimilate into our country. We believe to be a success in California and in the United States, you must be proficient in English. We want to cherish and preserve the ethnic diversity that adds strength and fiber to our society. Yet we remember the common thread binding us together as Americans is the English language. The melting pot has served this nation for 200 years. The ingredients may have varied, but this is no time to change the recipe. Vote yes on Proposition 63.

FRANK HILL
Member of the Assembly, 52nd District

SUGGESTIONS FOR DISCUSSION

1. Examine closely the "Text of Proposed Law." It is written in the formal and legalistic style of government documents and demands careful attention to read. Consider *SEC. 6*. How does (a) *Purpose* express the intent of the amendment? What assumptions does it seem to make? Now look at (c) *Enforcement*. What does the amendment entitle the state of California to do? What would "all steps necessary" actually look like in practice? Whom would it affect? What would be the consequences? Finally consider (d) *Personal Right of Action and Jurisdiction of Courts*. This section gives individuals the legal grounds to sue over breach of enforcement. Can you imagine a situation that would call for such legal action? Try to think of concrete instances of what suing would involve.

2. Consider the first set of argument and rebuttal. Notice that the argument in favor of Proposition 63 and the rebuttal invoke the notion of "our common bond" to make their case. But do they agree on what constitutes such a bond or who the "we" in "our" common bond might be? What fears or anxieties does each side seem to tap into? What is the significance of your answers that explain why the sides support or oppose Proposition 63?

3. Notice in the second set that the argument against Proposition 63 opens with the 100th anniversary of the familiar symbol of immigration, the Statue of Liberty, while the rebuttal begins by invoking the metaphor of the "melting pot" to describe the assimilation of immigrants. Both arguments tell the story of immigration to America, but they do so in very different ways. Describe the underlying narrative of immigration in each of the arguments. What purposes are these differing accounts of immigration meant to serve?

SUGGESTION FOR WRITING

Write your own analysis of how the two sides for and against Proposition 63 have posed the issues and sought to persuade voters to their views. What is the nature of the conflict? In what sense is it limited to questions of language use? To what extent does it raise larger questions about what it means to live in multicultural America? Draw on any of the readings in this chapter that seem useful to you in explaining your answers.

VISUAL CULTURE   *LANGUAGE POLICY*

The following two documents were designed to intervene in the English Only controversy. The first is a full-page ad that appeared in the *National Review*. As you can see, the group that sponsored the ad, U.S. English, founded in 1983 by Senator S. I. Hayakawa, is not only in favor of English Only legislation. It also opposes bilingual education. The second document is a pamphlet that presents the position on national language policy adopted in 1988 by the Conference on College Composition and Communication (CCCC), the leading professional association of college writing teachers.

SUGGESTIONS FOR DISCUSSION

1. The headline of the U.S. English ad compares immigrants of the past ("They knew they had to learn English") to those of the present ("today's immigrants are being misled"). The issue posed by U.S. English appears to be a simple matter of the truth on one hand (immigrants need "to learn English to survive") and a lie on the other ("you can make it without assimilating"). Are the issues, in your view, really so simple? What else might the ad suggest by its comparison of immigrants from the past to those of the present? Why do you think the ad designer pictures only immigrants from the past?

They knew they had to learn English to survive.

How come today's immigrants are being misled?

They learned without bilingual education. And without government documents in a multitude of languages. They knew they had to learn English before anything else.

But today, a whole new generation of Americans are being fed a lie by bureaucrats, educators and self-appointed leaders for immigrant groups. The lie says "you don't have to learn English because you can make it here without assimilating." The truth is this: without learning our shared language, an immigrant's dream of a better life will fade.

With nearly 700,000 members, we're the largest organization fighting to make English the official language of government at all levels. *Join us. Support us. Fight with us.* Because now more than ever, immigrants need to be told the truth.

Speak up for America. Call 1-800-U.S.ENGLISH

1747 Pennsylvania Avenue, NW, Suite 1100
Washington, DC 20006

2. The pamphlet "The National Language Policy" (page 549) has more space to develop its position than the English Only ad does. The CCCC pamphlet features no provocative headlines. What is the intended effect on readers of its understated tone and visual style? Notice how the pamphlet is divided into sections and how the sections are marked. How do the layout of the pamphlet and the way it organizes information contribute to its readability?

3. How do you imagine members of U.S. English would respond to the CCCC's "The National Language Policy"? What rebuttals and counterarguments might they make? Now ask the same questions about how CCCC might respond to the U.S. English ad. Do you see the English Only debate as hopelessly polarized with opposing sides deeply entrenched in their views? Can you imagine any common ground that they might share?

SUGGESTION FOR WRITING

Design a full-page ad or a pamphlet that presents your view for or against English Only legislation. Decide on a particular audience that you want to

SUPPORT THE NATIONAL LANGUAGE POLICY: WHAT YOU CAN DO

Strive to include all citizens of all language communities in the positive development of our daily activities.

Provide education, social services, legal services, medical services, and protective signing for linguistic minorities in their own languages so that basic human rights are preserved.

Emphasize the importance of learning second and third languages by all Americans so that we can:

- participate more effectively in worldwide activities
- unify diverse American communities
- enlarge our view of what is human

Recognize that those who do not speak English need time and encouragement to learn, but that their ability to prosper over the long term requires facility in the dominant American language.

Encourage immigrants to retain their first languages, to pass them on to their children, and to celebrate the life-supporting customs of their parents in the company of other Americans of differing backgrounds.

SELECTED TITLES

Adams, Karen L., and Daniel T. Brink, eds. *Perspectives on Official English: The Campaign for English as the Official Language in the USA.* New York: Mouton de Gruyter, 1990.

Baron, Dennis E. *The English Only Question.* New Haven: Yale University Press, 1990.

Butler, Melvin A., chair, and the Committee on CCCC Language Statement. "Students' Right to Their Own Language." Special Issue of *College Composition and Communication* 25 (Fall 1974): 1–32.

Crawford, James, ed. *Language Loyalties: A Source Book on the Official English Controversy.* Chicago: The University of Chicago Press, 1992.

Daniels, Harvey A., ed. *Not Only English: Affirming America's Multicultural Heritage.* Urbana, IL: NCTE, 1990.

Official English/English Only: More than Meets the Eye. Prepared for the National Education Association by John Trasvina. Washington, DC: National Education Association, 1988.

Piatt, Bill. *Only English? Law and Language Policy in the United States.* Albuquerque: University of New Mexico Press, 1990.

Smitherman-Donaldson, Geneva. "Toward a National Public Policy on Language." *College English* 49.1 (1987): 29–36.

BACKGROUND

The National Language Policy is a response to efforts to make English the "official" language of the United States. This policy recognizes the historical reality that, even though English has become the language of wider communication, we are a multilingual society. All people in a democratic society have the right to education, to employment, to social services, and to equal protection under the law. No one should be denied these or any civil rights because of linguistic differences. This policy would enable everyone to participate in the life of this multicultural nation by ensuring continued respect both for English, our common language, and for the many other languages that contribute to our rich cultural heritage.

CCCC NATIONAL LANGUAGE POLICY

Be it resolved that CCCC members promote the National Language Policy adopted at the Executive Committee meeting on March 16, 1988. This policy has three inseparable parts:

1. To provide resources to enable native and nonnative speakers to achieve oral and literate competence in English, the language of wider communication.

2. To support programs that assert the legitimacy of native languages and dialects and ensure that proficiency in one's mother tongue will not be lost.

3. To foster the teaching of languages other than English so that native speakers of English can rediscover the language of their heritage or learn a second language.

Passed unanimously by both the Executive Committee and the membership at the CCCC Annual Meeting in March 1988, the National Language Policy is now the official policy of the CCCC.

What raised the need for the Language Policy?

The English Only movement, which began in 1981 when Senator S. I. Hayakawa sponsored a constitutional amendment to make English the official language of the United States. Variations on his proposal have been before Congress ever since; there were five proposals in 1988 and three in 1990. The Language of Government Act has been pending before the House and Senate since 1991.

In 1983 an organization called "U.S. English" was founded by Senator Hayakawa and Dr. John Tanton, an ophthalmologist. That organization promotes English Only legislation, both in Congress and state legislatures. By June 1992, sixteen states had declared English the official language.

Some states, however, have taken stands against language protectionism. In 1989, New Mexico, Washington, and Oregon passed "English Plus" laws that protect the use of languages other than English and encourage the study of foreign languages. Both Hawaii and Louisiana have official policies aimed at preserving languages and cultures.

In February 1990, a federal district judge in Arizona ruled that the state's constitutional amendment making English the official language violated the First Amendment's protection of free speech.

What's wrong with English Only?

■ **It's unnecessary.**
English, the global lingua franca and the language of wider communication in this country, is not threatened. For two centuries, most immigrants learned English within a generation without any laws compelling them. Current immigrants are doing the same.

■ **It's unrealistic.**
Thousands of people are on waiting lists to enroll in English classes. Laws making English the official language do nothing to increase the number of such classes, nor do they teach a single person English.

■ **It's educationally unsound.**
English Only opposes bilingual and similar programs that help students build on their linguistic skills. When students cannot use their strengths, they experience alienation and failure. Prohibiting or discouraging diversity limits rather than expands learning opportunities.

■ **It's unfair and dangerous.**
When we pass laws that forbid health and safety information, street signs, court trials, and marriage ceremonies in languages people can understand, we deny them legal protection and social services.

■ **It's invasive.**
English Only laws violate the privacy of speakers of other languages. When Filipino hospital employees are told they cannot speak Tagalog in the lounge, or when a college employee is told he must not speak Spanish during lunch break, they are denied free expression.

■ **It's counterproductive.**
As members of the global community, we need speakers of different languages. It's shortsighted, anti-immigrant, and racist to demean and destroy the competencies of bilingual people.

■ **It's unconstitutional.**
The First Amendment guarantees freedom of speech. The Fourteenth Amendment forbids abridging the privileges and immunities of naturalized citizens. English Only laws violate these constitutional rights.

Who else opposes English Only?

The English Plus Information Clearinghouse (EPIC) was born in the fall of 1987. Housed at the headquarters of the Joint National Council on Languages in Washington, D.C., EPIC serves as a national repository for information helpful to the increasing number of scholarly, ethnic, and civil liberty organizations that oppose English Only legislation. *EPIC Events*, a bimonthly newsletter, keeps subscribers informed. According to EPIC's Statement of Purpose, the English Plus concept "holds that the national interest can best be served when all persons of our society have access to effective opportunities to acquire strong English proficiency *plus* mastery of a second or multiple languages."

More than forty civic, religious, and professional organizations have passed resolutions supporting the English Plus movement and supporting English Only. Supporters include NCTE, NEA, TESOL, MLA, American Council of Teachers of Foreign Languages, the Center for Applied Linguistics, the American Psychological Association, the National Council for Black Studies, and the National Council of Churches of Christ. Both NCTE and NEA have published books that explain their positions on English Only legislation and that provide background material necessary to guard against language restrictionism (see Selected Titles). For more information, contact EPIC, 220 I Street, NE, Suite 220, Washington, DC 20002.

CCCC
1111 W. Kenyon Road, Urbana, Illinois 61801-1096.

THE NATIONAL LANGUAGE POLICY

CONFERENCE ON COLLEGE COMPOSITION AND COMMUNICATION

Nonprofit Organization
U.S. POSTAGE
PAID
Champaign, Illinois
Permit No. 85

Lenguaje   Language   Sprache

reach—college students, teenagers, elementary school children, teachers, seniors, new citizens, business people, and so on. Then decide what you want your readers to do—vote, send money, be informed, come to a demonstration, change or reaffirm their beliefs, experience outrage. Design the ad or pamphlet so that it is geared to the needs and interests of your audience in terms of language level, amount of information, emotional appeals, and visual features.

CHECKING OUT THE WEB

The Lower East Side Tenement Museum maintains a website that can take you back to the experience of immigrants in New York City from the 1870s to 1935. Visit the site www.tenement.org for a glimpse of life on the Lower East Side. Originally built in 1863, the tenement at 97 Orchard Street housed over 10,000 people between 1870 and 1915. Sealed from 1935 to 1987, the restored tenement opened as a museum in 1994 and now offers tours and sponsors programs and exhibits. Through its website, you can take a video tour of two apartments—one occupied by the German-Jewish dressmaker Natalie Gumpertz and her family in the 1870s, the other by the Sicilian family Adolpho and Rosario Baldizzi in the 1930s. You can also visit each apartment in the tenement and meet the people who lived there in 1870 and 1915, peel through thirteen layers of wallpaper, and see some of the artifacts, such as advertisements, bank checks, medicine tins, and an infant's shoe, that have been recovered through excavation. The museum's exhibits often connect the old immigration to the new in interesting ways. When we visited, the museum was presenting a photographic essay on New York's Chinatown and an exhibit of shadow boxes with stories of recent immigrants put together by the museum's ESL program in collaboration with a local artist.

Mining the Archive

THE OLD IMMIGRATION, 1840–1920

Popular Song 1923. National Park Service Collection, Ellis Island Immigration Museum. Photo Chermayeff & Geismar MetaForm.

The U.S. English ad contrasts immigrants in earlier years of American history (who "knew they had to learn English to survive") to "today's immigrants" (who are "being misled" by bilingual educators and government bureaucrats). The photo of the mother and her three children recalls the millions of immigrants who crossed the Atlantic from southern and eastern Europe around the turn of the century. The ad asks us to imagine an era when the United States was a melting pot of different nationalities, and immigrants from the old country (unlike the immigrants of today) wanted to assimilate and learn English.

The historical archives, however, reveal a more complicated picture of the old immigration. From the 1840s, when the potato famine drove millions from Ireland, up to the early 1920s, when legislation severely restricted the numbers allowed to enter the United States, immigration has dramatically multiplied the foreign-born percentage of American residents, prompting anti-immigrant sentiments and fear for the country's national identity on the part of some native-born Americans. Racialist ideas were widespread in the late nineteenth century, and it was common to classify national and ethnic groups as separate races—Celts, Slavs, Hebrews, Mediterraneans, Alpines, Nordics, Asiatics, Negros, and so on—with the dominant Anglo-Saxon "race" at the top of the evolutionary scale. As historians have recently shown, nationality groups such as the Irish or Greeks or Italians were often viewed initially as separate races unfit to become Americans and only gradually became assimilated into American culture as Caucasians or "whites." (For more on this, see Noel Ignatiev, *How the Irish Became White*; David Roediger, *The Wages of Whiteness*; and Matthew Frye Jacobson, *Whiteness of a Different Color*.)

What these historians help us see is that the process by which the Irish, Germans, Slavs, Italians, and others worked out their places in American culture is a complex one—far more complex that the U.S. English ad allows for. You can get some sense of this complexity by consulting archival sources—to determine for yourself what this earlier era of immigration was like, how native-born Protestant Americans represented the Jews and Catholics arriving from eastern and southern Europe as racial groups, and whether the melting pot ideology we find in the U.S. English ad and elsewhere provides an adequate picture of the old immigration. Here are a few suggestions about places to look and issues to consider.

GOVERNMENT REPORTS

The Dillingham Commission on Immigration issued a series of *Reports of the Immigration Commission* (Washington, DC: Government Printing Office) in 1910 and 1911. The ninth volume, *Dictionary of Races or Peoples,* is especially interesting for its classification of forty-five races in the United States (thirty-six from Europe alone) that differ both biologically and culturally from each other. Arguments used at the time to restrict immigration (and preserve the racial integrity of Anglo-Saxon America) can be found throughout the Dillingham reports, as well as in testimony at later congressional hearings, such as Harry H. Laughlin, *Analysis of America's Melting Pot: Hearings Before the Committee on Immigration and Naturalization. House of Representatives, November 21, 1922* (Washington, DC: Government Printing Office, 1923).

BOOKS AND PERIODICALS

Madison Grant's *Passing of the Great Race: Or the Racial Basis of European History* (New York: Scribner's, 1916) was an influential polemic of its time that argued unrestricted immigration amounted to "race suicide" on the part of old-stock Americans. Henry Cabot Lodge's case that immigration is a bad biological investment on the part of the United States can be found in "The Restriction of Immigration" and "Lynch Law and Unrestricted Immigration," both of which appeared in the *North American Review* 152 (1891). You can find other statements on immigration in late nineteenth and early twentieth century periodicals such as *Harper's Weekly*, *Frank Leslie's Illustrated*, *Nation*, and *North American Review*. Pay special attention to the illustrations in *Harper's* and *Frank Leslie's*.

COURT CASES

The first U.S. naturalization law in 1790 limited citizenship to "free white persons." After the Civil War and the emancipation of slaves, in 1870 and 1875, legislation extended citizenship rights to "aliens of African nativity, and to persons of African descent." Legislation, however, did not really specify who was "white" or how to determine it. You can see the kind of tortured reasoning defining "whiteness" resulted in by looking at such judicial decisions as *Ozawa v. United States* 260 U.S. (1922) and *United States v. Thind* 261 U.S. (1923). In the first case, the judge ruled against the Japanese-born Takao Ozawa's petition for citizenship on the grounds that while he might be "white" (at least in the sense he wasn't black), he wasn't Caucasian. A year later, in the second case, the court ruled that Baghat Singh Thind, while he could be considered Caucasian, was not properly speaking "white" and therefore not entitled to citizenship. You can find these cases in law libraries or on Lexis-Nexis.

Credits

TEXT CREDITS

Chapter 4

Chapter 5

Chapter 6

Chapter 7

Chapter 8

Chapter 9

" 'Indians': Textualsim, Morality, and the Problems of History" by Jane Tompkins, from CRITICAL INQUIRY 13:1, 1986, pp.101-119. Copyright (c) 1986 by The University of Chicago Press. Reprinted by permission of The University of Chicago Press.

"The Tragedy of Vietnam" from AMERICA: A Narrative History, Brief Second Edition by George B. Tindall with David E. Shi. Copyright (c) 1989, 1988, 1984 by W. W. Norton & Company, Inc. Used by permission of W. W. Norton & Company, Inc.

"God's Country and American Know-How" from BACKFIRE by Loren Baritz. Copyright (c) 1985 by Loren Baritz. Reprinted by permission of Gerard McCauley Literary Agency.

"When Heaven and Earth Changed Places" from WHEN HEAVEN AND EARTH CHANGED PLACES by Le Ly Hayslip. Copyright ©1989 by Le Ly Hayslip and Charles Jay Wurts. Reprinted by permission of Doubleday, a division of Bantam Doubleday Dell Publishing Group, Inc.

"Private First Class Reginald 'Malik' Edwards" from BLOODS by Wallace Terry. Copyright ©1984 by Wallace Terry. Reprinted by permission of Random House, Inc.

From "Making A Memory of War" from CARRIED TO THE WALL: AMERICAN MEMORY AND THE VIETNAM VETERANS MEMORIAL by Kristin Hass. Copyright (c) 1998 by the Regents of the University of California. Reprinted by permission of the Regents of the University of California and the University of California Press.

Excerpt from the *Preface* "Whatever is foreseen in joy" from READING AMERICAN PHOTOGRAPHS: IMAGES AS HISTORY FROM MATTHEW BRADY TO WALKER EVANS by Alan Trachtenberg. Copyright (c) 1989 by Allen Trachtenberg. Reprinted by permission of Hill and Wang, a division of Farrar, Straus and Giroux, LLC.

Chapter 10

"America: The Multinational Society" from WRITIN' IS FIGHTIN' by Ishmael Reed. Copyright (c) 1994 by Ishmael Reed. Reprinted by permission of Lowenstein Associates Inc.

From CITY ON THE EDGE: THE TRANSFORMATION OF MIAMI by Alejandro Portes and Alex Stepick. Copyright ©1993 The Regents of the University of California. Reprinted by permission of University of California Press and Alejandro Portes.

"How to Tame a Wild Tongue" from BORDERLANDS/LA FRONTERA: THE NEW MESTIZA by Gloria Anzaldua. Copyright (c) 1987 by Gloria Anzaldua. Reprinted by permission of Aunt Lute Books.

"Home is Where the *Han* Is: A Korean American Perspective on the Los Angeles Upheavals" by Elaine H. Kim. Reprinted by permission of the author.

Reprinted by permission of the Modern Language Association of America from "Arts of the Contact Zone" by Mary Louise Pratt, PROFESSION '91.

"A Land With Rhythm and Beats for All" by Neil Strauss from THE NEW YORK TIMES, August 22, 1999. Copyright (c) 2000 by the New York Times Co. Reprinted by permission.

"In The End, Black Men Must Lead" by Touré from *The New York Times,* August 22, 1999.

PHOTO CREDITS

Introduction **Page 2:** © The Absolut Company.

Chapter 1 **Page 6:** *The Providence Journal*

Chapter 2 **Page 41 (top right):** Reprinted by permission, Motorola. **Page 41 (left):** Photofest. **Page 41 (bottom right):** Rob Lewine/The Stock Market. **Page 86:** "School Violence & Littleton Tragedy" from National Council of Teachers of English at http://www.ncte.org/special/violence.html, December, 1999. Copyright (c) 1999 by National Council of Teachers of English. Reprinted by permission. **Page 91 (top):** Photofest. **Page 91 (bottom):** The Kobal Collection. **Page 92:** Photofest. **Page 107:** Nina Leen/Life/TimePix.

Chapter 3 **Page 108 (right):** Jose Pelaez/The Stock Market. **Page 108 (top left):** New York City Board of Education Archives, Milbank Memorial Library, Teachers College, Columbia University. **Page 108 (bottom left):** From THE NEW FUN WITH DICK AND JANE by William S. Gray, et al., illustrated by Keith Ward and Eleanor Campbell. Copyright 1951 by Scott, Foresman and Company. Reprinted by permission of Addison-Wesley Educational Publishers, Inc.. **Page 163:** Courtesy of Hampton University Archives. **Page 164:** Jane Addams Memorial

Collection (JAMC neg. 613), Special Collections, The University Library, The University of Illinois at Chicago. **Page 165 (top):** "A New York Elementary School Classroom, 1942." *All the Children,* Annual Report of the Superintendent of Schools, City of New York (1942–1943). **Page 165 (bottom):** ©Apple Computer, Inc. **Page 172 (top):** From THE NEW FUN WITH DICK AND JANE by William S. Gray, et al., illustrated by Keith Ward and Eleanor Campbell. Copyright 1951 by Scott, Foresman and Company. Reprinted by permission of Addison-Wesley Educational Publishers, Inc. **Page 172 (bottom):** Public Domain.

Chapter 4   Page 173 (top left): Alinari/Art Resource, NY. **Page 173 (top right):** Cave painting 15000 BC. Caves of Lascaux, Dordogne/Bridgeman Art Library, London/New York. **Page 173 (bottom right):** Foto Marburg/Art Resource, NY. **Page 174:** Self Determination for D.C. **Page 175:** Courtesy of Coach. **Page 176:** The mark JEEP (r) is a registered trademark of Chrysler Corporation and is used with permission from Chrysler Corporation. **Page 178:** Billboard Using Graffitists Against Unhealthy Promotion. **Page 198:** Courtesy the National Fluid Milk Processor Promotion Board. **Page 199 (top):** Reprinted with the permission of The Pillsbury Company who has ownership of the Häagen-Dazs trademark. **Page 199 (bottom):** Courtesy: Altadis U.S.A. 2000. **Page 200:** Courtesy of the National Fluid Milk Processor Promotion Board. **Page 201:** Ad courtesy of State Farm Insurance Companies/ DDB Worldwide-Chicago. Photo by Redcat Productions/John Huet. **Page 202:** Courtesy of the United States Marine Corps. **Page 205:** Partnership For A Drug-Free America. **Page 206 (left):** Reproduced with permission. ©*Some Kinds of Abuses Start Early…Quit Smoking,* 2001. Copyright American Heart Association. **Page 206 (right):** ©American Lung Association, reprinted with permission. **Page 207:** Courtesy National Archives. **Page 208 (left):** Courtesy National Archives. **Page 208 (right):** RAJ Publishers, Lakewood, CO. **Page 209:** Paul Martin Lester. **Page 210 (left):** Edward Carreon. **Page 210 (right):** New York Times Graphics/NYT Permissions. **Page 211:** © Fallon McElligott/Rolling Stone by Straight Arrow Publishers, Inc. All Rights Reserved. Reprinted by Permission. **Page 213 (left):** *L.H.O.O.Q.* by Marcel Duchamp, 1919. ©2001 Artists Rights Society (ARS), New York/ADAGP, Paris/Estate of Marcel Duchamp. Cameraphoto/Art Resource, NY. **Page 213 (right):** Image courtesy of www.adbusters.org. **Page 214 (top):** Courtesy of Guerrilla Girls. **Page 214 (bottom):** *The Grand Odalisque* by Jean Auguste Dominique Ingres, 1814. Louvre, Paris, France. Giraudon/Art Resource, NY. **Page 226:** Alinari/Art Resource, NY. **Page 227 (top):** Reprinted by permission of *The Wall Street Journal* © 1997 Dow Jones & Company, Inc. All Rights Reserved Worldwide. **Page 227 (bottom):** © 1997, *USA TODAY.* Reprinted with permission. **Page 228:** Courtesy of Globe Editorial, Inc. **Page 229:** Private Collection

Chapter 5   Page 230 (right): Jeffery Dunn/Stock, Boston. **Page 230 (bottom left):** W. Hill, Jr./The Image Works. **Page 230 (top left):** Reprinted courtesy of Callard & Bower-Suchard Inc., ©1998. **Page 263:** Private Collection. **Page 264:** Reprinted courtesy of Callard & Bower-Suchard Inc., ©1998. **Page 265 (left):** Courtesy of The Gillette Company. **Page 265 (right):** Courtesy of Valentino Couture, Inc. **Page 269:** Source: Teenage Research Unlimited. Northbrook, IL. **Page 270:** "Main Page" and "Exhibitions/Past/Celebrating Elegance/Soiree de Paris" from Kent State University Museum at http://www.kent.edu/museum June 22, 2000. Copyright © 2000 by Kent State University Museum. Reprinted by permission.

Chapter 6   Page 271 (bottom right): Barbara Rios 1992/Photo Researchers. **Page 271 (top right):** Myron Wood/Photo Researchers. **Page 271 (left):** Joseph Szkddzinski/The Image Bank. **Page 300:** "La Familia" detail from "Chicano Time Trip" by East Los Streetscapers (Wayne Alaniz Healy and David Rivas Botello), 1997. 18' × 26' panel (total mural is 18' × 90'). Lincoln Heights, East Los Angeles. City Wide Mural Project. **Page 302:** "Pickers" by Judith F. Baca, 1990. Acrylic on plywood, 8' × 7'2", Leroy Park, Guadalupe, California. **Page 303:** "Uprising of the Mujeres" (detail), by Judith F. Baca, 1979. Acrylic on wood, 8' × 24', portable. **Page 309 (top):** Henry Chalfant, from "Subway Art," by Martha Cooper and Henry Chalfant. **Page 309 (bottom):** Diana George. **Page 310 (top):** Joseph Szkddzinski/The Image Bank. **Page 310 (bottom left):** Paul Martin Lester. **Page 310 (bottom right):** Myron Wood/Photo Researchers. **Page 313:** Hancock Historic Preservation Committee.

Chapter 7   Page 314 (top right): Richard Hutchings/PhotoEdit. **Page 314 (top left), (bottom left):** Photofest. **Page 360:** Photofest. **Page 361:** Photofest. **Page 367 (top):** Superman and all related elements are trademarks of DC Comics ©2000. All rights reserved. Used with permission. **Page 367 (bottom):** ©2000 Atlantic Syndication Partners. Reprinted by permission.

Chapter 8 **Page 368 (bottom left):** Photofest. **Page 368 (right):** George Eastman House. **Page 400:** DILBERT reprinted by permission of United Feature Syndicate, Inc. **Page 401:** DILBERT reprinted by permission of United Feature Syndicate, Inc. **Page 402:** DILBERT reprinted by permission of United Feature Syndicate, Inc. **Page 404 (top):** George Eastman House. **Page 404 (bottom):** Corbis-Bettmann. **Page 405:** Photography Collections, University of Maryland, Baltimore County. **Page 406:** Image courtesy of www.adbusters.org.

Chapter 9 **Page 415 (top right):** Rafael Macia 1988/Photo Researchers. **Page 415 (bottom right):** M.B. Duda/Photo Researchers. **Page 415 (left):** Library of Congress. **Page 476 (top):** Corbis-Bettmann. **Page 476 (bottom):** Library of Congress. **Page 477 (top):** Library of Congress. **Page 477 (bottom):** AP/Wide World Photos. **Page 478:** AP/Wide World Photos. **Page 481:** Archive Photos. **Page 482:** AP/Wide World Photos. **Page 483:** Edward Hausner/New York Times Co./Archive Photos. **Page 484:** Corbis-Bettmann. **Page 487:** Albany Civil Rights Movement Museum.

Chapter 10 **Page 488 (right):** AP/Wide World Photos. **Page 488 (top left):** Ellis Island Immigration Museum/NPS. **Page 549:** Courtesy U. S. English. **Page 550:** Courtesy Conference on College Communication, NCTE Permissions Dept. **Page 552:** Ellis Island Immigration Museum/NPS.

Index

Note to reader: All titles (of text selections, books, magazines, newspapers, television shows, movies, and songs) are printed in italic type. Names of authors of text selections are printed in bold type. Names of images are printed in regular type.